Environmental SCIENCE

How the World Works and Your Place in It

Jane L. Person

Second Edition

J.M. LeBel Enterprises
Dallas   New York   Toronto   Edmonton

Photographs:
Atomic Energy of Canada, Carolina Biological, Chemical
Manufacturers Association, Environment Canada, Environmental
Protection Agency, Exxon, Jean Farmer, Janet LeBel, Missouri Conservationist,
NASA Aerospace Education, New York City, Oxford University Press,
Payless Cashways, Jane L. Person, Pennsylvania Game Commission,
Sierra Club, Sterling International, Lonnie G. Thompson,
US Department of Agriculture, US Fish and Wildlife Service, Barbara Wagner.

Sidebars: Natalie Goldstein
Illustrations: Kim Robertson, Gavin Sedgewick, George Nishi
Composition: Heidi Palfrey
Design: Janet Zanette

Components:

- Textbook
- Teacher's Manual
- Issues and Investigations
- Study Guide
- Answers to the Study Guide
- Computer Test Program (ascii file)

Environmental Science   ISBN 0-920008-70-4

J.M. LeBel Enterprises
6420 Meadowcreek Drive, Dallas, Texas 75240
10335-61 Avenue, Edmonton, Alberta T6H 1K9

Brief Table of Contents

1   Introduction to Ecology — The Basics

2   The Atmosphere — Is the Sky Falling?

3 Food for the Table — Changes Through Science and Technology

4 Water — The Essential Fluid

Part I — Water as an Ecosystem — A Study of Aquatic Life

Part II — Water for the People

5 Energy — Past, Present, and Future

Table of Contents

1 Introduction to Ecology — The Basics

2   The Atmosphere — Is the Sky Falling?

3

Food for the Table — Changes Through Science and Technology

4   Water — The Essential Fluid

5   Energy — Past, Present, and Future

Preface

Environmental Science: How the World Works and Your Place In It is designed by a high school science teacher to introduce students in grades 9–12 to the major ecological concepts and the environmental issues that affect the world in which they live. Students will learn about technological developments that have created environmental problems as well as technologies that are helping to solve them.

The program provides a planned curriculum for a full year of science. It is specifically designed to provide a general science course for high school students. The reading level has been controlled to increase reading comprehension. At the same time, the writing style provides interesting reading that will hold the student's attention. No prior knowledge of science is assumed. This allows students with very different backgrounds in science to successfully complete the program.

There is an urgent need for environmental education at all levels in the K-12 curriculum. This program provides one way in which students can be become more aware of the interactions of people and their environment. The course is a real-life science course. It relates important environmental issues to the lives of the students and their families. It promotes awareness and understanding of practical everyday problems that affect their lives.

An Exemplary Science Program

The curriculum that was the basis for the 1990 edition of *How the World Works and Your Place In It* was chosen as an exemplary program in the 1986 Search for Excellence in Environmental Education conducted by the Office of Environmental Education, Pennsylvania Department of Education. The Excellence in Environmental Education Awards Program is sponsored jointly by the Pennsylvania Department of Education, the Pennsylvania Association of Conservation District Directors, Inc., and the Pennsylvania Alliance for Environmental Education.

It was also selected as an Exemplary Science Program by the National Science Teachers Association in the 1986 Search for Excellence in Environmental Education. The 1995 revised edition has been totally rewritten and updated. Every attempt has been made to maintain the same standards of excellence as in the original curriculum.

Design for Learning

The curriculum is organized in five units:

1   Introduction to Ecology — The Basics
2   The Atmosphere — Is the Sky Falling?
3   Food for the Table — Changes Through Science and Technology
4   Water — The Essential Fluid
5   Energy — Past, Present, and Future

Each unit is divided into sections that introduce major concepts. Unit 1 includes sections on ecology, succession, food chains and webs, flow of energy, and cycles. Sections in Unit 2 include composition of the air, weather, sources of pollutants, chemicals that pollute, effects of pollutants, and radiation as a pollutant.

Unit 3 includes sections that provide insight into the technology associated with food-getting prior to the development of agriculture, the development of agriculture, soil, soil erosion and its control, food for increasing populations, fertilizers, pests, and pesticides. Unit 4 is divided into two major sections: Water as an Ecosystem — A Study of Aquatic Life and Water for the People.

Water as an Ecosystem — A Study of Aquatic Life includes four sections: aquatic environments, creatures in the water, aquatic plants, and water quality. Water for the People includes sections on water supply, pollutants in the water, and the treatment of drinking water.

Unit 5 includes sections on the history of energy use, fossil fuels, and development of technologies that use alternative sources of energy.

The sections described above provide information that will help the students develop the basic concepts. Each section includes questions that test reading comprehension as well as questions that help students develop higher level thinking skills. This edition includes specific situations entitled "STS — Science Technology and Society Issues" that will help students develop decision-making skills.

Case Studies

Case studies provide an in-depth study of current environmental issues such as logging, endangered species, climate change, the clean-up of a Superfund site, damming rivers, and adding fluoride to drinking water. Through the study of specific situations, the student can better understand the concepts. In most cases, teachers will find the typical school year does not provide enough time for an in-depth study of the entire curriculum. It will become necessary to make choices. Teachers are encouraged to "localize" the curriculum. Some topics and activities can be used for enrichment.

Supplementary Materials

The course components include Textbook, Teachers' Manual, Issues and Investigations Manual, Study Guide with separate Answer Key and Test Program.

Some concepts, such as population studies, can best be developed through hands-on activities. Appropriate laboratory investigations have been developed for these concepts. Although field trips should be an essential element in an environmental science course, most of the activities included in the Issues and Investigations Manual can be completed with materials in a laboratory setting.

Teachers are encouraged to schedule field trips as often as possible. For example, although experiences observing aquatic organisms in the laboratory are valuable, students will gain an even better understanding and appreciation if they can see the organisms in their natural habitat.

The Teacher's Manual includes learning outcomes, answers to questions with supplementary information, suggested teaching tips, and suggested references for audio-visual and computer software. A bank of suggested test items, keyed to the learning outcomes, has been developed to accompany the textbook.

Acknowledgments

I would like to thank my family for understanding my commitment to this project and my commitment to my students. Most importantly, I would like to extend a special thank you to my husband, Richard, for his patience and understanding. I am indebted to him for agreeing to serve as consultant. His background and years of experience as a teacher of chemistry and nuclear science classes allowed him to provide constructive criticism that was essential to the improvement of the manuscript. His reviews and suggestions have been a very significant part of the development of this curriculum.

I am indebted to those teachers, especially Orval Johnson, Betty Burns, and Richard Person, whose commitment to students became a model for my own teaching. I owe much to those people at the Missouri Department of Conservation who wrote the articles, made the films and conducted the workshops that became the foundation for my approach to environmental education.

Thanks to former students who willingly field-tested activities and, through their responses, helped to fine-tune the curriculum. Thanks to my publisher, John LeBel, who has made it possible for many students across the United States and Canada to experience this curriculum and learn more about their world. This curriculum is for the students who as they learn about their world will be better prepared to help sustain it.

To the Student

This textbook is the basis of a course that will:

- give you a new way of looking at your world — that will inform you — to make you more aware of what is happening in your world.
- examine the physical and chemical processes that make the world work.
- study the relationships between you and other species that share your world.
- help you develop an awareness of how our actions are good and bad — of their risks and benefits.
- help you make more informed choices about things which you do that affect our environment — building dams and developments, disposing of toxic wastes, cutting forests, burning fossil fuels, driving automobiles, and selecting products in the marketplace.
- examine practical problems associated with daily living — the treatment of sewage, the supply of safe drinking water, the production of food, the use of chemicals, regulations for automobiles and wood stoves, and the effects of exposure to radiation.
- help you develop a philosophy that we must understand how the world works in order to make it a better world in which to live — a planet that will sustain a diversity of living organisms including humans.

UNIT 1

Introduction to Ecology — The Basics

First Image of the Global Biosphere

The image below shows the patterns of plant life, both on land and in the oceans, as observed from space. The ocean measurements indicate high concentrations of phytoplankton in the red and orange areas. Yellow and green areas represent moderate concentrations while blue and violet areas are the lowest concentrations.

The land measurements show dark green areas (rain forests). The lighter shades of green highlight tropical and subtropical forests, temperate forests and farmlands and some drier regions such as savannas. The yellow indicates areas of lower potential while snow and ice covered regions have no productive potential.

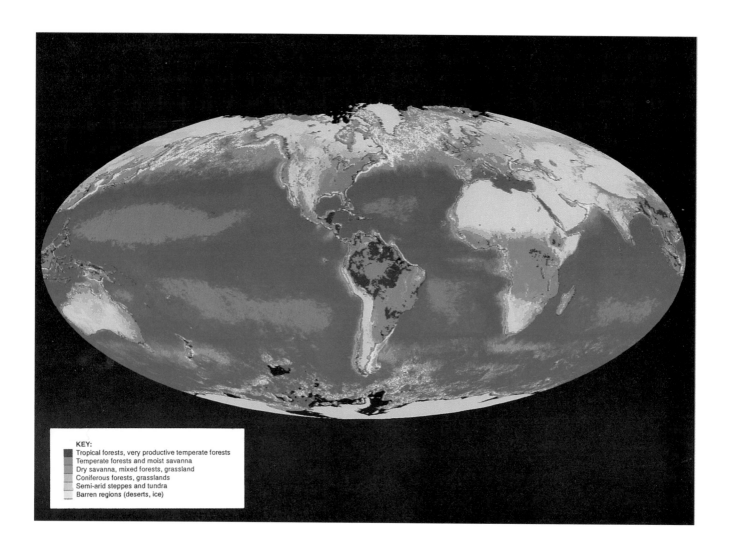

KEY:
- Tropical forests, very productive temperate forests
- Temperate forests and moist savanna
- Dry savanna, mixed forests, grassland
- Coniferous forests, grasslands
- Semi-arid steppes and tundra
- Barren regions (deserts, ice)

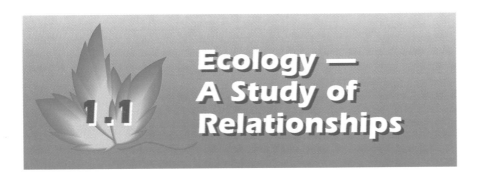
The term ecology comes from two Greek words meaning "the study of the home." Like biology, ecology is a science. While some biologists study organisms in a laboratory, others study organisms living in their natural environment. Wildlife biologists and conservation biologists study organisms interacting with their environment and other organisms. These biologists are sometimes called **ecologists**. **Ecology** is the study of organisms in their natural environment — their home.

Our home, the planet Earth, consists of large masses of air, water and land that support a thin layer of life — the **biosphere**. Everywhere that life exists on planet Earth — from the warm climate of the tropical forests to the cold waters of the Arctic ocean — scientists are seeking information that will help us better understand our world and how it works. While information is gathered by scientists conducting field studies here on Earth, instruments aboard spacecraft gather additional data.

September 1991 marked the deployment by the Space Shuttle of the Upper Atmosphere Research Satellite, or UARS.

Viewing Planet Earth from Space

In addition to instruments at ground level and aboard airplanes, scientists at NASA launch spacecraft to study the Earth and other planets. Although they are expensive to launch, satellites are an economical way to gather data. Instruments aboard satellites can quickly gather data from a very large region, and they continue to gather data for a very long time.

How can spacecraft gather information from the distant planet Earth? All objects absorb, reflect, and give off energy in the form of **electromagnetic radiation (EMR)**. Any type of object, whether living or non-living, can be detected by its distinctive pattern of electromagnetic radiation. Extremely sensitive instruments that detect this radiation allow scientists to monitor the health of planet Earth from outer space.

Images from remote-sensing equipment aboard spacecraft give us a global view of the biosphere. Computer enhanced photographs of the infrared radiation allow scientists to monitor the temperature

TRY TO FIND OUT

How a habitat provides an organism with shelter and food? Choose one animal in your neighborhood. Observe it for one week and record the conditions and resources found in its habitat that help it survive.

DID YOU KNOW?

Ecologists have long believed that species richness in an ecosystem, called biodiversity, maintains the ecosystem's stability. A study at the University of Minnesota examined different areas of prairie during the worst drought to hit the plains in 50 years, the drought of 1987-1988. They found that the prairie with the greatest diversity of plant species recovered much more quickly from the devasting drought than a species-poor patch of prairie. For each single species missing from an ecosystem, the destructive effects were magnified.

of the planet. Images that capture the visible wavelengths of radiation show the distribution and abundance of plant life on land and in the oceans. The distribution and abundance of human life are revealed by images that show our dependence on two forms of energy — electricity and fire.

Scientists also study the chemistry of the atmosphere. Using a **total ozone mapping spectrometer** (TOMS) aboard orbiting satellites, scientists monitor ozone levels in the upper atmosphere and predict possible effects of the changing levels. At the same time, other scientists monitor ozone levels in the lower atmosphere and study their effects on plant growth and human health.

Planet Earth is a complex environmental system with constant interactions among the atmosphere, the oceans, and the land. A better understanding of these interactions will help us more accurately predict the effects of human activity. Better predictions can help us manage natural resources in a way that will minimize the impacts on the environment.

Biomes — Climatic Zones of Life

When viewed from space, the biosphere appears to be a giant puzzle. But the pieces of the puzzle do not represent political regions. They represent biomes. A **biome** is a large geographic region determined by the climate and soil type. Each biome has a distinctly different type of plant life. Some of the major biomes are Arctic tundra, northern coniferous forest, temperate deciduous forest, grassland, and desert.

The **climate** of a region refers to its average weather. The major conditions that describe the climate are the amount and pattern of precipitation and the normal range of temperatures. The climate affects both the soil type and the plant life. The existing plant life creates an environment that supports a characteristic group of animals.

Ecosystem — A Functional Unit

While it is easy to identify biomes, they are too large an area for research. The functional unit of a biome that ecologists study is the ecosystem. An **ecosystem** is a group of organisms that live together and interact with each other and with their environment. Ecosystems may be natural or human-made.

The Sonoran desert, in the southwestern United States, is an example of a natural ecosystem. Equally famous ecosystems include the Ozarks, the Everglades, Yellowstone, the Badlands, the Amazon River, Chesapeake Bay, and the Great Barrier Reef. You can think of others.

Biome	Temperature	Precipitation	Soil Type
Arctic Tundra	• very low temp • cold winds • only surface of soil thaws • growing season 60 days or less	• often less than 10 in/yr (25 cm/yr) • falls mostly during summer months	• thin, acidic • few nutrients • **permafrost** — layer of permanently frozen soil
Northern Coniferous Forest or Taiga [TIE-guh]	• short summers; long, cold winters • above freezing for only 2-4 months	• 14-39 in/yr (35-100 cm/yr) • falls mostly during summer months	• thin, acidic soils • little **humus** — decayed matter • lacks nutrients • no permafrost
Temperate Deciduous Forest	• −30°C to +30°C • distinct seasons • growing season 5 months in North	• 29-59 in/yr (75-150 cm/yr) • snow in North • evenly spaced throughout year	• rich in humus • medium nutrient level • more decomposers than tundra
Temperate Grasslands or Prairie	• distinct seasons • moderate seasonal temperatures • hot summers and cold winters • continuous winds	• 10-39 in/yr (25-100 cm/yr) • mostly in spring and early summer; • growing season limited by rainfall • periodic droughts	• ten times more humus than deciduous forest • very rich in nutrients • deep topsoil
Desert	• cold, temperate, or tropical • daily temperature variation may be greater than seasonal	• usually less than 10 in/yr (25 cm/yr) • years of drought • dry winds; high evaporation rate • flash floods	• sandy • little ability to hold water • some rich in nutrients; others nutrient-poor.
Tropical Savanna	• cool and hot dry seasons separated by warm and rainy season • no cold season	• 39-59 in/yr (100 to 150 cm/yr) • wet spring and fall • long dry spells during hot months • heavy thunderstorms	• fertile soils • deep layer of topsoil • grasses prevent erosion
Tropical Rain Forest	• tropical • daily variation 9°F(5°C) is greater than seasonal • continuous growing season	• more than 78 in/yr (200 cm/yr) • seasons determined by amount of rain	• thin soils • few nutrients • if exposed to sun forms cement-like layer • rapid leaching

Natural ecosystems tend to be self-sustaining environmental systems. With the exception of water from precipitation and energy from the sun, the environment of a natural ecosystem contains all resources needed to support its community of organisms. Of course natural disasters, like volcanic eruptions, and human activities, like mining, can destroy natural ecosystems. Fires, considered disasters

Can you find the two ecosystems in this scene?

The Myriad Gardens Crystal Bridge in downtown Oklahoma City is a human-made tropical ecosystem. Inside this large cylinder, scientists have created both wet and dry tropical environments. In addition to the brightly colored birds, visitors may spot small brown lizards (anoles). Scientists introduced several kinds of lizards, insects and predatory mites to control certain pests. Replacing chemicals with natural predators is a part of the innovative integrated pest management (IPM) program. See Unit III for more information of IPM.

by humans, are essential to the maintenance of some forest and grassland ecosystems.

Human-made ecosystems include farms, cities, flower gardens, terrariums and aquaria. Unlike natural ecosystems, ecosystems created by humans are seldom self-sustaining systems. They usually require huge inputs of resources and energy.

Habitat — A Place to Call Home

It is important to remember that the living and non-living part of an ecosystem are dependent upon one another. "Nothing can live alone." Each living organism requires a certain set of physical and chemical conditions. Climate and soil conditions determine the types of plants that grow in an ecosystem. The plants determine the kinds of animals that live there.

If the correct sets of physical and chemical conditions exist, organisms thrive. Large herds of grazing animals exist only where grasses are abundant. If trees invade the area, animals that prefer trees become more common. Where trees produce too much shade, the growth of grasses is limited, and the number of grazing animals declines.

Although large animals are more obvious, an ecosystem includes many different kinds of organisms. Each organism has its own special "home" within the ecosystem. The place in an ecosystem where an organism prefers to live is its **habitat**. You might think of a habitat as the organism's address. It describes where the organism lives, but a habitat is more than just a place to live. It must meet all of the needs of the organism. Good habitat provides enough food and water, suitable living space, and cover.

Cover describes those places where animals hide to escape predators or where the young are protected from harm. Cover also provides the animals with shelter from harsh weather. If the cover

Relationships within an Ecosystem

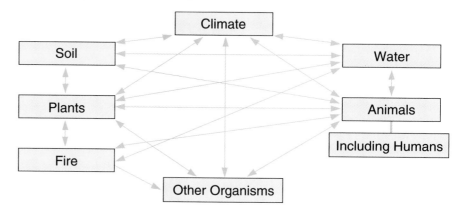

disappears, the wildlife will also disappear. The disappearance of cover may be due to natural changes in an ecosystem, or it may be due to human activities.

Populations of Woodpeckers

Organisms that are very much alike and breed to produce fertile offspring in their natural environment are members of the same **species**. Differences in structure or behavior prevent members of different species from breeding with each other. The downy woodpecker and the hairy woodpecker are members of the same family, but they are different species. Twenty different species of woodpeckers breed in North America.

The total number of a species living in a defined region is the **population** of that species. We frequently refer to the population of one species — humans, but the term population can refer to any species of plant or animal. The number of hairy woodpeckers in the forest is one population. The number of downy woodpeckers in the area is another population.

Both the downy and the hairy woodpeckers are **cavity nesters** — birds that build nests in holes within trees. Even though these two kinds of woodpeckers make cavities for nesting, they do not compete for housing. The preferred habitat of the hairy woodpecker is the interior of a deciduous forest. The downy woodpecker often chooses trees at the edge of the forest or a tree along a road.

Even if downy and hairy woodpeckers are found in the same area of the forest, it is unlikely that they will choose the same tree. The hairy woodpecker, with a longer and stronger beak, prefers to make its cavity in live wood or hard dead wood. The downy woodpecker always chooses soft dead wood.

More Cavities Needed

Bluebirds are cavity nesters, but they can't make their own cavity. Like the downy woodpecker, bluebirds prefer trees in open areas. The best habitat for bluebirds is an open area with scattered trees such as an old orchard. By clearing sections of forest to create fields and orchards, early settlers improved bluebird habitat. Bluebirds feed on insects on the ground, and insects were abundant in the fields and meadows.

In the early 1900s, eastern bluebirds were one of the most common songbirds, but by 1969 fewer than 100 bluebirds nested in Minnesota. Other states also reported severe declines in the populations of all three bluebird species.

Why did the populations decline? One factor may have been the widespread use of insecticides, but the most important factor was probably the loss of habitat. At first, fences were built with wooden

Hairy Woodpecker

Downy Woodpecker

THINK ABOUT IT

Figure out where in the food chain you fit in when eating each part of a cheeseburger: bread, cheese, beef.

Properly placed nesting boxes like this one provide much needed habitat for Eastern bluebirds.

Although the cavity is now too large, this old wooden fence post has provided a home for many bluebirds. Now it may provide protection for other cavity nesters.

This box is prime habitat for a female wood duck looking for a home.

Bluebird Nest

posts, and wooden posts develop cavities. While bluebirds like fence posts with cavities, farmers don't. Cavities make the fence post weak, and cattle escape through weak fences. After World War II, most farmers replaced wooden posts with new posts made of steel.

The invention of the chain saw made cutting of trees easier, and trees that were not cut were often destroyed by cattle. As the size of the farm machinery increased, farmers bulldozed rows of trees to make larger fields. Other trees disappeared during the construction of highways, shopping centers, and developments.

With less suitable habitat, the bluebirds were forced to compete with other birds for the few remaining nesting sites. More aggressive birds such as the tree swallow and house wren often drive the bluebirds from their nests. Starlings and house sparrows — both introduced to this country from Europe — also compete with the bluebirds for nesting sites.

All three bluebird populations — eastern, western, and mountain — declined nearly 90 percent between 1935 and 1985. The North American Bluebird Society and others are working to increase the number of bluebirds. The most successful method is to improve the habitat by providing the bluebirds with nesting boxes. Thousands of nesting boxes are in place and being monitored by individuals interested in helping the little bird that Henry Thoreau once said, ". . . carries the sky on its back."

If placed in the right environment, nesting boxes do attract bluebirds. Bluebirds prefer nesting boxes placed next to open and mowed areas. If placed near a brushy area, the box is more likely to attract house wrens. Tree swallows compete for isolated nesting sites in open areas. Competition from tree swallows will decrease if the boxes are placed in pairs, less than three feet apart. Boxes for mountain and western bluebirds must have slightly larger holes than those for eastern bluebirds, but if the hole is too large, starlings will nest in the boxes.

Another nesting box program aided the wood duck population. When house-hunting, the female wood duck looks for a cavity in a tree that is in or near the water. Often she chooses a cavity, excavated by a pileated woodpecker, with a hole too small for a raccoon to enter. Human activities — logging mature trees, draining ponds and hunting — threatened the wood duck population. In 1918 the United States and Canadian governments banned the hunting of this species. Groups of citizens and conservation organizations built nesting boxes and placed them on poles or in trees that are in or near the water. Today the wood duck population is greater than one million, and hunting is once again permitted.

Finding the Right Neighborhood

When the settlers came to America, much of the area east of the Mississippi River was mature forest. The large trees in a mature forest ecosystem provide too much shade for many low-growing plants. Due to the shade, mature forests do not provide suitable food or cover for a number of species including rabbits, ruffed grouse, and white-tailed deer. By clearing sections of the forest, the early settlers improved the habitat for these species.

As the forests were cut, new growth in the clearings provided plenty of food and good cover. The settlers not only improved the habitat, they also killed many of the natural predators. With better habitat, fewer predators, and restricted hunting, the populations of these species increased.

Today many of Pennsylvania's forests are once again mature. The shade of the mature trees and a large white-tailed deer population have reduced the low-growing plants that provide cover and food for rabbits and young grouse. In some areas, housing developments created openings that allow more sunlight to enter the forest. This encourages the growth of shrubs. In these areas the rabbit population may increase, but the ruffed grouse is shy and avoids areas where there is human activity. As a result, the ruffed grouse population is declining.

Clean water supporting fish and other aquatic life, in an area free from too much human activity, is good habitat for the river otter. As we develop wild areas, we destroy good otter habitat. In Pennsylvania the otter has been protected since 1952, but laws to protect a species can not save it if it has no space to live.

Living on the Edge

One species that benefits from human activity is the woodchuck, also called the groundhog. Groundhogs are mainly vegetarians, feeding

Wildlife Biologist

Wildlife biologists plan and carry out wildlife management programs. They identify conditions that affect wildlife, restore and manage wildlife habitat, conduct research to determine the best management methods, regulate hunting and fishing, and conduct programs to educate the public. A bachelor's degree with a major in wildlife studies or a closely related field is the minimum education required for employment as a wildlife or fisheries biologist.

Ruffed Grouse

Groundhog

on grass, leaves, and flowers. They are especially fond of alfalfa, clover and soybeans, but they may also find a meal in the garden or orchard. By cutting forests, clearing land, and raising crops, settlers provided a more suitable habitat for groundhogs.

The groundhog creates its own cover by digging a burrow with several rooms and openings. Since its ability to out-run its predator is limited, the groundhog prefers to stay close to home. It is important that the burrow be located close to a good supply of food.

Like the groundhog, most species do not travel far from home in search of food. One study showed that quail will not travel to a food supply that is more than two hundred yards (180 m) from their cover. When there was cover on only one side of a square forty-acre (16 hectare) field, the quail fed in only one half of the field. When there was cover on both sides of the field, the quail used the entire field.

The place where two ecosystems come together is known as the **ecotone** or the **edge**. An example of an ecotone is the place where the forest meets the field. The advantage of living on the edge is that it provides cover that is near a good food supply. Because of the available food and cover, the edge contains more species and larger populations of each species than either ecosystem. Ecologists refer to this as the **edge effect**. Humans frequently reduce the edge by making larger fields or building subdivisions, highways and industrial parks. The destruction of the edge means the destruction of valuable wildlife habitat.

To survive, animals need suitable habitat. Habitat is more than just a place to live. Good habitat provides enough food, cover, water and living space. The most critical threat to animals is often not a direct physical assault by humans. The greatest threat to most species of wildlife is the destruction of their habitat.

Limits to Population Growth

The size of a population that can exist in the ecosystem, at any given time, is the ecosystem's **carrying capacity**. There are a number of factors that limit the ability of the ecosystem to support a species. Anything that prevents the population size from increasing is a **limiting factor**. Possible limiting factors are:

- **Space**: Many species of animals establish territories for breeding. This includes most songbirds, as well as many mammals and fishes. Even species that do not establish territories often have less offspring when crowded.

  When the population becomes crowded, individuals may **emigrate** or move to other areas. The lemming, a small Arctic rodent, emigrates every four or five years. During an ordinary winter, lemmings are protected from their enemies by the snow, and if plenty of food is available, they continue to breed during the winter. As they become crowded, they move up or down the mountainside in search of food. Contrary to popular belief, they do not march to water to commit suicide. Lemmings are good swimmers.

- **Food**: When food supplies decrease, the size of the population depending on that source of food becomes smaller. In the tundra ecosystem of northern Canada, the only food for the lynx (*lingks*) is the snowshoe hare. When the number of hares decreases, the number of lynx also decreases. In the Florida Everglades, the snail kite population fluctuates with availability of its only source of food — the apple snail. Organisms that depend upon one food source are most vulnerable to population crashes.

  In the garden "good bugs" eat "bad bugs." If pesticides are sprayed to kill the "bad bugs," the population of "good bugs" also decreases. While some bugs — both good and bad — survive the spray, others move into the area from nearby gardens. The population of "bad bugs" must recover before there is enough food to support a large population of "good bugs."

What is the limiting factor for these Colorado potato beetles?

- **Climate and Weather**: Why is the coniferous forest biome in the northern reaches of the planet? Conifers can tolerate the extreme cold. Climate plays a major role in the distribution of plants and animals.

  Fewer animals survive when the winter weather is unusually cold, and the snow is deep. For certain species, such as rabbits, a cold and wet spring may decrease the number of young that survive. For other species, such as mosquitoes, an unusually wet spring provides ideal conditions for breeding and can result in a population explosion.

What are the limiting factors for these plants?

- **Cover**: If the habitat does not provide a good place to hide, individuals may become easy food for predators. On modern farms, the quail and rabbit populations are often limited due to a lack of brushy fence rows that would provide good cover. Farmers can improve the habitat by not mowing or harvesting certain sections of land.

- **Disease**: Organisms spread disease more readily if they are crowded. As the **population density** — number of a species per unit area of living space — increases, the distance that a disease organism must travel to reach its next victim is reduced. As a result, more organisms are infected with the disease. If the population density increases until the supply of food is limited, the weakened animals may die from diseases that they would normally survive.

Because it helps control the population of Mexican bean beetle larvae, the large Spined soldier bug is a "good bug."

- **Human Activity**: As wild areas become developed, the populations of those species that do not tolerate human activity will decline. Loons abandon their nests when disturbed by human activity. Bobcats and river otters leave the area in search of a more peaceful habitat. Successful breeding may depend upon the availability of a habitat without human disturbance.

Rabbits in Australia

THINK ABOUT IT

You have decided to alter your home and the area surrounding it to help animals. In short, you want to create a "wildlife refuge" around your home. What animals would you like to attract? What would you do? What plants would you put in? What kind of cover would you provide and how would you create it?

- **Shade**: The tops of the mature trees in a forest make a roof or **canopy**. The shade created by the canopy becomes a limiting factor. It prevents other trees of the same species from growing. Shade-tolerant species are more successful, and eventually become the dominant trees in the forest.

Population Explosions

In the absence of limiting factors, population explosions occur. This frequently happens when a new species is introduced to an ecosystem. Thomas Austin emigrated to Australia from England. He missed the sport of hunting, so he imported two dozen rabbits and released them on his estate. Hunters soon lost interest in the sport of shooting rabbits. Six years later 10,000 rabbits were destroying grasslands causing sheep to starve and even hired guns could not effectively reduce the population.

The rabbits destroyed much of the grassland, and the grass was replaced by less desirable plants including the prickly pear cactus. Why were the rabbits a problem in Australia and not in England? In England there were both predators and diseases that controlled the rabbit population, but in Australia there were no predators or diseases that killed rabbits. The rabbit population continued to increase until the food supply became a limiting factor.

Population explosions also occur when predators are eliminated from an isolated ecosystem. A classic example of what happens when predators are eliminated is the story of the Grand Canyon National Game Preserve. In 1906 President Theodore Roosevelt created the game preserve on the Kaibab Plateau in northern Arizona. The purpose of the preserve was to protect a splendid herd of mule deer.

In 1906 ranchers removed all domestic animals from the preserve, and government officials intensified their efforts to eliminate all major predators. Hunters and trappers killed 816 cougars, 30 wolves, 7,388 coyotes and 863 bobcats. There were probably fewer than 10,000 mule deer on the plateau when the intensive predator control began. In 1918, an estimate of the herd size was 40,000 deer. A census taken six years later reported 100,000 deer. The following winter, approximately 60,000 deer died of starvation.

The government replaced the predator control program with mule deer "killing program." At its peak, the population density was one mule deer per 7 acres. The deer had destroyed much of their habitat and reduced the carrying capacity of the land. Since 1939, the size of the herd has been controlled at about 10,000 — one deer per 68 acres. Controlling the population of mule deer has allowed the ecosystem to recover.

1. Define the following terms:

biome	electromagnetic
biosphere	radiation
canopy	emigrate
carrying capacity	habitat
cavity nesters	humus
cover	limiting factor
ecologist	permafrost
ecology	population
ecosystem	population density
ecotone	species
edge	total ozone
edge effect	spectrometer

2. What is ecology?
3. What do we call a scientist who studies ecology?
4. Describe the biosphere.

Viewing planet Earth from Space

5. What is the advantage of studying planet Earth from Space?
6. Describe how spacecraft gather data from planet Earth?
7. Explain why scientists feel that it is important to see a satellite's view of Earth in addition to all of the data being collected by scientists here on Earth.

Biomes — Climatic Zones of Life

8. Describe a biome and identify the factors that determine the type of plant life that exists in a biome.
9. Give three examples of biomes and identify unique characteristics of each.

Ecosystems — A Functional Unit

10. Describe an ecosystem and give examples of ecosystems where you live and ecosystems that you would like to visit.
11. Natural ecosystems do not need any input from humans, but they must have a supply of _____ and _____.
12. Compare a natural ecosystem to a human-made ecosystem.

Habitat — A Place to Call Home

13. Identify the two basic parts of an ecosystem.
14. Explain the statement: "Nothing can live alone."
15. List the physical factors which affect an organism's environment.
16. Explain how plants change the chemical and physical environment.

Population of Woodpeckers

17. What is another word that can be used to describe an organism's habitat? Compare the habitat of the downy woodpecker to the habitat of the hairy woodpecker.
18. Give three reasons why animals need cover.
19. Match the following terms with the correct description.

A. cavity in a tree	1. habitat
B. the number of hairy wood-	2. organism
peckers in a forest	3. population
C. any living thing	4. species
D. a group of organisms which can breed	
E. a school building	
F. the number of students in your high school	
G. humans	

More Cavities Needed

20. The bluebird is native to America. Describe the changes made by the early settlers that caused the bluebird population to increase.
21. What recent changes have caused a decline in the number of bluebirds?
22. How are some people trying to increase the bluebird population? Explain.
23. Explain how to increase successful nesting of bluebirds by decreasing the competition for nesting boxes from house wrens, starlings, and tree swallows.
24. Compare the habitat requirement of the bluebird to the habitat requirement of the wood duck.

Finding the Right Neighborhood

25. When settlers came, the populations of some animals increased. Identify three species that benefited from the activities of the settlers and explain why these populations increased.
26. In Sherwood Forest, a development in Pennsylvania's Pocono Mountains, trees are being cut and areas are being cleared for roads and houses. Will the clearing and development cause the grouse population to increase or decrease? Why?
27. Identify factors that could limit the population of river otters.

Living on the Edge

28. How did the arrival of the settlers affect the groundhog population?
29. Why did the quail feed on just one side of the field and avoid the other side?
30. A farmer removes a fence row to enlarge a field. Which species will be least affected — groundhogs, rabbits, or quail? Explain.
31. Why does the "edge" contain larger populations of certain species?

32. How are humans affecting the "edges"?
33. Identify the four factors necessary for good habitat.
34. Complete the following sentence. The greatest threat to many species is the . . .

Limits to Population Growth

35. Define carrying capacity. How do limiting factors affect the carrying capacity of an ecosystem?
36. Give some examples of limiting factors that affect the following species: quail, rabbit, lynx, loons, bob cats, river otters, ruffed grouse, white-tailed deer, blue birds, oak trees.

Population Explosions

37. Why do population explosions sometimes occur?
38. What limiting factors were missing when Thomas Austin introduced the rabbit to Australia?
39. What was wrong with the plan to protect the mule deer herd on the Kaibab Plateau?
40. Explain why population control is necessary.

Science **T**echnology **S**ociety

ISSUES

THE HUMAN POPULATION AND THE EARTH'S CARRYING CAPACITY

The population of planet Earth is 5.5 billion and growing. It took about one million years for the human population to reach 1 billion. At the current rate of growth, an additional 1 billion people are added every ten or eleven years. Think about the following questions in terms of the human species — **Homo sapiens**.

- At the current rate of growth, what will Earth's human population be when you are 30 years old?
- What is the carrying capacity of Earth for **Homo sapiens**? Can Earth support 10 billion people?
- What limiting factors control the human population?
- How have these limiting factors changed since 1800 when Earth's population was only one billion?
- How does the increase in the human population affect the carrying capacity of the planet Earth for other species? for the human species?

Indian Pipes

One of the most important relationships that exists between living organisms is based on their need for energy. Plants cannot make energy, but they can make their own food. To get energy they must compete with other plants for sunlight. Plants trap the sun's energy and use it to make food in a process called **photosynthesis**.

Green plants or algae are the foundation of nearly all ecosystems. They are producers. A **producer** is an organism that can use the sun's energy to make its own food. Mushrooms, fungi, and a few flowering plants, such as Indian Pipes, are not producers. Because they lack chlorophyll, they cannot use the sun's energy to make or "produce" food.

The word producer is used only when we speak of an organism that uses sunlight to create food molecules (sugar) from nonfood molecules (water and carbon dioxide). Producers are vital to the ecosystem because they make food for all other species. A cow produces milk, but cows are not classified as producers because they can not make food from nonfood molecules. In fact, no animal can make food from nonfood molecules.

All organisms must have food. Organisms are classified as producers or consumers. **Consumers** — organisms that cannot make their own food — depend on producers. There are several types of consumers. Those consumers that eat plants are called **herbivores** or "plant eaters." Consumers that feed on animals instead of plants are **carnivores** or "meat eaters."

Some consumers eat both plants and animals. They are **omnivores**. Bears and coyotes are omnivores. Their digestive system is not adapted for large amounts of plant material. However, when their

Can you identify the niche of these organisms?

Sea Otters

Condor

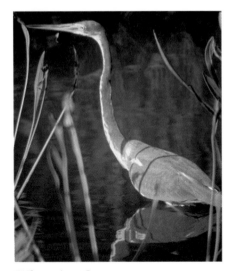

Whooping Crane

food supply is limited, they can digest plants well enough to keep from starving.

Another type of consumer is a decomposer. A **decomposer** feeds on the waste products or bodies of other dead organisms. Most decomposers are small. They include bacteria, fungi and a few flowering plants that lack chlorophyll. Decomposers have a very important role in any ecosystem. They recycle nutrients by changing the dead organisms and waste products into humus.

A **food chain** is a diagram that shows the flow of energy from green plants to consumer organisms. The food chain shows the niche of each organism. An organism's **niche** is its role or job in the ecosystem. The niche is usually described by the position of the organism in the food chain. While an organism's habitat can be compared to a person's address, the organism's niche can be compared to a person's occupation.

Some organisms have a very specialized niche. An example is the koala bear. They are herbivores feeding only on the tender shoots and leaves of eucalyptus trees. They can be compared to a surgeon who only performs heart surgery. Other organisms, such as brown bears, have a broader niche. Their varied diet includes both plants and animals. They can be compared to a farmer who may fill the roles of mechanic, heavy equipment operator, laborer, and businessman on any given day.

All animals classified as carnivores do not fill the same niche. Some carnivores are predators. A **predator** is an organism that feeds on other animals that it must first hunt and kill. The animal that is killed is the **prey**. **Scavengers** are carnivores that feed on organisms that either died naturally or were killed by other organisms. Vultures, flies, and crows are examples of scavengers.

Those consumers that feed on organisms that are still living are called **parasites**. The organism that is "eaten" is the **host**. During the summer you may be the host for a mosquito or tick. Your dog may be the host for several fleas. Mosquitoes and fleas are parasites. Since their host is an animal, they are also carnivores. If their host was a plant, they would be herbivores.

Building Food Chains

The first step in any food chain is always a producer. The second step is always an herbivore. Since the herbivore is the first consumer, it is sometimes referred to as the first-order or **primary consumer**. The second consumer in a food chain is a second-order or **secondary consumer**. The second-order consumer is a carnivore. It may be a predator or a scavenger. The third consumer is called a third-order consumer, and the fourth consumer is a fourth-order consumer. Decomposers may be at any step except the first, for like any other consumer they ultimately depend upon producers.

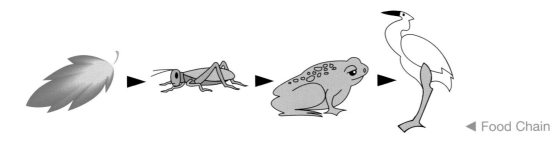

◀ Food Chain

The arrows in a food chain show what eats what. The arrow replaces the phrase "is eaten by." The direction of the arrow is very important. The arrow must point toward the "eater." "Grass is eaten by a cow" would be shown as:

Grass ⟶ Cow

The relationships in an ecosystem are more complex than those shown in a single food chain. Plants are not always eaten by insects, and the insects are not always eaten by frogs. The frogs are sometimes eaten by snakes instead of hawks. A **food web** shows the many possible food chains that exist in an ecosystem.

An ecosystem with a very simple food web is not a very stable ecosystem. Ecosystems with a complex food web — a web made of many chains — are more stable than an ecosystem with a simple web. This is due to the fact that the organisms have more choices of things to eat. If the population of one food source declines, the animal can feed on other organisms.

▼ Food Web

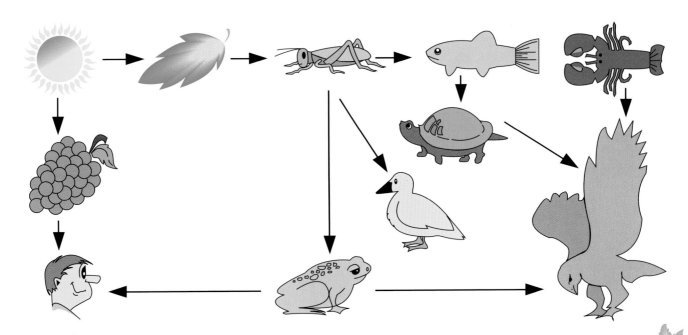

1. Define the following terms:

carnivore	parasite
consumer	photosynthesis
decomposer	predator
food chain	prey
food web	primary consumer
herbivore	producer
host	scavenger
niche	secondary consumer
omnivore	

2. Green plants "make" food. You might "make" a cake. The green plant is a producer. Are you a producer? Explain the difference between what a plant does and what a cook does in the kitchen.

3. In a sentence or two, describe the food chain shown below.

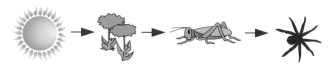

4. Identify the organism that fills each of the following niches in the food chain shown in question 3.

Predator	Primary Consumer
Herbivore	Producer
Secondary Consumer	Carnivore

5. Could the flowers in the picture be replaced with a picture of an Indian Pipe? Why or why not?

6. Why are producers said to be the foundation of all ecosystems?

7. We sometimes speak of vegetables and fruit as produce. A farmer takes "produce" to market. You buy tomatoes at a "produce" stand. Why do you think that vegetables and fruits are called "produce"?

8. Why are decomposers essential to an ecosystem?

9. What information can you learn from a food chain?

10. What is the niche of each of the following organisms?

koala bear	coyote
mosquito	vulture
brown bear	fungi
house fly	grass

11. What phrase replaces the arrow when describing a food chain?

12. A food (chain or web) best shows the relationships that exist in an ecosystem.

13. Do you think that the food web shown is a stable ecosystem? Explain.

Many people look at an aging tree with dead and dying branches as a waste. Such trees are frequently victims of a chain saw. Some of these trees are removed for firewood. Other trees may be removed because cutting every tree is a more cost-effective way of logging. Standing dead trees, often called **snags**, have become rare in some forests. A standing dead tree is worth a lot to wildlife.

Some birds nest among the leaves in the tops of trees while others prefer a nest with a view. The dead branches at the top of an aging tree provide an ideal nesting site for eagles and ospreys. Some birds prefer to nest in cavities. About one of every ten bird species in the United States is a cavity nester. Each cavity nester plays an important role — has a specific **niche** or job to do — in the ecosystem.

Woodpeckers are the excavators. The red-cockaded woodpecker makes a cavity in living pine trees, but almost all other woodpeckers make cavities in the soft wood of dead or dying trees. Most woodpeckers and other cavity nesting birds eat insects and are important members of the pest control force that protects the forest.

Some cavity nesters are very demanding. The American ivory-billed woodpecker needed large tracts — several hundred acres — of old-growth forest. The snags provided both cover and food. The large birds fed by removing large pieces of bark in search of insects. As their habitat disappeared, the ivory-billed woodpecker became an endangered species. It is probably extinct.

Another large woodpecker, the pileated, has become more common because it can survive in smaller tracts (about 160 acres/64 hectare) of less mature forests. The pileated also use snags for "drumming boards" to announce their presence to other birds intruding on their territory. The US Forest Service considers the pileated woodpecker an **indicator species**. This means that a forest with suitable habitat for a pileated woodpecker is a healthy ecosystem that provides for the needs of many other species including smaller woodpeckers.

Some cavity nesters adjust to changing conditions, but others are in trouble. The common flicker has been known to nest in utility poles and sometimes even in burrows made by other animals. The red-cockaded woodpecker lives in open pine forests in the southeastern part of the United States. Much of its habitat has been converted to pine plantations, and the woodpecker has not adjusted to the changing conditions.

Snag

Pileated Male Woodpecker

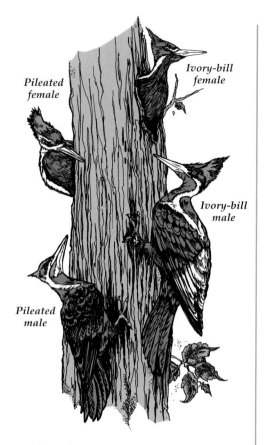

Pileated female

Ivory-bill female

Ivory-bill male

Pileated male

How does this tree provide protection for the forest?

The USFS Policy

It is the policy of the United States Forest Service (USFS) to save some trees for the insect-eating woodpeckers and other cavity nesters. In Missouri's Mark Twain National Forest portions of the forest have been left uncut for 200 years. California now leaves all snags that are not a fire or safety hazard. USFS biologists recommend that two or three snags per acre (0.4 hectare) be protected from cutting. Some **cull trees** — trees that will not yield high quality lumber — are left to become future snags. Lumber companies complain that the Forest Service leaves too many good trees standing on federal land.

Why do we need to leave good trees in the forest? It takes about 100 years for a tree to reach maturity, die, and become a snag. If all mature trees are removed, soon there will be no snags. Woodpeckers and other birds that thrive on tree-killing bark beetles and other forest pests may disappear if lumber companies remove all dead and dying trees. Foresters now believe that leaving snags for woodpeckers provides a forest with better insect protection. They also agree that it is possible to meet fire, safety and timber management goals and, at the same time, preserve the habitat of the cavity nesters.

Life in the Old Hemlock

During its long life, the 100-year-old hemlock tree has held the nests of a few species of birds. It has contributed its share of food and cover for the animals in the forest. Now it is showing its age, but the old tree still has much more to give before it is taken down by a winter storm. As a huge old dying tree, it is worth a lot to wildlife.

The aging tree is attacked by boring insects. They create tunnels that allow water, fungi and other insects to enter. As the wood begins to soften, new bird species are attracted to the tree. An eagle may choose the top of the old tree as a site for a nest. As branches die and lose their needles, they provide places for birds to sit and watch for flying insects. Bats also feed on insects near the tree.

As the bark becomes loose and the wood becomes softer, new species of birds can find food more easily. A brown creeper may nest behind loose pieces of bark. Insects that prefer solid wood move to a younger, firmer snag. Wood-peckers move into the old hemlock.

The pileated woodpecker selects a dead tree and makes a new nest each year. The perfect tree is 80 to 100 years old and about 12 inches (30 cm) in diameter. The snag needs to be somewhat decayed, but not spongy. Wood ducks, salamanders, flying squirrels, raccoons, and screech owls are a few of the animals that may move into old woodpecker homes. They will be followed by larger birds such as great-horned owls. The neighbors are constantly changing.

Eventually the tree falls and becomes a log where insects, snails and other small animals find food and a place to hide. Birds that prefer life on the forest floor to life in the canopy feed on the organisms living in the log. The rotting log continues to break down into **humus** — partly decayed plant material. Seeds fall on the rotted log. The moisture and nutrients in the humus provide the ideal conditions needed for the seeds to sprout. The log becomes a **nurse log** — a nursery for new trees. The life cycle begins again.

Should this tree be cut for firewood?

How many different animals might make their home in this tree?

Young tree growing from a decaying or "nurse" log.

2.2 QUESTIONS FOR STUDY AND DISCUSSION

1. Define the following terms:

   cavity nester   niche
   cull tree   nurse log
   humus   snag
   indicator species

2. What niche do cavity nesters fill?
3. Why are snags becoming rare?
4. Complete the food chain below.

   _____ → _____ → **Woodpeckers**

5. Give the niche of each organism in the food chain above.
6. Why has the ivory-billed woodpecker become an endangered species?
7. On a walk through a forest, you see a pair of pileated woodpeckers. What does this chance sighting tell you about the forest ecosystem?

8. Why isn't the common flicker endangered like the ivory-billed woodpecker?

The USFS Policy

9. Do lumber companies agree with the US Forest Service policy concerning snags? If not, explain how their policy differs.
10. Why is it important to allow some cull trees to grow and not remove them for firewood?

Life in the Old Hemlock

11. What relationship exists between the woodpeckers and the great-horned owls?
12. Explain how a healthy forest is dependent upon the presence of dead and dying trees.
13. Explain how a fallen log is important to the forest ecosystem.

Hawk Preying on a Mouse

Wolf

How did Hurricane Hugo affect the population of endangered red cockaded woodpeckers in South Carolina. What behavior of this woodpecker contributed to its own loss of habitat during the hurricane?

Predators survive by killing and eating other animals. Many animals, including humans, get all or at least part of their food this way. We don't often think of robins as predators, yet they prey upon insects and earthworms.

For some animals to live, others must die. It is the **niche** of some animals to be predators. Some predators are not always predators. Foxes sometimes eat grasses, berries and grapes. It is easier than catching a rabbit or ruffed grouse.

If chickens are easier for predators to catch than their natural food, they may eat chickens. When a predator makes a habit of killing chickens, the most practical answer may be to eliminate the predator. It may be necessary to kill certain predators to control the damage, but this does not mean that all predators are bad.

Most predators are valuable to us most of the time. Of the many creatures that get their food by killing and eating other animals, only a few individuals bother us.

We need predators to balance the reproductive power of most animals. A pair of field mice will produce offspring who will then produce offspring, and these offspring will produce more offspring. In only one year there could be one million field mice. Predators are nature's mousetrap. Without predators to control the populations, certain wild species, like mice, would crowd out other species. They would also destroy their habitat.

Predators control pest populations. They also get rid of the weak, the crippled, the stupid, the stunted, and the diseased individuals. They often kill the unfit before they can breed or spread disease. Those organisms that escape predators and breed make the population stronger. Their death is not wasteful because it provides food for other animals.

Research has shown that predators do kill **game species** — species that humans want for themselves, but they do not reduce the population drastically. During the 1940's, people were paid for killing bobcats, weasels, foxes, hawks, and owls. The money paid for the dead predator is a **bounty**.

Bounties were paid for predators in an effort to increase certain game species. The game populations did not increase as expected. The surplus animals died of disease, fires, floods, accidents, and lack of food or cover. It is the surplus animals that are the easy prey for the predator. When the surplus is gone, the predator usually turns to other, easier-to-get food sources.

If humans destroy the prey's natural cover, predators may kill too many of a particular species. When farmers remove the brushy fence rows and create bigger fields, they destroy the cover for the rabbits and other wildlife that used to live there. This increases the chances that the rabbits will become the prey of a coyote.

Where habitat is destroyed, hunting or trapping of coyotes may be necessary to protect the remaining rabbit population. But killing of coyotes will not restore the rabbit population to its original level. Without enough food and cover — good habitat — the population will not increase in size.

While farmers may have a right to destroy those predators that are killing the domestic animals, they must not set out to destroy all predators. Often it is a single animal that is causing damage. If a predator is a destructive individual, we may need to cancel our pest-control contract with it, but we will not profit by killing all predators.

Predators are not the only animals that cause damage. The animals that predators kill may be more destructive than the predators. These include rabbits, deer, crows, sparrows, mice, and insects. Any animal may be destructive if it becomes overabundant or out of place. The plant-eaters may be the most destructive of all. The animals we call predators are the best insurance we have against an overpopulation of plant-eating pests. Eliminating the predators will only cause more vandalism by the pests.

2.3 QUESTIONS FOR STUDY AND DISCUSSION

1. Explain the statement, "Being a predator is an animal's niche."
2. Explain the statement, "Some predators are not always predators."
3. In what way are most predators valuable to us?
4. How do predators make populations of animals stronger?
5. How does a game species differ from non-game species?
6. Make the connection between bounties, game species, and predators.
7. Did the bounty system work? Check with your state conservation department or game commission to determine if bounties are offered for any species in your area.
8. How do humans sometimes help predators kill more of a certain species?
9. In what way are predators an insurance policy for us?
10. Describe how your life might be different if there were no predators.

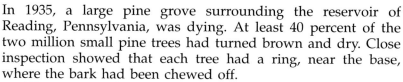

In 1935, a large pine grove surrounding the reservoir of Reading, Pennsylvania, was dying. At least 40 percent of the two million small pine trees had turned brown and dry. Close inspection showed that each tree had a ring, near the base, where the bark had been chewed off.

The grass in the meadow area between the trees had provided cover for rabbits, pheasants, meadow mice, groundhogs, weasels, and other small animals. The meadow mice are the main primary consumer in the meadow ecosystem. They are the major item in the diet of many predators: rough-legged hawks, short-eared owls, weasels, snakes, and sometimes crows.

In 1935 a deputy game warden shot many hawks. He may have been trying to protect the rabbits and pheasants, which are important game species. He may have had a dislike for predators. Some people feel that predators are our enemies.

A pair of meadow mice may have 17 litters in one year. Each litter will have between two to nine young. The young will begin to breed when they are 25 days old. In just one year one pair of mice can produce one million offspring.

In order for the population of meadow mice to remain the same, 43 mice must be destroyed each year for every mouse that survives. It is the job, or niche, of the predators to keep the population of meadow mice in balance.

Removal of the rough-legged hawks, by the deputy game warden, caused the population of meadow mice to grow so that there was a shortage of their normal food supply. In order to survive the winter, they began to feed on the bark of the pine trees.

How do we know the rough-legged hawks eat meadow mice and not pheasants or rabbits? The hawks shot by the game warden were sent to the Reading Museum. Examination of their stomach contents showed only the remains of meadow mice. Not one pheasant or rabbit was found.

In 1724 the colony of Pennsylvania offered a bounty for crows. Later hawks and owls were added to the list. In the 1930s the state of Pennsylvania offered a bounty for goshawks, a species that preys on birds. Farmers were concerned because goshawks also killed some chickens.

Most people cannot tell a goshawk from a red-tailed hawk. The bounty resulted in the killing of 76 goshawks and 295 other species of hawks. The farmer was the real loser since many of those species would have killed many thousands of rodents that feed on their crops.

Bald Eagle

WHAT DO YOU THINK?

Many ranchers graze their livestock on public land managed by different government agencies. This public land belongs to everyone. Yet ranchers pay rock-bottom prices for grazing their herds on this land. And it is primarily these ranchers who want predators on public land destroyed through the Animal Damage Control program ADC to protect their livestock. Do you think this is good land management practise?

1. What caused the death of the pine trees in Reading?
2. Draw a food web using a least six of the organisms found in the area around the Reading Reservoir.
3. How is the population of meadow mice normally controlled?
4. Meadow mice do not normally feed on pine trees. Why did they eat the bark of the pine trees at the Reading Reservoir?
5. How do we know what rough-legged hawks eat?
6. How does the offer of a bounty for killing predators affect the farm ecosystem? Explain.

2.5 CASE STUDY
Coyotes — An Opportunistic Omnivore

"Coyotes howling, yipping, barking, chanting in the brush this morning — that thrilling call of the wild. Like a loon's cry in the lake country, the song of the coyote . . . is the voice of the desert . . ."

Edward Abby

Many people associate coyotes with the West, but remains in prehistoric Indian villages tell us that they lived in the East during the Ice Age. Coyotes vanished from the East, perhaps 10,000 years ago. Their disappearance is probably related to the changing habitat and the presence of a larger predator — the wolf.

When the first settlers came, the Northeast was covered with forests. They found no coyotes, only timber wolves. Since the days of the first human settlements, the populations of most predators, including wolves, have decreased due to the loss of habitat and uncontrolled hunting.

Return of the Coyote

Coyotes are not like most predators; the coyote population seems to be increasing in the Northeast. The return of the Eastern coyote is thought to be due to the massive clear-cutting of forests and the disappearance of the Eastern timber wolf. Unlike the wolf, the coyote thrives in open spaces. They are very adaptable and can usually avoid humans. The coyote is filling an ecological niche that was left vacant in areas where the wolf and the mountain lion were eliminated.

The Eastern coyote is about the size of a German Shepherd, slightly larger than its western cousins. They make their nest in a room at the end of a long tunnel, often enlarging a burrow abandoned by a groundhog, skunk, or fox. They are opportunistic **omnivores** — eating almost any kind of plant or animal. They are smaller than wolves but larger than foxes. They usually hunt smaller animals, but they sometimes kill large prey.

DID YOU KNOW?

Black-footed ferrets hunt and eat prairie dogs. They almost became extinct without anyone noticing. Out west, ranchers poison prairie dogs because holes priarie dogs dig can trip up grazing cattle. When Black-footed ferrets ate poisoned prairie dogs, the ferrets were also poisoned. As prairie dogs were wiped out on the plains, ferrets starved for lack of prey. By the 1970s, scientists assumed the black-footed ferrets were extinct. Then in 1983, a rancher found a dead ferret on his ranch. An exhaustive search turned up a small population of ferrets. Through captive breeding programs, ferret numbers have increased. However, releasing them to the wild remains a problem. Though some black-footed ferrets have been released, the scientists are having difficulty finding habitats that still contain viable populations of prairie dogs and ranchers who are willing to allow these populations to exist.

Coyote

Without protection from dogs or humans, young calves and lambs may be easy prey for coyotes.

Rabbits are an important item on the dinner menu of an urban-dwelling coyote. They sometimes feed on garbage or on other scavengers such as raccoons and skunks. They also eat watermelon, berries, and corn. If grasshoppers are plentiful, they eat grasshoppers. They usually eat whatever gives them the most nutrition with the least output of energy. They prefer small animals — mice, chipmunks, and birds. In the country as well as the city, rabbits are an important food source — especially in winter.

The population of coyotes in Pennsylvania is small compared to the population in New York. This may be due to Pennsylvania's larger population of white-tailed deer. Deer feed on the low-growing plants that snowshoe hares need for food and cover. When there is a large white-tailed deer population, there is a small snowshoe hare population. The snowshoes are an important winter food source for the coyote. The snowshoe hare population is a limiting factor that determines the size of the coyote population.

The Persistent Predator

Ranchers have declared war on the coyote because of its reputation for killing livestock. Thousands of coyotes are poisoned, trapped, and shot each year in the western US. The Office of Animal Damage Control (ADC) reported that 76,050 coyotes were exterminated in the 1988. Most of the $12 million that ADC spends annually on lethal control methods goes to reduce coyote populations in the West.

In spite of the efforts to reduce the population, the western coyote population remains stable. Unlike wolves, coyotes have survived the war by adjusting their reproductive rate. When the coyote population reaches the carrying capacity of their habitat, the average litter size is two or three. When the population is reduced, the litter size increases to between five and eight, and the females become sexually mature at an earlier age. As a result, ranchers are faced with the same problem year after year.

It is true that coyotes sometimes kill large animals, but research shows that they are a much greater threat to the smaller ones. Examination of stomach contents from several thousand dead coyotes in the Western US has shown their diet to be mainly rabbits, mice, voles, and other small rodents. Many other foods are eaten: insects, birds, fish, beaver, skunks, grass, and nuts. Poultry and livestock make up only one eighth (1/8) of the stomach contents.

The coyote's bad reputation is probably due to the fact that they often eat **carrion** — dead animal carcasses. If coyote tracks are seen around a half-eaten sheep or deer, the coyote gets credit for killing the animal. The animal may have already been dead or was weakened before it was found by the coyote.

Stomach contents of 37 coyotes and 7 coydogs (across between a dog and a coyote) killed in Pennsylvania were examined. The stomachs of 15 contained the remains of deer. All but two of these were killed during or shortly after the legal hunting season. These coyotes had probably eaten the remains of deer left by hunters or wounded deer that had not been found by the hunter.

Maggots found in one stomach proved the coyote had been dining on a deer's carcass. One stomach contained hide from a Holstein cow and another contained hair from a pig. Both coyotes were probably acting as scavengers.

Coyotes eat whatever is available. If the watermelon is ripe, it is an easy dinner. If rabbits and rodents are plentiful, lambs or chickens are not bothered. If lambs or chickens are more available, the coyote will not pass up the opportunity. Coyotes are most frequently predators or scavengers, but they may also be the prey. They are hunted by wolves, golden eagles, and large cats, such as mountain lions.

A New Approach

Coyotes remain the number one problem for the sheep industry. Killing coyotes has not solved the problem. Realizing this fact, some farmers and ranchers are now turning to nonlethal methods to reduce their losses. Putting the sheep in corrals at night or fencing the pastures is effective, but not foolproof.

Keeping sheep in — and predators out — requires an expensive eight-strand high tensile wire fence, with two wires electrified. Fencing 5000 acres of land on a western ranch is prohibitively expensive. Rounding up sheep to pen them at night may not be practical. If fences are not an option, losses can be reduced with a few good security guards.

Certain breeds of European guard dogs — Great Pyrenees, Komandor, Maremma — have been bred to herd sheep. When the dogs are raised with the sheep, they bond to them and protect them from the coyote. Guard dogs are effective, but they are costly and they require care.

When raised with another animal, sheep become attached to the animal and follow the animal wherever it goes. Some farmers are bonding sheep with young donkeys. They require less care than guard dogs because they eat the same food as the sheep. Donkeys herd sheep like guard dogs, and attack coyotes if they get too close. Cattle don't herd sheep, but they instinctively charge coyotes.

Researchers trained sheep to graze among cattle by penning newly weaned lambs with young cattle for two months. Once a bond is established, the sheep graze among the cattle. Scientists put bonded sheep and cattle in one pasture, and

Dog guarding sheep

Returning a Predator to an Ecosystem

Between 1904 and 1935, 121 mountain lions, 132 wolves and 4,352 coyotes were killed in Yellowstone National Park. When predators were finally protected in 1940, only the coyotes were left. For more than 50 years, the coyote has been the major predator in the park. The park also is home to a small population of red foxes.

• Write an environmental impact statement describing how you think the park will change if the wolf is reintroduced to Yellowstone.

Shoould taxpayers money be used to compensate ranchers for livestock losses instead of to hunt predators? A privately funded program of this kind has been successful where wolves have been reintroduced. The money paid to ranchers comes from private wildlife protection organizations. A federal program like this would save taxpayers money and allow populations of threatened animals to rebound.

unbonded sheep and cattle in another. To be sure that the coyotes did not prefer one pasture over the other, the animals were switched each time a sheep was killed. The researchers stopped the experiment when 50 percent of the unbonded sheep had been killed. All of the bonded sheep survived.

Bonding sheep with cattle provides another advantage for ranchers. Cattle eat grasses and sheep prefer broad-leaved plants. The carrying capacity of the land — the number of animals the land supports — is greater for a mixed herd than it is for a single-species herd. The rancher's income is increased by a combination of two factors: the number of animals that the land can support, and the greater number of sheep that survive.

Coyotes take advantage of an easy food source. Farmers and ranchers make life easy for a coyote by providing an easy food source. When a guard dog (or donkey or cow) or an electric fence makes it more difficult for the coyote to prey on sheep, they begin to hunt rodents and jack rabbits. If farmers and ranchers win the war with the coyote, the cattle and sheep will have to compete with these herbivores.

2.5 QUESTIONS FOR STUDY AND DISCUSSION

1. What may have caused the coyote's disappearance from the East more than 10,000 years ago?
2. Have the populations of most predators increased or decreased? What are the two major reasons for the changes?

Return of the Coyote

3. The return of the coyote in the East is related to the disappearance of what two predators?
4. What changes in the eastern part of the US have made the area more suitable to the coyote than to the timber wolf?
5. Draw a food web that includes the coyote as an herbivore, predator, scavenger, and prey. Write the niche (herbivore, predator, scavenger, or prey) in parenthesis ( ) beside the name of the organism.
6. Make the connection between the snowshoe hare, the white-tailed deer, and the coyote populations.

The Persistent Predator

7. What means have ranchers used to control the coyote populations?

8. Describe the impact of the attempts to eliminate the coyote on the coyote population.
9. Explain why the ranchers are not able to eliminate the coyote.
10. Do you think that coyotes deserve their bad reputation? Explain.
11. The term "opportunistic omnivore" is used to describe the coyote. Explain why this term fits the "niche" of the coyote.

A New Approach

12. What methods are ranchers using to protect their flocks of sheep from the coyote?
13. Give two advantages of "bonding" sheep to cattle.

What If . . .

14. Predict the reaction of an orchard owner or owner of a Christmas tree farm to the announcement of a predator control program that focuses on coyotes.
15. What impact might a forest fire have on a coyote population?

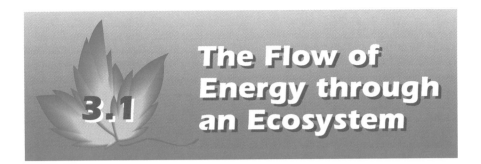

The Flow of Energy through an Ecosystem

3.1

When the sun shines on a grain of sand, it may make it so hot that you can not walk on it with bare feet. Yet when sun strikes a green leaf, it does not become hot. Why?

When sunlight — solar energy — strikes an object, the object either reflects or absorbs the energy.

- **Reflected** — approximately 30 percent of solar energy is reflected from the surfaces of water, land, clouds, air, plants, and human-made structures.
- **Absorbed** — approximately 70 percent of solar energy is absorbed by water, land, clouds, air, human-made structures, and plants.

Most of the energy that is absorbed by an object, living or non living, is changed to heat energy. If the object is a dry grain of sand, all of the heat energy is radiated back into air or, in the case of the sand particle, to your bare foot. If the sand is wet, it will probably not be uncomfortable because much of the heat energy is used in the process of evaporation.

The leaf is like wet sand. It is not hot to the touch, because most of the heat is used in the evaporation of water that is inside the leaf. The water vapor is then lost through openings in the leaf. This process is called **transpiration**.

Very little — between one and two percent — of the solar energy that reaches the Earth is absorbed by plants and trapped by chlorophyll. Once it is trapped by chlorophyll, solar energy is changed to chemical energy. In the process of photosynthesis, low energy molecules — carbon dioxide and water — are combined to make a high energy molecule — sugar. The sugar may be changed into other chemicals that form the structure of the plant (DNA, protein, cellulose), or it may be stored in energy-rich molecules (sugars, starch, oil). The energy, trapped in these molecules, is the foundation for the flow of energy through the ecosystem.

Building a Pyramid

The total mass of all organic matter at any level in a food chain is the **biomass**. To determine the biomass of the producers in an ecosystem, it is necessary to collect all plants in one unit area (one square metre), dry the plants and weigh them. Although it is a more difficult task, the biomass of herbivores and carnivores can also be calculated.

The biomass of the producers is always greater than the biomass of the herbivores. The biomass of the herbivores is always greater than the biomass of the carnivores. The biomass decreases with each additional step in a food chain. A diagram that shows this decrease in biomass is a **pyramid of biomass**.

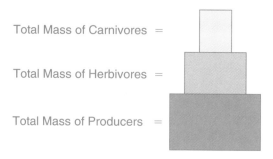

Total Mass of Carnivores =

Total Mass of Herbivores =

Total Mass of Producers =

Pyramid of Biomass ▶

Why does the biomass of organisms in a food chain always form a pyramid? Most of the energy trapped by the plant during photosynthesis is used by the plant to carry on its life processes. Only a small part of the energy trapped by the plant remains stored in the plant when it is harvested. This is the energy that is available to the herbivores.

If a plant receives 1000 Calories of energy from the sun, less than 5 Calories will be stored in the plant and be available to herbivores. If a deer eats the plant, only about 0.5 Calories will be converted to venison. What happens to the rest of the energy? More than half of the food eaten by the deer is changed to heat energy.

William C. Schultz kept 450 rabbits in a building next to his greenhouse. Rabbits give off excess body heat through their ears. Mr. Schultz designed a system to withdraw the warm air from the cages and blow it through plastic tubes on the greenhouse floor. He saved 13 percent of his fuel bill — 650 gallons (2,500 L) of liquid propane per day. He estimated that he could heat the greenhouse completely with 4,500 rabbits.

Most of the energy that is not converted to heat is used by the animal for daily activities. The need for energy increases when the animal is more active. Energy is used for digestion of food, making new cells, repairing injuries, mating, and reproduction. Every activity — even eating, sleeping, and breathing — requires energy.

Only a small portion of what is eaten at one level in the food chain is passed on to the next level. Only about 10 percent of the biomass at one level becomes biomass at the next level. Grasshoppers are only able to convert about 10 percent of the grass they eat into grasshopper biomass. The other 90 percent is uneaten, undigested, given off as heat, or used in grasshopper activities. The energy that

Grasshopper

remains trapped in the animal's wastes, or in uneaten parts of plants or animals, is available to decomposers.

Numbers in a Pyramid

Usually large numbers of organisms at the base of a food chain are required to support the smaller number of organisms at the top. This makes a **pyramid of numbers**, but the number of organisms at each level in a food chain does not always form a pyramid.

If the producer is very large, there may be a small number of organisms at the base of the food chain. The number of organisms does not always form a pyramid, but the biomass of a food chain always forms a pyramid. For example, a large number of gypsy moth larvae can feed on one large oak tree. The pyramid of biomass reflects the loss of energy that occurs at each step in the food chain.

The Population Connection

The number of organisms at the highest level in a food chain is directly related to the number of levels in the chain. More people can be supported if the food chain is shortened. If trout were eliminated from the food chain below, each person could live on 10 frogs per day. The ecosystem would then support 30 people. But who likes frogs?

If we eliminate the frogs and eat grasshoppers, nine hundred people could be supported by the ecosystem. They would each be allowed 100 grasshoppers per day — probably more than they would want.

Even more people could live off the land if they ate plants instead of growing plants to feed other animals. About 2,000 people, each eating three pounds of plants per day, could live on land that supports only one fisherman.

In America we produce 27,000 pounds (12,150 kg) of alfalfa to produce 3,300 pounds (1,485 kg) of beef. The 3,300 pounds (1,485 kg) of beef will produce 150 pounds (67.5 kg) of human tissue. Countries

Plants or algae form the base of the food pyramid. The producers are frequently eaten by insects.

How many insects will it take to support this fisherman?

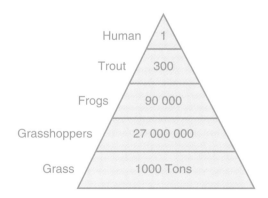

Human	1
Trout	300
Frogs	90 000
Grasshoppers	27 000 000
Grass	1000 Tons

◀ Pyramid of Numbers

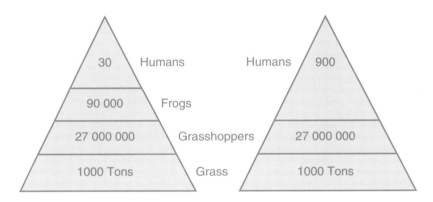

30	Humans		Humans	900
90 000	Frogs			
27 000 000	Grasshoppers			27 000 000
1000 Tons	Grass			1000 Tons

Reducing Links in a Food Chain ▶

of beef will produce 150 pounds (67.5 kg) of human tissue. Countries like India and China cannot support their large populations with this food chain. This explains why the main ingredient in traditional Chinese cooking is rice. The Chinese eat only small amounts of meat. By using the land to grow plants that people eat, the land can support more people.

Corn Fields and Coral Reefs

Ecosystems vary in the amount of plant matter they are capable of producing. The biomass of plants that an ecosystem can produce in a unit area (acre or hectare) is its **productivity**. The most productive ecosystem is an aquatic ecosystem. Coral reefs produce 70,000 pounds (31,500 kg) of algae per acre (0.4 hectare) each year. Some of our best corn fields produce only 13,000 pounds (5,850 kg) of corn per acre in a good year. Mountain meadows produce only one or two pounds (0.45-0.9 kg) of plants per acre in a year.

The amount of food available is a limiting factor for a population in an ecosystem. Energy is not recycled. It is lost at each step in the food chain. Therefore, organisms that are at a higher level in the food chain will have less biomass.

TRY TO FIND OUT

Biomagnification is the concentration of a substance, such as a pollutant, in organisms that are at the top of the food chain. The pollutant is passed from one feeding level of organisms to the next feeding level in increasing concentrations. How did biomagnification lead to the near extinction of bald eagles through agricultural use of the pesticide DDT?

3.1 QUESTIONS FOR STUDY AND DISCUSSION

1. Define the following terms:
   biomass   pyramid of biomass
   evaporation   pyramid of numbers
   productivity   transpiration
2. What happens to solar energy when it strikes an object?
3. Explain why the air temperature on a golf course is cooler than the temperature in the center of a city a few miles or kilometres away.
4. What percentage of the solar energy reaching Earth is absorbed by plants and trapped by chlorophyll?
5. Explain the statement: "Without chlorophyll, there would be no food chains."

Building a Pyramid

6. Describe how you would determine the bio-mass of your lawn.
7. Why does the biomass of the organisms at each level in a food chain always form a pyramid?

8. Very little energy received by a plant becomes available to the organisms at the next level of the food chain. What happens to the rest of the energy?
9. Why did Mr. Schultz keep so many rabbits?
10. What percent of the grass eaten by a grass-hopper becomes grasshopper?

Numbers in a Pyramid

11. All food chains don't form a pyramid of numbers. Why?

The Population Connection

12. Why is the total mass of carnivores in an eco-system always less than the total mass of herbivores?
13. How do food chains in China and India differ from food chains in the United States? Why?

Corn Fields and Coral Reefs

14. Rank the following ecosystems in order from most to least productive: coral reef, field of corn, mountain meadow.

Science
Technology
Society

ISSUES

MANAGING A MINK RANCH

Your science teacher plans to retire. For additional income, he/she plans to raise mink. In the wild mink eat muskrats and other rodents. Mink ranches normally feed the mink waste from meat processing plants. Your teacher's plan is to raise rats to feed the mink. Rats produce 100 babies each year. All of the rats not needed for breeding will be fed to the mink.

Rats are omnivores and will eat the mink carcasses after the pelt has been removed. To cut expenses, the mink carcasses will be fed to the rats. According to your teacher, an additional supply of food will not be necessary. Each population will provide the total food supply for the other. In other words, rats will eat mink, and mink will eat rats.

- Will this plan work? Why or why not? If not, how could you make it work?

Cycles in the Ecosystem
4.1

The source of energy for nearly every ecosystem is the sun. Once the solar energy is converted to chemical energy, it may be used for essential life processes. Much of it is lost as heat. Energy passes through an ecosystem in much the same way that cars travel on a one-way street. It travels in only one direction — from sun to producer to consumer. The energy that is lost from the ecosystem must be constantly replaced by the process of photosynthesis.

Unlike energy, matter can be recycled within an ecosystem. **Matter** may be defined as anything that takes up space and has mass. Matter refers to all of the chemicals that make up the earth, the air, and the organisms in an ecosystem. The chemicals can not be created or destroyed, but they can be changed from one form to another.

Nature Recycles

Ecosphere — A totally enclosed ecosystem.

Imagine an aquarium that doesn't require someone to feed the fish. In a closed ecosystem, matter is never gained or lost. Working for NASA, Dr. Joe Hanson developed a totally closed aquatic ecosystem. Dr. Hanson carefully selected species of shrimp, algae, and microorganisms, and then he sealed them in glass containers. No one ever needs to feed the shrimp or change the water in the aquarium.

With controlled light and temperature conditions, the sealed ecosystems continue to function without the loss or gain of any matter. The light provides the energy, and the microorganisms recycle the chemicals. Most human-made ecosystems are not closed ecosystems. They usually require huge inputs of matter. Zoos are an excellent example of an unnatural ecosystem where matter is not recycled within the system.

In natural ecosystems, some matter is gained or lost, but most matter is recycled. Although it is unusual, meteors and debris from outer space sometimes inject matter into an ecosystem. It is far more likely that matter entering an ecosystem was removed from another ecosystem by wind or water. Water sometimes removes large amounts of soil from an ecosystem and deposits it in an aquatic ecosystem. Wind picks up and carries small particles and gases great distances. Rain cleanses the air and deposits the matter in a distant ecosystem.

Human activities sometimes disrupt the normal flow of matter and threaten the continued existence of the ecosystem. The **biogeochemical cycles**, the flow of chemicals between the environment and organisms in it, are essential to the survival of all ecosystems. As you study each cycle, give particular attention to the potential environmental impacts of technology.

The Carbon-Oxygen Cycle

Carbon dioxide (CO_2) from the atmosphere is used by plants in the process of photosynthesis. Using light energy, plants combine carbon dioxide and water to form sugar. The sugar is both a source of energy and a building block for other compounds such as proteins, oils, and starches. The compounds produced by plants contain carbon and are called **organic chemicals**.

Plants give off oxygen (O_2) as a waste product. Although most of the oxygen in our atmosphere is produced by algae in the ocean, trees are also an important source. The oxygen is used by both plants and animals in the process of respiration. In **respiration**, the compounds containing carbon — the organic chemicals — are broken down, and carbon dioxide is released. When respiration occurs without enough oxygen, the organic chemicals are not completely broken down, and the new organic chemicals that result often have offensive odors.

The Carbon-Oxygen cycle is out of balance. There is more carbon dioxide being released into the atmosphere than is being removed from it. Most of the carbon dioxide is produced during the process of burning — **combustion**. When compounds containing carbon — coal, oil, or wood — are burned, the carbon is chemically combined with oxygen, and carbon dioxide is released. In a short period of time, combustion releases large amounts of carbon dioxide into the atmosphere. The use of carbon dioxide by plants during photosynthesis is a much slower process. As a result of the imbalance between these two processes, the level of carbon dioxide in the atmosphere is increasing. In Unit II we will examine the possible effects of the increasing levels of carbon dioxide.

Photosynthesis

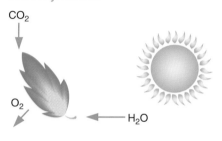

CO_2

O_2

H_2O

Smokestacks at coal-burning power plants and industries release huge amounts of carbon dioxide and water vapor into the atmosphere.

Algae, such as this seaweed clinging to the rocks and microscopic algae (phytoplankton) produce most of the oxygen in the atmosphere.

Carbon-Oxygen Cycle

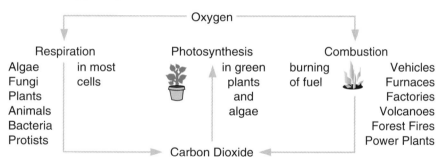

Oxygen

Respiration
Algae
Fungi
Plants
Animals
Bacteria
Protists
in most cells

Photosynthesis
in green plants and algae

Combustion
burning of fuel
Vehicles
Furnaces
Factories
Volcanoes
Forest Fires
Power Plants

Carbon Dioxide

D I D   Y O U   K N O W ?

Farmers use the nitrogen cycle to enrich the soil and help crops? Wise farmers rotate crops alternating crops that demand a lot of nitrogen with legumes, such as alfalfa. Planting legumes adds beneficial nitrogen to the soil. Before the legumes are mature, farmers plow them into the soil. The rotting plants also add needed organic matter to the soil. This process reduces the amount of fertilizer the farmer must add when planting the next crop.

When plants and animals die, the carbon compounds in their bodies are broken down by decomposers, and carbon dioxide is returned to the atmosphere. During the process of decay other chemicals are also returned to the soil or released into the air. One of these chemicals is nitrogen.

The Nitrogen Cycle

Without plants and decomposers, the carbon — oxygen cycle would stop. Plants and decomposers also make the nitrogen cycle go, but there is another group of organisms that is important to this cycle — the nitrogen "fixers." Plants and animals need nitrogen to make protein. The air is about 78 percent nitrogen, but plants and animals cannot use nitrogen (N_2) directly from the atmosphere.

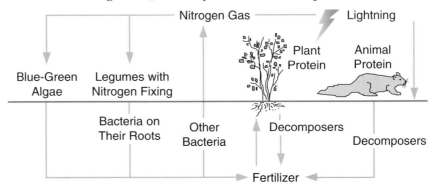

Nitrogen Cycle ▶

Special bacteria, in the soil and water, must change or "fix" nitrogen gas (N_2) into — nitrate (NO_3^-) or ammonium (NH_4^+) ions — nitrogen fertilizers that plants can use. These bacteria are called **nitrogen fixers**. Most nitrogen-fixing bacteria live in little houses, or **nodules**, on the roots of plants called legumes. **Legumes** are members of a large family of plants that includes peas, beans, alfalfa, clover, vetches, and locust trees. The plants provide food and cover for the bacteria. The bacteria convert nitrogen gas into fertilizer for the plant.

Animals get nitrogen from plants or from other plant-eating animals, in the form of protein. The nitrogen is recycled by special bacteria that break down the nitrogen compounds (proteins) in dead plants and animals, and in animal wastes. If the nitrogen fertilizers are not used by plants, the fertilizer may be recycled by special forms of bacteria. These bacteria convert the unused fertilizer into nitrogen gas that is released into the atmosphere. All natural ecosystems depend upon bacteria to keep the nitrogen cycle going.

Lightning plays a small role in the nitrogen cycle. The huge amount of electrical energy, that we call lightning combines nitrogen and oxygen (NO). Dissolved in the rain, the "fixed" nitrogen enters the soil where bacteria convert it into nitrate fertilizer.

To grow crops that require large amounts of nitrogen, farmers must add commercial fertilizers. Fertilizer manufacturers take nitrogen from the air and hydrogen from natural gas and combine them in a high pressure, high temperature environment. Since this process is very expensive, farmers often plant legume crops to take advantage of their ability to fix nitrogen.

Oxygen is needed for combustion, and the source of oxygen is the atmosphere which contains 79 percent nitrogen. The high temperature created during the process of combustion causes nitrogen and oxygen to combine forming nitrogen oxides. Motor vehicles, factories, power plants, forest fires, fireplaces and even grills are all sources of nitrogen oxides. While their fertilizing effect may benefit some crops, there are some disadvantages. These will be discussed in Unit II.

The Mineral Cycle

Most of the minerals in an ecosystem are stored in rock. They are released from the rocks by the action of wind, water, and changes in temperature. The process of physical and chemical forces releasing minerals from rocks is called **weathering**.

Wind sometimes acts as a sand-blaster breaking off small particles of the rock. Rocks are broken apart when water freezes and thaws. Rocks are also broken apart by the action of the roots. Plant roots exert a great amount of force as they grow. This can be seen when walking along a sidewalk on a tree-lined street. The tree roots often cause sections of the concrete to crack. The foundations of buildings and underground pipes are sometimes cracked by the growth of tree roots. This is physical weathering.

What forces will cause weathering of the rocks shown in this picture?

Chemical weathering occurs when acidic rain dissolves minerals in the rocks. Roots also produce chemicals that dissolve minerals in the rocks. Trees absorb some of the minerals. Others are carried away by water moving through the soil. This process is known as **leaching**.

Due to leaching and mining, the mineral cycle is a leaky cycle. **Mining** is the process of removing a natural substance from an ecosystem faster than it is replaced. Humans mine many minerals — aluminum, zinc, lead, gold, and phosphorous. You can think of others. We often remove these materials for use in our human-made

◀ Mineral Cycle

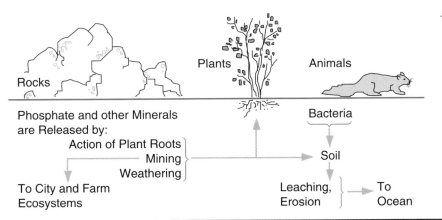

The tiny water droplets in these clouds are formed by the process of condensation.

ecosystems. Some of the minerals will be recycled and used over and over again. Others will be discarded in a landfill.

Mineral particles are also removed from an ecosystem by the action of wind and water. This process is called **erosion**. The mineral particles carried away by the flowing water may become a part of a sand bar in a large river or they may be deposited in the ocean. Whether they are removed from the cycle by leaching, mining, or erosion, the minerals are no longer available to the ecosystem.

The Water Cycle

Water enters the atmosphere by one of two processes — evaporation or transpiration. Water is lost from all surface water — rivers, lakes, streams, oceans — through the process of evaporation. Since the oceans cover more than 70 percent of the earth's surface, most water enters the air through the process of evaporation.

Water evaporates from the surfaces of cells within a leaf. The water then diffuses out of the leaf through openings called stomata. The loss of water from the leaves of plants is called **transpiration**. It is estimated that one acre (0.4 hectare) of corn may lose as much as 500,000 gallons (2 million litres) of water through transpiration during the growing season.

As the air cools, the water vapor collects into tiny droplets that form clouds. This process is called **condensation**. As the droplets become heavier, they begin to fall. The temperature of the air determines the form of moisture — rain, snow, sleet, or hail. All moisture falling from the atmosphere is collectively called **precipitation**.

Most of the precipitation falls into the oceans or other bodies of water. If the precipitation falls on land it either enters the soil or runs off the surface. Run-off flows into streams where the water begins its journey back to the ocean.

Infiltration is the process of water soaking into the soil. Water that enters the soil may be used by plants, or it may move through the soil until it reaches a layer of impermeable rock or clay. This layer of water is called **ground water**. Ground water is an important source

Water Cycle ▶

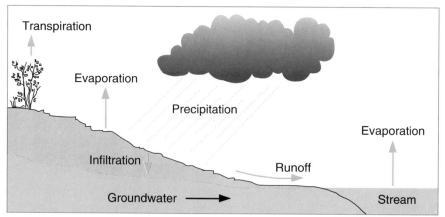

of drinking water for many people. It may flow from the ground at a spring or be pumped from a well.

The amount of precipitation is an important factor in determining the type of ecosystem and the population of organisms it can support. Unit IV investigates the water cycle in much more detail.

4.1 QUESTIONS FOR STUDY AND DISCUSSION

1. Define the following terms:

   biogeochemical cycles   nitrogen fixers
   combustion   organic compounds
   condensation   photosynthesis
   evaporation   precipitation
   ground water   respiration
   infiltration   runoff
   matter   weathering
   mining

2. Compare the flow of matter and energy through an ecosystem.

Nature Recycles

3. How did Dr. Hanson's ecosystems differ from most human-made and natural ecosystems?
4. Compare the recycling of matter in natural ecosystems and in human-made ecosystems.

The Carbon-Oxygen Cycle

5. What process uses carbon dioxide and produces oxygen?
6. What product of photosynthesis contains carbon?
7. What kind of organism produces most of the world's oxygen supply?
8. What two processes produce carbon dioxide? What process produces most of the carbon dioxide in the atmosphere?
9. By what process do decomposers return carbon dioxide to the atmosphere?
10. How is carbon dioxide produced during a fire?

The Nitrogen Cycle

11. What kinds of organisms are essential for the nitrogen cycle?
12. What two types of organisms are nitrogen fixers?
13. Identify plants that are legumes and explain how they are important to the nitrogen cycle.

14. Identify the form(s) of nitrogen that can be used by:
    A. plants   B. animals   C. decomposers
    D. nitrogen-fixing bacteria   E. blue-green algae
15. In what way is lightning important to the nitrogen cycle?
16. Explain how pesticides could stop the nitrogen cycle.
17. Why do farmers plant legume crops?
18. What is the connection between the oxygen cycle and the nitrogen cycle?

The Mineral Cycle

19. How are minerals removed from rocks?
20. Give examples of chemical and physical weathering.
21. Identify three processes that create "leaks" in the mineral cycle.

The Water Cycle

22. Identify the two processes that return water to the atmosphere.
23. Most water enters the air by which process?
24. What is the term that describes all forms of moisture leaving the atmosphere?
25. What is the process in which water vapor collects to form tiny droplets?
26. Identify the terms that describe what happens to water when it falls on land.
27. What term describes the water held in a layer of porous rock beneath the ground?

Think About It

28. What would happen if the amount of carbon dioxide in the atmosphere were to decrease drastically? to increase?
29. List some ways that industrial activity has changed the natural cycles.

5.1 Succession — Changing Ecosystems

TRY TO FIND OUT

How is fire an important regulator of ecosystem succession? Did human activity affect the devastating fires in Yellowstone National Park in 1988 or the terrible fires that destroyed parts of Los Angeles in 1993?

What would you see if you studied the same ecosystem year after year? One group of organisms will almost always be replaced by another. The series of changes that occur in an ecosystem with the passing of time is **succession**. It is the "aging" of the ecosystem.

Why does an ecosystem age? Organisms change the environment in which they live. The new environment is no longer a suitable habitat for the organisms that first lived there.

If a field is not mowed, trees begin to grow. As the trees get larger they shade the ground below. The grasses that grew well in the full sunlight will not survive in the shade. The animals that lived in the field, and fed on the grasses, will move to a new area in search of a better food source. Those organisms that cannot move will die as the environment changes.

Succession occurs in all ecosystems. In cold or dry climates the rate of succession may be extremely slow. The rate of succession may be altered by human activities. Ecologists have studied the changes that occur in various ecosystems. Sometimes they may interrupt the process in order to maintain the habitat for a rare or endangered species.

A pond is not a pond forever. As it grows old, it gets drier and drier. Ponds provide a particularly good example of succession. If you conduct a survey of ponds in your community, you may be able to locate ponds in each of the stages of succession described below.

When first formed, a pond has a sandy or muddy bottom. This "bare bottom" stage is the **pioneer stage**. The species of animals that live in the pond depend upon the "bare bottom." Mussels, a type of fresh water clam, cannot move across the bottom of the pond if plants are growing there. The caddis fly larva species that lives in a pond in the pioneer stage will not remain in the pond when the bottom is covered with plants. It uses sand from the bottom of the pond to build the case or "house" in which it lives.

Some species of fish make nests in mud that covers the pond's bottom. These fish will stop reproducing when the bottom of the pond becomes covered with plants. Animals that live in the pond during the pioneer stage feed on the small floating organisms — algae, protozoans, bacteria, and crustaceans.

Grass sprouts along the bank of this newly dug pond. What stage of succession is it?

When first formed, a pond has a sandy or muddy bottom. This is the pioneer stage.

Ponds weeds grow in the humus, but they don't reach the surface. This is the submerged plant state.

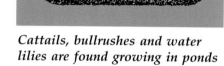

Cattails, bullrushes and water lilies are found growing in ponds which are in the emerging plant stage.

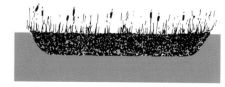

There are no large areas of open water. The pond has now become a marsh.

In time, the death and decay of organisms forms a layer of organic matter that covers the bottom of the pond. This layer of humus allows larger algae and small aquatic plants (pond weeds) to grow on the bottom of the pond. Since the plants do not reach the surface of the water, this stage is called the **submerged plant stage**.

The original fish are replaced by other species that lay their eggs on the leaves of the plants. Dragonfly and mayfly nymphs burrow in the muddy bottom. New species of mussels and caddis fly larva replace the species found in the bare-bottomed stage. The submerged plants and algae provide new habitats for organisms found in this stage.

As the pond continues to fill in, the thicker layer of soil on the bottom allows larger plants to become rooted. Cattails and bulrushes grow near the edge of the pond, and water lilies may be seen floating near the middle. This is the **emerging plant stage**.

At this point, organisms found in the pioneer stage are entirely gone. The emerging plants provide stems for those air-breathing organisms that need to climb to the surface for a breath of oxygen. The burrowing dragonfly nymphs are replaced by a new species that climbs on the submerged parts of the bulrushes. The gill-breathing snails are replaced by lung-breathing snails.

Diving spiders rest on the exposed bulrush and cattail stalks and feed on the abundant mayfly and dragonfly nymphs. The nymphs cling to the submerged stalks, then climb to the surface, shed their exoskeleton, and fly away. A species of caddis fly larvae, that is new to the neighborhood, makes its "house" from parts of water plants.

Worms live in the bottom mud, and aquatic insect larvae provide food for diving beetles. Frogs, turtles, and salamanders find plenty of food and places to rest. A few fish, such as catfish, may be found scavenging on the bottom. Leeches may feed on the fish or on an ecologist who wades in to study succession.

The stagnant water in the plant-choked pond has a low level of oxygen. Organisms that require a high oxygen level cannot survive. Crayfish solve this problem by carrying their eggs and young with them.

More years pass, and the pond becomes filled with plants, waste products, and bodies of dead organisms. When there are no longer any large areas of open water, the pond becomes a **marsh**. It is now

Drier than a marsh, the swamp supports the growth of trees that don't mind having wet "feet".

Soil carried by floods is deposited in the swamp. The drier ground supports a beech-maple forest.

On the prairie, flowers bloom in spring. Fires prevent the growth of trees.

Can you identify the stage of succession?

an area of shallow water with grasses and other rooted plants.

The truly aquatic animals die in the shallow, muddy water of the marsh. Frogs, salamanders, crayfish and leeches remain, but the fish cannot survive. Turtles and snakes may feed on the frogs or on dying fish. Often the adults cannot survive, but their eggs survive the summer and winter months and produce the species the following spring. This is why we may find many small organisms in temporary ponds each spring.

The water supply may come from springs or from a stream or lake. Some marshes are entirely dependent upon rainfall for their supply of water. The marsh may dry out completely during the summer. Salt water marshes depend on the tides to bring in water with a supply of food and oxygen. Only animals that can burrow in the mud or move with the tide can survive in a salt water marsh.

The marsh becomes drier as the organic matter continues to build up. Trees, such as the swamp maples, begin to invade the area. The marsh has now become a swamp. The swamp will be wet, maybe flooded, during spring and fall. The floods will deposit soil in the swamp. As the area continues to fill in, more trees invade, and the ecosystem is now a beech and maple forest.

On the western plains the marsh seldom enters the swamp and forest stages. Instead, the marsh becomes a grassland or prairie. Why don't trees invade? Fires swept by the strong winds frequently spread across hundreds of miles on the Great Plains. Fires and farm machinery (mowing machines and plows) don't give trees a chance to grow. In areas where farming doesn't occur and fires have been controlled, succession has reached the forest stage.

5.1 QUESTIONS FOR STUDY AND DISCUSSION

1. Define the following terms:
   succession   marsh
   humus   swamp
2. The kinds of organisms found in an old ecosystem are not the same as those found in a younger ecosystem. Why do some organisms disappear and others flourish in the area?
3. As you read, (1) identify the stage of succession shown in each of the diagrams, (2) identify the major types of plants that are present in each stage of succession.
4. A turtle enters a pond and starts to move across the bottom. What will the turtle find if the pond is in the pioneer stage?
5. Water lilies are floating on the pond. What does this tell you about the age of the pond?

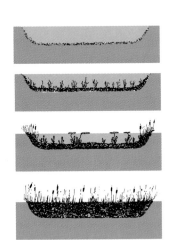

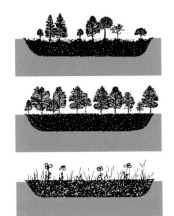

6. Identify the first stage of succession in which each of the following organisms would be found.

Stages
1. beech-maple forest
2. emerging plant stage
3. marsh
4. pioneer stage
5. submerged plant stage
6. swamp

Organisms
A. caddis fly larvae with cases made from plants
B. caddis fly larvae with cases of sand
C. dragonfly nymphs that climbs to the surface
D. mussels that move across the bottom
E. fish which lay eggs on leaves
F. fish which nest on the bottom
G. diving spiders
H. frogs and salamanders, but no fish

7. Arrange the stages listed in question 5 in the proper order in which they occur. Write the name of each stage.
8. How does a swamp differ from a marsh?
9. What happens to the level of dissolved oxygen in the water as the pond ages?
10. Explain how the emerging plants are important to some animals in the pond.
11. Explain why marshland sometimes becomes grassland or prairie instead of forest.
12. What natural event stops succession?

5.2 CASE STUDY
The Disappearing Lake

Ten thousand years ago, in much of the northern United States, snow would not stop falling. Summer never came. Large masses of ice called **glaciers** formed.

Glaciers slide along the ground like snow slides down a roof. Glaciers are very heavy, and as they move over the land, they scrape the rock and/or soil underneath. Pieces of rock are broken off. As these rocks are carried along by the glacier, they make scratches and grooves in the rock below. Glaciers sometimes act as snow plows or bulldozers pushing ridges of rock in front of them.

Kettle Lake

Kettle Lakes

Eventually, temperatures began to rise, and the glaciers started to melt. Rocks that had been carried or pushed by the glacier were left behind. The glaciers that pushed rocks in front of them left a ridge of rocky debris. While some deposits formed small ridges, other ridges were large enough to create a dam. Behind some dams, a deep hole with steep sides had been gouged out of the rock. When the ice in this hole melted, a kettle lake was formed.

Kettle lakes are different from other lakes; they have no entrances or exits. There are no streams that bring water to the lake. The water in the original lake came from the melting block of ice. Now the only sources of water are runoff from the surrounding land — the **watershed** — and precipitation that falls

Black Spruce

Orchid

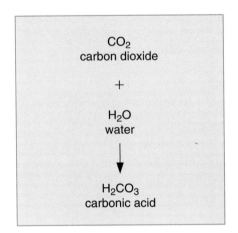

CO₂
carbon dioxide

+

H₂O
water

↓

H₂CO₃
carbonic acid

into the lake. Since there are no streams that drain water from the lake, most water is lost by evaporation.

Indians lived along the shores of these lakes and fished in their waters. The lakes were an important source of water for the Indians and for the animals that came to the lake. The area made an ideal hunting ground for the Indians. This new lake may not have seemed that different from other lakes where the Indians camped.

The Indians may have named the lake when it was in the pioneer stage — its bottom covered with glacial rocks. The fish the Indians caught may have fed on caddisflies. The sand, used by the caddisflies to make their cases, was transported from Canada by the glacier.

Freshwater mussels and fish fed on the small floating organisms that lived in the lake. As these organisms died, their decomposed bodies began to cover the rocky bottom of the lake. Where sunlight reached the bottom, larger plants and algae grew. The lake had now entered the **submerged plant stage**.

Like any other lake, the kettle lake began to "age." Without a flow of water, little mud is carried into the lake. The runoff from the lake's watershed is filtered by the leaves on the forest floor. Few nutrients enter the lake. Without mud and nutrients carried by a stream, the "aging" of the lake is a very slow process.

Without flowing water, there is little oxygen mixing with the water in the lake. As the organisms in the lake use oxygen, the level of dissolved oxygen decreases. Eventually the low level of oxygen becomes a limiting factor for fish, and the fish eventually disappear from the lake.

Without flowing water, the carbon dioxide produced by the organisms is trapped in the lake. It chemically combines with water to form carbonic acid (H_2CO_3). As the bacteria work to decompose the dying layers of sphagnum moss, they produce more and more carbon dioxide. The bacteria also produce another waste product — tannic acid.

The bacteria must work in an environment having a limited supply of oxygen. When your muscle cells work without enough oxygen, a waste product called **lactic acid** is made. When bacteria break down plant material, they produce a waste product called **tannic acid**. Tannic acid is an amber color, and it gives the water in the lake the appearance of a large cup of "tea." The increasing concentrations of carbonic and tannic acids make the water too acidic for most organisms.

A Floating Mat

A pond or lake with a flow of water becomes a marsh, then a swamp. In ponds and lakes without a good flow of water, the marsh and swamp stages are replaced by a stage of succession called a **bog**. The lack of oxygen and the increasing acidity are limiting factors that determine which plants and animals will survive in the bog ecosystem. Only a few species of plants can live in this harsh environment.

Along the shoreline of the lake, rooted plants began to creep out toward the open water. Willow trees, growing on the shore, dip the tips of their branches into the water. The tips act as floating islands that collect leaves and other debris. The lake is entering the **emerging plant stage**.

Sedges and other grasses invade the water at the edge of the lake. Sphagnum moss begins to grow around the sedges and other rooted plants near the shore. It also begins to grow on the floating islands made by the willow branches. Sphagnum moss is an evergreen plant that never dies. It continues to grow at the top, and as it grows, it extends outward, floating on the surface like a green raft.

The raft gradually begins to sink as its weight increases. As it sinks, the lower part of the moss dies and begins to decay. It doesn't decompose completely, because the high acid level in the deep water kills the bacteria that cause decay.

The mat of partly decayed moss is called **peat**. It becomes many feet thick and will eventually fill the entire lake. In countries, like Ireland and Denmark, peat is used for fuel. In other countries, where there is a better fuel supply, peat is sold at garden centers for mulching and potting mixes.

In a bog, the sphagnum mat acts as a gigantic sponge. It can absorb as much as 25 times its weight in water. It is said that the Indians used the sphagnum to line their back packs. Perhaps it was the papoose, the American Indian baby, who had the first disposable diapers!

Sphagnum was also important as a bandaging material. Since the acidity did not allow bacteria to grow, it made a clean dressing for wounds. The Indians and the American soldiers used it for bandages.

The Eye of the Bog

In the center of the bog is the last remnant of the lake. This last remaining area of open water is called the **eye of the bog**. Here the water is still deep enough to support the floating lily pads. While the lilies may be the dominant plant in the emerging plant stage, sphagnum moss is the dominant plant of the bog stage. As the mat grows thicker, it provides a place for other plants to grow. The sphagnum mat closes in on the eye, and the lilies are replaced by bog cotton, orchids and other plants that like to live in a slightly drier habitat.

Few kinds of plants can tolerate the high level of acidity and the low level of oxygen in the sphagnum mat. For those plants

Peat Mining

T R Y   T O   F I N D   O U T

Bogs are famous for their abundance of carnivorous plants—plants that trap insects as food. Sundew and the Venus fly trap are common bog plants that "eat" insects. How have plants growing in bogs adapted to this carnivorous lifestyle. Why do they need to trap insects for food? How do they lure insects to their death?

that can survive, the rate of growth is very slow due to the lack of nutrients. A few plants compensate for the lack of minerals by capturing and digesting insects. The sundew and pitcher plants are found in northern bogs. The Venus flytrap is common in bogs in the South where the temperatures are warmer.

The Invasion of Woody Plants

Several types of shrubs, including leatherleaf, blueberry, cranberry, bog rosemary, and bog laurel, begin to grow on the sections of the mat that are more solid. These plants are replaced by larger shrubs like witch hazel and poison sumac. Poison sumac is a shrub with a distinctive branching pattern, but it is easiest to identify after it has formed its white berries.

The bark of poison sumac contains a chemical that is far more irritating to the skin than poison ivy. Anyone planning to hike through a swamp or a bog should first learn to identify poison sumac. Poison sumac only grows in wet areas. Many people confuse poison sumac with the staghorn sumac. Since staghorn sumac likes to keep its feet dry, it is never found in a swamp or bog. It can easily be identified by its bright red seed clusters. Poison sumac has white berries.

Surrounding the zone of shrubs, near the original shoreline, trees begin to grow in the sphagnum mat. The type of tree is determined by the location of the bog. In addition to rocks, the glaciers also carried seeds. The constant evaporation of water from the bog makes it cooler than the surrounding area, and the plants of the bog may be species that are usually found in northern regions. Black spruce and tamarack, also known as larch, are species native to Canada, but they are found in **boreal** (northern) bogs in the northern United States.

The species of trees found in bogs are those that can tolerate the highly acidic and extremely wet conditions. The tree roots grow near the surface of the sphagnum mat. They do not provide the support of deeper roots, and the trees are easily blown over by the wind. Tree rings show that the trees growing in the bog are hundreds of years old, yet they are only a few inches in diameter. While the lack of nutrients in the moss mat doesn't prevent a tree from growing in a bog, it is the major limiting factor for the rate of growth.

Some birds, reptiles, amphibians, and insects make their home in the bog. Some species, such as the bog turtle, are only found in bogs. As succession continues in the bog, the bog becomes drier and less acidic. The trees of the bog are replaced by the hardwoods — beeches, red maples, and oaks — that grow in the woods nearby. The animals that live in the bog are replaced by their land-loving counterparts. In time, the bog changes into a hardwood forest.

1. How do glaciers change the land?
2. How are kettle lakes formed?
3. How are kettle lakes different from other lakes?
4. What are the sources of water for a kettle lake?
5. Describe the bottom of a kettle lake that is in the pioneer stage.
6. What is the second stage of succession?
7. Why does a kettle lake "age" more slowly than other lakes?
8. As the lake "ages" will the level of oxygen increase or decrease?
9. As the lake "ages" will the level of carbon dioxide increase or decrease?
10. When carbon dioxide combines with water it forms _____.
11. Identify another acid produced when the bacteria break down the dead plant matter.
12. Describe the appearance of water which contains tannic acid.

A Floating Mat

13. Lakes with water flowing through them become marshes and finally swamps. What do lakes without a water flow become?
14. What are two important limiting factors for the growth of plants in a bog?
15. What plants grow near the edge of the lake during the emerging plant stage?
16. Describe how sphagnum moss grows.
17. Why doesn't the dead sphagnum moss decay completely?
18. What is the name of partly decomposed sphagnum moss?
19. Describe at least three ways that sphagnum or peat moss has been used.

The Eye of the Bog

20. Describe the "eye of the bog."
21. What is the dominant plant in the bog? What plants might you find growing on the mat?
22. Why do some of the plants in the bog "eat" insects? Name some of the insect-eating plants that may be found in a bog.

The Invasion of Woody Plants

23. Name some of the shrubs that grow in the bog.
24. Which of these shrubs is poisonous?
25. Name the "northern" species of trees that are found growing in a boreal bog.
26. Explain why some species of trees aren't found in the bog?
27. How does the size of a spruce tree growing in the bog compare to the size of a spruce tree growing outside the bog? What causes this difference?
28. What is the final stage of succession for a bog ecosystem?
29. Name one species of animal that lives only in a bog.
30. Would you expect to find fish in the "eye of the bog"? If not, what limiting factors make the eye unsuitable habitat for fish.
31. The center circle represents the "eye of the bog." The largest circle represents the original shore of the kettle lake. Copy the diagram on your paper and write the number of each plant listed below in the zone where it would most likely be found. Some plants might be found in more than one zone.
    1. black spruce
    2. cranberry
    3. sphagnum moss
    4. lily pads
    5. pitcher plants
    6. leatherleaf
    7. bog cotton
    8. poison sumac
    9. tamarack
    10. sundew
    11. orchids
    12. red maple

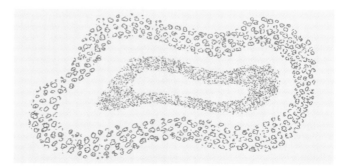

The Disappearing Lake

" . . . two hundred fifty years at least. That's old-growth bark, all kinds of animals can live in it. That's habitat."
Chris Maser
forest consultant

Most people, when asked to define a forest, would probably say "a place with trees," but a forest is much more than that. It is a complex ecosystem. When settlers came to America, they found much of it covered with **virgin forest** ecosystems. The word **virgin** refers to something that has not been altered by human activity. It is estimated that only 10% of the original forests remain. The future of the remaining **old-growth forests**, virgin stands of timber whose ancient trees have never been logged, is a hotly debated issue. Perhaps there is a lesson to be learned from the past.

Majestic trees grow in a virgin stand of timber in the Olympic National Forest.

Penn's Woods

There were 29 million acres (11.6 million hectares) of virgin forest in the colony founded by William Penn. The name of the Commonwealth — Pennsylvania — means "Penn's woods." The largest tract of virgin woods that remains in eastern Pennsylvania today is the 649-acre (260-hectare) Woodbourne Forest and Wildlife Sanctuary. It is owned by **The Nature Conservancy** — an organization whose goal is to preserve the best examples of a wide variety of unique ecosystems.

Indians saw the virgin forest as a source of food and a dwelling place of their God. The colonist's feared the forest and the animals that lived in it. This fear is reflected in *Little Red Riding Hood* and other popular children's stories. The colonists viewed the forest as an obstacle to agriculture, and they began clearing the land. Clearing was often accomplished with fire, and thousands of acres of forest were burned by fires that were often out of control.

For the first 200 years logging was primarily done to clear land for crops. The first sawmills were water-powered, and only a few existed. More than two-thirds of Pennsylvania was still covered with virgin forest in 1820. With increased demand for wood and improved technology, the rate of logging increased. By 1860 Pennsylvania had become the lumber-producing capital of the world.

WHAT DO YOU THINK?

Are "tree farms" forests? After clearcutting, lumber companies may plant the cleared area with a single species of tree, all lined up in neat rows. These single-species replantings are known as "tree farms." The logging industry prefers to call this "reforestation." Do you think this practice recreates a real forest? How do you think a tree farm differs from a forest?

Much of the wood was wasted. Frequently loggers removed only the prime log, and the remaining portion of the tree was left to decay. Hemlock was cut only for its bark. The bark, rich in tannic acid, was used in the tanning of leather. The log itself was not valuable, so it was left to decay on the forest floor. When owners sold the land, they often kept **bark rights** that allowed them to continue cutting trees and selling bark.

By 1900 the boom was over, and many towns became ghost towns. Hillsides were bare and gullies were filled with logs and branches. The young forests that grew would once again be cleared by forest fires and logging. Today the State of Pennsylvania owns and manages some two million acres of forest, but there are only a few isolated stands of virgin woods.

As the large stands of ancient trees disappeared in the East, the timber industry expanded westward. Today the lumber capital is somewhere in the Pacific Northwest — Washington, Oregon, or perhaps British Columbia. The logging communities in the Pacific Northwest are at the center of a national debate over the issue of logging the remaining old-growth forests.

Old-Growth Forests

The old-growth forests of the Pacific Northwest are noted for the many huge majestic Douglas fir trees that are hundreds of years old, but within the old-growth forest there are trees of all sizes and ages. While Douglas fir is the dominant species of tree, it is not the only species.

The variety of tree species and the different sizes and ages of trees in an old-growth forest help to make it a healthy ecosystem. A forest needs healthy mature trees to produce seeds that may grow into new trees or provide food for wildlife, but dead and dying trees also play important roles in the ecosystem. The standing dead trees or **snags** create habitats for insects and small mammals.

When a huge old snag topples during a storm, it opens up the canopy letting sunlight reach the forest floor. Fallen trees provide food and cover for wildlife and return nutrients to the soil. Some downed logs become **nurse logs** where young seedlings take root and grow. Nurse logs are evidence of the natural recycling processes that occur in an ecosystem.

The old-growth forest is a rich and diverse ecosystem. **Biodiversity** — the variety of plant and animal species in an ecosystem — determines the stability of the ecosystem. The greater the biodiversity of an ecosystem, the more stable the ecosystem will be. Ancient forests provide the unique habitats required by more than one hundred species of vertebrates. One massive tree supports an estimated 1,500 invertebrates — that's biodiversity!

Old-growth forests in the Pacific Northwest are noted for the huge majestic Douglas fir trees. Should this tree be cut?

Flying Squirrel Digging for Truffles

The northern spotted owl is an indicator species — a species whose presence indicates a healthy ecosystem.

Some species that need old-growth habitat are in trouble. Forest Service studies of California's Sierra Nevada forests found that the fisher, the Sierra Nevada red fox, the pine marten and the wolverine are at risk. All of these species are carnivores and need large areas of old-growth for hunting.

Some birds are also threatened with extinction. The marbled murrelet, a seabird that nests in the old-growth forest, is considered endangered and the northern spotted owl is listed as a threatened species. The northern spotted owl is an **indicator species** — a species whose presence indicates a healthy ecosystem. We know that the northern spotted owl needs large tracts of old-growth forests to survive. One study showed that a nesting pair of owls used more than 3,000 acres (1,200 hectares) of old-growth forest.

Can the old-growth forest survive without the owl? The owl is an important limiting factor for the small mammal populations. One of the owl's favorite foods is the northern flying squirrel, but it also feeds on red-backed voles and other small mammals. Flying squirrels, red-backed voles and other small mammals feed on truffles.

A **truffle** is a kind of fungus that produces a massive network of filaments that grow through the soil and penetrate the outer cells of the tree roots. The fungi help the tree absorb minerals, nitrogen and water from the soil. In turn, the root cells provide the fungi with food. The fungi also produce a chemical that stimulates the growth of the new root tips. Scientists say that these fungi are absolutely essential to the survival of trees.

Unlike mushrooms, the spore-filled reproductive structure of the truffles remains below ground. When the spores are ripe, the truffles give off an odor. Small mammals detect the odor, and dig for the golf ball-sized fungi that grow beneath the forest floor.

When squirrels, voles, and mice feed on these fungi, they carry the spores to new sites. The spores travel through their digestive system unharmed and are deposited with their wastes. Some animals deposit the spores nearby while others carry the spores to areas where trees have been cut. Here the fungus stimulates the growth of new trees. The relationships between truffles, flying squirrels, and the northern spotted owl is an example of the many interactions that occur in old-growth forests.

Streams in old-growth forests are among the cleanest streams in the world. They are ideal habitat for trout and salmon. The thick mat of decaying material on the forest floor holds and filters the water entering the streams. Streams in areas that are logged become choked with silt and woody debris. The fish populations of the northwest rivers have suffered from the effects of logging.

Multiple Use Management

Most old-growth timber on private land is already gone. Nearly all remaining old-growth wood is in National Forests that are managed by the federal government. Only those old-growth forests that are in National Parks or designated Wilderness Areas are protected. The US Forest Service can sell permits to log most of the remaining old-growth forests.

There are 191 million acres in 156 National Forests. The law requires National Forests and other federal lands to be managed for **multiple uses** — logging, mining, watershed protection, grazing, recreation, and fish and wildlife habitat. The local economy is often based on the "uses" that are permitted on the federally owned land. The Allegheny National Forest, in northwestern Pennsylvania, provides an example of "multiple use" forest management.

Streams in old-growth forests are among the cleanest streams in the world.

The Economic Impact of the Allegheny National Forest		
Use	Jobs Created	Value of Use
wood products	970	$48,400,000
oil and gas	950	$30,000,000
recreation	2,700	$91,000,000
Total	4,620	$169,400,000

Managing land for multiple uses isn't easy, and conflicts often occur. Pennsylvania Fish Commission data shows that the water quality of streams is being damaged by improper disposal of waste water from oil-and-gas production. The Forest Service admits that protecting ospreys and bald eagles during their breeding season is possible only "if the oil and gas operator is willing."

Sharp declines in the populations of bald eagles, black bears, river otters, pine martens, and Sitka black-tailed deer are expected due to logging in Alaska's Tongass National Forest. Critics of the Forest Service say that too often timber harvest is given priority over other uses. The Forest Service is quick to point out that the final decision on how much timber will be sold each year is made by Congress.

Conflict in the Northwest

The issue of logging old-growth forests is the most controversial environmental issue in the Pacific Northwest. Environmentalists are fighting to save the disappearing old-growth ecosystem.

A logger would say that this tree was overmature. What would an ecologist say?

Advances in technology have reduced the number of workers needed in the logging industry.

Ecologists believe the wood should stay in the forest. From an ecological point of view, there is no such thing as waste in a forest. The death and decay of a Douglas fir tree provide for the life of many other organisms.

Foresters, hired by commercial lumber companies, consider the old growth forest "overmature." To the forester, timber is a crop, and the crop is ready for harvest. Because of their size and mass, the old-growth trees provide valuable lumber. The clear, straight, tight-grained wood of an old-growth tree is far superior to wood from younger trees. Foresters hired by the timber industry believe it is wasteful to allow this valuable wood to decompose on the forest floor. They view the 200-year-old trees in terms of the board-feet of lumber the tree will yield.

Loggers and millworkers are fighting to save their jobs and the region's economy. Money from the sale of logging permits supports schools, libraries, and local governments. Some timber companies own no land and are totally dependent upon logs from National Forests. Some mills are designed for old-growth logs and cannot process smaller logs. Without permits to log, these mills must close. If loggers and millworkers are unemployed, every business in a logging town suffers.

While the spotted owl is an easy target for their frustrations, many other factors are working against the timber industry in the Pacific Northwest. The list below demonstrates why the logging industry in the Northwest is an endangered way of life.

- For many years, trees were logged but not replanted. In British Columbia more than one million acres are listed as "not sufficiently restocked."
- Advances in technology have reduced the number of workers needed, and even if logging continues at the current rate additional jobs will be lost to automation in the future.
- The export of logs to Japan and China has reduced the number of jobs in local mills.
- Some timber companies are moving south to take advantage of cheaper land, better soil and a longer growing season.
- A slow economy reduces the demand for lumber and wood products.
- Products must compete with cheaper imports.

While the timber industry is concerned about the loss of jobs because trees are "locked up," the commercial fishing industry is concerned that the destructive logging practices will cause a critical decline in the salmon runs. Erosion of treeless hillsides carries silt into the streams where it suffocates young fish and fish eggs. The lack of forest cover also increases the sunlight reaching the water, and the fish suffer when water temperatures rise.

How Much is Enough?

According to the National Audubon Society, timber companies were logging old-growth timber at a rate of 60,000 acres per year in 1987. If logging continued at that rate, the unprotected old-growth forests would be gone by 2010. The logging continues, but at a somewhat slower rate.

Congress passed the National Forest Management Act in 1976. This law requires that management plans be made for all national forests. The plan must provide sufficient habitat for all native vertebrate species. In 1992 a US District Court Judge ruled that a Forest Service plan was inadequate and extended a ban on logging a tract of old-growth forest. Court injunctions that ban logging in other areas continue to frustrate loggers as they wait for the results of scientific studies and court decisions.

If something is **sustainable** — it has the ability to keep in existence or maintain. Are old-growth forest ecosystems sustainable? How many more acres of old-growth forest can we safely cut and still sustain the virgin forest ecosystem? One problem is that we do not know how many acres of old-growth forest are necessary for the ecosystem to be maintained.

What we do know is that if we want old-growth forest ecosystems for our children and our children's children, we must protect these forests now. Satellite images of forests in the Pacific Northwest show a disturbing image. Habitats are being severely fragmented by logging, roads and development. A NASA research team warned that the Northwest forests are losing their "biological vitality." New management plans must protect blocks of ancient forest that are large enough to maintain biodiversity.

Tough decisions lie ahead because tough decisions were avoided in the past. The US Forest Service Chief is implementing a policy to establish a balance among demands for timber, wildlife habitat, recreational opportunities, and "long-term stability to the ecosystem." Are old-growth forest ecosystems sustainable? Only time will tell.

Some foresters believe that we can manage old-growth for sustained yield and at the same time maintain the old-growth forest ecosystems. A sustained yield of old-growth timber will be possible only if we define "old-growth" and allow trees to mature and reach an old age.

Whether the goal is to sustain old-growth ecosystems or old-growth timber production, we can not continue to manage our National Forests as we have in the past. Past decisions regarding the use of federal lands have too often been made on the basis of politics rather than science. Too many management decisions have favored short-term profits rather than long-term investments. Clearly sustainability has not been the goal.

Erosion from treeless hillsides carries silt into the streams.

1. Define the following terms:

   bark rights   snag
   biodiversity   sustainable
   indicator species   The Nature Conservancy
   multiple use   truffle
   nurse log   virgin forest
   old-growth forest

2. According to some estimates, how much of the original virgin forests remain?

3. What is the goal of The Nature Conservancy? Why did the conservancy buy the Woodbourne forest?

4. How do the children's stories like Little Red Riding Hood and the Three Little Pigs express the feelings of the colonists toward the forest?

5. Describe the change in the landscape that you would have noticed if you had visited Pennsylvania in 1820 and then again in 1920.

6. What were "bark rights" and why were they important?

Old-Growth Forests

7. What is the dominant species of tree in the old-growth forests in the Pacific Northwest? How old are the trees in an old-growth forest?

8. Forests are usually considered to be a renewable resource because when the trees are cut other trees will replace them. Some scientists do not consider the old-growth trees in a virgin forest to be a renewable resource. Why?

9. Describe the role of each of the following in an old-growth forest ecosystem:

   healthy mature trees
   standing dead and dying trees
   fallen trees
   nurse logs

10. What is the relationship between the biodiversity of an ecosystem and the stability of the ecosystem?

11. Is an old-growth forest ecosystem a stable ecosystem? Defend your answer.

12. Explain the statement, "A forest is more than a place with trees."

13. Identify 6 species that depend on old-growth habitat. Which of these species is considered an indicator species? What is the niche of all of these species?

14. Explain the relationships between the following organisms:

    northern spotted owls and old-growth forest
    northern spotted owl and red backed vole
    northern spotted owls and flying squirrels
    flying squirrels and truffles
    truffles and trees in old-growth forests
    small mammals and young trees growing in a cut or burned area of the forest
    trees in old-growth forest and salmon

15. Make a food web that includes the northern spotted owl, red backed vole, flying squirrel, truffles, and trees.

16. List the changes that might occur in the forest if the owl becomes extinct.

Multiple Use Management

17. Who is the largest owner of the remaining virgin forests?

18. Can trees in a National Park be legally cut? Can trees in a designated Wilderness Area be legally cut? Can the trees in a national forest be legally cut? List other possible uses of national forests.

19. Who makes the final decision on the amount of timber that is sold from federal lands each year?

Conflict in the Northwest

20. "Should trees in the old-growth forests be cut?" Give the position of each of the following groups on this issue and list the reasons for their position:

    conservationists   fisherman
    loggers   ecologists
    foresters

21. The northern spotted owl is a "threatened species." List several reasons why logging in the Pacific Northwest is a "threatened career."

How Much is Enough?

22. Does the National Forest Management Act protect the northern spotted owl?

23. Finish this statement: Old-growth forest ecosystems are not sustainable unless . . .

Science
Technology
Society

ISSUES

A SUSTAINED YIELD OF OLD GROWTH TIMBER

Nearly 20,000 women in the United States are diagnosed each year with ovarian cancer. **Taxol**, a chemical extracted from the bark of a Pacific yew, slows the growth of ovarian cancer, and it may be effective in treating breast cancer and lung cancer. The Pacific yew grows in the shady old-growth forest. The tree is considered a weed by loggers who destroy it when they clear-cut the forest.

The yew tree is rare, and slow-growing. The bark from at least three 100-year old trees is needed to treat one cancer patient. The forest can not produce enough of the chemical to treat the patients who need it, but maybe scientists can. Chemists are trying to synthesize taxol in the laboratory. Some scientists are using biotechnology techniques to extract taxol from Yew cells in tissue culture. Other scientists are investigating a taxol-producing fungus that grows on the inner bark of the tree.

What other life-saving drugs are in the forest? The issue of saving or logging the old-growth forest is far more complex than saving jobs or saving spotted owls.

According to a US Forest Service report, there are nearly 5 million acres of old growth in western Washington and Oregon. Nearly all of the old-growth is owned by the public. About 2.9 million acres has been declared unavailable for harvest in National Forest plans, or preserved in National Parks, designated Wilderness Areas or "natural research" areas.

- What is your opinion about harvesting the forest to produce life-saving drugs?
- What part of the remaining 2.1 million acres of old-growth do you think should be cut?
- What factors should be considered in the logging plan?

CASE STUDY
6.2 **Logging — Making Clearcut Decisions**

"Economic activities of man, such as logging can — if pursued relentlessly without regard for other forest values — do great harm to nature and her creatures."
The Living Forest — a report from
MacMillan Bloedel Limited
Vancouver, British Columbia

Is this good forest management?

It looks terrible. They go in with big equipment and log off all the beautiful old trees. The **felling** or cutting of every tree on a specific tract of forest is called **clearcutting** or **clearcut logging**. There is nothing left but big ruts and dead branches. The next spring brushy growth begins to appear. People who care about what happens to the land see changes, sometimes drastic ones, and they may get upset. A forester may see these changes as forest management.

Clearcut in a Mixed Oak Forest

A hunter may see a large section of old white oaks as a great place to hunt squirrels. It is also a place where wild turkeys may roost. To the squirrel, the turkey and the hunter this is good wildlife habitat. As the loggers move in, the squirrels, turkeys and other species that need mature trees for food and cover, crowd into the sections of forest that are left uncut. The hunter will follow.

In the spring new growth occurs, and the area becomes a tangle of brush. The adult turkeys will not find a place to roost, but the hen turkeys find the area ideal habitat for nesting. Ruffed grouse and rabbits are more plentiful. The young thrive in the dense tangles of brush where they find plenty of food and cover. Although there is no place for the hunter's deer stand, the young sprouts and grasses become favorite deer food.

As time passes, much of the low "brush" grows into young trees. After ten years or so, the clear-cut area supports a thick stand of young saplings. Later — in 60 to 100 years — the saplings will be mature trees that may be sawed for logs. The forester explains that, with proper management, this new stand of trees will be in a better condition than the old stand.

Goals for management of a forest should include production of quality wildlife habitat. Other goals for the same forest may include harvest of timber, protection of unique areas, protection of streams or lakes, outdoor recreation, and the mining of minerals.

Managing for Wildlife

In a forest where trees have reached maturity, some trees begin to die. Sometimes a whole tree dies during one growing season. More often the top of the tree dies leaving hollow sections in the trunk. These old trees provide snags for the cavity nesters and habitat for other species that nest and feed high within the **canopy**. More than 80 species of birds nest only in dead or dying trees. Some birds that are found in old-growth forests are not found in younger forests. To provide homes for these species, at least ten percent of a forest should be old-growth.

At least 40 percent of a forest should have trees that are capable of producing mast. **Mast** refers to acorns and other nuts and fruits that lie on a forest floor. Mast supports a large variety of wildlife, especially during winter when other foods are not available. Wildlife management plans often allow one half of the forest to remain in the mature mast-producing stage.

Another 20 percent of the forest must be capable of producing **forage** — those plants that are eaten by grazing or browsing animals. Clearcutting creates openings in the forest that allow sunlight to penetrate. By creating edges, clearcutting is beneficial to some species. Populations of rabbit, elk, deer, and other species that depend upon forage increase. Although bobcats are forest creatures, they thrive in areas with clearcuts. If the clearcuts are not too large, the forest provides plenty of cover while the clearcuts provide their preferred food — the rabbit.

A forest with all stages of growth ensures a diversity of wildlife. Timber companies can make a profit managing their forest lands for the production of wood and, at the same time, protecting other resources. If the management of a forest is well planned, it can provide both benefits for wildlife and resources for humans.

It will be 60 to 100 years before this brushy growth develops into a mature forest with sawlogs, but it provides quality habitat for certain species of wildlife.

If a Little Is Good, Is More Better?

While clearcutting destroys the habitat for some species, it improves the habitat for others. Clearcutting some areas produces an **edge effect** — an increase in the population of those species that depend upon the forest for cover and the clearings for food. But it is not always desirable to create an edge effect. The populations of **"deep forest" species** — that live in the interior of the forest — decline if too much of the forest is clearcut.

The size of clearcuts must be kept small, and the location must be carefully chosen to prevent fragmentation of the ecosystem. **Fragmentation** refers to the carving of an ecosystem into small isolated tracts. Activities that cause fragmentation include logging, road-building, developments and agriculture. These activities may create islands of plants and animals. If there are no corridors or passage ways between islands, it can spell trouble for the ecosystem.

Species that won't cross large open areas become genetically isolated populations. Inbreeding occurs in small isolated populations, and the species is threatened by a loss of genetic diversity. Some species may stop breeding because of an inadequate food supply or lack of space. With fewer species — less biodiversity — the stability of the ecosystem is threatened.

The Forest Cycle — Managing for Timber

In some regions, the number one agricultural crop is trees. When a forest is managed to produce a "crop of trees," the biodiversity is greatly reduced. In Canada's natural forest ecosystems there are 131 tree species, but only a few of these are considered commercially valuable. Both farmers and timber

Mast on Forest Floor

How does the management of this forest affect "deep forest" species?

companies plant and manage large tracts of land for the commercial production of a single species — a **monoculture**.

In many ways growing trees for harvest is much like growing and harvesting vegetable crops. The biggest difference is that a farmer planting a field of corn will harvest the crop in 60 to 100 days while a tree farmer planting a forest will wait 60 to 100 years.

To Log or Not to Log — That Is the Question!

When converting a forest to a tree farm, the first decision is how and when the existing trees should be harvested. All areas are not suited for logging. In some places the ecosystem may be irreparably damaged if any logging is allowed. In these areas the management plan must read "logging prohibited." The decision regarding logging and the method of cutting chosen should be based an analysis of the factors listed below.

- **Type and ages of trees** — Does the "taking" of these trees threaten the sustainability of the species? Is the wood that is "taken" replaced by new growth?
- **Slope of the land** — Is the land too steep for replanting? Can erosion be controlled and water quality protected?
- **Type of soil** — Will the soil support the regrowth of trees? The soil in the rain forest is baked into a hard, concrete-like surface when logging exposes it to the sun.
- **Climate** — Is there enough rain to support the recovery of the ecosystem? Is the amount and pattern of rainfall likely to cause severe erosion and flooding problems? Is the temperature too cold or too hot for germination and growth of seedling?
- **Wildlife** — Are there endangered or threatened species that will be affected by the logging? Is the ecosystem sustainable?
- **Location** — Will logging fragment the ecosystem endangering whole groups of species? Are the trees near a stream bank that will erode?

The Harvest: Which Trees to Cut?

- **Clearcut logging** — This method removes all timber regardless of size and condition. It is usually chosen for old-growth forests with many huge mature and "overmature" trees. It is often the preferred method of harvesting stands of **even-aged trees** where all trees are mature and ready for harvest at the same time. Clearcutting is also used in sections of forest that have been damaged by wind, fire, or insect infestations.

Clearcutting is necessary for the regeneration of certain tree species that are used in a large number of wood and paper products. In some regions, oaks are the most economically valuable species. In other regions timber companies grow pines, spruce, or fir. Without clearcutting, there would be fewer of these economically valuable shade-intolerant species. Clearcutting prevents maples and other less valuable species that can reproduce under shaded conditions, from taking over an area.

- **Selection logging** — This method, also called selective cutting, is used to harvest mature trees in a stand of **uneven-aged trees**. The logger may remove individual trees or small groups of trees. Mature high-quality trees are removed for sale as sawlogs. Lesser quality and smaller trees may be removed to improve the growing conditions for the remaining trees.

  When selectively cutting trees, care must be taken to protect the remaining trees. A University of Idaho study compared the use of horses and tractors as power sources in logging operations. The study found that 91 percent of the damage to standing trees was caused by the tractors. Mules and horses remove logs from selectively logged area with less environmental impact than heavy equipment.

- **Seed tree logging** — This method is much like clearcutting except that selected mature trees are left to provide seed for regeneration of the cut area. This method is used for sun-dependent species. It eliminates the need for replanting.

- **Shelterwood logging** — In this method, mature trees are harvested in a series of cuts over several years. The remaining trees provide a seed source and protection for shade-tolerant species such as Douglas fir.

After the Harvest: Planning for the Next Crop

The forest is restored by **natural regeneration** or germination of seeds from remaining trees after seed-tree, shelterwood, or selection logging. Small clearcut areas may recover with natural regeneration or by planting. Natural regeneration costs less than planting, but it requires more years until harvest. Planting may be necessary to grow a selected species. Preparation for planting often includes:

- **Mechanical preparation** — Debris on the forest floor makes replanting difficult and expensive. If the **duff** — blanket of twigs and needles — is too thick, the roots of the seedlings may die before they reach the moisture and nutrients in the soil below. The **slash** — limbs, tree tops, and other waste —

Tree farmers and timber companies often plant a single species of tree like these Douglas fir trees growing in Washington. What are the advantages and disadvantages of growing a single species — a monoculture?

Clearcut logging is the method often used to harvest stands of even-aged trees.

Slash burning clears the planting sites of brush and duff, making it easier to plant of seedlings.

Herbicides reduce the competition of "weed species" and the young trees grow faster.

and duff may be removed by heavy equipment. It is sometimes piled in rows and burned.

- **Slash burning** — This clears planting sites of brush and duff. The advantages of slash burning are low cost and suitability for steep slopes. It may be detrimental in sites where soil is thin and there is only a shallow covering of duff.
- **Herbicides** — These are used to kill the "weed" species. Though these species are a part of a natural forest ecosystem, they are considered "weeds" by the tree farmer. Competition for nutrients and water slows the growth of the commercially valuable trees. Herbicides are an efficient and effective way to remove weeds, but there are some concerns about their use. They destroy vegetation that could feed and shelter wildlife.

Planting: More and more forests are restored by planting genetically improved seedlings or plantlings. **Plantlings** look like seedlings, but they are produced by tissue culture from a few selected parent plants. Large areas in New Zealand have been re-forested using plantlings.

Thinning: Forests with the greatest commercial value contain trees that are tall and straight. After trees grow to pole size, six to ten inches (15-20 cm) in diameter, they are examined to see which trees should be removed. The best trees are given space to grow by removing poorly formed and overcrowded trees.

Fertilization: Many soils do not provide enough of the nutrients that trees need to grow. The growth rate is increased by applying fertilizers using helicopters or airplanes.

Protection: Forests need protection from fire and from pests. Protection from forest fires is an important part of forest management. In 1989, more than 12,000 fires burned 7.3 million hectares of Canada's forests. Pesticides are used to control outbreaks of pests and diseases. The problems caused by pests and diseases increase in areas that are large monocultures. This increases the need for pesticides. Both chemical and biological controls are used. There is concern about the use of herbicides and pesticides. Researchers continue to look for more biological controls.

Forests Forever

Our increasing demand for wood and wood products can not be met without intensively managed forests. **Intensively managed forests** — can produce nearly twice as much timber as unmanaged forests. Intensively managed forests require several procedures. These include promptly planting high-quality seedlings, controlling competition from weed species, enhancing

WHAT IS FOREST MANAGEMENT?

1. Pre-Harvest Planning

2. Logging

3. Site Preparation

4. Planting

5. Brush Control

6. Thinning

7. Fertilization

8. Protection

growth by thinning and adding fertilizers, and protecting trees from fire and insects. Our lifestyle depends upon intensively managed forests or tree farms, but there's a lot more than lifestyle at stake. The days of "cut-and-run" are long gone. "Forests forever" is a slogan of the British Columbia forest industry. The life of the industry depends upon sustainable timber production. What is more important is that the life of the planet depends upon sustaining our forest ecosystems. Sustaining planet Earth requires careful and intelligent decisions concerning clearcuts and other forest management practices.

6.2 QUESTIONS FOR STUDY AND DISCUSSION

1. Define the following terms:

   canopy
   clearcut logging
   deep forest species
   duff
   edge effect
   even-aged stand
   felling
   forage
   fragmentation
   herbicides
   intensively managed

   forest
   mast
   monoculture
   natural regeneration
   plantlings
   seed tree logging
   selection logging
   shelterwood logging
   slash
   slash burning
   uneven-aged stand

Clearcut in a Mixed Oak Forest

2. Why do foresters consider it necessary to clearcut some areas of a forest?
3. Give two species whose populations will increase if certain areas of the forest are clearcut.
4. After an area is logged by clearcutting, how many years must pass before large saw logs can be removed from the area again?
5. Good management of a forest must include an important goal. What is this goal?
6. List at least three goals of forest management in addition to the one listed in question 4.

Managing for Wildlife

7. Give the *minimum* percentage of the forest that should be in each of the following conditions when good forest management is practiced:
   old-growth
   healthy mature trees
   young brushy growth
8. List or describe the type of wildlife that will benefit from each of the stages of growth listed in question 7.

If a Little is Good

9. Explain why the edge effect is not always a "good" effect.
10. What changes may occur in an ecosystem that is fragmented? What is the effect of fragmentation on the stability of the ecosystem?

The Forest Cycle — Managing for Timber

11. How does the biodiversity of a commercial forest compare to the biodiversity of an unmanaged forest?
12. List at least three examples of conditions that should prohibit logging.
13. Select the type of logging that is preferred in each of the following situations:
    A. removing high-quality saw logs leaving smaller trees for later harvest.
    B. removing trees from an "overmature" stand.
    C. removing trees to create conditions needed by sun-dependent species and eliminate the need for replanting.
    D. salvaging trees after the eruption of Mt. St. Helens volcanic blast.
    E. removing poor quality trees to improve conditions for remaining trees.
    F. removing trees to prepare for planting oaks or pines.
    G. removing trees from even-aged stand.
    H. leaving trees as a seed source and protection for shade-tolerant species.
14. Give one advantage and one disadvantage of growing a forest by natural regeneration.
15. Describe two methods used to prepare the forest for planting young trees.
16. Give two reasons why it is necessary to remove slash and duff before planting.
17. Identify three types of chemicals that are used in commercial forests.
18. How do "tree farmers" increase the growth rate of trees?
19. What procedure is necessary to produce trees with the greatest commercial value?
20. Why are pests and diseases a greater problem in commercial forests than they are in unmanaged forests?

Forests Forever

21. Can we maintain our lifestyle without intensively managed forests? Explain.
22. How has the philosophy of the forest industry changed?
23. What is the connection between "Forests Forever" and sustaining planet Earth?

Have you ever seen a large flock of very noisy black birds? The birds are probably European starlings, imported from England in 1890. Supposedly, the starling was intentionally released, in New York City's Central Park, by a man who thought that America should have all of the birds mentioned in Shakespeare's plays.

Since their release, these aggressive black birds have spread throughout the United States and into Canada. Starlings are now one of our most common, if not most loved, birds. They congregate in large flocks, making noise and messing the sidewalks and buildings. They drive native birds from their nesting sites and compete with them for food. Although they are usually insect eaters, they sometimes feed on farm crops.

Now there are special rules for importing birds. The transportation of birds is regulated for two reasons:

- Some birds are protected by the Convention on International Trade in Endangered Species (CITES), and
- Birds carry serious diseases.

Parrots from South America probably carried the virus that caused an outbreak of Exotic Newcastle disease in southern California in 1971. Since the virus is highly contagious, 12 million birds — mostly laying hens — had to be destroyed. The cost to eradicate the disease was $56 million.

Today the importation of parrots, both legal and illegal, is a major problem. There is a big demand for pet parrots in North America, Europe, and Japan. Although many parrots enter the country through legal channels, the Fish and Wildlife Service estimates that more than 25,000 are smuggled into the US from Mexico.

Together with habitat loss, the "taking" of birds from the wild is causing serious declines in the populations of the most popular species. Another serious concern is that each illegally imported bird is a potential threat to US poultry industry and to native bird species.

Alien Plants

Plants growing in North America come from as many countries as the people who have settled here. Some plants were brought intentionally for use as food, medicine, or dyes. Other plants were accidentally brought in grain, straw, or soil. Whether the introduction was intentional or accidental, these "naturalized" plants have changed the landscape forever. Some of them are causing monumental problems.

Starling

This Fischer's Lovebird lives in a cage at the Crystal Bridge in Oklahoma City. It's native habitat is the tropical forest surrounding Lake Victoria in Africa, where it lives in small flocks.

Accidently introduced to this country from Europe, the tall brightly colored spikes of flowers make purple loosestrife a favorite in some flower gardens. It is readily pollinated by bees and other insects that feed on the nectar, but it is devastating to wildlife when it invades wetlands.

Plants native to North America can not compete with some introduced species, like purple loosestrife. Probably carried from Europe in soil used in a ship's ballast, purple loosestrife has invaded many of our wetlands. The dense stands of loosestrife are displacing the normal food supply of many wild animals. Very few animals feed on the loosestrife plant or its seeds. Some animals do use the loosestrife for cover but others, such as the muskrat, avoid it. By reducing the natural food supply and suitable cover for some species, purple loosestrife reduces the carrying capacity of the wetlands it invades.

Water hyacinth, possibly the most troublesome aquatic plant in the area bordering the Gulf Coast, is native to South America. Sold in the 1800s as an ornamental plant, water hyacinths were praised for their beauty and easy care. It escaped cultivation, and now it is a **weed** — a plant that is growing where it is not wanted. The water hyacinth is turning open waterways into wetlands and choking the life out of wetlands. Scientists have imported a South American weevil that feeds on the plant's juices. Weed-eating boats and herbicides are also needed to control the population of these fast-growing plants.

The Little but Mighty Mollusk

If a movie was made about the zebra mussel, it might be portrayed as a giant human-eating clam. In real life it is tiny, no bigger than your thumbnail, but it's probably a good idea to wear shoes when you go walking on a beach where they wash ashore. The shells are sharp, and they aren't kind to bare feet. That's only one of the problems caused by this tiny invader.

The zebra mussel is native to the Caspian Sea region of the Soviet Union. Sometime before the industrial revolution, the little mussel made its way to western Europe. On June 1, 1988, zebra mussels were first spotted in Lake St. Clair, between Lake Huron and Lake Eire. Scientists think that the mussel probably came as a stow-away aboard a European freighter in 1985 or 1986.

The zebra mussel was probably only one of many species that entered Lake St. Clair when the ship dumped the ballast water that it had taken in at a European port. In 1981, scientists (commissioned by Environment Canada) examined the potential problems that might result from foreign organisms in the water held in ships' ballast tanks. They examined the water in the tanks of 30 ships and found living organisms in every tank. The zebra mussel was one of the organisms identified, and the scientists predicted that they would cause problems.

Since they were released in Lake St. Clair, there has been a massive population explosion. A mature female zebra mussel can produce between 30,000 and 40,000 eggs each year. A zebra born early in the spring is sexually mature and reproducing by fall. The eggs hatch into free-swimming larvae that eventually develop adhesive threads and attach to a solid surface. They attach themselves to boats and barges and are transported upstream or carried to other bodies of water.

The fast-multiplying mussels have spread into all of the Great Lakes and are expected to invade all waterways connected to them. They have already been found in rivers in twelve states and two Canadian provinces. The zebra mussel is not the first organism to invade the Great Lakes and spread into other waterways, but it may cause the greatest economic and ecological problems.

Mussels could damage the fishing industry in the Great Lakes. They form large colonies with thousands of individuals per square metre. The colonies may completely cover the hard rocky surfaces that fish use for spawning. No one knows how this will affect the development of the fish eggs. Even if there isn't any negative impact on egg development, the zebras may still endanger fish populations.

Mussels are filter feeders, and a large colony of mussels filters a vast quantity of water. By removing algae and chemical pollutants, the mussels do improve water quality, but they may make it too clean for fish. If too many algae and other microscopic organisms are filtered from the water, zebra mussels may deplete the food supply of fish larvae. This could endanger walleye, whitefish, bass, perch, and other species of fish as well as organisms higher in the food chain.

Zebra mussels are creating enormous problems and huge expenses for cities and industries that use water from the Great Lakes. Filter feeders prefer moving water, and the intake pipes of industries and power plants become a nursery for the tiny zebra mussels. Detroit Edison spent $500,000 to clean the mussels from the cooling system of its power plant at Monroe, Michigan. The city lost its water supply for two days due to the mussels clogging the intake pipes.

The zebra mussel is not considered edible by humans, but they are eaten by diving ducks, crayfish and some species of fish (freshwater drum, carp, and sturgeon). The population of zebra mussels is expected to increase for three to five years and then level off.

Troubles for Trees

Diseases have attacked two of the most valuable native trees in the United States — the American chestnut and the American elm. In the 1800s one out of four hardwood trees, in forests from Maine to Georgia, was an American chestnut. It was probably the most valuable tree in the forest. Its beauty was described in

Escaping cultivation, the water hyacinth has become a weed that is choking the life out of wetland and filling in waterways.

D I D   Y O U   K N O W ?

Years ago the kudzu plant was introduced to the southeast to help control soil erosion. In no time, this weedy plant took over fields. Though its growth and spread are still more or less out of control, an important new use has been found for kudzu. Farmers whose fields have been taken over by the weed can now hope to sell the plant to drug companies that are extracting one of its chemical components found to be an effective treatment for people with alcohol dependence.

An isolated stand of American chestnuts in northern Michigan have so far escaped the blight. Trees like these once dominanted the eastern forest.

poems, its lumber used for building, and its nuts provided food for both humans and wildlife.

Chestnut blight — a fungus that grows beneath the bark and cuts off the flow of nutrients and water — was first seen in American chestnut trees in the New York Zoological Park, in 1904. It probably entered the United States on small trees imported from Asia. The spores of the blight are spread by the wind and carried by insects and birds. All efforts to stop the spread of the disease failed. By 1950 the disease had spread throughout the chestnut's natural range, and 3.5 billion trees had fallen victim to the disease.

The disease doesn't kill the roots, and new sprouts develop, but within a few years they too are taken by the fungus. Only isolated stands of the American chestnut remain. Scientists have discovered a non-lethal "hypovirulent" form of the fungus. Trees infected with this form of the disease seam to be recovering. Scientists hope to develop a biological control for the disease. Even if the species is saved from extinction, the American chestnut will never again be the dominant tree that it once was in the Eastern forests.

Another fungus, Dutch elm disease, produces a poison that clogs the sap-carrying tubes of the American elm. It is carried from tree to tree by the European elm bark beetle. Both the fungus and the beetle were probably imported from Europe with a ship load of logs.

Dutch elm disease was first reported in Ohio in 1930. By 1980 it had reached California. It kills as many as 400,000 American elms each year. Tree surgeons are making an effort to save the few remaining trees by injecting fungicides in the tree and the soil. They also remove the dead branches to prevent the beetle from breeding in the soft wood.

Like the populations of American chestnut and American elm trees, the population of American Indians was also reduced by the spread of disease. Blankets and other items that were traded to the Indians carried bacteria, and the American Indian had no resistance to the diseases of the European settlers. History repeats itself. During the 1980s, gold miners who entered Brazil's Amazon region introduced diseases to the Yanomami people. Three years later, 15 percent of the population had died of tuberculosis, influenza, mumps, malaria, and the common cold.

The Hitchhiker

The gypsy moth is probably the most serious insect pest in the forests of the Northeastern United States. It was introduced into Massachusetts from Europe in 1869, by a French scientist. He had hoped to breed a better silk-producing insect.

Some of the larvae escaped during his experiments, and they quickly found a new habitat in the surrounding forests. By 1902 they had spread throughout the New England States. Today they are still spreading south and west. The larvae are carried long distances by strong winds, but the prevailing wind direction has worked against the spread.

One moth was found in Sequoia National park in 1983. Inspectors think that it was carried from New England by campers. Other moths and egg masses have been found on campers in other states. The spread west will be hastened by these hitchhiking gypsies. Federal regulations now require movers to check for gypsy moths before moving outdoor equipment.

The gypsy moth prefers to breed on oak trees. As the population increases, the larvae feed on as many as 500 species of plants. Twelve million acres (4.8 million hectares) of forests in the Northeastern US were stripped of their leaves, in 1981. This was followed by 8.2 million acres (3.3 million hectares) in 1982 and 2.4 million acres (1.0 million hectares) in 1983.

Hemlocks that are completely stripped of their needles will die in one year. After two years of defoliation many hardwood trees die. Without new leaves, the gypsy moth population cannot find enough food to support the population. As food becomes a limiting factor, many larvae die of starvation.

When insects emigrate to this country, they usually leave their natural enemies behind. Without this limiting factor and with plenty of food, the population quickly reaches epidemic numbers. Limiting factors for gypsy moths in Europe included more than 100 parasites and predators. Few of these limiting factors were present in the United States. Some of the gypsy moths natural enemies have been introduced in the Northeast and have become important limiting factors in the size of the gypsy moth population.

How has the introduction of the gypsy moth affected the Northeastern forest ecosystem? Despite controls costing millions of dollars, the gypsy moth is alive and well. Many animals have learned to eat gypsy moths, and they have become an important food source for white-footed mice, shrews, skunks, frogs, lizards, spiders, ants, and as many as 40 species of birds.

As the larger trees die, the forest canopy is opened. With the additional sunlight, the low-growing plants in the forest become more dense. This increases the cover and food supply for the animals such as rabbits, grouse, and turkey.

The loss of acorns and other nuts does cause an immediate food shortage for some species, especially squirrels. Due to the increased growth of young woody plants, the deer soon have an increased food supply. Gypsy moth damage results in an

At one time many city streets looked like this. The citizens of Westmont, PA, spend thousands of dollars each year to protect this stand of American elm trees on Luzerne Street.

Many American elms are still found on college campuses. This magestic tree stands in front of the church on the campus of Hope College in Michigan.

Tree surgeons inject fungicides to protect the American elms from Dutch elm disease.

Egg masses on this tree indicate trouble for this mixed oak forest.

Once the oak leaves are gone, the gypsy moth caterpillar turns to other species of plants including grasses.

increase in the carrying capacity for some species and a decrease for others.

The Flight of the Bees

A scientist imported wild African bees to Brazil in 1956. He hoped that breeding them with European honey bees would make them more suitable to the tropics. When someone visiting the laboratory removed the cover, the bees escaped from the hives and bred with European honey bees. The hybrid offspring, Africanized honey bees, emigrated northward through Central America arriving in Hidalgo, Texas, on October 15, 1990.

Crew members and dock workers were alerted by the US Department of Agriculture to look for bee swarms that might be hitchhiking on ships coming to US ports from Latin America. More than twenty swarms have been destroyed. Although scientists knew that the bees would eventually enter the United States, the natural migration was slowed by trapping swarms in baited hives. This gave scientists more time to prepare for their arrival.

Honey bees are not native to the US; they were introduced by the European colonists. They are an important pollinator of crops and producer of honey. Only an expert can correctly identify a bee as an Africanized or a European honey bee. The Africanized bee is slightly smaller, and scientists use wing measurements for a fast identification. A computer analysis of many body parts confirms the identification.

Although Africanized honey bees are not the "killer bees" that movies describe, they are more aggressive and less predictable than the European honey bees. The venom of the Africanized honey bee is no more poisonous than the venom of the European honey bee. But they sting more often and follow the intruder farther. While they have caused both human and animal death, the chance that you will be fatally stung by any insect — including Africanized bees — is less than the chance you will be killed by lightning.

How will the Africanized intruders affect the existing bee population? Although scientists will not be able to stop the spread of the Africanized bees, they are working on ways to lessen the undesirable impacts by capturing bees and controlling breeding.

When Africanized honey bees enter European honey bee hives, they kill the queen and begin to lay eggs. The unpredictable and aggressive behavior of the Africanized bees may make it more difficult for beekeepers to manage the hives. Even if behavior is not a problem, there may be less honey for the beekeeper. Africanized bees use more of the honey they produce. European bees produce a surplus worth $150 million a year.

More important than the loss of honey may be the effect on pollination. Farmers depend upon bees to pollinate crops — including apples, almonds, blueberries, and cucumbers — worth about $10 billion a year. One third of the food we eat comes directly or indirectly from crops pollinated by European honey bees. We do not know how the interbreeding will affect pollination.

Africanized bees are not the biggest threat to the European honey bees. The two biggest threats are two species of parasitic mites. An Asian mite attacks bee larvae and pupae. A small European mite that lives, feeds, and reproduces inside the bee's breathing tubes was first found in Texas in 1984. It has spread to bee colonies throughout the country. The tracheal mite blocks the flow of oxygen and eventually kills the bee. Chemicals used by beekeepers to control the mites are effective but expensive.

In 1989 scientists brought bees to the United States from Eastern Europe. These bees are resistant to the tracheal mites and to other mites that attack the European honey bees. After 5 years of research, the Eastern European bees are being released to beekeepers to help them in the war against the costly mites.

The Medfly Attack

The Mayflower may have imported more species of pests than the number of humans it carried. The threat of introduced pests and diseases continues today with each illegal plant or animal that someone brings into the United States. The Mediterranean fruit fly, commonly called the Medfly, is a native of tropical Africa. It has become a serious pest in the Mediterranean area and in other countries. Introduced to the Hawaiian Islands in 1910, it continues to be a serious pest.

The small fly attacks more than 260 varieties of fruits, vegetables, and nuts. A female fly deposits one to ten eggs beneath the skin, and the fly larvae feed on the fruit pulp causing soft spots where the fruit begins to rot. The fly has been discovered in Texas, Florida, and California, but so far controls have been successful. In 1990 a Medfly outbreak threatened California's $18 billion agriculture industry. After a 16-month, $52 million campaign, the state Department of Food and Agriculture declared victory. Quarantines had been imposed to prevent the spread of the fly to other agricultural areas. In a previous outbreak, farmers had lost $100 million in crops.

USDA Animal and Plant Health Inspection Service (APHIS)

Every year, taxpayers spend billions of dollars to control imported pests. In addition, billions of dollars worth of crops

Except for their behavior, it is difficult to distinguish Africanized bees from European honey bees. The African bee is slightly smaller than the European honey bee but it is much more aggressive.

DID YOU KNOW?

A researcher from Clarkson University has discovered a way to find out if the bees nest in your backyard is Africanized or European. The technique involves taking a sample of the beeswax and testing to see what kind of hydrocarbons it contains. The beeswax of European and Africanized honeybees contain distinctly different amounts of several types of hydrocarbons.

TRY TO FIND OUT

Why do California Agriculture officials stop you at the State border and ask you if you have any fruit or vegetables in your car? What would they do if you said yes?

Beagle Brigade

The Escape of the Gerbils

Gerbils are not native to the United States. They are imported from Africa or Asia where they normally live in a desert eco-system. They are rodents that eat seeds and breed rapidly.

What do you think would happen if a gerbil owner released one or more pairs of gerbils in Southern California?

Would the result have been different if this gerbil owner had lived in the Northeastern US or in Canada? Explain.

A Spacecraft has Landed

- What are the potential effects of a spacecraft from Earth landing on another planet that has an organically rich "soil"?
- What, if any, cautions should be taken to minimize the impact of the event?

are lost because of these pests. The US Department of Agriculture restricts items brought to the US from foreign countries as well as items brought to the mainland from Hawaii, Puerto Rico, and the US Virgin Islands.

The Animal and Plant Health Inspection Service (APHIS) is responsible for guarding against the introduction of foreign plants and animals into this country. Anyone entering the country is required to declare any meats, fruits, vegetables, plants, animals, and plant and animal products they are bringing into the country. APHIS inspectors search luggage for undeclared products. In some air ports they use beagle dogs that are trained to "sniff out" contraband items. At other airports, low-energy x-ray machines scan luggage for fruits and meats.

Potted plants and soil from overseas cannot be imported because the soil might carry pests and diseases. Many plants and animals can be imported safely if the correct procedures are followed. Most fruit and lumber producing trees must go through inspection and testing procedures in quarantine. For some trees it may take as long as five years, because certain diseases aren't apparent until the tree begins to produce fruit.

Although quarantine procedures are good, they are not always totally effective. Why do we take the risk of a disease or pest hitchhiking on a plant and being accidentally released into this country? Few of the plants that are important food sources are native to North America. The only way to get new genes that might improve the varieties we grow here is to import plants from the mother country.

Know Before You Go

When you plan a trip, check the regulations and make the proper arrangements. The Agriculture Department recommends that you "Know before you go." You should also know the import and export restrictions for the country you are visiting. For example, if you're planning to take your dog with you when you visit England, you will need a permit. The permit requires that the dog be quarantined. England already has a population of dogs, so why must your dog be quarantined? The disease rabies is not present in England, but it could easily be imported by a rabid dog.

Your dog will be quarantined and observed for six months to assure that it is not rabid. Not only dogs, but all mammals entering England must be quarantined. This will prevent rabies from being introduced to England. It certainly pays to "Know before you go." A six-month bill for keeping your dog in quarantine is very expensive.

6.3 QUESTIONS FOR STUDY AND DISCUSSION

1. Of what benefit are starlings? Why may farmers dislike starlings?
2. What relationship may exist between starlings and bluebirds?
3. Give two reasons why it is necessary to regulate the importation of birds.

Alien Plants

4. Why did the early settlers import plants from their native countries?
5. Was purple loosestrife intentionally imported? If not, how was it introduced to this country?
6. Purple loosestrife is changing the habitat of the wetlands. Is this helping or hurting wildlife? Explain.
7. What introduced plant is causing problems in the waters along the Gulf Coast? What measures are being taken to control the growth of this plant?

The Little but Mighty Mollusk

8. Where and how was the zebra mussel introduced to the United States?
9. What are two ways that the zebra mussel may affect the fish populations?
10. What is the economic impact of the zebra mussels?

Troubles for Trees

11. Identify two diseases that have been imported, and name the tree that is affected by each.
12. Identify the way that each disease is transported.
13. What steps are scientists taking to save the American elm and chestnut trees?
14. In what way were the American Indians like the American chestnut and American elm trees?

The Hitchhiker

15. Why was the gypsy moth imported?
16. Do you think that the gypsy moth will eventually be found throughout the United States? Support your answer.
17. How did the number of acres affected by the gypsy moth change from 1981 through 1983? What natural factors may have led to this decline?

18. Identify two limiting factors for the gypsy moth population.
19. Which of these limiting factors is often missing when a population is introduced to a new environment?
20. Describe the changes that you will see in the appearance of a forest after several years with a large gypsy moth population.
21. Indicate whether the population of each of the following animals will increase or decrease and give the reason for the change:
    white-footed mice   squirrels
    rabbits   deer

The Flight of the Bees

22. Why did a scientist in Brazil import African bees? Describe what happened when the bees escaped the hive.
23. What kind of bee had been imported by the European settlers? How may the Africanized bees affect this bee population?
24. What other imported pest is affecting the colonies of European honey bee in the United States? Why are scientist importing bees from Eastern Europe?

The Medfly Attack

25. Explain why the Medfly is a serious threat the agricultural economy of the US?

USDA Animal and Plant Health Inspection Service (APHIS)

26. In what two ways do imported pests cost Americans money?
27. If you are planning to take living plant or animal material from one state to another, or from one country to another, what must you do to make sure you won't import a "pest"?

Know Before You Go

28. You are planning to take your award-winning dog to an important dog show in England. How far in advance of the dog show would the dog have to be sent to England? Why?

71

"The time to save a species is while it is still common."
Rosalie Edge, founder
Hawk Mountain Sanctuary

The **Endangered Species Act** requires the United States Department of Interior to identify and protect species that are in danger of extinction. A plant or animal is classified as an **endangered species** if its chances of survival and reproduction are in immediate jeopardy. A species may be listed as **threatened** if it is likely to become endangered. If a species that is endangered does not get help, it will probably become **extinct** — disappear from planet Earth.

The Endangered Species Act declared that endangered and threatened species "are of esthetic, ecological, educational, historical, recreational, and scientific value to the Nation and its people." The act prohibits killing, harming or in any way "taking" endangered or threatened species. This includes the "taking" of their habitat. The major goal of the Endangered Species Act is to restore populations of species so that they are self-sustaining members of their ecosystem. To meet this goal, the law requires that a "recovery plan" be developed for each endangered or threatened species.

The Department of the Interior maintains the official list of endangered and threatened species. According the US Fish and Wildlife Service, as of 1992, there were 523 endangered species and 144 threatened species on the official list. More than half (354) of the species listed are plants.

In addition to the species on the official list, there are 600 additional species that are known to be in trouble and more than 3,000 species that probably need help. Studies and procedures required for listing a species require both time and money. This limits the number of species that are added to the list each year. During the 1980's, 34 species became extinct while waiting to be listed.

Extinction — With or Without Humans

Plants and animals have disappeared from planet Earth long before humans existed. The most well known is, of course, the extinction of the dinosaurs. Fossils tell us that dinosaurs once roamed the earth, but they don't tell us why they became extinct. Was it due to climate changes caused by large asteroids crashing into the earth or perhaps massive volcanic eruptions? We do know that some 65 million years ago unknown events

Now listed as an endangered species, the Florida panther is getting help. Only time will tell if the help came soon enough to save the panther from extinction.

TRY TO FIND OUT

What is significantly different about the rate of extinctions today (due mostly to human activity) compared to the rate of extinctions in the past (due to natural phenomena)?

caused the extinction of many species, but others were somehow able to survive.

Fossil records suggest that the family tree of frogs and toads living today goes back perhaps 150 million years. Apparently these amphibians were better able to adapt to the conditions that caused the extinction of the dinosaurs. Today there is concern about declining amphibian populations. The National Academy of Sciences reports that there have been dramatic declines in populations of frogs, toads, and salamanders in at least 16 countries. According to the report, the major cause of the decline is drastic habitat modification. In some cases, scientists cannot identify the cause of the decline, and in other cases the cause is very obvious. It is human predators. In 1987, India banned the export of frog legs to protect its frog populations.

Extinction of species is a natural process, but human activities are causing species to disappear at a much faster rate than in the past. Many species are declining in numbers due to human population growth. In Africa, India, Asia, and South America the increasing human population is taking more and more space that was once available to other species.

Habitats are disappearing due to population pressure in North America as well. Rapid residential development in Las Vegas valley, together with other pressures, led to the emergency listing of the desert tortoise as an endangered species in 1989. The desert tortoise is an indicator species for the desert ecosystem.

The large cats — lions, tigers, leopards, and cheetahs — are robbed of their habitat and prey. Protection from hunting has not completely stopped the killing of these species. There has been a sharp increase in **poaching** — illegal hunting — of all tiger species to meet the demand for traditional Chinese medicines made of tiger bone. There are fewer than 7,000 tigers in the world. There is a real danger that tigers will be extinct in the wild in the near future.

A Little Fish versus a Big Dam

In 1967 construction began on the Tellico Dam in Tennessee. Construction of the dam had already caused much controversy when a 3-inch-long (7.6 cm) fish was discovered. The entire population of this small snail darter was thought to live in the Little Tennessee River. Building the dam would change the fast-flowing stream into a lake. The habitat of the snail darter would no longer exist.

Under the Endangered Species Preservation Act no federal projects are permitted that could destroy the habitat of an endangered species. Despite the fact that $100 million had

Aptosaurus (Dinosaur)

Some medicines are made from plant and animal matter.

Desert Tortoise

already been spent on the dam, construction was halted. A legal battle began over the dam and the Endangered Species Act.

In 1978 the Supreme Court ruled that the Endangered Species Act was constitutional. Later the same year Congress changed the law. The Act was amended to allow a panel of seven members to examine projects and decide if they should be exempt from the law. If the panel found that the project was more beneficial to the country than the environmental value of the species, the project could continue.

The panel reported that the Tellico dam was not necessary. They found that the electricity produced at the dam would save some money by replacing expensive electricity produced by burning fossil fuels. However the farm land that would be lost through flooding was of far greater value. The dam seemed to be dead, but Tennessee senators and representatives began a campaign that got the dam exempted from the Endangered Species Act. This was done by getting the issue included in another bill. While he disagreed with the building of the dam, President Carter felt other issues included in the bill made it necessary for him to sign the bill.

The completion of the dam did not result in the extinction of the snail darter. The United States Fish and Wildlife Service successfully transplanted the snail darter into a nearby river, and other populations of snail darters were discovered in other streams. The snail darter is no longer listed as an endangered species.

Will the Warblers Be Next?

Populations of passenger pigeons were once so large that they darkened the sky. The passenger pigeon was native to America and existed nowhere else in the world. Early settlers killed passenger pigeons by the millions, and then there were only a few. When the size of the flocks decreased, the bird's mating instinct was disrupted. The last passenger pigeon died in captivity in 1914.

The small (6 inch/15 cm) blue-gray and yellow Kirtland's warbler would not make such an easy target for a hunter. Its population was never large enough to darken the sky. In fact, the Kirtland's warbler is one of the world's rarest birds. The warbler population was not threatened by the gun. The population of about 400 birds is threatened by changing habitat and competition from the cowbird.

Kirtland's warblers nest only beneath stands of jack pines that grow in soil known as Grayling sand. The stands must be at least 80 acres. The bird's habitat is limited to a small area in north central Michigan. The nest is a hole, dug in the sandy soil at the base of a young jack pine tree, lined with bark and

Snail Darter

grasses. The sandy soil protects the nest from flooding during heavy rains. As the tree grows, the dense shade prevents the growth of plants that serve as cover for the nest, and the site is abandoned.

Although forest fires are destructive, they are essential to maintain the warbler's habitat. The cones of the jack pine only open when exposed to the heat of a forest fire. As our ability to control forest fires improved, the habitat of the warbler disappeared. Today a part of the Huron National Forest is being managed for the warbler. Mature stands of jack pine are burned, or stands of trees are cut and young trees are planted.

The clearing of forests for housing, highways, and agriculture fragmented the forest and encouraged the cowbird to expand its range from its original habitat in the Great Plains into the warbler's habitat. In the days when huge herds of bison roamed the plains, the cowbirds (sometimes called buffalo birds) followed the herds and fed on the insects that were disturbed by the large grazing animals.

This wandering lifestyle left no time for nest building or parenting, so the cowbirds laid their eggs in the nests of other birds. The young cowbirds are cared for by other species of birds as if they were their own. Although the cowbirds no longer follow bison herds, they still leave the parenting responsibilities to other birds. This practice is devastating for the young of the warblers and other host species.

The young cowbirds develop more quickly than the smaller Kirtland's warblers, and they take most of the food the adult warblers bring to the nest. As they grow, they often push the other birds from the nest. To improve the survival rate of the young warbler's, the US Fish and Wildlife Service trap and remove cowbirds from the areas where the warblers are nesting.

The California Condor

The California condor was known as "thunderbird" to the Indians living along the coast. Legends tell that the condor shot lightning from its eyes and made thunder by flapping its wings. Until the appearance of the gold miners, the condors were both feared and worshipped by the Indians. They fed on dead animals such as whales and salmon. They also cleaned up the carcasses of dead cattle belonging to the Spanish settlers.

The gold-miners began to shoot the condors because they thought such big birds must be dangerous. Then someone discovered that the quills of the wing feathers could be used as containers for gold dust, and the big birds were shot for their quills.

Condor eggs were sought by collectors. Adult condors do not lay eggs until they are six or seven years old. Normally a

The Kirtland's warbler habitat is protected during the breeding season.

The warblers nest only under young pine trees that grow in the soil type known as grayling sand.

The US Fish and Wildlife Service attracts birds to seed placed in an enclosed pen. Cowbirds are asphyxiated with carbon monoxide. All other birds are banded and released.

Condor

sexually mature female lays only one egg every other year. This makes condor eggs valuable; at least one condor egg was sold for $300, in 1900.

A study in 1972 estimated the condor population to be about 60, and confirmed that adult condors were not breeding. Only one or two young were being reared each season. The reason for the low rate of reproduction was not known. Was it loss of habitat? Condors are easily disturbed by human activity. If disturbed, they will desert a nest with an egg or chick. Was it a lack of food?

Another constant threat to the condor was the poison used by ranchers to kill coyotes. Since condors eat dead animals, they sometimes feed on poisoned carcasses left for the coyote. Poisoned carcasses, intended for coyotes, also kill other large birds. Both the bald eagle and golden eagle are killed by eating this deadly bait.

As an endangered species, condors are protected by law, but that did not stop the accidental poisoning of these birds. All of the four known condor deaths between 1983 and 1986 were due to poisons. Three died from lead poisoning caused by ingestion of bullets in animals that had been shot, and one died after eating a poisoned carcass set out for predators.

The reproduction of some birds, like the brown pelican, was affected by DDT. The pelican's eggs had thinner shells and were often broken. Often those that didn't break did not hatch. The shells of condor eggs collected between 1964 and 1969 were thirty percent thinner than the shells of eggs collected before 1943.

The low reproduction rate of condors was not totally due to broken eggs. Most condors were not breeding. In 1985 scientists observed only one breeding pair of condors. In April 1987 the US Fish and Wildlife Service captured all remaining California condors. The California condor was extinct in the wild.

With a very successful captive-breeding program at the San Diego Wild Animal Park and the L. A. Zoo, the population grew from 27 to more than 60 birds. Then in 1991 two radio-tagged condors were freed in Los Padres National Forest. For the first ten months the reintroduction of the condors seemed to be going smoothly, but then there was trouble. Hunters shot at the female condor. Fortunately she wasn't hurt. A short time later, the male condor was found dead. Scientists are not giving up. They still plan to release additional birds.

Back from the Brink

When the settlers arrived, the Great Plains ecosystem included the American bison (commonly called the buffalo) and the gray wolf. As the pioneers moved west, they slaughtered the buffalo because they competed with cattle for grassland and because they were the key to the survival of the Indians. "Hidemen" slaughtered whole herds taking only the hide and the choicest cuts of meat. The rest of the carcass was left to litter the plains.

By 1900 the population of perhaps 60 million bison that once roamed North America had been reduced to less than 1000 animals. There were about 550 bison near Great Slave Lake in northern Canada. About 200 were in the new national park at Yellowstone, Wyoming, and the remainder in private herds and zoos. Congress, realizing that they would soon be extinct, made it illegal to shoot bison. The US Army was assigned the task of protecting the bison at Yellowstone, and biologists began a breeding program to increase the size of the herd.

The American bison, once pushed to the brink, is no longer in danger of extinction. Today there are an estimated 120,000 bison, mostly in private herds. The Yellowstone herd, the only free-ranging herd in the United States, now numbers 3,000. During the winter when good grass is hard to find, some of the bison wander out of the park.

About half of the animals carry the disease brucellosis, and local ranchers are concerned that the bison will spread this disease to their cattle. Although it doesn't seam to affect the bison, brucellosis causes cows to abort their calves. To protect the cattle, bison that leave the park are shot. The killing of the buffalo is part of a highly controversial herd management plan.

Return of the Wolves

Wolves once existed throughout most of North America. The massive killing of the buffalo and the over-hunting of deer, elk and antelope eliminated much of their prey. The wolves turned to livestock, and ranchers turned to poisons, traps, and guns. Ranchers baited buffalo carcasses with strychnine. The poisoned carcasses were deadly to many animals, including the wolf. More than 100,000 wolves and their pups were killed in Montana between 1883 and 1942.

Today the only large populations of gray wolves are in Alaska, Minnesota, and Canada. There are 20,000 to 30,000 gray wolves in undeveloped areas of Canada. A small population of wolves exists in Isle Royale National Park, an island in Lake Superior. A few wolves have moved from Canada into Glacier National Park, in Montana, and into the Selway-Bitterroot Wilderness in Idaho.

The gray wolf was placed on the endangered species list in 1973. It is classified as endangered in every state except Minnesota, where it is listed as "threatened," and Alaska, where a healthy population of wolves is legally hunted. The Endangered Species Act requires that the US Fish and Wildlife Service

North American Bison (Buffalo)

develop recovery plans for endangered species. The Rocky Mountain Wolf Recovery Plan includes the reintroduction of ten breeding pairs of wolves in Yellowstone National Park. An earlier attempt to establish a population of gray wolves in northern Michigan wasn't successful. Within eight months, all four wolves had been killed.

Thousands of red wolves once called the Southeast home, but they too were nearly exterminated. By 1980 biologists had captured the last remaining red wolves from a coastal swamp along the Texas-Louisiana border. Some of the wolves were breeding with coyotes, and genetic studies identified only 14 red wolves. Now there are more than 200. While some remain in captive breeding sanctuaries, others are once again free to roam their native habitat.

Reintroduction of the red wolf was the first attempt to restore a carnivore species that was extinct in the wild. In 1987 four pairs of red wolves were fitted with radio collars and then released in the 120,000 acre Alligator River National Wildlife Refuge, in North Carolina. In 1991 breeding pairs of red wolves were reintroduced to Great Smoky Mountains National Park in Tennessee and North Carolina. Farmers are compensated for any livestock taken by the wolves, and landowners who allow the wolves to den on their property are paid bonuses.

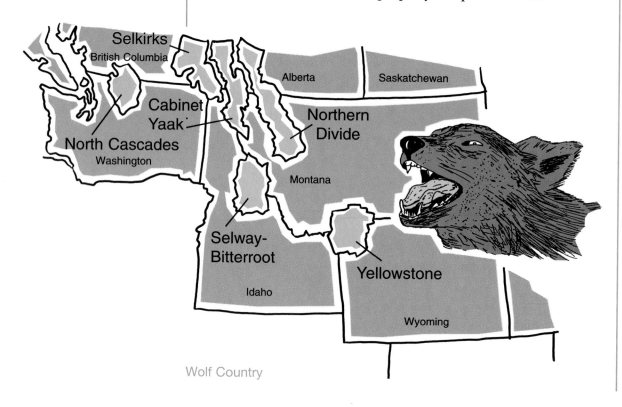

Wolf Country

Why Not Let Them Die?

Species have been dying out for generations, so why should we get concerned about losing a few more? Does it really matter whether the Kirtland's warbler or the California condor is extinct? Why should we be concerned about some plant that grows in another country and has yet to be discovered?

Scientists see plants as chemical factories, and some little known plants have produced some very important chemicals used to save lives. Plants and animals are the source for half of the prescription medicines we currently use. Drugs isolated from a decorative plant called rosy periwinkle are used to treat childhood leukemia and Hodgkin's disease.

Of the 240,000 plant species in the world, 85 percent of our food comes from only 20 species. None of the major crops grown for food (rice, wheat, corn, potatoes, beans, soybeans, cane, beets, bananas, and coconuts) are native to the United States. Seeds from plants growing in the wild may contain genetic messages that will improve the yield of these species or make them more resistant to drought, disease, or insect damage.

It is important that we protect all of the species in our "library of living things." The death of a species is a loss of genetic material. We do not know which of these species we will need in the future. Species that we have yet to discover may one day be vital to the production of our food, clothing, wood products, or medicines.

What is more important is that these species may be vital to the existence of ecosystems that sustain the planet. Biodiversity improves the stability of the ecosystem, and the loss of species reduces the diversity of the ecosystem. While every species may not be essential, some species play a vital role that stabilizes the ecosystem. Removal of a **keystone species** — a species that keeps the ecosystem in balance — will cause a chain reaction involving many other species in the ecosystem. There could be a major disruption in the ecosystem. Think of the ecosystem as the framework of a sky scraper. How many beams can be removed before the building collapses?

In the future, even more than in the past, the most critical threat to wildlife will be the destruction of their habitat. Future decisions about saving habitats and using (or not using) chemicals will play a major role in determining which species survive and which do not.

The Future of the Endangered Species Act

The Endangered Species Act was passed by Congress in 1973. Critics consider it a barrier to development and a threat to economic growth, and they vow to weaken it. One bill introduced

Rosy Periwinkle

Chemical Prospecting

Merck, the world's largest pharmaceutical company, agreed to pay $1 million to Costa Rica's National Institute of Biodiversity for samples of tropical plants, insects and microorganisms. Local people collected the organisms for the company. The company's chemists analyze the samples for chemicals that might be useful drugs. Royalties from any drugs developed by Merck will be used for science and conservation programs in Costa Rica.

- What do you think? Can there be sustainable development of a rain forest? Explain your position.

in Congress, the "Human Protection Act," would make the economic value of a species an important factor in decisions regarding an endangered species.

Supporters of the Endangered Species Act say the economy should not be the major issue. According to the US Fish and Wildlife Service, very few development projects are stopped because of an endangered species. A 1982 amendment to the act allows an "incidental taking" of some members of the species. The "taking" must be a part of a recovery plan that will ensure survival of the species.

Development of the Las Vegas Valley came to an immediate halt when the desert tortoise was added to the endangered species list in 1989 until a compromise was negotiated with the Southern Nevada Homebuilders Association. The developers agreed to pay $550 for each acre developed. The money funded the acquisition of 400,000 acres of prime tortoise habitat. In another case, an agreement allowed shrimping to continue but required shrimpers to use "turtle exclusion devices" to save the Ridley sea turtle.

Populations of some species — the bald eagle, peregrine falcon, American alligator, California condor, and red wolf — have benefited from recovery plans developed under Endangered Species Act, but other species became extinct while waiting to be added to the list. Critics argue that a few "glamorous species" get most of the money. *TIME* magazine referred to the California condor as the $25 million bird.

Many species are in trouble but they have not been identified as endangered species, and recovery plans have not been developed for many species that are listed. Many believe that the focus of the Endangered Species Act must be on saving entire ecosystems rather than individual species. Maintaining the stability of the ecosystems may be the key to maintaining the stability of planet Earth.

6.4 QUESTIONS FOR STUDY AND DISCUSSION

1. Define the following terms:
   endangered species   poaching
   extinct species   threatened species
   keystone species
2. The Florida panther is now listed as an endangered species. According to the Endangered Species Act, why is it important to save the Florida panther and other endangered species?
3. How does the Endangered Species Act provide help for endangered and threatened species?
4. What is the major goal of the Endangered Species Act.
5. Has the number of species listed as endangered increased or decreased? Explain why the number of species waiting to be listed as endangered or threatened is so large.

Extinction — With or Without Humans

6. How does the extinction of the dinosaurs show that extinction is a natural process?
7. According to the National Academy of Sciences, what is the major cause of the dramatic declines in the amphibian populations?
8. Make the connection between the decline in the population of the desert tortoise and other species and the human population.
9. What factors are causing the decline in the populations of large cats?

A Little Fish versus a Big Dam

10. Why was the Tellico Dam project stopped?
11. What was the purpose of the Tellico Dam?
12. If you had been a senator, would you have voted for the bill that allowed the Tellico Dam to be completed? Give reasons for your answer.
13. Is the snail darter still listed as an endangered species? Explain.

Will the Warblers Be Next?

14. List the major reasons for the decline in populations of the:
    passenger pigeon
    Kirtland's warbler
15. Make the connection between forest fires, pine trees, sandy soil, and the population of Kirtland's warblers.
16. Identify limiting factors for the Kirtland's warbler population.
17. Make the connection between human activities, cowbirds, and Kirtland's warblers.

The California Condor

18. What is the niche of the California condor?
19. List three reasons why the California condor was shot by the early settlers.
20. What was the relationship between the breeding pattern of the California condor and the price of condor eggs?
21. List factors that might explain the lack of breeding noted in the 1972 study.
22. Do you think that the reintroduction of the California condor to the wild will be successful? Justify your position.

Back from the Brink

23. Give two reasons why massive numbers of buffalo were killed by the pioneers.
24. What actions saved the American bison from extinction? Describe the change in the population of bison between 1900 and 1990.
25. Why are the bison leaving Yellowstone National Park? Why does this concern the ranchers?

Return of the Wolves

26. Identify the two areas of the United States that have large populations of wolves.
27. The Rocky Mountain Recovery Plan calls for reintroduction of the wolf into Yellowstone National Park. Debate this plan. What are the environmental and economic impacts of reintroducing the wolf? List information you need to make a decision on this issue.
28. Do you think that any of the species discussed in this section will become extinct? If so, which one(s)? What will cause the extinction of the species?

Why Not Let Them Die?

29. Give possible ways that a plant which has not yet been discovered or named might someday affect you.
30. Why is it important that we save plants like the rosy periwinkle and wild sugar beets?
31. Why is it important that we save a "library of living things"?
32. Explain how removal of a species from an ecosystem might cause the ecosystem to collapse. What term describes species that are essential to the balance of an ecosystem?
33. What is the most critical threat to most species of wildlife today?

The Future of the Endangered Species Act

34. Should a species be protected by the Endangered Species Act even though its economic value is low? Defend your position.
35. Should "incidental taking" of species be allowed?
36. Should the focus of the Endangered Species Act be the preservation of all species regardless of cost or should the focus be the preservation of ecosystems? Defend your position.

In the early 1930s, wildlife was in trouble. The activities of the settlers had destroyed much of the habitat. Some species had been nearly wiped out by uncontrolled hunting and trapping to supply furs, feathers, leather, and meat for commercial markets. Without changes, many species native to North America would soon disappear. To save species from extinction, there must be laws to regulate hunting and money to restore populations of animals.

Money for Wildlife

Hunting and trapping regulations were left to each state, but the federal government helped finance the restoration of wildlife with a new tax. The Pittman-Robertson Act placed a federal tax on hunting licenses, firearms, and ammunition, and it required that this money be used for wildlife conservation. In the early 1970s the P-R Act was amended to include taxes on archery equipment. Since 1937 these taxes have provided more than $1.7 billion for wildlife research and habitat restoration.

Each state has a conservation agency, department of natural resources, or fish and game agencies that are in charge of decisions concerning wildlife. Most of these agencies get little, if any, money from the state government. The taxes collected under the P-R Act provide up to 75 percent of the funds for all national wildlife restoration projects.

In 1992 wildlife in each of four states (Texas, Alaska, Michigan, and Pennsylvania) benefited from more than $6 million in P-R funds. States receive funds based on a formula that includes land area and hunting license sales. The money may be used to:
- Purchase and develop land for wildlife restoration.
- Maintain land in a manner that makes it suitable for wildlife.
- Conduct research to solve problems that affect wildlife.

A federal requirement for hunting migratory birds is the purchase of a Migratory Bird Hunting Stamp (the duck stamp). Money from the sale of the duck stamp has been used to establish the National Wildlife Refuge System. More than 30 million acres (12 million hectares) have been set aside for wildlife. Habitat loss is the biggest threat to wildlife, and the wildlife refuges provide habitat for many species. Populations of some endangered and threatened species are increasing because the refuges provide essential habitat.

Regulated hunting is allowed in some areas of the refuge, but most visitors are not hunters. Many of the people who visit

SCIENCE TECHNOLOGY & SOCIETY
I S S U E S

Saving the Earth's Biodiversity

Biodiversity refers to the variety of plant and animal species and other organisms living in an ecosystem, and the variety of ecosystems in the biosphere.

President Bush did not support efforts to save the Earth's biodiversity. The United States was the only leading power that did not sign the biodiversity treaty at the 1992 Earth Summit. Canada, France, Great Britain, Germany, Japan, and most other countries signed the treaty. After President Bush lost his bid for reelection, President Clinton signed the biodiversity treaty.

What do you think about saving the Earth's biodiversity?

How important is it that there be an international commitment to saving biodiversity?

What criteria would you use to assess the value of an eco-system?

wildlife refuges and lands bought with P-R money are hikers, bird watchers, wildlife photographers, or people who just enjoy being a part of "wild America."

Game versus Nongame

The Pennsylvania Game Commission is the "trustee" of all wild mammals and birds that breed in the state. The game commission's wildlife management programs are almost entirely funded with money from hunting and fishing licenses and money from P-R funds. Pennsylvania has 255 species of breeding birds and mammals, but wildlife management is largely confined to about 20 percent of these species — the game species. **Game species** are those species that can be legally hunted.

When hunters pay for wildlife management, and wildlife is managed by game agencies, the management plans often favor game species. When land is managed for game species, the habitat of some non-hunted or **nongame** species may be destroyed. In Pennsylvania, some of the non-game species of birds and mammals have suffered serious declines.

Some people would like to see game agencies replaced by conservation agencies. They feel that non-game species would benefit more if they are managed by conservation agencies that are supported by general taxes instead of taxes and fees paid by hunters. In some states, wildlife is managed by conservation agencies. One of the best in the nation is the Missouri Department of Conservation. In 1937 a voter initiative replaced Missouri's Game and Fish Department with a professionally managed Department of Conservation.

Citizens of the Show-Me State have shown that they care about all natural resources by voting for sales taxes that help fund conservation programs. Missourians (both hunters and non-hunters) support the programs of the conservation department with a one-eighth of one cent sales tax. The money improves and maintains habitats for both game and non-game species. Another one-tenth of one cent sales tax supports state parks and soil conservation programs.

The Return of the Whitetails

Many game species, including the white-tailed deer, would not be here today if it were not for management of their populations by conservation or game agencies. Minnesota, Wisconsin, Iowa, Illinois, Ohio, Pennsylvania, and much of New York, had no white-tailed deer by the late 1920s. There were only 395 deer left in Missouri. This was due to unregulated hunting and loss of habitat.

Duck stamp

White-tailed Deer

After the creation of state conservation or game agencies, refuges bought with money from hunting permits were stocked with deer from other states. Hunting was regulated, and there was strict enforcement of game laws. A high priority was placed on habitat restoration. Now there are more white-tailed deer than ever before. The population of whitetails in North America is more than 20 million.

Public hunting has been prohibited in Gettysburg National Military Park since 1895. The population of white-tailed deer in the park is estimated to be 1,200. In some areas of the park, there are 170 deer per square mile. The desired population density is 20-70 deer per square mile. The deer are eating 75 percent of all new growth in the 13 historic woodlots in the park, and they are causing tremendous damage to agricultural crops.

A three-year study concluded that the deer population is healthy, but the number of deer must be drastically reduced "to provide a satisfactory balance between deer and other resources." The report outlined options for herd management and recommended the use of deputized hunters or park rangers to remove the deer.

Nature's Way

The **carrying capacity** of a particular habitat determines the population that can be supported in a given area. In Pennsylvania, those counties that have dairy farms, and logging produce the largest deer. The counties with large areas that are closed to public hunting have smaller deer. Why? When the deer population remains high, there is greater competition for food. Deer in areas with a large population and a limited food supply will be smaller and have smaller racks (antlers).

As the number of deer increases, food becomes scarce, and reproduction decreases. Fewer does produce twins, and fawns with a low birth weight don't survive. Winter is the critical period, and food becomes the limiting factor. Fawns born the previous spring are the first to die because they cannot reach the higher buds and twigs. More adults will die from diseases and parasites, and they are an easy victim of any predators.

Game Management

In the absence of other large carnivores, humans have become the major predator. Some people feel that hunting deer, or other species, provides recreation for the hunter and keeps the populations from building to an unnatural high that is followed by a population crash. They feel that hunting is necessary to control deer populations in habitats where there are no natural predators. Others feel that it is better to let the population regulate itself.

Right or wrong, regulated hunting has become our primary method of wildlife management. The science of **game management** begins with a survey to determine the population density and the carrying capacity of the habitat. Then the managers set limits that allow "harvesting" of the surplus game.

The life expectancy of most small game and many fur bearers is less than one year. When the population finds good cover, food, and weather, the reproduction rate is high, and there is a "surplus" of animals. Unlike wood, the surplus cannot be stored. Eight out of ten quail hatched this year will not see next spring. If not killed by a hunter, they die of "natural causes." A study of ruffed grouse in Michigan found the same number of grouse in two populations — one with regulated hunting and one that was completely protected.

Mourning Dove

Doves in Indiana

On September 1, 1984, Indiana became the thirty-sixth state to allow a hunting season for mourning doves. The doves had been a protected song bird for 111 years. There were heated debates prior to the legislative action that created the dove season.

One letter sent by the Committee for Dove Protection began:"They are going to kill mourning doves again. They are going to kill mourning doves during their nesting season. They are, by killing parent birds that are still feeding their young, destroying nesting young as well." Other arguments of the dove defenders included:

- Doves ought to be protected because they are symbols of peace.
- Doves are closely related to the passenger pigeon which is extinct.
- Doves are mostly feathers and bone and are not good for eating.
- Doves relieve hay-fever sufferers by cleaning up ragweed seeds.
- Doves are the "prettiest thing I've ever seen."
- Hunters will bag two at a time because the dove always comes to the rescue of his or her mate.

Passenger Pigeon

Too Many Deer, Too Little Space

You are the manger of the 185 acre (74 hectare) Schlitz Audubon Center in Milwaukee. Here is the problem facing you.

The carrying capacity of the nature center is about 12 deer. During the last ten years the population of deer at the nature center has increased from 14 to 50. Twenty-seven fawns were born this spring. The deer are damaging the plants at the nature center. A survey of the sixty neighbors who live closest to the center revealed that 98 percent had deer visiting their yards. Seventy-seven percent of the neighbors had damage to their plants.

A few of the neighbors like having the deer in their back yards. One person built a feeder for the deer, but most of the neighbors are demanding that something be done.

- As manager of the nature center, you must present solutions to the board of directors for a vote. List at least three possible solutions, and give the advantages and disadvantages of each.

The Indiana Fish and Wildlife Division answered the pro-dove arguments with scientific data. A few doves, no more than ten percent, do nest during the hunting season. Both parents share the duties of feeding the young, so if one parent is shot the remaining parent can care for the young. Nesting doves will usually be on the nest, not flying over hunted areas.

Wildlife biologists say that when the shooting begins doves, like other game animals, think only of themselves. A dove will not fly to the rescue of its mate. Although doves may eat ragweed seeds, they also eat many other types of seeds, and they are not a major limiting factor of the ragweed population.

Doves weigh approximately four ounces (110 grams); they are not "mostly bone and feathers," but mostly breast muscle. According to John Madson, in his book *The Mourning Dove*, they are "rich meat and very special delicacies. Two doves per person provides an ample serving."

Although the mourning dove is related to the passenger pigeon, there are major differences between the two species. Passenger pigeons were not able to adapt to the changing habitat. The passenger pigeon fed only on a few types of forest mast and nested only in mature hardwood forests. The mourning dove eats almost any seed it finds and nests anywhere a site is available — trees, ground or buildings. A pair of passenger pigeons nested once each year and produced a single egg. A pair of mourning doves may nest six times a year and produce two eggs at each nesting. The hunting of mourning doves is regulated; their cousins were victims of unregulated hunting.

To Hunt or Not to Hunt

The days of market-hunting are long gone. Hunting is regulated, but some hunters ignore the regulations. Studies by wildlife agencies in Missouri, Washington, and New Mexico show that more animals are killed illegally than legally. Wildlife **poaching** refers to the taking of wildlife by any method that is illegal. This includes spotlighting of deer, netting of fish, and the taking of fish and game out of season.

Although some poaching may provide needed food, most poaching is done for "sport" or profit. Most states have major programs, some with undercover agents, to decrease poaching. It is poaching, not regulated hunting, that threatens certain wildlife populations.

There are many responsible hunters who follow the rules and, although they do take individual animals, they help the population by buying and improving the habitat. Habitat loss is the biggest cause of the decline in waterfowl populations. Ducks Unlimited has bought 3.5 million acres of wetlands, and raises millions of dollars each year to preserve habitat for waterfowl.

Hunters sometimes wound animals without killing them, but nature's way may not be less painful. A "natural" death may be more brutal than a death or even a crippling caused by a bullet. Starvation is not pleasant, but the dead animal does provide food for scavengers. Some people argue that hunters are not a part of the natural ecosystem, but in many cases we have altered the ecosystem and removed the natural predators from it. Humans have become the major predator in many ecosystems.

Every day some animals must die to allow others to live. Some people still hunt to put food on the table, but most people are far removed from the processes that produce our food. Most people are not hunters. They choose to let someone else be the killer of their domesticated prey — cattle, sheep, pigs, and chickens. Some people — vegetarians — choose to go lower on the food chain, but the use of pesticides to produce fruits and vegetables can also have a negative impact on some species of wildlife.

Our technological society allows the choice of hunting, but our technology often causes the accidental death of many kinds of wildlife — we call them road kills. With the exception of the hunting season, more deer are killed on the nation's highways than by any other means. More than 350,000 deer — and 100 motorists — are killed each year on our nation's highways in accidents involving deer.

Like any other controversial issue, there are two sides to the question of hunting. To some people, hunting is wrong — it's a value judgment. To others, hunting is a way of life — a tradition. Both sides have some valid arguments, but decisions regarding management of wildlife — both game and non-game species —must be based on facts, not on emotions. Symbols of peace and beauty are not valid arguments against hunting any more than symbols of evil and ugliness would be valid arguments for hunting.

Wildlife management involves much more than the issue of hunting. It also involves the issue of habitat destruction. Most human activities result in some negative impact on wildlife habitats. More wildlife is being destroyed by the developers, the dam builders, the road builders, and the swamp drainers than is destroyed by hunters. As the human population grows, the choices of land-use will be more and more difficult. Without habitat for wildlife, there will be no wildlife.

Deer Crossing

1. Define the following terms:
   game   nongame
   game management   poaching
2. What human activities had nearly wiped out much of the wildlife by the 1930's?
3. What was needed to restore wildlife to healthy populations?

Money for Wildlife

4. What was the purpose of the Pittman-Robertson Act? What was the source of the money?
5. List three appropriate uses of funds collected under the P-R Act.
6. What is the source of the money used for the National Wildlife Refuge system?
7. How does the National Wildlife Refuge System benefit endangered species?
8. How do wildlife refuges benefit people?

Game versus Nongame

9. What is the difference between a game and a nongame species?
10. Why do wildlife management plans often favor game species?
11. How does wildlife management in Missouri differ from wildlife management in many other states?

The Return of the Whitetails

12. Compare the population of white-tailed deer in the 1920s with the population in the 1990s, and explain the change.
13. What is the problem with the deer herd in Gettysburg National Military Park? What is the cause of the problem? And what is the recommended solution?

Nature's Way

14. What is the major limiting factor for deer?
15. What is the connection between the size of the rack (antlers) and hunting?

Game Management

16. What species is the major predator of the white-tailed deer?
17. State the argument for hunting as a game management tool.
18. State the argument against hunting as a game management tool.

19. What is the primary method of wildlife management?
20. What two facts do game managers need to know in order to determine how many white-tailed deer should be "harvested"?
21. Compare the population of quail or ruffed grouse in the spring when there is a regulated hunting season to the population in an area that is protected from hunting.

Doves in Indiana

22. Choose the correct word or phrase that reflects the information provided by the Indiana Fish and Wildlife Division during the legislative debates.
    A. (Most/Few) doves nest during the hunting season.
    B. The young are cared for by (the mother/both parents).
    C. The mourning dove feeds (mainly on ragweed seeds/on many types of seeds).
    D. The weight of mourning doves are mainly (bones and feathers/breast muscle).
    E. In states with hunting seasons, populations of mourning doves have (decreased/increased).
23. List the differences between the mourning dove and the passenger pigeon regarding food, nesting habitat, and offspring.
24. If you had been a member of the Indiana senate, would you have voted for or against the mourning dove hunting season? Defend your position.

To Hunt or Not to Hunt

25. Does hunting threaten any wildlife populations? If so, explain.
26. What is the biggest cause in the decline of waterfowl populations?
27. How do hunters help wildlife populations?
28. Explain the statement, "Everyday some animals must die to allow others to live."
29. In addition to hunting and fishing, how do humans kill wildlife?
30. List several human activities that cause declines in wildlife populations.

UNIT 2

The Atmosphere — Is the Sky Falling?

Nimbus-7 TOMS Images: The 12 octobers

The image below shows monthly average ozone levels during a 12-year period taken from NASA's Total Ozone mapping Spectrometer (TOMS) aboard Nimbus-7 satellite.

The color scale on the bottom of this image shows the total ozone values. The ozone hole development is indicated by low values (dark purple colors) apparent in the later years over Antarctica. This contrasts with the relatively higher ozone values over Antarctica in earlier years (1979-1982), when the hole is virtually nonexistent (blue green/green colors).

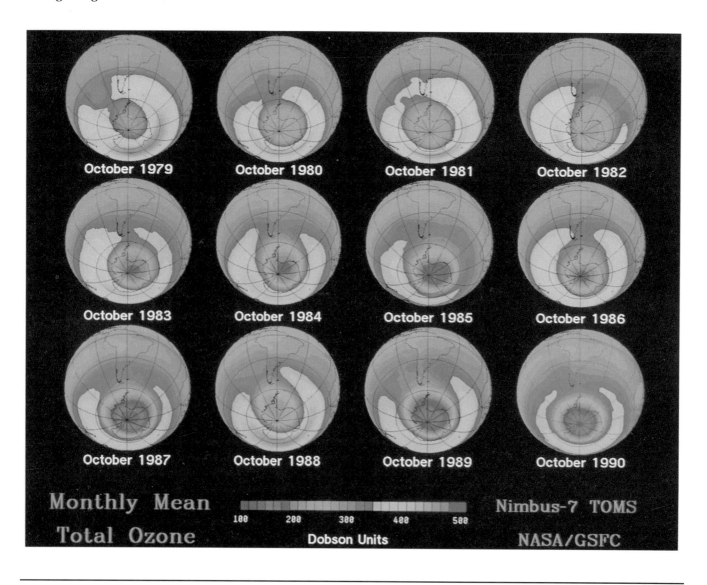

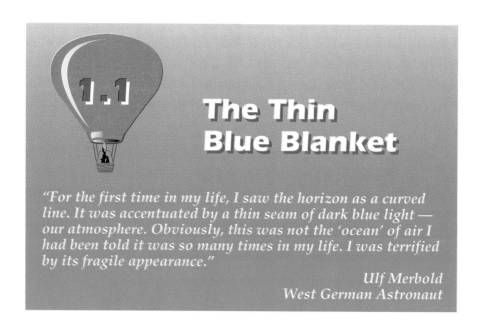

The Thin Blue Blanket

"For the first time in my life, I saw the horizon as a curved line. It was accentuated by a thin seam of dark blue light — our atmosphere. Obviously, this was not the 'ocean' of air I had been told it was so many times in my life. I was terrified by its fragile appearance."

Ulf Merbold
West German Astronaut

Photographs taken on trips to outer space give us new views of our world. Looking at Earth's horizon, it appears as if there is a thin blue blanket surrounding the planet. It is this blanket that makes it possible for humans and many other species to call this planet "home." This halo of blue is created when sunlight is scattered by Earth's atmosphere. The **atmosphere** is a mixture of gases — mostly nitrogen (78%) and oxygen (21%). It also contains argon, carbon dioxide, traces of several other gases, water vapor, and dust particles.

The thickness and colors of the blanket of gases surrounding a planet reveals information about its atmosphere and climate. The planet Mercury is small, and the force of gravity is too weak to hold even a thin blanket of gases. Without an atmosphere, Mercury's sky is black and the planet can't support life as we know it.

If astronauts travelled to Venus, they might describe a thick orange blanket beneath a thin blue one. The dense blanket of carbon dioxide (98%) helps create a climate that is far too hot — nearly 900°F (470°C) — for astronauts or other earthlings. Far from the sun, Uranus wears an extra-thick, blue-green blanket made of hydrogen, helium and methane. Its atmosphere is so thick that no sunlight reaches the planet.

Only Earth, with its atmosphere, provides the life-support system that we need. In proportion to the size of Earth, the atmosphere is no thicker than the skin on an apple. Most (99%) of the matter in the atmosphere is within 19 miles (30 km) of the Earth's surface. At higher altitudes the Earth's blanket is thinner. This is why airplanes flying at high altitudes must have pressurized cabins and also why the climate is cooler in the mountains.

Nasa's Nimbus-7 polar-orbiting satellite launched in 1978 has provided reliable TOMS (Total Ozone Mapping Spectrometer) of the global ozone layer.

The "hole" in the ozone layer over Antarctica is now known to damage one-celled plants called plankton living in the Antarctic ocean. Some species of plankton are sensitive to UV — others are resistant. There will likely be a change in the balance of species. Plankton are the primary producers at the base of the food chain. What will happen if the ozone "hole" keeps getting bigger, if UV rays get even stronger, and if the plankton population decreases?

Formation of Ozone

1. O_2 — UV light ⟶ $O + O$

2. $O + O_2$ — catalyst ⟶ O_3

Natural Destruction of Ozone

$O_3 + NO \longrightarrow O_2 + NO_2$

$2\,O_3 \longrightarrow 3\,O_2$

$3\,O_2 \rightleftharpoons 2\,O_3$ $3\,O_2 \leftharpoondown\!\rightharpoonup 2\,O_3$

Equilibrium   Nonequilibrium

The Earth's Atmosphere at Sea Level		
Selected Gases (in dry air)	Concentration percentage	(by volume) ppm
Nitrogen	78.08	780,800.
Oxygen	20.95	209,500.
Argon	00.93	9,300.
Carbon dioxide	00.0355	355.
Helium	00.00052	5.2
Methane	00.00017	1.7
Nitrous oxide (N_2O)	00.00003	0.3
Hydrogen	00.00005	0.05
Carbon monoxide	00.00003	0.03
Ozone	00.000025	0.025
Nitrogen dioxide (NO_2)	00.00002	0.02
Ammonia	00.000001	0.001
Sulfur dioxide	00.0000002	0.0002

If we could travel back to a time before there was life on this planet, we might find an atmosphere that was very different from the one that exists today. Some scientists think that planet Earth's primitive atmosphere contained large amounts of methane, ammonia, and water vapor. If this hypothesis is correct, our atmosphere has been drastically altered by events that we may never fully understand. One of these events was the formation of the ozone shield.

The Ozone Shield — a Natural Sunscreen

Most oxygen in the atmosphere exists in molecules formed by the reactions of two oxygen atoms (O_2). When ultraviolet light or bolts of lightning strike an oxygen molecule, it splits the molecule to create free oxygen atoms (O). Some of these atoms join other oxygen molecules to form ozone (O_3).

Most of the Earth's ozone (90%) forms a protective shield or filter within the stratosphere. Here ozone is constantly being produced, but the concentration is never more than a few parts per million by volume. Why is there so little ozone in the stratosphere? In the presence of certain chemicals, ozone easily breaks down. Nitric oxide (NO), a naturally occurring gas produced by volcanoes, eventually reaches the stratosphere. By destroying ozone, it counteracts the action of the sun's ultraviolet (UV) rays.

Usually the system is in balance, and the rate of ozone formation is equal to the rate of destruction. This is called an equilibrium. Scientists discovered that certain human activities are upsetting this equilibrium, and that is not good.

Biological Effects

The ozone shield is essential to life on planet Earth. Thus the ozone shield prevents most (99%) of the sun's harmful UV rays from reaching Earth. At a monitoring station in Argentina, significant increases in UV rays were detected during the summers of 1990 and 1992. Ultraviolet radiation can seriously damage plants, animals, and other forms of life. It also affects materials such as paints and plastics.

Ultraviolet radiation causes certain types of skin cancers and cataracts in humans. One in six Americans will suffer from skin cancer, and the incidence is increasing nearly 4 percent each year. The UN Environment Program predicts a 26% rise in nonmelanoma skin cancers — 300,000 additional cases a year — if there is a 10 percent worldwide drop in the ozone level. There could be 1.75 million additional cases of cataracts every year. There is some evidence that suggests the increase in UV light will lower the response of the immune system to infectious diseases.

While sunlight is necessary for photosynthesis, ultraviolet light is not. Studies show increasing levels of ultraviolet radiation decrease the rate of photosynthesis in sensitive plants. Some crops, including legumes, are extremely sensitive to UV light. Increased UV light slows the growth rate and lowers the yield of many crops that we depend upon for food.

Aquatic life is also very sensitive to ultraviolet radiation. Research shows that a moderate increase in UV light harms the one-celled algae that are the basis of the food web in the oceans. Experiments also show that frog eggs do not develop properly when exposed to increased levels of UV radiation.

NASA's Upper Atmosphere Research Satellite (UARS) launched September 1991.

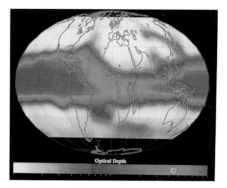

The above image shows aerosol particles in Earth's stratosphere acquired by Langley Research Center's SAGE II (Stratospheric Aerosol and Gas Experiment) satellite-based instrument. The map shows that, within a month following the Pinatubo eruption, a dense belt of material had encircled the globe in the tropics and optical depths in the tropics had increased by about a factor of 100 compared with measurements taken prior to the eruption.

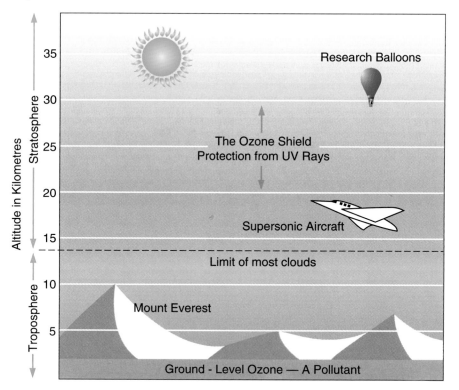

◀ Ozone in the Atmosphere

CFCs — The Risks and Benefits of Technology

Compounds containing carbon, fluorine, and chlorine are called **chlorofluorocarbons** or CFCs. CFCs are nontoxic and nonflammable. They are also inexpensive to produce. These characteristics made them ideal for several important uses that made life easier, more comfortable and even safer. Unfortunately, CFCs were found to harm the environment and were banned as propellants in the United States in 1978, although other countries continue to use them. Even the United States makes exceptions to its CFC ban. One exception to the ban is for medical use such as the inhalers used by people with respiratory problems. The following chart shows uses of CFCs as reported in 1992.

Worldwide Uses of CFCs	Percentage
• Blowing agents to make foam insulation, packing materials	24
• Solvents used as cleaning agents	24
• Air conditioning in vehicles	20
• Refrigeration	15
• Propellants in aerosol sprays	15
• Other uses	2

In the lower atmosphere CFCs are extremely stable chemicals. Eventually they rise into the stratosphere where the sun's UV rays split chlorine from the CFC molecules, and the chlorine attacks the ozone molecules. Each chlorine atom may destroy up to 100,000 ozone molecules before it is carried back into the lower atmosphere where it is washed out by the rain.

1. UV light splits chlorofluorocarbon (CFC) molecules releasing free chlorine (Cl).
2. The free chlorine atoms react with ozone molecules, forming chlorine monoxide (ClO) and oxygen (O_2).
3. A free oxygen atom (O) combines with the O in a ClO molecule, and the chlorine atom (Cl) is then free to remove an oxygen atom from another ozone molecule.
4. This is a repeat of equation 2 showing the continuous destruction of ozone. In this cycle the chlorine may destroy 100,000 ozone molecules.

CFCs Attack on Ozone

1. $CFCl_3 + UV\ light \longrightarrow CFC_2 + Cl$

2. $Cl + O_3 \longrightarrow ClO + O_2$

3. $ClO + O \longrightarrow Cl + O_2$

4. $Cl + O_3 \longrightarrow ClO + O_2$

Warning Not Heeded

The potential for the destruction of the ozone shield is not a recent discovery. As early as 1974, scientists studying the effect of CFCs on the ozone layer concluded that a "problem is well on its way . . . the present indication is the ozone layer is being destroyed."

The first action to stop the destruction of the ozone layer was not taken until 1977 when the UN Environmental Program drew up a **World Plan of Action on the Ozone Layer**. The UN action led the US, Canada, and several European countries to ban the use of CFCs in aerosols.

CFCs were essential industrial chemicals, and alternatives were not readily available. Politicians and scientists wanted more evidence before further restricting the use of such important chemicals. The evidence came in 1985, when a team of scientists reported a 50 percent decrease in the concentration of ozone over Antarctica — an ozone "hole." Scientists confirmed that the so-called hole was primarily due to the presence of chlorine monoxide (ClO), a by-product of the breakdown of CFCs.

Ozone is being destroyed at a much faster rate than it could be replaced by natural processes. Unique weather patterns during the spring season contribute to the great loss of ozone over Antarctica, but the loss is not limited to the South Pole. In 1993, scientists reported that ozone levels were 9 to 20 percent below average in the middle and upper latitudes of the northern hemisphere.

The Montreal Protocol

Is it too late to prevent damage to the ozone shield? Millions of tons of CFCs have been released into the atmosphere and many of them are still on their way to the stratosphere. As more CFCs reach the ozone layer, more ozone will be destroyed. The best we can do is reduce the future impact. We know that chlorine from CFCs and other related chemicals is the major cause of ozone destruction. The best way to limit damage in the future is to stop the production of these chemicals and reduce the amount released into the atmosphere.

The thinning of the ozone shield is a global environmental problem, and the solution requires the cooperation of all countries. On September 16, 1987, twenty-four countries signed the **Montreal Protocol on Substances that Deplete the Ozone Layer**. The goal was a 50 percent reduction in the use of CFCs. A 1990 amendment phases out the use of CFCs and other ozone-destroying chemicals. Now more than 92 countries are working together to protect the ozone shield.

New Technology

The CFCs in refrigerators and air conditioners are being replaced by hydrochlorofluorocarbons (HCFCs) that are less stable. HCFCs are less destructive to the ozone layer because fewer molecules reach the stratosphere. The 1990 Clean Air Act mandates that the production of HCFCs be stopped by 2030. The chemical industry is searching for replacement chemicals. The chemicals need to be nonflammable, noncorrosive, have low toxicity, and be reasonably priced.

In some cases, the CFCs used in cleaning electronic parts are being replaced by soap and water or citric acid and water solutions. One company is saving $200,000 per year by switching to a cleaning solvent made of citric acid (lemon juice) and water.

Halons are stable chemicals that contain bromine instead of chlorine. Like CFCs, they break down the ozone layer. The halons in

THINK ABOUT IT

Ozone is a pollutant in the lower atmosphere. A question that is often asked is "Why don't we ship the ozone up to the stratosphere to repair the ozone layer?"

TRY TO FIND OUT

CFCs are currently being replaced by HCFCs. Though HCFCs are an improvement, they still react with atmospheric ozone. Find out what new refrigerants are being developed to replace HCFCs. Are there any refrigerants that are completely safe?

hand-held fire extinguishers are being replaced by carbon dioxide, but carbon dioxide fire extinguishers are not suitable in all situations. In some military situations, carbon dioxide would not effectively reduce the danger of fire and explosion. The additional weight of carbon dioxide tanks creates a problem for airplanes. The search for a replacement for halons continues.

What You Can Do

- Auto air conditioners are a major source of CFCs. Make sure that the repair shop captures and recycles coolant when servicing or repairing your family's auto air conditioner.
- Refrigerator service companies are required to recycle coolant when making repairs. Have the coolant drained from a discarded refrigerator or air conditioner.
- Use carbon dioxide fire extinguishers rather than extinguishers that contain halon.
- Avoid spot removers and fabric protectors that contain 1,1,1 trichlorethane.
- Use sunscreen that blocks both UV-A and UV-B rays and avoid the sun between 10 a.m. and 3 p.m. if possible.
- Wear sunglasses that filter UV radiation.

1.1 QUESTIONS FOR STUDY AND DISCUSSION

1. Identify the two major gases that form 99% of Earth's atmosphere.
2. Explain why Earth has a thin blue blanket while Mercury has none.
3. What gas helps to create the hot climate on Venus?
4. Identify the environmental conditions that make life as we know it impossible on Uranus.
5. Explain why life is possible at sea level but life support systems are needed only a few miles or kilometres above Earth's surface.

The Ozone Shield
6. What are the sources of energy that split oxygen molecules in the atmosphere? What molecule is formed when three oxygen atoms join?
7. Identify the two layers of the atmosphere and describe the position of each layer in relation to the surface of the Earth.

8. Where in the atmosphere is the ozone layer found?
9. What is the concentration of ozone in the ozone shield? What prevents the concentration of ozone from increasing?

Biological Effects
10. Explain how the ozone layer protects life on planet Earth.
11. What are two effects of UV radiation on humans? Why may the occurrence of infectious diseases increase if people are exposed to increased levels of UV radiation?
12. How does ultraviolet radiation affect plants? Are all plants equally affected?
13. How might increased ultraviolet radiation affect aquatic food chains?

CFCs — The Risks and Benefits of Technology
14. What characteristics made CFCs ideal for use in a number of consumer products?

15. What percent of the CFCs produced was used as propellants in aerosol sprays? Do you think it was necessary to ban this use? Explain.
16. When CFCs were banned as an aerosol propellant an exception was made for medical uses. Do you agree with this exception? Support your opinion.
17. Describe the series of events that occur when CFCs reach the stratosphere. What eventually halts the destructive reactions?
18. What is the effect of CFCs on the chemistry of the stratosphere?

Warning Not Heeded
19. When did scientists first discover evidence that linked CFCs to the destruction of the ozone layer? When was the first action taken to stop the destruction of the ozone layer? What action was taken?
20. Why weren't other uses of CFCs banned in 1977?
21. What evidence did scientists collect in 1985 that confirmed the connection between the presence of CFCs in the stratosphere and the destruction of ozone?

22. Does the term ozone "hole" accurately describe what is happening to the ozone shield? Explain.

The Montreal Protocol
23. What actions will best protect the ozone shield?
24. What was the Montreal Protocol and why was it necessary?

New Technology
25. What chemicals are replacing CFCs in refrigerators and air conditioners? Why is this group of chemicals "safer"?
26. What are the desirable characteristics of chemicals that replace CFCs?
27. Are CFCs essential for cleaning electronic parts? If not, why do you think that they were used for this purpose?
28. What is the essential use of halons? Why can't halons be replaced by carbon dioxide?

What You Can Do
29. List one way you can help protect the ozone shield.
30. How can you best protect a small child from UV rays?

Science
Technology
Society

ISSUES

A PROPOSED RULE

In 1993, the EPA issued proposed rules prohibiting the venting of CFCs (chlorofluorocarbons) and HCFCs (hydrochlorofluorocarbons) during service or disposal of air conditioners and refrigerators. Landfill operators would be required to ensure that CFCs and HCFCs are removed before final disposal.

Violations would be punishable with a fine of up to $25,000 per day. EPA estimated that 110,000 metric tonnes of CFCs and HCFCs were being released each year in the United States during service and disposal of air conditioners and refrigerators.

- Should this proposed rule be adopted? Support your position.

2.1

Weather Patterns

"Achievable improvements in the atmospheric sciences (meteorology) are essential to the better understanding of the most fundamental environmental issues facing the world."
American Meteorological Society

Weather Predictions

Meteorology is the study of the physics and chemistry of the atmosphere. **Weather** refers to the atmospheric conditions that result from interactions among temperature, moisture, winds, and clouds. These components of the atmosphere behave according to scientific laws; therefore, weather can be predicted.

You may love it or hate it, but every morning when you look out your window there is weather. One or two extra weeks of cold weather in the mountains may mean additional income for ski resort owners. For the orchard or vineyard owner, it may mean the loss of this season's crop of peaches or grapes.

A rainy day may spoil a picnic or outing for someone who has a day off, but for the farmer, it may mean lost dollars because a field of hay is spoiled. If high winds come with the rain, it could mean the loss of a boat for a fisherman — and maybe a loss of life. Fishermen and farmers often begin their day by listening to the weather forecast.

People who spend much time out of doors have learned to use signs of nature for short-term weather predictions. Signs that occur because of physical changes in the atmosphere can accurately predict short-range weather forecasts. Some of these signs and their scientific explanations follow. You can probably think of others.

"A bright, silvery moon in late summer or fall means frost."
- **Explanation:** Clouds act as a blanket trapping the heat near the Earth's surface. If the sky is clear, Earth will lose more heat, and the chance of frost increases.

"Swallows fly high; clear blue sky. Swallows fly low; rain we shall know."
- **Explanation:** Before a storm, the barometric pressure is low and the birds adjust their flight to compensate for the change in air

Storms along the coast may cause erosion of sand and be dangerous for fishermen.

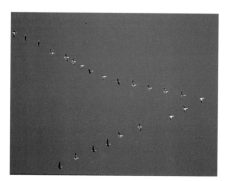

This sight may indicate the coming of cold weather or the approach of spring.

pressure. When the barometric pressure is low, flying is more difficult. Smoke follows much the same path as the birds. When the barometric pressure is low, smoke from a campfire hugs the ground. When it is high, the smoke rises straight from the fire.

"When spiders weave their web by noon, fine weather is coming soon."
- **Explanation:** Silk shortens and snaps when it absorbs moisture, so the spider must constantly repair the web. In dry weather silk is easier to spin, and the spider will have fewer repairs to make.

Wildlife behavior often provides clues to weather changes. Cats groom their coats more often when a storm is approaching. The increase in static electricity separates the hair and makes the extra grooming necessary. Deer and cattle feed earlier and longer than usual before a storm. If the elk suddenly begin to migrate out of the high country during late fall, it means that heavy snowstorms are on the way. These animals are probably responding to dropping barometric pressure and changing temperatures.

There are many "signs" of a coming bad winter, according to those who practice the folk art of forecasting, but these traditional long-range weather predictions are often wrong. According to folk lore, if the woolly bear caterpillar has a wide brown band, the winter will be mild. A narrow band indicates a harsh winter. Scientists tell us that the width of the band is determined by the genetic messages the caterpillar inherited, not by future environmental conditions.

The Weather Forecast

Today, weather forecasting is a complicated science that depends on sophisticated technology. Advances in science and technology make it possible to protect lives, if not property, against the forces of nature. The federal government spends millions of dollars each year on atmospheric research. Much of this money is spent on advanced satellites that collect information about the conditions in the atmosphere and supercomputers that interpret this information.

Weather satellites relay pictures of the cloud cover, temperatures, and wind speeds. Satellites offer two advantages to weather forecasters. They provide a global view of weather systems and they constantly monitor conditions. Twice each day, weather balloons are released from a limited number of weather stations. Tracked from the ground, they provide information about temperature, humidity, and pressure in the upper atmosphere. Weather balloons and aircraft are important sources of information because they provide more accurate data than satellites.

At rest areas along interstate highways travelers may find information about weather conditions.

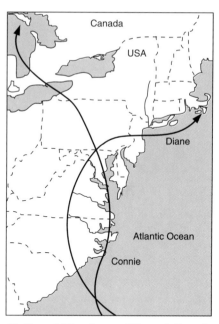

Paths of Hurricane "Connie" and "Diane"

WHAT DO YOU THINK?

Can you predict how clear-cutting of forests affects the weather? How will deforestation affect regional weather patterns such as rainfall, where rain forests once stood?

Storm Warnings

A new $3 million radar system is far more accurate than older radar systems. By bouncing microwaves off water droplets, Doppler radar can map the velocity of wind currents within a cloud. Using a Doppler radar system (sometimes called Nexrad for Next Generation Radar), forecasters can see inside a storm cloud, detect tornadoes in their embryonic stages, and issue warnings to people in the path of the storm.

Hurricanes were first spotted at sea by passing ships or by "hurricane-hunter" patrol planes. When Hurricanes Connie and Diane hit an unprepared East Coast in 1955, they caused billions of dollars in damage and many lives were lost. The destruction caused by these hurricanes led to the formation of the National Hurricane Center at Miami, Florida.

There were no satellite images of hurricanes Connie and Diane. The death toll was high because people had little, if any, warning. Then the first weather satellite was launched in 1960. Today a team of hurricane specialists relies on information from weather satellites, radar, and specially equipped aircraft. This information helps scientists determine the intensity of a hurricane, project the possible path, and issue public advisories. In 1992, hurricane Andrew hit Florida with a vengeance, causing $20 billion worth of property damage, but advanced warning allowed a massive evacuation that saved countless lives.

Improving the Forecast

With high-tech equipment, we have learned more about weather in the last fifty years than in all previous history. Still there is much to learn. Meteorologists can track the jet stream — a 200-mile-an-hour river of air that flows 20,000 to 30,000 feet above Earth's surface, but they do not understand why it moves the way it does. A poorly understood phenomenon known as El Niño — a dramatic warming of water in the East Pacific — may hold the key to seasonal forecasting.

Using information from hundreds of observation points, computers can predict the probable pattern of the upper atmosphere for the next 24 hours. Still, long-range predictions are very difficult to make because of the many variables that determine the weather. An improvement in the accuracy of long-range weather forecasts will require a better understanding of the connections between ocean water temperatures and weather patterns.

The Hydrogen Furnace

All weather is due to the interactions of four elements. The first of these is a giant star, the sun. The relationship between the Sun and Earth can be compared by a model in which Earth is the size and weight of a table-tennis ball. The Sun in the model would measure more than twelve and one-half feet (4 m) in diameter and would weigh about three tons. It is a *gigantic* hydrogen furnace using four million tons (3.6 million metric tonnes) of hydrogen fuel per second. At this rate, the sun has enough fuel to last at least 30 billion years.

Without the Sun, there would be no weather. The Sun produces energy by a process called **fusion**. The nuclei of two hydrogen atoms are fused to form one atom of helium. The helium atom contains less energy than the two hydrogen molecules. The "extra" energy is released as solar energy. This solar energy is the driving force behind all weather. Solar energy is converted by the atmosphere to wind.

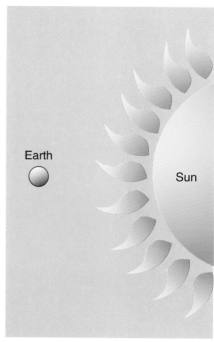

Earth and the Sun

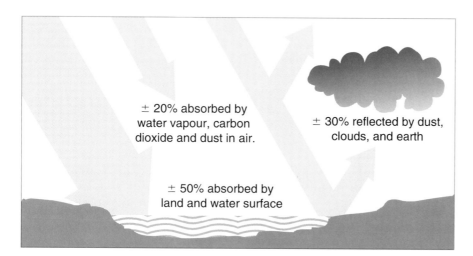

± 20% absorbed by water vapour, carbon dioxide and dust in air.

± 30% reflected by dust, clouds, and earth

± 50% absorbed by land and water surface

◄ Solar Radiation — What Happens to It?

The Air Around Us

The second factor that affects our weather is the atmosphere. The transfer of heat or light waves of energy is called **radiation**. As the light energy travels through the atmosphere, some of the waves are deflected by water droplets or dust particles. This is why we often see a rainbow when the Sun shines after a rain.

Much of the solar energy (30%) coming from the Sun is reflected by the air, the clouds and objects on Earth's surface. An additional 20 percent of the incoming solar radiation is absorbed by clouds, dust particles, water vapor, and other gases in the atmosphere. Thus only half of the solar radiation coming from the Sun is absorbed by Earth and objects on it.

When solar energy strikes an object, the energy that is absorbed is changed from a short wavelength form (light energy) to a long wavelength form of energy. We cannot see the long wavelengths of energy given off by the object, but we feel the energy as heat. It is the heat energy radiating from Earth's surface that warms the atmosphere.

DID YOU KNOW?

New technology has been developed to accurately predict tornadoes. Called DOTT (detection of tornadic thunderstorms), the unique combination of weather satellites and computer models has correctly predicted which thunderstorms are likely to spawn tornadoes. DOTT sends out its warning alarm up to 2 hours before the twister touches down. This advance warning gives people time to seek shelter and can reduce loss of lives.

WHAT DO YOU THINK?

Northern Siberia is so far from the equator that it receives no sunlight during winter months. Some Russian scientists have proposed putting a giant mirror in orbit above Earth. The mirror would be positioned so that it would reflect sunlight down on Siberia during the winter. What affect do you think this will have on the ecology of the Siberian tundra?

How does water vapor and carbon dioxide from stacks like these, affect the temperature of the atmosphere?

In a desert, where the air is clear and dry, 90 percent of the solar radiation reaches Earth and is changed to heat energy. While the daytime temperatures may be extremely high, the nights get cold because as much as 90 percent of the heat passes back into space. The desert is covered by only a very thin blanket of the major heat-trapping gas — water vapor.

Where the air is humid, the daytime temperatures may be warm, but they do not reach the extreme highs recorded in the desert. The water vapor in the atmosphere acts as a sheer curtain or screen that reflects light energy. The land may receive only 40 percent of the incoming solar radiation. At night, the water vapor acts as a thick blanket that prevents the heat from escaping, so the nighttime temperature remains warm.

Earth's atmosphere is like the glass in a greenhouse or car window. While the short wavelengths of light energy pass through the glass, most of the longer wavelength heat energy is trapped. Although the atmosphere does not trap heat in the same way a greenhouse does, the warming of the atmosphere is called the **greenhouse effect**. Planet Earth is a rather pleasant place to live because of the greenhouse effect that is created by its atmosphere.

Another important feature of the atmosphere is the cloud cover. Today, meteorologists are spending more time and money on the study of clouds than on any other area of research. **Clouds** are airborne masses of microscopic water droplets or ice crystals.

Smoke, whether from forest fires, chimneys, or automobiles, adds particles to the air. Winds pick up small particles of salt from the ocean or dust from exposed soil. All of these particles provide surfaces for the condensation of water vapor.

When moist air is pushed upward and is cooled, the water vapor begins to condense around these small particles. Water droplets or ice crystals will be formed, depending upon the temperature. The result of this process is the formation of clouds. The moisture in clouds will eventually be returned to Earth as precipitation.

The features of Earth's surface and the movement of its winds determine where the moisture will fall. The amount of moisture that is returned to Earth each year can vary from less than one inch, that falls in the interior of the Sahara Desert to as much as 50 feet, that fall on Mount Waialeale in Hawaii — the wettest spot on Earth.

Destruction of the tropical rain forest could affect weather over the entire planet. Transpiration from plants in the Amazon rain forest is an important source of water vapor for the formation of clouds. Clouds are an important factor in moderating Earth's temperature. They may be an effective sunscreen that reflects significant amounts of light energy. They also are an effective blanket that traps heat energy.

Change the chemistry of the atmosphere — the prevailing weather conditions — and the climate may change. The amount of water vapor and other heat-trapping gases in the atmosphere help to regulate the temperature of the planet. The mean temperature of planet Earth is 57°F (14°C). This temperature is significant because it allows water to exist as a liquid, and water in a liquid state is essential for life as we know it.

Seasonal Weather

The third factor that affects weather is the shape and movement of planet Earth. Earth is nearly spherical in shape. If you could squeeze a basketball so that both ends are somewhat flattened, then the basketball would be an appropriate model of Earth. If you shine a flashlight on the basketball, the light will be brightest where it is at a right angle to the ball. Other regions of the ball will be dimmer because the light striking an object at an oblique angle spreads out over more of its surface. Areas near the equator are always brighter and warmer than areas near the poles because they receive more direct sunlight.

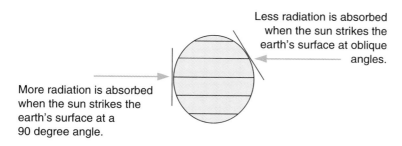

Less radiation is absorbed when the sun strikes the earth's surface at oblique angles.

◀ Solar Radiation

More radiation is absorbed when the sun strikes the earth's surface at a 90 degree angle.

As the air at the equator is warmed, it rises and is replaced by cooler, denser air. A flow of air is caused by the difference in temperatures at the poles and the equator. If Earth did not rotate, the movement of air would be from the poles toward the equator, but Earth rotates on its own axis from west to east. This rotation determines the direction of prevailing winds and ocean currents.

Earth is tilted on its axis. Regions of Earth are tipped toward or away from the sun. It is the tilt of Earth that creates the four seasons. In autumn and winter the northern hemisphere is tilted away from the sun. The decreased angle of the sun's rays brings shorter days

◀ Movement of Air

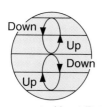

Down Up
Down
Up

Air Movement without Rotation

Prevailing Westerlies
Northeast Trades
Southeast Trades
Prevailing Westerlies

Prevailing Surface Winds due to Rotation

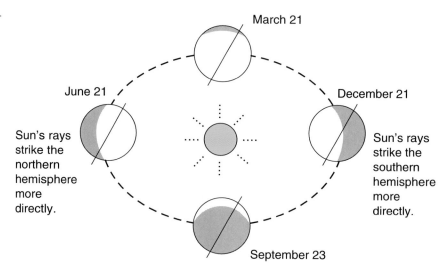

March 21

June 21

Sun's rays strike the northern hemisphere more directly.

December 21

Sun's rays strike the southern hemisphere more directly.

September 23

and colder weather. In spring and summer the northern hemisphere is tilted so that the sun's rays strike more directly. The weather becomes warmer.

Down to Earth

The fourth factor that influences the weather is the shape and make-up of Earth's surface. Due to its special chemical make-up, water needs a larger amount of heat to change its temperature than most other substances. When the sun is shining, the temperature of the oceans and lakes does not rise as fast as the temperature on the land. At night, when there is no sunshine, water loses its heat more slowly than the land.

Winds and waves easily mix the water and distribute the heat downward as far as 100 metres. Land is heated only on the surface. The heat can not easily be transferred to the deeper layers. Thus the water provides a much larger bank for heat storage.

Land gains and loses heat faster than water. The land "bank" loses its heat faster than the "bank" of water. This means that the land will be warmer in the daytime and cooler at night. This difference in the temperature of the land and the water creates a difference in air pressure that causes the movement of air.

People living near a body of water experience cooler temperatures in the summer and warmer temperatures in the winter than those who live far away from a body of water. This explains why many people like to spend week-ends and vacations at the beach or near a lake.

During the day, the land warms faster than the water. As the air above the land is warmed, it expands and rises. The cooler, more dense air over the water moves in and pushes the warmer air upward. At night the land cools faster than the water. The air above

THINK ABOUT IT

Global Problems

The atmosphere is a vital component of planet Earth's life support system. It is a moving envelope that receives substances from an ecosystem. It transports, transforms, and deposits those substances in another ecosystem. When pollutants enter the atmosphere, an environmental problem may become an international problem.

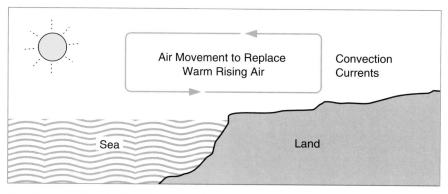

Daytime — Sea to Land

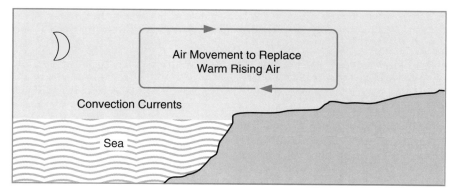

Nighttime — Land to Sea

the water is warmed as the water slowly gives up the heat it has stored. As the warm air expands and rises, it is pushed upward by the cooler, more dense air from the land.

Mountain ranges also help determine the weather. The Mississippi River Valley and the Great Plains lie in a depression between the Rocky Mountains in the West and the Appalachians in the East. Cold air masses sweep down from the North. When the cold air clashes with warm, moist air from the Gulf of Mexico, large storms and blizzards occur.

As the storm approaches a mountain range, the air is pushed upward. As the air rises it is cooled, and the water vapor condenses into some form of precipitation. In the United States, most of the precipitation falls on the western side of the mountains.

Humans can change the local weather pattern by adding buildings and other structures on the surface of Earth. Brick, concrete, asphalt, and other building materials absorb and hold heat. The vertical surfaces of buildings collect heat and reflect it to each other rather than back into the atmosphere. The mass of buildings makes the center of the city warmer than the surrounding area.

Early morning finds a valley in the Rocky Mountains covered with a layer of fog. The temperature inversion also traps air pollutants.

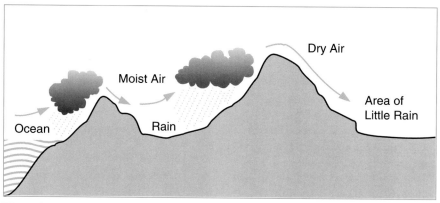

The Effect of Mountains on Weather

This creates an island of heat. If there is no wind, the air moves in a current similar to that of sea breezes. Think of the city as an island surrounded with water. The warm air rises and is replaced by cooler air from the edge of the city.

As the air — filled with tiny suspended particles — moves up over the city, it forms a ceiling. This can easily be seen as a haze. The particles reflect sunlight and the air circulation slows. On windless days the city's air becomes filled with pollution. Only a strong prevailing wind will move the pollution away from the city.

Under normal conditions the temperature of the atmosphere decreases with height. When there is no wind, an inversion may occur. An **inversion** is a condition in which a layer of warmer air covers a layer of cooler air beneath it.

Inversions frequently occur in valleys after the sun sets, and the cooler air flows down the mountain or hillside. In a valley, the cool air flows down along the mountain at night. The cool air becomes trapped by a warmer layer of air above. The inversion will disappear as the morning Sun heats Earth, and Earth warms the air. This may not happen until the Sun is directly overhead. During the winter months, Denver, Colorado often experiences inversions that last all day.

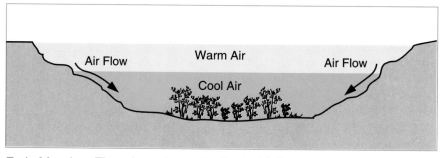

Early Morning: There is an Inversion in the Valley

Fall and winter generally have the longest-lasting and the greatest number of inversions. The major air pollution disasters of our time — Meuse Valley, Belgium, Donora, Pennsylvania, and London, England — were the result of inversions that occurred during the fall or winter months.

2.1 QUESTIONS FOR STUDY AND DISCUSSION

1. As you read and study this section, define the following words:

   cloud   jet stream
   El Niño   meteorology
   fusion   radiation
   greenhouse effect   weather
   inversion

Weather Predictions

2. Identify the four parts of the atmosphere that affect our weather.
3. List three careers that may be affected by the weather.
4. Give two signs that predict a coming storm.
5. On a clear September night, a gardener notices a bright, silvery moon. The tomato plants in the garden are still producing. Should the gardener cover the plants? Support your decision.
6. You and a friend are hiking the Appalachian Trail. You notice that the smoke rises straight above the camp fire. What kind of weather can you predict for tomorrow?
7. While on a hunting trip in the high country of the Rocky Mountains, the guide notices that the elk have started to migrate. Would it be a good idea to break camp and head down the mountain? What may happen if the hunters decide to stay?
8. On your way to school you see a flock of geese heading south. What kind of weather can you expect?
9. "The higher the weeds grow, the more it will snow." Does this "sign" accurately predict a coming bad winter? Explain why the statement is or is not a good long-range weather forecasting sign.

The Weather Forecast

10. List two advantages of satellites as sources of information for predicting weather.
11. Why do meteorologists still rely on weather balloons and aircraft to provide information for forecasts?
12. What types of information are collected by instruments on board satellites, weather balloons and aircraft?

Storm Warnings

13. What type of instrument allows meteorologists to gather information about winds within a developing cloud? What weather event can be identified using this technology?
14. What historic event led to the formation of the National Hurricane Center?
15. The cost of a new weather satellite is perhaps several billion dollars. If a new satellite was needed to replace an old satellite to maintain the accuracy of current forecasts would you defend or object to the expense? Support your position. Would you approve the expense if the satellite would improve the accuracy of forecasts?

Improving the Forecast

16. Today, because of modern technology, humans can make very accurate long range forecasts. (True/false)?
17. An understanding of two physical phenomena may be necessary for the accurate prediction of long-range weather patterns. What are these two phenomena?

The Hydrogen Furnace

18. Why is the sun sometimes called a hydrogen furnace? What is the waste product that is produced?

19. Is the sun likely to run out of fuel in your lifetime?
20. Is it technically correct to say that the sun "burns" hydrogen for fuel? How does the process used by the sun differ from the process of burning?
21. In the atmosphere solar energy is converted to what force that causes weather systems?

The Air Around Us

22. What two substances in the atmosphere scatter light waves?
23. Would there be rainbows if there were no atmosphere? Explain.
24. What happens to sunlight when it strikes an object on Earth?
25. How does the atmosphere affect the temperature of Earth? What is this effect on temperature called?
26. What is the major heat-trapping gas in the atmosphere?
27. Do you think an increase in the amount of other gases, such as carbon dioxide, in the atmosphere would affect the earth's temperature? If so, how?
28. If the air at high altitudes is closer to the sun, why isn't it warmer than the air near the surface of the earth?
29. Do molecules of water tend to stick together when they are in a warm or cool environment?
30. Identify three types of particles that are in the atmosphere. How do these particles affect the water vapor in our atmosphere?
31. Describe how clouds are formed.
32. Why do you think meteorologists are more interested in clouds than in other weather phenomena?

Seasonal Weather

33. Why is the equator always warmer than Canada or Australia?
34. How does the rotation of Earth affect the weather?
35. Explain why the northern states experience a distinct summer and winter season.

Down to Earth

36. On a hot summer day, how will the temperature of land near a lake differ from the temperature of land that is not close to any body of water? Explain the difference.
37. On a cold winter day, how will the temperature of land near an open lake or ocean differ from the temperature of land that is not close to a body of water? Explain the difference in temperature.
38. In many places the air seems to be motionless, but at the shore there is a gentle breeze. What is the cause of this movement of air?
39. What are the conditions that frequently cause storms in the Mississippi River Valley?
40. Western Pennsylvania often receives larger amounts of snow or rain from storms that originate in the Mississippi River Valley. What feature of the land causes the precipitation to fall before reaching the eastern part of the state?
41. Why are cities usually warmer than the surrounding countryside?
42. Describe the flow of air that occurs in a city when a wind is not blowing.
43. What effect does pollution have on air circulation in a city?
44. What conditions cause an inversion?
45. In what seasons of the year do most inversions occur? Why do they occur more often at these times?
46. Why are inversions sometimes dangerous?

2.2 CASE STUDY
Is the Earth's Climate Changing?

" . . . the next time you admire the spectacular sunsets created by nature's own volcanic smog, don't forget that this is her fiery reminder that we live and breathe in a thin veil of safety. Its ethereal future is now increasingly in our hands."

Stephen H. Schneider
National Center for Atmospheric Research

Climate is the long-term weather pattern of a place over a period of years.

Global Warming

Earth's atmosphere contains certain **greenhouse gases** that act as a blanket to trap heat and keep the planet warm. Without this blanket of gases, Earth would be ice-coated and unable to support life. This warming of Earth that is caused by certain gases in the atmosphere is the **greenhouse effect**.

For many years the natural greenhouse effect on planet Earth has created a comfortable place to live, but what about the future? Is Earth's climate changing? Many scientists think so. Obviously, Earth is warmer now than it was during the Ice Ages, but many scientists think that by 2070 the average temperature of planet Earth could increase 3° to 8°F (1.5° to 4.5°C). That is warmer than it has been in the last two million years.

The Ten Warmest Years Since 1880	
Year	Average Global Surface Temperature (°F)
1990	59.81
1981, 1988	59.64
1987	59.56
1980, 1983	59.51
1989	59.45
1973	59.31
1977, 1986	59.30

The 1980s were the hottest decade on record. During the 100 years that systematic weather records have been kept, the average global temperature has increased about 1.1°F (0.5°C). No one knows for sure if this change is due to global warming or is a natural variation in climate. But evidence indicates that **global warming** — an increase in the planet's average temperature — is likely over the next several generations.

SCIENCE TECHNOLOGY & SOCIETY
I S S U E S

Changing Climates Around the World

Bangladesh, a country about the size of Wisconsin, has a population greater than 112 million people. In contrast, Wisconsin's population is 4.9 million. The Ganges River flows through Bangladesh and into the Bay of Bengal. Approximately 10 million people — mostly fishermen and farmers — live along the coast.

- Contrast the impact of global warming on the people of Wisconsin and the people of Bangladesh.
- California normally has wet winters and dry summers. Water supplies in many areas come from melting snow. Predict the impact that global warming will have on California's water supply, assuming that there is no change in the amount of precipitation.

How might these clouds affect global warming?

Looking somewhat like growth rings in a tree trunk, annual dust layers in ice at the edge of the Quelccaya Ice Cap in Peru provide clues to the history of Earth's climate.

Scientist at the Byrd Polar Research Center drilled into ice caps in Peru and China to collect ice cores that are stored at −30°C.

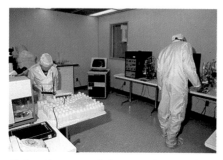

Scientists use laboratories with special clean room conditions to study the ice cores for evidence of climate change.

The Greenhouse Gases

Water vapor is the most important atmospheric greenhouse gas. The amount of water vapor in the atmosphere is controlled by the processes in the water cycle. It is usually one to two percent of a volume of air. The heat-trapping ability of water vapor is obvious from the lack of cooling that occurs at night during a spell of hot, humid weather.

While a mass of humid air may trap enough heat to make the weather uncomfortable, the amount of water vapor in the global atmosphere does not appear to be changing. Thus water vapor contributes to the natural greenhouse effect, but it is not responsible for **global warming** — accelerating the greenhouse effect. If the amount of water vapor in the atmosphere does increase, it could form low sun-blocking clouds that could have a cooling effect. Another possibility is that the water vapor will form high, ice-filled clouds that will contribute to global warming.

Of the greenhouse gases that are added to the atmosphere by human activities, **carbon dioxide** is the most important. Human activities have completely distorted the carbon cycle. A molecule of carbon dioxide that enters the air will remain there for about a century. Prior to the industrial revolution, the level of carbon dioxide in the atmosphere was probably about 270 ppm. Measurements indicate that the level of carbon dioxide has reached 355 ppm — an increase of 31% — and is increasing by about 0.5 percent each year.

Analysis of glacial ice cores shows a strong positive correlation between air temperature and the atmospheric concentration of two gases — carbon dioxide and methane — over the past 160,000 years. Scientists expect the carbon dioxide level to double within the next decade.

Where does all of that carbon dioxide come from? The major source of carbon dioxide is the burning of fossil fuels. Electric utilities produce 33 percent of the carbon dioxide; transportation produces 31 percent; industry adds another 24 percent; and heating of residential and commercial buildings is responsible for most of the remainder. Deforestation is also contributing to the increase in carbon dioxide.

Carbon dioxide is not the only greenhouse gas that is increasing. The level of **methane** in the atmosphere is about 1.7 ppm and is increasing at the rate of 1 percent each year. Most methane is produced by the decomposition of organic material in wet, oxygen-deficient environments, such as marshes, swamps and rice paddies. Other sources include cattle, leaking natural gas pipelines, and sanitary landfills.

CFCs (chlorofluorocarbons) not only destroy the ozone layer, but they are also important greenhouse gases. Although there are plans to stop production of CFCs, they will continue to be an important factor in global warming. CFC molecules are so stable that they remain in the atmosphere for more than 100 years.

Nitrous oxide (N_2O) is a potent greenhouse gas. Although it is present in the atmosphere in very small quantities [300 parts per billion (ppb)], it is 220 times more effective in trapping heat than carbon dioxide. Bacteria in the nitrogen cycle release nitrous oxide into the air from nitrogen fertilizers. It is also a product of burning fossil fuels and vegetation. It is produced during the manufacture of nylon, and tiny amounts are released from dental offices and whipped cream cans.

In the stratosphere (upper atmosphere), **ozone** blocks the Sun's harmful ultraviolet rays, but in the troposphere (lower atmosphere) ozone is a harmful pollutant. It is also an important greenhouse gas. As urban air pollution increases, the ozone level rises.

Turning the Thermostat Down

What difference might a few degrees make? Earth's average surface temperature is only about 1.8°F (1°C) warmer than the Little Ice Age. Then New York City was buried under 1000 feet of ice. Cooling by only a few degrees in the global average temperature can have a devastating effect.

The year 1816 is known as the "year without a summer." Summer temperatures dropped 1.8° to 4.5°F (1° to 2.5°C) below previous years. An eruption of an Indonesian volcano, Mount Tambora, had sent massive clouds of ash into the air. Killer frosts hit crops in Europe and North America. Snow fell in the New England states in July. The harvest was poor and the following winter was harsh. Other factors, such as a change in the normal pattern of the jet stream, may have contributed to the unusual snow and frost.

When Mount Pinatubo erupted in 1991, it spewed 15 to 20 million tons of sulfur dioxide into the stratosphere (upper atmosphere). It produced spectacular sunsets. The earth's surface cooled by 0.5°C (1°F). Scientists say the cooling is temporary. The pollutants that blocked the sunlight will disappear in three to five years and the warming trend will resume. Again, scientists do not know if other climate factors may have contributed to the cooling.

Living in a Warmer World

According to the World Resources Institute, "Greenhouse warming is the most serious and threatening problem of this century and the next." We know that the level of greenhouse

How are power plants and industries changing the composition of the atmosphere? Will this change cause global warming?

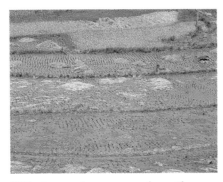

What greenhouse gas does the growing of rice contribute to the atmosphere?

Mount St. Helens

How might global warming affect Chicago. Will a warmer climate have the same impact on coastal cities?

It's not a pretty flower. It is food for more than 40 species of wildlife. How will these species be affected if the climat warms and the flowering dogwood cannot adapt to the change?

WHAT DO YOU THINK?

What would happen if predictions about global warming came true. Three separate scientific studies show that world food production would decline, especially in developing countries. Studies have also shown that up to 375 million people in the world could starve. What would the consequences of these events be for North Americans? How might these events affect you and developing countries.

gases in the atmosphere is increasing and if they continue to increase, global temperatures will rise. Most scientists agree that the build-up of carbon dioxide and other greenhouse gases has the potential to produce dramatic changes in the climate. Some of the possible consequences of global warming are described below.

Water: Global warming could cause the expansion of sea water and the melting of polar ice and snow. At the rate indicated above, global warming could cause the sea level to rise 0.2 to 1.4 metres by the year 2050. A one meter increase in sea level would threaten the homes of 200 million people. It will also threaten the homes of aquatic organisms that depend upon coastal wetlands.

The pattern of precipitation may change, threatening the water supplies in some areas. Water supplies in coastal regions may be affected by the intrusion of salt water. Some regions like the northern Great Plains are expected to be drier, and this could affect agriculture. Lower water levels in the Great Lakes could affect shipping. Lower water levels in some areas could seriously affect the generation of hydroelectric power.

Habitats and Wildlife: Climate zones could shift and some plants may not be able to adapt to the changes. Species that depend upon the plants will be affected. Hardwood forests are expected to expand. With every rise of 1.8°F (1°C), tree species will have to move 90 kilometers closer to the poles to survive. Preserves and National Parks may no longer provide the habitat for the wildlife that they normally protect. Food supplies may not be available when needed by migratory animals.

Agriculture: Carbon dioxide is often a limiting factor for plants. A doubling of the carbon dioxide level increased yields of major crops — cotton, wheat, soybeans, and corn — in laboratory experiments, but carbon dioxide is not the only variable. Plants must also adjust to changes in temperatures and moisture levels. Corn is particularly sensitive to heat during fertilization, and wheat will not mature at high temperatures. Problems with diseases and insect pests are expected to increase.

An international study indicates that crop yields may increase in temperate zones, but the warming may decrease yields in tropical zones. A longer growing season is expected to significantly improve Canadian agriculture. The US Department of Agriculture says that technology available in developed countries will allow agriculture to adapt to climate changes, but the demand for irrigation will probably increase in most areas. It is likely that the African nations will be hit the hardest.

Weather predictions: Scientists do not know what kind of surprises the weather will hold. Will warmer temperatures make the weather prediction more difficult? Storms are nature's way of balancing the energy in the atmosphere. Warmer sea surface temperatures will cause more frequent and more severe storms, particularly in coastal areas.

Humans: Heat waves could become more common in some areas. The heat will intensify the effects of other air pollutants such as ozone. The elderly are most susceptible to heat stress and would be most affected. Death rates from heat-related health problems will climb, especially in large cities and developing countries.

Must We Act Now?

Calculations based upon doubling the natural carbon dioxide level show that the mean global temperature of planet Earth will increase by at least 1.8°F (1°C) each decade. There is concern that organisms will not be able to adapt to such a rapid rate of change. Another concern is that the changes may be in sudden jumps rather than gradual increases.

Some computer models suggest that increased evaporation of water will cause a cloud cover that will moderate the temperature change. There has been an increase in cloud cover over 44 of 45 US cities studied by the National Weather Service, but no one knows why. Will evaporation of water and cloud formation counterbalance the warming trend? Possibly, but no one knows how much.

The computer models are not perfect. There are many uncertainties about the influence of ocean temperatures and clouds upon the climate. By the time we understand these relationships, it may be too late to stop global warming. Once the greenhouse gases are released into the atmosphere, they remain there for decades. It will take years to reverse the build-up of greenhouse gases.

Many scientists agree that, although we do not know how severe the climate changes will be, we must act immediately to reduce the risks associated with global warming. Even if global warming is not the threat that is predicted by some models, the actions taken will not be wasted. By reducing our use of fossil fuels, we will also begin to solve other serious environmental problems.

What Can You Do?

To decrease the threat of global warming, we must reduce the production of greenhouse gases. This can be done through increased energy conservation and alternative energy sources. Planting more trees to "soak up" some of the excess carbon dioxide will not, by itself, eliminate global warming, but it will help.

Change that light bulb! A 100-watt light bulb left on for 10 hours uses one kilowatt hour (KWH) of electricity. An average

In what ways may global warming affect this Chinese man?

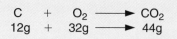

$$C + O_2 \longrightarrow CO_2$$
$$12g + 32g \longrightarrow 44g$$

New technology can reduce the threat of global warming. Most electricity is produced by burning coal. More energy efficient light bulbs reduce the production of carbon dioxide.

Using new fluorescent bulbs save energy as shown in this in store demonstration.

of 1.28 pounds (0.6 kg) of coal must be burned to produce each KWH of electricity. The carbon dioxide released during the combustion of the coal is 1.8 times the weight of the coal or 2.3 pounds (1.0 kg) for each KWH of electricity.

If all the households in the United States replaced one 100-watt light bulb with a compact fluorescent bulb that requires only 13 watts, the amount of carbon dioxide released into the atmosphere would be reduced by nearly 30 million tons (27×10^9 metric tonnes). The calculation assumes that the electricity is produced at a coal-burning power plant.

The burning of coal is the main source of carbon dioxide. Switching to oil or natural gas will produce less carbon dioxide than burning coal. Although there may be other significant environmental impacts, nuclear, hydroelectric, solar, and wind energy do not release any carbon dioxide.

Buy energy efficient models of appliances. Use mass transit, car pool, and when you purchase a vehicle make sure you select a model that gets good gas mileage.

Recycle. Recycling an aluminum can saves 95 percent of the energy required to make a new can. Conserving energy reduces greenhouse gases as well as air pollution that is responsible for $100 billion in annual health care costs.

Plant a tree. Obviously it will take more than one tree, but one tree will help. Planting one million square miles of fast-growing trees in the tropics would remove 2.5 billion tons (2.3×10^9 metric tonnes) of carbon from the air annually. That is nearly half of the carbon that is released by the combustion of fossil fuels.

A tree is half carbon. A 1989 survey showed that burning of tropical forests was releasing 2.4 billion tons (2.2×10^9 metric tonnes) of carbon into the atmosphere. Finding alternatives to the destruction of tropical forests will slow global warming. Each acre of tropical forest that is not cut will continue to remove four tons of carbon from the atmosphere each year.

The cost of planting one million square miles of trees is about $100 billion. Is it worth it? According to the US Environmental Protection Agency, the cost of saving the US East Coast from the projected sea-level rise caused by global warming could be as much as $111 billion.

International Cooperation

The increase in carbon dioxide and methane levels are directly related to the growth in the size of the human population and use of technology that depends upon energy from fossil fuels. Controlling the growth of the human population will slow the build-up of greenhouse gases and slow global warming.

People in industrialized countries contribute far more to global warming than people in developing countries. The average American generates 19 times as much carbon dioxide as the average Indian. Changing to technologies that reduce the use of fossil fuels is essential.

Global warming is an international problem, and a solution will require an international commitment. Some nations have made a commitment to a reduction in their contribution of greenhouse gases. Canada adopted a policy that plans to stabilize non-CFC gases at the 1990 level by the year 2000. Germany, Japan, Norway, France, and other developed countries are committed to stabilizing or reducing carbon dioxide levels. As of 1993, the United States was not committed to any policy to reduce carbon dioxide emissions.

This nuclear power plant near Berwick, PA, doesn't contribute any carbon dioxide to the atmosphere. Is nuclear power a good alternate energy source?

2.2 QUESTIONS FOR STUDY AND DISCUSSION

1. What is the connection between weather and climate? Give an illustration that describes the difference.

Global Warming
2. What is the characteristic shared by the greenhouse gases?
3. What is the greenhouse effect?
4. What is global warming? Do scientists have evidence that global warming is occurring on planet Earth?

The Greenhouse Gases
5. Identify five greenhouse gases.
6. What is the most important greenhouse gas? Is the level of this gas increasing? Is this gas causing global warming?
7. Explain how water vapor can sometimes cause warming of the atmosphere and at other times cause cooling.
8. What is the most important greenhouse gas that is being added to the atmosphere by human activity? How do scientists know that the level of this gas is increasing? What is the process that is producing this gas?
9. What humans activities are responsible for the increase in methane?
10. Compare the amount of nitrous oxide in the atmosphere to the amount of carbon dioxide.

11. Earth's climate is comfortable for humans and many other living things. How much lower would the average surface temperature have to fall to return Earth to conditions that existed during the Ice Ages?
12. What event caused the average surface temperature of Earth to fall in 1816 and 1991? Was the temperature change temporary?

Living in a Warmer World
13. What is the opinion of the World Resources Institute about the impact of global warming? Do most scientist agree with this position?
14. List the possible ways in which global warming may affect people.
15. List possible ways in which global warming may affect:
    wetland species forests
    endangered species
    migratory species.

Must We Act Now?
16. Why are scientists concerned about an increase in temperature of only 1°C over ten years?
17. Identify two weaknesses in computer models that predict the impact of global warming.

18. Give two reasons why many scientists think we should act now to slow the rate of global warming.

What Can You Do?

19. List actions you could take to help decrease the threat of global warming and for each action explain how the action will reduce the threat.

20. What is the connection between the human population growth and global warming?
21. What is the connection between technology and global warming?
22. What is the connection between lifestyle and global warming?

ISSUES

CLIMATE CHANGE: WHAT TO DO? WHEN TO DO IT?

The United States is the single largest producer of greenhouse gases, contributing about 22 percent of the gases released into the atmosphere each year. Canadians are responsible for 2 percent of the increase in greenhouse gases. Some nations have pledged to cut their carbon dioxide emissions. Australia, Austria, Denmark, and New Zealand have agreed to cut emissions by 20 percent within 10 or 15 years.

- What role should the US and Canada play in addressing the issue of global warming? Justify your position. While most experts on the subject of global warming feel that immediate action should be taken to curb global warming, some scientists are in favor of a 10-year delay before implementing any regulations that would reduce greenhouse gases.
- What is your position on this issue? Defend your position. Delegates at a conference on global warming recommended a tax on fossil fuels.
- If a so-called Carbon Tax is put on a ballot, would you vote for or against the tax?
- If the tax passed, with or without your vote, how could the money be spent to further reduce the threat of global warming?

ISSUES

CLIMATE CHANGE: PREDICTING THE EFFECTS

During the past fifteen years biologists have observed a sharp decline and "bleaching" in coral ecosystems.
- Do you think the decline is due to global warming? Support your position. It has been suggested that the Kirtland's warbler is the "canary in the coal mine" for climate change. [Refer to Unit I, Introduced Species for information on Kirtland's warbler.]
- Explain why the warbler may be an early warning alarm for global warming. The soil of the Arctic tundra contains a community of microbes.
- How might global warming affect these organisms?
- Could these organisms be a cause of global warming?

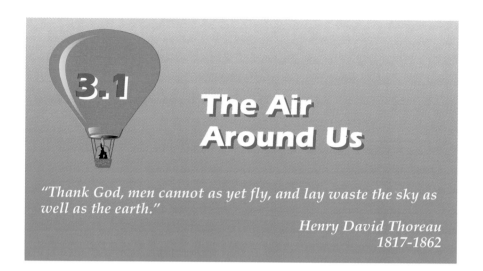

3.1 The Air Around Us

"Thank God, men cannot as yet fly, and lay waste the sky as well as the earth."

Henry David Thoreau
1817-1862

The air has never been pure. Sometimes it contains substances that are undesirable. Sometimes it contains substances that are harmful. These substances may be products of natural events such as volcanoes, forest fires, or decaying matter. Often the undesirable substances are by-products of modern technology. No matter the source, when a substance is present in an amount that is undesirable or harmful the substance is a **pollutant**.

Air pollution is not new. King Edward I tried to clear the sky over London in 1272 by banning the use of sea-coal. A man who sold and burned the outlawed coal was tortured and hanged. King Richard III heavily taxed the use of coal, but it did not help. London's skies remained dark and her buildings were blackened by the soot until the advent of gas and electric heat sources. The burning of coal continues to be a major source of air pollution in many areas of the world.

Processes that Pollute

Pollutants generally enter the atmosphere by one of three processes.

Attrition — From a Latin word meaning "to rub," attrition refers to the wearing or grinding of a substance by friction. Attrition includes sanding, grinding, and drilling. It also includes the breaking of a liquid into small droplets, as in spraying. Attrition creates small particles, sometimes called **particulates**, or fine droplets called **aerosols**.

Vaporization — This is the process by which a substance changes from a liquid to a gaseous state. Vaporization allows us to detect odors. Some liquids, such as perfumes and gasoline, vaporize at low temperatures. Other liquids vaporize only under high temperature or pressure.

> **DID YOU KNOW?**
>
> A new study shows that even in cities which meet air quality standards, people are getting sick and even dying from the effects of the polluted air. The six U.S. cities studied meeting air quality standards, were plagued by pollutants such as soot, sulfates, nitrates, and particulates. Industry and automobiles were usually the sources of the pollution. Studies have shown respiratory diseases and higher death rates can all be attributed to the pollution found in legally "clean" air.

These photographs show the air pollution problem in Beijing, China. Coal is the major source of energy for electricity and heat, and piles of coal like this one are found outside most buildings. What process produces most of China's air pollution?

Combustion — This is a chemical reaction in which substances combine with oxygen and release light and heat energy. This is the process we often refer to as "burning." One of the major sources of air pollution is the internal combustion engine.

If combustion of hydrocarbons is complete, the only waste products produced are carbon dioxide and water. For this to happen, three conditions must exist.

- The fuel must be a pure hydrocarbon or an organic compound with only hydrogen, carbon, and oxygen. A **hydrocarbon** is a chemical that contains only hydrogen and carbon. Gasoline, fuel oil, and coal are all hydrocarbons. However, they often contain other elements in addition to hydrogen and carbon. It is these elements, or impurities, that become pollutants when the hydrocarbon is burned. Alcohol is a clean-burning fuel because it contains only hydrogen, carbon, and oxygen.
- The fuel must be mixed with the correct amount of oxygen. If there is too much or too little oxygen, the fuel will not completely burn. Unburned hydrocarbon molecules and carbon particles (soot) enter the air as pollutants.
- The fuel must be burned at the correct temperature. At hot temperatures, nitrogen and oxygen in the air combine, forming nitrogen oxides. Nitrogen oxides are formed naturally when the energy in lightning heats up the atmosphere to extremely high temperatures. Nitrogen oxides are also formed in the internal combustion engine.

If these three conditions are met, the only products of combustion are water and carbon dioxide. Frequently one or more of the conditions are not met and combustion produces pollution.

Nature versus Man

The Clean Air Act, passed by Congress in 1970, forced industries to take steps to reduce pollution. Industry was somewhat hesitant to accept responsibility, perhaps because of the high cost of pollution control. Note the source of each of the following quotes.

"Nature emits air contaminants in far greater amounts than does man. Problems arise, however, when nature's self-cleansing capabilities are overwhelmed by man's excessive input from densely populated and industrialized areas."

Manufacturing Chemists Association
Air Pollution Causes and Cures — 1973

"Most air pollution, however, is man-made. The United States alone spews aloft over two hundred million tons of gaseous, solid, and liquid "aerial garbage" annually.

League of Women Voters of the United States
Facts and Issues — 1970

Nature Pollutes

There is no question that at certain times and in certain places, nature emits devastating amounts of air pollutants. Volcanoes may be the number one source of natural air pollution. On June 15, 1991, Mount Pinatubo, a dormant volcano in the Philippines, suddenly came to life emitting enormous plumes of dust, sulfur dioxide, and other chemicals. The Total Ozone Mapping Spectrometer aboard the Nimbus-7 satellite measured about 15 million tons of sulfur dioxide in the stratosphere. By the end of June there were 295 people dead and 39 missing persons. Early evacuation warnings had saved hundreds of thousands of lives.

Lake Nyos is a volcanic crater lake in the Republic of Cameroon in west Africa. Massive amounts of carbon dioxide, probably produced by volcanic activity, accumulate in the cold deep water at the bottom of the lake. On the night of August 21, 1986, some unknown event, possibly a rock slide, caused a sudden change in pressure within the lake. The lake "burped," releasing a large cloud of carbon dioxide.

Carbon dioxide is twice as heavy as air. The dense blanket of carbon dioxide and water vapor spread over the valley, killing 1,700 people, 3,000 cattle and uncounted numbers of wildlife. The only survivors in one village were women and infants in the hospital's second-floor maternity ward. Herdsmen on hillsides near the lake also survived. In 1991, scientists warned that the carbon dioxide levels are again building up in the lake making it "very dangerous."

Urban Pollution

Unlike the people who lived near Lake Nyos, most people are not exposed to unhealthy levels of carbon dioxide or other pollutants produced by nature. The major pollutants that affect most people are produced by the combustion of fossil fuels in automobiles, power plants, and industries. Although much progress has been made in improving the quality of the air we breathe, there is still work to be done. Consider the following examples.

The 23 million people of Mexico City breathe a mixture of pollutants including carbon monoxide, sulfur dioxide, nitrogen dioxide, and ozone. During the winter of 1991, there were only six days when the pollutants did not exceed danger levels. There was a 16 to 20 percent increase in the incidence of respiratory infections, nosebleeds, and emphysema.

Three-quarters of Mexico City's air pollution comes from the 15,000 buses, 40,000 taxis and nearly 3 million automobiles. Another major source of pollutants is a giant oil refinery that emits as much as 88,000 tons of pollutants into the atmosphere each year.

Winter also brings discomfort to the people of Prague, the capital of the Czech Republic. On good days, air pollution exceeds safety

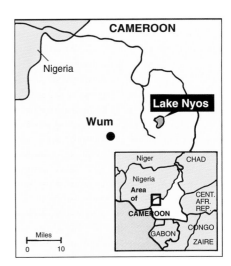

Lake Nyos is in a volcanic region.

WHAT DO YOU THINK?

Is the air you breathe clean enough? Should we live with air that has "acceptable" levels of pollutants in it? Find out why some states, notably California, have air quality standards that are far stricter than the federal standards.

thresholds for sulfur dioxide and airborne particulates. It also contains traces of arsenic, mercury, and lead. On bad days emergency alerts cancel school recesses.

The pollutants in Prague's air are by-products of the combustion of brown coal (lignite) that heats homes and powers factories. Pollution has destroyed nearly 50 percent of the forests and damaged nearly 70 percent of the rivers.

The air in many cities in the United States is not healthy. Six out of every 10 people in the United States live in an area that fails to meet air quality standards that are set by the EPA to protect human health. In 1991, ninety-six cities had not attained the national standard for ozone, 41 cities did not meet the standard for carbon monoxide, and 72 did not meet the standard for particulate matter. The biggest source of pollutants that plague urban areas is motor vehicles.

The 1970 Clean Air Act promised that people living in the United States could breathe clean air, and the air is much cleaner than it would have been without the 1970 law. There are signs that we are making progress. Southern California had less smog in 1991 than in any year on record and Kansas City met the federal ozone standard. The Clean Air Act was reauthorized in 1990. It set limits on the amount of pollutants that can enter the air and gave industries incentives to reduce pollution.

3.1 QUESTIONS FOR STUDY AND DISCUSSION

1. Define the following words:
   attrition   pollution
   combustion   vaporization
   hydrocarbon
2. When did air pollution begin?

Processes that Pollute

3. List the three processes that pollute the atmosphere.
4. Identify the process responsible for adding substances to the air in each of the following activities.
   Processes
   1. attrition   2. combustion   3. vaporization
   Activities
   A. a romantic evening with a candlelight dinner and a fire in the fireplace
   B. spray painting the Golden Gate Bridge
   C. setting the thermostat in your classroom at a higher temperature
   D. a classmate opens a bottle of perfume
   E. sanding a project in wood shop
   F. getting your wool sweaters out of their summer storage with mothballs
   G. burning the trash
   H. production of electricity at a power plant that uses coal
   I. using a household cleaner that is in a pump bottle or aerosol can
5. Which process is responsible for most odors?
6. List the three conditions that must exist in order for the only products of combustion to be carbon dioxide and water.

Nature versus Man

7. After reading the quotes from *Air Pollution — Causes and Cures* and *Facts and Issues*, what do you think is the major source of air pollution — nature or man?
8. Why do you think that the Manufacturing Chemists Association and the League of Women Voters had different views about the major source of air pollution?

Nature Pollutes

9. Identify two major air pollutants associated with volcanic eruptions.
10. What chemical caused the deaths of the people in the Lake Nyos valley? This chemical is not often thought of as a pollutant. Why was it so deadly?

Urban Pollution

11. Which process produces most human-made pollution?
12. What are the major air pollutants in Mexico City?

What are the major sources of human-made pollution in Mexico City?
What evidence is there that these pollutants are harmful?
13. What are the major pollutants in Prague? What is the source?
14. What are the major air pollutants in urban areas in the United States?
What is the biggest source of air pollutants in urban areas?
15. What evidence is there that things are getting better?

Areas Violating Ozone Standards

In 1991, 96 cities did not attain the national standard for ozone. Fewer cities (41) did not meet the standard for carbon monoxide.

Areas Violating Carbon Monoxide Standards

Source: Office of Air and Radiation, EPA

4.1 Chemicals that Pollute the Air

When the canary dies, it's time to get out of the mine!

Canary in Cage

Years ago, miners sent caged canaries down mine shafts to test the air. If the canary kept singing the miners knew the air was good, and they could enter the mine. But a silent canary meant trouble. Roger Tory Peterson refers to birds as an environmental litmus paper — indicators of the health of the environment. Since birds are smaller and have a higher metabolism rate than humans, they are affected by pollutants more quickly.

The New York Times reported that employees in Kuwait placed a cage with two brightly colored parakeets near the entrance of a hotel lobby soon after Iraq invaded Kuwait. Were the employees trying to keep the guest's minds off the war? No. They thought that if there was a gas attack, the death of the birds would be a warning to the people at the hotel.

Nerve gas and mustard gas are both deadly chemicals, and some people were fearful that Saddam Hussein might use these chemicals during the invasion of Kuwait. Chemicals used for chemical warfare are not widespread pollutants, but other toxic chemicals have spread around the globe.

The connection between agents of chemical warfare and pesticides is not an accidental one. Some of the chemicals developed for warfare were found to be deadly to insects. One of the first uses of DDT was to protect soldiers against insects that carry disease. We continue to use pesticides today because they eliminate pests and diseases, and they control crop losses.

The application of pesticides results in an unavoidable pollution of the air, even under the best conditions. Pesticides also enter the air during the manufacturing process and as they evaporate from the treated surfaces. Once in the air, pesticides may travel for thousands of miles before being deposited with rain or snow. DDT has been found in Antarctic penguins even though no DDT was ever sprayed in Antarctica.

Volatile Organic Compounds

Organic compounds refer to chemicals that contain carbon. Organic compounds that readily vaporize at normal temperatures are **volatile organic compounds (VOCs)**. DDT and other synthetic pesticides are volatile organic compounds. There are thousands of volatile organic compounds.

Refineries, chemical plants, dry cleaning businesses, furniture refinishers, and auto body shops regularly release VOCs into the atmosphere. There are also natural sources of VOCs. The "pine-fresh" scent of the forest and the odor of sweet-smelling flowers are both due to the vaporization of volatile organic compounds.

Hydrocarbons are volatile organic compounds. Three hydrocarbons commonly used as fuels are methane (CH_4), propane (C_3H_8), and butane (C_4H_{10}). Gasoline is a mixture of hydrocarbons including benzene (C_6H_6).

Hydrocarbons enter the air from the incomplete combustion of fuels, from the evaporation of fuels from the tank, and the escape of vapors during refueling. Most polluting hydrocarbons enter the air during the incomplete combustion of gasoline in automobiles.

Although sensitive detection equipment has replaced the canary, leaking methane gas still threatens underground miners. Large amounts of methane and other VOCs, produced by the action of bacteria on the sewage, are released into the air at sewage treatment plants. Some of the methane produced at sewage treatment plants and modern landfills is collected and burned to produce electricity or heat buildings.

In 1991, the 30 million people living in California released about 200 tons of VOCs a day from a variety of consumer products. Perfumes, hair sprays, deodorants, glues, inks, paints, charcoal lighter fluid and other consumer products contain VOCs. California has set standards to limit the amount of VOCs in consumer products.

Limits placed on the VOCs in thousands of consumer products sold in California will reduce the VOCs emitted by 60 tons a day. It will have the same effect as removing 7.5 million new 1991 model cars from California highways. California has also adopted strict motor vehicle emission standards. These measures are aimed at reducing the level of ground-level ozone. The formation of ozone is discussed later in this section.

California Standards for Volatile Organic Compounds in Consumer Products	
Products (1995 Standards)	Percent (by weight)
Aerosol carburetor choke cleaners, fabric protectants, aerosol household adhesives	75
Charcoal lighter materials, disinfectants	60
Aerosol automotive brake cleaners	50
Insecticides: foggers, crawling bugs, wasps, and hornets	40
Aerosol dusting aids	35
Insecticides: flying bugs	30
Insecticides: fleas and ticks, lawn and garden, all others	20
Aerosol cooking sprays	18
Nonaerosol household adhesives	10
Nonaerosol dusting aids	7
Hand dishwashing detergents	2

Nitrogen Oxides

The largest source of nitrogen oxides, 36 percent, is the burning of fossil fuels (coal, oil, and natural gas) at electric power plants. The second largest source of nitrogen oxides (NO_x), 31 percent, is transportation (trucks, buses, and automobiles). Bacteria, lightning, volcanoes, and forest fires are natural sources of nitrogen oxides.

$$2C + O_2 \longrightarrow 2CO \qquad C + O_2 \longrightarrow CO_2$$

Meat cooking is a major source of organic aerosol emissions. In the Los Angeles area meat smoke accounts for 21% of the fine organic carbon particles.

In the presence of sunlight and VOCs, nitrogen oxide (NO) reacts with oxygen to form **nitrogen dioxide** (NO_2). This brownish-red gas is responsible for the appearance of the smog that is a problem in Los Angeles and other major urban areas. This type of smog occurs only when there is enough sunlight and heat to provide energy for the chemical reactions. Because of this, it is known as **photochemical smog**.

Photochemical smog contains a mixture of up to 100 chemical compounds. One of the most important pollutants in smog is **ozone**. Ozone is a form of oxygen containing three atoms (O_3) instead of the usual two. It is normally found in the atmosphere in very small amounts. Ground-level ozone is sometimes called a secondary pollutant because it is usually produced by chemical reactions in the atmosphere.

A layer of ozone in the upper atmosphere absorbs some of the ultraviolet light rays that would normally cause skin cancer. Thus ozone is helpful to us when it is in the upper atmosphere. In the lower atmosphere ozone is a pollutant. Ground-level ozone increased 2 percent between 1970 and 1988. In 1992 Southern California exceeded the federal standard for ozone (0.12 ppm) 140 times.

Carbon Oxides

The incomplete combustion of fuels also gives off carbon monoxide (CO) and carbon dioxide (CO_2). The major source of carbon monoxide is the gasoline-powered motor vehicle. Industries and the burning of solid waste produce most of the remainder. Small amounts come from forest fires, burning banks of coal waste, and fires in underground coal mines.

Carbon dioxide is not usually considered an air pollutant, but it can be deadly in high concentrations. The United States produces more carbon dioxide than any other country. Scientists are studying its effect on Earth's climate.

Suspended Particulates

Suspended particulates include any solid particles or droplets that are small enough to remain in the air for long periods of time. Natural sources of particulates include sea salt, pollen, volcanic ash, and wind-blown dust. Dust also enters the air from mining, quarrying, farming operations, construction projects, and traffic on unpaved roads.

The incomplete burning of fuels releases small carbon particles known as **soot**. Burning also releases small pieces of minerals called **fly ash**. Fly ash may contain toxic chemicals such as lead and cadmium. Other pollutants in the atmosphere may become attached to the surface of the soot and the fly ash.

Both solid particles and **aerosols**, small droplets of liquid, are released to the air by industrial processes, agricultural practices, and in diesel exhaust. Air pollution from industries and the burning of fossil fuels is thought to be the source of mercury in remote lakes in Minnesota and Wisconsin. The presence of lead and pesticides in the polar ice caps provides evidence of how far suspended particulates can travel once they become airborne.

Sulfur Dioxide

Sulfur (S) is found in coal and fuel oil. When fuels containing sulfur are burned, the sulfur joins with oxygen from the atmosphere. Combustion of fuels is the major source of sulfur dioxide (SO_2). Two-thirds of sulfur dioxide comes from the burning of fossil fuels by electric power plants. About 20 percent comes from other industries.

Sulfur dioxide is a colorless gas that has a strong and irritating odor. It combines with oxygen to form sulfur trioxide (SO_3). This gas combines with water (H_2O) to form **sulfuric acid** (H_2SO_4). Small droplets of sulfuric acid create a haze that scatters the sunlight and reduces visibility.

Indoor Air Pollution

Shutting the windows will shut out some air pollutants, but it may increase the level of other air pollutants. Most Americans spend 90 percent of their time indoors. Energy conservation measures have sealed in air pollutants creating **sick building syndrome**. Symptoms of indoor air pollution include burning eyes, rashes, dizziness, difficulty breathing, headaches, nausea, and drowsiness.

Toxic indoor air pollutants are released by construction materials, home furnishings, heating and cooking appliances, tobacco smoke, hobby and craft materials, personal and home care products, and the people and animals that live in the home.

Formaldehyde is a colorless, flammable gas with a strong odor. Adhesives containing formaldehyde are used in many pressed wood products, such as particleboard and paneling. Formaldehyde is also found in carpeting, upholstery, and draperies.

Gas appliances, unvented kerosene heaters and poorly vented furnaces or stoves are sources of nitrogen oxide and carbon monoxide. Coal or wood stoves and cigarette smoke are major sources of VOCs and particulates.

Radon gas, pesticides, and tiny airborne fibers of asbestos are air pollutants in some buildings. In the following sections we will investigate the known and potential effects of the major types of air pollutants.

$$S + O_2 \longrightarrow SO_2$$
$$2S + O_2 \longrightarrow 2SO_3$$
$$SO_3 + H_2O \longrightarrow H_2SO_4$$

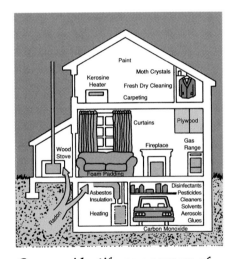

Can you identify any sources of air pollution in the home?

1. Why did the miners send canaries down the mine shafts?
2. Do you think that Roger Tory Peterson is right when he says that birds are good indicators of the health of the environment? Explain.
3. What group of chemicals commonly used today was the by-product of developing agents for chemical warfare?
4. Give three ways that pesticides enter the air.
5. What is the significance of finding DDT in Antarctic penguins?

Volatile Organic Compounds

6. What are the characteristics of volatile organic compounds?
7. List two natural sources and two human activities that release VOCs into the atmosphere.
8. Give two examples of hydrocarbons used as fuels and describe how they pollute the atmosphere.
9. Describe how sewage treatment plants and landfills pollute the air. How can the pollution be reduced?
10. List three types of consumer products that contain VOCs.
11. Which type of consumer products contain the most VOCs — aerosol or nonaerosol products?
12. Why is California limiting the amount of VOCs in consumer products?

Nitrogen Oxides

13. Identify the human activities that contribute most of the nitrogen oxides to the atmosphere.
14. List two natural sources of nitrogen oxides.
15. What physical conditions must exist for the formation of photochemical smog? What chemicals must be present?

16. **Secondary pollutants** are created by chemical reactions when other pollutants are present in the atmosphere. Identify two secondary pollutants that are in photochemical smog.
17. Complete the statement: Whether ozone is good or bad depends upon . . .

Carbon Oxides

18. Identify the major source of carbon monoxide.
19. When is carbon dioxide considered a pollutant?

Suspended Particulates

20. What are the two types of particulates that remain suspended in the atmosphere? Give an example of each.
21. Identify two natural sources and two human activities that produce "suspended particulates."
22. What evidence exists to indicate that particulates remain suspended in the atmosphere for long periods of time?

Sulfur Dioxide

23. What are the major sources of sulfur dioxide?
24. What secondary pollutant results from the release of sulfur dioxide into the atmosphere?
25. Explain how the production of sulfur dioxide, a colorless gas, can reduce visibility.

Indoor Air Pollution

26. What is sick building syndrome? And why are more people suffering from this syndrome?
27. Identify the types of pollutants that each of the following products may contribute to indoor air pollution.
   A. Kerosene heater
   B. Carpets
   C. Cigarette smoke
   D. Aerosol deodorizer
   E. Hobby or craft material

5.1 Air Pollutants and their Effects

"We are in somewhat the same position in regard to polluted air as the fish are to polluted water."

Allan V. Kneese

The Disasters

On December 4, 1952, a large mass of cold air began to spread across Britain. Late in the evening and early the next morning, fog began to form. At first it was just another London fog. But when the city awoke, tons of smoke from millions of coal stoves poured into the cold foggy air. Power plants added more smoke as people began to use more electricity.

As people went to work, the cars and buses added more pollutants to the cold, morning fog. Smoke poured from the smokestacks of the coal-burning furnaces at the factories and industries. The stagnant air was filled with a mixture of smoke and fog that later became known as **smog**.

It was difficult to see across the street. For several days, it was necessary to use the car's headlights to drive. Even street lights were needed. Within twelve hours, the first people began to die. By the time the winds came and carried the smog out to sea, many people were ill. The death rate climbed during the next few weeks, resulting in some four thousand deaths.

A similar weather pattern occurred again in 1956, and there were 1000 deaths. The British Parliament passed the Clean Air Act and began a program to reduce the pollution from the burning of coal. Stagnant air masses were blamed for 700 deaths again in 1962 and 1963.

The first disaster caused by air pollution was not in London. In December of 1930, the Meuse Valley in Belgium was trapped beneath a blanket of smog. The valley was filled with heavy industry, and the major fuel used by the industries was coal. Pollutants from the burning coal poured into the cold, December fog. During this temperature inversion, more than a thousand people became ill, and sixty people died.

Peppered Moths

Donora, a small town on the Monongahela River in Pennsylvania, lies in a valley surrounded by hills. There was a steel mill, a plant that made sulfuric acid, and a zinc reducing plant. The major source of energy for these industries was coal.

In October 1948, after three days of smog-filled air, many people complained of throat irritation, hoarseness, coughs, shortness of breath and nausea. Six thousand of the 14,000 people, living in Donora, became ill. Twenty people died. The normal daily death rate is two.

Stagnant atmospheric conditions caused several hundred additional deaths in New York City in 1953 and again in 1963. Both inversions occurred on week-ends. Had they occurred when the traffic was heavy and industries were operating, the death toll would have been higher. In each of these disasters the people most affected were the young, the elderly, and those who already had heart and lung problems.

The air pollution disasters are alarming, but most of us are exposed to much lower levels of air pollution from the day we are born. How does this affect us? In 1955 the federal government began to do research to determine the effects of air pollution. It was not until 1971 that National Air Quality Standards were established.

In the Laboratory

In science, a cause and effect relationship is usually proven in carefully controlled laboratory experiments. In a **controlled experiment** there is only one difference between two groups of subjects. The one difference between the two groups is the **variable**.

Mice exposed to nitrogen oxide in concentrations recorded in Los Angeles showed an increased death rate from pneumonia when compared to mice in control groups. Lung infections developed in caged animals that were accidentally exposed to diluted auto exhaust. In the laboratory next door where there were no fumes, no infections were noted.

Chemical analysis of tobacco and cigarette smoke show the presence of at least seven hydrocarbons that have produced cancer in laboratory animals. Lung cancers have not been produced in animals by the process of the animal "smoking." This may be due to the length of time the animal is exposed to the smoke or to the difference between laboratory animals and humans.

The Human Population — What the Studies Show

It is difficult to study the effects of air pollution in the human population because of the number of variables that exist. Yet a number of scientific studies have shown a relationship between long-term exposure to polluted air and diseases of the respiratory system.

- **Nashville, Tennessee:** A 12-year study, showed that more deaths from respiratory disease occurred among people living in the sections of the city where there is the greatest amount of air pollution.
- **Cumberland, Maryland:** A study showed that there were a significantly larger number of common colds among those living in the more heavily polluted section of town.
- **Seward, Pennsylvania:** A study compared Seward to New Florence, both towns with a population of about 1,000. The amount of air pollution was much higher in Seward. Respiratory tests were given to people over 30. Results showed people living in Seward were more often below the normal range for respiratory function.
- **Los Angeles, California:** Hospital records were examined for 223 consecutive days in 1961. There was a close correlation between high levels of various air pollutants and hospital admissions for allergies, respiratory distress, heart disease, circulatory problems, and flu.
- **St. Louis — Winnipeg:** Autopsies were performed on the lungs of 300 people from heavily polluted St. Louis and 300 people from much less polluted Winnipeg, Canada. The group was divided into cigarette smokers and nonsmokers. There was four times as much severe emphysema found in smokers from St. Louis as in smokers from Winnipeg. None of the nonsmokers had severe emphysema, but nonsmokers from St. Louis had three times as much mild to moderate emphysema as the nonsmokers from Winnipeg.
- **Longbeach — Glendora — Lancaster:** Long Beach, CA, is a heavily industrialized area. Glendora, CA, has some of the highest smog levels in the nation. Lancaster, CA, is a desert town with relatively clean air. An 11-year study compared nonsmoking, non-Hispanic residents of the three towns. Tests showed that long-term exposure to industrial air pollution and smog can seriously damage lung tissue. The small airways in the lungs were the most affected.

What the Surgeon General Says

The studies show that average smokers are ten times more likely to die of lung cancer, six times more likely to die of lung disease, and twice as likely to die from coronary heart disease. Scientists at the Centers for Disease Control found that tobacco smoke was the cause of nearly 25 percent of myeloid leukemia, a deadly form of cancer.

The age when smoking started, the amount inhaled, the number of years the subject has been smoking, and number of cigarettes smoked per day are all factors that increase the chance of cancer. As the length of time since smoking stopped increases, the cancer rates are lower.

DID YOU KNOW?

Indoor air pollution can be deadly. In 1976, 35 American Legion members died mysteriously at a convention. Long-term, persistent detective work led physicians to conclude that the deaths were caused by a bacterium that lived in the convention center's ventilation system. The air ducts had become a breeding ground for this new disease-causing bacterium. The strange new disease has been called "Legionnaire's Disease."

THINK ABOUT IT

You own a small woodlot. You cut trees for firewood to heat your home in the winter. It is autumn, and you go out to your woods to choose trees to cut. Do you cut living trees or dead trees? What determines your decision?

Some pollutants cause more damage if they are present with other pollutants than if they are alone. This is called a **synergistic effect**. When present together, cigarette smoke and air pollution have a synergistic effect.

The difference in cancer rates between city and rural non-smokers is small. Nevertheless city smokers have a much greater cancer rate than rural smokers. It appears that when city pollution is added to cigarette smoke, the effect of $1 + 1 > 2$.

Diseases Associated with Air Pollution

The air in major cities is unhealthy. The American Lung Association estimates that air pollution is responsible for $100 billion in annual health care costs and as many as 120,000 deaths each year. Certain pollutants cause changes in the respiratory system. These changes may result in one of the following diseases:

Chronic bronchitis results when the cilia, short, hair-like projections, in the bronchial tubes have been damaged. They normally sweep the mucus, which has trapped small particles and germs, out of the bronchial tubes. The cells lining the bronchial tubes produce more and sometimes thicker mucus. The mucus interferes with the exchange of air, causing a shortness of breath. A chronic cough develops because of the extra mucus.

Bronchial asthma is the result of an allergic reaction of the membranes lining the bronchial tubes. The membranes swell and make the air passages narrow. Extra mucus may also be produced. The smooth muscles in the walls of the bronchial tubes sometimes go into spasms. The spasms close the tubes, causing an asthma attack.

Emphysema results after years of irritation. The air sacs in the lungs, lose their elasticity. They are like an old balloon or worn out rubber band. They no longer have the ability to push the air out of the lungs. The air remains in the air sacs. Oxygen and carbon dioxide cannot diffuse across the damaged membranes as easily as they did across healthy ones.

Pneumonia and other infections occur more often when pollutants kill the bacteria-destroying cells which normally line the respiratory tract. More mucus is produced in response to the pollutants. The excess mucus limits the exchange of air and prevents the cilia from sweeping bacteria and other particles out of the lungs.

Lung cancer results when cell division goes haywire. Cells that wear out are normally replaced by division of the cells below. Inhaled smoke and pollutants cause normal cells to develop into cancerous cells. The cells grow and divide at an unusually fast rate. They may fill the air sacs and bronchial tubes. Air can not easily diffuse across the cancer cells as it does the normal lung tissue. Some of these cancer cells may break away and move to other sites in the lung or body.

Pollutants — How They Affect Humans

Carcinogens are substances that cause cancer. Some pollutants, including asbestos, arsenic, benzene, vinyl chloride, and radioactive substances are known to be human carcinogens. The EPA has concluded that environmental tobacco smoke, also known as secondhand smoke, is a human carcinogen responsible for about 3,000 lung cancer deaths each year in nonsmokers.

Respiratory Irritants irritate the lining of the respiratory system. Respiratory irritants include sulfur dioxide, nitrogen dioxide, chlorine, ammonia, formaldehyde, ozone, and other chemicals in photochemical smog and cigarette smoke.

Sulfur dioxide gas is only mildly irritating. When it combines with water in the atmosphere or the respiratory system, it forms sulfuric acid. Sulfuric acid is three or four times more irritating than sulfur dioxide.

According to the National Institutes of Health, exposure to ground-level ozone at levels above the 0.12 ppm standard is especially dangerous for asthmatics. Hospital admissions for asthma have increased in both the United States and Canada.

The EPA has concluded that environmental tobacco smoke (secondhand smoke) is responsible for 150,000 to 300,000 cases of bronchitis and pneumonia and other lower respiratory infections in children up to 18 months of age. Cigarette smoke also increases the risk of asthma and the frequency and severity of symptoms in children with asthma.

Particulates: Some air pollutants have a greater effect when there are tiny particles suspended in the air. The respiratory system has defenses against large particles. They are trapped by the mucus and swept out of the respiratory tract by the cilia. However, very tiny particles escape these defenses and are carried deep into the lungs. Some of these particles carry other pollutants into the lungs.

Studies in London, Chicago, and New York have shown when the sulfur dioxide level is .25 ppm and smoke are present, illness and death rates rise. According to the EPA, hydrocarbon particles can cause bronchitis, asthma attacks, respiratory infections, and cancer. On the basis of a study in Philadelphia, PA, scientists estimated that particulates are causing 60,000 deaths in the United States each year.

Carbon monoxide is absorbed by the blood. It combines with hemoglobin in the red blood cells more quickly than oxygen. Unlike oxygen, it is not given up to the body cells. This reduces the ability of hemoglobin to transport oxygen. Moderate concentrations cause fatigue, dizziness, and impaired judgment and impaired fetal development. The high concentrations from a leaky car exhaust or a malfunctioning furnace are fatal.

Mercury: Have you heard the expression "mad as a hatter"? In 1939, Lewis Carroll wrote about the mad hatter in the story of *Alice in Wonderland*. At that time most hatters were "mad." It was not until

WHAT DO YOU THINK?

Power plants upwind from the Grand Canyon have sometimes made the view more murky than magnificent. Smog and haze from power plants, and even from cities in the region, have often settled in the canyon. Would you favor closing power plants or forcing them to buy expensive pollution control equipment to preserve the view for tourists? What would be the cost to industry and its employees? If nothing is done, what would be the price paid in lost tourist revenue?

"Mad Hatter"

many years later that scientists realized the "madness" was a condition caused by their occupation.

Fur pelts were treated with mercuric chloride. Anyone who worked with the pelts, especially a hatter, was exposed to the fumes. Mercury is stored in the body and eventually builds up to levels that are toxic. At toxic levels it causes damage to the nervous system and the kidneys.

Lead is another heavy metal that interferes with the normal activity of the nervous system. There is a direct relationship between lead in gasoline and the level of lead in the blood. The amount of lead in the blood is measured in micrograms per decilitre ($\mu g/dL$). The EPA has set 10 $\mu g/dL$ as the maximum safe individual blood lead level for children. This standard is based on the following information:

70 µg/dl	Children with blood levels greater than this suffer from life-threatening brain damage, persistent mental retardation, kidney disorders, anorexia, severe abdominal pains, vomiting.
40-60 µg/dl	Effects of lead at this level include lower IQ, abnormal behavior, nerve disorders, and an inability to understand concepts. Children with these levels were seven times more likely to repeat a grade in school or be referred to a school psychologist for behavioral problems.
30-40 µg/dl	At this level lead causes a reduced number of red blood cells and interferes with nerve messages from the brain to the muscles.
12-20 µg/dl	Even at low levels lead prohibits the action of vitamin D that is necessary for normal growth and development in young children.

Why are children more affected by air pollution than adults?
- Children spend more time outdoors and interact more with the environment.
- They breathe up to three times as much air per pound of body weight as adults.
- They have fewer detoxifying enzymes in their bodies.
- Their bodies are still developing and their cells are dividing rapidly.

Effects on Animals

During the 1952 London disaster a cattle show was in progress. There were 350 cattle being exhibited. Five of these died, 52 became seriously ill, and 9 had to be destroyed. The sheep and swine showed no effects. The horses in London showed no effects. Cases of bronchitis and pneumonia increased among some animals at the zoo. This shows that different species of animals react in different ways to pollution.

Plants may become coated with air pollutants. As the animals feed on the plants they become sick. Air pollution events that were disasters for animals include:

1902   **Arsenic** from a copper smelter at Anaconda, Montana caused the death of sheep and horses.

1954   **Molybdenum** from a steel plant in Sweden poisoned cattle.

1955   **Lead and zinc** from foundries in Germany caused cattle and horses to become so lame that they had to be slaughtered.

1967   **Fluoride** from a phosphate fertilizer plant in Montana caused fluorosis in cattle and sheep. At first their teeth became discolored. Then they began to lose weight, they gave less milk, and growth was slower. Eventually their bones became deformed and they had to be killed.

1985   **Zinc oxide** from the New Jersey Zinc Co. at Palmerton, Pennsylvania, has accumulated in the soil. Where grass does grow, it contains enough zinc to cause lameness in horses.

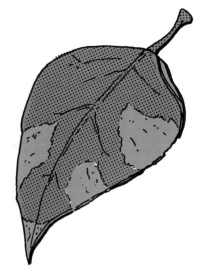

Leaf with Sulfur Dioxide Poisoning

Effects on Plants

Have you ever noticed the artificial plants used in landscaping some businesses? These businesses are frequently located near busy intersections. Plants show the effects of pollution before animals do. During the early 1900s the path of sulfur dioxide fumes from copper smelters could be traced by observing the death of plants.

Sulfur dioxide enters the pores in the leaf along with the carbon dioxide. As the cells die, damage can be seen as dried, whitened, or discolored areas on the leaf. Sulfur dioxide interferes with growth and decreases the yield of some plants, even when no damage is visible. Not all plants are injured by low concentrations of sulfur dioxide (0.3 ppm). Plants with thin leaves are more sensitive. Plants with fleshy leaves or needles are more resistant.

When there is dew or a light mist, the damage from sulfur dioxide is greater than the damage from sulfur dioxide alone. Very low concentrations of ozone are not harmful when it is the only pollutant. But in the presence of sulfur dioxide, the same low concentration of ozone becomes toxic. This is another example of the **synergistic effect**.

A seven-year study by the EPA and the US Department of Agriculture found that ozone is the most damaging air pollutant. The natural level of ozone is 0.025 ppm. Corn, soybeans, and winter wheat begin to show damage if the ozone level is 0.05 ppm for three weeks during the growing season. During the 1980s, ozone levels reduced crop yield in the United States by 5 to 10 percent. The Environmental Protection Agency estimates that air pollution costs farmers more than $500 million each year.

Experiments like this one at Penn State test the effects of air pollutants on plants.

Relative Sensitivity of the Leaves of Selected Plants to SO_2

SENSITIVE

Alfalfa	Barley	Endive	Cotton	Tobacco
Oats	Carrot	Chicory	Wheat	Rhubarb
Sweet Pea	Lettuce	Sweet Potato	Spinach	Radish
Squash	Bean	Broccoli	Clover	Pumpkin

INTERMEDIATE

Cauliflower	Parsley	Sugar Beet	Aster	Tomato
Parsnip	Apple	Cabbage	Zinnia	Marigold
Pear	Begonia	Grape	Peach	Apricot
Rye	Iris	Plum	Cherry	Gladiolus

RESISTANT

Rose	Irish Potato	Pine	Lilac	Chrysanthemum
Boxelder	Onion	Corn	Citrus	Virginia Creeper

Another gas that damages plants is **ethylene**, a pollutant in car exhaust. Ethylene leaking from "gas" lamps along city streets caused leaves to drop from trees. It also interferes with the opening of some flower buds in some plants. Other flowers wither or drop off when a few ppb (parts per billion) of ethylene are present. Higher concentrations retard the growth of tomatoes.

What does this mean to you? Of course it means that you may find plastic plants "growing" beside the curb. Plant nurseries must select resistant varieties of plants for landscaping. What is more important, it means you may have less selection or have to spend more money for food. For people who live in poverty, air pollution will reduce the amount of food they can buy. Air pollution may contribute to food shortages in countries where food is already in short supply.

Relative Sensitivity of Selected Plant Leaves to Smog

SENSITIVE

Endive (Romaine)	Tobacco	Spinach	Lettuce
Swiss Chard	Petunia	Sugar Beets	Celery
Barley (young)	Yellow Pine	Alfalfa	Oats

INTERMEDIATE

Barley	Eggplant	Tomato	Head Lettuce
Turnip	Rhubarb	Bean	White Pine
Onion	Parsley	Radish	

RESISTANT

Lettuce (old)	Two-Needle Pine	Cabbage	Cantaloupe
Cucumber	Pumpkin	Squash	Gladiolus

Property Damage

Air pollution affects both living and nonliving things. Metals corrode faster in industrialized areas. The degree of corrosion is proportional to the amount of pollution. Stone, like metal, is eaten away by pollutants in the atmosphere. Cleopatra's Needle has deteriorated more in the one hundred years it has been in Central Park in New York City than it did during the 3,000 years it spent in Egypt.

Sulfur oxides and **carbon dioxide** combine with moisture in the air to form acids. The **acids** dissolve metals, marble, roofing slate, and mortar in our buildings. They weaken the fibers in fabrics and leather. The **nitrogen oxides** and **ozone** destroy pigments in paint and fabrics. **Ozone** attacks rubber, making it brittle so that it cracks when stretched.

Even your textbook is not safe from pollution. Sulfur is used in the processing of wood into paper. The moisture in the atmosphere reacts with the sulfur compounds to form sulfuric acid. The **sulfuric acid** reacts with the paper, making it brittle. Historical libraries spend thousands of dollars each year for special air filters to control humidity levels and filter air pollutants.

The picture on top shows Shenandoah National Park on a smoggy day. The picture below taken from the same vantage point shows a clearer day.

Haze — Spoiling the View

Visibility, the greatest distance that one can see without the aid of technology, is being reduced by air pollution. In the West, the distance a person can see is often one-half to two-thirds of the natural visibility. Visibility in much of the East is reduced by four-fifths.

The major cause of reduced visibility is regional haze. The haze is caused by sulfur dioxide emissions, mainly from coal-burning electrical power plants.

5.1 QUESTIONS FOR STUDY AND DISCUSSION

1. Define the following words:
   bronchial asthma
   carcinogen
   chronic bronchitis
   controlled experiment
   emphysema
   lung cancer
   particulates
   photochemical smog
   pneumonia
   secondhand smoke
   smog
   synergistic effect
   variable

The Disasters

2. What was the major source of air pollution that caused the air pollution disasters?

3. Describe the geographic location of Donora, Pennsylvania. How did this location contribute to the 1948 air pollution disaster? See Section 2.1 Weather Patterns.

4. What groups of people were most affected by the air pollution disasters?

5. After a major air pollution disaster, countries have acted quickly to eliminate the problem. (true/false)

In the Laboratory

6. How many variables exist in a controlled experiment?

7. What happened to mice and other laboratory animals that were exposed to air pollutants? Were these valid experiments? Do you think that these studies can be applied to humans? Why or why not?

The Human Population — What the Studies Show

8. Why is it difficult to study the effects of air pollution on humans?
9. Studies have shown that the city you live in may affect your health. (true/false) What studies support your answer?
10. Studies have shown that the section of the city where you live may affect your health. (true/false) What studies support your answer?
11. According to the Los Angeles study, hospital admissions for heart disease were directly related to high levels of air pollution. (true/false)
12. Identify the variables that were present in the St. Louis-Winnipeg study. Do you think this was a good study? Why or why not?
13. What was the conclusion of the Longbeach-Glendora-Lancaster study?

What the Surgeon General Says

14. What diseases, in addition to those that affect the lung, are linked to tobacco smoke?
15. There is a direct relationship between the exposure to smoke and the chance of cancer. (true/false)
16. There is a direct relationship between the length of time since a person stopped smoking and the chance that the person will get cancer. (true/false)
17. Tobacco smoke is more deadly in some situations than in other situations. (true/false) Support your choice.

Diseases Associated with Air Pollution

18. What changes in the respiratory system bring about the chronic cough that is sometimes known as "smokers cough"? What is this condition called?
19. What changes occur in people who develop an allergic reaction to certain pollutants? What is this condition called?

20. What disease results when the air sacs remain inflated and can't help push the air out of the air sacs?
21. Pollutants cause changes in the respiratory system. Which changes will encourage the growth of bacteria?
22. Which changes will decrease the amount of air moving through the respiratory system?
23. How do cancer cells differ from normal cells found in the lung?

Pollutants — How They Affect Humans

24. What is the effect of a carcinogen? Name three substances that are carcinogens.
25. List several gases that are irritating to the respiratory system.
26. The gas, sulfur dioxide, is only mildly irritating, but in the respiratory system it can be deadly. What makes sulfur dioxide more irritating?
27. Why is sulfur dioxide more deadly in the presence of smoke?
28. Why are small particles more dangerous than large particles?
29. How does carbon monoxide interfere with the body's ability to get oxygen?
30. What pollutant caused hatters to become "mad"?
31. What two pollutants affect the nervous system?
32. Are children or adults more affected by air pollutants? Why?

Effects on Animals

33. Which animals were most affected by the air pollution disaster in London?
34. Air pollutants may enter the respiratory system of animals with the air that they breathe. Through what other body system may air pollutants enter the body of animals?
35. What type of air pollutants cause animals to become lame?

Effects on Plants

36. You own some land that you would like to use for growing a fall crop of pumpkins. The area is sometimes covered with a blanket of smog. Is it a good idea to plant pumpkins on this land?

37. Using the chart provided, identify the farmer(s) who would be most affected by sulfur dioxide pollution.

Kansas wheat farmer   Georgia peach grower
Midwestern hog farmer   Florida orange grove owner
Idaho potato farmer   South Carolina tobacco grower

38. If you were in charge of a tree-planting program in a large city, what type of pine tree seedling would you order?
39. When two pollutants are present, the effect of each one is greater than if either pollutant was present alone. (true/false)
40. Identify the conditions which intensify the damage caused by sulfur dioxide.
41. What is the most damaging air pollutant affecting agricultural crops?
42. Make the connections between air pollution and population.
43. Assume that you just inherited some money and have decided to open a florist shop specializing in fresh cut flowers that you will grow. You have two options:
    - buy land that borders a four-lane highway, at the edge of a big city or
    - buy land along a small country road, several miles away from the city.

    Which do you think would be the best buy and why?

Property Damage

44. What materials are damaged when certain air pollutants mix with moisture to form acids?
45. What materials are damaged when ozone is present?
46. Name 3 ways that air pollution costs you money.

Haze — Spoiling the View

47. What is the cause of regional haze? What problem does regional haze cause?
48. Do you think that regional haze is a serious air pollution problem that should be controlled? Why?

Summary Question

49. Identify the pollutant(s) that:
    (a) destroy rubber
    (b) destroy books
    (c) dissolve statues
    (d) interfere with growth of plants
    (e) interferes with the normal development of some flowers
    (f) cause animals to go lame
    (g) kill animals by combining with hemoglobin in the blood
    (h) affect the respiratory system of humans and some other animals, making breathing difficult

"We know our activities do affect various ecological systems."

— *Richard W. Hogeland, President*
The New Jersey Zinc Company
1975

The Franklin Ore

A **rock** is a collection of **minerals** — naturally occurring solids with specific chemical and physical structures. A rock mined to extract a useful mineral is an **ore**. Scouts, sent out from early settlements, searched for rocks with valuable mineral deposits. In the Franklin-Sterling area in northern New Jersey, they found an unusual ore that contained zinc, manganese, and iron.

Nearby they also found important deposits of copper and iron. The settlers successfully mined the copper and iron ores. They extracted the minerals by a process called **smelting**. Smelting involves heating the ores to high temperatures to separate impurities from **metals**, those minerals that conduct electricity and can be shaped or molded to a specific form.

Zinc Oxide — The First Product

For two hundred years after its discovery, no one mined the Franklin ore because no one knew how to extract the minerals. A small group of dedicated people worked for several years to develop a process to produce zinc oxide from this ore. The first use of zinc oxide was in the manufacture of paint. Paint made with zinc oxide pigment was whiter and brighter than paint made only with white lead. It also covered better. Adding zinc oxide to the white lead pastes also allowed paint manufacturers to produce paints in a thinned, ready-to-use form. This was the beginning of the ready-mixed paint industry.

Today there are many other uses for zinc oxide. Most zinc oxide is used in the enamel finishes on bathroom fixtures, kitchen sinks, refrigerators, and other appliances. Large amounts of zinc oxide are used by the rubber industry. In tires and other rubber products, it provides reinforcement against wear and prevents overheating. It is also an important additive used in the production of plastics and ceramics.

Check the labels and you'll find zinc oxide listed as an ingredient in a wide range of products sold in drug stores. A very pure form of zinc oxide is an important ingredient in face powders, adhesive tape, ointments, and mineral supplements.

Metal from the Franklin Ore

Eventually a process was developed to make metallic zinc from the New Jersey ore. Metallic zinc has many uses, but its main use is in the process of galvanizing. **Galvanizing** is the coating of iron or steel with zinc to prevent rusting.

Another important use of metallic zinc is the making of alloys. An **alloy** is a substance created by fusion of two or more metals, or sometimes a metal and nonmetal. **Fusion** occurs when the metals are heated to a liquid state. The best known of the alloys made with zinc is probably brass. **Brass** is made by fusing metallic zinc with copper and other metals including lead.

Another alloy, made mainly of zinc, is important in the die casting industry. A **die** is the mold or form that determines the shape of the object. **Die casting** — forcing heated metal into a die — produces many parts used in home appliances, office equipment, and vehicles. Many modern conveniences including dishwashers, light fixtures, typewriters, and even automobiles wouldn't work without die cast parts made of a zinc alloy.

Death on the Blue Mountain

In 1897, The New Jersey Zinc Company decided to build a new smelting plant. They laid out a community and named it Palmerton for Stephen S. Palmer, the company's president. Palmerton, Pennsylvania, was a company town. The first smelter began operating in 1898. The company built its second smelting plant, the East Plant, in 1911. For 82 years the smelters operated. They provided good jobs and supplied essential products for other industries.

The Blue Mountain was a picture postcard setting for the town of Palmerton. Dominated by oaks, American chestnuts, and white pines, the dense forest canopy shaded the mountain. In Palmerton, people planted vegetable gardens and grew flowers in their neatly trimmed lawns. They were proud hard-working people, and their life was good.

No one could have predicted that one day the picture on the postcard would show a mountain littered with the skeletons of dead trees and lawns with no grass. Unfortunately, the smelting of metals is not a clean process. Visit Ducktown, Tennessee, Sudbury, Ontario, or other sites where a smelter operated for many years, and the landscape provides evidence of the negative environmental impacts caused by the smelting of metals.

Trees in the original forest were cleared by loggers or destroyed by forest fires. Normally after a fire, the natural process of **succession** eventually produces a new forest ecosystem.

On the Blue Mountain the second-growth forest was missing one of the original dominant species. By 1930 the introduction of a fungus — the chestnut blight — prevented the regrowth of the American chestnut trees. [See Unit I Case Study 6.3 "Introduced Species"]

There were signs that the forest ecosystem nearest the smelters was ailing as early as the 1920s. The smelting operations continued and so did the decline of the forest. Aerial photographs of the area taken between the 1930s and 1980s show the gradual loss of the forest on the north slope of the Blue Mountain. By 1970 the forest ecosystem was gone. In some areas there were no signs of life. Other areas supported only scrubby growth — mostly sassafras, and its leaves showed signs of stress. What caused these changes? This question could only be answered by a detailed scientific study.

A Student Studies the Mountain

Dr. Marilyn Jordan, a graduate student at Rutgers University, conducted an extensive field study of the Blue Mountain's forest ecosystem. She identified the NJZ smelters as the probable source of pollutants. The only other industry, a small chemical plant, was located south of the Lehigh Gap. The location and the wind direction made it an unlikely cause of the changes on the mountain.

The prevailing winds blow from the northwest directly toward the Blue Mountain. Because the mountain intercepts the winds, it received a heavy dose of pollutants from the smelter's smoke stacks. The major pollutants were zinc, cadmium, copper, lead, and sulfur dioxide gas.

A census revealed that the density of trees and tree seedlings near the smelters was significantly less than the density at sites farther downwind from the smelters. Plots far from the smelters had twice as many tree species as plots close to the smelters. Could one or more of the pollutants be responsible for the difference in the number and kinds of trees growing near the smelters?

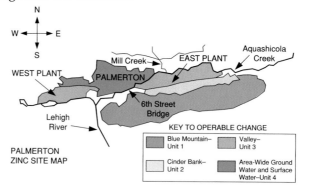

PALMERTON ZINC SITE MAP

The Blue Mountain — A Study of Trees		
Trees	Control	Lehigh Gap
Number per Hectare	809	544
Number of Species	13	7
Tree Seedlings	Control	Lehigh Gap
Number per Square Metre	4.5	2.4
Number of Species	11	5
The location of the Lehigh Gap plot was 2 km from the smelters. Control plots were more than 15 km from the smelters.		

Adapted from Jordan, Marilyn J. 1975.

Experiments in the Laboratory

Dr. Jordan thought that high levels of metals in the soil were preventing germination and/or stunting growth of seedlings. She suspected that the problem was either zinc or cadmium. To find out she designed a controlled experiment. She grew oak and pine seedlings in soil collected from the top of the mountain. Analysis of soil collected at sites near the smelter (2 km) showed high levels of zinc and cadmium. Soil samples collected far from the smelter (40 km) contained much lower levels of the metals.

Analysis of Soil Samples from the Blue Mountain				
Metals in Soil	Zinc (parts per million)		Cadmium (parts per million)	
Distance from Smelter	Near	Far	Near	Far
Organic Matter	20,000	300	500	3
Top Soil	2,000	100	10	2

Adapted from Buchauer, M.J. 1973.

The oak seedlings grown in the "near" soil produced less new twig growth and had fewer leaves. The average length of the leaf blades was shorter. The pine seedlings grown in the "near" soil produced fewer shoots and the shoots grew less. The needles on seedlings in the "near" soil were shorter and showed signs of yellowing. Both oak and pine seedlings grown in "near" soil produced very few new roots.

Were the plants being poisoned by the metals? Dr. Jordan analyzed oak leaves and pine needles to find out if the plants had absorbed toxic doses of zinc and cadmium. The only metal present at levels known to be toxic was zinc. Although the cadmium levels were not high enough to be considered toxic, cadmium might cause a **synergistic effect** — increasing the toxic effect of the zinc.

Dr. Jordan also collected seeds and acorns from the mountain. She studied the effects of zinc and cadmium on germination and found that zinc inhibits germination and growth of roots. While other environmental factors play some role, Dr. Jordan concluded that the "critical" factor preventing regrowth of the forest is zinc.

Life and Death on the Forest Floor

Dr. Jordan also studied microorganisms on the Blue Mountain. She found the total number of bacteria and fungi were greatly reduced near the smelters. Another scientist analyzed leaf litter on the forest floor at sites near and far from the smelter. He found thicker layers of leaf litter near the smelter ($8.1 kg/m^2$) than far from the smelter ($3.8 kg/m^2$). Other studies also show that there is a slower rate of decomposition in ecosystems polluted with metals.

A population census found the numbers and kinds of small arthropods, especially mites that are known to feed on leaf litter, are reduced at sites near the smelters. In a laboratory experiment, woodlice were fed samples of leaf litter collected from different sites along the Blue Mountain. The litter collected nearest the smelters was toxic to the woodlice. Leaf litter collected at sites further from the smelter was less toxic. A second experiment identified the probable cause of death as zinc poisoning.

Another study compared wildlife in an oak forest 10 km upwind from the zinc smelters with wildlife at a site 2 km downwind from the smelters. While earthworms, slugs and snails were common at the upwind site, none could be found at the downwind site. Frogs, toads and salamanders were also very rare or absent.

Much higher concentrations of metals were found in those species that feed on leaf litter. While tests show that some animals contain abnormally high concentrations of metals, it doesn't prove that the metals are killing these animals. A more important factor affecting some species may be the changes in the forest ecosystem.

Effects on Wildlife and Farm Animals

There is evidence that some species of small mammals and birds are being affected by high levels of lead, but most of these animals appear healthy. The lead concentrations in two cuckoos were as high as the levels associated with the death of bald eagles but lower than the levels known to kill some other species of birds. It is important to remember that the level of a pollutant that affects one species may not have the same affect on another species.

Little is known about the effects of heavy metals on wild mammals. Hunters cooperated with scientists from the US Fish and Wildlife Service to collect feces and tissues from white-tailed deer. Analysis of the feces, livers, and kidneys showed that many deer near the smelters are contaminated by zinc and cadmium. Examination of the hind legs of one deer revealed changes in joints that are associated with zinc poisoning. Cadmium levels may be high enough to cause kidney damage in older deer. Is the cadmium killing deer? Further research is necessary to determine the effects of these metals on the white-tailed deer population.

Farmers suspected that the smelters were causing lameness, swollen joints and a decline in the health of horses and cattle. Mature horses seemed healthy, but their foals became stiff-legged and stopped eating. Eventually the foals died, or their owners had them put to sleep. A postmortem examination revealed lesions similar to those found in the joints of animals fed high-zinc diets. One foal had severe osteoporosis and kidney disease. Both of these symptoms are associated with cadmium poisoning. One farmer found that he could raise foals if he bought feed grown outside the area.

Effects on Human Health

In 1975 the president of The New Jersey Zinc Company acknowledged that "our activities do affect ecological systems," and he pledged to "improve where possible the quality of life in and around our operations." Scientists have studied the effects of pollution on the mountain, but what about the health of people who were being exposed to high concentrations of metals? No one had studied the risks to human health.

The National Cancer Institute investigated a possible link between zinc smelting and lung cancer in white males. The results of the study indicated an increased lung cancer risk in those men exposed to high concentrations of arsenic and cadmium. Due to the limited number of individuals in the study, further research is needed to confirm a link between the smelting of metals and lung cancer in humans.

A special team of scientists reviewed the possible health risks at places where high concentrations of heavy metals have been found in the soil. Other communities included in the study were located near smelters in Texas, Arizona, Oklahoma, Montana, and Pennsylvania. People selected for the study donated hair, blood, and urine samples for analysis. They also completed a questionnaire to help identify other possible sources of metals.

DID YOU KNOW?

Researchers from the University of Tennessee have proven that creating "islands" of fragmented forest ecosystems lead inevitably to species decline and possibly even extinction. They found that ecological islands containing fewer than 15 pairs of breeding birds, for instance, would likely experience extinction of that population in a short time. Extinction would be due to factors such as inbreeding, death of offspring of one sex, or producing offspring all of one sex.

The study compared the levels of metals in the environment with the levels found in the body. Scientists concluded that people, especially children, living near smelters are exposed to higher levels of contamination. The study also showed that daily activities, such as smoking and time spent outdoors, affect exposure. It did not attempt to measure the health effects of the exposure to heavy metals.

The Environmental Protection Agency is concerned about possible health effects from high levels of heavy metals found in the soil near the smelters in Palmerton. In low doses cadmium can permanently damage kidneys. Lead also damages kidneys and interferes with the production of red blood cells and sperm. Children with blood levels at or above 10 micrograms per decilitre have significantly lower IQs.

During the summer of 1991, scientists conducted the first comprehensive health study of 211 families living near the smelters in Palmerton. The study also included a **control group** — families living in a town with similar characteristics but not near any smelting operations. The results of this study have not been released.

Heavy Metal Exposure in Populations Living near Smelters

- Communities near copper smelters had the highest levels of arsenic.
- Communities near zinc smelters had the highest levels of cadmium and lead.
- Sites nearest the smelters had the highest levels of metals.
- The 1-5 year olds had significantly higher levels of metals found in blood and hair than other age groups.
- In Palmerton, children living nearest the smelter had the highest levels of lead in their blood.
- Males had significantly higher levels of lead in blood and higher levels of all metals (cadmium, lead and arsenic) in hair.
- Many smokers had higher levels of metal in hair and blood than nonsmokers.
- In several cases, individuals who spent more time out of doors had significantly higher levels of metal in hair.

HRD — Hazardous Dust to Metal Products

The smelters shut down in 1980, and the West Plant of the New Jersey Zinc Company was dismantled. The zinc company, now called Zinc Corporation of America (ZCA), produces zinc products at the site of the east plant. ZCA no longer uses virgin zinc smelted from ores. The company buys recycled zinc — zinc recovered from parts in old cars and appliances — from its sister company HRD.

Horsehead Resources Development Company, Inc. (HRD) operates a metal recycling facility in Palmerton. Metals are recovered from EAF (electric arc furnace) dust, a hazardous waste product from steel mills. The dust is heated in high temperature (2,100°F) kilns to remove zinc, cadmium and lead. In 1991, HRD processed 345,000 tons of EAF dust, and recovered 66,000 tons of metals.

Recycling and the Environment

According to information provided by the company, HRD is a leader in the recycling of EAF dust. The company claims to have the only commercially proven high temperature metal recovery (HTMR) technology for processing EAF dust in the United States. The EPA has designated the HTMR process as the Best Available Demonstrated Technology for processing EAF dust.

Pollution control equipment at steel mills collects EAF dust to prevent the release of zinc, cadmium, and lead into the environment. EAF dust is listed by the EPA as hazardous waste. Due to the high zinc content (15 percent) EPA prohibited the landfilling of EAF dust where recycling is available.

Recycling of metals provides powerful environmental benefits. Recycling can cut energy required for the production of products from 50 to 90 percent. It also reduces pollution associated with mining and smelting the ores, and it eliminates the problems associated with solid waste disposal. To protect the environment we must recycle, but the proper procedures must be followed during the recycling process to minimize air and water pollution.

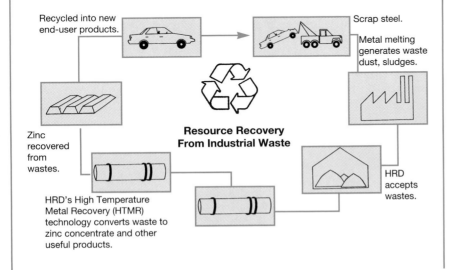

Recycled into new end-user products.

Scrap steel.

Metal melting generates waste dust, sludges.

Zinc recovered from wastes.

Resource Recovery From Industrial Waste

HRD accepts wastes.

HRD's High Temperature Metal Recovery (HTMR) technology converts waste to zinc concentrate and other useful products.

HRD versus the EPA

According to the company's 1991 Annual Report, modernization of the HRD facilities in Palmerton will "assure continued operations in Palmerton with maximum protection for our employees and the environment." But plans to modernize were not enough to satisfy the EPA. The agency is demanding action.

The Environmental Protection Agency says that there are serious problems with current operations at the plant. In January 1992, the EPA filed a lawsuit against HRD alleging repeated violations of the Clean Air and Clean Water Acts. According to the lawsuit, HRD:

- improperly stored hazardous wastes in piles exposed to wind and rain.
- allowed wastes to escape from storage facilities and open trucks.
- allowed illegal emissions from smokestacks and bag houses.
- discharged waste water with high levels of metals into the Aquashicola Creek.
- is operating without necessary permits.

Company officials maintain that the town is a relatively safe place to live. They say that current operations that involve recycling of metals are "an economic necessity" and that they are "relatively safe." The issue is not the value of recycling metals. The issue is the safety of the recyling operation at HRD in Palmerton.

Some citizens ignore the frequent headlines in the local newspapers that report the on-going negotiations between HRD and the EPA. Other residents follow the stories closely and closely monitor activities at the company. They are suspicious of the company's actions. Still other people display "NO EPA" signs in their windows.

HRD has a significant economic impact on the community. The company is the largest employer in the area, and it makes large charitable contributions to the community. HRD is "convinced that our technology will enhance the environment and will make us a significant leader in contributing to a cleaner environment." The EPA is taking enforcement actions to ensure that the environment is protected.

The Franklin Ore

1. Some — but not all — rocks are classified as an **ore**. What kinds of rocks are classified as ores?
2. The ore that became known as the Franklin ore contained a unique collection of minerals. List three minerals found in the Franklin ore.
3. You discover an important deposit of copper. Write a brief environmental impact statement that describes how you will make a profit from this discovery and identify the environmental impacts of your actions.

Zinc Oxide — The First Product

4. Identify 5 industries that use zinc oxide as an additive in their products.
5. List three products that you use that may contain zinc oxide.

Metal from the Franklin Ore

6. Explain how zinc is used in the processes of galvanizing, fusion, and die casting.
7. Make the connection among the following substances: brass, alloy, and zinc.
8. Think about it: Could you have come to school today without zinc and/or zinc oxide? Is zinc an essential element?

Death on the Blue Mountain

9. Compare the Blue Mountain in 1900 with Blue Mountain in 1970.
10. List positive and negative impacts associated with smelting of metals.
11. Identify the factors that led to the disappearance of the original forest ecosystem on Blue Mountain.
12. Identify the process that usually produces a new forest following a forest fire.

A Student Studies the Mountain

13. Explain why Dr. Jordan suspected that the NJZ smelters were the sources of pollutants affecting the mountain.
14. Identify the major pollutants produced during the smelting of the zinc ores.

15. Refer to the data in the chart "The Blue Mountain — A Population Census" and answer the questions below by inserting the symbol > "greater than" or < "less than."
    A. The population density of trees (number per hectare) at Lehigh Gap is _____ the population density at the Control sites.
    B. The biodiversity (number of species) of trees at the Control sites is _____ the biodiversity at the Lehigh Gap.
    C. The number of species of seedlings at the Control sites was _____ the number of species of seedlings growing at the Lehigh Gap.
    D. The distance between the smelters and the Control sites was _____ the distance between the smelters and the plots at Lehigh Gap.
    E. Both the number and kinds of trees growing in plots near the smelter is _____ the number and kinds of trees growing in plots at Control sites.

Experiments in the Laboratory

16. Soil samples collected near the smelter showed potentially toxic concentrations of two metals. What were these metals?
17. In the controlled experiment, Dr. Jordan compared soil samples taken from two locations. Identify the locations.
18. The greatest concentrations of zinc were found in the (organic matter/top soil). The greatest concentrations were taken from sites (near/far from) the smelters.
19. Compare the plants grown in the "near" soil to the plants grown in the "far" soil.
20. Identify the life processes that are inhibited or slowed by the pollutants in the soil near the smelters.
21. According to Dr. Jordan, what pollutant prevented the regrowth of the forest?
22. Dr. Jordan suggested that there may be a synergistic effect between zinc and cadmium. Explain how this affects the plants.

Life and Death on the Forest Floor

23. Explain why the dead leaves and dead trees accumulate on the mountain, but in other forest ecosystems they disappear.
24. Identify animal populations in the forest that appear to be suffering from the effects of the pollutants.
25. Make the connections: Trace possible pathways that pollutants might take from the smelter to the living organisms.
26. Explain why woodlice and earthworms are more affected by the pollutants than other small organisms.
27. Zinc is not equally toxic to all species. Explain why a species may be missing from the mountain even though it is not affected by zinc.

Effects on Wildlife and Farm Animals

28. Explain why it is difficult for scientists to predict the effects of the smelting operations on song birds.
29. Identify the heavy metals that may be affecting the white-tailed deer population and describe their effects.
30. The farm animals most affected by the pollutants were (young/old) horses. What pollutant probably caused the lesions found in joints? What pollutant probably caused the osteoporosis and kidney disease?

Effects on Human Health

31. Identify the weakness in the zinc smelter — lung cancer study.
32. List four groups of people who may be at the greatest risk because they are exposed to the highest levels of metals.
33. The EPA is concerned about the presence of two metals in the soil near the smelters. Identify the potential effects of these two metals.
34. The comprehensive health study includes a Control Group. What is the only difference between the Control town Jim Thorpe, and Palmerton?

HRD — From Dust to Metal

35. Identify the source of EAF dust.
36. Describe the recycling operation at HRD.

Recycling and the Environment

37. Identify the positive impacts associated with the recycling of EAF dust.
38. Identify the negative impacts associated with the recycling operation at HRD.

HRD versus the EPA

39. In Pennsylvania, it is illegal to store hazardous waste without a permit from the Department of Environmental Resources. If HRD applies for a permit to store the EAF dust, and it was your decision to issue or deny the permit, would you grant the company a permit? Justify your position.

CASE STUDY
The EPA at the "Palmerton Zinc Site"

There are few signs of plant growth on Blue Mountain in the vicinity of the zinc smelters. A build up of zinc in the soil is preventing the growth of most plants.

"Together, the problems form one of the largest and most complex Superfund sites in the nation."
— *Amy Barnett*
Environmental Protection Agency
community relations coordinator

In the 1970s, the United States made dramatic improvements in the quality of water and air. Not until the 1980s did the nation address the issue of hazardous wastes. The Comprehensive Environmental Response, Compensation, and Liability Act of 1980 (CERCLA) — commonly known as the "Superfund" law — was enacted to provide a nationwide program to address the threat of hazardous substances.

The law gave the US Environmental Protection Agency (EPA) the authority to respond to any situation involving a release or potential release of hazardous substances into the environment. It also created a federal trust fund ("Superfund") financed mostly by taxes on the manufacture and import of petroleum and 42 other chemicals. The funds are used by the EPA to "clean up" uncontrolled hazardous substances that may pose a risk to public health or to the environment.

Anyone who contributed to the release or potential release of hazardous substances is liable, and may be sued by the EPA for the cost of the clean up. "Potentially responsible parties" (PRPs) include former and current owners of the site, operators of the site, and anyone who disposed of or produced waste found at the site.

In 1982, the EPA identified approximately 2000 acres of the Blue Mountain in Carbon County, Pennsylvania, and a huge cinder bank near the NJZ East Plant (smelter) as a "Superfund" hazardous waste site. The EPA identified both current and former owners of the New Jersey Zinc Company as being "potentially responsible" for the contamination of the site. Working with the "responsible parties," the EPA is developing a detailed clean-up plan.

Due to the extremely large size of the Palmerton Zinc Site, it is divided into four units: the mountain, the cinder bank, the valley, and the water. Each unit addresses one area of concern.

For many years zinc was smelted at this plant in Palmerton, Pennsylvania.

Unit 1: The Blue Mountain

The mountain is covered with 4 million tons of toxic soil — an amount that can not easily be sealed in barrels and hauled away

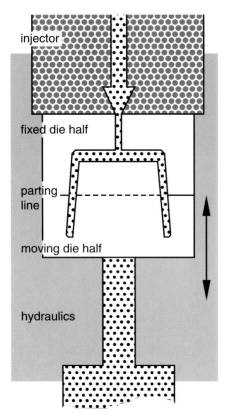

Die Casting Unit

for safe storage. Even if it was possible to remove the contaminated soil, it is unlikely that plants would grow in the rocky subsoil. Without plant roots to hold the soil in place there is massive erosion with each rainfall. The soil with its load of heavy metals is carried down the mountainside and into the Aquashicola Creek.

To reduce the threat from the hazardous chemicals in the soil, the "clean-up" must: (1) reduce erosion and runoff and, (2) restore the forest ecosystem. The plan, approved by the EPA, requires covering the north slope of the mountain with a synthetic soil. The artificial soil is a mixture of sewage sludge, lime and fly ash. **Fly ash** is the collection of particles captured by pollution control equipment at coal-burning power plants. **Sludge** is the solid material that is removed from the waste water at sewage treatment plants.

The sludge/lime/fly ash mixture is blended with grass and tree seeds then sprayed on the mountain. The revegetation project began in 1991. Several hundred acres have been revegetated, and the process will continue until the entire area is covered with a carpet of green plants.

Will a healthy forest ecosystem once again shade the mountain? Plants, including tomatoes that survive the human digestive system and sewage treatment, are growing in the synthetic soil. Will the trees grow once their roots reach the original soil? How well will the grass survive if trees don't grow? At the moment these are questions without an answer.

Unit 2: The Cinder Bank

The 2.5-mile-long cinder bank along the base of the mountain beside the Aquashicola Creek is 100 feet high, and in places it is 1000 feet wide. The EPA estimates that it contains 33 million tons of low-grade minerals including heavy metals that are **leachable** — soluble in water. Runoff from the cinder bank has carried heavy metals into the creek. Rain water percolating through the cinders leached heavy metals that contaminated a shallow aquifer.

In 1988 the EPA approved a plan to "clean up" the cinder bank. The plan included:
- regrading the cinder bank to increase runoff and decrease infiltration
- construction of a clay cap to decrease infiltration
- covering the cap with synthetic soil and planting grass and tree seeds
- collecting and treating runoff from the mountain and the cinder bank
- collecting and treating any precipitation that percolates through the cinder bank.

In 1991 the EPA amended the plan to include studies to investigate:

- potential environmental threats from fires in the cinder bank
- computer models to determine the effects of different "caps"
- new recycling technology.

Unit 3: The Valley

The clean-up plan for a Superfund site must be based on the most current scientific research data. The EPA reviewed the results of extensive soil tests conducted in 1988. At that time the dangers of lead were not fully known, and the EPA ruled that no immediate action was necessary. Then in 1991, the Federal Government reduced the amount of lead in blood that is "a threshold of concern" from 25 micrograms/decilitre to 10 micrograms/decilitre. Now, reducing the residents' exposure to lead and cadmium in soil and dust is the EPA's top priority.

In 1991 the Pennsylvania Department of Environmental Resources found high levels of lead, cadmium, and zinc in two homes in Palmerton. The EPA tested additional homes and found high levels of lead in the house dust and on porches. The agency ordered an immediate clean-up of 24 homes (with approval of the occupants).

The EPA is reviewing data from the 1988 soil tests. Meanwhile an investigation is underway to identify additional properties that contain high lead levels of lead, cadmium, and zinc. Another study is being conducted to identify the source or sources of contamination. Possible sources include the smelters, leaded gasoline, leaded paint, and current plant operations.

Results of Soil and Dust Samples Taken at Palmerton, Pennsylvania — May 1991		
	LOW	**HIGH**
Soil		
Cadmium	1 ppm	2 ppm
Lead	3 ppm	4 ppm
Vacuum Bag		
Cadmium	5 ppm	6 ppm
Lead	7 ppm	8 ppm
Exterior Porches		
Cadmium	9 ppm	10 ppm
Lead	11 ppm	12 ppm

Source: EPA

Once the sources are identified and the health study is completed, the EPA will assess the impact, if any, on human health, and select a "clean-up" plan. Until more information is available, the EPA suggests that people can protect themselves by vacuuming frequently and making sure that children wash their hands before eating. They also recommend that "citizens do not eat any vegetables or fruits grown in gardens with the original Palmerton soil."

Unit 4: The Water

In 1991, the EPA analyzed water samples from 211 homes in Palmerton and 135 homes in Jim Thorpe, Pennsylvania (the control group). The maximum contaminant level (acceptable level) of lead in public drinking water supplies is 20 ppm. Sixty-four samples had abnormally high levels of lead — 56 in Jim Thorpe and 8 in Palmerton.

In 1992, the EPA tested Palmerton's five public wells for lead, cadmium, arsenic, and zinc. One well showed a small amount of lead, but the amount was far below the "level of concern." None of the wells contained any of the other metals. The EPA suspects that the lead in the drinking water is being leached from the water pipes in the homes.

Although a shallow aquifer is contaminated, the EPA considers it unlikely that Palmerton's water supply is in any danger. The aquifer that supplies Palmerton's water is 200 to 300 feet below the ground. As water percolates through the soil, heavy metals become attached to soil particles. Thus heavy metals will probably be removed from ground water before it reaches the deep aquifer that is the town's water source.

Life Goes On

The residents of Palmerton deserve a clean, safe place to live. The children certainly deserve a clean and safe place to play. The ballpark across the street from the East Plant is owned by the school district and used by the girl's softball team. It is also used by 300 children who participate in the Booster Club programs. The Booster Club president described the field as ". . . like a rock garden when it rains. It has weeds, not grass. There are bare spots . . . (and) left field has craters like the moon's surface."

As a good will gesture toward the community, the Zinc Corporation of America agreed to landscape the field. The landscaping project included removing the contaminated topsoil and replacing it with soil from outside the contaminated area. The zinc company says that landscaping the field was a "beautification project." The Booster Club president says it is "a step in the right direction." The craters are gone, and the grassy field is far less dusty. The EPA says that a grassy field is safer than a bare field because the children are less likely to inhale dust that contains lead. The field of green is a better and, yes, a safer place to play. Breathing dust — even dust without lead — is not healthy.

The Clean-up Continues

The clean-up continues at the Palmerton Superfund Site. Amy Barnett, the EPA community relations coordinator says, "Together, the problems form one of the largest and most complex Superfund sites in the nation." To keep citizens informed, the EPA files technical reports and other information at the public library. Interested citizens and public officials may also attend hearings and receive "Superfund Update" fact sheets from the EPA.

Citizen's groups are actively involved. They ask questions and voice their concerns. One group of residents formed the Palmerton Citizens for a Clean Environment. Another group of citizens formed the Pro-Palmerton Coalition to combat negative publicity about Palmerton. Both groups monitor the current operations at the East Plant site and the progress of the clean-up.

5.3 QUESTIONS FOR STUDY AND DISCUSSION

1. What environmental problem was the target of the Comprehensive Environmental Response, Compensation, and Liability Act of 1980 (CERCLA)?
2. The Comprehensive Environmental Response, Compensation, and Liability Act of 1980 is know as CERCLA. What is the more common name for this law?
3. Tools are needed to do a job. The Superfund law gave the EPA two important tools that are needed to protect people and the environment from hazardous substances. What are these tools?
4. In which of the following situations might you be identified by the EPA as a "responsible party" and force you to pay for the "clean-up"?
   A. You operate a business that stores a hazardous waste product at the site. The EPA discovers that the chemical is threatening the ground water at the site.
   B. You are hauling a load of liquid fertilizer (ammonia) from the factory to the farm. There is an accident, and the ammonia leaks from the truck.
   C. You purchase land and find that barrels of toxic chemicals have previously been buried on the property.
   D. You are the owner of a company that produces batteries. A toxic waste is produced and sent to a treatment facility. The EPA discovers that the untreated waste was dumped into a stream.
   E. You invested money in a business that you did not operate. You grew tired of your investment and sold your interest in the business. Several years later the EPA declares that the business is a hazardous waste site.

5. Identify the "responsible parties" who must clean-up or pay for clean up of the hazardous waste at the "Palmerton Zinc Site."

Unit 1: The Blue Mountain

6. What type of hazardous substances threaten the environment?
7. A clean-up plan may include removal of the hazardous substances from the site. Explain why removal is not an appropriate clean-up method on the mountain.
8. Define the following terms: fly ash, sludge.
9. Describe how these two types of waste are being used to restore the forest ecosystem on the Blue Mountain.
10. What do you think about the clean-up plan? Will it restore the forest ecosystem? Will it protect the stream? Why do you think the plan will succeed or fail?

Unit 2: The Cinder Bank

11. In what ways does the cinder bank threaten the environment?
12. Describe how the clean-up will decrease infiltration and runoff.
13. Describe how the clean-up plan will further protect the stream and the ground water.
14. Why was the clean-up plan put on hold?

Unit 3: The Valley

15. Why did the EPA rule that no immediate action was necessary after reviewing the results of the soil tests taken in 1988?
16. What is the EPA's top priority now?
17. What steps is the EPA taking to clean-up the valley?
18. The current and former owners of the New Jersey Zinc Company have been identified as "potentially responsible" for the contamination of the soil. A study is being conducted to identify the source(s) of the contamination. Identify other possible sources of the lead found in the house dust.

19. If you lived in Palmerton and had young children, how would you protect them from the potential danger of exposure to lead and cadmium?

Unit 4: The Water

20. Water samples taken from homes in Palmerton and Jim Thorpe were analyzed. Which town had the largest number of samples with high levels of lead? According to the EPA, what is the probable source of the lead in the water?
21. The EPA concluded that the wells supplying drinking water for Palmerton's residents were (safe/unsafe).
22. A resident is concerned that the town's water supply may become contaminated 5 or 10 years from now. Explain to this resident why the EPA considers contamination of the wells unlikely.

Life Goes On

23. As the chairperson of the committee to oversee the landscaping of the ballpark, present a plan for the project. The goal of the plan is to provide an improved place for the area children to play sports. Justify the expense of the project to the Board Members of ZCA.
24. Do you think that the ballpark was dangerous before it was landscaped? Why or why not? Do you think it is safe now?

The Clean-Up Continues

25. The Palmerton Zinc Site was listed as a Superfund hazardous waste site in 1982. Why is the clean-up taking so long?
26. If you were a Palmerton resident, which citizen's group would you most likely support? Why would you choose this group?

"It came on the evening wind that drifted through the shantytowns . . . The lucky ones, alerted by the suffocating odor, escaped. Thousands did not. Some perished in their sleep. Others awoke, dizzy and nauseated, their eyes on fire and their lungs filling with fluid until they could no longer breathe, dying from exposure to a chemical few had heard of in perhaps history's worst industrial accident."

The New York Times

The site of the world's largest industrial accident was the Union Carbide pesticide plant in Bhopal, India. On December 3, 1984, water accidentally entered a tank containing methyl isocyanate (MIC), a chemical used in making pesticides. The chemical reaction caused the pressure in the underground storage tank to increase. The safety system failed, and the very toxic MIC gas filled the air.

The Human Cost

Some of the MIC broke down into hydrogen cyanide, a poison used in World War II. Unfortunately at the hospital no one realized the victims were suffering from hydrogen cyanide burns otherwise a cyanide antidote would have been used. The toxic gas killed more than 3,400 people, and nearly 200,000 people still suffer from the effects of the gas fumes. Some complain of chest pains, breathlessness, and pains in their muscles. Those with lung damage cannot get enough oxygen for hard physical labor.

Some people will require medical care for the rest of their lives. Their condition depends on how much gas they breathed. More than 2,500 of the women in neighborhoods affected by the leak were pregnant. More than 400 of these women had miscarriages — more than twice the average number for the area.

Safety Tests

At the time of the accident, information of the long-term effects of methyl isocyanate poisoning was limited. There are more than 80,000 chemicals sold in the United States. A study by the National Academy of Sciences revealed that the federal government does not have enough accurate health studies on most of these chemicals. Why isn't this information available?

The process of testing chemicals to determine their **toxic** or poisonous effects is very expensive. The testing procedure can cost millions of dollars and take several years to complete. The tests usually involve exposing laboratory animals to the chemical compounds. Exact scientific procedures must be followed.

Laws require manufacturers to submit the results of product safety tests to federal scientists. The test data is used to determine if a product is safe enough to market. The data is also used to determine safe levels of chemical residues on food, in drinking water, in air, and in the workplace. While testing has shown that the majority of chemicals on the market are not dangerous, some of chemicals are known to cause health and environmental problems.

In 1974, evidence presented during Senate hearings showed that test data is not always the result of good scientific work. Officials testified that some of the nation's major drug manufacturers have submitted inaccurate test results. These results were used by scientists at the Federal Food and Drug Administration to register seven new drugs. Why would a company submit inaccurate test results?

The Controlled Experiment

In every scientific study there is the potential for a serious mistake. Consider the problem of feeding 500 rats exact amounts of a chemical every day for two years. During this time several hundred more rats must be treated in the same way, except these rats do not receive the chemical. The group of rats that does not receive the chemical being tested is the **control group**. The group of rats that receives the chemical is the **experimental group**. Each animal's condition must be recorded daily. The weight of each animal must be recorded at least twice each week.

If a rat dies, its death must be recorded and samples of its body tissues preserved. At the end of the study, the remaining rats are killed. Slides of various body organs are prepared and analyzed. A two-year study will produce some 250,000 slides.

Consider some of the possible problems that might occur during this study. Over the weekend a technician failed to check the laboratory. In one cage the automatic watering system did not work, and some of the rats in that cage died of dehydration while others became weak and listless. A lab assistant failed to clean a cage, and some rats in that cage died of bacterial infection. Another assistant did not read carefully. The rats were fed the wrong substance.

All of these mistakes should be recorded and reported with the results of the study. Any mistakes in procedure must be evaluated with the data from the study. Some labs have found it easier to fake results. They know that repeating the study will cost the company time and money, and the people responsible may fear being fired.

Another problem is the fact that **toxicology** — the study of the effects of poisonous compounds — is a biological science. In physical science, objects act according to certain physical laws, such as gravity. Using these laws, scientists can predict the action of the objects. In biological sciences this is not always the case. The fact that rats develop cancer when exposed to a chemical does not necessarily mean that humans will develop cancer when exposed to the same conditions.

Different species of animals may have different reactions to a chemical. Even members of the same species may react differently to the same substance. These are the gray areas that lead scientists to have different opinions about the results of a scientific study.

Manufacturers can accurately predict how much money a new chemical can make for the company, how many jobs it can create and how useful it will be to society. These are the benefits. It is not as easy for scientists to predict the dangers or the risks of using the chemical.

A new technique is being developed so that the toxic effects of a chemical can be studied by using cells that are grown in laboratory dishes — a method called **tissue culture**. This will make testing much easier. It will also mean that testing can be done faster and with less cost. At the present time, testing animals is the only way we can predict the long term effects of chemicals.

Were tests faked by Union Carbide? Did Union Carbide build the plant in India so that it could avoid such expensive tests? The answer to both questions is no. Union Carbide also manufacturers nearly 20 million pounds of methyl isocyanate in the United States. They are required to submit safety tests, according to the Federal Insecticide, Fungicide, and Rodenticide Act.

A study conducted after the accident by the National Institute of Environmental Health Studies revealed that rats exposed to large doses of MIC develop scar tissue in the small air passageways of the lungs. Researchers think that these scars are permanent. They will make rats or humans more susceptible to respiratory disease and less able to do physical labor. The reproductive and immune systems of the rats were not affected by the MIC.

The Question of Safety

Could such a tragic event occur in the United States? Since many chemical industries are located in areas with a high population density, a major chemical accident could affect thousands of people. Although most chemical companies have good safety records, the potential for a major chemical accident in a densely populated area of the United States does exist.

In the past, federal inspectors did not seriously consider the possibility of major accidents, but since the Bhopal accident that has changed. An EPA study completed after the Bhopal disaster uncovered 11,048 accidents or "Acute Hazardous Events" that occurred in the United States between 1982 and 1988. The events caused 309 deaths and 11,341 injuries. There were 464,677 people evacuated from their homes and jobs. The EPA found that 17 of these events had the potential for more damage than the Bhopal accident.

Interviewed after the Bhopal accident, a chemical engineer who helped create a list of hazardous chemicals, said, "This country has been very lucky that it has not had a major chemical accident killing a lot of people. There have been many warnings. Those who try to minimize the hazards are totally wrong. And if there aren't many changes in the next couple of years, there probably will be a major accident here."

Preventing Accidents

Plant managers determine what safety precautions are taken. Prevention is better than any emergency plan. Managers have the responsibility to determine whether chemical processes are safe. They are responsible for installing proper equipment, such as temperature gauges and alarm systems, that will monitor reactions and warn of dangerous situations.

The federal **Occupational Safety and Health Administration** (OSHA) regulates 500 toxic chemicals in the workplace. Chemical plants are required to have certain safety equipment and limit exposure to toxic chemicals for workers in chemical plants. The massive size of the chemical industry creates problems. Only one in five chemical plants is inspected each year.

Safety during transport of chemicals is also a concern. Good safety measures cannot guarantee that an accident will not occur, but they can reduce the risk. A trailer carrying 3,000 gallons (1.1×10^4 L) of methyl isocyanate (the chemical that was released in Bhopal, India) nearly separated from the truck as it was being hauled from the plant in West Virginia to a pesticide plant in New York.

All shipments of MIC are accompanied by an emergency crew. The accident was prevented because the crew following the truck noticed sparks beneath the trailer and notified the truck driver. The driver was able to pull off the road. Another truck was sent to return the cargo to the plant in Virginia because Pennsylvania law prohibits shipments of hazardous chemicals, such as MIC, at night.

We are taking steps to make sure that we are better informed and ready to respond to an emergency situation. Experts agreed that better information about the location of hazardous chemicals was essential to reducing risks. If communities are to be properly prepared for a possible accident they have to know this information. In 1986, Congress passed the **Emergency Planning and Community Right-to-Know Act**. The act requires these actions by communities and companies:

- Chemical manufacturers must inform state and local authorities and make available to the public information on the quantities of hazardous materials they handle.
- Companies that make or use any of 313 listed hazardous chemicals must report amounts released to the environment.
- Companies must immediately notify national, state, and local officials when there is an unexpected release of certain hazardous substances.
- Local communities must develop an emergency response plan for chemical accidents.

The best way to reduce the chance of an accident is to avoid the use of toxic chemicals. Manufacturers are redesigning processes and improving procedures to minimize the risk of accidental releases of toxic chemicals. One paper company, Intertox America, has developed a way to bleach paper using hydrogen peroxide. The new procedure eliminates the use of toxic chlorine bleaching agents. Where toxics can't be replaced, a good emergency plan can reduce injuries and save lives.

5.4 QUESTIONS FOR STUDY AND DISCUSSION

1. What two events caused the accident in Bhopal, India?

The Human Cost

2. How did the poisonous compound methyl isocyanate affect people?

Safety Tests

3. What was the conclusion of the study done by the National Academy of Sciences?
4. Give two reasons why companies would like to avoid testing new chemicals.
5. Explain how chemicals are tested.
6. How are the test results used?
7. Are most chemicals on the market dangerous?

The Controlled Experiment

8. List some reasons why test data is sometimes faked.
9. What is the difference between the control group and the experimental group? Why is a control group needed?
10. Explain why the science of toxicology is more controversial than the science of physics.
11. What new technique is being developed that may some day allow us to study the effects of chemical compounds cheaper and faster?
12. What animal was the subject in experiments that studied the effects of MIC? What system was affected by the MIC?

The Question of Safety

13. Do you think that an accident like the one that happened in Bhopal, India, could happen in the United States? Justify your position.

Preventing Accidents

14. What is the role of the plant manager in the prevention of accidents at a chemical plant?
15. What is the role of OSHA in the prevention of accidents at a chemical plant?
16. How does Union Carbide try to insure the safety of people when methyl isocyanate is being transported in the United States?
17. How does Pennsylvania try to protect residents from the effects of chemical releases during transport?

18. What law, passed after the Bhopal accident, requires communities and companies to work together to reduce the risk from chemical releases?
19. List the 4 requirements of the Act passed by Congress in 1986.
20. Examine how the Emergency Planning and community Right-to-Know Act has affected your local community. Is there any evidence that your community is a safer place to live because of the Act?

"The clams go first, then the snails, then the crayfish . . . then out go the fish. . . . the lakes look like they have Astroturf on the bottom."

Harold Harvey
University of Toronto

Acid Rain: A Political Issue

The term "acid rain" was coined by a British chemist in 1872. It was not until one hundred years later that acid rain became an important scientific and political issue. At the 1972 United Nations Conference on the Human Environment, a Swedish scientist told the world about acid rain and acid snow in Sweden and Norway. He thought that the source of the acid rain was industry in Western Europe, and he suggested that acid rain was a kind of "chemical war."

Acid rain became a major environmental issue during the 1970s and 1980s. It has been a source of political disputes between Great Britain and the Scandinavian countries, between the United States and Canada, and between the midwestern and northeastern regions of the United States.

When President Reagan visited Canada in 1981, a crowd confronted him outside Parliament. They nearly drowned out the President's speech with chants of "Go home acid rain." A demonstrator held up a stuffed fish with the words "save me." It was the largest demonstration ever held against a foreign leader.

In 1982, the Canadian Film Board distributed a film concerning the issue of acid rain. The film's narrator says, "Winds do not respect political boundaries." The film describes pollution carried by winds from the United States to Canada. President Reagan's administration banned the film. Anyone showing the film in the United States was required by law to read a statement that said: "The Reagan administration has determined this film to be propaganda." Scientists, attending a conference sponsored by the National Wildlife Federation, declared the film to be "scientifically sound."

The controversy surrounding acid rain continued. Prime Minister Mulroney and President Reagan appointed Special Envoys to explore the issue of acid rain. In a speech at the New England Governors' Conference, Drew Lewis, President Reagan's special envoy said, "Saying [sulfur oxide] doesn't cause acid rain seems to me the same as saying smoking doesn't cause cancer. . . . I will recommend the administration acknowledge there is a problem."

The Special Envoy's joint report concluded that acid rain is a serious environmental and diplomatic problem requiring a US — Canada agreement. On March 19, 1986, President Reagan endorsed the report. This was the first time that the US Administration acknowledged that acid rain is an international problem that requires joint action by both countries. There was finally hope that the two governments could work together for the good of the common environment.

Acid Rain: Defined

The acidity of a substance is measured on a pH scale. The range of numbers on the pH scale is from 0 (very acidic) to 14 (very basic or alkaline). The pH value of 7, in the middle of the scale, is neutral. A change of one whole number on the scale represents a 10-fold change in acidity. A pH of 5 is ten times more acidic than a pH of 6. A pH of 3 is one thousand times more acidic than a pH of 6.

If no pollutants entered the atmosphere, rain and snow would be naturally acidic. Carbon dioxide, produced by natural processes, combines with water vapor in the atmosphere. When carbon dioxide combines with water, carbonic acid is formed. Although it is somewhat variable, the pH of natural rainfall is generally between 5.0 and 5.6.

$$CO_2 + H_2O \longrightarrow H_2CO_3$$
carbon dioxide + water → carbonic acid

The term **acid rain** is commonly used to describe any substance in the atmosphere that produces a pH lower than natural rainfall. Since these substances come in both wet and dry forms, scientists prefer the more accurate term **acid deposition**. Wet substances include rain, snow, sleet, hail, clouds, fog, dew, and frost. Dry substances are either gases or small particles that behave like acidic rain when they come in contact with any form of moisture. Acid rain is often ten times more acidic than natural rain (pH 4.0-4.6)

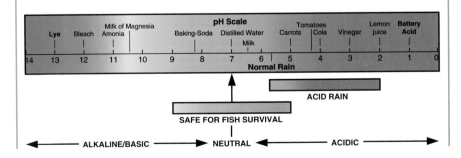

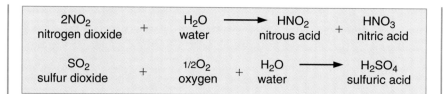

$$2NO_2 \text{ (nitrogen dioxide)} + H_2O \text{ (water)} \longrightarrow HNO_2 \text{ (nitrous acid)} + HNO_3 \text{ (nitric acid)}$$

$$SO_2 \text{ (sulfur dioxide)} + 1/2 O_2 \text{ (oxygen)} + H_2O \text{ (water)} \longrightarrow H_2SO_4 \text{ (sulfuric acid)}$$

TRY TO FIND OUT

How do scrubbers remove sulfur and nitrous oxides from industrial emissions? How costly are they? Compare the cost to industry of installing scrubbers to the loss of forests and lakes from acid rain.

Natural pollutants change the pH of precipitation. Wind-blown dust, from alkaline soils in prairie or desert regions, can raise the pH above 5.6. During thunderstorms, lightning changes nitrogen oxide into nitric acid. Sulfur from hot springs, volcanoes or decaying matter is changed into sulfuric acid. These acids can lower the pH to less than 5.0. Rain falling after the eruption of one volcano had a pH of 2.8.

Human Activities and Acid Rain

The major sources of chemicals that produce acid rain are human activities. Humans have been creating vast amounts of pollutants that cause acid rain since the Industrial Revolution. In North America, human activities produce 20 times more sulfur dioxide and 10 times more nitrogen oxides than all natural sources.

Fossil fuel combustion is the biggest single source of chemicals that form acids when released into the atmosphere. Fossil fuels — coal, oil, and gas — contain large amounts of sulfur and nitrogen. When these fuels are burned, sulfur dioxide (SO_2) and nitrogen oxides (NO_x) are released into the atmosphere. Chemical reactions with oxygen, water, and other chemicals in the atmosphere, convert these gases to sulfuric acid and nitric acid.

Smelters are the largest single source of sulfur dioxide emissions in Canada. In the United States, most sulfur dioxide is produced by electric power plants. The highest concentration of power plants and industries producing sulfur dioxide is in the Ohio River Valley.

In both the US and Canada, motor vehicle exhaust is the major source of nitrogen oxide emissions. On the west coast of the US, nitrogen oxides from vehicle exhaust seem to be the major cause of acid rain. In December 1982, the pH of a Los Angeles fog was 1.7. The pH of rain in the mid-continental states averages 4.4 to 5.0, while rain in the Northeast frequently has a pH of 4.0-4.5. A 1984 study showed the average rainfall in the state of New Jersey had a pH of 4.2. Individual storms are sometimes much worse. In Wheeling, West Virginia, one rainstorm had a pH of 1.5.

The state of Pennsylvania holds the record for the most acidic average rainfall in the nation (4.0-4.1). Some of the acid rain in Pennsylvania is caused by industries and power plants

The world's tallest smoke stack, Sudbury, Ontario, Canada.

in other states. Pennsylvania is located directly downwind from several states that are large producers of chemicals that cause acid rain, but Pennsylvania is also one of the largest producers of these same chemicals.

The Midwest-Northeast Controversy

For many years, scientists have believed "acid rain" comes from pollutants that pour out of the tall smokestacks in the Midwest, but this has been difficult to prove. The solution to pollution during the 1960s and 1970s was tall smoke stacks. Smoke stacks were built higher to carry pollutants farther away from their sources. It was thought that the pollutants would be diluted and destroyed if they were released high into the atmosphere.

Until now there was little scientific evidence to prove what really happens to the gases after they leave the stack. Now we know that the gases can react with water, oxygen, and other chemicals in the atmosphere. As the gases are carried by winds and weather systems, they are changed into sulfuric and nitric acids. These pollutants fall back to earth as acid rain hundreds of miles away from their sources.

How do you prove a chemical that lands in Toronto or Philadelphia came from a certain smoke stack in the Ohio River Valley? Experiments using tracer chemicals may eventually identify the exact sources of pollution.

Where does acid rain fall? ▶

Annual sulfate deposition levels measured in kilograms per hectare. Deposition levels exceeding 20kg/ha (18 lbs/acre) per year are generally regarded as threatening to moderately sensitive aquatic and terrestrial ecosystems.

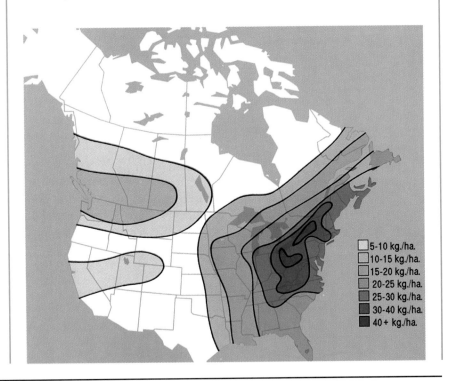

5-10 kg./ha.
10-15 kg./ha.
15-20 kg./ha.
20-25 kg./ha.
25-30 kg./ha.
30-40 kg./ha.
40+ kg./ha.

Tracers are chemicals that are not normally found in the atmosphere or chemicals that are found only in very small amounts. Some tracers are radioactive substances that can be detected by sensitive instruments. Others are unique chemicals that do not react with other chemicals in the atmosphere.

In 1983 scientists began an experiment that released a tracer substance from two different sites. One site was in the United States (Dayton, Ohio) and the other was in Canada (Sudbury, Ontario). The experiment was named **Captex** for Cross Appalachian Tracer Experiment.

The tracer substance was a mixture of carbon and fluorine. This gas — perfluoromonomethylcyclohexane — is normally found in the atmosphere in very small concentrations. For two weeks after the tracer substance was released, air currents were monitored by weather balloon stations. Air samples were taken at ground level and at different levels in the atmosphere. Scientists flying in airplanes collected air samples from clouds and from air masses. Computers plotted the path of the tracer chemicals and pollutants.

The experiment was originally designed to determine the path of pollution from a dangerous chemical explosion or a nuclear accident, but it also helped us learn more about the path of pollutants that cause acid rain. One of the largest experiments ever designed, Captex cost about $2 million, and the data took more than a year to analyze.

Acid Rain: Is It Deadly?

Living organisms cannot survive if the pH is too low or too high. The normal pH of human blood is 7.35-7.45. If the pH does not remain within this narrow range, a person becomes ill. Aquatic organisms become ill or die if the pH of their environment does not stay within an acceptable pH range.

The main concern about acid rain is the damage it is causing in aquatic ecosystems — especially lakes and streams. Like the canary in the coal mine, fish can tell us that something is wrong with their environment. In the Adirondack Mountains of New York State, many lakes are so acid that fish cannot live. Some species of fish are more sensitive to pH than others. Brook trout can live in water with a pH of 5.0 or lower; brown trout need a pH of 5.5 or higher; and rainbow trout need a pH of 6.0 or higher. Water with a pH below 4.3 is generally fishless.

When the pH falls below 6, many species of fish can't reproduce. Fewer eggs are released, and frequently they do not hatch. Even if the eggs hatch, the young fish cannot develop properly. It matters little that adults can live at this pH; without a new generation the species won't survive.

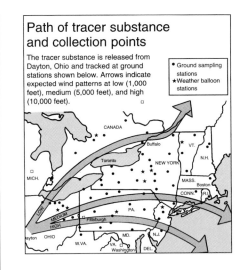

Path of tracer substance and collection points

The tracer substance is released from Dayton, Ohio and tracked at ground stations shown below. Arrows indicate expected wind patterns at low (1,000 feet), medium (5,000 feet), and high (10,000 feet).

- Ground sampling stations
★ Weather balloon stations

Acid rain and a lack of natural buffers in some regions threaten the survival of trout and other species.

Effect of Acid Shock on Fish

Most fish and amphibians breed in spring. Unfortunately this is also the time when lakes and streams receive all of the acid that has been stored in snow during the winter. The sudden increase in acid carried by the spring runoff causes a condition called **acid shock**. Acid shock sometimes kills entire populations of fish. Because of the heavier snow cover, acid shock is a greater problem in Canada than in the United States.

The salamander breeds in temporary ponds that are formed by melted snow or spring rains. A scientist at Cornell University hatched spotted salamander eggs in artificial pools. Ninety-nine percent of those eggs, in pools with a pH near neutral (7.0), hatched normally. Most of those eggs in pools with a pH less than 6.0 did not develop properly. Sixty percent of these salamanders died.

Many minerals are dissolved in the water of lakes and streams. These minerals are usually found in very small amounts. Researchers found that water with a low pH contains higher levels of some minerals. The acidic water dissolves aluminum and other minerals (cadmium, copper, lead, nickel, manganese, and mercury) from the surrounding rocks and soil. This process in which minerals are dissolved from rock and carried away by water is known as **leaching**.

The aluminum compounds collect in the gills of the fish. In response to the increased levels of aluminum, the gills become coated with mucus. The mucus prevents the exchange of oxygen and carbon dioxide across the gill membrane, and the fish suffocates.

The high level of aluminum also interferes with the absorption of calcium and sodium. Fish become deformed when they can't absorb enough calcium for a strong skeleton. A lack of sodium causes spastic muscle contractions that lead to death.

Fish and amphibians are not the only organisms affected. Mayflies, stoneflies, mussels, snails, and other organisms disappear at pH 5. A few species, such as the whirligig beetle and the water boatman, will survive and reproduce in water with a very low pH (3.5). These species are said to be **acid tolerant**.

As the lake becomes more acidic (the pH falls), many kinds of aquatic plants and algae disappear. Only a few kinds of mosses and algae survive, but the populations of these acid tolerant species increase.

Many people visiting Deep Lake, in Pennsylvania's Pocono Mountains, would not notice that the lake is sick and dying. The crystal clear water is misleading. Clear water is a sign that the many tiny organisms that normally cloud the water are dead. The many lively schools of Pumpkinseed sunfish seem healthy enough. It is not the presence of sunfish but the absence of other fish that indicates the lake is in trouble. A closer look at the sunfish indicates that their growth is stunted.

Deep Lake is an example of an acid lake. Its average pH is 4.0. Where many different kinds of organisms once lived, scientists now find only a few types of organisms. The few kinds of organisms that do survive are present in great numbers. An acid lake is not a dead lake, but it is not the healthy complex ecosystem that it once was.

Some species of mayflies, stoneflies and many bacteria feed on dead leaves that have fallen or blown into the water. In acid lakes there are few, if any, scavengers or decomposers. Leaves may lie on the bottom of the lake for years. The dead organisms do not decay. The nutrients in the lake or stream ecosystem remain trapped in the bodies of the dead organisms. They are no longer a part of the normal nutrient cycle.

The Buffer Factor

Some lakes become acid; others don't. Lakes that receive rainfall with the same pH may have very different pH readings. For example, the Great Lakes receive rainfall that is almost as acid as the rainfall in the Adirondacks, but the Great Lakes are not acid. Within the Adirondack Mountains, lakes that are only a few miles apart show different pH readings.

What causes this difference? Some lakes contain buffers; others do not. A **buffer** is a substance that, when placed in water, prevents large changes in the pH. The buffers are a natural Alka-Seltzer®. They neutralize the acids that enter the lakes. The drainage area, or **watershed**, around a lake contains rocks. The type of buffers that are found in a lake depends upon the kind of rocks and soil in the watershed.

The watershed around the Great Lakes contains a lot of limestone. Limestone is a soft rock. The minerals in limestone are easily dissolved in water. Water that contains low concentrations of dissolved minerals is called **soft water**. If the concentration of minerals is high the water is said to be **hard water**. Because hard water lakes contain many minerals, they are not readily affected by acid rain. This is because some of these minerals act as buffers.

Lakes and streams in a watershed that contain hard rocks — like granite — contain few minerals. Watersheds with hard rocks have soft water and are sensitive to acidic deposition because they do not have minerals that neutralize the acids. During storm events the pH drops. Eventually the lakes and streams lose the ability to support reproducing populations of trout and other fishes.

The Appalachian Mountains are made mostly of sandstone and shale. Sandstone and shale are not very good buffers. They contain few minerals that can neutralize acids. Still, sandstone and shale are better buffers than the granite of the Adirondack Mountains.

Buffer (Alka-Seltzer)

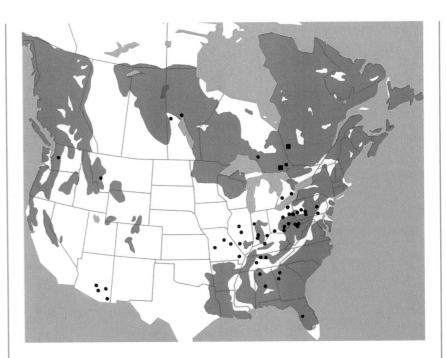

The sections maked in red are low in natural buffers and are susceptible to acidification. The black dots indicate sources with heavy concentrations of SO₂ emissions (between 100 and 500 kilotonnes per year). The squares indicate sources having SO₂ emissions of more than 500 kilotonnes per year. Smaller sources form a significant proportion of total emissions.

The watershed of some lakes in the Adirondack Mountains is covered with limestone that was deposited by glaciers. These lakes are not sensitive to acid rain. The water in these lakes has a pH of 7 even though the pH of the rainfall is 4.0. Other lakes without these limestone deposits are very sensitive to acid rain. Their pH can change quickly.

Four percent of lakes larger than 4 hectares (about 10 acres) and 8 percent of streams surveyed in a federal government study were acidic. Twenty percent of lakes and streams in the United States are very sensitive to acid rain.

According to the Pennsylvania Fish Commission, some populations of trout and small mouth bass have already been affected. They no longer stock some species of trout in streams that are acidic. Some pre-season stocking has been stopped because of acid shock. The commission considers acid rain the "greatest threat to future fishing." They predict that in another ten or twenty years some Pennsylvania streams will resemble those in the Adirondacks.

Can the Ecosystem Be Saved?

To save their lakes New York and Sweden are dumping tons of limestone into them. Limestoning is an expensive and temporary measure — a band-aid approach. More than 4,000 of Sweden's lakes are being limed. The estimated cost for 1985 was about forty million dollars. The Swedes are trying to buy some time until pollution controls reduce acid rain.

Limestoning of lakes is an experiment. Will the organisms that once lived in the lakes be able to live there again? No one really knows what the long term effects of this experiment will be. Sweden has found that in some lakes, the lime causes a population explosion of certain species of algae. The clear blue water of Sweden's Lake Gardsjon has changed to a green algal soup.

Impacts on Field Crops

Artificial acid rain has been sprayed on field crops grown in plastic cages. Most of the plants did not seem to be affected. Some plants did not grow as well as usual, while others seemed to benefit from the acid rain. This may be because sulfur and nitrogen are both plant nutrients (fertilizers).

Fertilizers are normally acids. The fertilizers that are necessary to grow the crops add far more acid to the soil than is added by acid rain. Farmers regularly add limestone to their soils to neutralize this acid.

One hypothesis suggests that acid rain may damage the leaves of plants and interfere with the process of photosynthesis. It is possible that this could result in reduced crop yields and slower growth of pastures and forests. At the present time there is little evidence to support this hypothesis. Scientists conclude that the nation's agriculture is not being damaged by acid rain.

Impact on Forests

What is causing the decline in growth of the shortleaf pines on the Coastal Plains of the Carolinas, the red spruce at high elevations in the Appalachian Mountains, the sugar maples in the northeastern United States and Canada, and the Norway spruce and silver fir in western Germany? Is acid rain killing our forests?

Forest decline describes a forest in which many trees show signs of stress: a thinning of the foliage, premature yellowing or loss of foliage, and an increase in the number of dying trees. Trees (mostly conifers) seem to be dying at unusually rapid rates in certain locations. About 8 percent of West Germany's forested area showed damage in 1982. By 1987 the damaged area had increased to 52 percent.

Many of the red spruce trees on Camel's Hump, a mountain near Burlington, Vermont, are more than 300 years old. About half of them are either dead or dying. Such a large loss of trees in such a short time period indicates that something is wrong. The damage is slowly spreading down the mountainside. Other species of trees are showing signs of damage. The tips of the branches of fir trees are brown. The hardwoods and beech are not growing at their normal rate. Young seedlings are not replacing the dying trees.

Healthy maple tree.

Maple tree showing decline due to a combination of factors including insects, climate and air pollution.

The forest on Camel's Hump has been studied by scientists for more than twenty-five years. One study showed that at several sites, the level of lead in the forest soil had doubled during a ten year period. The amount of organic matter — dead plant material — in the soil had also doubled.

At first, it may seem that this increase in organic matter is good. After all, gardeners want to increase the organic matter in their soil. Instead of being a good sign, the increase in organic matter shows that something is wrong with the decomposers in the forest ecosystem. The level of organic matter is increasing because the decomposers are not breaking it down and returning the nutrients to the soil.

Mountain soils are only a few inches deep and hold very few nutrients. Acid rain may be leaching nutrients, such as calcium and magnesium from the soil or leaves. It may also release toxic metals such as aluminum from the soil. Aluminum can enter the root hairs and inhibit the uptake of nutrients. Other toxic metals such as lead and cadmium may damage fine root hairs and kill decomposers.

Special stainless-steel augers are used to take core samples from trees. The growth rings provide a permanent record of how the tree grew in each year since the tree sprouted. The rings show that the growth rate of red spruce is declining. They also show that the aluminum content has tripled since 1950.

Scientists have found that acidic cloud water, in combination with other factors, increases winter damage in red spruce growing at high elevations. Also exposure to acid fog and sulfur dioxide affects root growth in ponderosa pine and Douglas fir.

Current research does not show a direct link between acid rain and widespread forest damage. However it is changing the soil chemistry. The US Forest Service concludes that these changes in soil chemistry will have negative impacts upon forests.

Scientists agree that ozone is a more important factor in causing forest damage than acid rain. Studies show that high levels of ozone from the Los Angeles basin, caused the decline of some species of trees in the San Bernadino Mountains of Southern California. Studies also show that ozone has damaged white pine trees in parts of the eastern United States.

The Forest Service suggests that forest declines are caused by a combination of factors. In addition to air pollution, trees are stressed by climate, insects, and diseases. The combination of factors varies for different species and different locations. Research on the decline of forests continues for there is still much to learn.

The Statue of Liberty

Steel bridges, tombstones, and statues — including the Statue of Liberty — show signs of damage. Many factors, including acid rain, may be responsible for this damage. Little research has been done to determine what damage is due to acid rain and what damage is due to other pollutants.

A study was conducted by the Environmental Protection Agency, the Brookhaven National Laboratory, and the Army Corps of Engineers. They estimated that acid rain causes $5 billion in damages each year in a region extending from Kentucky and Illinois to Maine. This damage is due to the corrosion of buildings and other structures. The study is important because it shows that acid rain is everybody's problem. It is not just a question of a few mountain lakes.

Can Acid Rain Harm People?

Sulfur gases can form "acid rain" within the lungs. They are associated with some respiratory diseases such as chronic bronchitis, asthma, and emphysema. Studies at the Harvard School of Public Health have found that acid aerosols may pose a significant public health risk.

Babies living on a farm in Sweden had spells of diarrhea caused by high levels of copper in the drinking water. The acid water from the well had dissolved copper from the plumbing. Blondes living in Sweden don't always have more fun. After washing their hair in water with high levels of copper, their hair is tinted green.

In Vermont, where pipes are frequently made of lead, people have higher than average levels of lead in their blood. High levels of lead (0.8 ppm) in the blood can cause brain damage, especially in children. The first five years of life are extremely important to the proper growth and development of the brain.

In the Adirondacks of New York, acid water causes plumbing to corrode, and the metals give an unpleasant taste to the water. Levels of both lead and copper are higher than normal in these water supplies.

Environmental scientists from New York's Department of Health give the following advice to people using these water supplies: When using the water for drinking or cooking, let faucets run a few minutes if they have not been used overnight. This will lower the concentration of metals.

The True Cost

We enjoy the benefits of burning fossil fuels. They provide energy for comforts like air conditioning, heating, lighting, appliances, transportation, and many forms of recreation. We need these forms of energy to maintain our present lifestyle, and we want the cost to be low. The fact is that we have not been paying the true cost.

The **true cost** of a product must include technology that will prevent pollution of our environment. We will pay the cost. The

Deciduous forest showing decline due to a combination of factors including insects, climate and air pollution.

The Statue of Liberty

only question is, how? We can pay higher utility bills to prevent the acid pollution or we can pay the higher cost of repairing structures and additional health care.

Some industries say the cost to prevent acid rain is too high. They say the damage caused by acid rain cannot justify spending millions or maybe billions of dollars to prevent it. The US Congress Office of Technology Assessment estimates that each American would have to pay $9 to $20 per year to reduce sulfur dioxide pollution.

Not all industries are against controlling stack emissions. One official for an electric utility, speaking at a conference on acid rain said, "I think we have dragged our feet . . . and we ought to get on with it."

Getting On With It

In 1980, Congress authorized a ten-year, $536 million study of acid rain. The **National Acid Precipitation Assessment Program** (NAPAP) study involved more than 1000 university and government scientists. While the study did not find acid rain to be the disaster that some had predicted, it did find a serious problem. The director of the study said, "The sky is not falling, but there is a problem that needs addressing."

By the time the final report was released, Congress was already at work hammering out the details of amendments to the Clean Air Act. The 1990 Clean Air Act Amendments, signed into law by President Bush, officially recognized acid rain as a serious environmental problem and set up an ambitious program to control air pollutants that cause it. Canada has made considerable progress in reducing sulfur dioxide emissions. A major reduction in sulfur dioxide emissions is now a goal of clean air regulations in both countries.

The Canada-US Air Quality Accord, signed in 1991, addresses the need to reduce another pollutant — nitrogen oxides. This agreement requires each country to reduce nitrogen oxide emissions from stationary sources such as power plants and industries. While this agreement is a step in the right direction, it does not address the major source of this pollutant. Transportation is the major source of nitrogen oxides in both countries (over 60% in Canada and 45% in the United States). Each country must also address the problem created by the growing number of vehicles contributing to the formation of acid rain and smog.

Finally the United States and Canadian governments are working together for the good of our common environment. The issue of acid rain will continue to be an issue that is discussed at meetings between the President of the United States and the Prime Minister of Canada.

1. Define the following words:

    acid deposition   hard water
    acid rain   leaching
    acid shock   pH scale
    acid tolerant   soft water
    buffer   tracer
    Captex   true cost
    carbonic acid   watershed
    forest decline

Acid Rain: A Political Issue

2. Why is acid rain a source of political dispute between countries?
3. What was the conclusion of the Special Envoys?

Acid Rain: Defined

4. Identify the following pH numbers as acid, base, or neutral.
    3, 8, 6, 7, 4, and 12.
5. A substance with a pH of 4 is 10 times more acidic than a substance with a pH of _____ and 100 times more acidic than a substance with a pH of _____.
6. What causes natural rainfall — without any pollutants — to be acidic?
7. What is the pH of natural rainfall?
8. Identify the wet forms of "acid rain."
9. Identify the dry forms of "acid rain."
10. Indicate whether the pH of rain is raised or lowered by each of the following events:
    A. dust blown from desert soils
    B. lightning during a thunderstorm
    C. sulfur oxide from hot springs
    D. eruption of a volcano
    E. decaying matter

Human Activities and Acid Rain

11. What two gases form the major pollutants in acid rain?
12. What is the biggest single human activity that is a source of chemicals that form acids when they are released in the atmosphere?
13. What is the major cause of acid rain in Canada? in the Ohio River valley? on the west coast?

14. What state has the most acidic average rainfall? Compare the acidity of the average rainfall to natural rainfall.
15. What method used to control pollution during the 1960s and 1970s actually led to increased levels of acids in the rain?
16. How can you prove that a chemical landing in New Jersey or Pennsylvania actually came from a certain smoke stack in Ohio? Give two types of chemicals that are used as tracers.
17. Explain the purpose of the experiment named Captex.
18. What can experiments like Captex tell us about acid rain?

Acid Rain: Is It Deadly?

19. Most fish cannot usually survive if the pH of water is below _____.
20. Why are many fish populations reduced if the pH is below 6?
21. Why are lakes and streams often more acid in spring than summer?
22. Fish often die because of the high levels of acid in water during the early spring. What is this condition called?
23. Spotted salamanders cannot develop properly if the pH is below _____.
24. Researchers have found that water with a low pH usually contain (lower/higher) levels of minerals than water with a high pH. Why is this true?
25. What mineral prevents the normal exchange of oxygen and carbon dioxide across the gills of fish?
26. What other organisms in addition to fish cannot survive in acid water?
27. Name two species of water insects that are acid tolerant.
28. Which species of trout is the most acid tolerant? Which species of trout is the most sensitive to acid waters?
29. If you examine a lake and find only a few species of mosses and algae and only a few species of aquatic invertebrates, what pH might you expect to find?

30. Which statement best describes an acid lake?
   A. An acid lake is a lake with only a few species of organisms, but large populations of each species.
   B. An acid lake is a lake with many different species of organisms, but smaller populations of each species.
31. Layers of leaves are often found lying on the bottom of an acid lake. The same situation occurs in bogs. What is the cause of this?

The Buffer Factor

32. Why do some lakes become acid while others do not?
33. What is the source of buffers that are found in a lake?
34. Which lake will contain more buffers — one with hard water or one with soft water?
35. Which lake is more likely to become acid — the lake with a watershed that contains (granite/limestone).
36. The lake which will contain the most buffers is a lake with a watershed that contains (granite/limestone/sandstone/shale).
37. What is the major type of rock found in the watershed of the Great Lakes?
38. The Great Lakes contain (hard/soft) water.
39. Cellar Pond in the Adirondack Mountains is an example of a lake that is sensitive to acid rain. It has a pH of 3.8. What type of rock would you expect to find in the watershed surrounding Cellar Pond?
40. According to the Game Commission, what is the greatest threat to future fishing?

Can the Ecosystem Be Saved?

41. Do you think that the best solution to the acid rain problem is treating the lakes with limestone? Support your position.

Impacts on Field Crops

42. Give a possible reason why some plants grow better when sprayed with acid rain.
43. Most acids in the soil of a corn field come from (acid rain/fertilizers applied by the farmer).
44. How do farmers prevent the soil in their fields from becoming acid?
45. What is one possible effect of acid rain that could reduce yields?

46. At the present time do scientists feel that our food supply is threatened by acid rain?

Impacts on Forests

47. Give evidence of forest decline on Camel's Hump?
48. The amount of organic matter is increasing on Camel's Hump. Is this good or bad? Why?
49. List three ways in which acid rain may be causing trees to die.
50. According to the Forest Service, what is causing the forest decline?

The Statue of Liberty

51. Acid rain is everyone's problem. Explain how acid rain costs you money.

Can Acid Rain Harm People?

52. What air pollutant forms "acid rain" within the lungs? What are the effects of this "acid rain" on the respiratory system?
53. Explain how acid rain sometimes causes high levels of metals, like copper and lead, in the drinking water.
54. What steps can people take to lower the level of lead in their drinking water?

True Cost

55. What is the true cost of a product?
56. Do you think you should be able to buy products without paying the "true cost"? Would you be willing to pay $20 more each year on your electric bill if it would reduce the amount of acid in the rain?
57. How can you justify additional expenses to someone who is against additional costs?

Getting On With It

58. What do you think should be done to solve the problem of acid rain? Which of the following actions should be taken?
   A. We should wait for more studies.
   B. We should start to reduce pollution from power plants even if it means we will have to pay more for electricity.
   C. We should require industries to reduce pollution and pass the cost on to the consumers.
   D. We should not force companies to install pollution controls if it means they may not be able to compete with imports.
59. What steps are being taken to address the problems caused by acid rain?

CASE STUDY
Clearing the Air — Stationary Sources

"The lesson of the Clean Air Act is clear: The nation need not give up its aspirations for a cleaner, healthier environment, or for other worthwhile social goals, even at a time of limited economic resources."

William K. Reilly
EPA Administrator, 1990

At one time people thought smoke pouring from factory chimneys and city streets lined with cars were signs of a better life. Today we know that emissions from both factories and vehicles contain pollutants that damage the environment and affect human health. At least for some humans and certain other species, a better life depends upon cleaner air.

Thousands of industries and millions of vehicles add pollutants to the air. Scientists think that air pollution is the source of 90% of the DDT, PCBs, and lead in Lake Superior. There is evidence that 25% of the nitrogen polluting the Chesapeake Bay comes from air pollution. Snowflakes deposit toxic chemicals in the Arctic ecosystem. Cleaning the air is a big job, but rain drops and snow flakes are efficient scrubbers. The only way to prevent the pollution of rain and snow is to reduce the load of pollutants entering the air.

Air Quality Standards

In 1970 the Nixon Administration established the **Unites States Environmental Protection Agency (EPA)**. Among other tasks, the agency is required to set and enforce air quality standards. An **air quality standard** is the maximum amount of pollutant allowed. There are two kinds of air quality standards. Standards are set for emissions and for ambient air.

Emissions include gases and particles entering the air from smoke stacks, chimneys and exhaust pipes. An **emission standard** is the maximum amount of a pollutant allowed to enter the atmosphere. Standards are set for the exhaust from certain stationary sources such as electrical power plants and other industries, as well as from mobile sources such as new motor vehicles and aircraft.

The Air You Breathe

Ambient air is the scientific term that refers to the air outdoors. It includes the air from ground level to about ten miles

WHAT DO YOU THINK?

At one time the EPA was criticized for not acting vigorously enough to eliminate asbestos from the human environment. Now it is being reproached for demanding sweeping action against the carcinogen. EPA mandates succeeded in getting more than 90% of schools in 40 states to remove asbestos building materials, at a cost of $3.8 billion. Yet if this mandate is extended to include businesses and public buildings, the cost will soar to about $150 billion for renovation of over 730,000 sites. Citing these high costs, experts question whether or not the actual public risk of exposure to this known carcinogen is worth the expenditure. Little data exist to substantiate the cancer risk from exposure to low levels of asbestos. Critics of the EPA further charge that total elimination of asbestos from the human environment is impossible. They advocate educating the public about the risks of asbestos, and leaving it at that. Are the risks of removal greater than simply ensuring that it is properly covered and not deteriorating?

How clean do we want the air? Do the benefits of grilled foods outweigh the risks?

(16 km) above Earth's surface. It is the air we breathe. The 1970 Clean Air Act required the EPA to establish **National Ambient Air Quality Standards** for six major air pollutants. These are:

sulfur dioxide   **ground-level ozone**   **particulate matter**
nitrogen oxides   **carbon monoxide**   **lead**

The 1977 amendments to the Clean Air Act required urban areas to meet air quality standards set to protect human health by 1987, but many areas did not meet the deadline. In 1991 the EPA reported that six of every ten people lived in areas that have excessive levels of one or more of these pollutants. Ninety-six cities failed to meet the ambient air quality standard for ozone — the primary ingredient in smog. Forty-one cities did not meet the standard for carbon monoxide, and 72 cities exceeded the standard for particulate matter.

Emission standards allow higher levels of pollutants than ambient air standards. This is based on the fact that people breathe ambient air rather than the exhaust from chimneys or motor vehicles. As the number of chimneys and the number of vehicles increases, it becomes more and more difficult for urban areas to meet the ambient air quality standards.

Setting Air Quality Standards

The EPA must set standards based on:
- the best available scientific evidence of the effects caused by the pollutant
- information gathered from citizens at public hearings — public opinion.

The standards must protect human health and prevent damage to the environment. They must also reflect the opinions and needs of the public. Can we enjoy the warmth of a fire in the fireplace on a cold winter night or cook a steak over coals on the grill in our backyard? Should pollution standards be set for restaurants that grill foods?

It is the job of the EPA to weigh the **risks** of pollution against the **benefits** of the product. For example:

Benefit: **Electricity** is needed for lighting, heating, cooling, and appliances.

Risk: Production of electricity causes increased levels of sulfur dioxide and particulates from electrical power plants that burn fossil fuels, OR the release of radiation from nuclear power plants, OR the loss of wildlife habitat for a hydroelectric dam, and the possible loss of life if the dam fails.

Benefit: **Wood** is the only source of energy for cooking food in many parts of the world. In some areas it is less expensive than other sources of energy for home heating. Burned in a fireplace or camp fire, it provides a desirable setting for a relaxing evening.

Risk: Burning wood produces carbon monoxide, soot and other particles, and cancer-causing chemicals. In some valleys, the carbon monoxide level exceeds the National Air Quality Standard for ambient air.

Controlling Air Pollution — Tall Stacks

The first attempt to control pollution was to send the pollutants up, up, and away. In the 1970s, to improve the local air quality, large industries and coal-fired electrical power plants increased the height of the smoke stacks. "Tall stacks" do not remove the sulfate particles or sulfur dioxide gas from the emissions. They simply send the pollution higher and spread it out farther. The pollutants come back to Earth, perhaps in another city, many miles from the power plant's "tall stack."

A nickel and copper smelting plant in Sudbury, Ontario, is the site of the world's tallest smoke stack. The smoke stack rises almost 1,300 feet (380 m). In 1970 the smelter released nearly 5 kilotonnes of sulfur dioxide for each kilotonne of metal the plant produced. As a part of the Canadian sulfur dioxide control strategy, the company installed additional pollution controls. By 1987, the smelter released only 2 kilotonnes of sulfur dioxide per kilotonne of metal produced.

The **Clean Air Act of 1970** made "tall stacks" illegal, but this part of the Act was not enforced. Citizens may take industries or government agencies to civil court if they allow pollutants to exceed EPA standards. Certain environmental groups, such as the **National Clean Air Coalition** and the **Natural Resources Defense Council** hire lawyers to argue cases in court.

In 1983, an environmental group filed a lawsuit against the EPA. As a result of the court's decision, the EPA was required to enforce the Clean Air Act. The agency may no longer allow the use of "tall stacks" to avoid the cost of more expensive pollution controls.

Pollution controls have made the air cleaner. Between 1970 and 1988, the amount of sulfur dioxide dropped 27 percent, and suspended particulate matter was down 63 percent, but nitrogen oxides increased 7 percent. The EPA says that the air is not clean enough. The goal of the 1990 Clean Air Act amendments is to make the air cleaner.

The 1990 Clean Air Act Amendments

A "grandfather clause" in the 1977 amendments to the Clean Air Act protected existing electrical power plants from the

The world's tallest smoke stack is in Sudbury, Ontario.

DID YOU KNOW?

Household woodstoves are stationary sources of air pollution. Burning wood releases carbon monoxide, soot, and other particulates into the air. Wood burning also contributes to the greenhouse effect. A tree is 50% carbon. When burned, one mature tree adds about 500 pounds of carbon dioxide to the atmosphere.

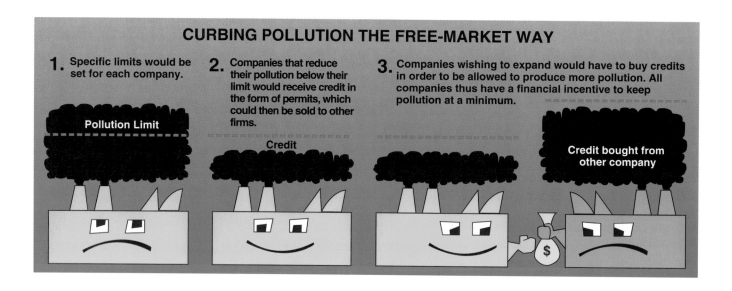

CURBING POLLUTION THE FREE-MARKET WAY

1. Specific limits would be set for each company.

Pollution Limit

2. Companies that reduce their pollution below their limit would receive credit in the form of permits, which could then be sold to other firms.

Credit

3. Companies wishing to expand would have to buy credits in order to be allowed to produce more pollution. All companies thus have a financial incentive to keep pollution at a minimum.

Credit bought from other company

$

expense of costly pollution controls. Only new power plants were required to install pollution controls. The new 1990 amendments to the Clean Air Act require annual sulfur dioxide emissions to be reduced to 8.9 million tons (8.1×10^6 metric tonnes) — 50% of the 1980 emissions — by the year 2001. To meet this goal, older power plants must clean up their emissions.

Beginning in 1995, more than one hundred coal-fired power plants, that are producing the most sulfur dioxide, must reduce the amount of sulfur dioxide in their emissions. Many of these power plants are located in the Midwest. An additional 200 power plants must comply with the law by the year 2000. While the EPA sets the standards, it allows the industries to choose the most cost-effective way to meet the standard.

The new law establishes an **emissions cap** — a maximum amount of sulfur dioxide that can be released in the atmosphere from all electrical power plants. Some power plants will be allowed to pollute more than others, but the total amount of pollution is limited to 8.9 million tons (8.1×10^6 metric tonnes). A company that reduces the emissions below the level required may sell its **"right to pollute"** to another company. Buying an available allowance gives a company the right to produce one ton of sulfur dioxide a year.

The 1990 amendments to the Clean Air Act will not be fully implemented until 2005. When the controls are in place, air pollutants entering the air each year will be reduced by 56 billion pounds — that's 224 pounds (102 kg) per person. The anticipated cost of air pollution controls is $25 billion per year. According to the EPA, that is 24 cents per person per day.

Why Burn Coal?

When **fossil fuels** (coal, oil, natural gas) are burned, the sulfur combines with oxygen forming sulfur dioxide. **(S + O₂ ⟶ SO₂) Soft coal** (bituminous) contains 0.5-4.5 percent sulfur by weight. A large electrical power plant may burn 10,000 tons (9080 metric tonnes) of coal each day. If a power plant burns coal that contains 3.0 percent sulfur, a smoke stack without pollution controls will send out approximately 900 tons (820 metric tonnes) of sulfur dioxide each day.

Why don't electrical power plants use fuels that contain less sulfur, if sulfur is causing a problem? **Hard coal** (anthracite) contains only 0.4-0.8 percent sulfur, but deposits of hard coal are very small compared to the deposits of soft coal. Oil contains much less sulfur than coal and natural gas contains even less sulfur than oil.

While some industries and power plants use these cleaner fuels, many choose to burn coal. Why? Soft coal is widely available and less expensive than other fuels. Depending upon the location of an existing electrical power plant and the cost of alternative fuels, soft coal may be the only available fuel. While there is enough coal on Earth to last 150 years, most of it contains large amounts of sulfur.

High sulfur coal can be burned without releasing large amounts of sulfur dioxide in emissions. Proven, reliable, and cost-effective technologies are available to remove sulfur. It may be removed before, during, or after combustion. The development and use of **clean coal technology** can create new jobs and preserve jobs in the coal mining industry.

Clean Coal Technology — Cleaning Coal

Sulfur and other impurities may be removed from coal prior to combustion. Washing the coal can remove 33 percent of the ash and 25 percent of the sulfur. In addition to reducing air pollution, coal washing decreases maintenance and increases the efficiency of combustion.

Other methods of cleaning coal are being investigated. Washing coal removes the inorganic sulfur but not the organic form. Scientists are investigating ways to break the chemical bonds. Scientists are using biotechnology techniques to try to develop bacteria that will eat the sulfur compounds in pulverized coal.

Clean Coal Technology — FBC

A new way to burn coal is **fluidized bed combustion — FBC**. A FBC boiler can burn low-grade fuels, including high sulfur coal, without producing large amounts of sulfur dioxide and

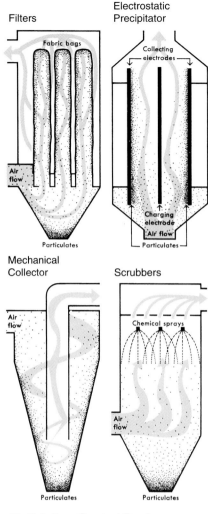

Air Polution Control Devices

nitrogen oxides. Other fuels that can be burned in FBC boilers include wood waste, sewage sludge, municipal waste, and tires.

Pellets of limestone (calcium oxide) and fuels are injected into the boiler along with air. The velocity of the air is controlled so that the force of the air lifts and mixes the small pellets forming a "fluidized bed" of burning coal. During combustion the calcium reacts with the sulfur to form gypsum. Some of the gypsum is removed as bottom ash. Smaller particles entering the stack are called **fly ash**. Fly ash is removed from the emissions by electrostatic precipitators or fabric filters.

FBC offers several advantages. The fuel is burned at lower temperatures, reducing the amount of nitrogen oxides formed. Since levels of both sulfur dioxide and nitrogen oxides in the emissions are low, scrubbers are not required. The crushed limestone used in FBC is less expensive than the powdered limestone needed for scrubbers. FBC also produces less solid waste than other coal-fired boilers. Another advantage is that the boilers are more compact and require much less space.

Clean Coal Technology — Wet Scrubbers

The flue gases may be passed over a special chemical called a **catalyst**. Catalysts are chemicals that speed up a chemical reaction. The catalyst encourages sulfur dioxide to combine with another oxygen atom to form sulfur trioxide. The gases now pass through a **scrubber**. In the scrubber, water is mixed with the gases. The sulfur trioxide combines with water to form sulfuric acid.

$$SO_2 + 1/2 O_2 \longrightarrow SO_3 + H_2O \longrightarrow H_2SO_4$$

This is the same process that would normally occur in the atmosphere when the sulfur trioxide combines with rain. When the sulfuric acid is formed in the stack, it is trapped and collected. Although the sulfuric acid is a product that can be sold, the cost of producing the sulfuric acid is much greater than its value. Wet scrubbers are very efficient, but they are expensive to operate because they require huge amounts of energy.

Removing Particles — Cyclones

In a cyclone, flue gases are forced through a vertical tube in which a whirlwind throws the larger particles against the sides of the tube. The particles fall to the bottom where they are collected, and the cleaner air passes upward through the center of the tube. Cyclones are less expensive than other methods, but they only remove the larger particles.

Wet scrubbers can be used with a cyclone to collect the smaller particles. The flue gases are passed through a chamber where water is sprayed to simulate rainfall. The artificial "rain" cleans the gases before they leave the stack.

Removing Particles — Electrostatic Precipitators

The electrostatic precipitator gives particles a strong electrical charge. The charged particles are attracted to metal plates with an opposite electrical charge. Periodically the plates are vibrated to remove the particles. Ninety-nine percent of the particles can be removed with this method. The precipitators are expensive to install, but they are much cheaper to operate than wet scrubbers.

Removing Particles — Filters

The process of filtering is used in coffee makers, furnaces, and vacuum cleaners. The filter must be designed for the specific use. Filtering is very efficient, but it is expensive to install. Operating costs vary with the type of material being filtered.

Removing Particles — Wood Stoves

In some areas smoke from combustion of wood in fireplaces, stoves, and furnaces can be a major source of particulate matter. By using EPA-certified stoves, performing routine maintenance, and burning dry wood, particulates can be reduced by about 70 percent. In many areas it may be necessary to prohibit the use of stoves and fireplaces when there is a stagnant weather pattern.

Removing Other Gases

Sulfur is only part of the air pollution problem. Nitrogen oxides (NO_x) contribute to the formation of ground-level ozone and "acid rain." Nitrogen and oxygen in the air combine at high temperatures during combustion. Newer electrical power plants are designed to reduce nitrogen oxide emissions. Pollution controls must be installed at older electrical power plants and other major stationary sources of NO_x.

Nitrogen oxides are reduced by controlling the flow of air and lowering the temperature of combustion. Recirculation of flue gases also reduces nitrogen oxides and hydrocarbons in the emissions.

Newer models of oil-fired furnaces also produce fewer nitrogen oxides. Because there are a large number of homes with older furnaces, it will be many years before there is a significant reduction in nitrogen oxides from this source.

Reduction in either nitrogen oxides or volatile organic compounds (VOCs) will reduce ozone levels. Motor vehicles are responsible for 50% of urban pollution. Controls for VOCs may be required for industries that use painting and coating processes and industries that use organic solvents in cleaning processes. VOC emissions in California will be reduced by 60 tons per day when new regulations on VOCs in consumer products take effect.

Environmental Planning

As a result of controls placed on stationary sources of pollution, our air quality is improving. There still are problems that remain, and the fight for clean air goes on. If we are to enjoy the benefits of electricity and the products of industry, we must pay a price. The price will either be the effects of air pollution or the cost of preventing pollution.

Environmental planning can play an important role in the design of new buildings and the remodeling of old ones. The EPA is encouraging corporations as well as state and local governments to install energy-efficient lighting. A Teflon-coated fiberglass roof that takes advantage of natural lighting and energy efficient lights reduced the demand for electricity at the Denver International Airport. Increasing energy efficiency reduces pollution and saves natural resources.

Changing to cleaner energy sources can also reduce pollution. Alternative fuels for vehicles are discussed in Case Study 6.2 Clearing the Air — Cars and Other Vehicles. Other alternative energy sources are discussed in Unit V.

6.1 QUESTIONS FOR STUDY AND DISCUSSION

1. Define the following words:

air quality standard	emissions cap
ambient air	EPA
catalyst	fluidized bed
clean coal technology	combustion
cyclone	fly ash
electrostatic	fossil fuels
precipitator	scrubber
emission standards	

2. Explain how air pollution is contributing to water pollution.

Air Quality Standards

3. What federal agency was created to control pollution? When was this agency established?
4. What is an emission standard?

The Air You Breathe

5. What term describes the air you breathe?
6. What are the 6 major air pollutants that have National Ambient Air Quality Standards?
7. Do most people living in the United States breathe clean air? Explain.
8. Why do the EPA emission standards allow higher levels of pollutants than the EPA ambient air quality standards?
9. Why is it getting more difficult for urban areas to meet air pollution standards?

Setting Air Quality Standards

10. Standards set by the EPA must be based on two types of information. What are the two sources of information?

11. Why does the EPA set ambient air standards for ozone and other pollutants?
12. Standards set by the EPA are sometimes controversial. Some people feel they are too strict, while others feel they are not strict enough. Why does the EPA allow any pollutants to enter the environment?
13. When setting air quality standards, the EPA must weigh the _____ against the _____.

Controlling Air Pollution — Tall Stacks
14. What was the first solution to air pollution from electrical power plants and industries? Why wasn't this a good way to control air pollution?
15. EPA sets and enforces standards. What can be done if these standards are not met?

The 1990 Clean Air Act Amendments
16. What was the "grandfather clause" in the 1977 amendments to the Clean Air Act? What changes were made in the 1990 amendments?
17. What is an emissions cap? How does the "cap" affect the building of a new electrical power plant?

Why Burn Coal?
18. Which type of coal contains more sulfur, soft or hard coal?
19. If sulfur is a dangerous pollutant, why can't we simply use fuels that are low in sulfur?
20. What are the benefits of clean coal technology?

Clean Coal Technology — Cleaning Coal
21. What are the advantages of washing coal prior to combustion?
22. Why doesn't washing remove all of the sulfur from the coal? What technology may increase the amount of sulfur removed?

Clean Coal Technology — FBC
23. In addition to coal, what other fuels can be burned in a FBC boiler?
24. How does the burning of coal in a FBC boiler compare to burning coal in a conventional boiler?
25. What are the advantages of FBC technology?
26. What additional pollution control must be used with FBC boilers?

Clean Coal Technology — Wet Scrubbers
27. Describe how wet scrubbers remove the sulfur dioxide before it reaches the atmosphere.
28. Since there is a demand for sulfuric acid, why don't industries jump at the chance to install catalytic converters and scrubbers?

Removing Particles
29. List four ways of removing particles from flue gases. For each method describe how the particles are removed.
30. Give one advantage and one disadvantage of each method listed above.

Removing Other Gases
31. Under what conditions are nitrogen oxides formed?
32. What two pollutants are reduced by recirculating flue gases?
33. One source of nitrogen oxides in our atmosphere is the oil or gas furnace in many older homes. Why will it take many years before this source can be controlled?
34. List other sources of VOCs that need to be controlled.
35. What environmental problems are caused by nitrogen oxides and VOCs?

Environmental Planning
36. What changes in the design of buildings can help to clear the air?

CASE STUDY
Clearing the Air —
Automobiles and Other Vehicles

6.2

Mechanic

Mechanics are responsible for repairing engines and inspecting vehicles to insure that they meet emissions standards. They may learn their skills by on-the-job training, but they often complete courses at vocational-technical schools or community colleges.

Futuristic Electric Vehicle

Where It All Begins

Most of the poisonous gases in automobile exhausts are waste products of incomplete combustion. **Combustion** is the burning of a mixture of fuel and oxygen. When there is not enough oxygen, combustion is incomplete and carbon monoxide and unburned hydrocarbons are formed.

A steam engine works by external combustion: the fuel (coal, wood, oil) is burned outside the engine. The first railroad locomotives, powered by steam engines, left a trail of thick black smoke. They hauled freight and any passengers who were brave enough to risk the hot fly ash that often flew into the passenger cars. Train rides were cleaner, if not safer, with the arrival of the internal combustion engine.

In the **internal combustion engine** the fuel burns or explodes inside a **closed cylinder**. A movable plunger called a **piston** is tightly fitted into the cylinder. Gasoline is fed to the engine along with air by either a carburetor or fuel injectors. Most internal combustion engines work on a four-stroke cycle. Power is delivered to the crankshaft once in each cycle.

First Stroke: As the piston moves down, the gas-air mixture is drawn into the cylinder.

Second Stroke: The valve closes. The piston moves up, compressing the air and gas mixture.

Third Stroke: The compressed mixture of gases is ignited by a spark plug. The burning fuel gives off hot gases that expand. The expanding gases push against the piston that is connected to a rod. The motion of the piston is transferred through the rod to the crankshaft and finally to the wheels of the vehicle.

Fourth Stroke: After the explosion, the cylinder is full of waste products including: carbon monoxide, nitrogen oxides, and unburned hydrocarbons. The exhaust valve opens, and the piston moves up to eject the waste products.

Too Many Cars, Too Many Miles

In 1970, the vehicles in the United States travelled 1 trillion miles. In 1990, the total vehicle miles travelled had doubled, from 1 trillion to 2 trillion. More than 80 percent of the total miles travelled are by automobile. It is expected that the total number of miles travelled will continue to increase. The total amount of pollutants produced will also increase.

The United States has strict regulations for emissions from vehicles. But controlling pollution is more difficult when more people are driving more vehicles more miles. The 8 million vehicles in Los Angeles produce 70 to 80 percent of the air pollutants (nitrogen oxide and hydrocarbons) that form photochemical smog in the LA basin. Vehicles are also the major source of carbon monoxide in urban areas.

The Government Steps In

California was the first state to require pollution controls on cars. All cars sold in California since 1963 have had some type of pollution control. Since 1966, cars sold in California were required to meet standards set for hydrocarbons and carbon monoxide.

The federal government adopted the original California standards starting with 1968 models. In 1970 Congress passed the Clean Air Act, setting strict standards for the three major air pollutants in car exhaust — hydrocarbons, carbon monoxide, and nitrogen oxides.

While the Environmental Protection Agency sets the standards, the auto makers must decide what technology can best be used to meet the standards. Before the new cars are sold, they must be certified by the EPA to insure that they do meet the emissions standards. The major improvement in the quality of our air during the last 20 years is due to pollution controls placed on automobiles.

Several methods can be used to reduce pollution from vehicle exhaust:

- Combustion can be improved by recycling the vapors and gases back into the engine.
- Additional air may be injected into the manifold to make combustion more complete.
- Catalysts may be used to encourage the complete burning of fuels.

The Catalytic Converter

Pollution can be reduced by chemically changing the pollutants before they leave the car's exhaust pipe. **Catalytic converters** are stainless steel containers about the size of a litre of soda. They contain a platinum catalyst. The catalyst allows more oxygen to react with the carbon monoxide and unburned hydrocarbons before the exhaust leaves the tailpipe. These dangerous compounds are changed to harmless carbon dioxide and water.

The platinum reduces two of the three major pollutants produced by the internal combustion engine. Another catalyst speeds up the breakdown of nitrogen oxides into nitrogen and

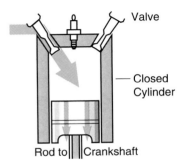

1. Intake

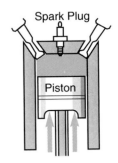

2. Compression

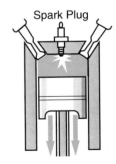

3. Power

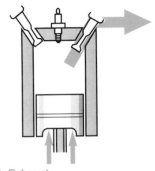

4. Exhaust

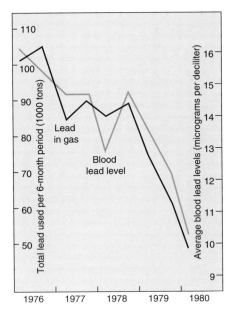

Lead use in Gasoline and Average Blood Lead Levels

oxygen. The Clean Air Act prohibits the removal or disabling of catalytic converters. When catalytic converters are removed or disabled, the level of hydrocarbons, carbon monoxide, and nitrogen oxide in the exhaust may increase up to 800 percent.

Lead in gasoline coats the platinum in catalytic converters. In addition to changing the catalyst so that it can not reduce the pollution levels of carbon monoxide and hydrocarbons, lead itself becomes a pollutant.

Get the Lead Out

Why was lead added to gasoline? Gasoline refineries did not have the ability to produce the amount of high octane gasoline they needed for the more powerful engines. By adding lead, the refineries could produce high octane fuel from low quality crude oil. Adding lead was the cheapest way to get the required high octane necessary to prevent the engine knocking. The lead also lubricated the valves.

Two factors forced refineries to find other ways of boosting octane. Studies linked the amount of lead used in gasoline to levels of lead found in the blood. The second factor was the introduction of the catalytic converter. Lead ruins the catalytic converter. EPA regulations make it illegal for someone who sells gasoline or operates a fleet of motor vehicles to put, or allow someone to put, leaded gasoline in a vehicle that is designed for unleaded fuel.

The EPA gradually lowered the amount of lead allowed in leaded gasoline. Lead levels in gasoline averaged 2.0 grams per gallon in 1975. The limit was 0.10 grams per gallon in 1988. A total ban on lead in gasoline will take effect in 1996. An immediate ban on lead would have forced older refineries to shut down. Leaded gasoline is still used in many European countries as well as China and South Korea.

Redesigning the Engine

Another way to reduce the amount of pollutants is to change the design of the engine. In a **diesel engine**, only air enters the chamber during the intake stroke. An exact quantity of fuel is injected into the cylinder during the compression stroke. Compression is greater in the diesel engine. The crowded molecules collide more often, and the heat created by the collisions ignites the fuel.

The diesel engine provides two advantages over the gasoline engine: less carbon monoxide and hydrocarbon emissions and better fuel economy. One concern about diesel engines is that they produce more particulates than gasoline engines.

The **stratified internal combustion engine**, introduced by a Japanese auto manufacturer (Honda), has two combustion chambers in each cylinder. The temperature of the burning gases in the main chamber is lower than the temperature in the conventional internal combustion engine. The result is fewer nitrogen oxides. The temperature in the second chamber is high enough and enough time is allowed for more of the fuel to completely burn. This prevents the formation of large amounts of carbon monoxide and hydrocarbons.

Is It Time for a Tune-up?

Most of the air pollution produced by automobiles on the road today comes from cars that are poorly maintained. A good engine tune-up is required to keep emission levels low.

More than 85 percent of the cars tested at a University of Michigan clinic showed a significant decrease in pollutant levels after a tune-up. The tune-ups included replacing spark plugs and ignition points, and adjusting timing and the carburetor. Some cars with seven to ten percent carbon monoxide in the exhaust had less than one percent after tune-up.

The chart, on page 188, identifies the normal function of structures associated with the internal combustion engine and describes conditions that can lead to increased air pollution.

Can We Meet the Standards?

Urban air quality has been improving steadily since the introduction of catalytic converters and unleaded fuel in 1975. Unfortunately, our reliance on automobiles as our primary means of transportation has made it difficult to control air pollution. Many urban areas still do not meet the National Air Quality Standards.

Vehicles built today emit 90 percent less carbon monoxide than those built in 1970. Still, 41 cities did not meet the carbon monoxide standard in 1990. Motor vehicles contribute 84 percent of the carbon monoxide in ambient air. The 1990 amendments to the Clean Air Act require states with areas that exceed the carbon monoxide standard to set up "enhanced" vehicle I/M (inspection/maintenance) programs to ensure that vehicles are not exceeding the emissions standards. The high-tech tests more closely simulate actual driving conditions.

States that do not meet the carbon monoxide standard must also provide "oxyfuels" during the winter months. **Oxygenated fuels** contain alcohol or other compounds that reduce the amount of carbon monoxide produced during combustion. Where carbon monoxide is a serious problem, transportation policies must be put in place to offset any increase in vehicle miles travelled.

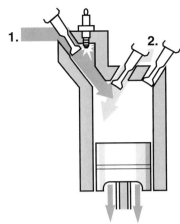

Intake:
1. A rich fuel-air mixture (more fuel/less air) enters the intake valve of the first chamber. It is ignited by a spark plug.
2. A lean fuel-air mixture (less fuel/more air) enters the intake valve of the second chamber. It is ignited by the flame of the fuel burning in the first chamber.

TRY TO FIND OUT

Are any experimental cars powered by photovoltaic cells, liquid hydrogen, ethanol, or other new forms of clean energy being produced. How do they work? Why are they less polluting? What problems with these technologies must be solved before the cars are practical for daily use.

AIR FILTER:	cleans the air that enters the carburetor.
Condition:	clogged with dust and grime; not enough air gets through
Result:	increased levels of hydrocarbons, carbon monoxide
CARBURETOR:	mixes the air and gasoline
Condition:	too much air; not enough gasoline
Result:	increased levels of hydrocarbons
Condition:	too much fuel; not enough air
Result:	increased hydrocarbon and carbon monoxide levels
CYLINDER:	contain pistons that compress the air-fuel mixture
Condition:	leaks between cylinder and piston
Result:	increases levels of hydrocarbons, carbon monoxide
PCV SYSTEM:	(positive crankcase ventilation system) recirculates the vapors that squeeze past the pistons
Condition:	clogged system
Result:	increases levels of hydrocarbons, carbon monoxide
IGNITION SYSTEM:	sends an electrical charge to the spark plugs
Condition:	improper firing of spark plugs
Result:	increased hydrocarbons
SPARK PLUGS:	ignites the air-fuel mixture in the cylinder
Condition:	worn or dirty plugs
Result:	increased hydrocarbons

Enhanced I/M (inspection/maintenance) programs are also required in areas that exceed the ozone standard. Ozone standards are not being met in 96 major urban areas including the LA Basin and the New York Metropolitan area. Gas stations may have to install vapor recovery systems. Vapor trapping canisters may be required on vehicles.

In order for the nation's most polluted cities to meet the ambient air quality standard for ozone, many vehicles must switch to reformulated gasoline and other cleaner-burning fuels. **Clean-fuels** include compressed natural gas, methanol (from natural gas), ethanol (from corn) and electricity. While clean fuels reduce the emissions of some pollutants, they may increase the emissions of pollutants. Some experts suggest that clean fuels will not solve the problem of air pollution in urban areas.

It is unlikely that southern California will meet federal standards before 2010. Southern California has the highest ozone levels in the United States. California has adopted vehicle emission regulations for 1995 model vehicles that are more strict than the federal regulations. Two percent of the cars sold in California must produce zero emissions of the three major air pollutants in 1998.

In 1990, there were 410,000 pre-1975 vehicles registered in the Los Angeles Basin. Replacing old cars with new ones cuts air pollution. Pollution controls and the improved fuel efficiency of new cars reduce pollution. The fuel economy of new US cars averages 27.5 miles per gallon (mpg). Some subcompact cars get nearly 55 mpg. With improved designs, use of lightweight materials and modification of engines, fuel efficiency can be improved.

There are 190 million motor vehicles in the United States. With many of these cars located in large cities, traffic congestion is a problem that is only expected to get worse. Each year, drivers stuck in traffic in Boston waste an estimated 300 million gallons of gasoline and add to the city's air pollution. Will the traffic congestion be reduced when construction of the expanded Central Artery — a $5 billion highway project — is complete? Some experts predict that the new highway will only attract more vehicles.

Well-designed mass transit systems can reduce pollution. More than 75 percent of commuters that work in downtown Toronto use public transportation. San Jose, California, built a trolley system that is attracting more and more passengers. In both cities, the design of the system and the location of parking facilities has made mass transit more convenient than driving.

Mass transit must clean up its act, too. Seventy-two cities did not meet the standard for particulate matter in 1990. Black clouds of diesel exhaust from trucks and buses are major sources of particulates. One diesel-powered bus emits as much particulate matter as 40-60 cars. The EPA has proposed regulations that would cut 95 percent of the particulates — 270 tons (245 metric tonnes) per year.

An alternative fuel for diesel-powered buses is **Biodiesel**. Research shows that buses using a 1 to 5 blend of biodiesel (made from soybeans) and petroleum diesel (made from crude oil) produce less pollution. Buses with catalytic converters using a diesel blend produced 31% less particulate matter, 21% less carbon monoxide, and 47% fewer hydrocarbons. SoyDiesel is currently in use in large-scale demonstration projects in several U.S. cities.

6.2 QUESTIONS FOR STUDY AND DISCUSSION

Where It All Begins

1. For each of the statements below, identify the choice that best completes the statement.
   A. Carbon monoxide and hydrocarbons are waste products of (complete/incomplete) combustion.
   B. In the (external/internal) combustion engine the fuel burns in a closed cylinder.
   C. The fuel burns outside the engine in an (external/internal) combustion engine.
   D. The steam engine is an example of an (external/internal) combustion engine.
   E. The (external/internal) combustion engine used coal or wood as fuel.

2. In your own words briefly describe what happens in the cylinder during each stage of the four-stroke cycle. In your description indicate if the valves are open or closed. (1) Intake (2) Compression (3) Power (4) Exhaust

Too Many Cars, Too Many Miles

3. During the last twenty years the total vehicle miles travelled has (decreased/increased).

4. If during the next twenty years the rate of change in total vehicle miles travelled is the same as it was during the last twenty years, how many miles will vehicles travel in the year 2010?

5. What air pollutants are causing problems in LA and other urban areas?

The Government Steps In

6. Identify the state that first required pollution control on automobiles. Identify the two pollutants that were controlled.

7. Identify the pollutants that were controlled by the 1970 amendments to the Clean Air Act.

8. Identify the party responsible for each of the following:
   A. sets standards for pollution control on automobiles
   B. makes decisions about the technology to meet the standards
   C. certifies that cars meet the standards

9. Give three changes in engine design that will improve combustion.

The Catalytic Converter

10. What is the purpose of the catalytic converter?

11. How does the platinum catalyst reduce pollution?

12. What happens to the nitrogen oxides in the catalytic converter?

13. Which type of gasoline should be used in cars with catalytic converters? (leaded/ unleaded). Why?

Get the Lead Out

14. Why did refineries add lead to gasoline?

15. What two factors forced refineries to eliminate the use of lead in the refining process?

Redesigning the Engine

16. Identify two engines that produce less pollution than the original internal combustion engine.

17. Explain how the ignition of the fuel in the stratified internal combustion engine differs from the ignition of the fuel in the original internal combustion engine.

18. What condition of the stratified internal combustion engine prevents the formation of nitrogen oxides?
19. What conditions in the stratified internal combustion engine prevent the formation of large amounts of carbon monoxide and hydrocarbons?

Is It Time for a Tune-Up?

20. Other than using the correct type of gasoline, what can car owners do to assure that their cars are not big polluters?
21. Describe two ways that an auto mechanic might "tune" your car engine so that it pollutes less.
22. Match the engine part with its function (job).
    Engine Part
    1. Air Filter   4. Ignition System
    2. Carburetor   5. PCV System
    3. Cylinder   6. Spark Plugs
    Function
    A. cleans the air
    B. contains pistons which compress air-fuel mixture
    C. recirculates vapors
    D. controls amount of air mixed with gasoline
    E. ignites fuel-air mixture
    F. causes spark plugs to fire

23. Match the major pollutant which will increase in each of the following situations.
    Pollutant
    1. increased carbon monoxide
    2. increased hydrocarbons
    3. both of these
    Situation
    A. dirty or worn spark plugs
    B. ignition system isn't working properly
    C. PCV system clogged or air filter dirty
    D. carburetor allows too much air to mix with gasoline
    E. leaks between cylinder and piston

Can We Meet the Standards?

24. Since newer vehicles pollute less, why are urban areas unable to meet the National Air Quality Standards?
25. What are the EPA requirements for urban areas that do not meet the NAAQ standard for carbon monoxide standard?
26. What are the EPA requirements for urban areas that do not meet the NAAQ standard for ozone?
27. Give two examples of clean-fuels and discuss the pros and cons of switching to clean fuels.
28. What steps has California taken to reduce the level of ozone? What additional steps should be taken?
29. Do you use mass transit? What changes would make mass transit a more attractive choice than the automobile?
30. What steps should be taken to decrease pollution from mass transit?

Science **T**echnology **S**ociety   **ISSUES**

HOY NO CIRCULA

Mexico City's pollution control efforts include a program "Hoy No Circula" [Don't Drive Today]. The system is based on the last digit of a car's license plate. The program includes taxis. The program reduces the number of private cars on the road each day by 20 percent.
- Should everyone who can afford a car be able to buy one?
- Should the price of cars be based on their emissions?
- Should cars with less than three passengers be prohibited from entering the major thoroughfares of big cities?

At one time, asbestos was considered a health risk only for asbestos workers. In 1971 the EPA listed asbestos as a hazardous air pollutant. In 1989 the EPA banned the manufacture of most asbestos products. Because of its widespread use, asbestos is an environmental problem that concerns every community in the nation. Exposure to asbestos may occur at home, at work, or at school. There is a potential danger for anyone who is exposed to asbestos fibers in the air they breathe.

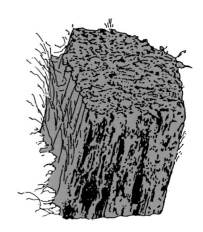

Asbestos Fibers Woven into Cloth

What Is It?

Asbestos is the name given to a group of natural minerals found in certain types of rock formations. Asbestos is mined and processed into fibers that are mixed with a binding material. Asbestos is heat-resistant, very durable, resists corrosion and insulates well. Because of these properties, asbestos became a common material used in construction as well as many other industries.

Asbestos has been widely used to strengthen material in a product, for thermal insulation, for fire protection, for deadening of sound, and for decoration on exposed surfaces.

How Can It Affect Your Health?

The problem is that products made with asbestos may release very tiny fibers that are 1,200 times smaller than a strand of human hair. These microscopic fibers remain in the air for a long period of time. If inhaled, the fibers can enter body tissues where they remain for many years. **Asbestosis** is a disease of the lungs that occurs when asbestos fibers remain in the lungs and make breathing difficult. It can be fatal.

Asbestos fibers are carcinogenic — causing several different forms of cancer, including lung cancer and **mesothelomia**, cancer in the lining of the chest and abdomen. These diseases take a long time to develop, sometimes 20 to 40 years. They are now being diagnosed in people who worked with asbestos during World War II.

The presence of asbestos does not always present a danger to health. The product is only dangerous if the fibers escape into the air. The danger of fibers entering the air depends upon whether or not the product is friable. An object is **friable** if it can be crumbled with the hand when it is dry. The products containing asbestos that are sprayed for fireproofing, insulation,

CAUTION
ASBESTOS DUST HAZARD
AVOID BREATHING DUST WEAR ASSIGNED PROTECTIVE EQUIPMENT DO NOT REMAIN IN AREA UNLESS YOUR WORK REQUIRES IT. BREATHING ASBESTOS DUST MAY BE HAZARDOUS TO YOUR HEALTH

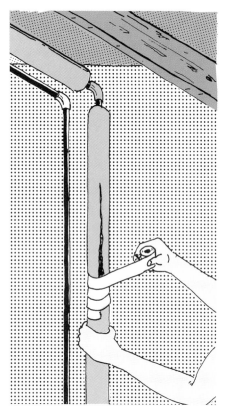

Repairing Asbestos Insulated Pipe

and decoration are often friable. Other products such as vinyl flooring, are not likely to lose fibers unless they are sanded or cut.

Schools and Other Public Buildings

Congress passed the Asbestos Hazard Emergency Response Act in 1986 to protect school children and school employees. It required all schools, both public and private, to inspect their buildings for any friable asbestos-containing materials. The Act also required an analysis of any material of an unknown composition. Schools are required to develop a plan to manage asbestos. Records are required and both students' parents and school workers are to be notified of any activities related to asbestos.

Nearly one third of the schools in a 1984 EPA study had potential asbestos problems, but many had already taken steps to correct the problem. Fines are given if the schools do not meet the requirements set by EPA.

Another EPA survey determined that 700,000 federal government buildings, private non-residential buildings and apartment buildings contain friable asbestos. Buildings built during the 1960's are more likely to contain asbestos than other buildings.

Is There Asbestos in Your Home?

Many single-family homes have products made with asbestos. See the list below for products that might contain asbestos.

Vinyl Floor Tiles and Flooring: Asbestos fibers may be released if the tiles are sanded, damaged, cut to fit in place, or severely worn. Do not remove old tiles. Instead cover with a new material.

Patching Compound and Textured Paints: Use of asbestos in these products was banned in 1975. Any old products should be properly discarded. For repair of old materials see the subheading "Safety Guidelines."

Friable Ceilings: If your home was built or remodeled between 1945 and 1978, the ceilings may be made of friable material that contains asbestos. Trained contractors should be hired to remove it or cover it with a coating.

Stoves and Furnaces: Cement sheet material around stoves probably will not release asbestos fibers unless scraped. Paper or milboard should be handled according to the safety guidelines. Furnace insulation should be replaced if it is in poor condition. See the safety guidelines for the proper procedure.

Walls and Pipes: If pipes were covered with insulation between 1920 and 1972, it probably contains asbestos. It is better to use wide duct tape to repair a damaged section than to try to remove the insulation. Wall and ceiling insulation installed between 1930 and 1950 may contain asbestos. It should be handled by trained contractors during remodeling or destruction.

Applicances: Appliances with asbestos are safe to use unless broken or misused. Unsafe models have been withdrawn from the market.

Roofing, Shingles, and Siding: In some of these materials, asbestos was used as a binding agent. If they are worn they may be spray painted to seal the fibers. Follow the safety guidelines when repairing or replacing these materials.

The manufacturer of a product may be able to tell you if the product contains asbestos. People who have worked with products containing asbestos, such as plumbers and building or heating contractors, may be able to make an educated guess about the composition of a product. Positive identification of asbestos requires analysis of samples by a qualified laboratory.

What Should You Do If You Find Asbestos in Your Home?

Any material that contains as little as one percent asbestos is subject to federal asbestos regulations. Most materials containing asbestos do not need to be removed. They should be repaired if there is any damage or deterioration. When maintained in good condition, building materials containing asbestos appear to pose relatively little risk.

When using or working with materials that contain asbestos, keep your exposure to a minimum by following the Safety Guidelines. If you hire a contractor, make sure that the contractor follows the same guidelines. Improper removal can actually increase rather than decrease the risk from asbestos fibers.

Safety Guidelines for Working with Materials that Contain Asbestos

1. Do not disturb any material that you think contains asbestos unless it is absolutely necessary.
2. Seal off the work area by using plastic and duct tape. Make sure that asbestos dust is not tracked into other areas.
3. Always wear an approved respirator. Also wear protective gloves, hats, and clothing. If possible, dispose of the clothing. If this is not possible, wash it separately.
4. Wet the material with a fine mist. Add a small amount (one teaspoon per quart of water) of a low-sudsing detergent to help the water penetrate the material.
5. If it is necessary to drill or cut material containing asbestos, do the work outside, if possible. Make sure the material is wet (see number 4).

THINK ABOUT IT

Setting Emissions Standards
- Should the EPA issue emissions standards for lawn mowers?
- Should people in areas that don't meet the ozone standard be required to use electric lawn mowers?
- Should emissions standards be issued for dune buggies and off-road vehicles?
- Should emissions standards be issued for construction equipment? farm tractors?

THINK ABOUT IT

Recycling Oil
- Is used oil recycled in your area?
- When the car gets an oil change, what happens to the used oil?
- Should we burn used oil?

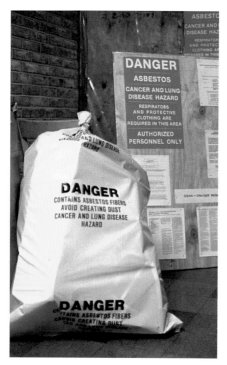

Proper disposal of materials containing asbestos is very important.

6. If it is necessary to remove the material, avoid breaking it into small pieces. Remove complete preformed pieces, if possible.
7. Place any material removed in plastic trash bags and dispose of it according to EPA regulations (see Disposal).
8. After removing the material, clean the area with wet mops, rags, or sponges. Repeat the cleaning a second time. Dispose of the cleaning materials in the container with the material removed. **CAUTION:** Do not dust, sweep, or vacuum particles suspected of containing asbestos. The asbestos fibers are small enough to pass through normal vacuum cleaner filters. Use wet mopping or specially designed vacuum cleaners.
9. If the work is to be done by a contractor, discuss these guidelines to make sure your exposure is minimized.

Disposal of Asbestos Wastes

EPA regulations control the disposal of asbestos wastes. Many states have programs for approving and licensing asbestos disposal sites. A waste hauler must notify a landfill of any load that contains asbestos wastes.

The load must be inspected to make sure that the wastes are in leak-proof containers and are properly labeled. If the wastes are not in the proper containers, the landfill operator must keep the wastes wet until they can be covered with a non-asbestos material.

There must be no visible dust during disposal. The EPA must be notified of any accidental releases of asbestos fibers. Within 24 hours a thick covering (at least six inches or 15 cm) of material that does not contain asbestos must be placed over the wastes.

Before the final closing of the area where asbestos is buried, 30 inches (76 cm) of non-asbestos material must be added to the six inches of cover already in place. The area must be properly graded and planted so that erosion is prevented.

1. Define the following words:

   asbestos   friable

   asbestosis   mesothelomia

   carcinogenic

What Is It?

2. What is asbestos?
3. What properties of this material make it a desirable ingredient in many products?
4. Give three reasons why asbestos might have been sprayed on a surface.

How Can It Affect Your Health?

5. What diseases are caused by asbestos?
6. How do asbestos fibers usually enter the body?
7. Some people who worked with asbestos during World War II have recently filed lawsuits against the companies for which they worked. Why do you think they waited so long?
8. Why is asbestos classified as a carcinogen?
9. Asbestos is dangerous only if it is friable. Why?

Schools and Other Public Buildings

10. Why was the Asbestos Hazard Emergency Response Act passed? What did the act require?
11. Asbestos has been found in government and privately owned buildings as well as multiple and single family homes. (True/False)

Is There Asbestos in Your Home?

12. The vinyl floor tile is very worn. What should be done?
13. You would like to paint a wall with textured paint. Do you need to worry about the paint containing asbestos?

14. You purchase a home that was built in 1960. You would like to remove a section of a ceiling to put in a stairway. Should you check first to see if the ceiling contains asbestos? If it does contain asbestos, how should you proceed with your planned remodeling?
15. You just learned that your furnace is insulated with asbestos. Should you consider replacing it?
16. You notice some insulation material is flaking off. You are not sure whether this material contains asbestos. Who could you contact that might be able to tell you if the product contains asbestos?

What Should You Do if You Find Asbestos in Your Home?

17. Try to find out if you have asbestos in your home.

Safety Guidelines for Working with Materials that Contain Asbestos

18. How should you dress when working with material that contains asbestos?
19. Before cutting material that contains asbestos, what should be done?
20. What should you do with the asbestos when it has been removed?
21. Describe the proper way to clean up the area after the asbestos has been removed.

Disposal of Asbestos Wastes

22. A truck containing materials with asbestos arrives at the landfill you operate. What procedures should you follow?
23. The landfill has been filled and no more wastes can be accepted. What must be done so that the asbestos will not become a pollutant?

7.1 Radiation — As a Pollutant

All matter is made of atoms. An **atom** has a nucleus that is surrounded by particles called electrons. It is the interaction of electrons between atoms that forms compounds. The nuclei are not involved in the making of new compounds.

The nucleus contains small particles called neutrons and protons. The neutrons and protons are held together by large amounts of energy. However, the nuclei of some atoms are not stable. The energy and/or particles released when these nuclei spontaneously disintegrate is called **radiation**.

Types of Radiation

Three types of radiation result from the breakdown of nuclei. **Alpha radiation** consists of particles that can be stopped by a sheet of paper. **Beta radiation** consists of faster moving particles that may require several inches of material to stop them. **Gamma radiation** consists of energy waves (rays) that travel at the speed of light. They may require several feet of material to stop them.

Radiation surrounds us. It is a part of our natural environment. Alpha, Beta, or Gamma radiation is **ionizing radiation** — high-energy radiation that can knock electrons from atoms. Some ionizing radiation enters Earth's atmosphere from outer space. We call this **cosmic radiation**. Solar radiation is mostly non-ionizing, low-energy light waves. It includes ultraviolet radiation that is not blocked by the ozone layer.

Radiation From Natural Sources

Radium is a naturally radioactive element. This means that the nuclei of radium atoms are so unstable that they spontaneously disintegrate without any outside force. This process is called "decay." When the nucleus of a radium atom spontaneously disintegrates or decays, it changes into a radon atom, and radiation is given off. The new radon atom is not stable. It decays and radiation is given off. This process continues until a stable atom is formed.

Radiation is given off by trace amounts of uranium-238 and radium found in soil and rock. Some rocks contain more uranium than others. This means that some parts of the world have higher levels of radiation than others. In one section of India, the average person receives 1,300 millirem of radiation per year — approximately 6 times the exposure of a person living in the United States.

The level of naturally occurring radiation is referred to as the **background level**. The average person in the United States receives approximately 300 millirem (mrem) of radiation from natural sources. The background level is affected by where the person lives and the person's lifestyle. As we move higher into the atmosphere, we encounter higher levels of cosmic radiation. Airline crews experience higher levels of cosmic radiation than fishing crews.

Natural background radiation differs considerably in different locations, due to differences in elevation and the radioactive elements present in the soil. People living in Denver, Colorado — the mile high city, are exposed to more cosmic radiation (350 mrem annually) than people living along the Florida coast where the typical person gets 280 mrem each year.

You will probably be exposed to less radiation in a building made of wood than in a building made of brick. Building materials such as granite, bricks, wallboard, and concrete contain small amounts of uranium. In the uranium decay series, radon gas is released. Solar heated homes that use sand, crushed rock, or concrete slabs for heat storage may contain more radon gas than homes without these materials. Other energy-efficient houses can also collect radon gas from the soil and rocks below, especially during the winter months when the house is closed.

All coal contains a small amount of naturally occurring radioactive materials. Most of this radioactive material is contained in the unburned residue and ash, but some is released into the atmosphere. The average coal-burning power plant releases more radioactivity into the environment than modern nuclear power plants. While nuclear power plants are closely regulated, there are no regulations regarding radioactivity released by coal-burning power plants.

Radiation from Human-Made Sources

Human-made radiation sources include all of those activities in which humans have concentrated radioactive materials. Nuclear weapons testing resulted in areas where radioactivity levels are higher than natural levels. Nuclear power plants release small amounts of radioactivity into the environment. People living nearest nuclear power plants in the United States are exposed to less than 0.1 millirem of radiation per year.

X-rays and radioactive substances are used in the diagnosis and treatment of disease. The average American gets about 55 millirem a year from x-rays and radioactive materials that are used for medical diagnosis and therapy.

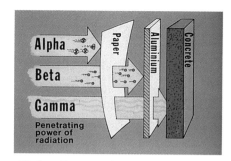

Alpha, Beta and Gamma Radiation

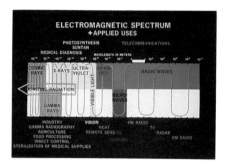

Electromagnetic Spectrum

DID YOU KNOW?

Plutonium has a half-life of 24,000 years. A half-life is the time it takes for half the atoms in a radioactive material to decay.

Product	millirem/year
Cardiac pacemaker (sealed plutonium)	5,000 (to chest)
Tobacco products	2,000 (to mouth)
Coal combustion	0.5-70
Oil combustion	0.002-0.04
TV receiver	0.5
LCD watch	1-3
Smoke detector	0.007

Biological Effects of Radiation

Radioactive substances enter the body when we eat and breathe. All humans normally have small amounts of radioactive materials inside their body. According to Nobel laureate Rosalyn Yallow, the amounts of radioactive potassium and carbon present in a normal human body would require the person — if he/she were a dead laboratory animal — to be disposed of as nuclear waste.

How does this radiation affect the human body? Most knowledge of the biological effects of radiation is gained through laboratory experiments involving large numbers of plants and animals, but not humans. Humans who have been exposed to radiation because of medical treatments, nuclear accidents, or nuclear weapons testing have also been studied.

The energy of radiation may cause changes in chemicals within the cell. The new chemicals may alter the structure of the cell or interfere with the cell's normal chemical reactions. The cell may no longer be able to carry out its normal functions. If these functions are vital to the life of the organism, the result is death of the organism. The extent of damage to the organism will depend on several factors that are described below:

Dose — Dose refers to the quantity of radiation given at one time. An example of a dose is 45,000 millirem of radiation received by people living near the Chernobyl nuclear power plant.

Dose Rate — The amount of radiation given per unit of time is the dose rate. An example of dose rate is 45,000 millirem/year. The effects are less damaging if the dose is spread out over a longer period of time.

Type of Radiation — Alpha radiation bombards the cells with large amounts of energy. It is more damaging than beta, X-ray, or gamma radiation that has less energy. Beta, X-ray, and gamma radiation are more hazardous due to their greater ability to penetrate into living tissues.

Type of Tissue — Cells that are dividing are more sensitive to the effects of radiation and the result is greater damage. This is why we often see changes in the skin, bone marrow, ovaries, and testes.

Age — Younger persons have more rapidly dividing cells, and exposure to radiation results in greater damage.

Health — The cells of a healthy person may be more capable of repairing the damage caused by radiation than the cells of someone who has other health problems.

A large dose of radiation may cause extensive and possibly fatal damage. Smaller doses cause less damage, and the damage may not be immediately observable. The period of time that is necessary before the damage can be observed is called the **latent period**. Often 10 to 20 years passes between the exposure to radiation and the appearance of some forms of cancer. The latent period is shorter for larger doses of radiation and longer for smaller doses.

Clinical effects of doses below 1,000 millirem are not measurable by current technology. These low doses only increase the probability, not the certainty, of any effect. When calculating risks, the assumption is made that any dose of radiation, no matter how small, involves some risk to human health. The risk, however, is very small when compared with other health risks, including poor diet, lack of exercise, and alcohol and tobacco comsumption.

In general we can say that the higher the dose, the more damaging will be the effects, and the quicker they will appear. The chart below shows the effects of specific doses of whole-body radiation given within a short period of time.

There is no evidence of any increase in cancer among people living in areas where natural background levels of radiation are several

---

Effects of an Acute Whole Body Exposure to Radiation

- 10,000,000 millirem — Person becomes comatose and dies within one or two days from damage to the central nervous system.
- 1,000,000 millirem — Person immediately experiences nausea, vomiting, and diarrhea. The number of blood cells made in the bone marrow will decrease. Death follows in one or two weeks from blistering of the small intestine.
- 350,000 millirem — One half of people exposed to this level of radiation will die in the first 60 days from damage to the blood and bone marrow. The people that survive will experience various degrees of nausea, vomiting, diarrhea, reddening of the skin, loss of hair, blisters, decrease in number of blood and bone marrow cells, and a decrease in resistance to infections.
- 100,000 millirem — Person will not notice any effects although there will be a decreased white cell count. There will be an increased probability of leukemia and life shortening.
- 10,000 millirem — There is no scientific evidence that humans are harmed by exposure to radiation below this level. Birth defects may occur if exposure during early embryo stages. Evidence may never be available because, if there are effects, they may be too small and occur too infrequently for detection.
- 1,000 millirem — No measurable effects. Statistical increase in tumors that occur before the age of ten, but only if exposure occurs during development in uterus.

times higher than average. Hereditary illness related to radiation has been observed in laboratory animals. Similar damage may occur in humans, but no statistically significant genetic effects were seen even with the high doses of radiation at Hiroshima and Nagasaki.

The risk of genetic effects in humans is apparently much less than the risk of cancer. Radiation above 50,000 millirem is a carcinogen though it is much weaker than many chemical carcinogens. Scientists have followed the health histories of nearly 76,000 survivors of the Hiroshima and Nagasaki bombings who were exposed to doses of radiation higher than 500 mrem. Between 1950 and 1985 more than 3,000 of the people died of cancer. This was several hundred cancer deaths above the expected rate. More than 60 percent of the people exposed were still alive 40 years after the bombing.

One year after the accident at the Chernobyl Nuclear Power Plant in Ukraine, the death toll was 31. All of the victims were workers at the power plant, firefighters or rescue workers. According to data released by the former Soviet Union, experts estimated that about 24,000 people received "fairly serious" radiation doses of about 45 rem (45,000 millirem). Scientists predicted an additional 100-200 additional cancer deaths among these people.

In 1992, the World Health Organization and health officials in Belarus, a former Soviet republic immediately downwind from Chernobyl, reported that childhood thyroid cancers had increased from four cases a year to about 60. Although previous studies have not linked thyroid cancer to nuclear accidents, radiation is known to cause thyroid cancer, and the release of radioactive iodine was a concern during the accident.

For information about the effects of radiation released during the accident at Three-Mile Island Nuclear Power Plant, see the Case Study: "Three Mile Island" in Unit V.

7.1 QUESTIONS FOR STUDY AND DISCUSSION

1. What is the basic building block of all matter?
2. What part of the atom is involved when a new compound is formed?
3. What part of an atom disintegrates, releasing radiation?

Types of Radiation
4. How do Alpha and Beta radiation differ from Gamma rays?
5. Which type of radiation would probably not damage the human body unless swallowed?
6. Which type of radiation is the most penetrating?

7. How does ionizing radiation differ from non-ionizing solar radiation?
8. Cosmic radiation is (ionizing/non-ionizing) radiation.
9. As the wavelength of radiation increases, the energy level _____.

Radiation from Natural Sources
10. You are told that iodine-135 is a naturally radioactive element. What does this tell you about the element?
11. What happens when a radium atom "decays"?

12. What is meant by the term "background level"?
13. What are the sources of background radiation?
14. Who receives more radiation — a person living in Denver, Colorado, or a person living in Miami, Florida?
15. Which type of power plant releases more radiation — a coal burning power plant or a nuclear power plant?
16. If the time in flight is equal, who receives more radiation — an airplane pilot or an astronaut?
17. Why do some people receive more background radiation than others?

Radiation from Human-Made Sources
18. How do human-made radiation sources differ from natural sources of radiation?
19. List four human-made sources of radiation.

Biological Effects of Radiation
20. Give two ways that radioactive substances enter the body.
21. Human bodies normally contain radioactive materials. (True/False)
22. Even with all the data available to scientists, they find it difficult to determine the effects of low levels of radiation on the human body. Give two reasons for this.
23. Explain how radiation damages the body.
24. Define the following terms: dose, dose rate, latent period.
25. From each of the following pairs, select the situation that would be expected to cause the most damage.
    A. 1. a single dose of 100 millirems
       2. a single dose of 1000 millirems.
    B. 1. 500 millirems per year
       2. 500 millirems per week
    C. Equal doses to the skin of
       1. Alpha radiation
       2. X-rays
    D. Equal doses of Gamma radiation striking
       1. muscle cells
       2. skin cells
    E. Equal doses of dental X-rays in a
       1. healthy young child
       2. a healthy adult
    F. Equal doses of the same type of radiation in a
       1. person who is healthy
       2. a person with AIDS.
26. Which of the following statements represents the most likely situation?
    A. If a person is exposed to a large dose of radiation, the latent period is likely to be very long.
    B. If a person is exposed to small doses of radiation, the latent period is likely to be very long.
27. Give the number of millirems of radiation that would most likely cause each of the following.
    A. loss of hair
    B. changes in embryo that might cause birth defects
    C. death within forty eight hours
    D blistering of the small intestine, leading to death
    E. increase in tumors in young children whose mothers were exposed to radiation while they were pregnant
    F. smallest dose that will increase chances of developing leukemia
    G. smallest dose that will decrease the num-ber of white blood cells
28. Is a dose of 10,000 millirems dangerous for an adult? Explain.
29. Airline pilots who regularly fly high-altitude New York-Tokyo flights receive 900 millirem per year cosmic radiation. If your friend was an airline pilot assigned to that route, and the friend told you she had just learned she was pregnant, would you suggest that she request a change in her flight assignment during her pregnancy? Explain.

A nuclear power plant was being constructed at Limerick, Pennsylvania. Radiation monitors had just been installed when Stanley Watras reported to work on December 17, 1984. As he walked past the monitors, he set off the radiation alarms. Officials found that the nuclear power plant was not the source of the radiation. They immediately began an investigation.

Danger at Home

Scientists went to the home of Mr. Watras to collect air, soil, and water samples. High levels of radon gas were found in all rooms in the home. According to one official, the level was "very high" — 165 times higher than the level allowed in uranium mines. The level of radiation was greater than the amount received from 455,000 chest X-rays. Following the advice of health officials, the family moved out of the house.

Radon is a naturally occurring radioactive gas. It is produced by the radioactive disintegration or "decay" of radium. Radium is formed in the uranium decay series and is found in certain types of rocks and soils. Houses can be contaminated when the radon gas rises through the soil and enters through cracks in the basement or foundation. In some regions well water contains high levels of radon. As water is used in washers, sinks, showers, and toilets, it releases much of the dissolved radon into the air.

The Watras' house is built over a layer of granite rock that contains 50 ppm of uranium. In order to conserve energy, the new house had been well insulated. The air-tight house trapped radon gas as if it were a huge bowl that had been turned upside down over the soil.

Scientific Studies

A granite rock formation — called the **Reading Prong** — runs from Reading to Easton, Pennsylvania. It continues through northern New Jersey and into southern New York State. In 1979 and 1980 a team of scientists, looking for commercially valuable deposits of uranium, studied the Reading Prong. An instrument similar to a Geiger counter was mounted on a Jeep. The scientists then drove the Jeep along 900 miles of roads within the prong and measured radiation coming from the ground. They marked road maps with colored pencils. Each color showed a specific level of gamma radiation detected on the roads.

The scientists did not locate any deposits that were commercially valuable, but they did find some locations with high levels of radiation. They gave this information to Pennsylvania's Department of Environmental Resources (DER), but it was another source of radiation that received the attention of DER and the news media. This was the 1979 accident at the Three Mile Island Nuclear Power Plant. Plans to check into the problem in the Reading Prong were put on hold, and the information was filed.

During 1980 and 1981, Pennsylvania Power and Light Company studied thirty-six homes to see if steps taken to conserve energy were affecting the air quality in the homes. One test measured the level of radon gas. They found some homes had levels beyond what is considered safe. Scientists were hired to study the radon levels. Their report was given to DER and EPA, but the DER officials were still too busy with the TMI accident to give it much thought.

Dr. Harvey Sachs, a geologist who worked on the Pennsylvania Power & Light (PP&L) study, tried to convince the Department of Environmental Resources that there was a problem. In a letter written in February, 1983, he warned that the radiation from radon was a more serious health problem than the radiation released during the TMI nuclear power plant accident. However, nothing happened until Stanley Watras walked passed the radiation monitors.

After high levels of radon (1,800-4,400 picocuries) were found in the Watras' home, maps were pulled out of file cabinets and studied. DER officials estimated that there were 20,000 homes in the part of the Reading Prong that lies in Pennsylvania. There may be as many as 250,000 homes built over the extension of the prong in New Jersey.

The Invisible Threat

The radioactive decay of radon gas produces solid particles called **radon daughters**. When these particles enter the lungs they give off radiation in the form of alpha rays. The energy bombards the lung cells, and the damage increases the risk of cancer. The danger from high concentrations of radon gas was first detected in miners. Studies of energy-efficient homes show that levels of radon in some homes are equal to those known to produce lung cancer in miners.

The EPA estimates that radon is responsible for 7,000-30,000 cases of lung cancer each year. Radon is the second leading cause of lung cancer; the leading cause is smoking. Experts say that 85 percent of the 140,000 deaths from lung cancer each year are caused by cigarette smoking. About one percent of all non-smokers develop lung cancer. It is thought that

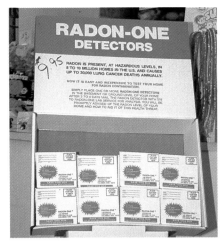

Radon detectors are available and can be used to determine the level of radon in your home.

Charcoal Canisters

Alpha Track Detectors

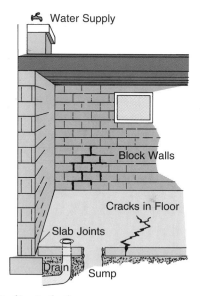

Indicated above are common radon entry points.

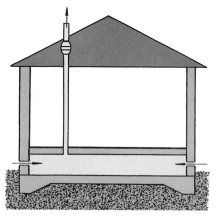

A system of pipes and exhaust fans may be used to reduce the level of radon in a home.

WHAT DO YOU THIŃK?

Finland and Canada have set the indoor radon limit at 20 pCi/L. The EPA's limit is 4 pCi/L. Do you think that the EPA limit is too strict? Explain.

as much as one-half of these cases may be due to indoor exposure to radon gas.

According to a US Surgeon General report, uranium miners who smoke have a risk of developing lung cancer that is ten times greater than the risk of smokers that are not exposed to uranium. Smokers who are exposed to excess levels of radon significantly increase their risk of getting lung cancer. This increased risk is due to the **synergistic effect** in which the damage caused by a pollutant is intensified if it is present with another pollutant.

Are You at Risk?

Scientists measure radon in picocuries per litre of air. A **curie** (named after Marie and Pierre Curie, the discovers of radium) is equal to the decay of 3.7×10^{10} atoms per second or the amount of radiation from one gram of radium. Pico means one-trillionth (1×10^{-9}) so a **picocurie** is the radiation given off by a trillionth of a gram of radium. A picocurie per litre is 2.2 atoms decaying per minute in a litre of air. The EPA suggests that the level of radon in your home should be lower than 4 picocuries per litre of air.

Of the 3,694 homes tested in the Pennsylvania section of the Reading Prong, sixty-six percent had levels of radon that exceeded 4 picocuries per litre of air. The problem is not limited to the Reading Prong. Anywhere there is uranium on Earth there is a potential problem. Uranium is usually found in granite rocks. Hot spots with high concentrations of radon have been discovered in Florida, New Hampshire, Maine, Pennsylvania, New York, New Jersey, Iowa, Tennessee, and Montana.

Not all homes built above granite rocks have high levels of radon gas. How the house is built determines whether or not it will trap any radon gas. Older homes have fewer indoor pollution problems because they have many cracks that allow air to enter. In many older homes the air is replaced with outside air one or more times each hour. In newer, tighter homes it may take two or more hours for the air inside the home to be replaced by outdoor air.

The EPA says that 10 percent of American homes have radon levels greater then 4 picocuries per litre of air. This means that as many as 9 million homes in this country have unacceptable radon levels. The agency believes that everyone should test their home for radon. Check with your state environmental protection agency to find out where to get a reliable test kit. Kits may cost from $15 to $50 dollars. There are two types of passive measurement devices in common use:

- One type of kit contains a small canister of charcoal that adsorbs the radon during a specific period of time, generally 2 to 7 days.
- Another kit — the alpha-track detector — contains a small piece of plastic that is sensitive to the alpha particles released by the radon and radon daughters. Exposure time is usually 2 to 4 weeks.

The kits are used as a screening measurement to provide a quick and inexpensive indication of whether occupants may be exposed to high levels of radiation. The tests are usually placed in the "worst case location" — usually the basement or lowest level of the home, with the doors and windows closed as much as possible.

Guarding Against Radon

What happened to Mr. Watras and his family? It took eight weeks of work and $32,670 to make the Watras' home safe. Their home was chosen as the site of a research project because it had the highest levels of radon in the area. The project was funded by the Philadelphia Electric Company's Engineering and Research Department. Approximately half of the cost of the project was spent for research.

After the radon-proof project was finished, the level of radon was less than 4 picocuries, the highest level considered acceptable by the Environmental Protection Agency. After the project was completed, the home was monitored periodically to ensure that the radon remained below the acceptable level. The levels had been reduced by using several methods:
- Installing a radon barrier and waterproofing the exterior basement walls,
- Sealing the interior basement wall and floor openings, joints and cracks,
- Installing a passive ventilation system.

Since the research project involving the Watras home, engineers have developed efficient methods to lower the radon level in a home. The cost of reducing the radon level in a home may be as low as $300 or as high as $3,000. Putting a radon reduction system into a home while it is being built costs $500-1000.

In 1993, the EPA proposed voluntary guidelines for home builders to protect a home against radon infiltration. On average, radon trapped in homes accounts for 55 percent of the radiation exposure (200 millirem every year) for people living in the United States. The EPA encourages state and local governments to include radon protection systems in building codes.

Radon Risk Evaluation Chart — Environmental Protection Agency

A	B	C vs D
200	440 to 770	1000 times average outdoor level
		More than 60 times non-smoker risk / 4 pack a day smoker
100	270 to 630	100 times average indoor level
		20,000 chest X-rays per year
40	120 to 380	
20	60 to 210	100 times average indoor level
		2 pack-a-day smoker
10	30 to 120	10 times average indoor level
		1 pack-a-day smoker / 5 times non-smoker risk
4	1350	200 chest X-rays per year
2	730	10 times average outdoor level
		Non-smoker risk of dying from lung cancer
1	313	Average indoor level
		20 chest X-rays per year
0.2	13	Average outdoor level

Legend
A Picocuries per litre
B Estimated number of lung cancer deaths due to radon exposure (out of 1000)
C Comparable exposure levels versus
D Comparable risk

1. Define the following words:
   picocurie   Reading Prong
   radon   synergistic effect
   radon daughters

Danger at Home

2. Why did the Watras family leave their home?
3. What was the source of the radon gas that was trapped in the Watras home?

Scientific Studies

4. Give the location of the Reading Prong.
5. Why were scientists studying the Reading Prong?
6. Why didn't the Department of Environmental Resources immediately investigate the problem in the Reading Prong?
7. What was the purpose of the study done by the Pennsylvania Power and Light?
8. According to Dr. Sachs, which source of radiation created the most serious health problem — radon or the TMI accident?

The Invisible Threat

9. What kind of radiation is produced by the radon daughters?
10. The presence of radon gas increases the chance of developing what kind of cancer?
11. Which causes more cases of lung cancer — cigarette smoking or radon gas?

12. What percent of non-smokers develop lung cancer? How many of these cases may be due to radon gas?
13. Uranium miners that smoke are (twice/five times/ten times) as likely to get lung cancer.
14. Radiation causes more damage in a smoker than a non-smoker. Why?

Are You at Risk?

15. What is the level of radon in your home that the EPA considers acceptable? (Be sure to include units.) At this level, how many atoms of radon are decaying each minute in each litre of air?
16. Why don't all homes built on the Reading Prong have high levels of radiation?
17. If you do not live in the area of the Reading Prong, should you be concerned about the level of radon in your house? Explain.
18. To test your home for radon, where would you put the detector? What time of year is the best time to test for radon? Why?

Guarding Against Radon

19. What measures were taken to radon-proof the Watras' home?
20. Should building codes require home builders to include systems that will protect a home against radon infiltration?

UNIT 3
Food for the Table — Changes through Science and Technology

Apollo 17 View of Earth

This photograph was taken when Apollo 17 was lined up with the Sun and the Earth, enabling the astronauts to take a full-disk view. Since it was taken in December, the beginning of summer in the Southern Hemisphere, the icecap that covers the Antartic continent was brightly illuminated. The land mass of Africa and Southwestern Asia appears in the northwest quadrant.

1.1 Food — Before the Big Mac

The Hunters and Gatherers

Humans have always needed plants for food, shelter, and for fire. Even when other materials are available for shelter and fire, plants are still needed for food.

Early humans did not raise plants and animals. They were hunters and gatherers who depended upon the wild plants and animals for food. It is said that the Shoshone Indians used one hundred different kinds of wild plants. Most of the gathering was done by women. The young girls soon learned from their mothers which plants could be eaten and which were poisonous. Most of their time was spent finding and preparing food. They had little leisure time.

During most of the time humans have lived on Earth their food has been supplied by hunting and gathering. If the time since humans first appeared on Earth was represented by 50 years, humans were hunters and gatherers for the first 49 of these years. **Agriculture**, the planting and harvesting of crops for food, did not appear until the very last year.

How Do We Know?

Archaeologists are scientists who study the things that early humans left behind. By studying the "dumps" of early humans, scientists can determine which kinds of plants and animals were important as well as how they were used.

The dumps must be carefully excavated. Each remaining piece of the people's trash is carefully removed, and its discovery is recorded. Later the pieces are examined more carefully. The items that once belonged to these early people are called **artifacts**. Artifacts are objects that were modified in some way by humans. Also found in the trash are bones, shells, and seeds. These things tell us something about the life of the people that lived at that time.

One of the things that archeologists want to know is the age of the items found. This tells them how long ago these people lived. The age of a once-living object, such as a bone or a shell, is determined by a process known as **radiocarbon dating**.

How the ability to create and control fire was one of early humans' major technological breakthroughs, and helped people use new kinds of food that could only be eaten after cooking? How did early humans make fire? When was flint first discovered and used?

Living	5800 Yr	11 600 Yr	17 400 Yr
Radioactive Material Remaining:	1/2	1/4	1/8

✗ Carbon-14 Still Present
✗ Carbon-14 Decayed
○ Other Atoms

WHAT DO YOU THINK?

Wild plants are genetically diverse and may contain genes we can use to improve commercial crops. Though many wild varieties have become extinct through habitat destruction, seeds of some wild plants have been saved in gene banks. Unfortunately, many gene banks are located in very poor, developing countries that don't always have enough money to fund their upkeep. A recent report issued by the National Research Council states, "Some minor seed banks are in fact seed morgues." Worldwide, sales of crop seed total more than $30 billion. Gene banks need at least $240 million to remain viable. Would you be willing to pay slightly more for food if a small tax was levied on food to help fund gene banks?

All living things contain two types of carbon: carbon-12 and carbon-14. Carbon-12, the most common form of carbon, is not radioactive. Carbon-14 is a radioactive form of carbon that is made by the action of cosmic rays on nitrogen in the air. As long as the organism is alive, the amount of carbon-14 remains the same. When the organism dies and no longer takes in carbon, the amount of carbon-14 decreases due to radioactive decay.

The age of the dead organism can be determined by comparing the amount of carbon-14 in the dead organism and the amount of carbon-14 in an organism living today. This method can be used to date organisms that are between 1,000 and 50,000 years old.

The amount of time it takes for one half of a radioactive element to break down is known as its **half-life**. Carbon-14 has a half-life of about 5,800 years. A dead organism is about 5,800 years old, if it has one-half of the carbon-14 found in a living organism. It will take an additional 5,800 years for one-half of the remaining carbon-14 to break down. If a dead organism has one-fourth of the carbon-14 found in a living organism, it is 11,600 years old. If a dead organism has one-eighth of the carbon-14 found in a living organism, it is 17,400 years old.

The Beginning of Technology

Early humans used the knowledge they had gained and the natural resources that were available to make products or develop processes that would improve their life. Today we call this **technology**. The technology used by early humans may seem very primitive, but sometimes it was as effective as our modern technology.

To improve the chance of a successful hunt, weapons were made from stone and bones. One type of stone used to make arrows was **obsidian**. Obsidian is a type of rock formed when hot volcanic lava cools very quickly. The quick cooling prevents the formation of crystals and the rock appears to be made of glass. The broken edges of this volcanic glass are very sharp. When scientists tested obsidian arrowheads, they found that the obsidian penetrated flesh better than arrows made with modern steel tips.

Before Wheat and Corn

Before there was wheat, flour was made from acorns. After the nuts were picked and shelled, they were put into a bowl-shaped container called a **mortar** and pounded into a coarse powder. The mortar was sometimes a "pot hole" in a ledge of granite rock. A smooth rock from the creek was used to pound the nuts against the sides of the mortar.

Acorns contain a bitter chemical called **tannin**. The tannin must be removed from the flour before it can be used to make bread or mush. A hole was made in the ground and lined with sand or cedar bark. The hole was then filled with the acorn flour, and water was added. The water dissolved the tannins, and they were carried away with the water as it slowly drained from the hole. This process in which chemicals are dissolved and gradually carried away by water seeping through the soil is known as **leaching**.

Hot water was used for the final leaching. To heat the water, rocks were first heated in the campfire and then dropped into baskets filled with water. Baskets made to hold water and cook mush were woven very tightly. The design and weave of the basket depended on how the basket was to be used.

Obsidian Arrowhead

A Waterweed: Wild Rice

Most of the plants we use for food today have been changed in some way. The science of **genetics** has provided us with bigger plants and fruits, fruits that ripen at nearly the same time, and plants that give us larger yields. There is one plant, however, that has resisted change. Many attempts have been made to tame it and grow it, but most of them failed. The Indians called it mahnomen, a word meaning "good berry." The botanist calls it *Zizania aquatica*; some call it wild rice.

If you want to eat as the Native Americans sometimes ate, you could buy some wild rice at the grocery store and cook it with a few quail, doves, or a rabbit. The flavors will taste the same as they did to the Native American. If you want to cook it as the Native American did, you will need a tightly woven basket, a campfire, some stones, and a specially bent twig to get the stones out of the campfire. You may want to substitute a little modern technology, such as a stainless steel pan and an electric stove.

Most of what is advertised as wild rice is produced in controlled paddies and is not truly wild. Naturally grown wild rice comes from lakes in Minnesota, Manitoba, and other states along the Canadian border. It is still gathered by the Chippewa Indians using canoes. Another kind of *Zizania* grows in Japan and China. The Japanese call it the "fruit-of-the-waterweed."

TRY TO FIND OUT

What characteristics do all grasses have in common? Grasses come in many different, often surprising, varieties. For example, Kentucky blue grass (on lawns), wheat, corn, bamboo, and sugarcane are all grasses.

Wild rice is not a true rice, although the grains look like grains of rice. It is a member of the grass family, a cousin of oats and rice. The stalks are rooted in water and stand ten to twelve feet tall. Near the top of these stalks are male and female flowers. The wind blows the pollen from the male flowers on one plant to the female flowers on another plant. When the seeds are ripe they drop off into the water and are buried in the mud. In spring they begin to grow.

Harvest time is in the early fall. The gatherers set up camp beside the lake. The rice stalks grow so close together that it is impossible to paddle a canoe, so the canoe is pushed with a pole. The first person in the canoe reaches out with a stick and bends the stalks into the canoe. A second stick is used to beat the stalks and knock the grains into the canoe.

Since all of the rice does not ripen at once, some of the rice will still be green and will remain on the stalks. Other grains will have already fallen into the water. This uneven ripening ensures the planting of next year's crop.

The rice grains must now be dried. Some of the Native Americans set the rice in the sun or built platforms of bark and kept a small fire underneath. Others stirred the rice in baskets with hot coals. Later, they traded with the settlers for metal kettles. Today, at modern mills this **parching** is done in large drums that rotate over slow gas fires.

The drying cracked the hulls of the rice. The rice was then put on clean skins and beaten with sticks to loosen the hulls from the grain. Some preferred to dig a shallow hole, line it with a clean skin, and then dance on the rice with moccasined feet. These may have been the first unofficial aerobics classes.

When the hulls are loosened they must be separated from the kernels. This process was known as **winnowing**. The seeds were placed on wide shallow baskets or trays of birch bark. With a gentle bouncing of the seed, the wind lifted the hulls from the grain. In today's modern mills, the hulls are taken off by big machines that have mechanical shakers and power fans.

Today the true wild rice sold at markets comes from the same rice lakes that it has for centuries. Much of it is still harvested by the Native Americans who make yearly trips to the rice lakes. Sometimes mechanical gatherers are used, but some states prohibit any mechanical devices. One company transports the hired Native Americans to the lake in planes which land on the water. The Native Americans camp at the lake during the harvest and the plane returns when the harvest is completed. This allows them to harvest rice at some lakes that cannot easily be reached by land.

Corn: Tamed by Humans

Today corn is a major source of food grown in most of North and South America. Scientists classify it as a kind of grass, but it is very different from other grasses. Most grasses have seeds that are light and easily scattered by wind. Some, with heavier seeds, have brittle stems that fall to the ground. Still others have seeds that are caught in the fur of animals.

The corn plant has several hundred seeds that are tightly held on a cob. The cob is wrapped in several layers of "leaves" and attached to a strong stalk that does not break easily. The protective wrapping prevents the seeds from being scattered. Even if the wrapping is removed, the seeds are too heavy to be carried by the wind and there are no projections that will catch in the fur of animals.

Corn is pollinated by wind. Directions in seed catalogs suggest that corn be planted in blocks of at least four rows, rather than in a single long row. This improves the chances of pollination and the development of cobs that are completely filled with kernels.

When corn is not harvested, the cob often remains securely attached to the standing stalk. If the stalk is knocked to the ground, several hundred seeds must compete with one another for space, minerals, and water. Few of them will survive to produce a mature corn plant. Few of the plants that reach maturity will be pollinated and few seeds will be produced. Without humans to plant the seeds of corn, this kind of grass plant would not survive.

Scientists have found other wild grasses from which humans have developed wheat, barley, and oats. They have not found any corn that has grown without the aid of humans. According to written records, corn did not grow in Africa, Asia, Europe, or in England. The Spaniards who traveled with Christopher Columbus were probably the first Europeans to see corn. They were given corn that was planted and tended by the Native Americans.

Corn on the Cob

Archeologists have concluded that corn was the main cereal crop that sustained the civilizations in the Americas. Many archeological digs have given us evidence of the importance of corn. It decorated pottery and was carved in the stone of sculptures. Golden stalks of corn decorated temples. Vessels thought to be corn poppers were made of pottery. Cobs of corn made from pottery were possibly used as toys. Real cobs of corn have been found in graves.

The search for the wild corn plants has so far been unsuccessful. On the bottom layer of a trash heap in Bat Cave New Mexico were tiny cobs of corn about the size of a penny. Radiocarbon dating showed their age to be 5,600 years. The kernels from the tiny cobs were small and hard like popcorn. Upper layers of the trash heap yielded larger kernels of corn.

Scientists think that each of the kernels was enclosed in a separate leafy wrapping. Corn that has each kernel wrapped separately is called **pod corn**. It sometimes appears as a freak in fields of corn today. The Native Americans considered it a sign of good luck. Scientists have experimented with crossing pod corn and a primitive kind of popcorn. They have managed to produce tiny cobs of corn similar to those found in Bat Cave. This proves that some of the traits of the corn found in Bat Cave are still found in corn today.

The corn in Bat Cave had probably lost the ability to scatter its seeds. No one knows what the wild corn plants looked like, but the pollen of corn plants has been found in dirt taken from a 200 foot (60 m) hole drilled for the foundation of a skyscraper. Corn pollen is the largest pollen of any grass plant and can be easily identified. The pollen is eighty thousand years old. How the wild corn seed was scattered remains a mystery. But the growing of corn appears to mark the beginning of farming as a way of life.

1.1 QUESTIONS FOR STUDY AND DISCUSSION

1. Define the following words:

   agriculture
   archaeologist
   artifact
   half-life
   hunters and gatherers
   leaching
   mortar
   obsidian
   parching
   pod corn
   radiocarbon dating
   tannin
   technology
   winnowing

The Hunters and Gatherers

2. List three ways in which humans use plants.
3. During most of the time that humans have been on Earth, food has been provided by (agriculture/hunting-gathering).
4. If humans had been on Earth for only one hundred years, how many of these years would they have practiced agriculture?

How Do We Know?

5. Early humans left no written records. How do we know what kinds of food were eaten by these early people?
6. Would a mortar be an artifact? Would an arrowhead be an artifact? Would a smooth flat stone be an artifact? Why or why not?
7. How can we tell the age of a tool made from bone?
8. Can this method be used to determine the age of a living organism? Why or why not?
9. If a dead organism has one-half of the C-14 found in a living organism, how old is it? If a dead organism has one-sixteenth of the C-14 found in a living organism, how old is it?

The Beginning of Technology

10. List some products of the technology used by early humans and give the natural resources used to make them.

Before Wheat and Corn

11. What type of seed was used to make flour before wheat?
12. Describe how the nuts were ground into flour.
13. Why was water poured into the flour and allowed to slowly drain away?
14. What is this process called?
15. Describe how Native Americans heated water.

A Waterweed: Wild Rice

16. What food can you buy today in the grocery store that is the same as the Native Americans ate?
17. Where does wild rice grow?
18. Describe how wild rice is gathered.
19. There is no danger that all of the wild rice will be taken at harvest and none will be left as seed for next year's crop. Why not?
20. Describe two methods used by Native Americans to dry the wild rice.
21. How is the wild rice dried today?
22. Describe how Native Americans removed the hulls from the wild rice.

Corn: Tamed by Humans

23. Give two reasons why corn seeds cannot be scattered without the help of humans.
24. How should corn be planted?
25. Why won't corn survive without the aid of humans?
26. Describe the corn found in Bat Cave. How old is it?
27. What evidence exists that proves that corn has been around much longer than this?
28. Why do scientists think that corn marks the beginning of agriculture?

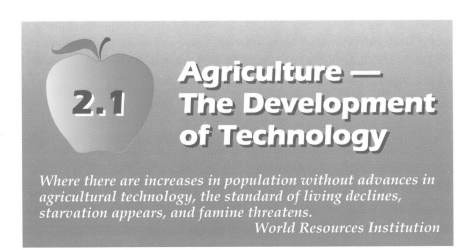

2.1 Agriculture — The Development of Technology

Where there are increases in population without advances in agricultural technology, the standard of living declines, starvation appears, and famine threatens.

World Resources Institution

Agriculture, the growing of crops for food, began with a very primitive technology. Hunting was still important to provide meat, but the crops that were planted promised a greater supply of food. Berries and wild seeds were still an important part of the diet and were necessary to provide certain vitamins and minerals.

Tools used by Native Americans were often made of sticks and bones.

Early Tools

The first farm tool was probably the **digging stick** that had been used for digging roots and bulbs. It was a strong, straight stick which had been sharpened at one end. Today in isolated parts of the world primitive farmers use only two farming tools: the digging stick and the **machete**, or big knife. Their method of farming today is probably very much like that of the first farmers.

Trees and brush are cleared with the machete, allowed to dry, and then burned. The stick is used to poke holes through the ashes and into the soil so that the seeds can be planted. The seeds are planted around the stumps and logs that still remain in the field. Two or three years later, when the crop is not so good, a new plot of ground is cleared.

Native Americans used the same kinds of tools and methods used by the stone-age people who had lived thousands of years before them. They had stone axes, fire-hardened sticks, and clam shells. Hoes were also used to prepare the ground for planting. Some hoes were L-shaped tree limbs with blades of stone or shell, while others had blades made from shoulder bone of deer or buffalo.

Bigger Machines to Prepare the Ground

After humans tamed animals, the hoe could be pulled through the fields. Egyptians used two oxen to pull this new invention that was called a **plow.** The first plows were made entirely of wood. They

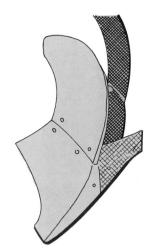

Moldboard Plow

This cast-iron plow was replaced by a plow made of hardened steel.

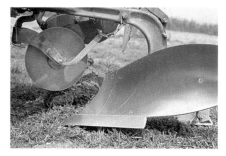

The newer plows have replaceable shins, plowshares and a coulter to cut through the sod.

were little more than big digging sticks that had been attached to a beam that was pulled by the oxen.

In 1797 a New Jersey farmer named Charles Newbold invented a cast-iron plow. The plow was not practical because the entire bottom had to be replaced when one surface was worn out. Using mathematical computations, Thomas Jefferson designed a **moldboard plow**. He was trying to design a plow that would work in all soils. The **moldboard** is a curved metal plate. At the bottom of the moldboard is the **plowshare** that cuts through the soil. A **shin** on the front edge of the moldboard also cuts through the soil. The plow rests on a **landslide** — a straight piece of metal that guides the plow.

An improved plow had the plowshare, moldboard, and landslide in separate pieces, so that only the worn parts would have to be replaced. At first people were afraid the cast-iron plow would poison the soil and cause weeds to grow. It would be twenty-five years before the plow was accepted.

A few years later John Deere, a blacksmith in Illinois, invented the steel plow. The cast-iron plow could not turn over the heavy, sticky soils of the prairie. Every so often the moldboard would have to be cleaned with a paddle. Some people thought the prairie was not fit for farming, but the new steel plow could cut through the heavy, sticky soil.

Modern plows have a circular steel blade, or **coulter**, which cuts through the sod or debris on the surface as a circular saw cuts through wood. The sod is then turned completely over by the **moldboard** — a curved blade of steel. Thousands of these plows were made in factories and sent out West to the "sod busters."

The first moldboard plows had one coulter and moldboard, and were pulled by a team of horses. Today **gang plows** with several coulters and moldboards are pulled by tractors, and they turn over the soil as if two to fourteen plows were being used at once.

The development of the country followed the development of the plow. It was the plow that allowed humans to change the earth. It brought some good changes as well as bad. The plow made it possible for fewer people to produce more food, but the plow has also caused the loss of much of our soil.

Before a field can be planted, the clods left by the plow must be broken up and the soil made level. This is done by dragging a **harrow** back and forth across the field. The first harrows were logs or tree branches. These were replaced with long boards that had wooden prongs along the bottom. Later iron spikes were pounded through the boards, and today the iron spikes are attached to iron frames. Iron or steel **discs** are sometimes used to cut through the clods before the harrow is used to smooth out the seed bed.

Machines for Planting

Wheat and barley were scattered by hand before the invention of the **hand-cranked broadcast seeder.** The broadcast seeder hangs by a strap over the shoulder. The seed sifts down on top of a small fan that scatters the seed over an area a few metres wide. The amount of seed planted is determined by how fast the person walks and how fast the seeder is cranked. Hand-cranked seeders are still used by people for lawns and gardens, and people only wanting to plant a few acres.

Grain drills are used on larger farms. The drill is a long box with planting tubes that carry seed to the ground. At the bottom of the tubes are discs that make a shallow trench for the seeds. Most drills also have boxes where fertilizer can be added. The first drills planted a strip of ground two metres wide. Modern drills can plant and fertilize a strip of ground six to eight metres wide. Some drills can cut through the sod and plant the seed without plowing and making a seed bed. These drills are known as **no-till drills.** (See Section 4.1)

Corn was planted by making a hole with a hoe, dropping in seeds, and covering the hole. This procedure was repeated every few steps until the field was planted. The first mechanical device used to plant corn was the **jab planter.** A steel blade was jabbed into the ground to make an opening. Then by moving the handles of the planter, three or four seeds were dropped through a tube into the hole. When the planter was pulled out of the ground the dirt fell in and covered the seed. Jab planters are still useful to the gardener and the research scientist.

Machines for Reaping

The first tool used for reaping was the **sickle**. A sickle is a curved blade on a short handle. The first sickle blades were made of sharpened stone; later blades were made of metal. The **scythe** was simply a larger blade with a longer curved handle.

Sometimes a **cradle** was attached to the scythe to catch the grain. It was made of pieces of wood fastened to the scythe. After each sweep of the blade, the stalks of grain were dumped to the ground. A few stalks were used to tie the grain into bundles, or sheaves, which were then stood in groups called **shocks**, and left in the field to dry.

A mechanical **reaper**, or binder, was perfected, manufactured, and marketed by a man named McCormick in 1831. It was a heavy machine made of wood and metal that was pulled by several horses. The inventor had studied the movement of the arms and legs as the wheat was cut with a scythe. A large reel with wooden blades pulled the grain toward the cutting blade. The cut grain was then carried on a canvas conveyer to a binding mechanism that tied the bundles of grain with a type of string called **binder twine.** Workers followed the reaper and stood the bundles into shocks.

Most farmers thought that they couldn't afford such a machine, even though it could cut six acres (2.4 hectare) in a day. This was six times as fast as anybody could work with a scythe. McCormick per-

Today farmers use gang plows. This 3-bottomed gang plow is pulled by a 50 horsepower tractor.

Grain drills pulled by horses made planting easier. Today farmers use no-till drills to plant corn and grains such as wheat and barley. No-till planting eliminates the need to prepare the soil, but it requires the use of herbicides to control the growth of weeds.

217

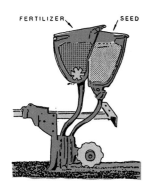

FERTILIZER   SEED

Grain Drill

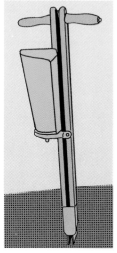

The hand-operated jab planter replaced the digging stick and the hoe for planting corn.

Shocks of corn and grains are left in the field to dry.

suaded the farmers to buy the machine by allowing them to pay with several installments. This may have been the first installment-buying plan.

Now it took only a few workers to reap the miles and miles of wheat that could be grown on the plains. During the Civil War, when many men were fighting instead of farming, more wheat was grown than ever before. The invention of the reaper helped provide the money, food, and labor necessary for the North to win the war.

Now that grain could be reaped quickly, there was a greater demand for the **threshing machine.** Until the threshing machine had been invented, the grain had been separated from the straw by beating it with flails on the floor of the barn. This particular floor of the barn became known as the **threshing floor.** A **flail** is a long stick with a heavy beater-stick fastened to the end. With ten hours of hard work, a man could beat out seven or eight bushels of wheat.

The first **threshing machines** were pulled and powered by horses; later ones would be powered by steam engines that burned coal. The threshing machine separated the grain from the straw and the **chaff,** or protective sheaths that covered the individual grains. It took several workers to operate the threshing machine, but 300 bushels (10.6 m³) of wheat could be threshed in one day, unless the machine broke down.

Today self-propelled **combine harvesters** are used to harvest all types of grain, including wheat, rice, soybean, and corn. The machine got this name because it is a combination reaper and harvester. Some combines can harvest a strip of grain more than 24 feet (8 metres) wide. These huge machines are moved from farm to farm as the grain ripens on the Great Plains. More than a million combines are in use today.

Of course the Native Americans and Pilgrims used their bare hands to husk the cobs of corn from the stalks. Farmers invented a variety of **corn pegs** to make the husking easier. The first peg was a thin piece of wood or bone that had been sharpened to a point at one end. A piece of string or leather bound it to the middle joint of the fingers on the right hand.

The peg was used to slash open the husk that was then pulled back from the ear of corn. The best corn peg developed was a kind of fingerless leather glove with a steel hook that ripped the husk open. A good husker could husk a bushel of corn in less than one minute.

Corn was often harvested with a binder, and the bundles of corn stalks were placed in shocks until they were needed. Binders were later replaced with a mechanical corn harvester, commonly called a **corn picker.**

A **header** on the corn picker guides the stalks toward rows of revolving, snapping rollers. The rollers pinch and snap the cob from the stalk. As the picker moves down the row, the ear of corn is husked and tossed into a wagon. On large farms the corn picker has been replaced by the combine harvester that picks, husks, and shells the corn.

Corn that is picked by hand or by a corn picker must be shelled. Small farms in Africa, that grow only a few hectares of corn, still shell the corn by hand. Shelling is done by one of the following methods:

- The cob is held in the palm of the hand and the kernels of corn are removed with the movement of the thumb.
- A shelled cob is rubbed on another cob to remove the kernels of corn. This method is faster than using the bare hands, but it requires more energy and skill.
- The husked cobs are put in a bag and beat with a stick while the bag is turned. The cobs are removed and any kernels of corn left on the cob are removed by one of the first two methods.
- The cobs are spread on a raised platform made of sticks and bamboo poles. The cobs are beaten with a stick, and the kernels of corn fall through spaces in the platform. Any kernels left on the cob are removed by one of the first two methods.

A **shelling board** made with U-nails (called staples) is three times more efficient than any of the methods listed above. Two rows of nails are placed 0.8 inches (2 cm) apart on a wooden board, and a space of 1 inch (2.5 cm) is left between the nails within each row. The cob of corn is rubbed against the nails to remove the kernels of corn.

Several **hand-cranked corn shellers** have been invented and are still used by small-scale farmers. Some models have a large flywheel that makes the sheller more powerful, and reduces the amount of human energy needed to turn the handle of the sheller. The handle is turned to start the rotation of the flywheel. Once the flywheel is turning, the hand crank can easily keep the gears in the sheller moving, and corn can be shelled as fast as it can be fed into the opening.

Two combine harvesters make harvesting this wheat an easy task. After changing the header, the combine harvester will be used to pick and shell the corn.

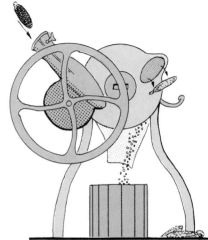

Burral's Hand-Cranked Corn Shellers (1840)

Horse Drawn Mechanical Reaper

In most of the world planting and harvesting is still done with animals and human labor. Cows are used in the rice field in China to prepare the soil for planting.

Farmer

Farmers or farm managers are responsible for planning schedules for planting and harvesting. They must be aware of signs that indicate potential problems caused by pests or diseases and take the correct steps to minimized the damage. They are also responsible for decisions concerning buying and selling of farm products, employing workers, and keeping financial records. Although there are no educational requirements, graduation from high school and vocational courses in agriculture or horticulture are desirable. Some employers prefer to hire managers with a bachelor's degree while others consider experience more important.

A spring adjustment allows the sheller to adapt to cobs of different sizes. The cobs pass between toothed, cast-iron shelling plates. As one of the plates rotates, the cobs are forced against the teeth that remove the grains of corn. The cob is ejected out of an opening, and the kernels of corn fall through another opening into a container.

Some hand-cranked corn shellers have been adapted with motors that turn the flywheel. One type of sheller used a treadle and flywheel to move the gears. It could shell 300 to 350 bushels (10.6-12 m³) of corn per hour. New models of corn shellers are adapted to the power take-off shaft of a tractor. They can shell 350-500 bushels (10.6-12 m³) of husked corn per hour.

A number of machines have been developed to harvest root crops. The simplest and oldest machine for harvesting potatoes is still in use by small-scale farmers. The **potato digger** has a modified moldboard that digs and raises the potatoes onto prongs. The potatoes are carried to a metal elevator chain. The soil is shaken from the potatoes and falls through the links of chain as the potatoes are moved toward the back of the machine. They either fall to the ground or are placed on a cart. Stones and other debris must be removed before the potatoes are placed in bags.

Harvesters have been invented for many different crops. A celery harvester moves through a field at a rate of five or six feet (1.5-1.8 m) a minute. Twenty-four rows of celery are cut, trimmed, washed, sorted, and packed in crates as the harvester moves across the field.

More Food with Less Labor

Gasoline and diesel tractors are used with many different machines. Bigger and better machines meant that fewer people could farm more land, and provide food for more people. Machine power replaced the power of millions of work horses. The 27 million head of mules and horses used in the early 1900s have been replaced by the horsepower of the internal combustion engine. The millions of acres needed to grow food for the animals can now be used to grow food for humans

In 1880, it took 180 hours of labor to produce 100 bushels of corn. In 1978 it required only four hours. Wheat production required 373 hours in 1880 compared to 10 hours in 1978. The labor needed to produce a bale of cotton was reduced from 300 to 11 hours by 1978.

In 1880, twenty-two million people, or 44 percent of the U.S. population lived and worked on farms. By 1979, there were only 6.2 million, or less than 3 percent of the total population living and working on farms. Today one farmer produces food for an additional 35 people.

This reduction in farm labor is not totally due to the use of bigger and better machines. Without the development of better varieties of seeds, effective chemical fertilizers, chemicals for controlling diseases, weeds, and insects, there would be no need for the mechanical technology. This agricultural technology along with the technology needed to transport, process, and sell the products of agriculture provides nearly 25 percent of all available employment in the United States.

In Other Parts of the World

Farming in the US is not like farming in many other countries. In most countries farming methods have not changed much for hundreds of years. Wooden plows are still used, and seeds are still scattered by hand. On the farms in many countries, more than 90 percent of the power is still produced by humans and other animals. Bigger and better machines are not always the answer to food shortages in these countries. The production of food is also dependent upon good soil.

2.1 QUESTIONS FOR STUDY AND DISCUSSION

1. Define the word agriculture.

Early Tools

2. What are the tools that are used by primitive farmers, in isolated parts of the world today?
3. What materials did Native Americans use for the blades of their hoes?

Bigger Machines to Prepare the Ground

4. Rearrange the following list so that the plows are in the order in which they were invented.
   steel plow
   cast-iron plow
   wooden plow
   gang plow
5. Match each of the following plow parts to their function (job).
   Plow Parts
   1. coulter 2. landslide 3. moldboard 4. plow share 5. shin
   Functions
   A. a curved metal plate that turns the soil.
   B. a piece of metal which cuts through the soil and is attached to the bottom of the moldboard
   C. a straight piece of metal which is a guide for the plow
   D. a piece of metal that cuts through the soil and is attached to the front edge of the moldboard
   E. a circular steel blade that cuts through the sod or debris on the surface

6. Identify how each of the following inventors improved the plow.
   Charles Newbold
   Thomas Jefferson
   John Deere
7. The plow can be considered both a good invention and a bad invention.
   Describe the "good" changes that occurred because of the plow.
   Describe the "bad" changes that occurred because of the plow.
8. Identify the two types of farm equipment that are used to prepare the seedbed after the field has been plowed.
9. Complete the following statement to describe each of the changes that were made to improve the harrow.
   A. The first harrows were simply made of . . .
   B. These were replaced by harrows made of with . . .
   C. The wooden prongs were replaced by . . .
   D. Modern harrows are made completely of. . . .

Machines for Planting

10. How does the planting of seed with a broadcast seeder differ from the way seed is planted with a grain drill?

11. What was the first invention that made corn planting easier?
12. What is the advantage of the no-till drill?

Machines for Reaping

13. Blades for cutting were first made of.... These were later replaced with blades made of....
14. How does a scythe differ from a sickle?
15. What attachment was sometimes used with the scythe? What was the advantage of using this attachment?
16. What is another name for the reaper? What two jobs did the reaper do?
17. What piece of equipment was replaced by the threshing machine?
18. What was the source of power for the first threshing machines? for later ones?
19. How many bushels of wheat could be threshed in one day using a flail? using a threshing machine?
20. What machine has replaced the reaper and threshing machine today?
21. What materials were used for the first corn pegs? Describe one of the corn pegs that was developed later.
22. What was the first machine that was used to harvest corn?
23. What machine is used today by smaller farms to harvest corn? by larger farms?
24. How do corn pickers remove the cob of corn from the stalk?
25. What process is done by combine harvesters that is not done by the mechanical corn picker?
26. If you had to shell a bushel of corn, which of the four methods listed would you choose?

27. Do you think a shelling board would make the shelling easier?
28. What mechanical device makes some hand-cranked corn shellers easier to turn?
29. How does the hand-cranked corn sheller remove the kernels of corn from the cob?
30. What source of power has replaced the human hand for many corn shellers used today?
31. How does a potato digger differ from a plow?

More Food with Less Labor

32. Why do we have more food available today even though fewer people are farming?
33. Explain how the internal combustion engine made more food available for people.
34. What percent of the total population lives and works on farms today? How many people can one farmer feed?
35. What improvements, other than machines, have enabled farmers to produce more food?
36. What percent of jobs in the US are provided by "off-the-farm" agricultural technology?

In Other Parts of the World

37. What provides the power for most farming that occurs outside the US today? Do you think we would help developing countries most if we sent them some of our modern equipment?
38. If you were given the money from a large benefit concert, and you were asked to spend it to benefit the people in countries that do not have enough food, how would you spend it?

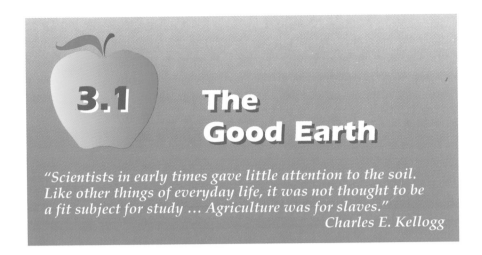

3.1 The Good Earth

"Scientists in early times gave little attention to the soil. Like other things of everyday life, it was not thought to be a fit subject for study … Agriculture was for slaves."

Charles E. Kellogg

Better seeds and human-made chemicals have made it possible for us to produce more food than this country can use. Advances in agricultural technology allow us to produce this food with less effort. Some food is produced in greenhouses with the plant roots suspended in a solution of nutrients (fertilizers) — a method called **hydroponics.** However most plants are still dependent upon the soil for their nutrients.

The Formation of Soil

Soil is sometimes called "black gold" because it is so valuable, but soil is not always black. **Soil** refers to that thin layer on Earth's surface that is made by the interaction of five factors:

- rocks
- sunlight
- living organisms.
- water
- air

The formation of a metre of soil may take as little as 100 or as many as 100,000 years. In some locations, soil may be only one or two centimetres deep, but it may be several metres deep in other places. On mountain slopes some rocks are not covered by any soil at all. The soil that might have formed there has been blown away by the wind or carried away by water.

Soil formation occurs faster in a climate with higher temperatures and more rainfall than it does in colder and drier climates. The rainfall provides water needed for chemical reactions and the warmer temperature increases the speed of the reactions.

The type of soil formed is determined by the climate as well as the material available. The same type of rocks in New York and Montana will produce different types of soil. The greater amount of rain in New York will cause leaching of certain minerals. The Montana soils will have higher concentrations of these minerals because of the drier climate.

Soil Conservationist

Soil conservationists study soil and water conservation problems and develop programs for the proper use of these resources. Most soil conservationists are employed by the SCS and the EPA. They work with private landowners, public utilities, government agencies, and other groups concerned with conserving soil and water resources. They conduct surveys and prepare maps of soils. They recommend methods of farming which help conserve soil. They also develop plans for soil conservation during the building of highways and developments. Soil conservationists must earn a bachelor's of science degree.

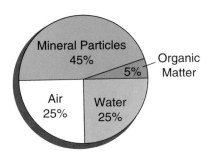

Composition of Soil: Weathering of rocks produces mineral particles. Chemical weathering of these particles releases essential nutrients that are needed by plants.

$$4\ FeO + O_2 \longrightarrow 2\ Fe_2O_3$$
ferrous iron   ferric iron (iron
(bluish-gray)   oxide or rust) (red)

$$H_2O + CO_2 \longrightarrow H_2CO_3$$
(carbonic acid)

The Parent Material

Rocks are the parents of the soil. The rocks are broken apart by the physical and chemical forces in nature. These smaller pieces of rock become a part of the soil. Rocks contain certain compounds called **minerals**. The minerals found in the soil are those that were present in the rocks. The color of some soils is partly due to the minerals it contains.

Weathering

The process of breaking rocks apart or removing minerals from them is called **weathering**. The **weathering agents** are the chemical and physical forces that break rocks apart and/or remove minerals from them. They include water, ice, wind, temperature changes, sand, glaciers, and the roots of plants. The weathering agents work in the following ways:

Temperature changes cause rocks to expand and contract. These changes may cause the rocks to crack producing small particles containing minerals.

Freezing water (ice), expanding within the cracks, forces the rocks apart like a wedge.

Tree roots act as a wedge breaking rocks apart as they grow into the cracks in the rock.

Plant roots produce chemicals that dissolve minerals from the rocks.

Sand and rocks carried along by moving water scour the soil and rocks beneath.

Glaciers can carry much bigger rocks that file and scrape the rocks below.

Wind-blown sand acts like a sandblaster on the rock surfaces.

Chemical Changes in Rocks

The minerals in many rocks contain a compound called ferrous iron (FeO). When these rocks are first broken the new surfaces have a bluish-gray color. Once the new surfaces are exposed to the air, chemical weathering occurs. The chemical produced in this reaction is iron oxide (Fe_2O_3). We recognize it by the rusty color of the rock's surface. It is the same chemical that is formed when a piece of metal containing iron is changed to rust.

Soil that has poor drainage and lacks air may contain ferrous iron and appear bluish-gray. This is typical of soil in many swamps and bogs. A red color indicates that the soil is well drained and contains pores filled with air.

Another type of chemical weathering occurs when acids react with certain types of rocks. Carbon dioxide is produced by the roots of plants. When the carbon dioxide combines with water in the soil, it forms carbonic acid.

The carbonic acid dissolves the calcite in limestone and marble. The calcium and bicarbonate ions are soluble in water. The calcium can now be absorbed by plant roots. Similar reactions are also caused by acid rain. Other minerals are also dissolved from rocks by carbonic acid. A mineral that is common in soils is aluminum. If too much aluminum is released from the rocks, it can be toxic to the plant roots.

Virginia, Kentucky, and Missouri are states that have many caves. The caves are formed when carbonic acid dissolves the calcite from the limestone rocks. **Stalactites** hang, like icicles, from the cave ceilings. They are formed as the dripping water evaporates and leaves behind the calcite that it had been carrying. Sometimes they join the **stalagmites** that have built up as the mineral-laden water evaporates from the cave's floor. Other minerals in the water may color these formations.

$$H_2CO_3 + CaCO_3 \rightarrow Ca^{++} + 2HCO_3^{-}$$
(calcite)

Texture of the Soil

The mineral particles that are a part of soil may be classified by their size. The size of the particles determines the **texture** of the soil. Particles larger than a grain of wheat or corn are not generally considered a part of the soil, even though they are found within the soil and on its surface.

Size of Mineral Particles in Soil		
Size	**Diameter (mm)**	**Can be seen with**
Gravel	greater than 2.0	naked eye
Coarse Sand	2.0-0.2	naked eye
Fine Sand	0.2-0.05	naked eye
Silt	0.05-0.002	light microscope
Clay	less than 0.002	electron microscope

Different **soil textures** are produced by the combination of sand, silt, and clay in different proportions. **Loam** is a term used to describe soils which are made of a mixture of sand, silt, and clay. Often other terms are also used with loam to give a better description of the soil's composition. Some of the common **soil textures** are listed below:

Sand: contains 85% or more sand; 15% or less silt and clay particles
Sandy loam: may contain 60% sand; 30% silt; and 10% clay
Loam: may contain 40% sand; 40% silt; and 20% or less clay
Silt loam: may contain 30% sand; 60% silt; and 10% clay
Clay: contains 60% or less silt and sand particles; 40% or more clay
Clay loam: may contain 30% sand; 40% silt; and 30% clay

Stalactites hang, like icicles, from the ceiling of Crystal Cave in southern Missouri. As the dripping water evaporates, the mineral deposits form stalagmites seem to grow from the cave's floor.

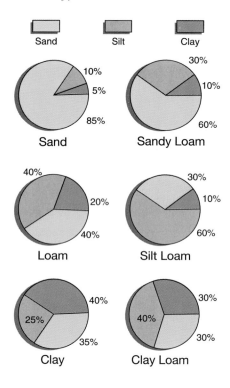

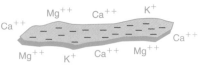

Clay Particle

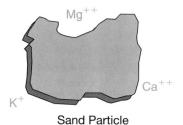

Sand Particle

The pie charts shown above represent different soil samples. The correct texture of any soil sample can be easily determined by the use of a "Soil Triangle" that is published by the US Department of Agriculture. First you must find the amount of each particle size present in the sample. This is done by a simple laboratory procedure. (See Investigation Manual)

Too many clay particles in soil can make it difficult to work, but they are an important part of the soil. Clay particles increase the soil's ability to hold both water and nutrients. Nutrients enter the soil from the processes of weathering and decay. The nutrients are dissolved in water and may be carried away as the water drains through the soil. This process is known as **leaching**.

Clay particles attract and hold nutrients. The clay particles have a negative charge. Essential plant nutrients like calcium, magnesium, and potassium have a positive charge. They are attracted to the negative charge of the clay particles where they are stored until they are needed by the plants.

Humus

The "moon dust" brought back by the astronauts contains some of the same minerals found in the soil on Earth. The dust consists of particles from rocks like those found on Earth. Soil on planet Earth contains more than broken pieces of rock. It contains another very important substance called humus. Since there is no life on the moon, moon dust does not contain any humus. The absence of humus means that there is no soil on the moon, for there can be no soil without life.

Humus is the partly decomposed organic matter that was once living, or was produced by a living thing. The more plants and animals that lived and died in the soil, the more humus the soil contains. Dead leaves and stems of plants on top of the soil, and dead roots within the soil will become humus. Waste products and dead bodies of animals will also become humus.

Many species of bacteria, fungi, protozoans, insects, spiders, centipedes, millipedes, snails, slugs, earthworms, and other animals feed on the dead plant and animal matter. These organisms help to change the dead matter into humus. The activities of the animals in the soil also help to mix the humus with the soil.

Like clay, humus also has the ability to attract and hold both water and nutrients. We can increase the water-holding capacity of the soil by increasing the amount of humus in the soil. As the process of decay continues, humus releases its nutrients to the soil.

Can There Be Too Much Humus?

Most soils contain between 1 and 5 percent humus by weight. Desert soils have very little humus, often less than 1 percent. Peat or bog soils may contain close to 100 percent humus. **Muck soils** have been formed by the decay of peat moss that lies above the water level. They contain 20 percent or more of humus and are black in color.

Muck soils are easily worked and have a good structure. Because of the large amount of organic matter, muck soils usually contain high levels of nitrogen and phosphorus. In Wisconsin a record 600 bushels of onions per acre have been produced and potatoes have yielded up to 800 bushels per acre — four times the national average.

There are some disadvantages of muck soils. They often lack the minerals that are normally supplied by the usual parent material — rocks. Because they are formed in swampy areas, the water level must be lowered through a series of ditches or drain tiles. Laws protecting wetlands may make it illegal to drain muck soils. If muck is allowed to dry, it is easily carried away by the wind.

Structure of the Soil

Many organisms in the soil produce chemicals that act as a "glue." As the animals feed on the dead material, they also take in sand, silt, and clay particles. Bacteria and fungi produce a slimy substance that contains enzymes that break down part of the dead material. The mineral particles and the partly digested organic matter (humus) are glued together forming small clumps. The result is a loose crumbly soil.

When individual particles are glued together to form larger pieces, they give the soil a physical characteristic called **structure**. If the particles are glued together into rounded clumps with a diameter of less than 1.5 cm the structure is called **granular**. If the clumps are irregular instead of rounded, it is called a **crumb** structure.

A crumb structure is created when making pie dough or biscuits. Flour and salt are mixed together and then a kind of fat is cut into the mixture with a blender or two knives. The fat glues the flour and salt mixture into small clumps or crumbs the size of peas. When bakers see this structure they know it is time for the next step in the dough making process.

If soil particles are glued into thin horizontal plates, the structure is **platy**. Other arrangements give structures called prismatic, columnar, and blocky. Some types of soil do not have any structure. Desert sand consists of individual grains that do not stick together. Soil with large amounts of clay may stick together in large masses. Structure can be developed in both types of soil by adding humus.

Spaces in the Soil

Plant roots are made of living cells. The soil must supply these cells with both water and air. Between the particles or clumps of soil are spaces. Forty to sixty percent of a volume of soil is normally pore space.

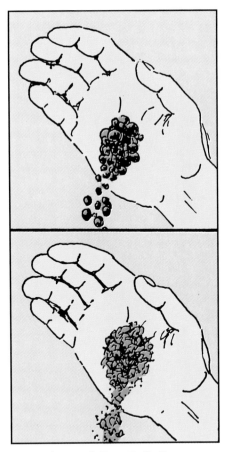

Granular and Crumb Soil

These spaces allow water and air to travel through the soil. If there are no spaces, the roots cannot get the air and water they need. If the spaces are too big, the water will quickly drain through the soil. Soil with big spaces cannot hold the water that will be needed by plants during dry periods.

The pore space determines the amount of rain that will run off and the amount of rain that will enter the soil (infiltration) and move downward through the soil (percolation). The ability of air and water to move downward through the soil is measured in inches per hour.

Description of Percolation Rate	Downward Movement of Water (per hour)
Very slow	less than 0.06 inches (0.15 cm)
Slow	0.06 to 0.20 inches (0.15-0.5 cm)
Moderately slow	0.2 to 0.6 inches (0.5-1.5 cm)
Moderate	0.6 to 2.0 inches (1.5-5 cm)
Moderately rapid	2.0 to 6.0 inches (5-15 cm)
Rapid	6.0 to 20 inches (15-50 cm)
Very rapid	more than 20 inches (50 cm)

The size of the spaces in the soil depends upon the soil's texture. Smaller spaces are found in soils with smaller particles. Larger spaces are found in soils with larger particles. The chart below shows the relationship between these soil characteristics:

- **soil texture** — size of mineral particles
- **infiltration** — the ability of water to soak into the soil
- **water-holding capacity** — the ability of the soil to store water
- **aeration** — the ability of air to move through the soil.

Texture	Infiltration	Water-Holding Capacity	Aeration
SAND	Good	Poor	Good
SILT	Medium	Medium	Medium
CLAY	Poor	Good	Poor
LOAM	Medium	Medium	Medium

Since spaces in sandy soils are large, water and air move through the soil very quickly. Sandy soils dry out rapidly after a rain. The spaces in soils with a large amount of clay are small, too small for water to move through. If the land is level, water will stand on the surface and prevent air from entering the soil. The roots will die because of a lack of oxygen.

The pore space is also affected by the amount of humus and the structure of the soil. By adding humus and creating a crumbly soil structure, we can increase the amount of water that will enter clay soils. Adding humus to sandy soils will increase their water-holding capacity.

A soil conservationist and a farmer survey a sloping field to determine the location of a terrace.

A Soil Profile

Since most of the plant and animal materials that form humus are located near the surface of the soil, the top layer is normally darker than the soil below. This top layer of humus-rich soil is called **topsoil**.

The layer of soil beneath the topsoil does not contain humus. It is called the **subsoil**. Subsoil has a higher clay content than the soil near the surface. Water moving through the soil picks up clay particles from the topsoil and carries them down into the subsoil layer. The color of the subsoil is determined by the minerals it contains.

Beneath the subsoil is the weathered **parent material** — the pieces of rock that lie on top of the bedrock. Not all soils have a well-developed profile.

A soil profile shows the darker layer of topsoil and lighter subsoil.

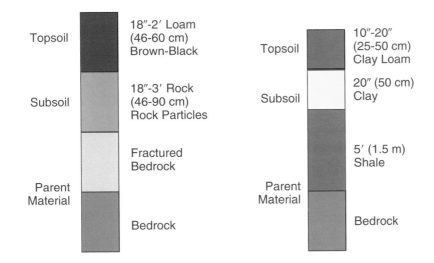

Topsoil	18"-2' Loam (46-60 cm) Brown-Black
Subsoil	18"-3' Rock (46-90 cm) Rock Particles
	Fractured Bedrock
Parent Material	Bedrock

Topsoil	10"-20" (25-50 cm) Clay Loam
Subsoil	20" (50 cm) Clay
	5' (1.5 m) Shale
Parent Material	Bedrock

◀ Typical Soil Profiles

3.1 QUESTIONS FOR STUDY AND DISCUSSION

1. Define the following words:

aeration	parent material
humus	soil
hydroponics	subsoil
infiltration	structure
leaching	texture
loam	topsoil
mineral	weathering
muck soil	weathering agent

2. Which term refers to the process of growing plants without soil? If plants can be grown without soil, why is it so important that we study and protect our soils?

The Formation of the Soil

3. List the five things that are needed to make soil.
4. Explain why:
   A. Soil forms faster in a warmer climate.
   B. The same type of rocks may produce different soils in two different climates.

The Parent Material

5. Why are rocks sometimes referred to as the "parents of the soil"?

Weathering

6. Explain how freezing water and temperature changes cause weathering.

7. Give two ways that roots cause weathering.
8. Explain how sand and rocks cause weathering.
9. What is produced as a result of the weathering of rocks?
10. How are the nutrients released from the mineral particles?
11. What percent of soil is made up of mineral particles?

Chemical Changes in Rocks

12. If the soil is a rusty red color what compound is probably present?
13. Why does the blue-gray color of rocks containing iron change to a red color when the rocks are broken?
14. What does a red color tell us about the water-holding ability of the soil?
15. How do plants increase chemical weathering?
16. What mineral is released by the action of carbonic acid? What type of rock is weathered by the action of this acid?
17. Explain how caves are formed.

Texture of the Soil

18. What determines the texture of the soil?
19. Rearrange the following particles in order, from largest to smallest.
    Clay, Gravel, Sand, Silt
    A. Which particle can be seen only by using an electron microscope?
    B. What is the smallest particle that can be seen with the naked eye?
    C. Which particle would not be considered a part of the soil?
20. How does sandy loam differ from sand?
21. How does clay loam differ from sandy loam?
22. Give one disadvantage and one advantage of clay particles.

Humus

23. How is "moon dust" different from soil?
24. We know that plants depend on the soil for their life, but the soil is also dependent upon plants. Explain this statement.

25. Explain how earthworms, bacteria, and fungi are important to the soil.

Can There be Too Much Humus

26. Give the amount of humus found in the following types of soil.
    A. desert soil   C. garden soil
    B. peat or bog soil   D. muck soil
27. Which do you think would be the best use for land with muck soils — a housing development or truck farming? Why?

Structure of the Soil

28. Explain how structure is developed in soils.
29. What do the names of various soil structures describe?
30. How can structure be developed in clay or sandy soil?

Spaces in the Soil

31. What part of soil is normally pore space? Why is it important to have this amount of pore space in the soil?
32. What is the relationship between pore size and particle size?
33. Which of the following soil textures has the best infiltration rate? (clay/clay loam/sandy loam/silty loam)
34. Which of the following soil textures has the best water-holding capacity? (clay loam/silty loam/sandy loam/sand)
35. Aeration will be best in which of the following soil types? (clay loam/silty loam/sandy loam/sand)
36. Often plants do not grow well in sand or in clay. What is the cause of the problem in each soil type?
37. What can be done to improve the sand and clay soils?

A Soil Profile

38. Describe the differences between topsoil and subsoil. Consider the following characteristics.
    A. humus content.   C. color
    B. clay content

4.1 The Soil Disappears

"The nation that destroys its soil destroys itself."
Franklin Roosevelt

The Land Provides

Native Americans thought of Earth as their Great Mother who provided for their needs. Some Native American tribes cleared small areas of land to grow maize (corn). If the land was not productive, they moved on to other areas. The type of farming practiced by Native Americans had little effect on the land. There were few Native Americans, and there was plenty of land.

The Native Americans did not like the farming methods used by the colonists. They felt that plowing the earth was like wounding their Great Mother Earth with a knife. Neither the settlers nor the Native Americans realized how much the plow would change the land.

In Europe there was little land, and there were many people. When they came to America, the colonists saw miles and miles of land that they could own and use as they wanted. It seemed that there would always be plenty of good land for everyone.

Erosion occurs when the soil is moved by wind or water to some new location. Before the colonists came, erosion was a slow and natural process. Three hundred years later much of the good soil is gone. The colonists did not intend to destroy the land. They did not realize that the soil was lighter than the soil they had farmed in Europe, or that the rains were sometimes heavier and the winds stronger.

The Debts Must Be Paid

There had been so much land that the colonists did not see the need to care for it. They did not know that more and more colonists would come to America to live off the land. Many were able to come because trading companies paid their transportation costs. In return they were expected to provide the trading companies with goods that could be sold in Europe. People living in the New England colonies provided fish, furs, and lumber. Those living in the southern colonies paid their debt with tobacco.

These fields of wheat and cotton are evidence that erosion is still destroying our farmland.

This field of soybeans growing on a farm in the Midwest is an example of a monoculture.

Tobacco grows well only if the soil is rich in nutrients. As soon as they were settled, the colonists cut and cleared the forests to grow tobacco. The humus in the new fields provided the nutrients the tobacco needed. Each year the colonists planted the same crop on the same land. This practice of growing only one type of plant on a large area is called **monoculture**. After only three or four years, the soil was light in color because there was no humus left. When no profit could be made, the land was abandoned.

By the end of the seventeenth century, it became obvious that the land was wearing out and washing away. After the trees had been cut, the heavy rains made gullies (deep ditches) in the slopes. Farming practices also created gullies. The gullies got bigger and bigger.

Westward Ho!

The colonists moved west in search of better land. The Western Movement finally brought people to the area called the Great Plains. The grassy plains that had belonged to the Native Americans and buffalo became the property of the settlers and their cattle. Soon there were too many cattle, and not enough rain. The little grass that remained could no longer support large herds of cattle, so the cattlemen sold out or moved further west.

The native prairie grasses that grew on the plains were tough and could tolerate long dry periods; they were **drought-resistant**. The grass had developed thick root systems that soaked up the rain and held the soil in place. The thick sod prevented evaporation of water from the soil. Below the sod was some of the richest soil in the world. The "sodbusters" used steel plows to cut through the soil and turn over the sod. The Indians looked at the sod and muttered "wrong side up," but the settlers were pleased with how well their plows cut and turned the sod.

The Dirty Thirties

Europe was at war and needed wheat. More of the Great Plains was turned "wrong side up." For several years there was enough rain, and the plow continued to cut and turn more and more sod. Sometimes the rains did not come when needed, and the winds always blew.

The early 1930s brought several years of extremely dry weather. The corn and wheat that the farmers planted were not drought-resistant like the native grasses that had grown in the dry prairie soil. The crops failed.

With no roots to hold it in place, the dry soil was easily picked up by the wind. The **black blizzards** began as strong winds. They carried the top soil east. In the nation's capital the sky grew dark. Dust settled on desks in New York City and engulfed ships at sea. On the Great Plains the topsoil drifted like snow along fence rows, buried farm machinery, gravestones, and sometimes buildings.

The southern part of the Great Plains, where Kansas, Oklahoma, Texas, New Mexico, and Colorado meet had become known as the **Dust Bowl**. Hugh Hammond Bennett from the US Bureau of Soils, spoke to Congress about the need for a national program to save the soil. As he spoke, a large cloud of dust from a storm in Oklahoma darkened the sky. He pointed to the window and said, "There, gentlemen, goes Oklahoma."

A National Plan to Save the Soil

It was 1935 and finally there was a new concern about saving the land. Although the Dust Bowl had not been the first or the only major loss of soil, it led to the first national program to save the soil. Congress created the **Soil Conservation Service (SCS)** within the US Department of Agriculture. Hugh Hammond Bennett became its first Chief. Conservation specialists were employed by the SCS to help people better understand and protect their land. Another federal agency, the **Agricultural Stabilization and Conservation Service (ASCS)**, was established to provide money to help pay for the cost of the conservation work.

Today the Soil Conservation Service still helps individuals, organizations, cities, counties and states to protect their land and water resources. States have been divided into soil conservation districts that usually follow county lines. A group of locally appointed or elected individuals is responsible for planning, approving, and implementing the conservation projects within the district.

Conserving soil and water is not a simple task. There are more than 70,000 different types of soil on planet Earth. Since 1935 the SCS has surveyed and mapped the soil types found throughout most of the United States. Information from these **soil survey maps** is used to plan the methods of conservation that will be used.

The major goal of the Soil Conservation Service is to protect our soil and water. Conservation of soil and water cannot be achieved without reducing the rate of erosion.

Black Blizzard (Dust Clouds Approaching House)

Types of Erosion

Although erosion is a natural process, human activities increase the rate at which it occurs. Most erosion is caused by rain. There are three types of soil erosion that are caused by the force of moving water:

Gully Erosion is the most obvious form of erosion. It occurs on steep slopes where there is little or no plant growth. The fast-moving water collects in channels and cuts away the soil, forming small ditches. With each rain the ditches become wider and deeper, and big ditches or gullies are formed. Gullies eventually become too wide for animals or vehicles to cross.

Rill erosion occurs on gentle slopes with little or no plant growth. Water collects and runs off in small channels. The rills or small ditches are only a few inches or centimeters deep.

Rill Erosion

Gully Erosion

A Landslide — Mass Erosion (Slumping)

Sheet erosion occurs on land that has a very gentle slope with enough plant growth to prevent rill erosion, but not enough to completely prevent erosion. Sheet erosion is the very gradual removal of a thin layer, or sheet, of topsoil. It can often be seen as muddy runoff water.

When water is absent, wind often causes sheet erosion. Soil particles become air-borne when the soil is dry, the wind speed is high, and the land surface is not covered with plants. The largest area of land subject to strong prevailing winds and a lack of moisture is the Great Plains, although these conditions may occur in nearly any location.

Although gully erosion is the most obvious, most topsoil is removed by rill and sheet erosion. Many farmers that have fields without gullies may not realize that their fields are losing topsoil. Traditional farming methods can easily cause a loss of five or more tons (4.5 metric tonnes) of topsoil per acre, each year. If this amount of topsoil is evenly spread over an acre of land, the depth of the layer would be 1 mm or about the thickness of a dime.

Another type of erosion occurs when certain types of soil become saturated with water and move down a slope due to the force of gravity. This movement of soil is known as **mass erosion** or **slumping**. Mass erosion is seen as a landslide on a steep slope or a cave-in of a bank that overhangs a stream. Although this mass erosion occurs in many places, the most famous examples are the mud slides of southern California that damage homes and close roads.

Slowing the Rate of Erosion

Soil scientists think that natural weathering processes can replace topsoil on most farmland in the United States at a rate of five tons per acre per year. The rate at which topsoil can be replaced is called the **tolerance value**. The rate of erosion during the dirty thirties far exceeded the tolerance value.

Scientists from the Soil Conservation Service help landowners reduce the rate of erosion on their land. A conservation plan, designed by a soil scientist might include several of the following conservation practices:

Contour planting refers to plowing and/or planting across the slope rather than up and down the slope. Thomas Jefferson called it "horizontal plowing." The plow furrows and rows follow the curves of the hills on a level. The rate of erosion is slowed because the furrows and rows slow the speed of water as it flows down the slope.

Strip-cropping also slows the speed of moving water. Strips or bands of close-growing plants (clover, alfalfa, grasses, wheat, oats) are planted next to crops that are planted in rows (corn, soybeans). Strip-cropping works best when the strips are planted on the contour.

Diversion terraces are needed on steep slopes. Diversion terraces are ridges of soil that are constructed along the contours. This creates a series of stair steps that make the slopes shorter and slow the speed of the flowing water. The terraces are planted with permanent grasses or with crops that will be harvested.

Waterways are used to prevent gullies on steep slopes. A waterway is a wide ditch that is planted with a permanent grass cover. It allows surplus water to run off without creating gullies.

Crop rotation refers to the practice of planting a series of different crops in the same field. For example, wheat may be planted in a field after the corn is harvested. Then clover is grown before corn is planted again.

Data gathered during a fourteen year experiment at the Missouri Agricultural Experiment Station showed that land planted with a corn-wheat-clover rotation lost an average of 2.7 tons (2.4 metric tonnes) of topsoil per acre each year. Similar fields where corn was planted year after year lost 19.7 tons (17.7 metric tonnes) of topsoil per acre (0.4 hectare) each year.

Windbreaks are strips of trees, shrubs, or tall grasses that are planted in rows that are perpendicular to the direction of the prevailing wind. They reduce the speed of the wind, and help to reduce wind erosion. Other benefits of wind breaks include trapping blowing snow, reducing moisture loss, and protection of plants and animals.

Conservation tillage includes several methods that reduce the amount of tilling and avoid the use of the moldboard plow. The soil is not "turned upside down." This allows the root structure to remain in the soil and the stems of plants to remain as a mulch, or covering, on the soil surface.

Some kind of conservation tillage is used on about one-third of the nation's farms. The United States Department of Agriculture (USDA) predicts that by the year 2000, 80 percent of the nation's farmland will be planted with conservation tillage.

One method of conservation tillage uses a **chisel plow** instead of the moldboard plow. The chisels loosen the soil without turning under the sod or other plant material. Another method is called no-till planting. A **no-till planter** prepares the soil and plants the seed in one operation. A no-till planter has a **cutting colter** that cuts a slit in the soil. A **double-disc opener** pushes the silt open, and a **planter** drops the seed in the soil. Then the **press wheel** closes the soil over the seeds.

There are several benefits of no-till planting:
- Since it requires fewer trips across a field, it reduces compacting of the soil by heavy farm equipment. This increases the infiltration of rain and reduces erosion.
- No-till planting also requires fewer pieces of machinery, and less energy is needed to plant the crop.
- On well-drained soil, fertilizers are used more efficiently. This results in higher yields (more food per acre) and less water pollution.
- The mulch reduces the amount of moisture lost by evaporation.

Contour planting in this field helps prevent erosion of a sloping field.

This farmer is using a no-till planter to plant soybeans. Can you identify the parts of the no-till planter in the picture above.

Centre — Pivot Irrigation

Centre — Pivot Irrigation Fields

- No-till planting decreases the amount of soil lost to wind erosion.
- The plant debris provides cover and food for wildlife.

No-till planting also has its disadvantages:

- Before the plants begin to grow, the field looks "trashy." Because of this no-till planting will not be accepted before education changes some farmers' attitudes. Formerly, straight rows and clean bare fields were signs of a good farm.
- Planting must be delayed in the northern part of the United States
  because the soil temperature is cooler when the soil has not been plowed. This may be a problem for some plants that require a long growing season, and greater management and planning.
- No-till planting requires greater use of herbicides and pesticides. It is estimated that no-till planting of corn requires 50 percent more pesticides. However, chemicals are much more likely to remain in the soil instead of being carried away with runoff water.

Cover crops are grasses or legumes that are planted to hold the soil in place. Field corn is planted in rows that are about 30 inches apart. It is picked late in fall when the temperatures are too cool for another crop to grow. Even if the corn field is not plowed, much of the soil is left exposed to the wind and the rain during the winter months. Some farmers hire a helicopter to seed rye in the field before the corn is picked. The rye grows during the cool fall weather and its root system helps hold the soil in place until the spring planting.

We've Learned Our Lesson — Or Have We?

It was December 1977. In Bakersfield, California, there was a drought the second year in a row. Fields were plowed and ready for spring planting. The cattle had stripped the rangeland of any grass they could find. It was a cold day in the San Joaquin Valley when a wind storm approached.

One hundred mile-per-hour winds lifted topsoil, sand and rocks the size of nickels. The rocks broke windshields and were embedded in telephone poles. The sand sawed through fence posts and sand-blasted the finish on cars as well as anything else that was exposed. Cattle suffocated and people experienced bronchitis and other lung problems.

The two feet (0.6 m) of topsoil blown from freshly plowed fields fell as red rain hundreds of miles away. Geologists estimate that the winds removed 25 million tons (22.5 million metric tonnes) of soil from the freshly plowed fields in the valley and an additional 25 million tons (22.5 million metric tonnes) from overgrazed rangeland. When rain finally came, it washed soil onto highways and into lakes and streams. Pesticides and herbicides attached to particles of clay were carried into drinking water supplies.

In 1977 wheat fields in eastern New Mexico lost three feet of topsoil to strong wind storms. Although 1977 was a year with less rain and stronger winds than normal, much of the erosion would not have occurred without the changes that had been made by humans. For example, over-grazed lands lost far more topsoil than land that was properly managed.

In 1972 the United States sold wheat and other grains to the Soviet Union. Farmers were encouraged to plant more grain. Any extra grain produced would be sold to other countries. The Secretary of Agriculture, Earl Butz, advised farmers to "plant fence row to fence row." Grasslands and hillsides that should never have been plowed were planted in wheat, corn, and soybeans to "feed the world."

Many of the soil conservation practices that had been developed after the Dust Bowl are now ignored. Farmers have torn out windbreaks and fence rows so that they can use bigger machinery. Some farmers have abandoned the practice of farming on the contour. With such big machinery it is much easier to go in a straight-line.

The benefits of crop rotation are often ignored. Hay and pasture land once planted for grazing is now planted with crops increasing erosion. The market and climate determine which grain will be grown. On 60 percent of all farmland the same crop is planted in the same field year after year.

Some farms are losing more topsoil today than they lost during the Dust Bowl. The USDA reports that one-third of the nation's farmland is eroding at a faster rate than their tolerance value. An average of one inch of topsoil is disappearing every eight to ten years, but some areas of the country are losing topsoil faster than others.

One tenth of the wheat-growing area of eastern Washington has lost all of its topsoil. Each year Missouri loses an average of 12.2 tons (11 metric tonnes) of soil from every acre (0.4 hectare) of farmland. In the last one hundred years half of the state's topsoil was lost. Some western Tennessee farms are losing 150 tons (135 metric tonnes) per acre (0.4 hectare) each year.

In many parts of Iowa the deep black topsoil that was once fourteen inches (35.6 cm) deep now measures only six to eight inches (15-20 cm). The tops of some hills are gray and their slopes are much darker. The dark topsoil has moved down the slope leaving the subsoil exposed on the top of the hill.

Loss of topsoil is not only a problem for the American farmer. Scientists in Hawaii can tell when spring plowing begins in northern China. Soil particles removed from fields in China by wind erosion travel 4,000 miles (6,400 km) to Hawaii. Farming practices in all of the major food-producing countries cause billions of tons of topsoil to be lost each year.

It's Not Just the Farmers

Studies show that many other activities also increase the rate of erosion. See chart on the right.

Off-road vehicles removed more soil in some areas than nature will make in the next 1,000 years. A hillside near Salt Lake City, Utah,

Salination (Salt Patch)

Another form of irrigation — pipes supported by wheels move through the crop.

Activity	Rate of Erosion (compared to natural rate)
Highway construction in Virginia	200 × faster
Building a shopping center in Maryland	100 × faster
Surface mining in Wyoming	11 × faster
Logging in Oregon	4 × faster

Wes Jackson is a plant scientist, and recipient of a MacArthur "genius" award, who is trying to save the soil and the people of the Great Plains. His research involves cross-breeding native prairie grasses with agricultural crops to produce a high-yield grain that enriches and holds the prairie soil. His task is not easy.

All plants get energy from sunlight. Native prairie grasses use most of this energy to produce roots that enrich and maintain the fertile soil of the plains. Native grasses are perennials; their roots live in the ground all year. Their genes make them drought-resistant. Native grasses produce some seeds, but not many. Agricultural grains, on the other hand, use most of their energy to produce lots of seeds that we eat as grain. Their roots are shallow because they have little energy left over to put into root growth. The roots die during the winter, and the ground must be plowed and the annual crops replanted each spring. Wes Jackson is trying to develop a seed-rich, perennial that is drought-resistant and whose roots hold and enrich the soil. It's a tall order.

slid into a residential subdivision after off-road vehicles had destroyed the plant cover. The US Geological Survey estimates that landslides cost Americans a billion dollars a year.

Unfortunately, the steel plow has caused more erosion than any other single piece of modern technology. Soil that should never have been plowed is being carried away by the rain or the wind. Sometimes government policies have allowed and even encouraged big business interests to become "sodbusters." Changing highly erodible land from grasslands or forests to cropland increases the rate of erosion.

More money can be made from an acre of cropland than from an acre of grassland. The short-term cost of reducing erosion is three times greater than the benefits the farmer will realize. Because of these economic factors, big businesses and poor farmers often do not practice soil conservation.

The Effects of Erosion

Though humans may gain short-term benefits, fish and other aquatic life will suffer from the effects of erosion. The silt carried from the land builds up in lakes, reservoirs, streams, and rivers. Soil is out of place in a body of water — it is a pollutant. It smothers the eggs of fish and other aquatic organisms. It clogs storm sewers and irrigation canals, clouds our drinking water, increases the chance of flooding, and the need for dredging our navigable waterways.

Most plants get nutrients from the top few inches of soil where most of the organic matter and microorganisms are found. As the topsoil gets thinner, the **productivity** — the amount of food produced per acre — declines. American farmers use products of technology, such as hybrid seed, chemical fertilizers, pesticides, and herbicides to make up for any loss of productivity caused by erosion.

Crop yield declines as topsoil is lost. Products of agricultural technology have continued to increase the yield per acre and have hidden the effects of erosion. In the 1980s, farmers produced more food than was needed. The surplus was due to the increased use of technology as well as an increase in the number of acres farmed.

The production of our food and the quality of our environment depend upon the wise use of our soil. Soil erosion is decreasing the productivity of farms on every continent. As the natural fertility declines, greater amounts of oil must be used to supply the fertilizers needed. We must remember that oil is not a renewable resource — its supply is limited. Soil is a renewable resource only if we use it wisely.

Irrigation Destroys the Soil

Take an airplane flight over the dust bowl today and you will see green circles that look like checkers on a huge game board. New technology allows farmers and ranchers to farm the dry land of the Great Plains. Today corn, which requires vast quantities of water, is grown on land that was once only good for grazing cattle.

Turbine pumps pull water from deep wells and feed it to "walking water" or **center-pivot irrigation systems**. Center-pivot irrigation systems have self-propelled sprinklers which "walk" in a huge circle and spray water on land that normally gets less than 20 inches (50 cm) of rain each year.

The source of water is the Ogallala Aquifer that runs deep beneath the soil, from South Dakota to Texas. This aquifer was formed thousands of years ago and geological changes have shut off its major source of water — the Rocky Mountains. Like oil deposits, the Ogallala water deposit is a nonrenewable resource. The water is being "mined" and some people are becoming concerned about the possibility of another dust bowl when the water runs out.

Today the Ogallala supplies water to irrigate two million acres (0.8 million hectare) of land in Kansas. Corn grown on this land is fed to cattle in large feed lots. Not far away, in Garden City, Kansas, is the world's largest beef-packing plant. The automated plant can convert a minimum 550 pound carcass into "boxed-beef" in less than one hour. The plant slaughters 5,000 cattle a day — 1.5 million each year. Forty percent of the beef produced in the United States depends upon water from the Ogallala Aquifer.

There is no shortage of corn-fed beef steaks in the grocery stores today because technology allows us to draw water from the Ogallala and feed and process beef with very little labor. But the water in the Ogallala will not last forever. During the next twenty-five years 80 percent of the Ogallala's water will be gone. Already farmers that use electricity to pump the water are finding it too expensive to continue irrigation.

What will happen to our beef supplies when water is gone? More important, what will happen to the land? Topsoil losses to wind erosion are higher on irrigated land than on land that is farmed without irrigation. What will happen when the sprinklers are turned off? Some say it will become the Great American Desert. Then tumbleweeds will be the biggest crop produced.

Gary Baker, chief of Kansas's Groundwater Management District #3 put it this way: "The time will come when we'll be real sorry that the Sandsage Prairie was ever developed. I sure don't want to live here when these hills go dry, 'cause they're never going to stop blowing."

Before the mining of the Ogallala Aquifer began, irrigation had produced large yields of grains in other regions of the world, but it also destroyed the soil. The area between the Tigris and Euphrates Rivers was once known as the Fertile Crescent. Six thousand years ago farmers irrigated the land, and crops grew abundantly. Eventually **salinization**, the buildup of salts in the soil, ruined the land.

Dense residue from no-till farming provides a winter source for many wildlife species such as Canada geese.

DID YOU KNOW?

In 1950, the Ogallala Aquifer under many parts of Kansas was 8 feet deep. Due primarily to irrigation, today it is only 6 feet deep. The Ogallala Aquifer is estimated to have held about 2,000 km³ of water, the largest aquifer in the world. If the Ogallala Aquifer is depleted, it will take about 6,000 years for it to naturally recharge.

Today, six thousand years later, farmers there struggle to grow crops. Water carries soluble salts in solution. The water evaporates but the salts (sodium, calcium, and magnesium chlorides) remain in the soil. Unless the salts are flushed from the soil, they build up and harm the plants. In some areas, poor drainage prevents the salts from being flushed through the soil, and drainage pipes must be installed to prevent the soil from being "salted-out."

In other areas there is not enough water available to use for the flushing process. In these areas **subsurface drip irrigation** can be used. The water is run through underground pipes directly to the roots of plants. The distribution of water can be controlled by computer. The technology for irrigation processes that do not ruin the soil is available, but it is very expensive and most farmers cannot afford it.

Irrigation has turned thousands of acres of desert in the southwestern United States into some of the world's most productive farmland, but salinization is now ruining many of those acres. California's agricultural valleys are slowly becoming "salted-out." One third of California's irrigated farmland — 1.5 million acres (0.6 million hectares) — may be destroyed by the year 2000. What will this mean to us? California's agricultural valleys supply nearly half of the nation's fruit, nuts, and vegetables.

4.1 QUESTIONS FOR STUDY AND DISCUSSION

1. Define the following words:
   Agricultural Stabilization
        and Conservation
        Service (ASCS)
   black blizzards
   center-pivot irrigation
   conservation district
   crop rotation
   conservation tillage
   contour planting
   Dust Bowl
   diversion terrace
   drip irrigation
   drought-resistant
   erosion
   gully erosion
   mass erosion
   monoculture
   Ogallala Aquifer
   productivity
   rill erosion
   salinization
   sheet erosion
   slumping
   Soil Conservation
        Service (SCS)
   soil survey maps
   strip-cropping
   tolerance value
   waterway
   windbreak

The Land Provides/The Debts Must Be Paid

2. Describe the Native Americans' method of farming.

3. Describe two methods of farming destructive to the land that were used by the colonists.

Westward Ho

4. Buffalo had roamed the Great Plains for years, and it had been a constant food source for them. Cattle are very much like buffalo. Why was the grass on the Great Plains destroyed by the cattle but not the buffalo?

5. Explain why the native prairie grasses could withstand long dry periods.

6. Do you think that when the Native Americans used the expression "wrong side up," they were aware of the erosion that would result from the colonists' farming? If not, why did Native Americans think plowing was wrong? Not all Native American tribes practiced farming, some tribes were still wanderers. Which of these methods of living was the lifestyle of the Plains Indians?

The Dirty Thirties

7. The early settlers could not use all of the wheat they grew. Why did they plant it?

8. Some people might say the "black blizzards" were caused by the weather, others contend that they were caused by humans. What were two weather conditions that were necessary for the "black blizzards"? How did humans help create the conditions that led to the "black blizzards"?

   Do you think there would have been a Dust Bowl during the 1930s if the Great Plains had not been settled?

9. What was Hugh Hammond Bennett referring to when he said, "There, gentlemen, goes Oklahoma."?

A National Plan to "Save the Soil"

10. There are two federal agencies that work to save the soil. List the agencies and explain their role in soil conservation.

11. What is the purpose of a soil conservation district?

    Who is responsible for projects within the district? (Check your phone book under United States Government, Department of Agriculture.)

    Is there a soil conservation district in your county? Where is it located? What is the phone number?

12. The SCS continues surveying and mapping the soil types found in the US. They have been working on this project since 1935. Do you think this is necessary, or is it a waste of federal money? Explain.

13. Explain how soil conservation also protects our water resources.

Types of Erosion

14. Match the descriptions given with the correct type of erosion.

    Type of Erosion
    1. gully erosion
    2. rill erosion
    3. sheet erosion

    Descriptions
    A. is frequently seen on land with steep slopes and little or no plant growth.
    B. occurs on land with little or no slope.
    C. occurs on land with gentle slopes.
    D. is caused by both water and wind.
    E. causes small ditches.
    F. causes streams to be muddy after a rain, even though a loss of top soil was not obvious.
    G. is the most obvious form of erosion.
    H. might cause a road to be closed.

15. Traditional farming methods often cause a loss of _____ or more tons of topsoil per acre per year.

    This amount of topsoil represents approximately _____ mm of soil, over an acre.

16. Rill and gully erosion are caused by running water. Another type of erosion that damages houses, roads, and the banks of streams is caused by soil saturated with water. This is called _____.

Slowing the Rate of Erosion

17. The tolerance value for most farmland in the United States is _____ tons per acre per year. During the 1930s the soil was being "mined" because the rate of erosion was (greater than/less than) the tolerance value.

18. Identify the conservation practices used in the following situations.
    A. A wide shallow ditch that is planted with a permanent grass cover
    B. Horizontal plowing or planting
    C. Planting methods that allow the root structure of the previous crop to remain in the soil
    D. Bands of close-growing crops alternating with bands of crops planted in rows
    E. Runoff is decreased by removing water beneath the soil in order to allow more infiltration of water
    F. Making a ridge of soil along the contour of a slope
    G. Following a crop with a different crop during the next growing season. Example: wheat, soybeans, corn
    H. Using a chisel plow
    I. Planting across the slope rather than up and down the slope
    J. Planting rows of trees or shrubs

K. When this method is used, fields may appear as a patchwork quilt
L. When this method is used, fields may appear to be a series of stair steps
M. Instead of running off the surface, water is carried to a stream by a series of pipes
N. Allows water to runoff without creating gullies
O. It is anticipated that by the year 2000, 80 percent of the nation's farmland will use this conservation practice

19. Explain how a chisel plow prepares the ground for planting.
20. List the four parts of a no-till planter and describe their role in planting.
21. Explain how no-till planting:
    A. improves the soil structure
    B. benefits the farmer
    C. benefits the plants
    D. benefits wildlife
22. Give two reasons why farmers may not like no-till planting.
23. No-till planting requires the use of (less/more) herbicide and pesticide. Chemicals used with no-till are (less likely/more likely) to pollute water supplies.

We've Learned our Lesson — Or Have We?
24. Describe how the 1970s were like the 1930s.
25. Explain why some farmers don't use the conservation practices that will reduce the loss of topsoil.
26. How long will it take for an average farm to lose one inch (2.5 cm) of topsoil? If a farm has only eight inches (20 cm) of topsoil and nothing is done to reduce the rate of erosion, how many years will it take to lose all of the topsoil?
27. According to the USDA one-third of the nation's farmland is eroding at a faster rate than their tolerance value. What does this mean?
28. How could you tell that erosion had occurred on a hill by simply looking at the plowed land?

29. It is said that some of the soil in the Midwest is silt from Asia. Do you think this could be true? If so, how did it get there?

It's Not Just the Farmers
30. List five human activities, other than farming, that increase the rate of erosion.
31. What single piece of equipment has caused the most erosion?
32. Why do farmers plant crops on hillsides and dry grasslands even though they know it will increase the rate of erosion?

The Effects of Erosion
33. List six reasons why soil is a water pollutant.
34. How does erosion affect productivity?
35. If so much topsoil has been lost, how is it that the United States continues to produce a surplus of food?
36. How does the loss of topsoil make us more dependent upon oil from the Middle East?
37. Is oil a renewable resource? Is soil a renewable resource?

Irrigation Destroys the Soil
38. What development of modern technology allows corn to be grown on the Great Plains today?
39. What is the source of water for irrigation?
40. Is the Ogallala Aquifer a renewable resource? Why?
41. How is the Ogallala Aquifer important to your food supply?
42. The Fertile Crescent was once one of the most productive areas of irrigated farmland in the world. Although water is still available, little will grow there. Why?
43. Give two conditions that cause the salt concentration of the soil to increase on irrigated farmland.
44. How can this salinization be avoided? If the technology is available to prevent the land from being ruined, why isn't it used?
45. In what way will the salinization of the California soil affect your diet?

Native Americans called it mako (land) sica (bad); South Dakotans know it as the Big Badlands.

The region of South Dakota known as the Badlands lies between the Black Hills — with its famous Mount Rushmore — to the west and the Missouri River to the east. The Native Americans thought this wilderness of rock and grass had been created by a terrible storm. Now we know that it has been carved by the natural forces that cause erosion. Today the carving process continues to change the shape of the badlands.

This part of the United States had once been covered by the sea. Mud and organic matter from the bodies of dead organisms were deposited on the sea floor. Year after year new layers were added, and the old layers were pressed into a kind of black rock, called shale.

The earth began to push gently upward; the movement was very slow. As the internal forces continued to push, the sea gradually drained into the Gulf of Mexico. Just as it had taken millions of years for the muddy material to collect on the bottom of the sea, it took millions of years for the sea to be drained.

The movements within the earth pushed a big mass of granite rock upward. The rock was beneath the black shale that had once been the ancient sea floor. Eventually this mass of granite rock with its covering of shale became the Black Hills of South Dakota.

The soft shale rock was now exposed to the agents of weathering. As the shale weathered, bits and pieces of the rock were carried down the mountain sides and deposited at the base. These deposits of eroded rocky material at the base of the Black Hills began a building process that would eventually form the Great Plains.

Silt and clay particles were carried and deposited by streams. Sometimes volcanic eruptions, forming the Rocky Mountains, sent ash high into the air and the winds spread it over large areas. The ash was deposited in layers, as if it were icing on a cake. As the Rocky Mountains became higher, layer after layer of sand, clay, silt, and volcanic ash was added.

The building of the plains finally came to an end. Once erosion had removed the shale from the Black Hills, the harder granite was exposed. Now erosion was much slower. The volcanoes that had built the Rockies quit belching out a supply of ash. Seeds, carried by the wind, were deposited in the newly formed soil. Gradually grasses began to grow on these new

---

TRY TO FIND OUT

Why are the Great Plains plagued by drought? Why do the prairies get so little rainfall? What is the **rainshadow effect**, and how does it affect the climate of grasslands?

TRY TO FIND OUT

Farmers on the Great Plains actively prevent and fight fires on their land. What effect do you think this has on soil regeneration in this agricultural region?

The famous sculpture on Mount Rushmore is carved in granite that is much more resistant to erosion than the clay bluffs that form the Badlands. In some places ridges of rock that resist erosion form dikes that look like miniature mountain ranges.

plains that stretched from Canada to Texas, and from the Rockies to the Mississippi Valley.

At some places the Great Plains were 5,000 feet (1.5 km) above sea level. Now erosion would begin to wear them down, just as it had the Black Hills. Streams of water with their load of eroded material moved toward the lower elevations. The rock that had built the plains was very soft. As the water cut through the soft rock below, gullies were formed and sometimes the gullies became deep ravines.

Today one of the highest elevations on the Great Plains is Sheep Mountain Table that stands nearly 3,300 feet (1 km) above sea level. Sheep Mountain Table is a part of the Badlands National Monument. This National Monument has been created by the weathering agents and the resulting erosion.

Erosion caused drastic changes in the appearance of the Great Plains. It began to look like a miniature mountain range. Geologists now call any area with this appearance a "badland." In some places there are **dikes** — ridges of harder rock that is resistant to erosion. In other places there are **pedestals** — odd mushroom shapes that are formed when rocks that are more resistant to erosion protect a column of softer material below.

Two hundred feet below Sheep Mountain Table is the White River. Sometimes it carries only a small stream of water; often the riverbed is dry. The river's name refers to the chalky white clay particles that are carried by its water.

The annual rainfall average is only 16 inches (40.6 cm). It doesn't rain often, but violent summer rainstorms cause the river to flood and the floodwaters eat away the land. The heavy cloudbursts and strong winds send walls of water against the clay bluffs. The water tears the shallow roots of the grasses from the thin topsoil. Once the grass is removed, the water cuts through the layers of soft rock.

The climate is extremely hot and dry in summer, cold and dry in winter. The record high of 116°F (47°C) was recorded in 1910 and the record low of -42°F (-41°C) in 1916. It is not unusual for the temperature to be 110°F (43°C) in the afternoon and 50°F (10°C) at midnight. It is this quick change in temperature that causes the local thunderstorms.

The size of Sheep Mountain Table and other grasslands continues to decrease each year as streams eat away its soft sides. Some areas of the Badlands are being cut away at the rate of one half inch (1.3 cm) each year. This is a very fast rate of erosion. In some other parts of the country it may take 500 or even 1,000 years for this amount of erosion to occur.

A strong wind almost always blows from the west across the Badlands. It is always a dry wind. Any moisture it held was lost as it was forced up and over the mountains on the west. The wind is a strong weathering agent. With the force of a baseball pitcher, it hurls the particles of sand that it carries against the soft rocks of the Badlands. This giant sandblaster produces new sand, silt, and clay particles that will be carried away by the wind or the water. Many of these particles that were once a part of the Badlands are a part of the fine silty soils in Iowa, Illinois, Minnesota, and Wisconsin.

Some people tried to farm the Badlands, but had no success. Finally after the Dust Bowl years, homesteads were abandoned or were sold to the government. Some talked of making the threatened wilderness into a national park or monument. Others thought the idea was ridiculous.

Finally in 1939 the Badlands National Monument was established. It is not intended to be a lasting monument that should be polished and repaired. Rather, it is a monument designed, created, and destroyed by natural processes. For those who take the time to observe and study, it is a monument that helps us understand and appreciate the natural processes at work on planet Earth.

4.2 QUESTIONS FOR STUDY AND DISCUSSION

1. Where are the Badlands located?
2. Were the Badlands created by bad farming practices? Explain.
3. Describe how the Black Hills were formed.
4. What was the soft rock that was eroded from the Black Hills?
5. Since much of the Black Hills has eroded away, why is it that the famous carvings of the Presidents still remain?
6. Describe the two events that built the Great Plains.
7. Once the Great Plains were formed, what began to happen?
8. Explain what causes dikes and pedestals to form.
9. How did White River get its name?
10. Why is erosion so severe in the badlands when the annual rainfall there is only 16 inches?
11. What types of erosion (See Section 4.1) occur in the badlands? Where did the soil from the badlands go?
12. What makes the Badlands different from many other National Monuments?

5.1 Can Technology Feed the World's Hungry?

"The Earth cannot support a larger population of any species than it can supply food for."

Isaac Asimov

Agronomist

An agronomist designs and conducts experiments to develop better ways of growing crops. Agronomists study the effects of planting, cultivating, and harvesting crops. They investigate methods of controlling weeds, pests, and diseases. They also investigate the effects of weather and pollution on crop production. Agronomists may be employed by agricultural corporations, governments, or universities. A bachelor's degree in agronomy or agricultural science is required.

The Population Connection

About one billion people were living on planet Earth in 1800. The world population doubled by 1930. In 1960 it reached 3 billion; in 1974 four billion. In 1987 the population reached 5 billion, and it continues to climb.

Ninety-one million people were added to the world's population in 1991, boosting the world population to nearly 5.4 billion. The World Watch Institute predicts that by the year 2005 the population will reach 6.7 billion. If the growth rate remains at the current level, the population could reach 8.5 billion by 2025. Current trends suggest that the world population may stabilize at about 11 billion by the year 2100.

The growth rate of the world's population is currently 1.7 percent. The **population growth rate** is the percentage change in the population over time. For example, Italy's population declined by an average 0.03 percent each year between 1985 and 1990. For the same period of time, the United States' population increased by an average 0.81 percent each year. The **natural increase** is due to a greater number of births than deaths, but the population growth rate of a country is also affected by migration. Net immigration adds about 500,000 people to the United States' population each year.

During the 1970s the growth rate of the world's population was declining, but the slowdown in the growth rate came to a halt in the 1980s. In some regions the growth rate is increasing. There are two major factors that cause the population growth rate to increase.

- Birth rates have remained high, while improvements in health care and sanitation have caused death rates to drop.
- There are more women reaching the childbearing age, especially in the developing countries. Even though each woman is having fewer children, there are more women giving birth.

The chart, on page 247, shows the average annual population change for the world and its major geographic regions. Although most countries in Europe have reached a population growth rate near zero, about 40 countries still have a population growth rate greater than 3 percent. Most of these countries are in Africa, Asia, and Central America.

Why People Go to Bed Hungry

The number of humans continues to increase, with about ninety-one million people added to the world's population each year. That means there are ninety-one million more people to feed. By 2100 the demand for food will double. The increasing population puts greater pressure on our forest, grassland, soil and water resources. There is a severe lack of fuel in some areas. One-third of the world's people still use firewood as the major source of fuel for cooking.

In nearly a third of the world, hunger is a constant problem. During the last 20 years more than 11 million people died in famines. Famines during the 1960s led China's government to promote a "one-child family" policy. The government's efforts to reduce the population growth rate and to increase food production have reduced the problem of hunger in China.

The number of hungry people increased in many countries in southern Africa during 1992. Pictures of starving children accompanied news stories of severe drought and famine, but weather was not the only factor that caused the severe shortage of food. Political problems in Somalia disrupted the distribution of food by relief workers. Political stability is essential if efforts to feed the world's hungry are to be successful.

Misuse of land is also an important factor causing food shortages. Throughout history there are many cases where increases in population have led to the cutting of forests and the farming of land that is not suited for farming. The farming methods increase the rate of erosion and remove the humus from the soil. Soil without humus lacks the ability to hold water, and rain quickly percolates through the soil or runs off the land. The land that was once covered by forest or grassland becomes a desert.

The World's Tillable Land

The former Soviet Union, India, China, the United States, and Canada have more than one half of the world's cropland and produce more than one half of its food. In spite of this India, China, and the countries of the former Soviet Union do not have the ability to produce all of the food they need. Only the United States and Canada produce a surplus of food.

The amount of food produced per person is declining because the supply of tillable land is limited. Sixty percent of Earth's land area is covered by ice and snow, mountains, or deserts and is not productive. About 30 percent of the land is tillable. The rest is covered by forests or is suitable only for grazing.

Average Annual Population Change (percent)			
	1975–80	1985–90	1995–2000
World	1.73	1.74	1.63
Africa	2.88	2.99	2.98
North & Central America	1.47	1.29	1.09
South America	2.28	2.01	1.71
Asia	1.86	1.87	1.68
Europe	0.45	0.25	0.23
USSR (Former)	0.85	0.78	0.64
Oceania	1.49	1.48	1.24

A billboard in Xiamen, China, promotes the government's "one-child family" policy.

DID YOU KNOW?

About 50 percent of Mexico's population is under the age of 15, a situation typical for many developing countries. How does the age of a country's population affect population growth? Do you think such exponential population growth can be supported with current or even projected food supplies? What, if anything, do you think can and should be done about the growing human population?

With 22 percent of the world's population, China has only 5 percent of the world's tillable land. Much of the land is too steep and rocky for farming. In some places bench terraces held in place by rock walls create small plots for growing crops.

The regions of the world with the largest populations do not have equally large areas of tillable land. For example, China has 22 percent of the world's population, but it has only 5 percent of the world's tillable land. The United States and Canada have only 5 percent of the world's population, but they each have 4 percent of the world's tillable land.

If all of the tillable land on Earth had been equally divided among all of the world's people in 1950, each person would have had about one half an acre (0.23 hectare) — less than one half the area of a football field. In 1992 the amount of cropland per person was about one quarter acre (0.13 hectare). As the population continues to grow, the cropland per person continues to shrink.

Each acre of tillable land is not equally productive. The productivity of about two-thirds of the cropland in India has declined due to erosion and loss of nutrients. Climate and soil type determine what types and how much food can be grown on the tillable land. Some areas have little rainfall and without irrigation this land is not very productive. In other areas the cold means that fewer crops can be planted and short-season varieties of seeds are needed.

Japan

Japanese farms are usually no larger than 5 acres (2 hectares), yet Japanese farmers have the highest yields per acre in the world. The high yield per acre is due to three factors:
- the development of seed varieties that produce high yields,
- the use of large quantities of fertilizer, and
- labor that does not depend on the use of large equipment.

Bigger is not always better. Very few Japanese farmers own a tractor or any other piece of large equipment that is essential to the American farmer. The largest piece of equipment used by most Japanese farmers is a two wheeled roto-tiller.

Large equipment does not increase the yield per acre. Mechanical planters waste seed. Since the ground is not completely level, mechanical planters often drop seeds that are not planted at the proper depth. Mechanical pickers cannot distinguish between green and ripe produce. Although varieties of fruit have been developed which ripen at nearly the same time, the ripening is not perfect and some fruit is lost. Mechanical harvesting also increases the amount of fruit that is bruised and will spoil during storage.

The Green Revolution

To prevent hunger, farmers in developing nations must increase the amount and quality of food they can grow. Scientists from developed nations serve as advisors to farmers in developing countries. They help the farmers improve their methods of farming so that they can improve the yield.

Better farming methods do not depend on importing expensive farm equipment. The lack of available fuel and spare parts in many developing countries would make the equipment useless. The technological development that has done the most to help the hungry is the production of high-yielding seed varieties.

During the 1960s new varieties of wheat and rice that produced higher yields were developed. This was called the **Green Revolution.** An American scientist, Dr. Norman Borlaug, was awarded the 1970 Nobel Peace Prize for his role in the development of the high-yielding, disease-resistant varieties of wheat. Many countries improved their production of wheat and/or rice by using the new varieties.

The Green Revolution did not solve the problem of hunger. Even Dr. Borlaug did not believe that the development of new varieties of wheat and rice was the solution to world hunger. He said the Green Revolution is simply "buying 20 to 30 years of time . . . in which to bring population into balance with food production." About population growth, he said, "Unless tamed, it will one day wipe us from Earth's surface."

India

Many people in India and other developing countries are poor. In 1980 the World Bank estimated that 730 million people living in poor countries did not have enough money to buy food to give them the energy needed for a day's work. The Green Revolution did not help the poor farmers. They cannot afford the new varieties of seed or the fertilizer needed for the seeds to grow.

Many people live in parts of India that lack trees. They cannot afford to buy coal or oil for cooking. They sometimes travel for miles up the sides of mountains to the nearest wood supply. The destruction of the forests increases the problem of erosion.

Some Indian women follow the cows and collect the dung. After it is dried, the dung is burned to supply the heat for cooking. This natural source of nutrients is used for today's fuel instead of next year's fertilizer.

Bangladesh

Fertilizers and higher-yielding varieties of seeds are useless without water. Farmers in northern Bangladesh need low-cost irrigation technology. An example of this type of technology is the bamboo tubewell with a twin cylinder bamboo treadle pump. If the farmer supplies the bamboo, the cost of the pump is about 325-400 taka ($13-16). A hand pump for drinking water can be added for an additional 92 taka ($3.70).

The treadle pump is run by human power. It can deliver 20-35 gallons (76-133 L) of water, depending on the depth of the water table that may be 10-20 feet (3-6 m). Farmers that are using bamboo pumps are now harvesting three crops a year instead of the one or sometimes two that can be harvested without irrigation. The treadle pump was developed and first used in 1980. This type of modern

Small farms like this one in Japan produce the highest yields per acre because of intensive farming methods.

Tilapia Fingerling

technology is important to the production of food in a country that has one of the highest population growth rates in the world.

More Protein Needed

Some scientists estimate that two-thirds of the world does not get enough protein. Without enough protein in their diet, children die or are crippled for life and adults lack the energy needed for normal daily activities.

Although the Green Revolution increased the amount of food available and decreased the amount of hunger, it reduced the amount of protein in the diet. In many rice fields, fish were grown in the irrigation canals. Fertilizers and pesticides used to grow the new varieties of rice killed the fish.

The best way to provide low-cost protein is through foods that are already familiar to the people. In Tanzania, farmers are being taught to raise fish in hand-dug ponds. The ponds are dug and filled with water from springs. They are stocked with Tilapia fingerlings. The fish are fed garbage, cornmeal, and bran. Rotting fruit and other plant material thrown in the pond provides nutrients for algae and food for small organisms that the fish eat. Six months later the fish have grown to eight inches and provide much of the protein in the family's diet.

Plants are the main source of protein for most of the world's hungry. In some areas, farmers found that they could make more money by growing wheat instead of soybeans that are higher in protein. Scientists continue to develop new varieties of wheat and other plants that contain more protein.

The United States — Always a Land of Plenty?

The new varieties of wheat have increased the yield in the United States as well as in other countries. Most of the wheat imported by many countries comes from the surplus produced by the United States and Canada. People in other countries drink milk and eat foods produced by animals fed corn and soybeans that are grown in the United States. Soybeans are also used to make a high-protein mixture that is similar to milk. Seven ounces (12 ml) of this mixture supplies the daily nutritional requirements of a child.

Will the United States always be able to produce more food than its population needs? In 1992 the population of the United States was 256 million. The US population has grown by almost 100 million in the last 40 years. Each year it takes more of the food produced in the United States to feed people living in the United States.

Farmers have increased food production by increasing yield and expanding the land area planted. There are only 475 million acres (1.8×10^8 hectares) of cropland in the United States. There are 604 million acres (2.4×10^8 hectares) of permanent pasture and 736 million (2.9×10^8 hectares) of forest and woodland. While some of this land

WHAT DO YOU THINK?

China must find a way to feed a growing population while still encouraging economic growth to raise its people's standard of living. In 1950, 0.4 acres of rice were grown for every person in China. By 1990, that figure had shrunk to 0.2 acres of rice per person. China is rapidly industrializing. Industrial development is gobbling up arable land around population centers. As the standard of living rises, the people are demanding development of new and better housing. As a result, scarce cropland is being taken out of production. How do you think China, and other developing countries, can plan for industrial development, housing, and preserve farmland in the process?

might be converted to cropland, it would mean a loss of wood production, wildlife habitat, and grazing land.

Unfortunately prime farmland is also prime property for development. Land development, office buildings, and parking lots now stand where wheat and corn once grew. Many of our most productive farms are being developed. The National Association of Conservation Districts estimates that 320 acres (128 hectares) of farmland are being developed every hour. In addition more than 3,500 acres (1,400 hectares) of rangeland and forests are being developed daily.

Preserving Farmland

Can technology make up for the acreage lost to development? We cannot guarantee advances in future technology. But we can guarantee that future generations will have productive farmland if we protect our tillable land. Protecting farmland requires the cooperation of politicians and landowners, and possibly a change in our way of life.

Two methods are currently used to protect agricultural lands. Property is taxed on the basis of its development value. Land used for farming and grazing is taxed at a low rate. Residential and commercial lands are taxed at higher rates. Some states require penalties if land that has been taxed at an agricultural rate is developed. In some states, inheritance taxes are also lower if the land continues to be used for agriculture. These laws can delay the development of land, but they cannot prevent it.

The second method prevents development and ensures the land will remain as agricultural land. The state, county, or a conservation group buy **development rights** to the land. Selling of "rights" is not a new idea. Timber rights, mineral rights, oil rights, and hunting and fishing rights have been sold for many years.

After selling the development rights, the owner still owns the land, and can live on it and farm it. A restriction is placed on the deed to ensure that the land will always be used for agricultural purposes. The land can be sold, but it cannot be developed.

The development rights are usually sold for the difference in the agricultural and development value of the land. This compensates the owner for taking away the right to develop the land.

The Hamburger-Rain Forest Connection

People in the United States are fond of many foods that do not grow here. Pineapples, coffee beans, cocoa, and many other foods are imported by the United States. Although many animals are raised in the United States for the purpose of slaughtering, the American markets also sell ham from Denmark, lamb from New Zealand, and beef from Central America.

There are a number of reasons why animal products raised in the United States are also imported from other countries. Artificial cases are used for some sausage links, but some sausage is stuffed in casing

Agricultural Extension Agent

Do you have a question concerning the use of a pesticide? Call your agricultural extension agent. The agent will be able to answer your question, or he/she will be able to find the answer for you. This is just one of the ways that an extension agent can help you. Although the agents work mostly with farmers, they provide information for anyone with a problem related to agriculture. Each spring the agents get many calls from gardeners and homeowners concerning soil testing, planting and cultivating techniques, and pest control. The extension agent may inform interested readers through a column in the local newspaper. Agents must have a bachelor's degree in agriculture or agricultural education.

Prime farmland is being developed at an alarming rate. Farmland preservation programs in Pennsylvania and other states protect farmland from development.

Slash-and-Burn Agriculture

made from the outer membrane of the hog intestine. In the United States these casing are cleaned by machine; in Denmark they are cleaned by hand. Some butchers feel the casings cleaned by hand are better, so they import sausage casings.

Beef is imported because it is cheaper than beef grown in the United States. Brazil and Central American rain forests are cleared to make cheap grazing land for large cattle ranches. A farmer in Panama cuts and burns the trees. When the spring rains come, the farmer sows grass seed and then sells the land to cattle ranchers for about $32 an acre. This is the farmer's way of earning a living.

The warm temperatures and high amount of rainfall cause the rapid decay of organic matter into the soil. The native tropical plants develop dense shallow root systems that absorb nearly all of the nutrients released by the decaying matter. Once grasses are planted, the nutrients released by decay are leached from the soil because the roots of the grasses cannot absorb them quickly.

Two-and-one-half acres (1 hectare) of land must be cleared for each head of cattle. Five years later, because of the loss of nutrients, erosion, and competition from insects and weeds, the productivity of the land (growth of grass) is reduced so that 12-17 acres (5–7 hectares) of land are needed per head of cattle. At this point the beef operation is no longer profitable, and the rancher must move on to other cleared land.

This type of **slash-and-burn agriculture** is the single largest cause of tropical forest loss around the world. One-half of Central American jungles have been destroyed since 1900, much of them since 1950 when the demand for beef in Central America and the United States suddenly increased. In the United States, the growth of the fast-food industry was the cause of the increased demand for cheap, lean beef. Central American beef is used in convenience foods — hamburgers, hot dogs, chili, soups, beef stew, frozen pot pies, baby foods, and pet foods.

The demand for Central American beef continues to increase. Central American population has doubled since 1950 and will double again by the end of the century. Central Americans eat 30 pounds (13.5 kg) of beef per person per year; much of it from the rain forest pastures. Some countries in Central America are importing beef to meet the demand of their growing population.

Americans eat about 105 pounds (47.3 kg) of beef per person per year; nearly half of it in restaurants and fast-food outlets. How much of the beef that you eat comes from Central America or Brazil rain forests? Labeling laws allow all beef to be labeled "domestic" once it has been inspected. It may be difficult for someone buying boned and frozen beef to determine its original source.

The Sea as a Source of Food

Seventy-one percent of Earth is covered with oceans. Will the oceans be the solution to the world's increased need for food? Technology increased the harvest of fish between 1950 and 1989, but the fish catch is no longer growing. Many species of edible fish — salmon, tuna, sardines, flatfish, and others — are already being threatened by intense fishing pressure.

Fishing vessels equipped with modern technology have the ability to take more fish from the oceans than the oceans can produce. Countries are restricting fishing rights to stop over-fishing and maintain a sustainable yield. Canada and the European Community have both suspended cod fishing off Canadian coasts. The capacity of the ocean to produce fish is limited, so as the human population grows, the fish available per person is declining. Your share of fish declined from 43 lb (19.4 kg) in 1988 to 40 lb (18 kg) in 1991.

Land development along the coasts also threatens fish populations. Marshlands were cheaper than other land. Developers bought, filled, and built on thousands of acres of marshlands. The food chain of many deep water fish begins in the marshlands. The estuaries are the nurseries for many species of fish. The small fish produced in one acre (0.4 hectare) of estuary will produce 240 pounds (108 kg) of edible fish. Protecting the marshlands and estuaries is essential to our food supply.

Pollution of the ocean is another threat to our food supply. Fish, oysters, crabs, and other organisms accumulate poisons in their body fat. The area of the ocean that produces the most food is the area nearest the coast. This is also the area most likely to be polluted.

Will the sea provide? Fishermen from a small fishing village in China cast their nets upon the water. Their methods are primitive compared to the high-tech fishing vessels from developed countries.

Can Earth Feed 11 Billion People?

As world population increases, the amount of cropland per person decreases. Some experts think that Earth can feed 11 billion people if we use our cropland wisely, protect our oceans and coastal wetlands, share our knowledge and resources with other countries, and transport food products to areas where they are most needed. Unfortunately, social and economic differences may always ensure that some people will go hungry.

5.1 QUESTIONS FOR STUDY AND DISCUSSION

The Population Connection

1. Graph the population growth for the years given in the two paragraphs of this section. Plot the years along the base of the graph (x-axis). Mark the population size along the left side of the graph (y axis).
2. During which period of time did the world's population grow the fastest?
   1800–1930   1960–1974
   1930–1960   1975–1987

3. How fast is the world's population growing each year?
4. The doubling time is the number of years required for a population of an area to double its present size at the current rate of population growth. To calculate the doubling time, divide the number 70 by the percent growth rate. What is the doubling time for the world's population at the current growth rate?

5. In 1990, the birth rate in the United States was 16 per 1,000 and the death rate was 9 per 1,000. What was the Natural Increase in population?

6. In 1990, the total United States population was 251 million (251,000,000). This is 251,000 groups of 1,000 people. Calculate the Natural Increase in the United States population during 1991. [Number of Groups x Natural Increase/Group = Natural Increase]

7. What two factors determine the growth rate of a country? Calculate the total number of people added to the US population in 1991.

8. How does the growth rate of the United States compare to the growth rate of the world?

9. In what region of the world is the growth rate approaching zero? What regions have the highest growth rate?

Why People Go to Bed Hungry

10. How has the population growth affected our natural resources?

11. The total world population is (decreasing/increasing). The demand for food is (decreasing/increasing).

12. What is the Chinese government doing to reduce the number of hungry people? What event led to this action?

13. Why do people go to bed hungry? List at least four reasons.

14. What is the relationship between the increasing population and the increasing amount of desert?

The World's Tillable Land

15. List the five regions that have most of the world's cropland and produce most of the world's food. Which of these countries have a surplus of food?

16. What part of the world's land is tillable?

17. How does the amount of tillable land in China compare to the amount in the United States and Canada? How does the population of China compare to the population of the United States and Canada?

18. How much tillable land exists for each person in the world?
How does the amount of tillable land available per person in 1992 compare to the amount available in 1950?
What will happen to this number in the future?
If you were to be assigned your portion of land and are expected to grow your own food, would it make any difference which acre you were given? Why?

19. The US and Canada both have 4 percent of the world's tillable land. Which country grows the most food? Why?

Japan

20. What is the typical size of Japanese farms? What type of equipment do they use?

21. How does the yield per acre on Japanese farms compare to other farms? Give three factors that increase their yield.

22. Give two ways in which equipment reduces the yield per acre.

The Green Revolution

23. Identify those statements that are true and those that are false.
Solving the problem of world hunger is dependent upon:
A. developing countries being able to grow more of their own food.
B. developing countries importing farm equipment from other countries.
C. improving the methods of farming in developing countries.
D. farmers from developing countries coming to the United States to see how food is grown here.
E. scientists going to developing countries to help farmers.
F. developing countries controlling their population growth.
G. the success of Dr. Norman Borlaug's Green Revolution.

24. The term Green Revolution refers to what technological development?

India

25. Why didn't the Green Revolution help the poor farmers?
26. In what two ways does the lack of fuel in India harm the soil?

Bangladesh

27. Describe the modern technology that is increasing the production of food in Bangladesh. What is the source of energy?
28. Why is this technology so important to a country like Bangladesh?

More Protein Needed

29. What part of the world's people have diets lacking the proper amount of protein? How does this lack of protein affect these people?
30. What is the best way to increase the protein in the diet of people in other countries? How is this being accomplished in Tanzania?
31. How did the Green Revolution decrease the amount of protein in the diets of people who grew rice?
32. What is the main source of protein in the diets of most of the world's people? What plant is a good source of protein? What crop was grown instead? Why?

The United States-Always a Land of Plenty?

33. How did the Green Revolution affect the United States?
34. What two countries supply most of the wheat exported to other countries?
35. Soybeans are a major crop exported by the United States. Give two ways that other countries use soybeans.
36. Give two ways that farmers in the United States have increased food production. Do you think that the United States will always be able to produce enough food to meet the needs of people in this country and have excess to export? Explain.
37. What is happening to prime farmland?

Preserving Prime Farmland

38. How can tax laws encourage people to use land as farmland instead of developing it?
39. What other method is used to preserve farmland?
   How does this method ensure that land will always be farmed?
   What determines the cost of the development rights?
40. Which of these two methods do you think will work the best?
   If you owned land that was considered prime farmland, would you sell the development rights? Explain your answer.

The Hamburger-Rain Forest Connection

41. If we grow a surplus of food in the United States, why do we import food?
42. What type of land is being developed into ranches in Central America?
   After the first few years, what happens to the carrying capacity of the land?
   What causes this change?
43. What is the major cause of habitat loss in rain forests?
   Why do farmers practice this method of agriculture? Do you think that the forest habitat could be saved if the farmer could sell the "development rights"? Explain.
44. What products might you buy that would be made from Central American beef?
45. Some fast-food chains claim to sell only domestic beef. Is it possible that this beef was raised in Central America? If this is true, why isn't this false advertising?

The Sea as a Source of Food

46. Give three reasons why the ocean is not the answer to the food shortage problem.
47. Why is it important to protect the land along the coasts?

Can Earth Feed 11 Billion People?

48. What do you think? Can Earth provide food for 11 billion people? Explain.

Long before scientists understood the nutrient cycles, people observed that plants grew well in some soils and poorly in others. The soils in which plants grew well were said to be fertile. After plants had been grown in the same soil for a few years, they no longer grew as big or looked as healthy. The soil was "worn-out."

By trial-and-error people learned how to make the soil grow better crops. Ancient writings refer to the practice of applying manure when crops were planted. The American Indians taught the colonists to put fish heads in the mounds with their corn seeds. Manure and fish heads provided something that made the plants grow better.

Scientists experimented by growing plants in water or clean sand instead of soil. These experiments proved that plants need certain chemicals for proper growth. Other experiments showed that fertile soils are rich in the chemicals that plants require for growth.

In a natural ecosystem the nutrients — chemicals needed by the plants — are returned to the soil when the plant decays. Some nutrients are lost from the ecosystem by erosion and leaching, but most are recycled.

Plants "rob" the nutrients from the soil. Each year that plants are grown and harvested, more of the same chemicals are removed from the soil's "nutrient bank." Many of the nutrients are transported from the farm ecosystem to the city ecosystem. Farming increases the amount of erosion. Erosion and leaching also remove nutrients from the soil. Soon the soil's supply of certain chemicals is exhausted. The soil is now infertile — unable to support good plant growth. It is "worn out."

Essential Nutrients

Scientists learned that the fertility of the soil depends upon the presence of at least thirteen chemical elements. Plants require large quantities of three nutrients: nitrogen (N), phosphorus (P), and potassium (K). These are the primary nutrients. Smaller amounts of other nutrients are needed. These secondary nutrients are calcium (Ca), magnesium (Mg), and sulfur (S).

Seven additional elements have been identified as being necessary for plant growth. Since only very tiny amounts of these nutrients are needed, they are referred to as micronutrients. The micronutrients are iron, manganese, boron, copper, molybdenum, zinc, and chlorine.

The Primary Nutrients

Nitrogen is frequently the limiting factor for plant growth. It is necessary for proper growth of leaves and stems. Plants with plenty of nitrogen grow fast in warm, humid weather. They have a rich green color. Even with plenty of moisture and warmth, lack of nitrogen results in slow growth and leaves that are yellow-green in color.

Sometimes the elements needed by the plants are present in the soil, but they are not in a form that plants can use. Nitrogen is a good example of this. The air spaces between soil particles contain nitrogen gas (N_2), but it cannot be used by the plants unless bacteria change it into the proper form: ammonium ions (NH_4^+) or nitrate ions (NO_3^-).

Plants remove large amounts of nitrogen from the soil. Since the forms of nitrogen used by plants readily dissolve in water, they are easily leached from the soil. Some forms of nitrogen escape into the air. We are aware of this each time we open a bottle of ammonia or change a baby's diaper.

Just as a lack of nitrogen causes problems, too much nitrogen also causes problems. If too much nitrogen is present the stems of plants grow very tall, but they are not strong. These stems are easily broken by heavy winds or rain. An excess of nitrogen also makes plants more susceptible to fungal diseases and to frost.

Although plants are larger, they do not taste as good if too much nitrogen is present in the soil. Cows do not eat the large clumps of grass that grow on the piles of old manure droppings. During dry weather, high levels of nitrogen (nitrates) can accumulate in plants if too much nitrogen is present in the soil. Cattle eating these plants may develop **nitrate poisoning**.

Phosphorus is necessary for the formation of good root growth as well as flower and seed formation. If the proper amount of phosphorus is not available, plants produce fewer blooms and less fruit. A lack of phosphorus results in slower growth and makes plants more susceptible to disease.

Potassium is also necessary for proper growth and resistance to disease. Potassium forms strong stems, and it is necessary for the development and ripening of fruit.

Nutrient deficiencies are not always easily recognized. Plants develop purple-tinged leaves when they are lacking phosphorus, but plants turn purple when temperatures are cool and purple is a natural color for some plants. A lack of potassium may cause "firing" or browning of the edges of leaves, but the edges of leaves on some plants turn brown if there is not enough humidity.

Plants lacking potassium or phosphorus appear stunted in growth. Ears of corn have rows of kernels that are crooked or incom-

History

A hundred years ago only natural materials such as manure, compost (a mixture of decayed plant materials, leaves, stems and roots), and peat mosses were thought to be capable of fertilizing soils. These natural materials were spread on the soil by farmers.

Then Justis von Liebig, a German scientist, set out to show that any materials which replaced the essential elements would act as a fertilizer and improve plant growth. Using a small plot of land, von Liebig added chemicals containing the essential elements. Thus began the fertilizer revolution. Today chemical fertilizers are used around the world. Food production has risen dramatically wherever fertilizers have been applied.

One hundred bushels (3.5 m³) of corn contain 78 pounds (35 kg) of nitrogen, 16 pounds (7 kg) of phosphorus, and 22 pounds (10 kg) of potassium.

plete when potassium is deficient. A lack of phosphorus prevents the kernels of corn from filling out, and results in "nubbins" instead of well-developed ears of corn.

Potassium and phosphorus are present in some soils, but they are "fixed" in chemical compounds that are not soluble in water. Other forms of potassium readily dissolve in water and are quickly leached from the soil. In both instances the minerals are not available to plants and nutrient deficiencies may occur.

The chemical compounds in the soil are affected by the **pH** of the soil. If the soil has the proper pH, chemicals are in forms that can be absorbed and used by the plants. If the pH of the soil is too high or too low, the nutrients are locked in compounds that plants cannot use.

Soil Testing

Farmers and gardeners must make sure that the soil has the proper amount of each nutrient available for the plants. The nutritional quality of vegetables, fruits, and grains is determined by the nutrients present in the soil. The yield-per-acre is increased if the proper nutrients are present in the soil.

You can tell something about the physical structure of the soil by looking at it and feeling it, but how can you tell if there are enough nutrients for the crop that is being planted? To find out the level of nutrients in the soil, a soil sample is taken and chemical tests are made. There are several ways to do this:

- Send a soil sample to the laboratory at your local university's College of Agriculture. The instructions and kits for mailing the sample are available from the university's Cooperative Extension Office in your county. Check the telephone book.
- Send a soil sample to a private laboratory.
- Buy a soil testing kit from a local garden supply and test your own soil.

The first two methods provide the most accurate and detailed information. Private laboratories are more expensive than universities. The cheapest and quickest method is a soil test kit but it will not be as accurate, and it will not provide as much information.

A Choice of Fertilizers

Once the test results are known, the farmer or gardener must decide which fertilizers to use. The term fertilizer refers to any substance, natural or manufactured, that is added to the soil in order to supply one or more plant nutrients.

Synthetic fertilizers are human-made products. Their production involves chemically changing the nutrients so that they are readily available for the plants.

Organic fertilizers are natural products made from dead organisms or their waste products. Their production may involve physical changes such as grinding, but any chemical changes are through natural processes. Bone meal is considered an "organic" fertilizer because it is natural bone that is simply ground into a powder.

Organic fertilizers are not always organic chemicals. Rock phosphate is considered to be an "organic" fertilizer because it is a natural rock. It is crushed into a powder, but it has not been chemically changed.

Superphosphate is classified as a synthetic fertilizer because the rock phosphate has been treated with a chemical (sulfuric acid) to make the phosphate more readily available to plants.

Scientists discovered how to change nitrogen gas into chemical compounds that plants can use. In the late 1930s they manufactured the first synthetic fertilizers. Natural gas is needed to make the fertilizer, and large amounts of other fossil fuels are used to supply the energy needed for the chemical reactions. In the 1930s the low price of fossil fuels allowed manufacturers to produce and sell synthetic fertilizers at a relatively low cost.

The nitrogen removed when protein is broken down in the liver becomes a part of a compound called urea. The **urea** and other waste products are filtered out of the blood by the kidneys. When straw used as animal bedding is dug into the soil, it is an important source of fertilizer. The compound urea is also synthesized from atmospheric nitrogen and natural gas. Urea is an organic chemical, but whether it is a synthetic fertilizer or an "organic" fertilizer depends upon its source.

Farmers found that they could dramatically increase the yield-per-acre by using synthetic fertilizers on the "worn out" soil. The increased use of synthetic fertilizers, along with other technological advances such as better seeds and pest control, improved both the yield and the quality of the crops.

An Unlimited Supply?

A constant supply of nitrogen is insured by the action of the nitrogen cycle. But the availability and cost of synthetic nitrogen fertilizers are directly dependent upon the supply of natural gas and crude oil. Fossil fuels are not renewable resources, so the supply of natural gas and crude oil will one day be exhausted. Long before these supplies run out, a shortage of synthetic nitrogen fertilizers may occur because of political actions. Oil imports were limited by the Arab oil embargo during the 1970s.

Phosphorus, potassium, and all of the secondary nutrients are minerals that are found in rocks. Rocks that contain calcium, magnesium, sulfur, and potassium are common, but few rocks contain phosphorus.

Plants we grow for food crops require more phosphorus than the grasses or trees that originally grew in the soils. The soil needs applications of phosphate fertilizers to produce food crops. Ninety-seven

SCIENCE TECHNOLOGY & SOCIETY
BIOTECHNOLOGY

Water Hyacinth

Water hyacinths obtain their nutrients through their roots which hang directly in the water allowing a maximum and continuous contact with the nutrients or other materials dissolved in the water. The principal plant nutrients are phosphorus, nitrogen, and potassium. These are also the major components of commercial fertilizers present in waterways due to agriculture runoff as well as sewage and industrial effluent. Water hyacinths will absorb these and other chemicals.

Sewage Water Treatment with Water Hyacinth

Water hyacinths absorb and digest nutrients and minerals from sewage water. The protein-rich hyacinths must be harvested at intervals, but can be dried and used as fertilizer, animal feed, or as a source of energy.

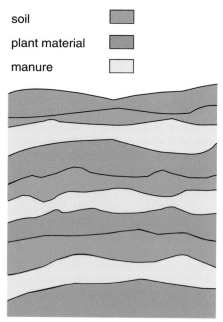

soil

plant material

manure

Compost

percent of the rock phosphate is located in the United States and Russia. Early in the next century all of the known deposits of rock phosphate will have been mined, and the phosphate will have been scattered over farmland or used for other purposes.

The phosphorus is either removed from the soil by the plants or is carried away by erosion. The phosphorus in the body is not recycled, since it is either absorbed by our bones or carried through out digestive systems to become human waste that is sent to sewage treatment plants. Humans also lose the phosphorus that is in uneaten plant parts that pass through to garbage disposals.

Some of the phosphorus is carried into streams with the treated wastewater. Here it joins the phosphorus carried away by erosion, and the journey continues to the ocean. It will take millions of years before the phosphate being deposited in the ocean will accumulate into new rock deposits that could once again be mined.

The loss of potassium by the same pathway is not as critical because there are more rocks with potassium. A potassium shortage will not occur for five generations.

The Organic Way

The organic method of farming and gardening tries to duplicate the continuous recycling of nutrients that occurs in a forest ecosystem. Although the organic method does not eliminate all loss of phosphorus and potassium, it decreases the loss. For example, organic gardeners recycle plant material instead of "feeding" it to the garbage disposal.

Organic materials must be broken down by bacteria before they can be used by plants. The bacteria "rob" the soil of nitrogen during the time it takes to break down the organic matter. Organic gardeners speed up the process of decay by making compost piles. The pile is made with alternating layers of soil, manure, and plant material. It is kept moist and turned frequently to provide air. The resulting compost is a mixture of soil and decomposed organic materials (humus).

Organic matter feeds the organisms in the soil and provides nutrients for the plants. The fungi in the soil help the plant roots to absorb nutrients. When farmers depend entirely on synthetic fertilizer, the level of organic matter in the soil decreases and the fungi disappear. Without the help of the fungi, larger amounts of fertilizer are needed so that plants can get the same amount of nutrients.

The organic matter also helps maintain good soil structure. The humus increases the water-holding capacity of the soil. This decreases erosion and leaching. The humus particles also increase the ability of the soil to hold nutrients until they are needed by the plants.

More than two billion tons of animal feces, slaughterhouse waste, and other organic waste products are produced each year. Putting the material in a land fill takes up valuable space and removes nutrients from their natural cycle. Some of this material is already used as fertilizer. Dried blood and bone meal are two examples.

Some farmers use treated sludge (organic wastes from sewage treatment plants) as a soil conditioner and a source of nutrients. Sewage sludge from Chicago, Illinois, is shipped to the coal mines in southern Illinois. It is plowed into the poor soil that remained after the coal was removed by strip-mining, and grass is planted. New topsoil is being created by the addition of organic matter to the eroding subsoil.

New Jersey no longer allows sewage sludge to be dumped in landfills. The sludge must be tested for heavy metals and treated to prevent harmful bacteria from entering the soil. The crops grown on the land cannot be used directly for human consumption. The amount of sludge applied is determined by the amount of nitrogen required by the crop that will be grown on the land. This prevents water pollution from excess nitrogen.

Green manure crops are grown for the purpose of adding organic matter to the soil. If clover is used, the level of nitrogen in the soil is also increased. Rye is a grass that is often sown in the fall for a winter cover crop. The clover or rye is plowed under or killed with herbicides when another crop is planted in spring. By planting rye or clover, the farmer also decreases erosion.

Which Is Better — Organic or Synthetic?

Both forms of fertilizer provide nutrients for plant growth. The plant cannot tell the difference between natural and synthetic sources. Both types of fertilizer have advantages and disadvantages.

Advantages of Organic Fertilizers

- Most organic fertilizers are not as concentrated and will not harm the plants. There are some exceptions such as fresh poultry manure and dried blood.
- Organic materials are available for a longer period of time and are less likely to be lost from the soil.
- Many organic fertilizers add humus to the soil.

Disadvantages of Organic Fertilizers

- If you must buy organic fertilizer they are more expensive than synthetic fertilizers.
- Nutrient levels of N, P, K in most organic materials are usually low, and large amounts of material are required to provide proper plant nutrients.
- The nutrient levels will vary with the materials used.
- Organic materials must be composted before their nutrients are available to the plants.

WHAT DO YOU THINK?

In January, 1994, stringent limits were set on commercial fishing off the New England coast to prevent the total collapse of fisheries. The 50% reduction in commercial fish takes will be cushioned by $2.5 million in aid to affected fishermen and communities. Though the restrictions will hurt the fisheries, there is unanimous agreement that they are necessary to prevent a total collapse of fish species such as cod, flounder, and haddock — species all on the verge of collapse due to overfishing. To further protect fish populations, the original 800 square mile region set aside for spawning haddock will be increased to 2,600 square miles. As one fisheries expert put it, "If we don't act now, the resource will be totally lost." Do you think this policy is justified and fair to all concerned?

Advantages of Synthetic Fertilizers

- Synthetic fertilizers are more economical than organic (if you must purchase the fertilizer).
- The nutrients are concentrated and only small amounts of fertilizer are needed.
- The concentration of nutrients can be easily determined by reading the label and must meet industry standards.
- The nutrients are quickly available; plants do not have to wait.

Disadvantages of Synthetic Fertilizers

- If too much fertilizer is used, or it is placed too close to the plant, the concentrated chemicals will harm the plant.
- Since very small amounts are needed, people often apply too much.
- Since the nutrients are very soluble in water, they are easily leached from the area of the plant roots.
- They do not increase the humus content of the soil.

6.1 QUESTIONS FOR STUDY AND DISCUSSION

1. Define the following words:
compost	nutrients
fertile soils	organic fertilizers
fertilizer	primary nutrients
green manure crops	secondary nutrients
micronutrients	synthetic fertilizer
2. How did people know which soils were good?
3. What materials were first added to the soil to make plants grow better?
4. How did scientists prove that plants need certain chemicals to grow?
5. Give three ways that plant nutrients are lost from the soil.
6. What is another name for soil that is "worn out"?

Essential Nutrients

7. Name three chemical elements plants must obtain from the soil. Plants need three other chemical elements. Name them. (Hint: remember photosynthesis.)
8. List the three primary nutrients.
9. List the three secondary nutrients.
10. Iron is called a micronutrient. What does this mean? List the six other micronutrients needed by plants.

The Primary Nutrients

11. Which primary nutrient is frequently a limiting factor for plants? How do plants appear when they lack this nutrient?
12. Identify the two forms of nitrogen used by plants. How is the nitrogen in the soil changed into these forms?
13. If these forms of nitrogen are not absorbed by plants these are easily lost. What happens to them?
14. What happens if too much nitrogen is available to a plant?
15. Why do plants need phosphorus? Why do they need potassium?
16. What is a sign that plants are lacking phosphorus? What is a sign that plants are lacking potassium? Why are nutrient deficiencies difficult to diagnose?

17. In one field a farmer finds many ears of corn with crooked or incomplete rows of kernels. In another field she finds many very small cobs of corn that are not filled out with plump kernels. What nutrient may be lacking in the first field? in the second field?
18. How does the pH level in soil affect the ability of the plant to use the nutrients in the soil?

Soil Testing

19. Give two reasons why farmers, gardeners, and orchard owners are concerned about the nutrient levels in their soil.
20. Give three places where you can obtain a soil test.
   Which test(s) will be the most accurate?
   Which test is the most expensive?
   Which test is the quickest?
   Which test will provide the least information?

A Choice of Fertilizers

21. Since all of the chemical elements in fertilizers are found in the environment, why do humans make fertilizers?
22. What kind of human-made changes are allowed in fertilizers classified as organic or natural?
23. Why isn't superphosphate classified as a natural fertilizer?
24. Some urea in fertilizer is synthetic while other urea is organic. Explain the difference.
25. Explain the role of fossil fuels in making fertilizers.
26. Identify the three technological advances that improved the quality and the yields of farmer's crops.

An Unlimited Supply?

27. What is the limiting factor for the supply of nitrogen fertilizers? What caused the shortage of nitrogen fertilizers in the 1970s?
28. Identify the primary nutrient that is most limited in supply.
29. What happens to the phosphorus and potassium lost from the soil?
30. Explain why nitrogen is not as readily lost from the nutrient cycle.

The Organic Way

31. How do organic farmers and gardeners reduce the loss of phosphorus and potassium?
32. Why do organic gardeners make compost piles?
33. Describe a compost pile. How would a gardener take care of a compost pile?
34. After a few years of organic gardening less fertilizer is needed. After a few years of synthetic gardening more fertilizer is needed. Explain the difference.
35. Explain why an organic gardener would have less need to irrigate the garden.
   Explain why an organic gardener would not need to fertilize as often.
36. Give three examples of natural fertilizers made from waste.
37. How is sludge from the city of Chicago being used?
38. What regulations are required when sewage is applied to farmland?
39. What is the purpose of growing a green manure crop? What two crops are frequently grown as green manure crops? Which of these crops also increases the level of nitrogen in the soil?

Which is Better?

Copy the items below and indicate the description that applies to organic fertilizers, with an O.
Indicate the description that applies to synthetic fertilizers with an S.
Indicate the description that applies to both organic and synthetic with a SO.
40. provide nutrients for plant growth
41. contain more concentrated chemicals
42. are available for a longer period of time
43. nutrient levels are standard and can be easily determined
44. are more expensive if purchased
45. nutrient levels are low
46. plant may have to wait for nutrients
47. people often use too much
48. increases the humus content of the soil
49. nutrients are more easily leached away

Pests and Pesticides — They Both Cause Problems

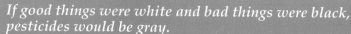

If good things were white and bad things were black, pesticides would be gray.

Mosquito

Pest, a word that comes from the Latin word for plague, refers to any troublesome, destructive or annoying organism. Insects and other pests have bothered humans for generations. Some insects carry disease and others compete with humans for food.

The bacterium that causes bubonic plague is carried from rats to humans by fleas. A graph of the human population reflects the fact that more than one-fourth of the population of Europe died of the plague in the 14th century. Mosquitoes are not just another annoying pest. They carry malaria and yellow fever. These two diseases have killed more people than all the wars throughout history.

Large quantities of food are destroyed each year by insect pests. In the 1840s more than half a million people starved when a fungus struck the Irish potato crop. Millions of people avoided starvation by emigrating to other countries. So many people died on ships leaving Ireland that they were called coffin ships.

One of the worst insect pests is the grasshopper. Since the beginning of history, plagues of grasshoppers have been attacking the crops which humans grow for food. Grasshoppers were an enemy the settlers faced as they moved West.

The year 1874 was known as The Year of the Grasshopper. Grasshoppers ate almost everything except the native grass. Great swarms of grasshoppers moved across the Great Plains destroying crops and stopping trains. The bodies of the dead grasshoppers made the rails so slick that the engine couldn't pull the train. Farmers began to expect a plague of grasshoppers about every ten years. Grasshoppers are still serious pests.

According to the Agricultural Research Service, grasshoppers do $400 million worth of damage each year. When the density of grasshoppers is eight per square yard (0.8 m²), the grasshoppers damage the plants eaten by livestock and game animals. In 1985, a state of emergency was declared in 14 western states. Idaho farmers fought a two-mile-wide (3.2 km) band of grasshoppers. In some places the population density was 1800 grasshoppers per square yard (0.8 m²)

The land appeared as if massive lawn mowers had cut the plants off where they came out of the ground.

Cotton plants are not only a source of fibers for clothing, but also a source of oil for shortening and meal for livestock feed. The boll weevil entered the United States from Mexico in the 1890s. The quarter-inch (0.6 cm) weevil drills into the cotton bolls and lay its eggs. The boll of cotton provides a home and a source of food for the larvae.

In the early 1900s the boll weevil was such a destructive pest in Coffee County, Alabama, that farmers tried to raise peanuts instead of cotton. The peanut crop was so successful that a fountain was built and dedicated to the boll weevil. Had it not been for the boll weevil, peanuts might never have become the major cash crop in Coffee County.

The boll weevil is not the only enemy of the cotton plant. Farmers that continue to plant cotton must battle aphids, army worms, bollworms, pink bollworms, leaf worms, cutworms, webworms, tobacco budworms, ground beetles, grasshoppers, cabbage loppers, leaf rollers, leaf perforators, leafhoppers, fleahoppers, nematodes, salt-marsh caterpillars, spider mites, stink bugs, tarnished plant bugs, Lygus bugs, thrips, and whiteflies. It is little wonder that cotton growers became dependent upon pesticides.

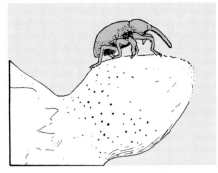

Boll Weevil on Cotton Plant

Miracle Chemicals

People tried magic and banging drums, but they did little to scare off the swarms of insects. Then humans discovered chemicals that kill — **avicides** (bird killers), **insecticides** (insect killers), **fungicides** (fungus killers), **nematicide** (nematode killers), and **herbicides** (weed killers). Collectively these chemicals are called **pesticides**.

The first pesticides came from naturally occurring minerals. These included arsenic, copper, lead, mercury, sulfur, and zinc. During the 1800s, arsenic compounds were used to control the potato beetle. The **Bordeaux mixture**, a mixture of calcium hydroxide and copper sulfate, is still sometimes used as a fungicide. Wine makers still use sulfur compounds to kill bacteria and wild yeast on fruit they use for making wine.

Other early pesticides were naturally occurring chemicals that were produced by plants. **Pyrethrum** came from the dried flowers of chrysanthemums, **nicotine sulfate** from tobacco plants, and **rotenone** from legumes that grow in the Indian subcontinent. These natural chemicals proved to be expensive, and they were not highly effective in controlling certain types of insects.

The fact that human-made chemicals could be used to kill insects was discovered during World War II. Insects were used to test chemicals (nerve gases) which were being developed for chemical warfare. Two groups of chemicals tested were chlorinated hydrocarbons and organic phosphates. Important insecticides were developed from both types of chemicals.

The boll of cotton has escaped damage from the boll weevil. No doubt pesticides provided the needed protection.

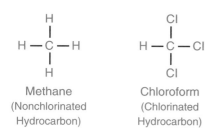

Methane
(Nonchlorinated
Hydrocarbon)

Chloroform
(Chlorinated
Hydrocarbon)

The chlorinated hydrocarbons became the most important group of insecticides. They were successful because they were cheap and easy to use, they killed many different kinds of insects, they continued to kill insects long after they were applied, they weren't washed away by the rain, and they were not toxic to humans. The first chlorinated hydrocarbon was the chemical dichloro-diphenyl-trichloro-ethane, more commonly known as **DDT**.

To understand chlorinated hydrocarbons we must look at some chemical formulas:

A carbon atom with four hydrogen atoms attached is a hydrocarbon molecule called methane. It is the major chemical in natural gas. When hydrogen atoms are removed and chlorine atoms are added, new compounds called **chlorinated hydrocarbons** are formed. A simple example is chloroform — an anesthetic.

Chemists built larger, more complex chlorinated hydrocarbons. All of these molecules are made of carbon, hydrogen, and chlorine atoms. By changing the number and arrangement of atoms, chemists made different insecticides.

Chemists found that by using other atoms such as phosphorus, and sometimes nitrogen or sulfur, instead of chlorine, they could make other types of pesticides. Today chemical companies produce more than 35,000 different products to control insects, weeds, fungi, nematodes, and other pests. Although ninety percent of Americans use pesticides around their house and yard, most of these chemicals are used by farmers.

Some of the common insecticides are listed below. It is important to note that today we use more herbicides than insecticides.

Class of Insecticide	Name
Organochlorides (chlorinated hydrocarbons)	Aldrin • Chlordane • DDD • DDT • Dieldrin • Endrin • Heptachlor • Lindane • Toxaphene
Organophosphates	Diazinon • Malathion • Parathion
Carbamates	Sevin® (carbaryl) • Maneb
Naturally occurring (organic pesticides)	Nicotine Sulfate • Pyrethrum • Rotenone

Not All Are Pests

It is important to remember that all insects, rodents, worms, and fungi are not pests. In fact most are helpful. Of the 82,500 insects that exist in North America, about 10,000 are considered by humans to be pests. This means that only one out of eight insects is a pest. Several of the remaining seven insects are beneficial to humans.

Many worms and fungi are found in "healthy" soil and are important for the process of decay. Penicillin, streptomycin, and other antibiotics come from fungi in the soil. Certain molds are responsible for the different flavors of cheeses. Some fungi are necessary for the production of certain foods. Yeast is used in the making of wine, beer, and bread.

One-third of our diet consists of crops that are pollinated by honeybees. The major food in the diet of dairy cattle is alfalfa. The flower structure of some plants, like alfalfa, prevents pollination by wind or other insects. These crops have become dependent upon pollination by honeybees.

Before adding chemicals to the environment, it is important to study their effects upon organisms in the soil, insects, birds, fish, and mammals. If this is not done, we may wipe out organisms that are helpful to humans when we only intended to kill an organism we considered a pest.

Monoculture — An Invitation to a Picnic

At a picnic you might hear someone say, "Who invited the ants?" It seems ants have an excellent ability to find food, and there is always plenty of food at a picnic. Farmers and gardeners grow plants that seem to create a picnic for ants and other insects. Because of this we call the insects pests.

Growing one crop over a large area provides an abundant food supply for the insects. When there is more food available, more insects survive and reproduce. Scientists have estimated that in some corn fields there have been more than 60,000 European corn borers per acre (0.4 hectare).

Humans also create monocultures on golf courses and lawns. Golf courses are treated with large amounts of chemicals to control sod webworm and other pests that feed on turfgrass. Well-manicured lawns that support only one kind of grass must also be heavily treated with chemicals to control pests.

The farmer who spends long hours in the field and does not have time to pay much attention to the lawn is less likely to have problems with pests or diseases. A closer look at the lawn will probably show that, unlike the corn field, it is not a monoculture. It has many different types of grasses, and probably some broad-leaf weeds.

Problems Caused by Pesticides

When synthetic pesticides first appeared, doctors had visions of eradicating diseases spread by pests and farmers imagined a day when no pests would harm their crops. Unfortunately, these visions were only pipedreams.

At first it was easy to see the significant benefits of synthetic pesticides. DDT saved many lives that would have been lost because of diseases carried by pests. The quantity and quality of food were dramatically improved by the use of pesticides. Without the use of pesticides, an estimated 30-35 percent of a crop is lost before harvest. Another 10-15 percent is lost while the food is in storage.

In this picture agricultural pesticides are being applied by truck.

In 1962 the book *Silent Spring* was published. Rachel Carson wrote the book so that the public would be aware of the problems associated with the use of pesticides. The book caused quite an uproar. The publication of *Silent Spring* stimulated an evaluation of the risks of using pesticides. Today we are much more aware of some of the problems caused by pesticides. One of problem is the creation of superbugs.

Superbugs: People expected the pesticides to eliminate all pests. That didn't happen. Even before it was approved for public use in 1947, some houseflies were surviving when sprayed with DDT. Why were some flies surviving when others died? Changes occur in the DNA of some flies that enable them to produce enzymes that detoxify or make the pesticide harmless. These genetic changes make the insect **resistant** — immune to the pesticide.

1. When insects are sprayed, a few of the insects become resistant to the pesticide.
2. The resistant insects may mate with other resistant insects that survived the spray, or they may mate with insects that arrive from areas that have not been sprayed.
3. The new generation of insects will have many more resistant insects. Unaffected by the spray, they breed and produce offspring.
4. More of the insects in the next generation are resistant to the pesticide. When a new spray is used, the process begins again.

Each time a pesticide is used, more insects become resistant to it. These resistant insects breed and produce offspring that are resistant to the pesticide. The life cycle of an insect is short, and they reproduce quickly. During one season there may be as many as six generations of boll weevils in the cotton fields of the southern United States. Most pests develop resistance to a chemical within five years, but sometimes it takes only one season.

Today more than 400 species of insects and mites are resistant to pesticides. This number has doubled since 1965. Ten species of insects are resistant to every group of insecticides known. As the use of herbicides increases, resistance is becoming a serious problem in weeds. Scientists have identified more than twenty weeds that have developed resistance to one class of herbicides.

Persistent Pesticides: Plastic is persistent; paper is not. If we bury plastic, we can come back years later and dig it up. It will be very much the same as it was when we buried it. If we bury paper, organisms in the soil will break it down, and later when we dig, we will find nothing that looks like paper.

Chemicals that can be broken down by organisms in the environment are **biodegradable**. Like paper, some pesticides are biodegradable. Other pesticides are not easily broken down by organisms in the environment. Like plastic, these pesticides are found in the soil many years after they were used. We say these pesticides are **persistent pesticides**.

Some pesticides are more easily broken down than others. Some are broken down in a few days. Others are broken down more slowly and remain in the soil for a few weeks or months. The more persistent a pesticide is, the longer it will remain in the environment.

Class of Pesticides	BIODEGRADABLE to PERSISTENT
Time to break down	days → weeks → months → years

The pesticides classified as chlorinated hydrocarbons are extremely persistent. They remain in the environment for many years after they are used. DDT was the pesticide most frequently found in a 1984 survey of fruits and vegetables grown in California. The use of DDT was banned in the United States twelve years before the survey.

DDT evaporates from the fields where it is sprayed and is carried by wind and water. Some of the pesticide hitchhikes on dust particles until it is brought down by the rain or snow. DDT has been spread by the winds and deposited throughout the world by rain and snow. It has been discovered in birds, seals, and fish in Antarctica. Like other animals, humans carry DDT and other chlorinated hydrocarbons in their body fat.

Chemicals Found in Human Body Fat		
Compound	Use of Chemical	Mean Amount (micrograms/kilogram)
PCB	electrical insulator	907
DDE	breakdown product of DDT	2095
DDT	insecticide	439
Dieldrin	insecticide	69
Heptachlor epoxide	insecticide	43
Hexachlorobenzene	fungicide	62

At first it had seemed that persistence was good because farmers would not need to reapply the pesticides so often. This would save them both time and money. Then we began to learn of another problem — bioaccumulation.

Bioaccumulation: Only very small amounts of the pesticides that are chlorinated hydrocarbons dissolve in water, but they easily dissolve in fat. This was first thought to be a major advantage because the pesticides would not be easily washed away by rain.

When pesticides like DDT are carried into lakes and streams, much of the chemical is deposited in the soil at the bottom of the water or absorbed by organisms living in the water. Cell membranes are made out of protein and fat. The chlorinated hydrocarbons are easily absorbed through the cell membranes of the aquatic organisms.

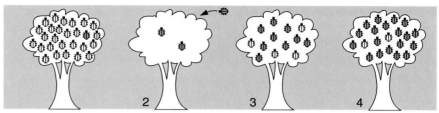

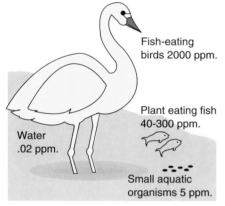

Insect Resistant to Pesticide
Insect Not Resistant to Pesticide

1. When insects are sprayed, a few of the insects become resistant to the pesticide.
2. The resistant insects may mate with other resistant insects that survived the spray, or they may mate with insects which arrive from areas that have not been sprayed.
3. The new generation of insects will have many more resistant insects. Unaffected by the spray, they breed and reproduce.

Fish-eating birds 2000 ppm.

Plant eating fish 40-300 ppm.

Water .02 ppm.

Small aquatic organisms 5 ppm.

Example of Bioaccumulation

Few organisms have the enzymes needed to break down pesticides. Since the chemicals dissolve in fat more easily than water, they are stored in the body fat rather than being excreted with wastes through the kidneys. The pesticides accumulate in the organism's body tissues. As the pesticide moves up the food chain, it becomes more and more concentrated. This is called bioaccumulation.

In 1957 a study at California's Clear Lake showed that the water contained DDD, a pesticide similar to DDT. Examination of the organisms revealed the amounts of pesticide shown in the following diagram. The small aquatic organisms absorb DDD and stored it in their body fat. The fish convert 10 grams of small aquatic organisms into 1 gram of fish. Since the fish could not break down the DDD, all of the pesticide from the 10 grams of food was stored in the 1 gram of mass the fish gained.

The populations of some species of fish-eating birds, such as ospreys and eagles, began to decline. One colony of ospreys in Connecticut declined from 200 breeding pairs in 1938 to 12 pairs in 1965. Scientists frequently found broken eggs and eggs that did not hatch. The egg yolks in the unhatched eggs contained high levels of DDT. The fat in the egg yolk provides energy for the developing bird. Evidently the DDT interfered with the normal development of the egg. High levels of DDT had also been found in fish eggs that did not develop normally.

Scientists obtained eggs that had been laid before DDT was used as a pesticide from collections in museums. When they compared these eggshells to the broken eggshells collected from the nests, scientists found that the broken eggshells were much thinner. Apparently DDT was preventing the deposit of calcium in the eggshell.

Since most uses of DDT were banned in 1972, the level of DDT in the water has declined and the populations of fish-eating birds are once again on the rise. During the 1970s bald eagles were seen in only 39 states. Today they can be found in every state except Hawaii, and their populations have increased significantly.

Other food chains were also affected by DDT. Elm trees were sprayed with DDT to control Dutch elm disease. DDT was used to kill the elm bark beetle that spreads the Dutch elm fungus disease. Scientists hoped that this would stop the spread of the disease.

Since DDT is not easily dissolved in water, rains did not wash it away. As the leaves fell and decayed, the DDT accumulated in the layers of organic matter under the trees. When earthworms fed on the decaying matter, they absorbed and accumulated DDT. Robins returned in the spring and began feeding on the worms. Birds that fed in areas that had been sprayed soon died of insecticide poisoning. In areas that had not been sprayed, the robins were not affected.

Pesticides Create Pests: There are two approaches to killing pests — the rifle approach and the shot gun approach. Imagine yourself as a tiny hunter. Armed with a tiny rifle, you climb aboard your tiny airplane and take off for the nearby potato field. As your copilot flies around the plants you take careful aim and fire. One after another, the striped potato beetles fall from the plants. Selective pesticides are like this hunter. **Selective pesticides** kill only one type of organism. Other types of organisms are unaffected by the pesticide.

Many pesticides are not selective. They do not search out and destroy just one kind of pest. They are like the tiny hunter with a shotgun. Some pellets hit the potato beetle while others hit ladybird beetles, or other beneficial insects. **Broad-spectrum** pesticides kill many different kinds of pests. It is easy to see the advantage of using just one kind of pesticide to get rid of several kinds of pests that are attacking a cotton crop, but there is also a disadvantage. While broad-spectrum insecticides kill many different pests, they also kill beneficial insects.

Pesticides sometimes make a major pest out of a minor one by eliminating its predators. This was the case with the bollworm. The boll weevil was a major pest in cotton fields. As farmers attempted to destroy the boll weevil, they also destroyed the natural predators of the bollworm. Without predators, the bollworm became a major pest. By studying the graph on the next page, we can better understand how this can happen.

1. Insect pests have predators that keep the population in balance. As the pest population increases, the population of predator insects also rises.
2. The rise in the population of predators occurs more slowly because the predator population depends upon the pests for food.
3. When the food supply of the pest (the plants) becomes limited, the pest population begins to decline. Fewer pests mean less food for the predator insects, and the predator population declines.

Robins
Earthworms
Leaves

Bioaccumulation of DDT in the Food Chain

This rise and fall of insect populations continues to occur until it is upset.

4. Such an upset occurs when a broad-spectrum insecticide is used. The populations of both kinds of insects experience a drastic decline when the pesticide is used. The surviving pests find themselves in a world with few natural enemies. The pests multiply quickly, and a pest population explosion occurs.

Pest-Predator Populations ▶

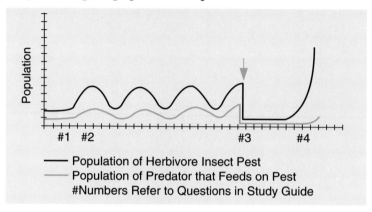

Population of Herbivore Insect Pest
Population of Predator that Feeds on Pest
#Numbers Refer to Questions in Study Guide

7.1 QUESTIONS FOR STUDY AND DISCUSSION

1. Define the following words:
   Bioaccumulation
   Biodegradable
   Bordeaux mixture
   Broad-spectrum pesticide
   Chlorinated hydrocarbon
   DDT
   Nicotine sulfate
   Persistent pesticide
   Pest
   Pesticide
   Pyrethrum
   Resistant
   Rotenone
   Selective pesticide

2. Give two reasons why some insects are classified as pests.
3. Identify the two pests that must be eliminated in order to decrease the spread of bubonic plague.
4. Identify the two diseases spread by the mosquito.
5. Identify the following pests that:
   A. destroyed the potato crop in Ireland in the 1840s.
   B. was probably the worst insect pest of the early settlers in the western US.
   C. entered the US from Mexico in the 1890s.
   D. was responsible for the destruction of rangeland and grassland in the western US in 1985.
   E. destroyed the cotton crop in Coffee County, Alabama, in the early 1900s.
6. List five different insects that damage cotton plants.

Miracle Chemicals
7. In what ways are nematicides, insecticides, and fungicides alike? What is an herbicide?
8. What was the source of the first pesticides?
9. What type of pesticide is the Bordeaux mixture?
10. Identify the natural pesticide that comes from these plants:
    A. chrysanthemums
    B. legumes growing in the Indian subcontinent
    C. tobacco plants
11. Give two disadvantages of the natural pesticides.
12. When were synthetic insecticides first used?
13. Identify the two types of insecticides that were developed from nerve gases.

14. Give six reasons why the chlorinated hydrocarbons were such successful pesticides.
15. How do scientists make chlorinated hydrocarbons?
16. What percent of Americans use pesticides? Which people use the largest amounts of pesticides?

Not All Are Pests

17. Are most insects pests? What percent of insects are pests?
18. Give three ways in which some fungi are helpful to man.
19. A decrease in honeybees might mean a decrease in milk production. Explain.

Monoculture

20. What is monoculture?
21. How does the practice of monoculture increase the population of insects?
22. Why are some lawns and golf courses often attacked by pests and disease?

Problems Caused by Pesticides

23. How was DDT helpful to man?
24. Without the aid of pesticides, how much of a farmer's crop might be lost before it reaches the consumer?
25. Why was *Silent Spring* such an important book?
26. What changes occur in some insects that enable them to survive when sprayed with a pesticide?
27. Increasing the number of times the spray is used during a season will only make the situation worse. Explain.
28. Explain why insects develop resistance to pesticides more quickly than other pests such as "weeds"?
29. How will the number of pest resistant species change in the next 20 years?
30. A pesticide that is not persistent is _____.
31. Chlorinated hydrocarbons are (biodegradable/persistent).
32. Why do we find DDT and other pesticides in places in the world where they were never used?
33. Is it likely that we will find biodegradable insecticides in Antarctica? Explain.

34. The organophosphates and the carbamates are biodegradable. Would you expect to find these pesticides in your bloodstream?
35. Why did people first think that it was good that DDT was persistent?
    Why did people first think that it was good that DDT did not easily dissolve in water?
36. What characteristic of DDT and other insecticides makes them so easily stored in the body?
37. Since DDT is not easily dissolved in water, what happens to it when it is carried into a lake with runoff during a storm?
38. Give two ways that DDT decreased the population of some fish-eating birds.
39. How were robins affected by DDT?
40. Why do people, robins, and fish-eating birds have more pesticide stored in their bodies than other organisms such as crabs and earthworms?
41. Explain how a selective pesticide works.
42. What do we call pesticides that are not selective?
43. In a natural environment what are the two limiting factors which limit the number of pests?
44. Refer to the * beside each number on the graph of Predator-Pest Populations for the following questions.
    *1. What is happening to the pest population?
    *2. Is the predator population changing? If not, give a reason why not.
    *3. What is happening to both the pest and predator populations? What caused this change?
    *4. Which population is increasing?
45. Why does the use of a broad-spectrum pesticide lead to an increased pest population?

Review Questions

46. Explain the statement, "If good things were white and bad things were black, pesticides would be gray."
47. Explain why farmers in the Great Plains began to expect a plague of grasshoppers about every ten years.
48. Why is it important to study the effects of pesticides upon organisms in the environment other than "pests"?

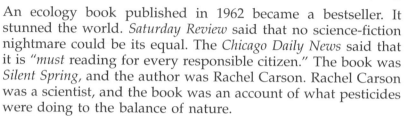

"By their very nature, chemical controls are self-defeating, for they have been devised and applied without taking into account the complex biological systems against which they have been blindly hurled."

Rachel Carson
in *Silent Spring*

An ecology book published in 1962 became a bestseller. It stunned the world. *Saturday Review* said that no science-fiction nightmare could be its equal. The *Chicago Daily News* said that it is *"must* reading for every responsible citizen." The book was *Silent Spring*, and the author was Rachel Carson. Rachel Carson was a scientist, and the book was an account of what pesticides were doing to the balance of nature.

Rachel Carson had been editor-in-chief of the US Fish and Wildlife Service's publications. As she read about the accomplishments of DDT, she became concerned about the possible long-term effects the pesticide might have on organisms in the environment. In the 1950s research indicated that pesticides were causing problems, but most of the public was not yet aware of this information.

Rachel Carson felt the public should know, and she set out to write a book about the use of pesticides. Her goals were to inform the public and to get the attention of government officials. It took her five years to research and write *Silent Spring*

Ms. Carson was known as a responsible scientist, and the list of references that supported her statements filled 30 pages. When one chemical company asked the publisher to reconsider its plans to publish the book, the publisher hired an independent scientist to check the facts. The facts were confirmed, and the book was published.

Any discussion of pesticides prior to the publication of *Silent Spring* had been based on economics. Greater use of pesticides allowed farmers to grow bigger and better crops. Pesticides were cheap and easy to use, and they increased the profits for the farmer. Chemical companies and the Department of Agriculture promoted pesticides with the claim that "Unrestricted use of pesticides is necessary to grow the food to feed and the fibers to clothe the world's millions of people."

The problems caused by the unrestricted use of pesticides was a very controversial subject. Rachel Carson was the first person to approach the issue from an ecological point of view.

Rachel Carson

Some scientists supported Ms. Carson; others referred to her as "an emotional woman from the garden club." Rachel Carson was not just "an emotional woman." She was a professional who had done her homework and knew her subject.

Her book survived the controversy and became the stimulus for amendments to the Federal Insecticide, Fungicide, and Rodenticide Act — the law that regulates pesticide use. Before her death in 1964, Rachel Carson offered these recommendations about pesticides to a senate subcommittee:

- that all community, state, and federal spraying programs be legally required to give adequate advance notice to citizens who will be affected.
- that citizens who are inconvenienced or damaged by their neighbor's spraying be able to "seek appropriate redress."
- that new programs in medical research and education of the medical profession be supported.
- that registration of chemicals be determined by all agencies concerned rather than only the Department of Agriculture.
- that new pesticides be approved only when there is no chemical already available or no other method that will work.
- that the government give full support to research on new methods of pest control which will reduce or eliminate the need for chemicals.

Rachel Carson did not campaign against the use of all chemical pesticides, nor did she feel that all environmental problems are due to the misuse of pesticides. If she had been one of the authors of the Bill of Rights, she would have included "the right of every person to be free from poisons distributed by private or public individuals." She felt that this right had been left out only because our predecessors could not foresee the problems that would accompany pesticides (and other toxic chemicals).

Perhaps no other person has influenced environmental policies as much as Rachel Carson. When she died, two years after the publication of *Silent spring*, Senator Abraham Ribicoff paid her tribute from the floor of the United States Senate with these words: "...this gentle lady who aroused people everywhere to be concerned with one of the most significant problems of mid-twentieth century life — man's contamination of his environment."

With the publication of *Silent spring*, Rachel Carson had accomplished both of her goals. She had also gotten the attention of government officials. Ten years after the publication of *Silent spring*, DDT was banned and a new government agency had been created. It is called the Environmental Protection Agency.

1. What is the name of the book written by Rachel Carson?
2. What is the topic discussed in the book?
3. Why did Ms. Carson write a book on this subject?
4. Are the statements in Ms. Carson's book supported by fact?
5. Why do farmers use pesticides?
6. According to the USDA and the chemical companies that manufacturer pesticides, are pesticides needed? If so, what for?
7. How was Rachel Carson's book different from other books that discussed pesticides?
8. Select the one statement from each pair that best describes the position that Rachel Carson supported?
   1A. Only natural pesticides should be used because they are not dangerous to wildlife.
   1B. A new pesticide should be approved only if there is no other way to get rid of the pest.
   2A. Citizens should be warned when their area will be sprayed.
   2B. Spraying should not be done because it contaminates the environment.
   3A. The Department of Agriculture should register pesticides.
   3B. Other government agencies should be involved in the registration of pesticides.
   4A. All environmental problems are due to the use of pesticides.
   4B. The government should support research that would reduce pesticide use.
9. A substance called agent orange was sprayed on some of the forests in Vietnam. It contained an herbicide that caused the trees to drop their leaves. The herbicide was used so that the enemy could be spotted more easily. Some of the Vietnam veterans filed a law suit because of health problems they claim are due to their exposure to agent orange. Would Rachel Carson have supported their right to file a law suit?
10. If Rachel Carson had been one of the authors of the Bill of Rights, what right would she have added?
11. What were Rachel Carson's goals? Did she accomplish her goals?

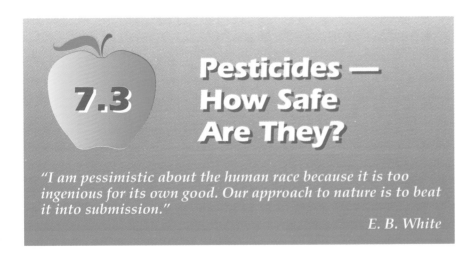

7.3 Pesticides — How Safe Are They?

"I am pessimistic about the human race because it is too ingenious for its own good. Our approach to nature is to beat it into submission."

E. B. White

The 1970s gave us a new awareness of the problems that were caused by the use of human-made pesticides. Laboratory tests showed some pesticides were causing tumors, liver disorders, and changes in the chromosomes of laboratory mice. But the problems extended beyond pesticide resistance, broken eggshells, and tumors in mice.

Pesticide Poisoning

There are an estimated 20,000 to 300,000 poisonings of agricultural workers a year. There may be 1000 deaths each year due to pesticide poisoning. No one knows for sure because record keeping is poor and workers don't always report poisoning.

There are several reasons why poisoning may not be reported. Many farm workers in the United States do not speak English, some are illegal aliens and fear being deported, and others fear losing their job. Doctors may not identify an illness as pesticide poisoning because the symptoms of pesticide poisoning — nausea, headaches, diarrhea, vomiting, and skin rash — are also the symptoms of other illnesses.

The EPA issued regulations that require that employers train workers in pesticide safety, post safety information, and place warning signs that prohibit entry into sprayed areas for between 12 to 72 hours, depending upon the pesticide used. The notices must be posted in English and Spanish.

Parathion is an inexpensive pesticide that is highly effective against a broad range of insects. It is one of the most acutely toxic pesticides registered by the EPA. A few drops of parathion on the skin of an orchard worker can be fatal. It has made thousands of farm workers ill and has been linked to the death of more than 70 workers. The EPA restricted its use to only 9 crops to reduce the number of workers poisoned by parathion.

THINK ABOUT IT

Not all misuse or overuse of pesticides can be blamed on agriculture. In the United States, homeowners use five times more pesticides per acre on their lawns than farmers do on their own fields. About 67 million pounds of pesticides are applied to lawns every year.

Most agricultural pesticides are applied by airplanes.

Most agricultural pesticides are applied by airplanes. A study of aerial spray pilots (crop dusters) conducted by the Federal Aviation Agency (FAA) showed most of the pilots had mild to moderate symptoms of pesticide poisoning. Another study showed that pilots of planes spraying pesticides had a high number of auto accidents on their way home from work.

Improper use of pesticides on plants grown for food has also caused pesticide poisoning. During the summer of 1985, some California-grown watermelons were contaminated with the pesticide aldicarb. Although no one died, nearly 300 people in five western states suffered from nausea, diarrhea, and tremors due to aldicarb poisoning.

In 1989 and 1990, 11 out of 15 babies born in a village in a southwestern Hungary had severe birth defects. The cause of the defects was the improper use of the pesticide trichlorphon at a local fish farm. The new director of the farm disregarded directions and bathed fish in the undiluted pesticide. Fishing had been banned, but many people were not informed of the ban and ate the treated fish. All of the mothers of the affected children had eaten the contaminated fish while they were pregnant. The level of pesticide in the fish was 1,000 the recommended maximum level.

The Banning of Pesticides

Until 1970 the control of pesticide use was the responsibility of the US Department of Agriculture (USDA). The USDA promoted the use of chemical pesticides as an effective way to increase yields and make greater profits. In 1970 the responsibility for regulating pesticide use was removed from the USDA and assigned to the Environmental Protection Agency (EPA).

By the end of the 1970s most of the first group of pesticides — the chlorinated hydrocarbons — had been banned or their use severely restricted by the EPA. Federal regulations were tightened. Some of the new regulations were based on laboratory studies and effects on wildlife, but restrictions were placed on some pesticides because of possible effects on humans.

One pesticide known as DBCP (dibromochloropropane) was found to be the cause of sterility among male workers at a plant where the pesticide was manufactured. The EPA banned the manufacture of DBCP. The herbicide 2,4,5-T is contaminated with a very toxic substance known as dioxin. The EPA banned some uses of 2,4,5-T after it was linked to a high rate of miscarriages among women living near heavily sprayed commercial forests in Oregon. The EPA ban was based on the "suspected effect" of the herbicide.

There is still much we don't know about many of the chemicals that we use. A 1984 report from the National Academy of Science found that sufficient data existed to determine the health hazards of about 10 percent of the pesticides in use. The reason for this lack of information is many of the pesticides we use were registered during the 1950s and 1960s, before health and safety tests were required.

Tests are now being conducted on some 1400 chemicals used as pesticides. We are learning more about the effects of the chemicals being used, but the process is slow. Only about 25 to 30 of these chemicals can be tested each year.

The Rules Have Changed

New pesticides that are marketed or used in the United States must be registered by the EPA. Before a pesticide can be registered, the EPA must evaluate the risks and benefits of its use. The risks include danger to humans and the environment. The benefits include protection of crops from pests and the protection of animals, including humans, from disease. The EPA is required by law to balance the risks to the environmental and human health with the benefits of using the pesticide.

Manufacturers spend several years and several million dollars on testing programs. The decision to register or not to register a pesticide is based on tests that determine the possibility that the pesticide will cause cancer, birth defects, nerve damage, or changes in chromosomes. Studies must include the effects on mammals, birds, fish, and shellfish.

Pesticides in Our Food

The manufacturer must provide complete instructions that describe how a pesticide is to be used and information concerning the risks of using the pesticide. If the pesticide is to be used on a food crop, the EPA must establish a tolerance level. The **tolerance level** is the maximum amount of pesticide residue that is allowed in or on food, or in drinking water.

Once tolerance levels are set, the Food and Drug Administration monitors the pesticide levels in foods to be sure that they are below the tolerance level. The FDA inspectors find their job is similar to that of the state highway patrol. Like the police who can't stop all speeders, the food inspectors can't stop the sale of all food with unsafe levels of pesticides.

When pesticides are used on crops that will be eaten by humans or other animals, it is important to follow the directions concerning "days to harvest." Days to harvest refers to the number of days between the last application of the pesticide and the day the crop can be legally harvested. Crops that are harvested too quickly after spraying may have pesticide residues that exceed the "safe" tolerance levels.

The farmer must allow the proper amount of time for the pesticide to break down before harvesting the crop. The time needed var-

WHAT DO YOU THINK?

The National Residue Program tests meat for only 41 of the 600 pesticides used in agriculture. Though dangerously high levels of pesticides in meat are recorded by the agency, the monitoring takes so long that by the time the test results are available the meat has already been sold and eaten. Do you think meat packers should be required to keep meat off the market until all test results are in? Do you think meat should be tested for all agricultural pesticides used? Would you be willing to pay more for meat to cover the cost?

ies with the type of crop grown and the pesticide used. For example, a certain pesticide may be applied one day before harvesting potatoes, but not within four days of harvesting spinach. The manufacturer must include this information with the pesticide when it is sold.

Pesticides in Our Water

Some water supplies in agricultural areas contain pesticides. The following warning is on the label of an herbicide made by Shell Chemical Company. "Bladex is a pesticide which can move (seep or travel) through soil and can contaminate ground water that may be used as drinking water. Bladex has been found in ground water as a result of agricultural use. Users are advised not to apply Bladex where the ground water is close to the surface and where the soils are very permeable — well drained soils such as loamy sands."

In Suffolk county, Long Island, New York, the soil is sandy, and the ground water is only a few feet below the surface. Well water is the only source of drinking water on the island. In 1979 more than 2,000 wells were found to contain Temik, a pesticide is applied to the soil to control nematodes. Since its approval in 1975, the pesticide had been used to spray many of the 22,000 acres (8,800 hectares) of potato fields in Suffolk county.

The active ingredient in Temik is aldicarb, the same chemical that contaminated watermelons in California in 1985. It had been thought that Temik would break down in the soil before reaching the ground water. Now we know that, at least in some situations, this does not happen. Since Temik was found in the wells on Long Island, it has been found in the ground water near Florida's citrus groves and in potato-growing regions of 12 other states.

The tolerance level set by the New York State Department of Health for Temik in drinking water is 7 ppb. More than 1,000 wells had levels of Temik above 7 ppb. One well had 515 ppb. The sale of Temik was banned in Suffolk County, and the manufacturer provided filters for the contaminated wells. Three years after the ban of Temik, the pesticide was still present in the water from the contaminated wells. These wells could remain polluted for the next one hundred years.

How Safe Is "Safe"?

Scientists cannot always agree on which pesticides should be registered. Some pesticides that are registered by the EPA have been banned by some states. This action can protect the ground water supply, but the pesticides are also found in food that is shipped from other states or imported from other countries. About 40 percent of grains and grain products, 50 percent of fruits, and 30 percent of vegetables produced in the United States in 1991 contained pesticide residues.

While only 0.5 percent of foods sampled exceeded the "safe" levels, some scientists believe that it is impossible to define a "safe" level of pesticide. The EPA is criticized for setting tolerances when there has not been enough data collected to determine what is really "safe." Some states have set tolerance levels that are lower than those set by the EPA. Tolerance levels are lower for water than for foods because they are based on the total amount consumed. It is expected that you will consume more water than broccoli, so water is not permitted to contain as much pesticide as broccoli.

According to a report released by the National Academy of Sciences, there is "a potential concern" that some children may be ingesting unsafe amounts of pesticides. Tolerance levels for pesticides are based on danger to adults, not children. While the academy found no evidence that children have been harmed by pesticides in food, the scientists say that children may be a greater risk than adults.

Foods containing pesticides make up a larger portion of a child's diet than an adult's diet, and developing bodies may be more sensitive to changes caused by pesticides. Even though the risk is small, the National Academy of Sciences recommends that new test procedures be developed for evaluating pesticide toxicity in children, and more data needs to be collected on the amount of food children eat.

Another concern is the effect of pesticides that are combined with other pesticides. Laboratory studies test the effects of pesticides individually. The foods we eat may have been sprayed with several pesticides. More than 300 different pesticides have been licensed for use on food crops. At least 50 pesticides have been registered for use on apples.

Little is known about the effects of pesticides when they are combined with other pesticides. A study conducted by the Natural Resources Defense Council found 19 different pesticides on fresh fruits and vegetables grown in California. The analysis of samples from supermarket warehouses found two or more pesticides on 66 percent of oranges and 44 percent of apples. Some fruits and vegetables had residues of six or more pesticides.

What affect do you think these barrels of waste will have on groundwater?

Risk versus Benefits

While products of technology provide certain benefits, they also carry certain risks. Airplanes and cars provide the benefit of speed, but there is always the risk of an accident. For every product of technology, we could make a list of risks and benefits.

There is no question that pesticides have saved millions of lives and billions of dollars worth of crops. It has been suggested that overpopulation would not be the problem it is today if pesticides had not saved so many lives. Pesticides benefit us by protecting us from disease and hunger, but the use of pesticides also carries certain risks.

When the EPA approves a pesticide they must consider both the risks and the benefits of the product. Many people think the benefits

Genetically Engineered Pesticides

The EPA has given conditional registration to two pesticides that are produced by genetically altered DNA in a naturally occurring microbe. The pesticides are proteins that are naturally made by the bacteria Bacillus thuringiensis (Bt). Using recombinant DNA techniques, scientists insert the message for production of the pesticides in the bacteria Pseudomonas fluorescens.

Using heat the Pseudomonas bacteria are killed and made into pesticides called M-One Plus and MVP. What is the advantage of using Pseudomonas bacteria as a factory to make the pesticide? The Pseudomonas bacteria are enclosed in a capsule. The capsule extends the time that the pesticides are effective.

- What are the risks of using genetically engineered pesticides?
- What are the alternatives?
- Do the benefits outweigh the risks?

of using pesticides justify the risks taken. Others think the risks are too great. While the risks from using poisonous chemicals can not be eliminated, they can be reduced.

Reducing the Risks

Although the chlorinated hydrocarbons (DDT, chlordane, lindane) were not very toxic to humans, they are **persistent pesticides** — non-biodegradable. This persistence increased the risk of damage from their continued use, and their use was banned or restricted by the EPA. Trace levels of these pesticides remain in the environment posing a risk for wildlife and humans.

Manufacturers produced new **biodegradable pesticides** (pyrethroids, carbamates, and organophosphorus compounds) that break down more easily. These pesticides were promoted as "safer." The risk of bioaccumulation in the food chain is reduced, but accumulation is not the only risk.

At first scientists thought that since the pesticide breaks down quickly the risk to the consumer would be very small. Now scientists are learning that some of the breakdown products are more toxic than the parent chemical. Still, the use of biodegradable pesticides presents less risk to the consumer than the use of persistent pesticides that will accumulate in the fatty tissues.

To reduce the risk during application of the pesticide, the EPA has restricted the use of some pesticides. Pesticides classified as **restricted** are only available to farmers and commercial applicators who have been certified by the state's department of agriculture. To be certified a person must take a course in the proper use of chemicals and pass a written examination. They must demonstrate their understanding and ability to use information on the label.

> **STOP!**
> **ALL PESTICIDES CAN BE HARMFUL TO HEALTH AND THE ENVIRONMENT IF MISUSED.**
> **READ THE LABEL CAREFULLY AND USE ONLY AS DIRECTED.**

Workers using a restricted pesticide are also required by federal law to follow the directions on the container. This includes wearing protective clothing and sometimes a respirator and goggles. Some pesticides are easily absorbed through the skin even when washed with soap and water immediately after spraying. Wearing protective clothing to prevent pesticide poisoning can sometimes lead to other problems. When applying pesticides in hot weather, workers face two problems — pesticide poisoning and heat exhaustion.

Since 1982 the EPA has required the use of **Signal words** and **Precautionary Statements of Hazards** on the labels of pesticides. The words used are determined by EPA, not the manufacturer of the pesticide.

EPA Toxicity Category	EPA Required Signal Word	EPA-Required Precautionary Statements for Acute Oral Ingestion and Skin Absorption Hazards
I	**DANGER** (Skull and Crossbones) **POISON**	Fatal if swallowed or absorbed through skin. Do not get in eyes, or on clothing. Wear protective clothing and rubber gloves. Wash thoroughly with soap and water after handling and before eating or smoking. Remove contaminated clothing and wash before reuse.
II	**WARNING**	May be fatal if swallowed or if absorbed through skin. Do not get in eyes, on skin, or on clothing. Wear protective clothing and rubber gloves. Wash thoroughly with soap and water after handling and before eating or smoking. Remove contaminated clothing and wash before reuse.
III	**CAUTION**	Harmful if swallowed or absorbed through skin. Avoid contact with skin, eyes, or clothing. Wash thoroughly with soap and water after handling.

Following the directions also includes using the correct amount or "dose" of the pesticide. Manufacturers must prove that the concentration of pesticide recommended will kill the pest. Some people think "if a little is good, more will be better." When the amount of pesticide used is greater than the amount given in the directions, the pesticide present on the food may exceed the "safe" tolerance levels. Using more pesticide also increases the risk that the water supply may become contaminated, and wildlife may be poisoned.

Pesticide applicators need to check the weather report before applying pesticides.

- Plants may be damaged by some pesticides if the temperature is too warm.
- Pesticides should not be sprayed when the wind will carry the chemical away from its target. Even when there is no wind, some of the pesticide enters the air by evaporation.
- If it rains soon after the pesticide is applied, the pesticide may be washed off the plant before it can kill the pests. If the pesticide is washed off the plant too quickly, it may contaminate bodies of water nearby.

When pesticides are sprayed on crops in the flowering stage, honeybees may be poisoned. In some states bees are protected by laws that prevent the spraying of pesticides while crops are in bloom. More than 400,000 colonies are destroyed or damaged by pesticides each year. The following steps can be taken to decrease the number of bees killed:

- Select pesticides that are not so toxic to bees.
- Spray in the evening or at night when the honeybees are not collecting pollen.
- Alerting the owner of the beehives so that the hives can be moved or closed.

These apples have not been sprayed with pesticides. Would you eat these apples?

Even if these precautions are taken, some pesticides will kill bees. Manufacturers prepackage some pesticides in small capsules. The pesticide is slowly released as if it were a timed-release capsule. The pesticide is effective for a longer period of time. This is an advantage to the farmer. It protects the workers from the poison, and it reduces the number of times they must spray, but it is more deadly to bees. The insecticide pellets are about the same size as pollen. They are picked up by the bee and carried back to the hive. Stored with the pollen, the pesticide continues to kill bees.

The Perfect Apple

Does the grower really need to use so many pesticides? At first, pesticides were used to protect crops from pests that might destroy them. Some pesticides are still used for that purpose. Other pesticides are used to improve quality because consumers demand perfection.

It is not likely that the corn ear worm will eat more than one or two rows of corn kernels. The rest of the ear of corn is still safe for human consumption, but many people are not willing to cut away the bad part. Consumers want perfect ears of corn, and growers spray with pesticides to provide them.

Some insects that attack fruit do not affect the taste of the fruit, only the appearance. An example is a small insect called a thrip. Thrips cause small rusty spots on the skin of oranges. They do not affect the fruit itself, but farmers may not be able to sell the oranges with rusty spots.

Some buyers will not accept fruit if it has more than one percent cosmetic damage. If the growers do find a buyer, they may have to accept a lower price for the blemished fruit. So the spraying continues, even on fruits and vegetables that are going to be crushed into juice.

Is There a Better Way?

At this time there is little evidence that the levels of pesticides generally found in the environment are hazardous to human health. This lack of evidence makes some people feel safe. Others are not so secure. They worry about exposing people to small amounts of pesticides. There is little reliable data on the long-term effects of exposure to small amounts of pesticide. Most health studies used short-term exposure to larger amounts of pesticide.

Some people feel that we are wasting time debating which level — 10 ppb or 30 ppb — of a pesticide is a "safe" level. They feel that the best policy would be to reduce pesticide use as much as possible. Some pests can be controlled without the use of chemical pesticides. Where these methods are used, the use of pesticides has been drastically reduced. Some alternative methods of pest control are discussed in Section 7.4 IPM-A Better Way to Control Pests.

1. What problems were revealed by laboratory studies of pesticides?
2. What problems were being caused by pesticides in the environment?

Pesticide Poisoning

3. How many people suffer from pesticide poisoning each year? Approximately how many people die?
4. List several reasons why a farm worker who is a victim of pesticide poisoning might not report it.
5. Explain why doctors may give the wrong diagnosis to a victim of pesticide poisoning.
6. How is the EPA protecting farm workers from pesticide poisoning?
7. How is the EPA protecting farm workers from parathion?
8. How are most of the agricultural pesticides applied? In what way do pilots who apply pesticides show the effects of the exposure to pesticides?
9. Workers are not the only people who are sometimes poisoned by pesticides. Describe how your food might become contaminated with pesticides.

The Banning of Pesticides

10. What agency regulated the use of pesticides before 1970? What agency has been responsible for regulation since 1970?
11. What group of pesticides was banned in the 1970s?
12. Why was the use of the herbicide 2,4,5-T restricted?
13. When were most pesticides registered? Were health and safety tests required?
14. How many different chemicals are used as pesticides? How many of these chemicals can be tested each year? How long will it take to test all of these chemicals?

The Rules Have Changed

15. Identify the kinds of information that the EPA must evaluate before a pesticide can be restricted.

16. Identify four types of changes that might be observed in laboratory animals being tested for pesticides.
17. What types of organisms are tested for pesticides?

Pesticides in Our Food

18. What information must the manufacturer include on a pesticide label?
19. Which pesticides are required to have a tolerance level?
20. Define the terms tolerance level and days to harvest.
21. Where can you find information about the number of days to harvest?

Pesticides in Our Water

22. Explain why the use of Bladex has been restricted.
23. Identify two situations in which pesticides should not be used.
24. Why didn't the pesticide Temik break down in the soil before reaching the ground water in Suffolk County, Long Island?
25. What tolerance level has been set for Temik in the state of New York? How long are the wells expected to remain contaminated? Would you classify Temik as biodegradable or persistent?

How Safe Is "Safe"?

26. Do scientists agree on which pesticides should be registered? Do scientists agree on the level of pesticide that is considered "safe"?
27. Why are levels of pesticides allowed in food higher than those allowed in water?
28. Is it possible that the apple you eat was sprayed with more than one pesticide? Why are some people concerned about the presence of more than one pesticide on food?

Risk versus Benefits

29. In order to enjoy the benefits of technology, we must also take certain _____.
30. What are the benefits of pesticides?

31. When the EPA approves a pesticide, they must consider both the _____ and the _____.

Reducing the Risks

32. What risk was reduced by banning or restricting the chlorinated hydrocarbons?
33. Parathion is an organophosphorus compound.
    Is it persistent or biodegradable? What is the greatest risk associated with the use of parathion — immediate toxic effects or bioaccumulation in the food chain?
34. Who takes the greatest risk when parathion is used — the worker or the consumer?
35. What is required of people who apply pesticides that are classified as restricted use?
36. Which of the following people can apply a "restricted use" pesticide?
    homeowner
    all farmers
    farmers who have passed a written exam
    certified commercial applicators
37. Give two reasons why workers may refuse to wear the required protective clothing when applying pesticides.
38. Which of the following words — CAUTION, DANGER or WARNING — is required on labels of the most toxic pesticides? Which word would probably be found on a pesticide used by the typical homeowner?
39. List three risks that are increased when the amount of pesticide applied is greater than the concentration recommended on the label.
40. What weather conditions are needed for application of pesticides?
41. Pesticides are used on some plants, especially fruit trees, several times during a growing season. Which of the following spraying times is most harmful to bees — pre-bloom, full bloom, post-bloom, or post harvest? How can the danger to bees be reduced?
42. "Microencapsulation" of the pesticide parathion reduces the risk to the worker applying the pesticide. What is another advantage of "time-released" pesticides?
43. Why is microencapsulation of a pesticide more harmful to bees?

The Perfect Apple

44. Explain the statement "You are one of the reasons why farmers use so many pesticides."
45. Would you be willing to use oranges with "rust spots" if the damage was only skin deep and the fruit was not affected?
    Would you consider eating corn-on-the-cob that had minor insect damage?
46. You are given a choice of a salad made with fresh pineapple or one made with canned pineapple. If you knew that the fresh pineapple had been dipped in a fungicide solution to prevent fresh fruit rot and the canned pineapple had not been treated, which would you select? Explain why.
    Do you think foods should have labels that reveal the pesticides that have been used? If you had a choice of buying food that was labeled at a higher price than food that was not labeled, which would you select?
47. Do you think it would make a difference if consumers refused to buy frozen orange juice that was made from oranges treated for thrips or other insects damage that does not affect the fruit quality?

Is There a Better Way?

48. Are the pesticides in the environment today harmful to human health? Are you sure? Explain.
49. Do you think that scientists can really determine "safe" levels of pesticides? Explain.
50. Do you think that the amount of pesticides used should be reduced?
    Would you be willing to pay more for food grown without pesticides?
    Would you be willing to use food that was not as perfect if it meant that fewer pesticides would be needed?

IPM — A Better Way to Control Pests

7.4

"We should no longer accept the counsel of those who tell us that we must fill our world with poisonous chemicals; we should look about and see what other course is open to us."
Rachel Carson
in Silent Spring

We have doubts about the safety and long-term effectiveness of insecticides, yet we must control insect pests. Pests still take about one-third of our food every year. According to the Office of Technology Assessment, if all farmers quit using pesticides, there would be no commercial production of apples, lettuce, and strawberries.

Despite the use of chemicals, corn is still attacked by 70 different insect pests. The chlorinated hydrocarbon mirex was used against red fire ants for 15 years, but they are still a major pest in the South, from Texas to the Carolinas. Mirex was banned in 1978.

A new approach called **IPM** for **Integrated Pest Management** involves the use of not one, but several different methods of insect control to reduce the population of a particular insect pest. The farmer selects a combination of the most effective methods described below.

Resistant Varieties

Some plants are naturally resistant to insects. Some produce their own pesticides. The odor of herbs and evergreens comes from chemicals that discourage pests from attacking the plants. Some plants produce chemicals similar to caffeine and nicotine which interfere with the flow of messages in the bug's nervous system. Tannins and other chemicals found in some plants make the bug unable to digest food.

Scientists are developing varieties of crops that are resistant to attack by specific pests. Resistant varieties have some type of built-in protection. It may be a natural pesticide, or it may be a physical barrier such as spines or hairy leaves. This is an ideal solution to insect control because it reduces the need for spraying synthetic pesticides.

Imagine getting a package in the mail, and when you open it you find it contains 4,000 wasp larvae. Dairy farmers are finding that mail-order wasps can do the job that poisons once did — control the fly population. The ant-sized wasps insert their eggs in the fly larvae. One cow patty can hide as many as 2,000 fly larvae, and an insect control program using two species of parasitic wasps can reduce fly breeding by 99 percent.

Varieties of wheat have been developed that are resistant to the Hessian fly. The Hessian fly is one of the most serious pests of wheat. Varieties of alfalfa are being developed that are resistant to attack by weevils. Scientists are also interested in developing varieties of crops that are resistant to attack by insects while the food is in storage.

The development of resistant varieties is a time consuming and expensive process. Plant breeders began a program to develop apple varieties that are resistant to the major apple diseases — scab, rust, fire blight, and mildew. The resistant varieties developed must also produce high-quality fruit. No one wants a disease resistant apple tree if the fruit tastes like cardboard. The breeding program that began in the 1940s finally produced apple trees resistant to these diseases in the 1970s.

New processes developed in the field of genetic engineering may someday reduce the time needed to develop new varieties. We still have a lot to learn about the chemical messages (genes) inside the plant cells. Scientists have found that it is difficult to transfer genes from one plant cell to another. Recently they were able to transfer genes from bean plants into sunflower and tobacco plants. One day they hope to transfer the genes from plants that are resistant to pests into plants that are an important source of food.

Imagine a plant that secretes a sticky chemical that traps and kills mites. Some plants do excrete chemicals that make the plant resistant to mites. Scientists have identified the chemical excreted by some varieties of geraniums and are now working on biosynthesis of the chemical in the laboratory. Perhaps one day scientists will identify the genes responsible for this resistance and be able to transfer it to other plants.

Beneficial Insects

Wasps are the most useful insect for control of other insects. The beneficial species of wasps are much smaller than the familiar wasps that build paper nests and are feared for their sting. Most live alone and the females hunt insects to provide food for their young.

The female wasp lays her eggs inside the eggs or larvae of insect pests. The wasp eggs hatch, and the wasp larvae feed on the egg or the inside of the host larva. When they are mature, they eat their way out of the host and spin a cocoon. In the cocoon they gradually change into adult wasps. Parasitic wasps and some parasitic flies help control the populations of important insect pests like the gypsy moth larvae, cutworms, boll weevils, and tobacco hornworms.

Other adult insects are predators. An adult ladybug may eat more than 50 aphids in one day. Both the larvae and adult green lacewings feed on aphids. The larvae are often called aphid lions. The maggots of some species of flies also feed on aphids.

All insect predators are not good biological controls. The praying mantis has a big appetite for insects, but it is not selective. Beneficial insects, insect pests, and other praying mantises become a part of its diet. Buying praying mantises for your garden will do little to reduce the population of insect pests.

Other Natural Enemies

Viruses, protozoa, bacteria, fungi, parasites, and predators can be used to control certain insect pests. Some harmful nematodes in the soil are strangled by certain types of fungi. *Nosema locustae* is a one-celled protozoan that lives as a parasite in grasshoppers. As it feeds and multiplies in the stomach of the grasshopper, the grasshopper slowly becomes ill and dies.

A very small rod-shaped bacterium *Bacillus thuringiensis* (Bt) may be the safest insecticide that is used today. It does not harm honeybees or other beneficial insects, spiders, fish, birds, or humans. Vegetables sprayed with Bt may be eaten immediately after spraying. There is no required waiting period or "days to harvest." Bt is also exempt from the requirement of a "safe" tolerance level.

Bt is a very selective insecticide. The bacteria produce a chemical that is toxic to caterpillars (larvae of moths and butterflies). Some types of larvae killed by Bt are the larvae of gypsy moths, tobacco hornworms, imported cabbage worms, cabbage loopers, tobacco budworms, and armyworms.

When these caterpillars feed on leaves that have been sprayed with Bt, the toxic chemical produced by the bacteria begins to break down the insect's stomach wall. The caterpillar stops feeding within 24 to 48 hours and will die within several days. When the caterpillar dies and decays, the Bt bacteria also decay. This prevents any build-up of the bacteria in the environment.

A new variety of Bt discovered in Israel (BtI) produces poisons that affect many species of mosquito larvae. When the larvae mistakenly eat it as food, it causes the cells of their digestive system to explode.

Japanese beetles can be controlled by another bacterium that causes milky spore disease (*Bacillus popillae*). It is sprayed on the soil where the beetle larvae live. When the larvae die, the spores of the bacteria are released into the soil. These spores continue to control the beetle larvae once they have become established. There are two disadvantages to control with milky spore disease. It is expensive to establish the spores and they are effective only if used in the entire neighborhood.

Some insect-eating birds, such as the purple martin, can effectively control some insects. Some fish are being tested for their ability to control populations of mosquito larvae and certain aquatic weeds. Fish that eat mosquito larvae are commonly used in California rice paddies.

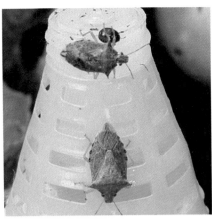

To the RESCUE! soldier bug attractor is a major breakthrough in biological insect control. The spined soldier bug is a natural predator of over 100 destructive insect pests. The yellow cone contains a sex attractant that lures the bug to the area where insect control is needed.

This apple tree shows signs of damage from Japanese beetles.

Male Japanese beetles are attracted to a chemical that smells like a female beetle. They cannot cling to the slick plastic surface and are trapped when they fall into the bag.

Birth Control

Birth Control is another method of controlling insect populations. Males that have been sterilized by radiation are released in the fields. When these males mate with untreated females, the females lay eggs that do not hatch. This reduces the population of the new generation.

The screwworm fly, a parasite that lives in the open wounds of cattle, was eliminated from Florida and is controlled in the Southwest by releasing masses of sterile male flies. This method of birth control is also used to eliminate introduced pests before their populations become large. This technique works only when the pest population is small and is not widespread.

Creating Confusion with Chemicals

Some insects can be attracted to and caught in traps that are baited with **sex attractants**. Male insects often find a female of the same species by the way she smells. The females produce a chemical that can be identified by a male when the male is a mile or more away. This sex attractant increases the chance of reproduction.

Researchers have isolated and identified several of the chemicals that produce these odors and can now make synthetic sex attractants. In 1957 bait containing a sex attractant and an insecticide were used to eliminate the Mediterranean fruit fly from Florida. Since then, it has been used to control fruit flies introduced in Florida and California. Experiments with sex attractants produced by the gypsy moth have not been very successful.

The artichoke that is grown in California has only one destructive insect pest, but in 1981 it cost $300 per acre to control the pest. The sex attractant of the female plume moth has been identified and synthesized. California's artichoke farmers are hoping that its use will reduce the amount of insecticide needed to control the moth.

Research continues on synthetic **hormones** that trigger insect development at the wrong time or prevent insect larvae from maturing into adults. Such hormones could cause insect pupae to change into their adult form during the winter when it is too cold for them to survive.

Other hormones being tested stop the development of insect larvae and produce freaks that can't eat or reproduce. The insect hormones tested are not toxic to humans or other animals, but they have affected some beneficial insects.

Cultivation Practices

The western corn rootworm is now resistant to the pesticides once used to control it. The practice of monoculture has allowed the rootworm to affect thousands of acres. Planting corn in the same field year after year insures a food supply for the rootworm. Crop rotation can remove the food supply and reduce the pest population.

Damage to some crops can be reduced by timing the planting and the harvest to avoid the insect. In some cases planting should be delayed until the region is free of the insect pest. Delaying the planting of wheat prevents Hessian flies from laying eggs on the young wheat plants. Faster growing varieties of cotton allow harvest before the pests arrive. Plowing covers crop residue eliminating winter habitat for some insect pests. This reduces the population of pests and the damage to the crop in the next growing season.

Pesticides

Pesticides are an important part of an IPM program. Biological controls have significantly reduced the amount of pesticides used to control certain pests, but they have not replaced the use of pesticides entirely. The state of California used 600,000 pounds (2.7×10^5 kg) of pesticides to control mosquitoes in 1970. Thanks to new methods of biological control, they used only 40,000 pounds (1.8×10^4 kg) of pesticides in 1983.

The control of certain insect pests by IPM has been very successful. When resistance to insecticides threatened the cotton industry, growers turned to IPM techniques. During the 1960s, 20 million pounds (9×10^6 kg) of insecticides were used to grow cotton in Texas. Since 1976, the use of insecticides for Texas-grown cotton has decreased by 90 percent, and at the same time yields have increased.

Farmers using the calendar as a guide, spray at regular intervals even though few insects may be present. Computer programs are helping farmers reduce the amount of pesticide they use. Texas farmers can use an IPM program called BUGNET. Farmers sweep the cotton fields with bug nets and report the number of boll weevils found. A computer at Texas A & M University uses this information to determine when the weevils will reach damaging levels. This allows the farmer to spray only when necessary.

The spring flight of the codling moth, a devastating apple pest, begins on the first day when there is a 62°F (17°C) temperature at sunset. Control of this pest is accomplished by spraying when the insect is in the larval stage. Farm advisors enter the date of the first spring flight in a computer, and the program calculates the dates for each stage in the life cycle. With this information, the farmer can avoid spraying after the larva has spun its cocoon, when it is too late.

Some insects develop only when the temperature is within a specific range. The development stops if the temperature is too low or too high. An IPM program at the University of California is linked to the National Weather Service. Using the average daily temperature and the minimum and maximum temperatures for the development of the species, a computer program calculates the **growing degree days** — the daily accumulation of heat — and tells farmers when the insect will be in each stage of its life cycle. The farmer can select the most appropriate time to spray.

WHAT DO YOU THINK?

Biofac, Incorporated breeds bugs — 100 million a day. Their cheapest bugs sell for ten cents per thousand; their top-of-the-line insects go for 25 cents a piece. Biofac breeds bugs that feed on or otherwise kill agricultural insect pests. They are doing a brisk business. At first, government agencies banned the bugs because, they said, they were an "adulteration" of food products. It is ironic that Biofac, a leader in Integrated Pest Management, only received approval of their products when the FDA and EPA reclassified the beneficial bugs as pesticides and then approved them for agricultural use. Among Biofac's best sellers are pricey lacewings ("they just suck bugs' blood right out") and parasitic wasps that control weevils.

What kinds of insect pests grow in your area? What kind of IPM business could you start to help farmers and gardeners in your region control destructive insects?

The Benefits and Disadvantages of Biological Controls

It would cost two hundred dollars an acre to control citrus red scale insects using chemical insecticides. The cost of control using the Aphytis melinis wasp is $20 per acre. Biological controls are usually cheaper to use than chemical controls, and biological controls don't pollute the environment.

Biological controls kill only the pest, not the innocent insects that may offer a beneficial service to humans. With these advantages, why are chemical controls still used?

Here are some of the reasons:

- Biological controls are often more expensive to develop than chemical controls. Our most destructive pests have been imported from other countries. It is necessary to travel to the country where the pest originated to find its natural predators and diseases. The natural predators or diseases must be brought to the US and studied under strict quarantine to make sure it will attack only the pest. This makes research on biological controls very expensive.

- Companies may not be able to make large amounts of money selling biological controls. Without a financial incentive, most companies will not invest the time and money necessary to research biological controls. Most biological control research is conducted by universities and the federal government.

- Although biological controls may exist for most insect species, the research has not been done to identify and test them. Effective biological controls are not yet available for many insect pests.

- In order for biological controls to be effective, farmers must identify the pest and plan a course of action to prevent a population explosion. Some farmers are not planners. They find it easier to use chemical pesticides.

- Some biological controls are not effective unless they are applied over a large region. This requires the cooperation of the surrounding neighbors. Milky spore disease is not effective against the Japanese beetle unless used over a wide area.

- Chemical pesticides are fast-acting and biological controls are slow-acting. It may take a few days or weeks for a biological control to reduce the pest population. A worm may quit eating within an hour of being sprayed with bacteria, but it remains upon the plant for several days before dying. This leads some people to think that the bacteria don't work. A chemical pesticide kills a worm almost instantly.

Pest Control Does Not Mean No Pests

An insect is a pest only when its population is large enough to damage or at least bother other organisms, including humans. The goal of IPM is not to eliminate the pest, but to reduce the pest population.

WHAT DO YOU THINK?

Should companies research biological controls? How can they be encouraged to do so?

DID YOU KNOW?

Scientists at the University of Wisconsin have incorporated a natural biological pesticide into the common baking potato. The gene inserted into the potato came from Bt, a soil bacterium. It produces a protein that is harmless to people but deadly to the Colorado potato beetle. Most of the "insecticidal" protein occurs in the plant's leaves rather than in the edible tuber, that researchers have pronounced unchanged in taste and quality.

For IPM to be acceptable to the farmer, the money lost because of the surviving pests must be less than the cost of using pesticides to eliminate them.

The presence of insects does not always mean there is a problem. It has been shown that one insect "pest" is actually helpful when its population is small. A large population of lygus bugs decreases the yield of a cotton crop, but a small population of these bugs increases the yield. The bugs remove some of the cotton bolls that would normally drop off anyway. This early removal allows the remaining bolls to grow larger. The bug is like a gardener who removes some pumpkin flowers so that the remaining flowers can produce larger fruit.

7.4 QUESTIONS FOR STUDY AND DISCUSSION

1. According to the Office of Technology Assessment, what foods would not be found in the grocery store if no pesticides were used?
2. Give two pieces of evidence that tell us pesticides are not eliminating the pests.
3. What is IPM? What is the goal of IPM and how does the farmer reach this goal?

Resistant Varieties
4. Identify two types of plants that produce their own pesticides.
5. Identify three chemicals produced by plants that may be pesticides.
6. Identify the two body systems in bugs that may be affected by pesticides.
7. Resistant varieties of each of the following crops have been developed. Identify the pest or pests that attack varieties of these crops that lack resistance.
   A. wheat   B. alfalfa   C. apples
8. Often when plants are in storage they are attacked by insects or fungi. What is one way we could avoid loss of our food crops during storage without using pesticides?
9. Give two reasons why we have not developed more varieties of crops that are resistant to pests.
10. Plant breeders are trying to develop a peach tree that is resistant to the peach borer. What other characteristic must this peach tree have in order to be acceptable to the consumers? How long might it take scientists to develop this tree?

11. Explain how genetic engineering may reduce the time needed to develop a variety of plant that is resistant to a certain pest.

Beneficial Insects
12. What type of insect is the most beneficial insect for controlling pests? Where do the females deposit their eggs? Why do they choose this location?
13. List three kinds of insects that are good biological controls for aphids.
14. Why isn't the praying mantis a good choice for insect control?

Other Natural Enemies
15. Identify each type of organism listed below, and give the pest(s) that it helps control.
    Nosema locustae
    Bacillus thuringiensis (Bt)
    Bacillus popillae
16. Why is Bt thought to be the safest insecticide used today?
17. How many days must you wait before harvesting a vegetable that has been sprayed with Bt?
18. List two disadvantages of using milky spore disease to control the Japanese beetle?

Birth Control
19. Explain how radiation is used as a form of birth control for some insect pests.
20. What are two limitations of this means of pest control?

21. Identify the two types of chemicals that are used to confuse insects.
22. Explain how sex attractants are used to control insect populations.
23. What insect has been successfully controlled by using sex attractants?
24. Some California farmers are using the sex attractant of the _____ in an attempt to decrease the pesticides used on the _____ crop.
25. Explain the possible ways that synthetic hormones can reduce a population of insects.
26. Give one advantage and one disadvantage of hormone treatment.

Cultivation Practices

27. List three cultivation practices that will help reduce the population of insect pests.

Pesticides

28. Have biological controls reduced the use of pesticides or have they replaced the use of pesticides?
29. Which state has significantly reduced the amount of pesticides used to control mosquitoes? Which state has significantly reduced the amount of pesticides used to control pests on the cotton crop?
30. A computer program at Texas A & M University will tell farmers when it is necessary to spray their cotton crop. What information must be fed into the computer?

31. How can a computer program help an orchard owner control the population of codling moths on apple trees?
32. Why is it more important for a farmer to know the number of growing degree days than to know what day of the year it is?

The Benefits and Disadvantages of Biological Controls

33. List three advantages of biological controls.
34. Why are biological controls often more expensive to develop than chemical controls?
35. Why aren't more private companies interested in developing biological controls?
36. Why is it difficult to convince some farmers that biological controls really work?
37. Briefly list five reasons why biological control of insects has not entirely replaced chemical control.

Pest Control Does Not Mean No Pests

38. Complete this statement. An insect is only a pest when _____.
39. What is the goal of IPM?
40. Complete this statement. A farmer will probably accept an IPM plan if he can be convinced that the amount of money he will lose because of damage done by the pest is less than _____.
41. Why shouldn't a cotton farmer kill all lygus bugs?

BIOTECHNOLOGY: NATURE'S PESTICIDES

Green Grapefruit — Did you know that Caribbean fruit flies (and other insects) are attracted to the color yellow? A scientist has discovered that a natural growth hormone (gibberellic acid) disapppears as a grapefruit turns yellow. When scientists spray grapefruit with a solution containing 10 ppm of the hormone, it prevents the grapefruit from losing its chlorophyll and turning yellow. The fruit flies tend to ignore the green fruit. The fruit continues to ripen, and growers already treat the grapefruit with another growth hormone, ethylene, to turn grapefruit yellow during storage. The growth hormone doesn't harm beneficial insects.

Biosoap — The sweet potato whitefly attacks more than 600 plant species. The fly not only sucks the energy from the plant, it also carries viruses, and other disease-causing organisms that attack the plant. The USDA's Agricultural Research Service has found a natural, nontoxic chemical that kills nearly 100 percent of the whiteflies. It is an extract of a plant that is related to tobacco and grows in Australia. The chemical, called a biosoap, is a plant-produced detergent. It dissolves the hard waxy coating that protects the fly, and the fly dies of dehydration.

The Sweet Smell of a Raspberry — Buy a pint of raspberries, put them in the refrigerator and forget them for three days. If you do, you probably won't want to eat them. They will be covered with a heavy growth of mold. Molds attack soft fruit causing decay within five days of the time the fruit is picked, even when it is refrigerated.

Scientists, at the USDA's Bioactive Constituents Research lab, heve identified five chemicals that may reduce the growth of mold on soft fruits. The naturally produced chemicals contribute to the smell of strawberries and raspberries, but they are not in a high enough concentration to be an effective fungicide. One of the odor-causing chemicals, 2-nonanone, is a federally approved flavoring. A timed-release capsule of 2-nonanone, place in a sealed box of berries, inhibits the growth of mold and extends the shelf-life of the berries.

- What are the risks of using natural chemicals as pesticides?
- What are the alternatives?
- Do the benefits outweigh the risks?

"No one says you shouldn't worry about people first; but if you really do, you need to protect fish and wildlife. Fish and wildlife are more sensitive; they always die first."

Ted Williams

The Law is Changed

Most of our pesticides, including DDT, were approved under the Federal Insecticide, Fungicide, and Rodenticide Act of 1947. This 1947 Act required the manufacturers to test the pesticide for short-term or acute effects. In 1972 the US government banned the use of DDT because of its effects on wildlife and because of evidence that it caused cancer in some species. That year Congress also amended the 1947 Act to require testing for the long-term or chronic effects of the 50,000 pesticides that were registered.

Since 1972, more than 15 other pesticides have been banned, or their use has been suspended while more studies are conducted. Guidelines for the 1972 amendments were not established until 1983. Since then the EPA has begun a review of the 1400 ingredients in the pesticides that remain on the market. It may take an additional 20 years before this review is completed. Meanwhile, most people are not aware that many of the products that they buy have not been tested for long-term effects.

A Partial List of Pesticides that Have Been Banned

1972 **DDT banned.**
Reason: Adverse effects on wildlife and a potential carcinogen.
Update: A recent study (1985-1991) of women in New York showed that women with just 19 ppb of DDE (a breakdown product of DDT) faced 4 times the risk of having breast cancer as women with only 2 ppb DDE.

1974 **Aldrin and Dieldrin banned.**
Reason: Bioaccumulation and carcinogenic.

1975 **Chlordane banned. Heptachlor ban proposed.**
Reason: Caused cancer and liver disorders in laboratory mice.
After nearly five years of hearings, the EPA decided to allow the use of existing supplies of heptachlor, if certain

restrictions were followed. Heptachlor would be phased out over the next five years. Some exemptions to the ban were allowed where no alternative pesticide was available. The tolerance level for food was set at 0.3 ppm. Later, exemptions were allowed in some states for the use of chlordane to control termites.

1976 **Mirex withdrawn voluntarily. Banned in 1978.**
Reason: Carcinogenic, bioaccumulation in humans, contamination of the Great Lakes.
Kepone withdrawn.
Reason: Death of workers exposed to kepone. Some workers suffered severe nervous system disorders. A spill in the James River caused the river to be closed to commercial fishing.

1980 **DBCP banned.**
Reason: DBCP was identified as the cause of sterility among workers in a pesticide plant in California's San Joaquin Valley. Since then, it has been discovered in drinking water in the San Joaquin Valley and has been linked to cancer in a study done by the state of California.

1983 **Heptachlor production banned.**

1984 **EDB banned.**
Reason: Linked to cancer and genetic mutations.

1986 **Dinoseb sale and use immediately suspended.**
Reason: High risk of birth defects and a potential cause of human male reproductive disorders from occupational exposure.

1987 **Heptachlor and chlordane sale banned.**
Velsicol Chemical Corporation agreed to stop selling their pesticides that contain chlordane and heptachlor primarily used to control termites.

1991 **Carbofuran banned in Virginia. EPA signs agreement with FMC.**
Granular carbofuran (Furadan 15G) immediately banned in certain ecologically sensitive areas. A phase out of all but a few minor uses. By 1994, only 2,500 pounds may be sold annually in the United States. Production is not banned.
Reason: Acute toxicity to birds including bald eagles and other birds of prey. This is the first pesticide to be banned solely because of its effects on wildlife.

An Exemption Caused Trouble in Hawaii

The state of Hawaii was granted an exemption from the original EPA ban of the insecticide heptachlor. More than 11,000 acres (4,400 hectares) of pineapples are raised in Hawaii. The mealy bug is an insect pest that damages the pineapple plant. The bug

Sugar Cane being harvested in Louisiana.

WHAT DO YOU THINK?

Would a few spots or worm holes on fruit or vegetables prevent you from buying the produce? Do you think chemicals should be used solely to improve the appearance of produce? What about Alar? In 1968 it was approved for use on apples. In 1973, tests indicated it might cause cancer. In 1984, the EPA issued a statement that Alar is a carcinogen. In 1985, EPA proposes a ban on Alar, but an "advisory panel" calls for more testing while Alar use is continued. Alar makes apples look good. Do you think catering to consumers' preference for "perfect produce" outweighs the potential health risks the EPA discovered Alar may pose?'

feeds on the pineapple plant and produces a substance called honeydew that is a favorite food of a certain species of ant.

The ants protect the mealy bug from their natural predators, which are ladybird beetles, wasps, and lacewings. No insecticide was effective against the mealy bug, so pineapple growers attacked the ants. The growers said heptachlor was the only insecticide effective against the ants, so the EPA gave the growers permission to continue using heptachlor.

When the pineapple was harvested the leaves of the plant were chopped and fed to the dairy cows. The EPA set certain guidelines for growers to follow. The maximum amount of heptachlor that could be sprayed was less than two pounds per acre. The chopped leaves were to be stored for one year before feeding. The EPA also stipulated the chopped leaves and the milk must be tested for pesticide levels.

The leaves were never tested, and the milk was only tested twice a year. In 1982, samples of milk were found to contain 2.7 ppm heptachlor. This was far above the .03 ppm tolerance level that had been set. Dairy products were recalled. The sale of contaminated milk, butter, ice cream, cottage cheese, and yogurt was banned.

Since then the feeding of the pineapple leaves "green chop" has been stopped and the use of heptachlor has been banned. A year later, the cows were still producing milk with high levels of heptachlor. Scientists did not know how long the pesticide would remain in the cow's bodies.

What will be the long-term effects of heptachlor? It may be difficult to identify heptachlor as the cause of any future health problems that occur. Tests of milk from Hawaiian women showed the presence of several other pesticides including DDT, DDE (a breakdown product of DDT), chlordane, and dieldrin.

A Costly Mistake in the Midwest

It was March 1986, three years after the production of the pesticide heptachlor had been banned. Approximately 100 dairy farmers in Arkansas, Oklahoma, and Missouri were told that they could no longer sell their milk. It was contaminated with the pesticide heptachlor. Thousands of gallons of milk were recalled from a region that included portions of eight different states.

The dairy farmers were surprised to learn about the contamination because none of them had used heptachlor. The FDA discovered the heptachlor in a feed supplement during routine tests on feed produced by Valley Feeds in Van Buren, Arkansas. The supplement is normally a cheap source of feed for dairy cattle, but this time buying the less expensive feed was a costly mistake.

The grain used to make alcohol had been contaminated with the pesticide. The alcohol was not intended for human consumption. It was used in the production of gasohol. The part of the grain that remains after the alcohol is produced is called mash. The mash still contains nutrients and is used as a supplement for cattle feed. Valley Feeds bought the mash and then sold it to the dairy farmers.

The farmers were concerned about the health of their families and about the possibility of losing their farms. Unless they could sell their milk, the farmers would have no income. The heptachlor contamination did not produce any short-term health effects in humans. Those infants whose liver and immune system were still developing have the greatest risk of long-term health effects.

Keeping the Grass Green

The lush green grass that grows on golf courses and lawns is grown with the aid of a number of toxic chemicals. Waterfowl such as Canada geese, ducks, and herons that like grassy areas are frequent victims of pesticide poisoning. Large numbers of the birds have been found dead on golf courses and sod farms.

Seven hundred brant geese died after feeding on a Nassau County, New York, golf course that had been treated with the pesticide diazinon. More than 150 bird die-offs caused by diazinon have been documented by the US Fish and Wildlife Service. The EPA banned the use of diazinon on golf courses and sod farms.

The EPA also requires commercial applicators using diazinon to be certified, but an exception is made for lawn care companies. Diazinon is still available at supermarkets and lawn care centers for use on lawns and gardens, and is widely used by homeowners who are not certified as pesticide applicators. The company that makes diazinon claims that the pesticide can be used safely if it is applied properly.

The Fish and Wildlife Service prosecutes applicators when bird kills occur. One lawn care company claimed to have followed instructions when applying diazinon to the lawn of a condominium development, yet 47 mallards died. The company was fined $4,700. Homeowners can be held liable for birds killed when using pesticides.

Made in the USA

A pesticide banned by the EPA cannot be sold for use in the United States, but the EPA has no authority to ban the export of pesticides. If the EPA does not ban the production of a pesticide, the manufacturer can continue to produce the

T H I N K   A B O U T   I T

Exemptions to a Pesticide Ban:
- Should the EPA permit exemptions to already banned pesticides?
- If so, what circumstances should warrant an exemption?
- If not, what might be the positive and negative impacts of the exemption?

WHAT DO YOU THINK?

New IPM methods have been proposed for controlling destructive grasshopper infestations on grazing lands in the western United States. They involve importation from Australia of a predatory wasp and a parasitic fungus. Do you think that the likelihood that these introduced species will eradicate grasshoppers is worth the risk involved in introducing alien species into the grassland ecosystem?

pesticide and may legally export it to other countries. About 30 percent of the pesticides exported are chemicals that have been banned, severely restricted, or have not yet been approved for use in the United States.

Exporters are required to notify the buyer of any restrictions that the US government has placed on the chemical. They must also make sure that the containers are labeled according to US laws. Unfortunately, this has little effect on how they are used in other countries. One problem is the difference in language and another is that the farmers are often poorly trained. Even those pesticides that are acceptable by US standards may result in poisoned food and poisoned people if not properly stored or used.

Why do people in other countries use DDT after the EPA banned its use in the United States? The varieties of high-yield rice and wheat developed during the Green Revolution are dependent upon the use of agricultural chemicals — fertilizers and pesticides. Cost is an important factor. The chlorinated hydrocarbons are much cheaper than many of the newer pesticides.

People in the United States are concerned about the persistence of DDT (and other chlorinated hydrocarbons) and the long-term effects upon the environment. People in third world countries are more interested in the short-term effects of starvation and the immediate threat of disease.

The use of pesticides in other countries has a widespread effect. Many of the countries that import pesticides export food. A pesticide that is banned in the US may be used in another country to grow food, and that food may be exported to the United States. About one-fourth of all fruits and vegetables that are sold in the United States are imported from other countries. Nearly one-half of all imported fresh and frozen produce comes from Mexico.

Tolerances have been set for 487 pesticides used in the United States and/or Mexico. The Federal Food and Drug Administration monitors the pesticide levels in foods. About 11,000 samples are analyzed each year. Tests have shown that pesticide residues are lower in foods that are grown in the United States than in foods that are grown in other countries.

Only a few samples of food are taken for several million pounds of imported produce. In 1982, fourteen orange samples were taken for each 200 million pounds (9×10^7 kg) of oranges imported. Why were so few oranges tested? The FDA must buy a crate of oranges in order to test for the presence of pesticides. Testing requires expensive equipment and trained personnel. The number of food samples that can be tested is limited by the amount of money that congress approves for the FDA budget.

The Law is Changed

1. What type of tests are required by the 1947 Federal Insecticide, Fungicide, and Rodenticide Act?
2. What type of tests are required by the amendment that was added in 1972?
3. What was the first pesticide to be banned?
4. Have most of the chemicals that are in pesticides sold today been tested for long-term effects?
5. How long may it take to test all the chemicals in the pesticides that are currently sold in the United States?

A Partial List of Pesticides that Have Been Banned

6. List three reasons why the EPA banned or restricted the sale and/or use of certain pesticides.
7. Why were exemptions allowed for heptachlor? chlordane?
8. Which pesticide contaminated the Great Lakes?
9. Which pesticide contaminated the St. James River?
10. Which pesticide caused disorders of the nervous system?
11. Which pesticide was linked to genetic mutations?
12. Which pesticide caused sterility?
13. Which pesticide was found in the drinking water in the San Joaquin Valley?

An Exemption Caused Trouble in Hawaii

14. Which pesticide caused problems in Hawaii?
15. What crop was sprayed with the insecticide?
16. What pest was damaging the pineapple crop?
17. Why didn't the growers use natural predatory insects instead of the pesticide?
18. Why did the EPA allow the growers to use a pesticide that had been banned?
19. Explain how milk was contaminated with heptachlor.
20. What tolerance level was set for heptachlor in food?

21. What level was found in milk?
22. We may never know if any health problems are caused by heptachlor. Why?

A Costly Mistake in the Midwest

23. What pesticide was found in the milk in the Midwest?
24. Explain how the Valley Feed Company made the feed supplement that it sold to the farmers.
25. What were the two major concerns of the farmers?
26. Were there any short-term health effects?
27. Which humans were at the greatest risk of damage from the pesticide in the milk? Why?

Keeping the Grass Green

28. Which pesticide has caused the death of ducks and geese on golf courses?
29. Some of the chemicals used to treat lawns and plants can be dangerous to people or animals if they come in direct contact with them. Should neighbors be notified when the lawn next door is treated with pesticides?
30. Some lawn-care companies are investigating alternatives to pesticides. How might they control pests without using pesticides?

Made in the USA

31. Chemical companies can sell pesticides that have been banned or restricted, and pesticides that have not been approved by the EPA. Who buys them?
32. List two ways that the government regulations try to protect people in countries that buy the pesticides.
33. Give two reasons why the exported pesticides are often the cause of pesticide poisoning.
34. Why do farmers in other countries use pesticides like DDT when less persistent pesticides are available?
35. Why do you think some people in developing countries are not as concerned about the long-term effects of pesticides as some people in developed countries?

36. Furadan 15G has been banned in Virginia and its use is being phased out in the United States. Are you concerned about other countries using this pesticide and other pesticides that are banned in the United States? Why?

37. How might pesticides that are used in other countries affect you and your environment?

38. What agency is responsible for monitoring the pesticide levels in food? Do you think one sample out of 14 million pounds of oranges is enough? If not, how many samples would be enough? Why aren't more samples taken?

Science
Technology
Society

ISSUES

SHOULD AZM BE BANNED?

The sugar in products that satisfies our craving for something sweet comes from sugar cane or sugar beets. Although sugar is the most obvious product of sugar cane, it is possible to produce more than 30 other products including paper, chemicals, and biodegradable plastic. Sugar cane can produce energy — electricity and ethanol — without any net increase in carbon dioxide.

The pesticide endrin protected the sugar cane crop from the corn borer. When endrin was banned, it was replaced with the pesticide azin-phos-methyl (AZM). It appears that AZM may be causing problems, but pesticides may be used if the benefits outweigh the risks. Are the problems severe enough to justify the banning of AZM? That is the question that must be answered.

Some of the most massive fish kills in US history occurred in Louisiana in 1991. One estimate places the loss at one million fish. The cause of death was pesticide poisoning. The pesticide AZM was responsible for 15 separate fish kills in 1991 and 6 fish kills in 1992. No one was prosecuted for the fish kills. One pilot was cited for spraying in the rain, but the charges were later dropped. The fish kills were declared 'acts of God' because runoff following heavy thunderstorms washed the pesticide into the bayous around the sugar cane fields.

AZM is a neurotoxin. It interferes with the normal flow of nerve impulses and causes muscles to contract in random motion. The body of an affected fish appears to vibrate in the water. Death comes from respiratory failure. There were 27 AZM-related health complaints filed with the Louisiana Department of Agriculture and Forestry (DAF) between July 10 and September 19, 1991. One complaint represented a number of people who reported symptoms of pesticide poisoning within hours of spraying near their village. Symptoms reported included acute asthma, eye irritation, severe rashes, and vomiting.

The use of AZM was temporarily suspended. The suspension came late in the season, and the cane borer was not much of a threat.

If you were in charge, would you further restrict or ban the use of AZM?

- Consider the environmental and economic impacts of your decision.
- What additional information would you need to know before making the decision?

Global Sea Surface Temperature

This diagram of Earth's sea surface temperature was created from two weeks of infrared observations by the Advanced Very High Resolution Radiometer (AVHRR), an instrument on board NOAA-7 during July 1984.

Temperatures are color coded with red being warmest and decreasing through oranges, yellows, greens, and blues.

Temperature patterns seen in this image are the result of many influences including the circulation in the ocean, surface winds and solar heating. Major ocean currents such as the Gulf Stream off the United States East Coast, the Kuroshio off the East Coast of Japan, the mixing of the Brazil and Falkland currents off the eastern coast of South America, and the Agulhas off southern Africa appear as meandering boundries of cool and warm waters.

Images of sea surface temperature such as this help scientists to better monitor and ultimately understand the changes to Earth caused by events such as El Niño.

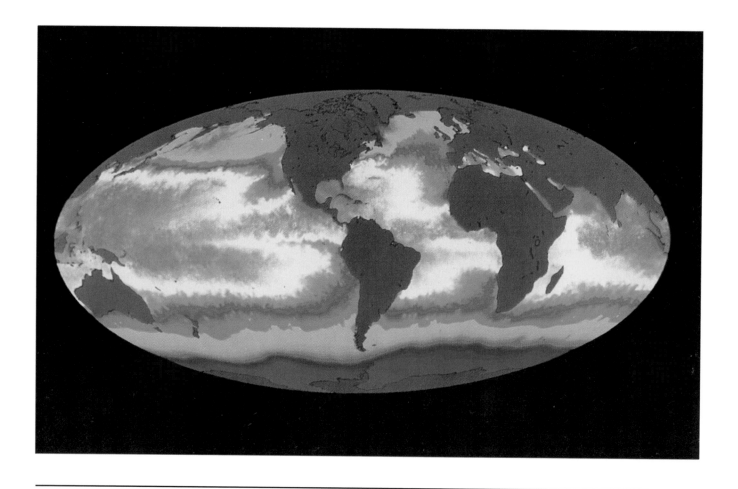

Aquatic Environments

There are many types of aquatic environments. There are freshwater ecosystems and saltwater ecosystems. Freshwater ecosystems can be divided into two groups: those with moving water and those with standing water. Standing bodies of water include lakes and ponds. The major difference is that a **lake** is a standing body of water with an area that is too deep for rooted plants to grow. Unlike the lake, a **pond** is so shallow that rooted plants grow across the entire bottom.

Flowing waters include rivers, streams, brooks, creeks, and human-made channels through which water moves. **Streams** are bodies of flowing water that are usually more shallow than a pond. Streams are sometimes called creeks or brooks. A body of flowing water that is much larger and deeper than a stream is called a **river**. The large volume of water in a river or lake comes from the many streams that flow into it. These streams are called its **tributaries**.

Human-made channels are straight box-like ditches that have been dug to move water more efficiently. Human-made channels do not offer wildlife the variety of habitats that can be found in natural streams and rivers. There are several different **habitats** or places where organisms can live in an aquatic ecosystem. Aquatic habitats include:

- **Surface film** — the place where the water meets the air. Animals found here include air-breathing insects that may walk on or hang from the surface of the water.
- **Open water** — the area where the rooted plants do not reach the surface of the water. It is the habitat for large fish, turtles, and birds. Microscopic plants and animals float in the open water. These organisms are known collectively as **plankton**.
- **Bottom** — the area of rocks, sand, or mud that is the habitat for a variety of small organisms including bacteria, snails, worms, sponges, crayfish, and the larvae of some aquatic insects.
- **Water's edge** — where the water meets the land. This area is home for the greatest number of species of plants and animals. Many small organisms can be found on the leaves and stems of plants. The plants provide many hiding places where small fish and other organisms find some protection (cover) and a place to breed.

This river receives water from many tributaries.

Channels — box-like ditches are dug to move water more efficiently. Although they provide habitat for some species, like this anhinga, they do not provide the variety of habitats found in a natural stream.

The great blue heron walks slowly through the shallows at the water's edge looking for prey that might be hiding beneath the vegetation.

The habitats found in streams depend upon the volume of flowing water and the slope of the stream bed. Streams are divided into three different regions — upper reaches, middle reaches, and lower reaches.

The **upper reaches** include the regions of the stream with the greatest slope. Often the water appears white because its surface is broken as it flows over rocks. These areas are called **rapids**. There are many shallow areas of swiftly flowing water. These areas are called **riffles**. Rapids, riffles, and waterfalls are abundant in the upper reaches of a stream. The fast-moving water causes constant erosion. The bottom of the stream is covered by rocks that are too large to be carried by the water. The rocks are worn by the force of the water and the load of sand and gravel that it carries.

Organisms that live in the upper reaches must constantly fight the fast current of water. Rocky projections create small **pools** or areas of slower moving water. Although the fish living in this region of the stream are strong swimmers, they spend most of their time in these pools. They dart from the pool to feed on insects that are carried by the current and then return to the pool to wait for the next meal.

Organisms that are not good swimmers must hold on. Algae, insect larvae, and other organisms attach themselves firmly to the surfaces of rocks so that they will not be washed away. The small animals either strain microscopic food from the flowing water, or they feed on the algae that is growing on the rocks.

The upper reaches of the stream contain fewer species of plants and animals than other regions of the stream that have slower moving water. The populations of those species in the upper reaches are smaller than populations found in regions with slower moving water.

The **middle reaches** include the sections of the stream with less slope than the upper reaches. There is less erosion, and silt (fine particles of soil) may be deposited in some pools. The pools are larger

Are these scenes found along the upper, middle, or lower reaches of a river?

and more plentiful than in the upper reaches. Rooted plants growing along the stream's edges provide food and shelter for some species.

The number of species found in the middle reaches is greater than the number found in the upper reaches. The population densities are also greater — there are more organisms per unit area. Most organisms are found in the shallow areas of the stream rather than in the deeper water.

The **lower reaches** include the sections with a gentle, steady flow. There are no rapids, riffles, or waterfalls. The eroded material from the upper and middle reaches is deposited here. The bottom of the stream is covered with mud or sand.

Bushes and trees grow along the edges. Flat areas known as swamps or flood plains border the stream. Seasonal flooding deposits sand and soil over this land. The community of plants and animals of the lower reaches is very much like the community of a pond.

Each ecosystem has its own community of organisms. Each species has a **niche** to fill — a job to do. It is the complex interactions among the species that keeps the ecosystem in balance.

1.1 QUESTIONS FOR STUDY AND DISCUSSION

1. What characteristic is used to classify a body of water as a pond instead of a lake?
2. What characteristic is used to classify a body of flowing water as a river instead of a stream?
3. Identify the habitat of the pond or lake which will contain the most species and the largest populations.
4. What term refers to the streams which flow into a river or a lake?
5. How do human-made channels differ from natural streams and rivers?
6. Match the stream habitat listed in column II with the correct description given in column I.

Column I	Column II
Description	**Stream Habitat**
A. region with greatest slope	1. lower reaches
B. region with gentle, steady flow	2. middle reaches
C. community of organisms most like a pond	3. upper reaches
D. rocky bottom; constant erosion	
E. region with least slope	
F. some areas of erosion and some areas of silt deposits	
G. stream bordered by flood plains	
H. region with waterfalls	
I. region with small pools; many riffles and rapids	
J. region with fewest species	
K. muddy or sandy bottom	
L. region with large pools; some riffles and rapids	

Creatures that Live in the Water

What kind of organisms can be found in aquatic environments? A survey of organisms in an aquatic ecosystem reveals much about the quality of the water. The aquatic insects and other small organisms are the best indicators of water quality because they do not move very far or very fast. Chemicals dumped in the water may be carried quickly downstream.

As you study these creatures you will learn that some are "clean water" organisms while others are "pollution tolerant." Certain organisms are called **index species** because their presence in large numbers can tell us whether the water is clean or polluted.

Tubifex Worms "sludge worms" (Segmented Worms)

Habitat: Tubifex worms inhabit the muddy and/or sandy bottoms of aquatic habitats including lakes, swamps, ponds, rivers, and streams.

Activity: They burrow head first into the bottom sediment. The tail-end waves back and forth in the water increasing the exchange of oxygen between the water and the body of the worm. Tubifex worms use very little oxygen.

Eat and Eaten By: Like their cousin, the earthworm, *Tubifex* worms feed on small organic particles and bacteria. They are eaten by waterfowl, fish, and many invertebrates including leeches, midge larvae, dragonfly nymphs, flatworms, and water mites.

Environmental factors: *Tubifex* worms can tolerate organic pollution, and their presence in large numbers indicates large amounts of organic matter — sewage or decaying vegetation. They are an index species — indicators of organic pollution. They can tolerate low levels of dissolved oxygen and high levels of heavy metals, insecticides, herbicides, and fungicides. Their tolerance and uptake of these dangerous chemicals can result in large amounts of these chemicals in organisms that feed on the *Tubifex* worms.

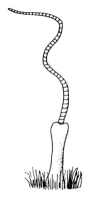

Tubifex Worm (Sludge worm)

Leeches (Segmented Worms)

Habitat: Leeches live in quiet water, especially ponds in northern states.

Activity: Leeches are sensitive to light and to vibrations. They move toward vibrations. They are usually attached to aquatic plants unless they are searching for food.

Eat and Eaten By: Leeches are sometimes parasitic. They may attach themselves to turtles, fish, salamanders, frogs, and tadpoles. When blood is not available they feed on snails, worms, and insect larvae. Some species are scavengers feeding on dead organic matter.

Environmental factors: Leeches are seldom found in acidic waters.

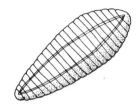

Bloodsucking Leech

Free-living Flatworms

Habitat: All types of fresh water.

Activity: Flatworms cling to plants and stones in shallow water. They are sensitive to light and avoid it by hiding under objects.

Eat and Eaten By: A few species feed on certain types of algae. Most are carnivores, feeding on small animals either living or dead. They are eaten by other worms, insects, and crustaceans.

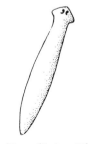

Planaria (Free-living Flatworm)

Crayfish (Crustaceans)

Habitat: Crayfish inhabit wet meadows, ponds, streams, and rivers; they are seldom found where water is more than 5 feet (1.5 m) deep.

Activity: They spend the day in burrows that can be identified by "chimneys" made of mud balls piled high from digging the burrow. They are active at night.

Eat and Eaten By: Crayfish are omnivores, eating fish, aquatic insects, plants and dead organic matter. They are eaten by fish, wading birds, frogs, turtles, raccoons, otter, mink, and humans.

Environmental Factors: In the southern part of the US they sometimes become a pest feeding on grain, sugarcane, and cotton seedlings. They also burrow into dams and dikes. If eaten, they must be cooked thoroughly because they are sometimes a host for a lung fluke that is a parasite in man.

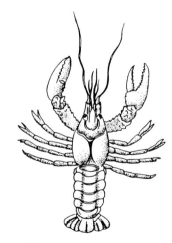

Crayfish

Scuds "Sideswimmers" (Crustaceans)

Habitat: Scuds live in ponds, deep water of large lakes, streams.

Activity: Scuds swim on their sides. They avoid light and usually live close to the bottom.

Eat and Eaten By: Scuds are scavengers on dead plants and animals. They are eaten by fishes that feed near the bottom.

Environmental Factors: Scuds are found in large numbers in clear, clean waters.

Scud (Sideswimmer)

Water Flea

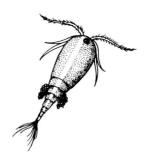

Female Cyclops (A Common Copepod)

Seed Shrimp

Fish Spider

Water Fleas (Crustaceans)

Habitat: Water fleas are abundant in all fresh water.

Activity: Water fleas sweep food into their mouths with their "legs." They swim with a jerky motion using their antenna.

Eat and Eaten By: They feed on algae, microscopic animals including smaller water fleas, and decaying organic matter. Water fleas provide 90% of the diet of small fish. They are also eaten by hydras, insects and wading birds.

Environmental Factors: Water fleas are abundant in all types of water except rapid streams and polluted waters.

Copepods (Crustaceans)

Habitat: Copepods are common in all quiet waters, and they can sometimes be found in running water.

Activity: Some species form cysts when conditions are not favorable. This helps them survive during droughts. The cysts are often spread by the wind.

Eat and Eaten By: Copepods feed upon organic matter, algae, and bacteria. Several species are parasites on fish, but they rarely do any damage. They are eaten by hydra, fish, and other animals, but they are not as important a food source as water fleas.

Seed Shrimps (Crustaceans)

Habitat: Seed shrimps inhabit all types of fresh water.

Activity: Seed shrimp are commonly found in mats of algae and in bottom mud. They lay their eggs on the stems of plants and the roots of duckweed.

Eat and Eaten By: Seed shrimp are scavengers. They are eaten by small fish.

Spiders (Arachnids)

Habitat: Some spiders live near the shore while others live beneath the surface of the water.

Activity: The fisher spider can dive and remain below the surface of the water, for long periods of time. It is covered with body hair that traps a coat of air around its body. Other spiders live near the shore and may be seen skating across the water.

Eat and Eaten By: Spiders feed mainly on insects, but they sometimes eat a small fish or tadpole. They feed by sucking the fluids from the body of the chosen victim.

Water Mites (Arachnids)

Habitat: Water mites are found in quiet pools of streams as well as ponds and lakes. They are also found in temporary pools and hot springs.

Activity: Most water mites crawl about on submerged plants or on the muddy or sandy bottom. They must surface for air.

Eat and Eaten By: Most water mites feed on worms, small crustaceans and insects; some are parasites. They are the prey of hydras, insects, and fish. Sometimes they are the main food found in a fish's stomach.

Environmental Factors: Some biologists feel that water mites are valuable as a control for mosquitoes. A mosquito with several mites will not feed, and without blood the mosquito cannot reproduce.

Water Mite

Mosquitoes (Insects)

Habitat: Mosquito larvae and pupae live in any standing water.

Activity: Mosquito **larvae** cling to the surface of the water and breathe air through small tubes. They are often called "wrigglers" because of the wriggling motion they make as they move through the water while feeding.

After seven days of feeding, they change into a **pupa** that is shaped like a question mark. The pupae cling to the surface of the water for two days while changing into the adult form. The female mosquito returns to the water where she deposits a small raft of eggs.

Eat and Eaten By: Mosquito larvae feed on algae, microscopic organisms, and organic matter. The pupae do not eat. The adult females need a dose of protein for development of the eggs. Thus, it is only the females that feed on human blood. The adult males may not eat at all, or they may feed on the nectar of flowers and ripe fruit.

Mosquito larvae and pupae become food for some small fish. One mosquito-eating fish, the gamusia or mosquito fish, has been released in the California rice fields and the Reflecting Pool in Washington, D.C.

Environmental Factors: Mosquitoes carry the parasites that cause malaria and the viruses that cause yellow fever and encephalitis. They also carry organisms that cause diseases in other animals, such as heartworm in dogs. In Africa, every year one million deaths are caused by malaria. Other countries such as India, Pakistan, Asia and Central America also have a large number of deaths caused by malaria. In North America five different kinds of encephalitis are caused by viruses carried by mosquitoes.

Mosquito Larva

Phantom Midge Larva

Cranefly Larva

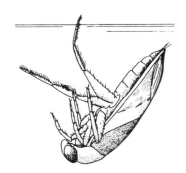

Backswimmer

Water Boatman

Midgeflies (Insects)

Habitat: Midge flies may live in any body of fresh water. Some species live in the water of pitcher plants.

Activity: Some species of midge flies build tubes and others live in the stems of plants. They spin nets to catch their food.

Eat and Eaten By: Most midge fly larvae eat algae and decayed plant matter caught by their nets. They may be the most important source of food for young fish and other aquatic carnivores.

Environmental Factors: No other single genus of insects is so important as a food source for so many different fish.

Craneflies (Insects)

Habitat: Some cranefly larvae live among decaying plants and mud at the edge of ponds and lakes. Some live in fast moving water, while others live in very moist places such as a wet meadow, damp moss, or decaying wood.

Activity: Adult craneflies are often seen swarming near ponds. They are poor fliers and often become food for a carnivore. The larvae breathe by pushing a disk through the surface of the water.

Eat and Eaten By: Cranefly larvae feed on leaves and roots of aquatic plants and on algae. A few species feed on *Tubifex* worms and small insect larvae. Pupae and new adults are eaten by spiders. The larvae are eaten by trout, frogs, salamanders, and birds. The adults are eaten by birds, amphibians, spiders, and other insects, especially dragonflies.

Backswimmers (Insects)

Habitat: Backswimmers are common in most quiet ponds.

Activity: When resting, backswimmers hang head-downward from the surface of the water, or they hold onto plant stems with their front legs. They must come to the surface for a new supply of air. They carry the air underneath their wings and on the lower side of their body. The air appears as a silver film. They have a beak that can inflict a painful bite.

Eat and Eaten By: Backswimmers are predators, usually feeding on small crustaceans that they hold with their front legs. Sometimes they attack small fish. The young are eaten by other insect predators.

Water Boatman (Insects)

Habitat: Water boatmen inhabit the shallow water of ponds, lakes, streams, and muddy pools.

Activity: Water boatmen must surface for air, but they always break the surface of the water with their head-end, and they always swim with their backs up. They must cling to water plants to remain submerged.

Eat and Eaten By: Water boatmen are omnivores. Their major source of food is dead plant matter or filamentous algae. They pierce the cell wall with their beak and drink the liquid from the cell. They also feed on mosquito larvae and other small organisms. Water boatmen are eaten by fish.

Water Scorpions (Insects)

Habitat: Water scorpions usually can be found among the muddy leaves and stems of plants at the edge of the pond or stream.

Activity: They remain underwater lying in wait for their prey. They often back up a stem of a plant and breathe through the long air-tube made with the long tail filaments.

Eat and Eaten By: Water scorpions are predators. They feed upon mayfly and damselfly nymphs, snails, and crustaceans. They clutch the prey with their powerful front legs and suck the juices from the body.

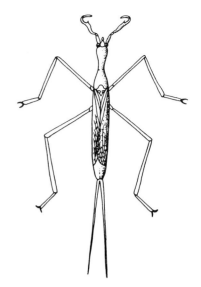

Water Scorpion

Water Striders (Insects)

Habitat: Most water striders live on the surface of quiet or gently flowing water.

Activity: Water striders or pond skaters skim rapidly over the surface. They sometimes collect in schools. A water strider's body is covered with short hairs. This provides an envelope of air when they dive beneath the surface to capture their prey.

Eat and Eaten By: Water striders are predators. They feed on insects that fall into the water, and they catch crustaceans and small aquatic insects (backswimmers and emerging midges) that come near the surface. They are often hosts for the larvae of parasitic water mites.

Water Strider

Giant Water Bugs (Insects)

Habitat: Giant water bugs live among the plants or on the bottom of ponds and quiet pools.

Activity: They often rest on the bottom, or they sit with the tip of the abdomen extended above the surface of the water. Air fills a system of air tubes and is carried in the space beneath the wings. Giant water bugs are good fliers. One species that is attracted to lights is known as the electric-light bug. Swimmers sometimes are bitten by these bugs.

Eat and Eaten By: Giant water bugs are fierce predators. They feed on dragonflies and other insects, crustaceans, tadpoles, frogs, and fish.

Environmental Factors: Giant water bugs can become a serious pest in fish hatcheries.

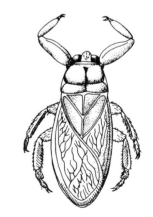

Giant Water Bug

Larva

Predaceous Diving Beetle

Whirligig Beetle

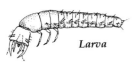

Larva

Scavenger Beetle

Dragonfly Nymph

Predaceous Diving Beetles (Insects)

Habitat: Diving beetles live in weed-grown areas of lakes, ponds, and streams.

Activity: Adult diving beetles often hang head down. Only the tip of the abdomen is above the surface of the water. The larvae are called "water tigers." Both larvae and adults are very active predators. The adults use their hind legs as oars when swimming.

Eat and Eaten By: Diving beetles feed upon any small animals they can catch. Both the larvae and the adults attack tadpoles, leeches, snails, insects (including other water beetles), and small fish. They become food for reptiles, amphibians, fish, wading birds, raccoons, and skunks.

Whirligig Beetles (Insects)

Habitat: Whirligig beetles inhabit quiet ponds, lakes, puddles, or backwater of flooded streams.

Activity: Whirligig beetles are easily recognized by their whirling motion. The larvae hide and hunt on the bottom. The larvae look like centipedes.

Eat and Eaten By: Adult beetles feed on insects caught on the surface of the water. Some are scavengers. The larvae are predators, feeding on *Tubifex* worms, insect nymphs and small fish.

Scavenger Beetles (Insects)

Habitat: Scavenger beetles live in weedy ponds and flooded areas with emerging plants.

Activity: Scavenger beetles are covered with a silver film of air when submerged and are sometimes called "silver beetles." To get air they stick their club-shaped antenna through the surface of the water. They have oar-like hind legs like the diving beetles. Unlike the diving beetles, they alternate legs as if "walking" through the water. This trait may be useful in identification.

Eat and Eaten By: The adult beetles are scavengers feeding mainly on dead plant material. The larvae are mainly predators. The hundreds of young larvae that hatch from the eggs feed on each other.

Dragonflies (Insects)

Habitat: Dragonflies inhabit ponds, lakes, and streams often covered with silt and with emerging vegetation.

Activity: Adult dragonflies hold their wings in a horizontal position when at rest. Damselflies fold their wings when at rest. This difference can be used to identify the adults. Adult dragonflies are predators. They fly about, patrolling the weedy edge of ponds. The nymphs patrol the muddy bottoms of ponds and seize their prey with an extended lower lip that has hooks. The lip is used as a long arm.

Eat and Eaten By: The nymphs feed on insect larvae, worms, snails, small crustaceans, tadpoles, and small fish. Both the nymphs and adults feed on mosquitoes. In some areas of the country, the adults are called "mosquito hawks." Although they compete with young fish for food, they are important food in the diet of adult fish.

Damselfly (Insects)

Habitat: Damselflies make their home in ponds, lakes, and streams, often covered with silt and with emerging vegetation.

Activity: Damselflies are much more delicate-looking than dragonflies, but looks don't tell the entire story. Their activity is very much like that of the dragonflies except that they fold their wings when at rest.

Eat and Eaten By: The prey and predators of the damselfly are the same as for the dragonfly.

Damselfly Nymph

Mayflies (Insects)

Habitat: Mayflies thrive in clean fresh water. Mayflies can live in almost any water habitat unless it is polluted.

Activity: Mayfly nymphs can most easily be recognized by the seven pairs of gills along the abdomen and two or three long tail filaments. They have a single claw on each foot. Clouds of adults are often seen on early summer evenings. The adults have only one purpose in life — to reproduce. A few hours or days after becoming an adult, they mate and deposit eggs in the water. Death soon follows.

Eat and Eaten By: Mayfly nymphs are herbivores. They feed on algae and sometimes the leaves of rooted plants. They are an important food source for larger aquatic insects and fish. The adults do not eat. They are frequently the prey of birds, frogs, fish, and dragonflies.

Environmental Factors: The mayfly is an indicator species — an indicator of clean water. They cannot survive in polluted water. Mayflies are an important link in the food chain.

Mayfly

Stoneflies (Insects)

Habitat: Stonefly nymphs can be found on the dark side of stones in clean running water.

Activity: Both the nymphs and the adults prefer shade. The flattened nymphs cling to rocks with two strong claws. The adults hide among leaves of shrubs close to the water. Neither the nymphs or the adults are very active.

Eat and Eaten By: The nymphs of most species feed on algae and dead plant matter. A few species eat other insects. The adults of most species do not feed. Stoneflies are an important food for fish. They are considered the most important food item in the diet of young trout.

Environmental Factors: The presence of stoneflies indicates clean water and high levels of oxygen. They are very seldom found in polluted water or water with low levels of oxygen. They can only be kept in an aquarium if an air pump is used to oxygenate the water.

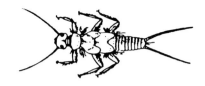

Stonefly Nymph

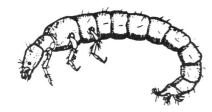

Caddisfly Larva

Hellgrammite (Dobsonfly Larva)

Springtail

Riffle Beetle

Water Pennies (Beetle Larvae)

Caddisflies (Insects)

Habitat: Caddisflies occur in every aquatic ecosystem.

Activity: Most caddisfly larvae live in cases made of mud, sticks, and stones. They usually creep along the bottom in search of food. Some species that live in streams build nets to catch food. The adults are active at night and are attracted to lights, but they are not very strong fliers.

Eat and Eaten By: Most larvae feed on algae and dead plant matter. They also eat crustaceans, insects, and worms. They are an important food in the diet of trout and other fish. The adults do not feed.

Dobsonflies (Insects)

Habitat: Dobsonfly larvae live under stones in the fastest part of swift moving streams.

Activity: The larvae, commonly called **hellgrammites**, avoid the light and are seldom seen unless stones are quickly pulled from the stream. When threatened they often swim backwards. The adults are often attracted to lights and often fall to the ground after circling the light several times.

Eat and Eaten By: The larvae are predators and feed on other aquatic insects. They are eaten by fish.

Springtails (Insects)

Habitat: Springtails inhabit the surface of water along shorelines of ponds and streams.

Activity: Springtails have six legs, but they often jump by using a tail-like structure similar to the spring of a mouse trap.

Eat and Eaten By: They feed on dead plant and animal matter. References do not indicate that they are an important source of food for other organisms.

Water Pennies (Insects)

Habitat: These insects live in rapid currents. Most beetles live in quiet waters with submerged or emerging plants where they hide while waiting for their prey. They also lay their eggs among the plants. Unlike other beetles, **riffle beetles** lay their eggs on stones in the swiftest part of the current.

Activity: The flat, copper-colored larvae, called a water penny, cling to the underside of rocks in the rapids. When a rock is pulled from the water, the water penny remains motionless and can easily be overlooked. They must be removed from the rock and turned on their back in order to see their legs and gills.

Eat and Eaten By: Both the larvae, called a water penny, and the adult riffle beetle are herbivores, feeding on the algae that grows on the stones. They are food for the dragonfly larvae, other predaceous beetles, water birds and even turtles.

Snails (Mollusks)

Habitat: Most species live in the shallow water of ponds, streams, lakes, and rivers.

Activity: Snails glide slowly on their muscular foot over the surfaces of all objects beneath the water.

Eat and Eaten By: The snails feed on algae and plant parts. They are eaten by most larger animals. Some of their predators include dragonfly nymphs, giant water bugs, fishes, frogs, salamanders, turtles, muskrats, and raccoons.

Winkle (Snail)

Mussels (Mollusks)

Habitat: Larger mussels burrow in the muddy bottoms of rivers or lakes. Some smaller species are found on the rocky bottoms of clear streams.

Activity: Mussels have a foot that they use for digging into the river bottom. They have siphons that take in water and small particles of food. The larvae (glochidia) develop in the gills of the female clam.

Once they develop their first shell, they leave the female through the siphon and attach to the fins or gills of a specific species of fish. If they attach to the wrong species they drop off.

Eat and Eaten By: The larvae remain as parasites on fish for several weeks. The adults feed on microscopic plankton and organic matter. Mussels are eaten by fish, muskrats, and raccoons.

Environmental Factors: Because mussels live long lives and their movement is limited, they are excellent indicators of water quality. All species require flowing water and a stream with a stable bottom. Some species can live in a wide range of water quality conditions, while other species have more specific needs that must be met.

Fingernail Clam

1.2 QUESTIONS FOR STUDY AND DISCUSSION

1. What groups of organisms are the best indicators of water quality?
2. Why are living organisms sometimes better indicators of water quality than chemical tests?
3. Match the habitat listed in Column II with the correct description given in Column I.

Column I Description	Column II Habitat
A. Tubifex worms	1. bottom
B. spiders	2. water's edge
C. water striders	3. surface

4. Match the organism listed in Column I with the correct habitat given in Column II.

Column I Organism	Column II Habitat
A. predaceous diving beetles	1. bottom
B. larvae of whirligig beetles	2. water's edge
C. dragonfly nymphs	3. surface
D. stonefly nymphs	
E. mosquito larvae	

5. Large numbers of these organisms are found in water with very low levels of dissolved oxygen and high levels of organic pollution:
a. leeches b. scuds c. Tubifex worms

6. Which of the following is *not* a niche of a leech?
   a. herbivore   b. parasite   c. scavenger
7. Large numbers of scuds and water fleas indicate:
   a. clean water   b. polluted water
   c. low level of dissolved oxygen.
8. The niche of a seed shrimp is:
   a. herbivore   b. parasite   c. scavenger
9. Which of the following is the most important fish food?
   a. copepods   b. seed shrimps   c. water fleas
10. Which of the following adaptations allows a water spider to remain submerged for long periods of time:
    a. large book lungs   b. body hairs to trap air
    c. gills
11. Which of the following insects carries the organism that causes malaria?
    a. cranefly   b. midge   c. mosquito
12. Which of the following is an omnivore?
    a. backswimmer   b. water scorpion
    c. water boatman
13. Which of the following insects breathes through long air tubes?
    a. predaceous diving beetles
    b. water scorpions   c. water striders
14. What is the common source of food for the mayfly nymphs, water pennies, and snails?
    a. algae   b. crustaceans
    c. small insect larvae
15. Which of the following insects are indicators of clean water?
    a. damselfly and dragonfly nymphs
    b. cranefly and midgefly larvae
    c. mayfly and stonefly nymphs
16. Which of the following insect larvae is also known as a hellgrammite?
    a. damselfly   b. dobsonfly   c. dragonfly
17. The larvae of this aquatic organism is a parasite on fish:
    a. mussels   b. snails   c. water pennies
18. Which of the following insect larvae live in cases they have made?
    a. caddisfly   b. mayfly   c. stonefly
19. Water mites are valuable because they:
    a. help control insects
    b. they are an important food for fish
    c. both
20. Which insect becomes a pest at fish hatcheries?
    a. predaceous diving beetles
    b. water scavenger beetle   c. giant water bug
21. This insect nymph can be recognized by its seven pairs of gill filaments along the abdomen and two or three tail filaments:
    a. damselfly   b. mayfly   c. stonefly
22. Which of these insects is the most important item in the diet of young trout?
    a. mayfly nymph   b. stonefly nymph
    c. caddisfly larvae
23. Which of the following organisms is most likely found in an open water habitat?
    a. small fish   b. large fish   c. crayfish
24. Give three ways in which plants along the water's edge are important to other organisms living there.

Plants in an Aquatic Ecosystem

1.3

In biology class you probably learned that algae are members of the kingdom Protista. Although biologists classify most algae as protists, many people refer to algae as plants. Many references include algae as a type of aquatic plant. Whether algae are classified as protists or plants is not an issue that concerns the ecologist. The ecologist is most interested in the role that algae play — their **niche** — in the ecosystem.

Types of Algae

Very small, usually microscopic types of floating algae are known as **plankton algae**. When present in large numbers, plankton algae give the water a brown, yellow, red, or pea-soup green color. Although they are not flowering plants, when enough algae are present to color the water it is called an **algal bloom**. When there is an algal bloom, each milliliter of water contains thousands, or even millions, of alga cells.

Pond scum is a floating mat of filamentous algae. **Filamentous algae** grow as long strands or filaments instead of individual floating cells. Some filamentous algae form a green fur-like covering on stones in fast-moving streams.

Another type of alga, sometimes mistaken for a flowering plant, is often found on the bottom of ponds or lakes in areas with limestone soil. **Stonewort algae**, easily identified by a central stem with whorls of branches, may grow to a length of 2 or 3 feet (0.6-1 m). It is sometimes called **muskgrass algae** because of its appearance and odor.

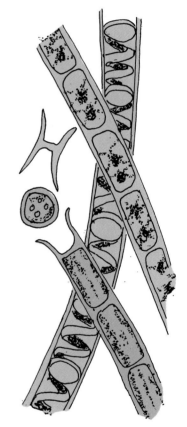

Filamentous and Plankton Algae

The Importance of Algae

Algae are the most important **producers** in any aquatic ecosystem. Some species of algae serve as the first link in many food chains. Another important role for algae is the production of oxygen. Algae use carbon dioxide and produce oxygen during photosynthesis. They produce most of the dissolved oxygen in standing or slow moving water. Much of this oxygen escapes into the atmosphere. However, some remains as dissolved oxygen (DO) to support life in the water.

Most organisms, including algae, use oxygen for respiration. When there are too many algae competing for a place in the sunlight,

The algae bloom in this aging pond is due to millions of microscopic cells in each milliliter of water.

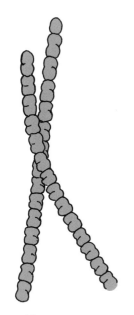

Anabeana Algae

many of the algae die and decay. The demand for oxygen increases. When the weather brings a series of warm, calm, and cloudy days, the algae cannot produce enough oxygen to meet the needs of all the aquatic organisms.

Some fish require high levels of dissolved oxygen. When the amount of dissolved oxygen in the water is not sufficient to meet their needs, the fish die. A **fish kill** — the death of many fish at one time — may be caused by too many algae. The cause of the fish kill may be the lack of oxygen, or the algae may produce toxic chemicals.

Some species of algae damage the gills of fish. Excessive concentrations of certain algae can be a problem for other animals as well. Algal blooms have caused the deaths of sheep, horses, dogs, ducks, and cattle.

Some types of algae make swimmers sick. Some algal blooms are toxic to humans. *Anabaena*, a blue-green alga, can cause an allergic reaction. Swallowing water with high concentrations of *Anabaena* causes cramps, diarrhea, nausea, headaches, muscle pain, weakness, and sore throats. Water with a pea-soup green color is not safe for swimming.

Many lakes and reservoirs have large populations of certain species of algae that cause taste and odor problems. A fishy odor in a water supply is frequently due to the presence of certain algae rather than fish. One species of algae gives the water the odor of a pig pen.

Water treatment plants remove algae and other particles by filtering the water through sand. As water passes through the filter, the particles are trapped in the spaces between the grains of sand. When algae are present in large numbers, the filters become quickly clogged.

As the particles fill the spaces between the grains of sand, the flow of water slows. The direction of the water is reversed to remove the algae and other particles. This process is called a **backwash**. Normally filters are cleaned every twenty-four to thirty-six hours. During an algal bloom, the filters must be washed more frequently. An algal bloom can add several thousand dollars a day to the cost of cleaning the water in a big city like Detroit.

Types of Flowering Plants

There are three types of flowering plants that grow in aquatic ecosystems.

- **Submerged plants** — These plants grow in deep water and usually are rooted in the muddy bottom. Except for the flower, these plants grow entirely below the surface of the water.
- **Emerging plants** — These plants grow in shallow water. Most of the stems, leaves and flowers grow above the water.
- **Floating plants** — These plants have floating leaves and flowers, or their leaves and flowers rise only slightly above the surface.

The Importance of Flowering Plants

The submerged stems and leaves of flowering plants provide habitats for many small organisms. The surfaces of leaves and stems provide homes for bacteria, fungi, algae, diatoms, protozoa, insect larvae, aquatic worms and other small organisms. Fish and amphibians deposit their eggs among the plants. The plants provide protection from predators and a source of food for the young.

The emerging plants along the shore prevent erosion and provide cover for fur-bearing animals such as beaver, muskrats, and mink. Muskrats and beavers feed on the roots and stems of plants such as cattails and water lilies. The plants at the water's edge provide nesting sites for many species of waterfowl and other birds, such as the red-winged blackbird. The seeds provide an important source of food.

It is easy to see the benefits of a large pond. A large pond increases the value of a property. Potential buyers can anticipate hours of relaxation fishing, swimming, or simply watching the activity of the wildlife.

What if the pond is only a small pond that dries up in the middle of the summer? Ponds less than four feet deep may dry up during the summer, freeze solid in winter, or both. Such temporary ponds cannot support a population of fish. They are too shallow and weedy for swimming, and too small for ice skating.

A small, shallow, weedy pond provides excellent salamander and amphibian breeding habitat. The "weeds" provide places for egg-laying as well as hiding places for the larvae. It is the lack of fish in these temporary ponds that makes them the ideal place for salamanders and amphibians to breed. Fish eat eggs and larvae, and they compete with reptiles and amphibians for food. The absence of fish greatly increases the chance that an egg will survive to become an adult.

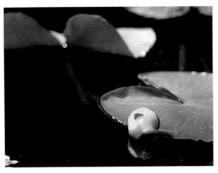

The surfaces of leaves and stems of these water lilies provide cover and food for many small aquatic organisms.

Emerging plants along the shore of a pond provide food and cover for birds, mammals, and fish.

Water Pollution and Plant Growth

Some pollutants inhibit the growth of aquatic plants while other pollutants stimulate growth. Both types of pollutants can create serious problems. Chemicals that affect the growth of aquatic plants may enter an aquatic ecosystem when there is an industrial accident or from daily operations at an industrial plant — **point sources** of water pollution. Herbicides and fertilizers enter aquatic ecosystems in storm water runoff from lawns and farms — **nonpoint sources** of water pollution.

Many aquatic ecosystems, especially ponds and lakes, are polluted with chemicals that stimulate plant growth. This is due to increased levels of certain chemicals that are plant nutrients (fertilizers). The primary chemicals that stimulate growth are nitrates and phosphates. Major sources of nutrients are sewage treatment plants, developments with individual home septic systems, food processing plants, the application of fertilizers, and animal wastes.

Water Use and Plant Growth

The intended use of a body of water determines whether the growth of plants is desirable. For some uses, there may be too many plants. If the major use for a body of water is recreation that includes boating, swimming, and water skiing, too much plant growth is undesirable and may be hazardous.

Too many aquatic plants interfere with operations at fish hatcheries. Excessive plant growth slows the flow of water in irrigation systems, and the plants steal water intended for farm crops. Pipes in industries and water treatment plants may become clogged with floating plants. Certain species of algae give water an unpleasant odor and flavor.

For some uses, plant growth is essential. Aquatic plants attract ducks and geese. People who fish like a limited number of aquatic plants that provide cover, food, and a spawning site for the fish. Plant growth at the water's edge is also needed to control erosion.

Controlling Plant Growth

When the presence of aquatic plants interferes with the planned use of the water, it is necessary to control their growth. Control of submerged plants is not necessary in ponds that are more than ten feet (3 m) deep. There is not enough sunlight at this depth to allow much plant growth. Consideration of this fact when building a pond can prevent problems later. When necessary, the following methods can be used to control plant growth:

Physical Removal — This method is most effective for small quantities of plants at the water's edge. Pulling or cutting must be repeated to prevent new growth. The physical removal of submerged plants is often not practical because fragments of the stems left in the water will frequently grow into new plants.

Animals — Animals that eat aquatic plants are not usually very helpful in controlling plant populations. Fragments left behind develop into new plants. Ducks and geese feed on certain floating and submerged plants, but their wastes provide fertilizers that cause algal blooms.

Some exotic species of fish have been promoted to control aquatic vegetation. Their total impact upon the ecosystem is not fully known. The release of these fish is prohibited in some states.

Chemicals: Many aquatic weeds can be controlled with chemicals. Chemicals that kill unwanted plants are called **herbicides**. The following steps must be taken to provide the most effective control and the least damage to the environment:

- Identify the plants causing the problem.
- Select the correct herbicide.
- Determine the time of application that will provide the most effective control. It is usually late spring or early summer.

- Calculate the surface area and the average depth of the pond or lake. This is necessary to determine the amount of the chemical to be used.

In some states, permits are required to chemically treat any waters. In Pennsylvania, permits for the use of aquatic herbicides must be approved by both the Pennsylvania Fish Commission and the Department of Environmental Resources.

Many herbicides are toxic to fish and other animals. Many organisms may be affected by the lack of food and oxygen that results from the death of the plants. Fish may be poisoned by a chemical used to control plant growth, or they may die because of a lack of other organisms that serve as food. The decay of the dead plants may lower the dissolved oxygen content of the water to a level that is harmful to fish causing a fish kill.

1.3 QUESTIONS FOR STUDY AND DISCUSSION

1. As an ecologist which of the following true statements do you consider most important?
   a. Algae are protists.
   b. Algae are **not** plants.
   c. Algae are producers.

Types of Algae
2. Match the type of algae in Column II with the proper descriptions in Column I.

Column I Descriptions	Column II Type of Algae
A. cells are arranged in long strands	1. filamentous algae
B. microscopic, floating algae cells	2. stonewort algae
C. pond scum	3. plankton algae
D. grows on the bottom of lakes in limestone soil	
E. fur-like covering on stones	
F. the water is colored when large numbers of these microscopic algae are present	
G. a population explosion of this algae is called an "algal bloom"	
H. forms floating mats	
I. algae has a stem with whorls of branches	

The Importance of Algae
3. Algae are not flowering plants. Describe what you would see in a lake with an "algal bloom."
4. Give two reasons why algae are so important in an aquatic ecosystem.
5. On cloudy days and at night fish and algae must both compete for _____.
6. Give four problems caused by excessive concentrations of algae.
7. What is a backwash? Why do water treatment plants have to do more backwashes during the summer months?

Types of Flowering Plants
8. Classify each of the following plants as submerged, emerging, or floaters.
   • Cattail and bulrush may grow 2 to 3 feet (< 1m) above the surface of the water.
   • Lotus and duckweed both have flat leaves that lie on the surface of the water.
   • Curly and leafy pondweed — only the flower peeks above the surface of the water

The Importance of Flowering Plants
9. Briefly explain how flowering plants are important to each of the following organisms
   bacteria   insect larvae
   fish and frogs   muskrats
   waterfowl

10. Why is a temporary pond may be a better habitat for frog eggs than a bigger permanent pond.

Water Pollution and Plant Growth

11. Name the two chemicals that are plant nutrients. Name three different types of wastes that would contain these nutrients.
12. Give an example of a **point source** and a **nonpoint source** of nutrients.

Water Use and Plant Growth

13. Identify three uses of water that might make it necessary or at least desirable to control plant growth.
14. In addition to providing food and cover for wildlife, it is desirable to have plants growing along the water's edge. Explain why.

Controlling Plant Growth

15. How deep should a pond be in order to prevent too much growth of submerged plants?

16. What type of plants can sometimes be controlled by physical removal?
17. Why isn't physical removal a successful method of controlling submerged plants?
18. Give two reasons why the use of ducks and geese is not a successful method to control plant growth.
19. Why is the release of fish that feed on aquatic vegetation prohibited in the state of Pennsylvania and some other states?
20. List five steps to be followed when using herbicides to control growth of aquatic plants.
21. A pond owner sprays his pond with chemicals that will stop the growth of aquatic plants. According to the directions given on the container it would not harm the fish, yet a few days later there was a fish kill. The pond owner has carefully followed the directions on the container. Give two possible reasons why the fish died.

Science
Technology
Society

ISSUES

IMPORTED FISH TO CONTROL IMPORTED PLANTS

Lake Istokpoga is a shallow, nutrient-rich 27,000-acre (10,900 hectare) lake in south Florida. Federal, state, and local governments have spent nearly $4 million on herbicides to control a weed problem in the lake. The weed is hydrilla — an aquarium plant imported from Africa — that escaped into the wild in the late 1950s. Hydrilla was discovered in Lake Istokpoga around 1980.

In 1992, nearly 2,500 acres (1000 hectare) of the lake were treated with the hydrilla-killing herbicide Sonar. The herbicide slowly kills the hydrilla by interfering with its growth process. It does not affect fishing or other recreational uses of the lake. Farmers, who use water from the lake for irrigation, were notified to avoid using the water for seven days after the herbicide was spread.

Other attempts to use herbicides, to control the growth of hydrilla, were not effective. After each treatment, the hydrilla grew back. To prevent the hydrilla from bouncing back, and stop wasting money, the Florida Game and Fresh Water Fish Commission (FG and FWC) decided to add a biological control — fish.

After the herbicide reduced the growth of hydrilla, the state released 125,000 Chinese grass carp. The hydrilla-eating fish live for about 10 years and grow to about 70 pounds. The fish were sterilized so that they will not reproduce. Regulations make it illegal for fishermen to keep the carp if they are caught. If the fish are effective, more fish will have to be stocked in about five years.

- What plant is causing a problem in Lake Istokpoga? Why do you think this plant has become a problem?
- Identify the methods of control used by the (FG and FWC) to control plant growth.
- Evaluate the action that has been taken to control the growth of hydrilla in Lake Istokpoga. Do you think this plan will work? Do you think this is a good idea?
- If you ran a local agency, under what conditions would you permit herbicide use in bodies of water?

1.4 Water Quality — Chemical and Physical Factors

How do we determine quality? Factors such as size, color, and flavor might be used to determine the quality of an apple. "Use" is another factor that is important when judging the quality of apples. Some apples are good for baking, others for eating, and still others are good for making applesauce.

Water quality is determined by a number of chemical, physical, and biological factors. "Use" is also important when judging the quality of water. High quality drinking water with 1.4 ppm chlorine would not be high quality water for a goldfish. Most fish cannot live in water with even small amounts of chlorine. Brook trout and brown trout cannot survive in water with more than .02 ppm chlorine.

The ability of an organism to survive and reproduce in an aquatic ecosystem depends upon the quality of the water. The water quality depends on certain physical, chemical, and biological conditions. When substances are present in the water in amounts that are harmful to the organisms living in or using the water, the water is **polluted**.

In this section we will study some of the conditions that affect the water quality of aquatic ecosystems. Such studies are not simple. Changing one condition will often cause other conditions to change. For example, a change in temperature will affect the amount of dissolved oxygen that the water can hold. **Synergistic effects** also occur. Some chemicals are more poisonous when certain other chemicals are present. Keeping this in mind, let's investigate water quality.

Dissolved Oxygen

Aquatic organisms do not break apart water molecules to get oxygen for respiration. The oxygen they absorb, through their skin or special respiratory structures, is oxygen gas (O_2) that is dissolved in the water — **dissolved oxygen (DO)**.

Dissolved oxygen enters water by **diffusion** from the atmosphere. When water is mixed with air as it falls over rocks and waterfalls, the level of dissolved oxygen is greatly increased. Standing or slow-moving bodies of water have lower dissolved oxygen levels than fast-flowing water or bodies of water with wave action.

TRY TO FIND

Overfishing of Chesapeake Bay has been blamed on the fact that it is a **commons**. A commons is public property and preserving it is everybody's responsibility—that is, it's no one's responsibility. Visit your library and find the essay by Garrett Hardin entitled "The Tragedy of the Commons." Find out why resources that are part of a commons are almost always degraded beyond repair. How does the tragedy of the commons apply to many of our environmental problems?

At certain times, dissolved oxygen is a limiting factor for the presence of organisms in a pond or lake, but it is not usually a problem for organisms living in a rapidly flowing stream with clean water.

Photosynthesis in algae and aquatic plants increases the level of dissolved oxygen during daylight hours. At night and on cloudy days, the oxygen level falls as all organisms, including algae and aquatic plants, use oxygen for respiration. The water at the bottom of a deep lake has very little dissolved oxygen. Any oxygen that reaches the bottom by diffusion is used by decomposers.

Water that is polluted with organic matter has less dissolved oxygen than clean water because the bacteria and other decomposers use much of the oxygen for the process of decay. When there is not enough oxygen for decomposers that require oxygen, other decomposers that do not use oxygen take over the job of decomposition. The waste products produced by these organisms cause the "smell" of polluted water.

Dissolved oxygen may be the most important factor affecting aquatic organisms. A large variety of organisms usually indicate water with a high level of dissolved oxygen. Fewer types of organisms are found in water with a little dissolved oxygen. Many of these, such as the water boatman, must come to the surface to breathe.

A balanced aquatic ecosystem probably contains between 5 and 10 ppm of dissolved oxygen near the surface. Only a few species of fish can survive in water with less than 4 ppm dissolved oxygen. Carp can survive in water with only 1 or 2 ppm dissolved oxygen. Trout require much higher levels of dissolved oxygen, usually more than 6 ppm.

Temperature and Dissolved Oxygen

The solubility — ability of a substance to dissolve in a liquid — of a gas decreases as the temperature of the liquid increases.

At 32°F (0°C) water can hold 14.6 ppm dissolved oxygen.
At 59°F (15°C) water can hold 10.1 ppm dissolved oxygen.
At 86°F (30°C) water can hold only 7.5 ppm dissolved oxygen.

As the water temperature increases, the water retains less dissolved oxygen. In contrast, cooler water can hold more dissolved oxygen. Fish, such as trout, that require high levels of dissolved oxygen are found in cold water. Warm water fish, like carp and catfish, can survive in water with very low levels of dissolved oxygen.

Fish are cold-blooded animals. As the temperature of the water rises, the body temperature of cold-blooded animals increases. As the temperature increases, more oxygen is needed to maintain their normal body functions. The warmer water may not hold enough oxygen to supply the fish's needs.

Gas Bubble Disease

Most water used by industries, especially electrical power plants, is used for cooling. Pollution occurs when hot water is dumped into aquatic ecosystems. The warmer water cannot hold as much dissolved oxygen. Water quality standards strictly limit industrial activities that increase the temperature of a natural aquatic ecosystem. To meet the requirements, some companies build cooling towers or holding reservoirs that permit the water to cool before it enters the natural aquatic ecosystem.

Can There Be Too Much Oxygen?

We have already seen that the amount of gas that can be dissolved in the water is dependent upon the temperature. When a liquid holds all of the gas that can be dissolved at a given temperature, it is **saturated**. If it holds less than it can possibly hold, the amount of gas dissolved is described as the percentage saturated. For example, if water holds half of the gas it can hold at a given temperature it is 50% saturated.

Under certain conditions more gas is dissolved in water than normally would be dissolved at a given temperature. When this occurs the water is supersaturated. Supersaturation of water occurs below dams in rivers. As water falls over the dam, it is mixed with too much air. Fish get too much air in their blood, and the gases form bubbles. This is known as gas bubble disease. The problem is the greatest in spring when large amounts of water flow over the dam. Fish that do not die of gas bubble disease are frequently in a weakened state and often die of other diseases.

If the level of dissolved oxygen and the temperature of a body of water is known, the percentage saturation of a water sample can easily be determined using a Saturation Monogram. [See Investigation Manual] A healthy aquatic ecosystem should have water that is 80-125% saturated with air. If the saturation level is below 60% the fish may die from lack of oxygen.

pH

Few organisms live in water with a pH lower than 4 or higher than 9. Although some organisms live in water with a very low or very high pH, most species have a narrow range of pH where they can grow and reproduce. Scientific studies have provided the following information:

> The best range for the growth of algae is 7.5 to 8.4.
> The best range for fish is between 6.7 and 8.6.
> The best range for animals in the ocean is between 7.8 and 8.5.

The pH of water often determines the kinds of animals and plants that can live there. Water with a pH between 6.5 and 8.5 usually supports a good variety of plant and animal life.

The pH of the water is affected by several factors. Lakes and ponds are usually basic (alkaline) when they are first formed. Living organisms produce carbon dioxide during respiration. When organisms die more carbon dioxide is produced during the process of decay. Carbon dioxide forms **carbonic acid** when it combines with water. When large amounts of carbonic acid are dissolved in the water, it lowers the pH.

$$CO_2 + H_2O \longrightarrow H_2CO_3$$
$$H_2CO_3 \longrightarrow H^+ + HCO_3^- \longrightarrow 2H^+ + CO_3^{--}$$

Water entering aquatic ecosystems from industries may contain chemicals that alter the pH. Accidents involving trains and trucks sometimes result in chemical spills that affect the pH of the water. One accident involved a truck that was carrying detergent. Although the detergent did not affect the aquatic insect life in a small creek nearby, it caused the death of more than 32,000 fish.

There are many places where coal has been removed from the ground by strip mining. Some coal deposits and the surrounding rock formations contain sulfur. When the sulfur is exposed to air and water, **sulfuric acid** is formed. For many years after the mining has ceased, sulfuric acid is produced with each rain.

$$S + O_2 \longrightarrow SO_2$$
$$SO_2 + \tfrac{1}{2}O_2 + H_2O \longrightarrow H_2SO_4$$

Acid lakes are formed in the old strip mine pits. During heavy rains, these lakes overflow and drain into nearby creeks. Old strip mine lakes lie in the watershed of Cedar Creek, a tributary of the Missouri River. As many as sixty thousand fish have been killed when a lake overflows, and a slug of acid moves down the creek. Once the acid is diluted, fish once again move up the creek from the Missouri River. They will be the victims when heavy rains cause another acid lake to overflow.

Strip mining can be done without damage to nearby streams. To prevent the formation of acid, the sulfur minerals left behind must be covered with soil. This reduces the amount of acid in the runoff. These new lakes can be stocked for fishing, and plantings can be made to provide more habitat for wildlife.

Hardness

The rocks and soil in the watershed determine the hardness of a body of water. If the area contains granite rocks that do not dissolve easily, the water will contain few minerals. Water which lacks certain minerals is said to be **soft water**. In areas where there is much limestone, the carbonic acid in the water dissolves the calcium and magnesium compounds from the rocks. Water that contains calcium and magnesium is said to be **hard water**.

The total hardness test is the water test most used by industry. Minerals in the water interfere with many industrial processes. The manufacture of steel and synthetic rubber require water with less than 50 mg/L calcium carbonate.

Hard water also contains mineral compounds that act as buffers. Aquatic ecosystems in streams and lakes with hard water are less affected by acid rain than those in streams and lakes that contain soft water. The buffers prevent large changes in pH that would harm the aquatic organisms.

Nitrates and Nitrites

Most fertilizers used by farmers and homeowners contain nitrates. When it rains, the nitrates from fields and lawns are carried with storm water into nearby streams and lakes. Another major source of nitrates is sewage produced by humans and other animals. One cow produces waste equal to the sewage produced by 4.5 humans.

The nitrates in a body of water are nutrients for algae and aquatic plants. The increased growth of algae eventually lowers the dissolved oxygen level of the water. Excess algae may also cause undesirable odors and tastes. The algae clog filters in water treatment plants and industries.

Some algae are toxic and excess growth may prevent the use of water for swimming. Even though algae are not flowering plants, excessive growth of algae is referred to as an **algal bloom**. Algal blooms may occur if the total inorganic nitrogen (nitrate, nitrite and ammonia) levels are above .30 ppm.

More than 45 ppm nitrate is hazardous to most animals. The nitrate is changed to nitrite by special bacteria in the baby's digestive system. Nitrites enter the bloodstream causing a condition called **methemoglobinemia**. When nitrites are present, oxygen can not combine with hemoglobin. The "blue baby" condition that results is sometimes fatal. Nitrate levels in the water of some farm wells, and wells in areas with septic systems, is high enough to cause the death of infants. Well water should be tested for nitrates.

Phosphates

Phosphates also enter the water from fertilizers used by farmers and homeowners. Other sources include human and animal wastes and certain industrial processes. Phosphates don't harm humans and other animals unless they are present in very large amounts.

Phosphates are plant nutrients and increase the growth of algae and aquatic plants. A level of 0.025 mg/L increases the growth of algae and plants in ponds and lakes. The maximum level of phosphates recommended for rivers and streams is 0.1 mg/L. Excessive levels of nutrients — nitrates and phosphates — cause algal blooms.

The excess growth of algae in this stream indicates a high level of nutrients. The nutrients are supplied by both human and animal wastes upstream.

1. List three types of factors that affect water quality.
2. What chemical might be present in high quality drinking water, but would be considered a pollutant in an aquarium or stream ecosystem?
3. Most organisms need oxygen. Under what conditions would oxygen be considered a pollutant?
4. Why are studies of aquatic ecosystems often complicated?

Dissolved Oxygen
5. What is the source of oxygen used by aquatic organisms?
6. What are the two major sources of the dissolved oxygen in water?
7. For each of the following situations, indicate whether the amount of oxygen in the water is best described as HIGH or LOW.
   A. water flowing rapidly in a stream
   B. water standing in a puddle
   C. pond on a sunny day
   D. ponds at night or ofter a series of cloudy days
   E. deep water in a lake
   F. water with a high level of organic matter
   G. water with only a few types of organisms
   H. water with a large variety of organisms
   I. water with only carp and mostly air breathing invertebrates
   J. water with trout
8. Several species of fish are found in a stream and a large variety of macroinvertebrates are present. What is the minimum amount of dissolved oxygen that you would expect to find?
9. Explain why the level of oxygen is low in each of the following situations:
   A. Water polluted with organic matter
   B. Early morning in a pond with a large algae population

Temperature and Dissolved Oxygen
10. As the temperature of a liquid increases the amount of gas that can dissolve (decreases/ increases).

11. What is the maximum water temperature where a fish could live, if it required 10 ppm of dissolved oxygen?
12. Which of the following fish would probably not be found in a reservoir built to receive water from a power plant? (carp/catfish/trout)
13. Give two reasons why fish may not be able to get as much oxygen as they need if the water is warm.
14. Give two ways that industries prevent thermal (hot water) pollution.

Can There Be Too Much Oxygen?
15. Describe the condition which exists when fish get gas bubble disease.
16. Give the location and the time of year when gas bubble disease usually occurs.
17. What is the range of saturation levels that indicate a healthy aquatic ecosystem?
18. If water holds less than 60% of the gases that it can normally hold at a given temperature, what has probably happened to the oxygen?

pH
19. Most organisms live in water with a pH above _____ and below _____.
20. Would you expect to find a large algae population if the pH is 6? _____
21. Would you expect to find a large variety of fish if the pH was 10? _____
22. The pH range that will support a good variety of plant and animal life is between _____ and _____.
23. The pH of new ponds and lakes is usually _____.
24. As a pond or lake ages the pH decreases due to a build up of _____ which is a waste product of _____.
25. Chemicals such as detergents sometimes cause fish kills because they alter the streams _____.
26. Why do fish kills sometimes occur in streams near old coal mines?
27. Why would this problem occur at some coal mines but not others?

Hardness

28. What determines the hardness of a body of water?
29. Bodies of water in areas with granite rocks will be (hard/soft).
30. Bodies of water in areas with limestone rocks will be (hard/soft) due to the presence of _____ and _____.
31. Why is the total hardness test the most frequently used test in industries?
32. Why will hard water be affected less by acid rain than soft water?

Nitrates and Nitrites

33. What is the major nutrient used in fertilizers?
34. Name another major source of this nutrient.
35. How will excess nitrates affect a body of water?
36. List three problems caused by excess algae growth.
37. Define the terms algal bloom and methemoglobinemia.
38. What water supplies are most frequently affected by high levels of nitrates?

Phosphates

39. What is the major source of phosphates in water?
40. How do excess phosphates affect lakes and streams?

2.1

CASE STUDY
Changing the Flow — What it Does to Wildlife

Nature's Engineers

Although they are not highly intelligent animals, beavers are excellent engineers. They create their own ponds by damming a stream until it overflows. Their building supplies consist of mud, stones, and small trees — willows, aspens, or poplars. Beavers sometimes dig canals in order to float logs to the pond site.

Beaver dams help conserve both water and soil. A series of beaver dams on a mountain stream helps to hold back water during the flood season. By allowing more time for infiltration, the ponds also increase the amount of water returned to the ground water supply.

Beavers left southwestern Wyoming after cattle destroyed the trees they needed for food and dam building. Without beaver dams to slow the flow of water, the free-flowing streams carved deep ditches in the meadows. Scientists measured the amount of silt carried by the water in free-flowing streams and in streams with beaver dams. In one stream with beaver dams, the water carried away four tons (3.6×10^3 kg) of silt each day. In an undammed stream nearby, the water carried a much heavier load — 109 tons (9.8×10^4 kg) of silt daily.

The Bureau of Land Management tries to slow erosion by building rock chip dams, but building and maintaining these dams is expensive. One day a biologist noticed a beaver had moved into the area and was trying to build a dam with the

Beaver Dam

only material available — sagebrush. The biologist transported beavers to the area and provided them with trees. The beavers not only build, but constantly survey and repair the dam. The cost of transporting beavers and providing trees is far below the cost of government built rock chip dams.

While the beaver dams help reduce erosion, they also improve the habitat for many species of wildlife. Beavers bring large amounts of plant materials to a pond. The decay of these materials provides nutrients for algae and plants. These nutrients increase the productivity of the stream, and many organisms benefit from the increased food supply. In addition to providing food, the plant material deposited by the beavers also provides protective cover for small fish. In some river systems, most fish depend upon a few streams that are shaped by beavers to provide nurseries for their young.

Some property owners love beavers; others hate them. Beavers don't seem to mind a few people nearby, but people often don't like the way that beavers alter their habitat. Property owners and lumber companies object when beavers cut down trees. City officials object when beavers block storm sewers. Why are more beavers moving to suburban areas? Populations of beavers are increasing and the beavers are expanding their range because natural predators have been wiped out.

Danger Below the Dam

Supersaturation — too much air dissolved in water — caused the worst fish kill recorded in Missouri. Nearly 500,000 fish were killed in the first two years following the completion of the Harry S. Truman Dam on the Osage River. There were no previous reports of supersaturation causing the death of fish below dams on large rivers in the Midwest. The engineers probably did not consider the possibility of supersaturation in designing the dam.

Water pressure increases with depth, and the amount of air that can be dissolved in the water increases as the pressure increases. At a depth of thirty feet (9m), the amount of air that can be dissolved in the water is twice the air normally found in water. As it tumbles over the dam, the water is mixed with air. The water captures air bubbles, carries them deep into the pool below the dam, and the water becomes supersaturated.

Most aquatic organisms need some dissolved oxygen (DO) in the water, but too much dissolved oxygen can be as dangerous as too little. If the amount of DO in water is 10 percent more than is found in the water naturally, it can be harmful to aquatic life. The amount of dissolved oxygen in the water below Truman dam was more than 30 percent above natural levels. At this level, fish cannot survive more than a few hours.

The dissolved oxygen is absorbed by the blood as water passes over the gills. Small bubbles of air form in the blood when some of the air comes out of solution. The fish develop a condition similar to the bends called **gas bubble disease**. Biologist can easily identify the problem by blisters formed by the air bubbles under the skin. Another symptom, called popeye, occurs when bubbles collect behind the eye and push it out of its socket. If air bubbles cause blood vessels in the eye to burst, the fish will be blind. It will die if air bubbles block blood vessels carrying blood to the heart or other vital body organs.

Barriers for Fish

Supersaturation is not the only problem that dams create for fish. Although the adults live in salt water, some fish must have access to fresh water streams for reproduction. Salmon, shad, and other species of fish migrate from the ocean to spawn in the same fresh water stream where they were hatched. The instinct to return to their native stream is so strong that the fish fight powerful rapids and jump over waterfalls twelve feet high.

As they return from the Pacific Ocean, salmon must detour through fish ladders built around nine dams on the Columbia River. **Fish ladders** are pools of water arranged as a series of steps. Some water is diverted around the dam and flows through the pools. Fish can jump from one pool to the next as they make their way around the dam.

Fish can bypass low dams by using fish ladders, but fish ladders cannot move fish over high dams like Grand Coulee. Even though the words are not written on the massive concrete or earthen structure, high dams and low dams without ladders are a "dead end" for fish. Dams on the Columbia River prevent salmon from using almost one-half of their original spawning areas.

Dams can be even more deadly to the young fish as they migrate downstream. The power turbines on hydroelectric dams kill millions of young fish as they make their way to the ocean. Biologists estimate that as many as 15 percent of the fish in a stream are killed as they pass through a dam. This loss can be prevented by installation of screens. Unfortunately they are expensive to install and maintain.

Between 1960 and 1980 the number of wild salmon on the Columbia River decreased from 187 million to 72 million. During that time four dams with fish ladders were constructed. A study showed that several major dams in the Northwest are costing more in lost fish and recreation than they are providing in irrigation or power supply.

Savage Run Dam on Oregon's Rogue River was built to provide irrigation water for agriculture, but most of the farms have

Engineers designing large hydro-electric dams, like this one in Washington State, must consider the possibility of supersaturation.

This fish ladder allows salmon and other migratory fish to bypass the dam that forms Lake Washington.

Machinery at the old mill is silent and the dam is no longer needed. Many old dams, like this one prevent fish from migrating up streams in the Northeast.

been replaced by developments. Although the dam has two fish ladders, biologists say the old dam is a real fish-killer. A government study shows that it will cost millions of dollars to remodel the ladders in order to improve fish passage.

The alternative to remodeling the ladders is to dynamite the dam. The Fish and Wildlife Service calculate that if the dam were removed, 26,700 more fish would return to the river in a typical year. This would add more than $6 million to the local economy.

Many rivers in the United States are blocked by old dams that no longer serve their original function. Although these old dams block fish migration, they have been there for so long that we have forgotten the potential of the undammed river to support fish.

It is not likely that many of these old dams will be removed. In most cases the benefits would not be great enough to justify the expense. In the future we will likely see more dams built to provide electricity. In 1985 there were 50 small hydroelectric dams proposed for Idaho's Salmon River. If migratory species of fish are to survive, the location and design of new dams must be given careful consideration.

Channeled Streams and Wildlife

The natural bed of a stream or river where the water usually flows is called the **channel**. The natural channel of an old river twists and turns as it wanders to the sea. The channels are often deepened and straightened to increase the flow of water and prevent flooding. Rivers are also channeled to make them better highways for transportation.

Channels are generally not good for wildlife. As channels are dug, the trees and shrubs along the stream's banks are usually removed. Channeled streams have few, if any, trees to shade the water and protect it from the hot summer sun. Some species of fish are not able to tolerate the warmer temperatures.

Fish in channeled streams also face other problems. The roots of trees and shrubs growing along the stream bank help hold the soil in place. Once they are removed, there is nothing to protect the stream bank from the force of the flowing water. The rate of erosion increases. As the stream banks are eaten away, the gravelly bottom becomes covered with silt.

Silt and clay increase the **turbidity** — cloudiness — of the water. The clay and silt particles cover the bottom of the stream and fill the deep pools. The lack of food, oxygen, and good breeding places become limiting factors for some species of fish. The turbidity also makes it more difficult for predators, such as otters and herons, to locate their prey.

The making of channels decreases the productivity of the aquatic ecosystem. It also destroys the habitat of deer, squirrels, wood ducks, otters, eagles, and other wildlife species. Figures, released by the Fish and Wildlife Service show that straightening the Missouri River resulted in the loss of 127 miles (203 km) of shoreline and destroyed 475,000 acres (190,000 hectares) of wildlife habitat.

The Kissimmee — Repairing a River

The Kissimmee River once meandered nearly 100 miles (160 km) through the central part of Florida. That was before Congress approved a major project to convert wetlands along the river to farmland. The project included a 200-foot (60 m) wide, 30-foot (9 m) deep channel with five gates to control the flow of water. The Army Corps of Engineers took the natural bends out of the river and changed it into a 56-mile-long (90 km) canal.

Along the river's natural channel were 45,000 acres (18,000 hectares) of wetlands. More than three-fourths of these wetlands were drained by the canal. The wetlands that remain are changed. Plants that grow in the pools created by the engineers are not a good source of food and cover for wildlife. Gone are the small fish and freshwater shrimp that were food for the birds. Many species have nearly disappeared. Water fowl populations have declined by 90 percent. Nesting bald eagles have declined 70 percent.

After many years of draining wetlands and reducing wildlife habitat, we have begun to realize the importance of wetlands. Changing the winding river into a straight canal was a big ecological mistake. Now, as part of the "Save Our Everglades" program, canal C-38 is being changed back into a river. Cattle pastures are being changed back to wetlands. It will take time and millions of dollars, but they have begun to put the bends back into the Kissimmee River.

Restoring the river will benefit wildlife, but it will benefit people, too. The program to save the Everglades is also a program to save the water supply for the people of southern Florida. Without the wetlands to absorb the water and return it to the earth, the people of Miami are in danger of running out of fresh water.

What Have We Learned?

Changing the natural flow of water affects both the quality and the quantity of habitat available to wildlife. It also affects the quantity and quality of water available for our use. When we plan changes in the ecosystem, we must remember that the ecosystem is a complex puzzle, and we must carefully study how all the pieces fit together.

Channeling the Kissimmee River resulted in great ecological damage. The goal of a $1.4 million demonstration project is to see if the river ecosystem can be restored.

Nature's Engineers

1. What animal is a natural engineer?
2. What natural materials do they need to build their dams?
3. In what way is the beaver a conservationist?
4. Explain how the beaver dams affect the water cycle.
5. The amount of silt is greater in a stream (with/without) beaver dams.
6. Give two ways that beaver dams are better than government-built dams.
7. Give two ways that the beavers help other organisms.
8. Explain why many humans consider the beaver a pest.

Danger Below the Dam

9. Define supersaturation.
10. Describe how water becomes supersaturated.
11. Describe the symptoms of a fish with gas bubble disease.
12. What causes the death of a fish with gas bubble disease?

Barriers for Fish

13. Give two ways that dams decrease the population of fish.
14. Give a possible solution to each problem listed in question 12.
15. Do you think that dams that are no longer serving their original purpose should be removed to help the migration of fish? If so, who do you think should pay for their removal?
16. If you were in charge of issuing permits for small hydroelectric dams on the Idaho River, how many of the 50 proposed dams would you approve? Why this number?

Channeled Streams and Wildlife

17. What is the channel of a stream or river?
18. Describe the channel of an old river.
19. Describe how the channels are changed when a river or stream is channeled.
20. Give three reasons why rivers and streams are channeled.
21. Describe four ways in which channelizing a stream might affect fish.
22. Describe how channelizing a stream affects other wildlife.

The Kissimmee — Repairing a River

23. How did the COE change the Kissimmee River?
24. Although the river was only 100 miles long, the changes made by the Army Corps of Engineers affected thousands of acres. Explain how this was possible.
25. What changes are being made in the Kissimmee River as a part of the "Save Our Everglades" program?
26. Explain how the changes will affect wildlife and how they will affect people.

What Have We Learned?

27. How does changing the natural flow of water affect wildlife?
28. How does changing the natural flow of water affect humans?
29. How is an ecosystem like a puzzle?

CASE STUDY
Trouble at Mono Lake

"We've already lost in California most of our wetland habitat, and with that an incredible diminishment of birds and other wildlife . . . So with increasing population pressures, I think places like Mono Lake are going to be cherished because they are the last of the last."
Martha Davis, executive director
Mono Lake Committee

Just east of Yosemite National Park, on the eastern slope of the Sierra Nevada Mountain Range, is a large depression called Mono Basin. Here in the desert climate, not far from Lake Tahoe, is the largest natural lake that lies entirely in the state of California.

The Inland Sea

For at least 700,000 years, water from the melting snow has tumbled down the mountainside into Mono Lake. In winter, clouds of steam rise from the lake at places where water bubbles out of hot mineral springs beneath the lake's surface. At other places, water enters the lake from cold freshwater springs.

Water entering the lake reached a dead end, for there are no rivers or streams that carry water from the lake. The water remains in the lake until it evaporates, leaving behind its load of minerals. Except for the water from the freshwater springs, water in the lake is not fit to drink. It is about 5 percent salt.

Life in Mono Lake

Mono Lake has been called the Dead Sea of California. Although it is too salty for fish, the lake is not dead. In spring, the growth of algae makes the lake look like a large bowl of green soup. Then in May, brine shrimp hatch and begin to feed on the algae. By August they have reduced the algae population so much that the lake is once again clear blue.

A company called Jungle Labs harvests some of the brine shrimp to feed tropical fish and hatchery trout, but most of the brine shrimp are harvested by birds. More than one hundred species of birds depend upon the brine shrimp and larvae of brine fly in the lake.

Prepare for Take Off

Mono Lake is an essential resting and feeding stop for water birds migrating across Mono Basin. After spending the summer at their breeding grounds in the northern US and southern Canada, birds like the Wilson's phalarope, a member of the sand-

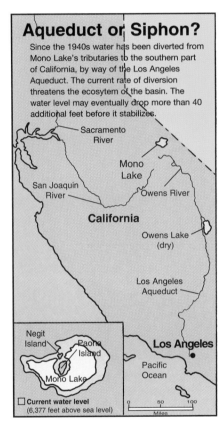

Diversion of water from Mono Lake's tributaries threatens the wildlife that depends upon the lake ecosystem.

Diversion of water from Mono Lake's tributaries threatens the wildlife that depends upon the lake ecosystem.

Wilson's Phalarope

piper family, come to Mono Lake. It is here that they prepare for their nonstop flight to their wintering grounds in South America. Birds come to Mono Lake.

The birds stay at Mono Lake a month or more, feeding on the brine shrimp and larvae of brine fly. The unlimited food supply provides the energy the birds need for their long journey. Some of the adult birds double their weight before they head south.

As the birds put on the layers of fat, they also shed their summer coat and grow new feathers. This process, called **molting**, also requires large amounts of energy. The birds spend much of their day feeding and grooming their new coat of feathers. As August approaches, the birds depart for their winter lake-front home in the Andes Mountains of South America.

Don't Step on the Eggs

Mono Lake is the primary nesting site for more than 80 percent of California gulls. Islands in the lake provide the ideal habitat for the nesting gulls. The freshwater springs provide drinking water and the lake provides plenty of brine shrimp to eat. The islands provided protection from coyotes. It was an ideal habitat, but things have changed.

Since 1941, water that would normally flow into the lake has been diverted causing the level of the lake to drop more than 40 feet (12.2 m). In 1979 a land bridge appeared connecting Negit Island to the lake's shore. The National Guard tried to destroy the bridge with explosives, but they were not successful. Coyotes crossed the land bridge, the gulls panicked, and most of the 34,000 chicks were killed.

In 1980 the state erected a chain linked fence across the bridge, but only a few gulls returned to Negit Island to nest. After a series of wet winters the land bridge was flooded in 1985, and gulls began to return. The water level is shallow, and if the lake level decreases the island may once again be connected to the shore.

Tourists at Mono Lake — Then and Now

Mono Inn and other motels were busy in the 1950s. About 300 guests stayed at the motels each night. There were conventions, meetings, and boat races. Tourists could enjoy a boat ride and a tour of Paoha Island. Some people came to swim and water ski. Other people came to enjoy the cool evening breeze from the lake.

Tourists no longer come to Mono Lake for boat races, but they do come to see the wildlife and the unique landscape left by the shrinking lake. The National Forest Service has declared the Mono Basin a National Forest Scenic Area. More than 145,000 people visit the area each year.

The lake is less than half the size it was in 1958. At some places, the new shoreline is nearly a mile (1.6 km) from the lake's original edge. **Tufa towers**, irregular columns of calcium carbonate, like stalagmites found in a cave, stand along the lake's shores. The columns were formed beneath the water when fresh water mixed with chemicals in the lake. As the level of the lake has fallen, some of the columns have been exposed.

As the lake shrinks, the old lake bottom is exposed to the air. Nothing grows near the lake because of the high concentrations of minerals that accumulated in the lake bed. Winds pick up the alkaline dust, and a dust storm makes seeing difficult and breathing dangerous. Air quality on the eastern shore is often below state and federal air quality standards.

Tufa Tower

Where Did the Water Go?

The city of Los Angeles lies in the southern part of California. An average of 15 inches (38 cm) of rain falls on the city each year. This is not enough to meet the needs of the city's growing population. In the early 1900s, the city bought land in the Owens Valley and built a 200 mile (320 km) aqueduct to provide additional water for the city, but that was not enough.

A study made in 1920 concluded that the city could continue to expand if the Owen's Valley Aqueduct was extended into the Mono Basin. Most of the land in the basin is owned by the federal government, and the government gave the water rights to the city. Some owners were poor and very willing to sell their land to the city. The land owned by people who would not agree to sell was condemned.

Now water from four of the five creeks that once flowed into Mono Lake has been diverted into aqueducts that carry water to the city of Los Angeles. The fifth creek is too small to divert. Each year the 340-mile-long (544 km) aqueduct delivered 32 billion gallons (1.3×10^{11} l) of water from Mono Basin to LA — 17 percent of its water supply.

Most of the water used in Los Angeles comes from the Owen's Valley, and the diversion turned Owen's Lake into a dry lake bed. Another 7 percent of water used in LA is purchased from the Metropolitan Water District. Water sold by the MWD comes from northern California and the Colorado River. Only seven percent of the city's water supply comes from its own wells.

A Day in Court

Most of Mono Lake is owned by the federal government. It is the opinion of some that the government, as owner, should care for the lake in a way that would benefit "the people." In other words, land owned by the public should benefit the public, not one city.

Lawyers for National Audubon Society, Friends of the Earth, the Mono Lake Committee, and several residents of the Mono Lake area asked the court to decide the question: "Does the Los Angeles Department of Water and Power (LA DWP) have the right to divert water from Mono Lake if it will destroy the lake?" On the other side of the issue, the LA DWP defended the right of the city to divert water from Mono Basin.

In 1983 the California Supreme Court ruled that the LA DWP must consider the environmental effects of the diversion of water from the Mono Basin. It was the opinion of the court that a state must balance the commercial value of water and the interest of the public trust when granting water rights. The decision was appealed to a higher court.

In 1989 a Superior Court Judge ordered the LA DWP to temporarily halt diversions from the Mono Basin. He also ruled that the lake level must be raised nearly two feet. The California Legislature voted to create a $60 million fund to help Los Angeles find new water sources.

The Need for Water

How badly does LA need the water from Mono Basin? The state-federal task force recommended LA cut its diversion of Mono Basin water from 100,000 to 15,000 acre-feet. An **acre-foot** of water is the amount of water that covers one acre of land to a depth of one foot. According to the task force, water conservation and a wastewater recycling program could reduce the city's need for water.

Additional water needed could be purchased from the Metropolitan Water District (MWD). Why does LA prefer water from the Mono Basin when other sources are available? Water from Mono Basin flows by gravity to LA. Water from the MWD must be pumped over the mountains, and this makes it more expensive. Mono Basin water offers another advantage. As the water flows to the city, it passes through hydroelectric generators. These generators provide two percent of the city's electricity. Using other sources of electricity would be more expensive.

Will the Lake Survive?

The groups working to save the lake are willing to allow Los Angeles to divert some water from Mono Basin, but they want enough water to flow into the lake to maintain a healthy ecosystem. Mono Lake is now one-half the size and twice as salty as it was in 1958. If the lake continues to shrink, and the salt concentration increases, the water will become too salty for the algae and brine shrimp.

Now that court decisions have forced Los Angeles to restore some of the natural flow of water to the lake, there is hope that the lake ecosystem will survive. There is some concern that the problems created at Mono Lake may be transferred to other ecosystems if the potential environmental impacts are not carefully considered.

2.2 QUESTIONS FOR STUDY AND DISCUSSION

1. Give the location of Mono Lake.
2. Explain why the climate of the Mono Basin is desert. [See Unit II: Weather]

The Inland Sea

3. Identify the three sources of the water in Mono Lake.
4. Explain why the lake is sometimes called the Inland Sea.
5. If you hiked to Mono Lake and had forgotten to take water along, would you be able to find water to drink? Explain.

Life in Mono Lake

6. Draw a food web that includes only the producers and consumers found in and around the lake.
7. What commercial product is harvested from the lake? Draw the food chain that includes this product.

Prepare for Take Off

8. Explain the importance of Mono Lake to the existence of the Wilson's phalarope and other migratory birds.
9. What are two important changes that take place during the birds' stay at Mono Lake?
10. Give the summer and winter addresses of the Wilson's Phalarope.

Don't Step on the Eggs

11. Identify the bird that nests at Mono Lake.
12. Give three reasons why the islands on the lake provide ideal habitat.
13. What changes have occurred in the past to make the island habitat less suitable for nesting?

Tourists at Mono Lake

14. Describe the changes in the lake that make it less suitable for some tourists.
15. Explain how tufa towers are formed.

Where Did the Water Go?

16. Describe how the city of Los Angeles obtained water rights for the Mono Basin.
17. List the four sources of the water supply for the city of Los Angeles.
    Rank them in order beginning with the source that supplies the most water.

A Day in Court

18. Who is the major landowner in the Mono Basin?
19. How did court rulings in 1983 and 1989 affect the Mono Lake ecosystem?

The Need for Water

20. List the three recommendations made by the state-federal task force to reduce LA's need for water from the Mono Basin.
21. Explain why water from Mono Basin is cheaper than water supplied by the Metropolitan Water District from the Colorado River .
22. In addition to cost, give another advantage of using water from the Mono Basin.

Will the Lake Survive?

23. What changing condition in the lake could make the lake unsuitable for life?
24. Assume that you are a federal court judge who has been assigned the case of the Mono Lake Ecosystem versus the City of Los Angeles. You must answer the question "Does the Los Angeles Department of Water and Power have the right to divert water from Mono Lake if it will destroy the lake?" Give your answer and write a brief statement to support your opinion.

"The preservation of our soil and water resources must be one of our national priorities. History has shown us that when the soil or water resources of a society diminish, so does that society."
Charles S. Robb, former Governor of Virginia

The area where fresh water from a river mixes with salt water from the ocean is called an **estuary**. The largest estuary in North America is the Chesapeake Bay. People living in Maryland and Virginia simply call it the Bay, as if it were the only one. There are many other bays, but no other bay is as complex or as productive as the Chesapeake.

The Bay receives water from nearly 50 rivers. Its 64,000 square-mile (166,000 sq. km) watershed lies in six different states (Delaware, Maryland, Virginia, West Virginia, Pennsylvania, and New York) and the District of Columbia. Although the Bay does not reach into Pennsylvania, almost half of Pennsylvania is in the Chesapeake Basin (watershed). The Susquehanna River flows 440 miles (700 km) from Cooperstown, New York, through Pennsylvania, and into Maryland. It supplies one-half of the Bay's freshwater. In the upper region of the Bay, 90 percent of the water is supplied by the Susquehanna.

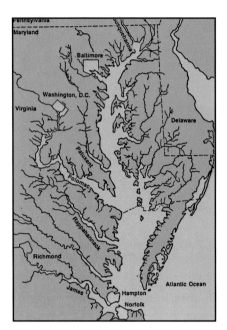

Chesapeake Bay

The People's Bay

The Bay extends for almost 200 miles (320 km) from southern Virginia to northern Maryland. Two major shipping ports on the Bay are connected with many smaller ports farther inland. The ease of transportation has encouraged the development of many industries including shipbuilding, agriculture, steel-making, paper manufacturing, and chemical production. Jobs provided by these industries have attracted many people to the area.

The Bay also supports a large recreational industry that attracts many tourists to the area. More than 180,000 licenses are sold each year for sailboats and motorized pleasure boats. The edges of the Bay provide habitat for so many humans that the Bay is sometimes called the "People's Bay." Since 1950, the population along the Bay has more than tripled, and it continues to grow. Nearly fifteen million people live in the Chesapeake Bay watershed. Much of the land that was once forests or pastures is now urban or residential.

Habitat for Wildlife

The wetlands along the 8,000 miles (12,800 km) of the Chesapeake Bay's shoreline provide critical habitat for many wildlife species that are permanent residents and for many migratory birds. The grasses that grow in the shallow water provide essential food and cover for many organisms. Fresh water flowing from the land provides the grasses with the nutrients and minerals needed for growth.

In the past wetlands were considered worthless unless they could be drained, filled in, and used for farmland or developed. Today scientists see wetlands as important nurseries for fish and vital habitat for wildlife. On the basis of the ability to produce food, wetlands are more valuable than the best, most productive, farmland.

Estuaries are important protein factories. Two-thirds of the commercially important fish and shellfish harvested along the Atlantic Coast depend on estuaries and their wetlands. Of the ten most commercially valuable species (shrimp, salmon, tuna, oysters, clams, menhaden, crabs, lobsters, flounders, and haddock), seven species depend on estuaries. Only tuna, lobsters, and haddock do not. For some species the estuary is a good source of food. For other species the estuaries provide places to spawn and nurseries for their young.

Fish and Wildlife in Trouble

The Chesapeake Bay supports more fish and wildlife than any other estuary. More than 2,700 species of animals live in the Bay itself. Although it still provides most of the seafood for the Atlantic coast, the Bay is no longer producing as much protein as it once did. As the human population has increased, the quality of water in the Bay has declined.

The oyster population is suffering from poor water quality, parasites, and overharvesting. Thirty years ago 3.3 million pounds (1.5×10^6 kg) of oysters were taken from the Bay per year. Today the catch is less than 1 million pounds (5×10^5 kg) per year. Blue crabs are still plentiful, but scientists worry that the population cannot withstand the pressure from crabbers who are still trying to make a living from the Bay. Crabbers take about 95 million pounds of crabs from the Bay each year.

The catch of valuable fish is also declining, and commercial fisheries are in difficulty. In 1969, more than one million pounds (4.5×10^5 kg) of shad were taken from the Chesapeake. Ten years later the take was only 20,000 pounds (9×10^3 kg). The commercial harvest of striped bass fell from nearly 15 million pounds (6.8×10^6 kg) to less than 2 million (9×10^5 kg) in a decade. In 1984,

Development and human activities along Chesapeake Bay and the rivers and streams which enter the Bay are threatening its ability to produce food for people and wildlife.

The Susquehanna River supplies one-half of the Bay's freshwater and 90 percent of the water in the upper Bay.

Submerged aquatic plants that grow in the shallow water of the Bay are the most important producers in the Bay's food chains. Much of the submerged vegetation has disappeared.

This shellfish taken from Chesapeake Bay is contaminated with bacteria from human waste.

the striped bass, or rockfish, was listed as a threatened species. The states of Maryland, Delaware and Virginia banned striped bass fishing.

Although overfishing with commercial nets is partly responsible for the decline in fish populations, another problem is the poor quality of the water in the Bay. The Chesapeake was once the spawning habitat for as much as 90 percent of the striped bass. As the water quality declined, fewer adult fish spawned, fewer eggs hatched, and fewer young survived. The ban on fishing has helped to rebuild the population and a limited fishing season is once again permitted.

Fish like menhaden and bluefish that spawn in salt water are not in difficulty. Menhaden is now the most economically important finfish in the Bay. It continues to be one of the world's most abundant sources of fish meal, which is used in fertilizer and cat food.

Submerged aquatic plants are the most important producers at the base of many of the Bay's food chains. More than 60 percent of the Bay's submerged aquatic vegetation has disappeared. The result is a loss of habitat for fish, shedding soft crabs and many smaller organisms. The loss of plants also reduces the food supply for some species of waterfowl. While some waterfowl have adapted by eating farm crops, other populations have declined.

Identifying the Problems

In 1975 the US Congress asked the Environmental Protection Agency to begin a major study of the Bay's water quality and its wildlife. The following major questions were to be answered:
- How serious is the decline in water quality?
- What is causing the decline?
- What can be done?

In September 1983 the EPA published the results of the seven-year study. The study confirmed the theory that the Bay acts like a sink without a drain. Some pollutants that enter the Bay are attached to particles of clay. As the water flows through the Bay to the ocean, the clay particles sink to the bottom of the Bay. Studies were conducted on two types of pollutants — nutrients and toxic substances.

Nutrients

Population growth and farming practices have increased levels of nutrients, mainly nitrates and phosphates, in the upper and middle parts of the Bay. Nutrients come from both point and nonpoint sources. **Point sources** are those that are discharged through a pipe or ditch — mainly sewage treatment plants and industries.

Nonpoint sources are those that flow directly from the land. Nonpoint sources include runoff from farm land, residential lawns, real estate developments, construction sites, and abandoned mines. Precipitation is also an important nonpoint source of pollution. Precipitation deposits nutrients (nitrogen oxides), pesticides, and toxic chemicals such as mercury and lead into the Bay.

In Maryland, the major source of nitrogen (48%) and phosphorus (62%) comes from point sources, mostly sewage treatment plants. The rest comes from nonpoint sources, mainly agriculture. The nutrients fertilize the Bay and stimulate the growth of algae. The increased growth of algae and particles of soil suspended in the water, reduce the amount of sunlight that passes through the water. Without sunlight the submerged aquatic plants die, and an important link in the food chain is gone.

When the algae die, they sink to the bottom and begin to decay. The process of decay uses the dissolved oxygen faster than it is replaced by photosynthesis. The low level of dissolved oxygen (DO) becomes a limiting factor for fish and shellfish. In the 1930s, during the months of July and August, low levels of oxygen occurred in some areas of the Bay. Today the upper and middle regions of the Bay have low levels of oxygen from May until September.

Toxic Substances

Toxic substances are chemicals that can harm living organisms. Toxic metals include arsenic, cadmium, chromium, copper, lead, and zinc. Organic compounds that are toxic include hydrocarbons, pesticides, and other industrial chemicals that contain carbon.

More than 5,000 point sources are dumping wastewater into the rivers and creeks that flow into the Bay. Much of the wastewater contains low levels of nutrients and/or toxic chemicals. Toxic chemicals accumulate in the Bay, and in some areas high concentrations of certain toxic chemicals are threatening organisms.

The highest levels of toxic chemicals are found in the upper Bay. According to EPA water quality standards, the region above Baltimore is contaminated. Bethlehem Steel Corporation's Sparrows Point Plant on the Chesapeake is Baltimore's largest polluter. The Federal District Court in Baltimore found Bethlehem Steel liable for illegally dumping dangerous industrial wastes —acids, cyanide, chromium, oil, grease, and phosphates — into the Bay. The company violated the water quality permit on average more than once a week between 1978 and 1983.

Toxic chemicals also enter the Bay through storm drains that carry runoff away from urban areas. It is estimated that two out

Point sources like the pipe shown here dump toxic pollutants into rivers that flow into the Bay.

WHAT DO YOU THINK?

The United States has drained more than 50 percent of its wetlands. Yet farmers are draining prairie potholes, wetland oases in the arid Midwest that are crucial to waterbirds, in order to add this arable land to their fields. One defense farmers put forward for this practice is that maneuvering gigantic farm machines around the potholes is too expensive. It is a fact, farm machinery uses more fuel making turns (to avoid a prairie pothole) than it does moving in a straight line. Using less fossil fuel is environmentally sound. Saving prairie potholes for waterbirds is ecologically necessary. What do you think can be done to solve this problem?

What are the environmental impacts of this oil sprayed along a Pennsylvania highway? Some of the toxic chemicals evaporate, but some of the oil is carried by runoff into the storm drain. Eventually it will have an impact on an aquatic ecosystem system like the Chesapeake Bay.

of ten automobile owners change their own oil and illegally dump it into the nearest storm drain. Oil poured into a storm drain eventually enters an aquatic ecosystem. Experts think that the amount of waste oil that flows into the Chesapeake Bay in one year equals that of the *Exxon Valdez* oil spill.

The four quarts (3.8 L) of oil from a car engine can form an oil slick that covers nearly 8 acres (3.2 hectares) of an aquatic ecosystem. An **oil slick** — a layer of oil on the surface of the water — reduces the amount of dissolved oxygen that can enter the water from the atmosphere. The oil also suffocates fish by coating the surfaces of their gills. Bottom dwelling organisms and submerged aquatic plants are suffocated when mixtures containing oil settle to the bottom of the Bay.

Oil dumped into the bay contains certain toxic chemicals that slowly dissolve in the water. Some of these chemicals are carcinogens while others, like lead, produce other toxic effects.

Many households, auto, lawn, and garden products such as paints, paint thinners, pesticides, antifreeze are improperly dumped or flushed down the drain. These toxic substances are not removed by the standard sewage treatment process, and they flow into the bay with the treated wastewater. During heavy rains, many of the chemicals used on lawns and gardens are carried into storm drains with the runoff. Chemicals clinging to particles of soil are also carried into the Bay by erosion. Some of these chemicals are toxic to organisms living in the Bay.

Areas of the Bay contaminated with toxic chemicals support fewer types and numbers of bottom-dwelling organisms. Some toxic chemicals are stored in body fat. As these chemicals are passed through the food chain they become more and more concentrated. This is called **bioaccumulation**. Even though the levels of some toxic chemicals present in the aquatic ecosystem are low, much higher levels are found in fish.

Acid rain may be dissolving aluminum in the soil and carrying it into creeks used by some fish for spawning. This may be one factor causing the decline of some species of fish. In areas with high levels of toxic chemicals, fish tissue contains abnormal cells.

Working Together to Save the Bay

Government officials and the public were alarmed by the information revealed by the EPA study. If the living resources of the Bay were to be saved, immediate action was needed. In December 1983, officials from Maryland, Virginia, Pennsylvania, the District of Columbia, and the EPA signed the **Chesapeake Bay Agreement**. The agreement was the beginning of a cooperative effort to "improve and protect the water quality and living resources of the Bay."

The states and the Environmental Protection Agency worked together to develop a plan for the entire Chesapeake Basin. The plan includes changes in the following areas:

Industry: Industries must stop dumping wastewater with higher concentrations of toxic chemicals than those allowed by their wastewater discharge permit. Toxic chemicals must be removed by pretreatment of wastewater before it is sent to the sewage treatment plant or discharged directly into the Bay. It is essential that we keep as much of the toxic chemicals as possible out of the estuary.

Storm Water Control: Projects are being implemented to slow the velocity of storm water runoff and reduce erosion. This will help protect aquatic life from being suffocated by sediment. In some places it is necessary to pretreat storm water to reduce the levels of toxic chemicals like nitrogen, and phosphorus.

Agriculture: Much of the nitrogen enters the Bay as nitrates that are leached from crop land and animal waste. Most of the phosphorous is carried into the Bay as phosphates on eroded soil particles. Soil and water tests in southeastern Pennsylvania show that farmers often apply more nutrients than their crops need. The excess is carried into the Bay.

Pennsylvania, Maryland, and Virginia have nutrient/manure management programs. These programs are beginning to reduce nutrients entering the Bay through use of the **Best Management Practices (BMPs)**. These practices not only help reduce pollution in the Bay, but they also reduce the cost of raising a crop. BMPs include the following:

- using soil tests to determine the actual amount of nutrient needed
- timing the application of nutrients to correspond to the crop's needs
- reduced tillage
- crop rotation
- contour farming
- strip cropping

Land Use: Human activities including agriculture, logging, and development, on land along streams increase runoff and contribute to erosion. Forests provide the best protection against erosion. Planting a buffer strip to separate human activity from streams can reduce erosion and decrease the sediment and nutrients carried into the stream. Maryland has restricted development by requiring a thousand-foot (76 m) buffer zone along most remaining natural shorelines.

Sewage Treatment Plants: Construction and improvement of existing sewage treatment plants will reduce the load of nutrients entering the Bay. Repair of some sewage systems is needed to prevent storm water from flowing into the sewage pipes. As storm water increases the volume of sewage to be

Many of the nutrients in Chesapeake Bay come from farm animals like these dairy cows.

THINK ABOUT IT

The bog turtle once ranged over a vast area of eastern wetlands. It is now endangered, threatened, or extinct in most places where it used to live. When town planning boards have allowed wetlands to be drained for development, scientists have in some cases moved any bog turtles that lived there to other wetlands nearby. However, bog turtles seem to be imprinted by their original wetland habitats. Scientists have often found the tiny turtles laboriously trekking along roadways from their new habitat back to their original (now destroyed) wetland homes. It seems the turtles cannot get used to a new or newly created wetland. What implications does this have for wetland development and human-made marshes?

All species of sea turtles are endangered or threatened. Sea turtles swim through hundreds of miles of ocean to lay their eggs on native beaches. Most beaches along U.S. coastlines are severely eroded. Yet turtles' instinct for returning to their native beach is so strong, that they lay their eggs on the eroded beaches. The eggs are doomed. Seabirds or raccoons eat the shallowly buried eggs. Thus, sea turtle populations are unable to recover due to poor reproductive success caused by human coastal development.

treated, the quality of treatment is reduced and more nutrients flow into the Bay.

Monitoring: Physical and chemical conditions in the Bay must be measured and recorded in order to determine how the Bay responds to natural variations caused by changing seasons, storms, and droughts. The data collected will also reveal how the Bay is responding to the attempts to restore it. In 1984, the EPA began measuring 19 water quality variables at 50 different stations on the Bay. The states are responsible for monitoring the same variables on the major rivers that empty into the Bay.

Restoring Declining Populations: Submerged aquatic plants are being replanted in some areas of the Bay. Hatcheries are helping to restore populations of striped bass and oysters.

It may take many years before water analysis and population studies reveal trends that reflect the changes in human activities. We must remember that it has taken years to pollute the Bay, and it will take years to restore it. Scientists cannot predict the outcome of the program to save the Bay, but they expect the living resources to increase as the water quality improves.

Lessons Learned

Lesson 1: The solution to pollution is **NOT** dilution; the solution is control of contaminants at their source.

Lesson 2: When you no longer want it you can't simply throw it or wash it "away." There is no "away." It will go somewhere.

Lesson 3: Political boundaries do not stop pollution. Eroded soil from New York and Pennsylvania, sewage from Washington, D.C., toxic chemicals from Baltimore, and acid rain from power plants in the Midwest all affect the quality of the water in the Chesapeake.

You Can Make a Difference

It has taken us a long time to learn these lessons, and hopefully it is not too late for the Bay. You can help. You may be contributing toxic chemicals to the Chesapeake Bay or another aquatic ecosystem. By following the suggestions listed below you can help keep toxic chemicals out of aquatic ecosystems.

• Do not pour oil or other toxic substances down the drain.
• If possible, use substances that are not toxic.
• Recycle oil and antifreeze by taking it to a service station or an oil recycling center.
• Check the phone book for the phone number of a government agency that can provide information about how to dispose of toxic substances. The Cooperative Extension Service in your county may be able to provide the information you need.

1. According to former Governor Robb, what must a society do to ensure that it will remain a strong society?
2. Define estuary.
3. What river supplies the Chesapeake Bay with most of its fresh water?
4. Most of the Chesapeake (Basin/Bay) lies in the state of Pennsylvania.

The People's Bay

5. Explain why many industries are located on the Bay.
6. Give two reasons why people are attracted to the Bay.
7. How has the increase in population changed the Bay ecosystem?

Habitat for Wildlife

8. What two needs do the grasses in the wetlands provide for wildlife?
9. Plants need fertilizer to grow. Where does the grass growing in the wetlands get the fertilizer it needs?
10. Wetlands produce (more/less) food per acre than the best, most productive, farmland.
11. Wetlands are (more/less) productive than the best, most productive, farmland.
12. Give two ways that fish depend upon estuaries.
13. List three species of fish that depend upon estuaries.
14. If you were a commercial fisherman, would you encourage the development of wetlands near estuaries? Explain.

Fish and Wildlife in Trouble

15. Why is the Chesapeake Bay sometimes considered the most important estuary?
16. How has the quality of water in the Bay changed as the human population has increased?
17. Some oystermen can no longer make a living on the Bay. Explain why.
18. Name two species of fish whose populations have declined during the last ten years.
19. Which species are illegal to take in the parts of the Bay that border the states of Maryland and Delaware?

20. Identify two factors that have caused the decline in fish populations.
21. Why is the striped bass population in greater difficulty than the menhaden?
22. What is the major use of menhaden?
23. Give two ways that the submerged aquatic plants are important to organisms in the Bay.

Identifying the Problems

24. What three questions did Congress ask the EPA to answer?
25. How long did it take the EPA to complete the study?
27. Explain why the level of certain types of pollutants in the Bay has increased.
28. Identify the two major nutrients in the Bay.
29. What two activities have caused this increase?
30. Explain the difference between point sources and nonpoint sources.
31. Give two examples of point sources and two examples of nonpoint sources.
32. What major activity is responsible for the high levels of nitrogen and phosphorus in the upper Bay? How do these nutrients enter the Bay?
33. Explain how the increased nutrients cause the submerged aquatic plants to die.
34. Explain how soil erosion also leads to the death of submerged aquatic plants.
35. Explain how the increased nutrients affect the amount of dissolved oxygen in the Bay.
36. Explain why increased growth of algae can create problems for fish and shellfish.
37. Dissolved oxygen levels in the Bay have (decreased/increased).
38. Define toxic substance.
    Give two examples of toxic metals and two examples of toxic organic compounds.
    Give two sources of toxic chemicals that enter the Bay.
39. What is an oil slick? Give two ways that oil suffocates fish.
    Identify two other types of organisms that are affected by oil in the water.

40. Used motor oil may present another danger for aquatic organisms. Explain.
41. Give two ways that household and lawn products may enter the Bay.
42. What evidence makes scientists think that toxic chemicals may be affecting bottom dwelling organisms?
43. Even though the level of some toxic chemicals present in the water is low, much higher levels are found in fish. Explain why.
    What term describes this increase in concentration of toxic substances at higher levels in the food chain?
44. Explain how acid rain may be increasing the level of aluminum in the creeks leading into the Bay.
    Explain how the increased level of aluminum may be causing a decline in certain fish populations.
45. What other changes in fish have been seen in areas with high levels of toxic chemicals?

Working Together to Save the Bay

46. What is the goal of the Chesapeake Bay Agreement?
47. Why was the state of Pennsylvania included in the agreement?
48. Explain how industry can help clean up the Bay.
49. Describe what can be done to reduce the level of these pollutants in storm water:
    A. sediment   B. toxic chemicals
    C. nitrogen and phosphorus

50. Why will reducing erosion also reduce the level of phosphorus in the Bay?
51. What is the major type of pollution entering the Bay from Pennsylvania?
52. What is the goal of the Best Management Practices program?
53. How will the Best Management Practices program help farmers?
54. List four of the Best Management Practices that a farmer might use.
55. What is the best way to protect streams from human activity?
56. How will construction and improvement of sewage treatment plants improve the quality of water in the Bay?
57. How will we know if the steps taken to restore the Bay are improving the quality of water in the Bay?
58. What populations are being "restocked" or "replanted" in some areas of the Bay?

Lessons Learned

59. Explain what is meant by each of the following statements:
    "The solution to pollution is not dilution."
    "There is no 'away'."
    "Political boundaries do not stop pollution."

You Can Make a Difference

60. What should you do with oil or antifreeze that you no longer want?
61. What should you do if you have a toxic substance that you want to get rid of, but you don't know the safe method to dispose of it?

The Clean Water Act, passed by Congress in 1972 and strengthened in 1977, created several programs to control water pollution. Congress gave the US Environmental Protection Agency (EPA) the responsibility of enforcing the programs. **Section 404** of the Clean Water Act requires anyone planning to place dredged or fill materials in the waters of the United States to first obtain a permit from the US Army Corps of Engineers (COE).

Often it is not easy to determine where land ends and water begins. The **"waters of the United States"** are defined as navigable waterways, streams and lakes that flow into navigable waterways, and wetlands that lie beside these bodies of water. **Wetlands** are defined as those areas with plants that are adapted for life in soil that is saturated with water. The EPA and COE identify wetlands by studying the plants, the soil type, and water in the area.

Wetlands are not always wet. **Prairie potholes** are shallow basins that are found in the Great Plains states. They are filled with water each spring just at the time when ducks and other water birds are migrating through the region. The potholes often dry up before fall. **Wet meadows** are seldom flooded, but the soil is usually water-logged. Although **bottomland hardwood forests** (often called swamps) are periodically flooded, they may be dry for half of the year.

Water or Land?

Should wetlands be considered a part of the water or the land? The Corps of Engineers concluded that wetlands should be protected under Section 404 because they affect the water quality and aquatic ecosystems in the following ways:
- Wetlands slow the flow of runoff helping to prevent erosion.
- Wetlands store floodwater helping to prevent flooding downstream.
- Wetlands protect the shoreline from erosion during storms.
- Wetlands filter and purify water that drains into lakes, rivers, or streams. Wetlands have been called "nature's kidneys."
- Wetlands provide spawning, nesting, rearing, and resting sites for aquatic species. Two-thirds of US commercial fishes depend on estuaries and salt marshes.

Until recently, people thought of wetlands as wastelands. The **Swamp Lands Acts**, passed by Congress in the mid-1800s, gave 65 million acres (26 million hectares) of federal wetlands

Although they may be dry for long periods of time, wetlands like this cypress swamp support plants that are adapted for soil that is saturated with water.

Federal, State and Local Regulations

In 1986 the US Corps of Engineers began granting blanket approval — a nation-wide permit — to anyone who wants to fill wetlands up to one acre in size.

Nearly half of the potholes in the "duck belt" across Minnesota and the Dakotas are less than a quarteracre (0.1 hectare) in size. One study showed that 75 percent of the prairie country's breeding ducks and 96 percent of its breeding shorebirds are raised on these seasonal ponds.

A study in Massachusetts revealed that during the spring and summer black bears spend 60 percent of their time feeding in small forested wetlands.

Many state and local governments have recognized the importance of small wetlands and have passed laws that regulate activities in wetlands. Some of these regulations are more restrictive than federal laws.

- Check the regulations in your area
- If you owned a prairie pothole or a small forested wetland, could you fill it?

to states for the purpose of "reclaiming." Wetlands were considered useless, unless they were drained and filled to create land for housing developments, industry, or farming. Wetlands have sometimes been used for landfills or garbage dumps.

Now we know that wetlands are not wastelands. In addition to improving water quality, wetlands also:

- provide habitat for wildlife and plants. According to the World Resources Institute, wetlands provide habitat for as many as 600 wildlife species and 5,000 plant species. At least 45 percent of the animals and 26 percent of plants listed as endangered need wetlands.
- recharge the ground water.
- provide timber including bottomland hardwood, black spruce, and cypress.
- provide recreation including hunting, fishing, bird watching, canoeing, and hiking.

Loss of Wetlands in Selected States		
State	**Acres Lost**	**Percent***
California	4,546,000	91
Ohio	4,517,200	90
Missouri	4,201,000	87
Illinois	6,957,500	85
Oklahoma	1,892,900	67
Pennsylvania	627,986	56
Texas	8,387,288	52
Florida	9,286,713	46
New Jersey	584,040	39
Maine	1,260,800	20
New Hampshire	20,000	9
Alaska	200,000	0.1

*of estimated original wetlands

More than half of the wetlands in the lower 48 states were "reclaimed" before we recognized that wetlands are not wastelands. According to the World Resources Institute the wetlands remaining in the lower 48 states cover 5 percent of the land surface. Wetlands cover 14 percent of Canada's land surface. In both the United States and Canada, agriculture has been responsible for 85 percent of the wetlands lost. In the United States, thousands of acres of wetlands are still lost each year, but the rate of loss is slower now. The following examples show how Section 404 has slowed the disappearance of wetlands in the United States.

Riverside Bayview Homes, Inc.

Riverside Bayview Homes, Inc. owned 80 acres (32 hectares) of low-lying, marshy land near Lake St. Clair in Michigan. In 1976 as they prepared to start the construction of houses, they began placing fill material on their property. The developer did not obtain a 404 permit from the Corps of Engineers.

The Corps of Engineers filed suit in US District Court to stop the developer from filling the wetlands without a 404 permit. The court ruled that the property was a wetland and a 404 permit was required. The developer appealed the decision.

The Court of Appeals reversed the lower court's decision. The court ruled that the developers were not required to obtain a 404 permit because the wetlands were not subject to flooding by navigable waters. This decision was appealed to the US Supreme Court.

The US Supreme Court ruled that Congress wrote the Clean Water Act to protect water quality and aquatic ecosystems. The court concluded that it was the intent of Congress to include wetlands next to navigable waterways as "waters of the United States." The court also found that the land owned by Riverside Bayview Homes, Inc. had been properly identified as wetland. In addition, the court found that the wetland extended to Black Creek, a navigable waterway. The court ruled that the developers were required to obtain a 404 permit from the US Army Corps of Engineers before placing fill on their property.

Moving a Marsh

The purpose of Section 404 of the Clean Water Act is to protect water quality and aquatic ecosystems, not to prevent development of wetlands. Less than 5 percent of all requests submitted for permits are denied each year. The permit process is designed to make sure that each project is carefully evaluated. Where possible, the Corps of Engineers tries to find alternatives to development of wetlands. When this is not possible, they work with the developer to make sure damage to the wetlands is minimized.

Before the Clean Water Act was passed, road builders simply hauled truckloads of fill and built roads across wetlands. Highways in many states, including a section of four-lane highway in Wisconsin, are built through wetlands. When the Wisconsin Department of Transportation (DOT) needed to expand the highway to six lanes, a 404 permit was required. The Corps of Engineers required the Department of Transportation to submit a plan that showed how they would minimize damage to the marsh.

The DOT proposed a plan that included hiring an environmental scientist to construct five wildlife ponds and create 25 acres (10 hectares) of new marshland. After evaluating the plan, the COE agreed that there was no alternative to developing the marsh. They issued a permit to fill the marshland and expand the highway.

Wetland Refuge Manager

A manager of a wetland or other refuge is responsible for protection of the ecosystem. He/she supervises and monitors activities on the refuge. In some cases the manager may be responsible for buying additional land and restoring or improving the habitat for certain species. Managers are responsible for supervising employees, directing population studies, and developing education programs. Decisions concerning hunting at some refuges may be the responsibility of the manager. Managers must have a bachelor's degree in wildlife management or some related field. On-the-job training is also necessary.

Coastal Development

More than 100 beach-front homes damaged by a storm cannot be rebuilt. New federal and state laws prohibit rebuilding homes in coastal wetlands under the following conditions:

1. the damage is more than 50 percent of the home's value, and
2. when septic and water systems have been affected.

Consider the environmental impacts and the economic impacts of these laws.

• Is this law fair to property owners?
• Are there alternatives?
• Should the law be changed?
• What additional information do you need to know to make these decisions?

The road builders dug up and moved 22 acres (8.8 hectares) of the Upper Mud Lake Marsh. The peat contained roots of wetland plants. Plants and topsoil were removed from the area of the new marsh and replaced with the peat. The road was built and the impact on the marsh was minimized.

Swamp or Shopping Center

Pyramid Companies of Boston owned land near Interstate 95 in Attleboro, Massachusetts. Locally the area is known as Sweeden's Swamp. The COE refused Pyramid's request for a permit to build a 150-store shopping center on 50 acres (20 hectares) of the swamp. The decision made by the New England COE office was overruled by the COE headquarters in Washington. Washington instructed the New England Office to issue the permit, with the requirement that Pyramid minimize the loss of swamplands by building an artificial swamp nearby.

The Environmental Protection Agency is required by law to review decisions made by the Corps. After reviewing the permit application, they vetoed the request for a permit. The request was vetoed because another site was available for the proposed shopping center. The available site was only one mile away from the swampland owned by Pyramid. Under current law, a permit cannot be issued to fill a wetland if another environmentally less sensitive site for development is available.

Put It Back the Way It Was

Cases in which owners or developers have placed fill in wetlands without obtaining the required 404 permit, they may be ordered by the courts to restore the site to its original condition. This requires the removal of the fill, restoring the normal flow of water, and replanting of wetland plants. The goal of the restoration plan is to re-create the wetlands.

Destroying 86 acres (34 hectares) of wetlands in Maryland cost one landowner $2 million in fines. The landowner, a wealthy New York businessman, was charged with negligent violation of the Clean Water Act. He pleaded guilty. He had hired a project manager to convert his 3,272 acre estate into a private retreat for duck hunting. The Army Corps of Engineers notified the manager that permits were needed, but the manager allowed the work to continue without obtaining the proper permits. When the landowner was notified, he fired the project manager and hired a conservationist to restore the wetlands. The retreat is now recognized as a model for wetland development.

Can Humans Imitate Mother Nature?

Ecologist Joy Zedler is monitoring a new wetland created to replace a part of San Diego's Sweetwater Marsh. The marsh was disturbed to build a new interchange for Interstate 5 and a flood-control canal. The 404 permit required the road builders and ditch diggers to create a new marsh in another location.

Zedler has studied the new marsh for 5 years, and she concludes that it is not functioning like the original marsh. Why? Creating a functioning marsh required finding all the parts, and we do not know all of the parts. When an important predatory insect is missing in the new marsh, there will be a population explosion of insects that feed on marsh plants. The Sweetwater Marsh is home to the endangered light-footed clapper rail. Although birds still nest in sections of the marsh that weren't disturbed, they are not nesting in the newly created marsh. No one knows why.

The National Research Council has also concluded that restoring wetlands is a "trial-and-error" process. While it may work in some places, replacing wetlands is not always a success. The council recommended that restoration projects should not be used to justify the destruction of other wetlands. It is difficult to stop development, especially when the human population has increased 24 percent in only ten years.

2.4 QUESTIONS FOR STUDY AND DISCUSSION

1. What department of the federal government is responsible for enforcing the Clean Water Act?
2. Who must obtain a Section 404 permit? What department of the federal government is responsible for granting Section 404 permits?
3. When is a body of water classified as "waters of the United States"?
4. What is a wetland? What are the three factors that the EPA and COE study in order to identify an area as a wetland?

Water or Land?

5. List the ways that wetlands improve water quality.
6. What was the purpose of the Swamp Lands Acts?
7. We know that wetlands improve water quality. List four additional reasons why wetlands are valuable.

8. What percent of the wetlands in the lower 48 states have been reclaimed? How does the loss of wetlands in Canada compare to the loss in the United States? What is the major reason for wetland loss in both countries?

Riverside Bayview Homes, Inc.

9. Why did the Corps of Engineers file suit against Riverside Bayview Homes, Inc.?
10. Why did the Court of Appeals reverse the decision of the District Court?
11. According to the decision of the US Supreme Court, are wetlands a part of the "waters of the United States"? Was the land owned by Riverside Bayview Homes, Inc. wetland? Were the developers required to obtain a 404 permit?

Moving a Marsh

12. What is the purpose of Section 404 of the Clean Water Act?
13. Most requests for section 404 permits are denied. (True/False)
    If there is no alternative, development of wetlands is allowed. (True/False)
14. Describe how the Wisconsin Department of Transportation built a road through a marsh without destroying it.

Swamp or Shopping Center

15. Why did the Environmental Protection Agency veto a permit that would have allowed Pyramid Companies of Boston to build a shopping center in Sweeden's Swamp?

Put It Back the Way It Was

16. What if a developer or private landowner fills in the "waters of the United States" without a permit?
17. What three requirements must be met in order to restore a wetland that has been damaged by placing fill in the wetland?
18. Do you think the fine for violations of the Clean Water Act at the Maryland estate was appropriate? Explain your answer.

Can Humans Imitate Mother Nature?

19. What makes it difficult to create a new wetland that functions like the old one?
20. Why don't we "just say no" to the development of wetlands? Do you think we should?

Science **T**echnology **S**ociety

ISSUES

DEFINING A WETLAND

In 1992 there was an attempt to rewrite wetland identification manuals and redefine wetlands. Compare the 1989 and the proposed 1992 definitions of "what is a wetland?"

The 1989 Definition:

Land is classified as a wetland if any one of these conditions exists:

- Water floods the area for 7 consecutive days during the growing season.

- Certain types of water-loving plants are found.

- The soil is flooded or saturated with water at or near the surface (within 18 inches).

A Definition proposed in 1992:

Land is classified as a wetland if all of these conditions exist:

- Water floods the area for 15 consecutive days during the growing season and number of days in defined growing season are reduced.

- Fewer types of plants are classified as water-loving plants.

- Soil must be saturated at the surface for 21 consecutive days.

An important goal has been "no net loss of wetlands". If the proposed definition in 1992 is adopted, will there be a net loss?

Compare the environmental and economic impacts of the two definitions.

2.5 Dam the Rivers or Let Them Run Free

The river is an ever-changing environment dominated by flowing water. At least it was until someone decided to build a dam.

The Army's Dam Builders

One of the first schools of engineering was the army's military academy at West Point. The United States government depended on the West Point engineers for their technical knowledge needed to harness the nation's rivers. Today the US Army **Corps of Engineers** is the largest engineering firm in the world.

Many of the nation's rivers are no longer the wild, free-flowing rivers that were discovered by the early explorers. With the approval of Congress, the rivers are dammed, dredged, and straightened by the Army's engineers. The Corps has been given the responsibility of maintaining the nation's navigable waterways and protecting its wetlands.

Rivers are often the subject of controversy. Wars have been fought over rivers. More recently the courtroom has become the scene of battles fought over the use of rivers. Projects planned by private developers and industries have been challenged in court by individual citizens and environmental organizations.

Groups of interested citizens have challenged dams and other projects proposed by the Corps of Engineers. Some of the projects have been stopped. For other projects, the court case only delayed the completion date and increased the project cost. Critics claim the Corps of Engineers often underestimates the cost of a dam and the value of the land to be flooded, while they overestimate the benefits and the useful life of the dam.

Making changes in an ecosystem may offer certain benefits for humans. Unfortunately these benefits always carry a price tag. Along with the cost in dollars, the price tag includes another cost — the value of the ecosystem that is lost. The question that must always be asked, "Which is greater, the cost or the benefit?"

Thanks to the Army Corps of Engineers the Mississippi River is navigable for most of its length.

This Dam was built along the Little Miami River in Ohio. Its purpose is flood control for the cities downstream.

Dams provide flat-water recreation such as sailing, but opponents of the Meramec Dam questioned the need for additional flat-water recreation facilities.

Dams Provide Flood Control

Dams are often a part of flood control plans. Frequently dams flood areas that are sparsely populated in order to protect areas downstream that have a greater population density. The Flood Control Act of 1936 included plans for 243 dams as a part of the Comprehensive Flood Control Plan for the Ohio and Mississippi Rivers.

Two of the dams would be built on the Meramec River in Missouri. Located near St. Louis, the valley along the lower reaches of the river supports a steadily increasing population. Towns that have been built on the broad floodplain are frequently flooded. The dams would help protect the densely populated region of the Meramec Valley.

Congress first voted funds for the **Meramec Dam and Meramec Park Lake** proposal in 1968. Construction of the first dam was to be completed in 1978, but the dam was never built. Missouri citizens fought long and hard to keep the flow of the Meramec River from being blocked by dams. It was their opinion that the costs were greater than the benefits.

The Corps of Engineers has often proposed dams for flood control in areas that have been devastated by major floods. Monroe County, Pennsylvania, sustained $28.5 million in property damage during the 1955 flood. Seventy-eight people in the county were killed by the flood.

In 1960 the Corps recommended the construction of 14 small dams on tributaries of the Brodhead Creek. Another dam was to be built at Tocks Island on the Delaware River. This dam would permanently flood land in Monroe County, but it would decrease flood damage for eight communities on the lower reaches of the Delaware. Only two of the proposed dams were built.

Save the River

Dams create lakes, and lakes provide an opportunity for flat-water recreation. The lake created by Meramec Dam would have provided 12,600 acres (5,040 hectares) of flat-water recreation near the densely populated St. Louis area. Figures provided by the Corps of Engineers showed that the lake could support 3.7 million visitors annually. According to the Corps, recreational opportunities offered by the lake would include motor boating, water skiing, bird-watching, picnicking, sightseeing, fishing, swimming, camping, field sports, and ice skating.

Opponents of the dam suggested that the undammed stream already provided most of the recreational activities that would be offered by the lake. They questioned the need for additional flat-water recreation facilities. Lakes within a 100 mile radius of St. Louis already provided 134,000 acres (53,600 hectares) of flat water for recreation. According to Missouri's Statewide Outdoor Recreation Plan (1976), the supply of flat-water recreation already exceeded the demand. In addition the plan suggested that the demand for free-flowing streams would soon exceed the supply.

The Meramec River was one of only seven free-flowing streams remaining in the state. The Corps of Engineers pointed out that more than 30 miles (49 km) of streams above the lake would still be available to canoeists. They also suggested that the uniform flow created by the dam would increase the number of days that canoeists could float the 108 miles (173 km) of river below the dam. The project, they said, would also improve public access to the river. Opponents argued that the dam would flood the most beautiful stretch of the free-flowing stream.

The Corps of Engineers also planned to build **Tocks Island Lake and Dam** on the Delaware River. It was to be a multi-purpose project that would provide recreation, flood control, hydroelectric power, and water supplies. The environmental cost of the Tocks Island Project would be the loss of one of the few unspoiled free-flowing sections of river in the northeastern United States. Interested citizens and environmental groups rallied to "Save the Delaware" as Missourians had rallied to "Save the Meramec."

The weather cooperated with the plan to save the Delaware River. During the years of debate about the dam, there were no floods, and there were no major water shortages. An evaluation showed that the need for additional power supplies was uncertain, and a need for free-flowing recreational facilities was demonstrated. In addition, federal money that was once available for dams and other federal projects was needed for the Vietnam War.

Finally Congress voted to shelve the $325 million Tocks Island Project and protect the river. They declared the 37-mile (59 km) section, that would have been covered by the reservoir, a part of National Wild and Scenic Rivers System. Land purchased for the project was transferred to the Delaware Water Gap National Recreation Area. The Tocks Island Project was finally killed in 1992 when Congress deauthorized the proposed dam.

Dams Provide a Water Supply

Had the Meramec Dam been built, the lake behind the dam could have supplied 207 million gallons (7.9×10^8 L) of water per day for communities nearby. Opponents of the dam said this additional water supply was not needed. According to the Missouri Geological Survey, ground water supplies in the area are sufficient to meet the needs of the area until the year 2076. The Corps of Engineers argued that drilling deep wells is expensive and Meramec Lake would provide growing communities with a cheaper source of water.

Lakes that store a supply of water for future use are often called **reservoirs**. Many communities depend upon reservoirs to provide their water supply. More than 22 million people, or about 10 percent of the nation's population, live in the region extending from New

Tocks Island on the Delaware River

The proposed dam at Tocks Island was not built. This section of the river and its floodplain are now a part of the Delaware Water Gap National Recreation Area. Visitors still enjoy canoeing the free-flowing river.

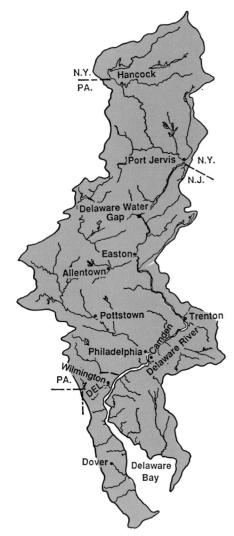

Delaware River Basin

York City to Philadelphia. Most of these people depend upon the 12,765 square mile (33x10⁹ km²) watershed of the Delaware River for their water supply.

The area that drains into a river is the river's watershed or basin. Water in the Delaware River Basin is shared by four states: New York, New Jersey, Pennsylvania, and Delaware. Disputes over the water shared by the four states in 1931 and 1954 were settled by the Supreme Court.

In 1961 the governors of the four states signed the **Delaware River Basin Compact**. The Compact recognized the Delaware River Basin as a regional resource, and it created the **Delaware River Basin Commission** to manage the resource. The Commission consists of the four governors and a commissioner who is appointed by the President of the United States.

The Compact requires the Delaware River Basin Commission to adopt a comprehensive plan for managing the water resources in the Delaware Basin. The Commission also sets policy for the floodplain, sets water quality standards, and approves projects that would affect water resources in the basin. An important part of this plan has been the building of dams to increase the basin's capacity to store water supplies.

New York City's 9 million residents use about 1.5 billion gallons (5.7x10⁹ L) of fresh water each day. While some residents of Queens pump water from their wells, most people living in New York City obtain their water from the 18 reservoirs and 4 controlled lakes owned by the city.

Although New York City is not in the Delaware River Basin, the city owns three reservoirs on the upper reaches of the Delaware River. The 1954 decision of the US Supreme Court allows New York City to divert 800 million gallons (3.0x10⁹ L) daily from the Delaware Basin. This is about one-half of the water needed by the city.

New York City is not the only city to divert water from one watershed to another. The Colorado River is about the same size as the Delaware River, and it is the only major source of surface water in the Southwest. Water held behind dams on the Colorado River is diverted to cities like Los Angeles, Phoenix, and Denver. Some of the water flows into irrigation canals in southern California.

Because it lies east of the Cascade Mountain Range, the Columbia Basin in the eastern part of the state of Washington receives less than twelve inches of rain a year. Although the soil in the Columbia Basin is fertile, farming is not be possible without irrigation. The water needed for irrigation is pumped from a reservoir behind Grand Coulee Dam. The dam forms a 151 mile (242 km) lake on the Columbia River.

In Canada where the Columbia River begins, it snows almost every day during winter. By winter's end the Rockies are covered with 30 or 40 feet (9-14 m) of snow. Most of the water flowing in the high reaches of the Columbia River comes from the melting snow. Grand Coulee Dam blocks the flow of water, and stores it for the farmer's thirsty crops.

Dams Provide Water to Increase the Natural Flow

Droughts during the mid-1960s and again in the early 1980s created water shortages for many communities throughout the northeastern United States causing low flow in the Delaware River. The drinking and industrial water supplies of Camden, New Jersey, and Philadelphia, Pennsylvania were threatened. The problem was not the absence of water but the presence of salt.

The flow of fresh water in the Delaware River normally keeps the **salt front** — the line where fresh water from the river meets the ocean water — near Wilmington, Delaware. In January 1981, the Delaware River Basin Commission declared a drought emergency. The salt front had moved 30 miles (48 km) upstream near Camden, New Jersey.

Philadelphia's Torresdale water treatment plant takes water directly from the Delaware River. Removing salt is expensive, and the water treatment plant is not designed to remove salt. An advancing salt front threatens the city's water supply. Even though Camden draws its water supply from wells, when the river's flow is low, the ground water may be contaminated by salt and other chemicals in the river water. Water from the river moves through the ground to the aquifers that provide Camden's water supply.

High salt content in a water supply damages pipes, plumbing, and machinery. It ruins products produced with the water, and it is a threat to human health. The 1954 Supreme Court ruling that allowed New York City to divert water from the Delaware River also required the city to release water from its reservoirs during periods of low natural flow. The city must release enough water to guarantee a minimum flow of 1,750 cubic feet per second (49 cubic metres per second) at Montague, NJ.

Before New York City built the reservoirs and releases were made to increase the natural flow, the flow at Montague was sometimes only 175 cubic feet per second (4.9 cubic metres per second). Thus during droughts, the release of water from New York City's reservoirs helps to maintain a minimum flow of water in the Delaware River. Dams on the Delaware help to keep the salt front at a safe distance downstream during low-flow periods.

Drought conditions, a growing population, and a rising sea level are factors that have led the Delaware River Basin Commission to conclude that the existing reservoirs did not have adequate water storage capacity. In order to insure the ability to control the salt front the commission recommended the following:

- Enlarge New York City's Cannonsville reservoir.
- Enlarge two flood-control dams in Pennsylvania's Pocono Mountains to provide water storage and recreation.
- Construct a reservoir in New Jersey.
- Hold the Tocks Island project in reserve for development after the year 2000 if it is needed for a water supply.

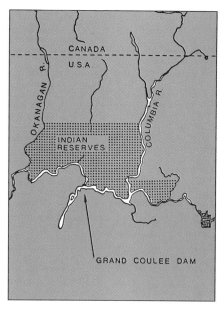

Grand Coulee Dam and Reservoir

WHAT DO YOU THINK?

To accommodate peak electricity needs in Las Vegas, enormous amounts of water held behind the Glen Canyon Dam on the Colorado River are released periodically each day. These sudden releases often raise the river by 13 feet. Surging currents have eroded campsite beaches, destroyed Native American archeological sites, and ruined wildlife habitat (some inhabited by endangered species). Scientists, environmentalists, and tour guides support stabilizing the release of water from the dam, though this might result in a slight electricity rate increase in Las Vegas. What would you do?

Barges move through the locks at a dam on the Mississippi River. Dependable navigation on the nation's large rivers provides the least expensive means of transporting products.

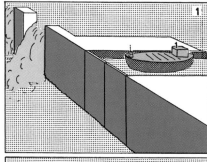

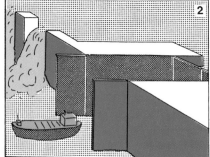

Operation of a Lock

After the Tocks Island Project was shelved by Congress, the Delaware River Basin Commission ordered seven electrical utility companies that draw water from the river to build a reservoir to hold water that can be released into the river during low flow. Construction of the dam forming the Merrill Creek Reservoir in Harmony township, New Jersey, was completed in 1988. Water is pumped from the Delaware River when the flow is high and re-released into the river at times of low flow. The reservoir diminishes the threat of salt water intruding into the lower sections of the river.

Dams for Navigation

The cheapest way to ship cargo is by water. The Allegheny and Monongahela Rivers meet at Pittsburgh, Pennsylvania, to form the Ohio River. In 1977 more freight was hauled on the Ohio River, between Pittsburgh and Cairo, Illinois, than was hauled through the Panama Canal. The city of Pittsburgh claims to be the largest inland port in the United States.

Travel on the Ohio River has not always been smooth. At Pittsburgh, the Ohio River is 700 feet (210 m) above sea level while at Cairo it is only 250 feet (75 m) above sea level. The natural river elevation sometimes changes abruptly with the water forming rapids and waterfalls. Early settlers traveling the Ohio River met an obstacle near Louisville, Kentucky — a mile (1.6 km) long area of rapids known as "The Falls." The elevation dropped 19 feet (5.7 m) at The Falls making it the greatest hazard to navigation on the Ohio River.

In 1824 Congress directed the US Army Corps of Engineers to improve the nation's rivers for navigation, and six years later the Corps finished a dam and a canal around The Falls. The dam controls the river's flow, and the canal is fitted with a series of locks. A **lock** is an area between two massive steel gates. Barges enter the lock, and the water is raised or lowered to meet the river on the opposite opening of the lock.

By 1929, the Ohio River had been channelized to a depth of nine feet (2.7 m) and fitted with 46 locks and dams. Today powerful diesel tugboats push as many as seventeen barges from Pittsburgh to Cairo, in less than a week. At Cairo the barges are joined with others and are pushed down the Mississippi by larger tugboats.

Dams for Hydroelectric Power

Dams may be used to change the energy of moving water to electrical energy. Some of the newer hydroelectric dams are 90 percent efficient. Although less than 40 percent of the hydroelectric potential in this country has been developed, it is not likely that many new dams will be built for hydroelectric power. Most new hydroelectric generation will come from the installation of generation equipment at existing dams.

There are more than 30 reservoirs along the 1,214-mile (1942 km) length of the Columbia River. All but 80 vertical feet (24 m) of the river has been dammed to provide power for the Northwest. Power stations along the Columbia River can provide 80 percent of the electricity in the Pacific Northwest. The Columbia River represents one third of all the potential hydroelectric power produced in the US

Computers monitor and regulate the flow of water in the river. At one time the ability of the Columbia River to provide water and electricity may have seemed unlimited, but today there is competition for both of these resources. When water is taken from the river for agriculture or other uses, it reduces the power that can be produced down-river.

The competition for water and power has become the limiting factor in the Pacific Northwest. Industries that once considered moving to the area have made other plans because of the uncertain power supply. The Snake River is the largest tributary of the Columbia. Additional dams along its length could provide additional power for the Northwest. Conservation Groups have fought power company proposals for dams that would flood the section of the Columbia River known as Hell's Canyon. According to some people Hell's Canyon provides the best white water rafting in the United States.

Hydroelectric dams are deadly to fish populations. To get to the spawning areas, salmon must use fish ladders to by-pass 8 dams on the Columbia and Snake Rivers. The journey downstream is a treacherous one for the juvenile salmon. Millions of young fish are killed as they pass though the powerful turbines at the hydroelectric power plants.

Before the era of dam building on the Columbia River, the river was home to 16 million salmon. Now the population of salmon in the river and its tributaries is about 2.5 million, and most of these fish are hatchery fish. More than 200 Columbia River wild salmon and steelhead runs are now extinct, and 76 others are near extinction. The Snake River's sockeye salmon was added to the endangered species list in 1991.

Saving the salmon is important to the Northwest fishing industry. Salmon fishing is an important part of the Northwest's economy, but so is cheap electricity. The aluminum smelters were drawn to the Northwest by the promise of cheap electricity, and changing the flow of water to protect the salmon could decrease the efficiency of hydroelectric power plants and increase the cost of electricity.

In Canada, Hydro-Quebec has built a series of dams on rivers that empty into the James Bay. The dams produce as much energy as 30 nuclear power plants. Six percent of the electricity is sold to other Canadian provinces and the northeastern United States. Native Cree Indians are fighting a proposal by Hydro-Quebec to dam the Great Whale River. They claim that the dams will make it impossible to support themselves with fishing, hunting and trapping.

TRY TO FIND OUT

If there are private dams on rivers or streams in your region. Are they licensed by Federal Energy Regulatory Commission? Do the dams still serve a useful purpose? Do they damage the environment? If you have such a dam near you, find out about when its license comes up for renewal. Learn about the dam and decide if you think the license should be renewed or should the dam be removed.

Dam Safety

Dam failures in the late 1970s caused national concern over the safety of dams. The disasters resulting from the dam failures led the President to direct the Corps of Engineers to inspect the nation's fifty-thousand dams for potential hazards.

The safety of dams is dependent upon the geological features of the area and the structure of the dam. There are some places where dams should never be built. These include earthquake-prone areas and areas where the rock is porous.

Over a period of many years, water flowing beneath the earth dissolves limestone rock leaving openings called caves. Some of the passageways may be filled with clay. If a lake lying over this type of porous rock structure develops a leak, the water pressure may force the clay plug out of the cavity. If the plug is removed, the lake may be emptied in the same manner as a bathtub.

2.5 QUESTIONS FOR STUDY AND DISCUSSION

The Army's Dam Builders

1. How did the US Army Corps of Engineers (COE) improve transportation in America?
2. List two responsibilities that Congress has assigned to the COE.
3. In the past, wars have been fought over rivers. Where are battles over rivers fought today?
4. List two factors that, according to critics, are *under*estimated by the engineers.
5. List two factors that critics claim are *over*estimated by the engineers.
6. What question should always be asked when plans are being made to change an ecosystem?

Dams Provide Flood Control

7. Dams have often been proposed to protect areas from floods. What area would have been protected by the Meramec dams? What areas would have been flooded?
8. What event caused the COE to propose 14 dams on tributaries of the Brodhead Creek in Monroe County, Pennsylvania?
9. If the dams had been built, would they have provided flood protection for Monroe County?

Save the River

10. In addition to flood control, what additional benefits would have been provided by the Meramec Dam?
11. Why were some people opposed to the dam?
12. What benefits would have been provided by the Tocks Island Dam on the Delaware River?
13. What valuable resource would have been lost if the dam had been built?
14. List the reasons why the dam at Tocks Island was never built.
15. What did Congress do to protect the river and the surrounding area?

Dams Provide a Water Supply

16. What is the source of water for people living in the Meramec River valley?
17. What would be the advantage of getting water from a lake?
18. What percent of the nation's population depends on the Delaware River watershed for its water supply?
19. List the four states that share the water in the Delaware River Basin.
20. How were disputes over water use in the Delaware River Basin settled before 1960?
21. Why was the Delaware River Basin Compact important?

22. What are the four "jobs" of the Delaware River Basin Commission?
23. What is the source of drinking water for most people in New York City?
24. Is New York City in the Delaware River Basin? Explain the relationship between New York City's water supply and the Delaware River.
25. What is the only major source of surface water in the Southwest? What major cities depend on this source for their water supply? Are any of these cities in the Colorado River Basin?
26. Why does the Columbia Basin receive so little rain each year?
27. What is the source of water that flows in the upper reaches of the Columbia River?
28. Explain the following statement: Without snow in the Canadian Rockies there would be no farms in the Columbia Basin.

Dams Provide Water to Increase the Natural Flow
29. During a drought people living in Camden, New Jersey, and Philadelphia, Pennsylvania, are concerned that their water supply will become contaminated. What chemical may enter the water supply?
30. What is a salt front? Where is the salt front normally located?
31. Why doesn't the city of Philadelphia simply remove the salt at the water treatment plant?
32. What is the source of drinking water for the people of Camden, New Jersey? Why are they so concerned about the salt front?
33. Why would industries that do not use the water for drinking or in food products be concerned about the salt content of the water?
34. Would the salt front remain further downstream if New York City did not divert water from the Delaware River Basin? Explain.
35. List three factors that might cause the Delaware River Basin Commission to bring the Tocks Island Project back to life.

Dams for Navigation
36. Why have rivers been such an important means of transportation? What city claims to be the largest inland port? What river begins at this port?
37. What made the area of the Ohio River near Louisville, Kentucky, so dangerous? How was navigation through this section improved?
38. How was the Ohio River changed to improve transportation?

Dams for Hydroelectric Power
39. New fossil-fueled power plants are 40 percent efficient. How do hydroelectric power plants compare?
40. In what region of the country is most of the hydroelectric power produced?
41. What are the two limiting factors for development in the Pacific Northwest?
42. What would be the environmental cost if additional dams were built along the Snake River?
43. Do you think that additional dams should be built so that more industry can move into the Pacific Northwest? Justify your position.
44. Electricity produced at dams on Quebec's Great Whale River would be exported to the northeastern United States. Evaluate the environmental and economic impacts of the proposal.

Dam Safety
45. What events caused the President to call for an inspection of the nation's dams?
46. Who is responsible for the inspection?
47. List two factors that determine the how safe a dam will be.
48. List two places where dams should not be built.
49. What may happen if a dam in built in an area with a porous limestone rock structure?

"We need to start giving land back to the river. If we don't, sooner or later the river will take it back."
Larry Larson, Director Wisconsin's Floodplain Program

Sometimes rain falls gently and disappears into the soil, but often it strikes the earth with great force loosening tiny particles of silt and clay from the earth. If the earth cannot absorb the water, it begins a journey across the land carrying some of the particles with it.

The force of the moving water loosens more particles, and the water cuts a path as it moves across the land. The water with its **load** — the clay and silt particles that it carries — flows into a stream. The streams dump the water into a river until the river can hold no more, and then there is a flood.

The Water Drops Its Load

Floods occur when water reaches the top of the banks of a river or a stream and flows across the low, flat land that lies along the body of water. The low, flat land that is periodically flooded is called the **floodplain**. Some of the standing water slowly sinks into the soil restoring the supply of ground water. Much of the floodwater slowly returns to the river as the water level drops.

As the water stands on the floodplain, it drops some of the silt and clay particles that it carried. When the water is gone, a thick new carpet of fertile loam soil is left behind. Some of the world's best farmland is found along the banks of rivers where frequent floods bring a new supply of fertile soil to the land.

Along the coast where the rivers reach the ocean, the slope of the land is often gentle and the velocity of the water is slowed. Here, at the mouth of the river, the water drops its load of silt and clay forming an area of land called a **delta**. During the last 6,000 years the load dropped by the Mississippi River has added some 30,000 square miles (7.8×10^4 km²) to the state of Louisiana. But now, because of structures built to protect New Orleans from floods, the Mississippi Delta is shrinking.

Cities Along the River

The valleys along rivers and streams are the most convenient and profitable places to live, especially in mountainous areas. Two-thirds of the state of Pennsylvania is mountainous. Of the 2,800 communities in Pennsylvania, 2,468 are located on floodplains that lie along rivers and streams in the valleys.

WHAT DO YOU THINK?

Your ancestors built a business and a family home on a flood-plain when they settled on a river in the late 1800s. They thought the location ideal, because at that time most transport of goods was done by boat. However, since then the area has been struck by devastating floods. The town where you live has decided to tear down its flood walls and restore floodplain wetlands. This will require your home to be demolished or moved to an upland site. How would you feel about this policy? Under what conditions would you cooperate?

WHAT DO YOU THINK?

The director of the Association of State Floodplain Managers said, "For too long we've tried to adjust rivers to human needs. Then we wonder why our rivers are messed up and why we continue to get flooded. We need to adjust human behavior to river systems."

People chose to live along rivers because the river provided a cheap and easy means of transportation. The river also provided a source of water, and the rich level land of the floodplain was the most suitable land for farming. Farmers cleared timber and sometimes dug ditches to drain water from the swampy lowlands.

The river also provided water power that attracted industry to the river communities. The force of flowing water was first used to turn water wheels that provided the power to grind grain. Later dams were built, and now water flows through turbines to turn generators that make electricity. Although most electricity is not produced by water power, large power plants still require huge amounts of water. The 33 coal-fired power plants along the Ohio River withdraw more than twice the amount of water withdrawn by cities and industries from the river by all other users.

In regions with a good supply of raw materials, small communities grow into large cities. One of the world's most productive industrial and agricultural regions is the Ohio River Valley. The valley supplies clay, limestone, sandstone, and coal for industries. The river supplies the water and an efficient means of transportation.

The population of a river community declined when the supply of raw materials was exhausted, or the river changed its course. In the 1920s, 15,000 people lived in Cairo, Illinois. Barges transported lumber from the saw mills and wood products from the industries in Cairo. Today the once abundant forest is gone, and the population of Cairo is less than 6,000.

Raindrops Falling on the City

As more land is developed, the amount of water that can be absorbed by the earth decreases. Buildings, streets, and parking lots cover the land and prevent infiltration of the water. When it rains, the run-off now flows through large pipes beneath the ground called **storm sewers**. The storm sewers, which replaced the natural streams, carry the run-off water to the nearest river.

More development means more run-off. When the storm sewers can't carry the water away fast enough, city streets are flooded. When storms bring large amounts of rain, any natural streams that remain in the developed area are quickly filled, and low-lying areas of the city are flooded.

Straight and Narrow Channels

To carry away the excess water, the meandering paths of rivers or streams are sometimes replaced with **human-made channels.** The channels are shorter, straighter and have a steeper slope than the natural channels of the river or stream. This increases

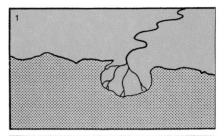
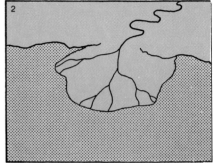
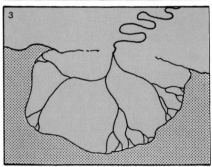

River Delta Formation

the amount of water that can be carried away. In the area where there are human-made channels the amount of flooding is reduced.

Channels may solve the problem of flooding for one area, but they increase the risk of flooding in other areas downstream. As the increased flow of water reaches an area that has not been channelized, its flow is slowed, and any low-lying areas are likely to be flooded. As more miles of the river are channelized, larger areas downstream are flooded.

Johnstown, PA — City on a Floodplain

The city of Johnstown, Pennsylvania, is located at the point where two mountain streams meet to form the Conemaugh River. The city quickly became an important manufacturing area in western Pennsylvania. By 1889, its population had reached 30,000. Like other towns built on floodplains, Johnstown was regularly flooded.

The area of Johnstown has received national attention because of the many lives lost in three major floods. Of the 3,500 Pennsylvanians who died in major floods during the last 100 years, at least 2300 people were killed in floods that hit the Johnstown area.

What caused the Johnstown area floods, and why were so many lives lost? The first major flood occurred on May 31, 1889, when six to eight inches (15-20 cm) of rain fell in a 24-hour period. Normally a three-inch rain was enough to cause flooding in Johnstown. It had been the wettest May on record, and the soil was saturated. Even then, it would probably have been "just another flood" except for an old earthen dam on the south fork of the Little Conemaugh River.

The 900-foot (270 m) long and 70-foot (21 m) high dam held water in a 500-acre (200 hectare) lake. The dam was originally built to provide water for the state's canal system, but the system was no longer used. A group of wealthy business owners from Pittsburgh bought the lake and a large area of land. The dam needed repairs, and the new owners hired a contractor with no experience in dam construction to rebuild the dam. For several years the new owners enjoyed their private lake. Then the heavy rains came.

The repairs made on the weak dam did not meet the engineering standards for a large earthen dam. Little water could flow from the lake because the spillway had been partially blocked and a fish gate installed. Soon the water began to flow over a low area in the center of the dam. After a few hours, it burst through the weakened dam, and a 40-foot (12 m) wall of water moved toward Johnstown. In just a few hours 2,100 people were drowned.

Johnstown, Pennsylvania, has been flooded many times and many lives have been lost.

Monuments in the cemetery's Unknown Plot honor the memory of those whose bodies were never recovered after the flood of 1889.

The city rebuilt, and each time the river flooded the residents cleaned up the silt and clay that the floods left behind. Then on March 17, 1936, an unusually heavy rainstorm melted the snow covering the mountains. The resulting flood killed 25 people. The city once again rebuilt.

After the city cleaned up and rebuilt, the US Army Corps of Engineers straightened the channels of the two mountain streams and built **dikes** — massive sloping concrete walls — to protect the city. The engineers thought this would put an end to the city's flood problem, and Johnstown began to promote itself as flood-free.

Johnstown remained flood-free for 41 years and 124 days — until July 19, 1977. Then during a 12 hour period, thunderstorms dropped nearly 12 inches (30 cm) of water in the Johnstown area. This large amount of water caused five small earthen dams built on streams above the town to collapse. The human toll was 75 people dead and 26 people missing.

Just before the flood, one of the dams had been inspected and declared safe. Why did a dam that was declared safe collapse? Dams are not built to withstand unusual storms like the 12-inch (3 cm) in 12-hour rainfall. A storm like this is likely to occur in any given place only once in 500 years. Officials tell us that it would be too expensive to protect against the risk of such rare storms.

The US Army Corps of Engineers flood protection project had been designed to protect the city of Johnstown from a flood like the one seen in 1936. The 1977 flood was a bigger flood. The engineers said the flood protection project had protected the city. Without the deeper, straighter channels and the concrete walls, flood damage would have been even greater.

The Value of a Floodplain

Some people feel the floodplain belongs to the river. The floodplain provides a natural storage area for the excess water that the river cannot carry. It is also an important recharge area for the ground water supply. Although these are extremely important functions, they do not help the landowner pay the mortgage.

In our society, the value of land is not determined by the role it serves in its natural ecosystem, but by the money that can be gained if the land is sold or developed. An acre (0.4 hectare) of swampy forested land along a river might be worth $350. The same acre (0.4 hectare) that has been cleared and drained for farmland might sell for $1,350.

If this land is located near a large city and has potential for residential or commercial development, it might sell for $2,350 per acre (0.4 hectare). After it is developed, it may be worth

Water cascading over the broken dam on the South Fork of the Little Conemaugh River. In only a few hours the wall of water hit the city of Johnstown.

Now the National Park Service Flood Museum overlooks the site of the broken dam and the dry lake bed.

The natural channel of the river has been straightened and massive concrete dikes have been built to reduce the chances of flooding within the city.

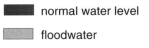

normal water level

floodwater

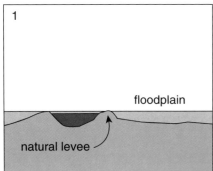

Stream (Before and After Development)

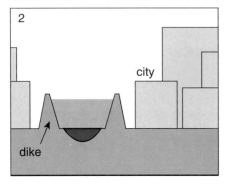

$23,500 per acre (0.4 hectare). Unfortunately when floodplains are developed, the value of property damaged during a flood also increases. Buildings may be destroyed, or a building and its contents may be damaged by a flood.

The Cost of Using a Floodplain

By 1986, 50 years after the adoption of a national flood control policy, the federal government had spent $23 billion dollars for flood protection. In spite of this fact, losses from floods continue to increase. The Johnstown flood of 1889 caused $17 million worth of property damage. In 1936, the developed area had doubled in size and damage was $41 million. In spite of the $7 million flood protection project, the 1977 flood caused an estimated $350 million worth of property damage.

Floods are the major cause of disasters. A major flood occurs somewhere in the United States nearly every year. A region is eligible for federal assistance if it is declared a disaster area by the President of the United States. After four days of heavy rains, in November of 1985, the Governor of Virginia asked President Reagan to declare eleven regions of his state disaster areas. He estimated that floods had caused $551 million in property damage and taken 20 lives. Floods in West Virginia had caused $200 million in property damage and taken an additional 20 lives.

Spring was unusually wet, and the summer months that are normally dry were filled with frequent and sometimes violent thunderstorms that dropped unbelievable amounts of water in the upper Midwest. It caused the Great Flood of '93. The floods began in April and continued through August. More than 40 lives were lost and property damage exceeded $10 billion. Counties in 8 states were declared disaster areas by President Clinton.

The cost of using the floodplain is determined by the land use selected. Many large cities — including Boston, Kansas City, St. Louis, Pittsburgh, and New Orleans — are built on floodplains and depend upon floodwalls or levees for protection from flood waters. The national flood control program that began in 1936 involves channelizing streams, building upstream dams to store run-off water and building levees to protect developed areas. But channels, dams, and levees cannot guarantee the protection of developed areas.

In 1951, over 200,000 homes were lost in levee-protected areas. A new $8 million levee protected Mark Twain's hometown of Hannibal, Missouri, during the Great Flood of 1993, but other town's weren't so fortunate. In spite of efforts to strengthen levees with millions of sandbags, many levees gave way. In some places, the force of the water breaking through the levee uprooted trees, demolished houses, and moved grain bins and propane tanks off their foundations.

In addition to property damage and loss of life, floodwaters also disrupt normal functions such as transportation. Floods destroy bridges, railroads and roads. More than 300 roads in Missouri were impassable during the flood of '93, and barge traffic was halted on the Missouri and upper Mississippi Rivers. Industries shut down when they ran out of parts or could not deliver their products.

Another problem in flooded areas is the lack of a safe supply of drinking water. Floodwaters often carry raw sewage, dead animals, and toxic chemicals that contaminate community water supplies. A flood along the Raccoon River in July 1993, knocked out the water treatment plant that serves the 250,000 residents of Des Moines, Iowa. Although operators restored water service within two weeks, it was another three weeks before the water was again safe to drink.

Property Damage from Flooding on Floodplain

Different Approaches to Flood Control

Some people feel that the best kind of flood protection is restricting land use so that floods cause less damage. When floodplains are used for agriculture, the cost of flood damage is relatively low. Floods destroy growing crops, but the farmer's loss is reduced by the nutrients in the silt and clay particles that are deposited by the flood. The financial loss that occurs when cropland is flooded is much less than when developed land is destroyed by floods.

It might seem that a simple answer to prevent the high cost of damage from floods would be to prevent farming or development of the floodplains. Let the floodplains remain as wetlands. The problem especially in urban areas is that wetlands and wildlife compete with people for the limited space available. Wetlands and wildlife do not provide as many jobs or generate as much money from taxes as farms, industrial parks, and housing developments

In 1960 St. Louis County, Missouri, adopted a land-use plan in which all land subject to flooding by major rivers or streams, including the Meramec, Missouri and Mississippi Rivers, was zoned as open space. The use of this land for open space, agriculture, or parks would not be severely affected by periodic flooding. The planners felt that the floodplains would best serve humans if they were left to fulfill their natural role of flood control.

In 1970, a development corporation asked the St. Louis County government to rezone a 1,200 acre (480 hectare) site on the floodplain of the Missouri River. The developer's proposal included an industrial complex and housing for 16,000 residents. The new development would be named **Earth City**,

Equipped with levees, holding ponds, and pumping stations, Earth City avoided flood damage during the great flood of 1993. How do you think this affected areas downstream?

and it would be protected by levees, drainage ditches, and pumping stations.

St. Louis County hired two engineering firms to study the technological and environmental aspects of the proposed city. In its report to the county government, one of the firms concluded that it was technologically possible to build Earth City. They suggested that the question was not whether it could be done, but should it be done? Modified plans were finally approved, and the industrial complex was built on the floodplain along the Missouri River.

In 1965 Congress asked the Corps of Engineers to develop a plan to control flooding along the Charles River in eastern Massachusetts. The river flows through Cambridge and Boston where it empties into the harbor. All of the marshes along the bay have been filled and developed. Walls have been built along the river to protect the cities, but storms still bring floods.

After a five-year study, the Corps recommended that the best way to control flooding was to buy 8,500 acres (3,400 hectares) of undeveloped wetlands in the Charles River watershed. If left in their natural state, the wetlands would absorb excess water and provide better protection than any additional levees or reservoirs. Purchase of the wetlands would also be less expensive than construction of flood-control structures. Congress approved the **Natural Valley Storage Plan**, and the federal government began to buy wetlands in order to guarantee that they will remain in their natural state.

An Act of Congress

The loss of life and property to floods continues to increase each year. Structures built to control floods fail to hold back floodwaters. The presence of flood control structures gives people a false sense of security and may encourage them to build on the floodplain.

In 1973 Congress responded to the increasing cost of flood damage by passing the Federal Flood Disaster Protection Act. The new law encourages communities to use floodplains in ways that will not result in the loss of life or property damage when floods do occur.

Buildings in areas that are prone to flooding must be elevated or flood-proofed. Floodways must be constructed so that water can pass through the community without causing damage. Communities must follow federal regulations for floodplain development in order for developments to be eligible for federal funding and federal flood insurance.

In a pamphlet celebrating the 50th anniversary of the Flood Control Act of 1936, the US Army Corps of Engineers includes the following statement: Many flood control experts today advise that structural flood control projects should be built only if a nonstructural solution is not feasible. The nonstructural solutions generally involve moving people rather than controlling water.

The Missouri and Mississippi Rivers and their tributaries reclaimed much of their floodplains during the Great Flood of '93. After the floodwaters returned to the rivers, private property owners and government officials were left with difficult decisions concerning reclaiming the land or giving the land back to the river.

2.6 QUESTIONS FOR STUDY AND DISCUSSION

1. What load is carried by the water?

The Water Drops Its Load
2. What is a floodplain?
3. Explain why some of the best farmland lies along the banks of rivers.
4. Explain how a delta is formed.

Cities Along the River
5. List three reasons why the early settlers chose sites along rivers.
6. Why did industries choose sites along rivers?
7. Why do coal-fired and nuclear power plants often build along rivers?
8. Give two reasons why the Ohio River Valley has become one of the most productive industrial areas in the nation.
9. Explain why the populations of some river towns like Cairo, Illinois, have decreased.

Raindrops Falling on the City
10. What is the relationship between developed land and infiltration of water?
11. What structures replace natural streams in cities.
12. Why do low-lying areas of cities flood faster than low-lying areas in undeveloped areas?

Straight and Narrow Channels
13. How do human-made channels differ from the natural paths of rivers or streams?
14. Why are natural paths sometimes replaced by human-made channels?
15. How do human-made channels affect the amount of flooding in the area where the channels were made? How do they affect the amount of flooding in the area downstream from the channels?

Johnstown, PA — City on a Floodplain
16. Why has the city of Johnstown become famous?
17. Why were so many lives lost in the flood that occurred in 1889? How could the disaster have been prevented?
18. What caused the killer flood of 1936?
19. What changes were made in the river to reduce the risk of flooding?
20. How many years passed before another killer flood hit the Johnstown area? What events caused this flood to be so destructive?
21. Why did the supposedly safe dams collapse?
22. Do you think that dams should be built to withstand storms that occur only once in five hundred years? If not, how should the people be protected?
23. The city was flooded and lives were lost after the Corps of Engineers flood protection project was completed. How could the engineers claim that the project was a success?
24. Do you think that there can ever be a flood-free city built on a flood plain? Explain.

The Value of a Floodplain
25. List two natural functions of a floodplain.
26. Why do developers insist on developing floodplains?

The Cost of Using a Floodplain
27. Compare the amount of property damage in the Johnstown floods of 1889 and 1936.
28. Did the COE flood protection project reduce the amount of property damage in the 1977 flood? If not, why?
29. What is the major cause of disasters?

30. Why did the governor of Virginia ask the President to declare areas in his state disaster areas after they had been hit by floods in 1955?
31. List three large US cities that are built on floodplains.
32. Describe three ways in which these and other cities have been protected from floods.
33. What evidence indicates that these flood protection measures cannot guarantee protection from floods?
34. List three ways that your family's life might be disrupted by a flood even though your home was not destroyed and no lives were lost.

A New Approach to Flood Control
35. List at least three uses of floodplains that will not result in costly damage when flooding occurs.
36. How does a flood partially compensate a farmer for the crops that are lost when flooding occurs?
37. Give three reasons why flood plains are developed.

38. Describe the floodplains land-use plan that was adopted by the St. Louis County planners in 1960.
39. If you had been a voting member of the St. Louis County government in 1970, would you have voted to rezone the 1,200 acre site on the floodplain of the Missouri River? Why or why not?
40. Describe how the Corps of Engineers' Natural Valley Storage Plan provided further flood protection for Cambridge and Boston.

An Act of Congress
41. Describe how flood control structures may increase the loss of life and property.
42. Describe two ways that the 1973 Federal Flood Disaster Protection Act will decrease the amount of federal money spent for damages from flooding.
43. Explain this statement: The river and the land are partners.
44. In your opinion, what criteria should determine which levees will be repaired after they are breached in a major flood and which levees should be removed?

Science
Technology
Society

ISSUES

RETURNING SALMON TO THE ELWHA RIVER

Washington's Elwha River was home to large populations of 8 species of salmon and trout. Dams have devastated the populations. The Elwha's king salmon population is extinct. Construction of the Elwha dam in 1913 violated state law because it did not include any mechanism to allow fish to pass.

The construction of Elwha and Glines Canyon dams have left fish with only 5 miles of their original habitat. Dale Crane, the Pacific Northwest regional director of the National Parks and Conservation Association, says the only way to restore the biodiversity of the river is to remove the dams. Federal studies have concluded that fish runs cannot be restored without removal of the dams. Experts say, removal of the dams could restore the fish populations to their historic levels.

There is increasing pressure from local residents, environmentalists, and Native Americans to restore the fish runs. The dams provide electricity to a pulp and paper mill owned by a Japanese company. The Glines Canyon Dam's license expired in 1976. The Federal Energy Regulatory Commission has issued a temporary license for it each year.

Consider the question: Should the dams be removed?
- What factors must be considered in making this decision?
- What additional information is needed?
- If you had to make a decision, would you relicense the dams or remove them?

The Mississippi River flows from a lake in northern Minnesota for some 3,700 miles (5,900 km) to the Gulf of Mexico. It receives water from 31 states and two Canadian provinces.

The River as a Highway

Today the Mississippi River and its floods are not like those described by Mark Twain in *The Adventures of Huckleberry Finn.* At one time there were no barriers to slow the flow of the river. During the last one hundred years the river has been remodeled. Dams have been built, channels have been dug, and both industries and cities have polluted the Mississippi.

When Mark Twain lived along the Mississippi, he watched as hogs, cattle, tobacco, corn, wheat, flour, and concrete were loaded on steamboats at Hannibal, Missouri. Hannibal once had the largest concrete plant in the world. It supplied most of the concrete that was used to build the Panama Canal. Today barges and tug boats have replaced the steamboats, but the economy of the Midwest is still linked to the traffic on the Mississippi.

Today the "monstrous big river" that Huck Finn enjoyed is managed by the Army Corps of Engineers. The COE is assigned the task of preventing floods and assuring that the Mississippi River is navigable from Minneapolis to the Gulf of Mexico. The Corps has built levees to prevent flooding and cut nine-foot (3 m) deep channels in the river bed to allow barge traffic. The COE built 29 locks and dams between Minneapolis and St. Louis, to keep the flow of water constant.

Changing Rivers

In the spring of 1865 the steamboat Sultana was traveling up the Mississippi River. It carried a load of cattle and hogs, sugar in wooden barrels, and passengers. Most of the passengers were Union soldiers who had been freed from Confederate prisons in the South. Seven miles (11 km) up river from Memphis, Tennessee, a boiler on the overloaded steamboat exploded. The boat sank and many people drowned.

Attempts to salvage the boat were unsuccessful. Later the river cut a new path, leaving the boat partly buried in the old river bed. Today the boat is buried beneath tons of silt and clay that has been deposited by the annual spring floods. Each year, an Arkansas farmer plants and harvests crops in the rich soil that has covered the boat.

Minnesota's Lake Itasca forms the headwaters of the Mississippi River.

Rivers that flow across land with a gentle slope naturally move back and forth, changing their path every hundred years or so. There have been at least six major changes in the path of the Mississippi, and it is once again trying to shift its course. Many years ago the Mississippi shifted its course making a large curve or meander connecting the Mississippi to the Atchafalaya River in Louisiana.

Each year the amount of water flowing into the Atchafalaya increased. Instead of following the Mississippi to the Gulf of Mexico, the water followed the shorter, steeper route of the Atchafalaya. By the 1950s, 30 percent of the Mississippi's water was flowing into the Atchafalaya. If nothing was done, most of the Mississippi would eventually take the new route.

The River versus the Corps

Although it is normal for old rivers to change their flow, the Army Corps of Engineers is trying to keep the river in its present bed. Seventy miles (112 km) north of Baton Rouge, Louisiana, the COE has built a set of levees and water control gates — a **river control structure** — that is designed to keep the water in the Mississippi River bed.

Why not allow the Mississippi River to change course? A 1980 study by Louisiana State University pointed out some of the changes that will occur if the Mississippi shifts its course:

- Barge traffic between New Orleans and the Midwest will be cut off unless the silt deposited by the river is removed.
- Salt water will move up the river channel and contaminate New Orleans' water supply.
- Morgan City, Louisiana, an oil town of 20,000, and the surrounding area where an additional 30,000 people live would be flooded, and would become part of the Gulf of Mexico.
- Broken pipelines will cause a shortage of natural gas in several eastern states.

It is not an easy task to keep a big river from taking a new path. The engineers must constantly fight erosion that would cause the river control structure to collapse. The cost of maintaining the structure is $5 million a year. Some people think that no matter what the Army Corps of Engineers does the Mississippi will eventually take the easier route to the Gulf.

The Mississippi demonstrated its power during the Great Flood of 1993. Water reached record levels and caused billions of dollars in damage. The likelihood of a flood like that occurring is once in 500 years. Will the river control structure hold if a 500-year flood hits the lower Mississippi Basin? Only time will tell who will win this battle — COE or Ol' Man River. One engineer studying the problem remarked, "Man cannot change the work of water."

1. Where does the Mississippi River begin?

The River as a Highway

2. List four ways that humans have changed the Mississippi River during the last 100 years.
3. List the two jobs which have been assigned to the Army Corps of Engineers.

Changing Rivers

4. Explain how a steamboat called the Sultana was buried on a farm in Arkansas.
5. Identify a Louisiana river that receives water from the Mississippi River.

The River versus the Corps

6. What is the purpose of the river control structure built by the Army Corps of Engineers?
7. How would a change in the path of the Mississippi River affect the Midwest?
   How would it affect the people of New Orleans?
   How would it affect the people of Morgan City, Louisiana?
   How might it affect people living in the East?
8. Do you think that maintaining the flow is worth the high cost of maintenance?

2.8 CASE STUDY
Cleaning up the Rivers

For many years our rivers were used to carry wastewater away from the cities. The Industrial Revolution and the invention of the water closet (the first indoor toilet) increased the river's load of wastes. Rivers that smelled of sewage and water-borne diseases — diseases caused by organisms in the water — were common.

Reviving the Thames

In London, conditions were so bad that draperies were dipped in disinfectant and hung in the windows of Parliament to protect members from the smell of the Thames River. In the mid-1800s some 25,000 people living in the vicinity of London died of cholera. After the epidemic, sewers were built to take the waste out to sea. Sewers did not solve the problem. They only moved it from one location to another.

Sewage treatment plants built in the 1930s were damaged by bombs during World War II. By 1950 the Thames River was declared dead. Salmon had disappeared, and only a few eels remained in the river. Following a ten-year study, the sewage treatment plants were rebuilt. Wastewater was treated before it entered the Thames, and the solid waste was dumped at sea.

Today pollution in the Thames has been reduced by 90 percent, and salmon have returned. More than 100 species of fish have been recorded in the Thames. Some people believe that

The Thames River as it flows through London is no longer a sewer. Today it is home to many species of fish including salmon.

The Northeast Water Pollution Control Plant serving the Philadelphia area.

where the Thames River meets the North Sea is the world's cleanest urban estuary.

Restoring America's Rivers

Not long ago America's rivers were a lot like the Thames. The first sewers were constructed in New York City during the 18th century. They carried untreated sewage and dumped it into the rivers. Every day during the 1970s, 290 million gallons (11x10⁸ L) of raw sewage flowed into the Hudson and East Rivers.

The price of progress in Boston was the death of the Charles River. People were warned about the dangers of falling into polluted rivers such as the Hudson and the Charles. Members of Harvard's rowing teams practiced on the river. Their friends joked that if the boat overturned, they should not yell for help because "if a teaspoon of the Charles gets in your mouth when you open it, you're done for." But it was no joke. The river was not a healthy environment for humans or for fish. By 1900 the river was so polluted that shad had disappeared.

Forty years ago the Delaware River was black with untreated sewage and chemical wastes. Chemical fumes often overcame dock workers in Philadelphia. In the early 1950s the level of dissolved oxygen in the Delaware Estuary was zero, and the fish populations in the river had declined drastically. Now, human sewage flows through wastewater treatment plants before entering the river, and shad catches are increasing every year.

In 1927 workers refused to work on construction along the "ugly and filthy" Willamette River in Oregon. All major cities along the river discharged untreated sewage directly into the river, and there was no treatment for industrial wastes. Between 1947 and 1967, the state's population doubled. Two-thirds of the people living in Oregon live in the valley along the Willamette River. It is also the site of most of the state's industrial development.

The citizens of Oregon were fed up with the polluted river. With strong citizen support the State Legislature passed laws to control pollution. By 1967 most cities had built plants to provide primary and secondary treatment of their sewage. Although the sewage was treated, the river bed was still lined with decaying matter, and globs of slimy material floated down the river. At a public hearing, the river was described as a "stinking, slimy mess, and a menace to public health — a biological cesspool."

A study reported that the dissolved oxygen level in the Willamette River was 2.5 ppm. This is comparable to someone trying to breathe without an oxygen mask at 20,000 feet (6,000 m) above sea level. The study also found that 90 percent of the oxygen-demanding wastes were coming from pulp and paper industries. The state required that all pulp and paper mills treat primary and secondary waste. The slime disappeared, and fish now thrive in water that has 5 ppm dissolved oxygen.

Lobbyists and some lawmakers objected to the first laws passed to improve the quality of water in Maine's rivers. They feared that the paper companies would be forced to shut down and thousands of jobs would be lost. It cost cities and industries in Maine more than one billion dollars to build the needed wastewater treatment plants. The paper companies spent millions of dollars for larger, more modern plants.

Was it worth it? Today the rivers are clean, Atlantic salmon have returned, and none of the paper companies closed their doors or left the state. Recreational use of the rivers brings millions of dollars to Maine's economy. The problem facing the legislature today is not how to control pollution, but how to regulate the use of the state's restored rivers.

Fishable and Swimmable Rivers

There is no river too small or too polluted that it is not worth saving. The water in all rivers should be "fishable and swimmable." This was the belief of Congress when it passed the 1972 Clean Water Act. The new federal water quality standards required cities to treat their sewage before dumping it into rivers and streams. Industries were also required to use the "best possible" technology to stop pollution.

To meet the new water quality standards, the City of New York added two modern secondary treatment plants. To make the best use of limited space, one of the treatment plants was built below ground level, and the rooftop of the 30 acre (12 hectare) treatment plant is now a city park.

Much of the wastewater that once flowed into our rivers from point sources — mainly industries and sewer pipes — is now being treated to remove the pollutants. Since 1972, more than $75 billion has been spent to build wastewater treatment systems. In the majority of cases, rivers and streams are safe for fishing and swimming. A survey of more than 650,000 miles (1×10^6 km) of rivers and streams, in 1990, found that 80 percent met the standards for fishable waters and 75 percent met the standard for swimmable waters.

Some communities have yet to meet the Clean Water Act's goal of fishable and swimmable. One of the most polluted coastal areas is Boston Harbor. The Massachusetts Water Resources Authority (MWRA) serves 2.5 million people in 60 communities. Courts found the authority in violation of state and federal clean water laws. Because of out-dated sewers and treatment plants, 500 million gallons (1.9×10^9 L) of improperly treated sewage pours into the harbor each day.

At the sewage treatment plant in Plymouth, MA, large beaters mix air with the sludge. Is this primary or secondary treatment?

The MWRA is now constructing a massive sewage treatment plant on Deer Island in Boston Harbor. Completion of the project is scheduled for 1999. When completed, the treatment facilities on Deer Island will treat primary and secondary sewage from 43 communities.

At the Sewage Treatment Plant

Primary treatment: As sewage enters the sewage treatment plant, it may flow through large **screens** that remove rags, sticks and other large items. At some sewage treatment plants the water passes through a **grinder**, something like a gigantic garbage disposal. The sewage is then piped to huge settling tanks where it is allowed to stand for an hour.

Primary treatment involves physical separation of liquids and solids. One-third of the suspended solids (organic matter) settles out of the water in the **primary settling tanks**. The solids that sink to the bottom of the tank are called **sludge**. Floating grease and scum are skimmed off the surface of the water. Both the sludge and the **effluent** — treated waste water — are piped to other tanks for further treatment.

Primary Treatment ▶

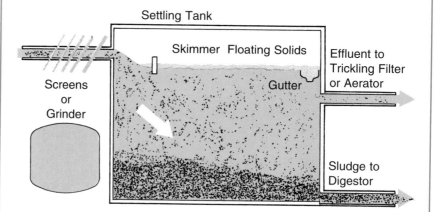

Secondary treatment: Secondary treatment is required in all US municipal sewage treatment plants. Some cities must treat large volumes of sewage in a very limited space. Although it is more expensive, the **activated sludge process** is often used for secondary treatment because it requires less space than the trickling filter process.

The waste water is piped to large tanks, and air is pumped into the sewage. The air supplies bacteria with the oxygen they need to breakdown the organic matter in the sewage. After several hours in the aeration tanks, the wastewater is then pumped to **secondary settling tanks** where the remaining solids settle out. Some of this sludge, which contains millions of bacteria, is returned to the aeration tanks where the bacteria help "eat" the organic matter in the wastewater.

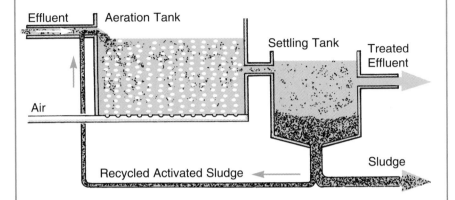

◀ Activated Sludge Process

Where space is not a problem, trickling filters are used for secondary treatment. A **trickling filter** is a bed of stones that is between three and ten feet (1-3 m) deep. The effluent from the primary settling tank is sprayed over the stones. Algae and bacteria growing on the stones remove most of the organic matter and nutrients from the water, as it trickles down through the bed of rocks. The purpose of primary and secondary treatment is to remove organic matter and nutrient — food for algae and bacteria — from the sewage. Primary and secondary treatment can remove 90 percent or more of the organic matter and nutrients from the sewage.

Sludge from the primary and secondary settling tanks is piped to **digesters** — large heated tanks where the sludge is held for 15 to 20 days. During this time, more of the organic material is digested by bacteria that do not use oxygen. Natural gas or **methane** is a waste product of this digestion process.

Some of the methane gas is burned to provide heat for the digesters. At large treatment plants, the excess gas produced also supplies heat for buildings nearby. The digesters at the world's largest sewage treatment plant in Chicago produce enough natural gas to heat more than 3,000 homes.

Sludge — It's Not a Dirty Word

What to do with the sludge once it is digested can be a problem, especially for large cities. In 1928 New York City began loading the digested sludge on special barges and dumping it in the ocean. The EPA approved a site 12 miles (19 km) off the coast

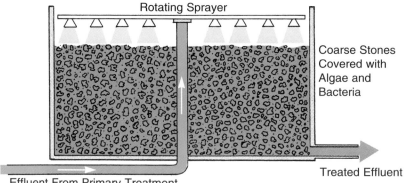

Rotating Sprayer

Coarse Stones Covered with Algae and Bacteria

Treated Effluent

Effluent From Primary Treatment

The algae and bacteria growing on the bed of rocks in this trickling filter remove the nutrients from the water sprayed over them.

as a dump site for sewage sludge from treatment plants on Long Island and in New Jersey.

The EPA closed the 12-mile site in 1988, and approved a new Deepwater Municipal Sludge Dump Site 106 miles off the coast of New Jersey. The City of Boston asked the EPA for permission to dump its sludge at the new Deepwater Dump. The EPA said no to Boston and required New York City and other communities to phase out the dumping of sludge. On June 29, 1992, the final load of New York City's sludge was dumped at sea.

Sludge may be incinerated or used as fertilizer. If space is not a problem, the sludge may be spread on drying beds of sand and gravel. The water drains through the sand. In cold and wet regions the drying beds are located in glass houses, and the "greenhouse effect" helps to dry the sludge.

Space is a problem in Chicago, and the city found drying sludge too expensive. They solved the sludge disposal problem by buying several thousand acres of land in Fulton County, Illinois. The land had been ruined by the strip mining of coal. Chicago's sludge is now shipped to Fulton County and stored in reservoirs. During the spring and summer months, the sludge is sprayed on the land and crops are planted.

Farmers can reduce their fertilizer costs by applying sludge, but the sludge must be properly treated and tested to make sure that it is safe. It is unlikely that sludge that has been "digested" will cause disease. Most disease-causing organisms and parasites can't survive the no-oxygen environment in the digester. Although it is unlikely that diseases could be caused by using treated sludge, it shouldn't be used on food crops that are to be eaten by humans.

Sludge used to grow crops should be tested for nutrient (N-P-K) content. If too much sludge is applied to the land, the excess nitrogen leaches into the water supply or nearby streams. The farmer must know the nutrient level of the sludge and the soil in order to calculate how much sludge can be safely applied.

Sludge can also be used to make compost. In 1970 a treatment plant at Holland Landing, Ontario, began using earthworms to compost sewage sludge and food processing wastes. Worms are used in Japan to compost sludge from the pulp and paper industry. At the sewage treatment plant in Lufkin, Texas, earthworms live in beds of aged sawdust and feed on sewage sludge. Sludge is sprayed over the sawdust beds for 3 to 5 minutes once a day. Fresh bedding, lime, and water are added as needed. The compost is used by the Department of Parks and Recreation.

What is New York City doing with its sludge? Once the facilities are constructed, the sludge will be dried at high temperatures and converted to fertilizer pellets. Until the facilities are ready, the dewatered sludge is being hauled out of the city to composting facilities, farms, and to modern landfill in Virginia.

The Need for Pretreatment

Since heavy metals prevent normal plant growth, sewage sludge must be tested to determine the levels of heavy metals it contains. Soil tests must also be taken to find the level of heavy metals in the soil. If the soil already contains high levels of heavy metals, sludge should not be applied to the land. Most heavy metals interfere with plant growth at levels well below those that are toxic to humans and other animals, but this is not true of cadmium. Plants are not affected by levels of cadmium that are toxic to humans.

Industry produces most of the heavy metals found in sludge. To prevent high levels of heavy metals in sludge, industries must pretreat wastewater before dumping it into the sewers. Heavy metals combine with the organic matter and become concentrated in the sludge. Proper pretreatment and laboratory testing can ensure that the sludge is safe.

The purpose of primary and secondary sewage treatment is to reduce the organic matter and lower the biological oxygen demand (BOD) of the effluent (treated waste water). Sewage treatment plants are designed to provide an ideal environment for the bacteria present in the sewage. The bacteria break down the organic matter, but they do not have the enzymes that are necessary to break down toxic wastes. Toxic wastes flushed into the sewer may kill the bacteria and stop the treatment process. Industries are required to pretreat wastewater so that toxic wastes don't interfere with the treatment process.

Chlorination

After secondary treatment, the wastewater is usually disinfected. The least expensive and most common method of disinfection is chlorination. Chlorine added to the effluent kills any disease-causing bacteria that might remain in the water. If properly used, more than 99 percent of the harmful bacteria are killed.

One disadvantage of chlorination is that chlorine reacts with organic compounds in the water to form **trihalomethanes** which are carcinogenic. Another disadvantage is that chlorine is also toxic to organisms in the aquatic environment. Since bacteria are less likely to survive in cold weather, some regions do not require chlorination during the winter months. Year-round chlorination is required if the effluent is discharged into waters that contain shellfish beds.

Combined Sewers

Combined sewers carry both sewage and storm water. When combined sewers were built, no one anticipated the problems they would eventually cause at sewage treatment plants. During average rainfalls the volume of water entering the sewers can be 5 to 15 times greater than the normal flow. Sewage treatment plants are not designed to process this massive volume of water.

When storms hit cities with combined sewers, untreated sewage and storm water may flow directly into the river. One hundred combined sewer overflow pipes dump untreated water into Boston Harbor. This makes the harbor one of the worst polluted bays in the US. New sewer systems must have separate storm and sanitary sewers.

The Effluent — Additional Treatment

Secondary treatment at some sewage treatment plants produces effluent that does not meet EPA standards for nitrates and phosphates. Without further treatment, the effluent will pollute streams and cause algal blooms, but it can be a valuable resource as irrigation water for golf courses, farmland or forests. Natural or artificial wetlands can also be used to remove nitrates and phosphates from effluent.

Effluent from the new treatment facilities on Deer Island in Boston Harbor will be piped through a 9.5 mile-long (15 km) tunnel into Massachusetts Bay. This part of the Boston Harbor clean-up plan is controversial. There is some concern that the effluent may cause algal blooms. One thing is certain — if there is a problem there won't be any easy solutions.

Lagoons and Aquaculture

Where land is available, wetlands may replace trickling filters or activated sludge processes. Another method that provides primary and secondary treatment is a lagoon. Although lagoons require large amounts of land, they are much less expensive to build and maintain than the conventional sewage treatment plant. A **lagoon** is a shallow pond where sewage is held for 20 to 30 days. In warm climates, algae and bacteria in a series of lagoons can provide acceptable primary and secondary sewage treatment.

Water in a lagoon may have to be recirculated to prevent odors that are produced when there is a lack of oxygen. Mosquitoes cause problems at lagoons, but this problem may be reduced by adding fish that eat mosquito larvae and bats that feed on the adults. Water hyacinths were added to lagoons to help control odors. These lagoons produce cleaner wastewater because the hyacinths use the nitrates and phosphates, and the roots filter the water.

Water hyacinth treatment ponds are being used in several southern states. The hyacinths can be used as food for cattle. Although hyacinths can only be used in warm climates, other aquatic plants such as duckweed, watercress, or cattails can be used in areas with cooler climates.

One of the most popular spots for bird watchers in western Michigan is the Muskegon Wastewater Treatment Facility. More than 10,000 acres (4,000 hectares) of land around the treatment facility has been cleared and planted with crops. The fields are fertilized and irrigated with the recycled wastewater that is stored in two 800-acre (320 hectare) lagoons.

It may look like a lake, but it is one of two lagoons that provide primary and secondary treatment for sewage from the Muskegon, MI, area.

After several months of treatment in the lagoon, the wastewater flows through ditches to fields where crops are growing.

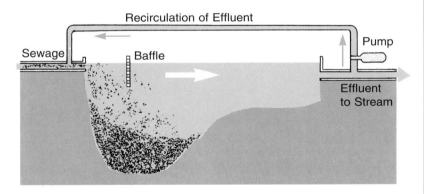

Recirculation of Effluent

Sewage

Baffle

Pump

Effluent to Stream

◀ Lagoon

On-Site Sewage Treatment

Septic tank-soil absorption systems are the most common type of wastewater treatment used in rural areas. One-third of housing units in the United States use this form of wastewater treatment. A **septic tank** is simply a large tank buried in the ground to treat sewage from an individual home or business. Solids settle to the bottom, bacteria break down organic matter, and the effluent flows through pipes into the **soil absorption field** (drain field).

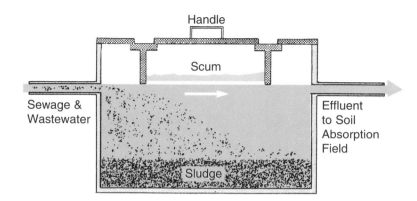

Sewage should remain in the tank for at least 24 hours to allow solids to settle out of the wastewater. The size of the septic tank is based on the number of bedrooms in the home. In Pennsylvania, the formula for calculating tank size assumes a minimum daily flow of 400 gallons (1.5×10^3 L) per day for a home with three or fewer bedrooms. An additional 100 gallons is added for each additional bedroom. The flow rate assumes the use of automatic washing machines, garbage disposals, and dishwashers.

Water Hyacinths

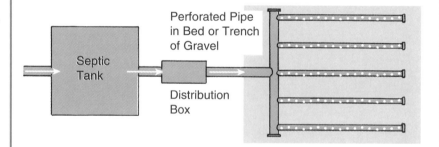

Septic Tank and ▶
Soil Absorption Field

The effluent from the septic tank flows through a system of perforated pipes in the absorption field. The size of the soil absorption field is determined by the size of the house and the soil's percolation rate. The soil must be a good filter — not too porous and not impermeable to water. The **percolation rate** — the rate at which water moves through the soil — must not be too fast or too slow. For a subsurface absorption field, the rate of water movement must be between 6 and 90 minutes per inch (2.5 cm).

In Pennsylvania, a minimum soil depth of 60 inches (120 cm) is required for a subsurface absorption field. If the site selected for the absorption field does not meet the requirements for a subsurface system, the absorption field must be placed in a

After several months in the lagoon, the treated wastewater is used to irrigate field crops like corn.

mound above the soil's natural surface. A layer of sand is placed on the soil to increase the depth of the absorption area. The depth of the sand required is determined by the depth of the natural soil.

The drain pipes are placed in a layer of gravel. Building paper is placed over the gravel before the field is covered with top soil. This prevents the soil from clogging the system. Grease should never be poured down the drain since it will also clog the absorption field.

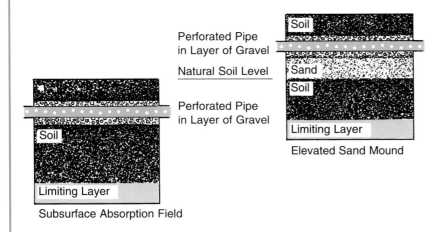

Perforated Pipe
in Layer of Gravel

Natural Soil Level

Perforated Pipe
in Layer of Gravel

Soil

Sand

Soil

Limiting Layer

Elevated Sand Mound

Soil

Limiting Layer

Subsurface Absorption Field

◀ Cross Section of Soil
Absorption Fields

Inside the Septic Tank

About 50 percent of the solids that remain in the tank are normally digested by the bacteria; the remainder will accumulate in the bottom of the tank as **sludge**. Large amounts of disinfectants may kill the bacteria and stop digestion of the sludge.

Unless it is regularly removed from the tank, sludge will build up and clog the absorption field. The frequency of pumping depends on the size of the tank and the number of people in the household. Garbage disposals may double the amount of solids to be digested, and should not be used with septic systems. If garbage disposals are used, the size of the tank should be doubled.

The mixture of fluid and solids (3 to 5 percent) pumped from the tank is called **septage**. Septage contains disease-causing organisms and can contaminate water supplies. The usual method for disposal of septage is to spray it on farmland.

Farmland used for septage disposal should be in one of the following USDA soil texture classes: sandy loam, sandy clay loam, silty clay loam, or silt loam. The site must also meet the following requirements:

- There must be a soil depth of at least 20 inches (50 cm) to bedrock.
- The water table must be at least 4 feet (1.2 m) below the surface.
- The slope of the field must not exceed 12 percent.
- There must be no visible sinkholes.
- It must not be subject to flooding or erosion.
- It must be more than 300 feet (90 m) from a water supply and 100 feet (30 m) from a spring.
- The soil must not be frozen.

Livestock should not feed on the crops that have been sprayed with septage for at least 60 days after application. The septage applied on dairy farms must be plowed under before crops are planted. Dairy cows are not allowed to feed on crops sprayed with septage. Septage should not be used on home gardens or land that is used for commercial production of food that will be eaten raw. If applied properly, septage can be beneficial. If it is not applied properly, it can be dangerous.

In more densely populated areas, with limited farmland, the usual method of septage disposal was lagoons. The groundwater in many communities is polluted by nitrates leaching from the lagoons. The use of lagoons for septage disposal is being phased out. The septage from septic systems in Harwich, Massachusetts, is being treated in a solar aquatic greenhouse with artificial wetlands and aquaculture ecosystems. The effluent is treated with UV light to kill any harmful microorganisms. According to the Massachusetts Department of Environmental Protection the effluent met Class I drinking-water standards.

Is It Worth the Cost?

Wastewater entering the river upstream becomes drinking water downstream. Improperly treated wastewater not only makes water unfit to drink, it also makes it unfit for fish and other aquatic organisms. Effective wastewater treatment is essential to human health. Effective treatment of wastewater and proper disposal of sludge is essential to meet the goal of "fishable and swimmable" waters.

Modern treatment methods are expensive. New York City water and sewer rates increased by 20 percent and more increases are expected. While it cost $20 million a year to dump sludge in the ocean, the first year of the city's land disposal was $250 million. While there are some scientists that believe that the oceans can assimilate our wastes, others disagree. New regulations, like the ban on ocean dumping, provide increased protection for the ocean ecosystem. The ocean is a source of food, and in some places, drinking water. Like the rivers and the streams, the ocean water quality needs to be fishable and swimmable.

2.8 QUESTIONS FOR STUDY AND DISCUSSION

1. Identify two major events that increased the river's load of wastes.

Reviving the Thames

2. What disease carried by the water caused the death of many people living in London in the 1800s?
3. Describe England's first attempt to clean up the dirty river.
4. Compare the condition of the Thames River in the 1950s with the condition of the river today.
5. What is responsible for the change in the condition of the Thames?

Restoring America's Rivers

6. Would salmon have survived in the Hudson or East Rivers in the 1970s? Explain.
7. What fish disappeared from the Charles River in the 1900s?
8. Identify the two types of pollution that created problems in the Delaware River in the 1950s. How did this pollution affect the level of dissolved oxygen and the fish populations in the river?
9. Identify the two types of pollution that created problems in Oregon's Willamette River. What action was taken to clean up the river?
10. After the treatment plants were built, what was the level of dissolved oxygen in the river? What was the source of the pollution that caused the low DO level?
11. What action was taken to solve the problem? What is the level of dissolved oxygen in the river now?
12. What major industry in Maine polluted the state's rivers?
    Why did some people object when laws were passed to improve the water quality?
    What other industry benefited from the clean rivers?

Fishable and Swimmable Rivers

13. What was the goal of the 1972 Clean Water Act?
14. What did the federal water quality standards require of cities? of industries?

15. Are the water quality standards being met by all cities?

At the Sewage Treatment Plant

16. What processes occur in the primary treatment of sewage.
17. Distinguish between sludge and effluent.
18. Is primary treatment of sewage a biological or physical process?
19. Give one advantage and one disadvantage of the activated sludge process.
20. What is added to the wastewater during the activated sludge process? Explain how the wastewater is cleaned in the activated sludge process.
21. What process is sometimes used instead of the activated sludge process? What are the advantages of this alternative method of treatment?
22. Describe a trickling filter.
23. What is the purpose of primary and secondary treatment of sewage? How effective is primary and secondary treatment?
24. Compare the way in which organic matter is removed from the waste water in the activated sludge process with the way it is removed in the trickling filter process.
25. What part of the sewage receives further treatment in the digesters? What is the purpose of this digestion process?
26. How do the bacteria working in the digester differ from the bacteria working in the activated sludge or trickling filter processes?
27. What waste product is produced by the action of bacteria in the digesters? How is it used?

Sludge — It's Not a Dirty Word

28. How did the city of New York dispose of its sludge prior to 1992? What does the city do with its sludge now?
29. Describe a bed used for drying sludge. Why are these beds sometimes enclosed in glass houses?
30. How does the city of Chicago dispose of its sludge?

389

31. Why is it unlikely that sludge from a digester will cause disease?

32. Should you use sludge on your garden?
Would you buy vegetables from a farm that used sludge to raise these crops?
Would you buy pork from a farmer who used sludge as a part of the fertilizer needed to grow corn to feed the pigs?

33. What tests must a farmer have before using sludge as fertilizer?
What dangerous situation may result if a farmer applies too much sludge to the field?

34. What organism is being used in several countries to compost sewage sludge?
Identify two other types of wastes that can be composted by the same process.

The Need for Pretreatment

35. Explain why sludge should be tested for heavy metals. Why are soil tests also needed?

36. What heavy metal might cause problems for humans and other animals at levels which are too low to affect plant growth?

37. What is the source of most heavy metals found in sludge? How can the problem of heavy metals in sludge be avoided?

38. Explain why toxic wastes are not removed by primary and secondary sewage treatment.
Explain how toxic wastes may interfere with the primary and secondary sewage treatment processes.

Chlorination

39. Why is chlorine added to the effluent?

40. How effective is chlorination? What are the disadvantages of chlorination?

41. During what time of the year are some sewage treatment plants allowed to release effluent without chlorination?
Since effluent may contain bacteria that cause disease, why is this allowed?
Why are other sewage treatment plants with a similar climate required to chlorinate effluent all year-round?

Combined Sewers

42. How do combined sewers contribute to the pollution of Boston Harbor?

43. What is the advantage of separate storm and sanitary sewers?

The Effluent — Additional Treatment

44. Despite primary and secondary treatment, the effluent from some sewage treatment plants still contains excessive levels of nitrates and phosphates. How will these chemicals affect the stream?

45. Identify a beneficial use of effluent that has excessive levels of nutrients.

46. What is the advantage of pumping effluent which doesn't meet the water quality standards for nutrients into a wetland?

47. What problem may be caused by the effluent from the Deer Island sewage treatment plant?

Lagoons and Aquaculture

48. Describe how lagoons provide primary treatment of sewage.

49. Describe the secondary treatment which occurs in lagoons.

50. Describe how the following problems associated with odors and mosquitoes in lagoons might be eliminated.

51. Identify the plant that is being added to lagoons in warm climates to aid the treatment processes. What plants could be used in colder climates? Describe how these plants purify water.

52. Explain how farmers might use lagoons to solve pollution problems and lower feed costs.

On-Site Sewage Treatment

53. Identify the most common type of sewage treatment found in rural areas.

54. Identify the two parts of a septic system. Briefly describe what happens to the wastewater as it passes through the system.

55. Is the treatment of sewage in a septic tank more like the treatment that occurs in a digester or an activated sludge tank? Why?

56. How is the size of the septic tank determined?

57. What two factors determine the size of the soil absorption field?

58. Describe a subsurface soil absorption system.
59. Why is the percolation rate in the absorption field important?
60. List the two factors that determine if a soil absorption field may be buried below the natural ground level.
61. Describe how a soil absorption field is made if the natural soil level does not meet the minimum depth requirement.
62. What type of material should not be poured down the drain if the drain leads to a soil absorption field? Why?

Inside the Septic Tank

63. What type of material might interfere with the normal digestion processes in the septic tank?
64. What will happen if a septic tank is not emptied regularly?
   List three factors that determine how often the septic tank should be emptied.
65. What is septage? What is the usual disposal site for this material?

66. List several factors that determine if land is suitable for septage disposal.
67. Is it acceptable for a farmer to allow beef cattle to graze in a pasture where septage has been sprayed?
   Is it acceptable for a farmer to allow dairy cattle to graze in a pasture where septage has been sprayed?
68. Is it acceptable for a farmer to grow tomatoes in a field where septage has been sprayed?
69. What problem can occur when lagoons are used for disposal of septage?
70. Describe the technology that is being used in Harwich, MA, to purify the septage from septic systems. How pure is the effluent?

Is It Worth the Cost?

71. Is it possible to have rivers that are "fishable and swimmable"? Explain.
72. Do you think that the ocean should be used as a disposal site for human wastes? Justify your position.

3.1 Poisons in the Water

"Sand, gravel, and silt through which water travels do filter out harmful bacteria. But the soil is almost helpless against many man-made organic chemicals."

Andrew Hogarth
Michigan Department of Natural Resources

Synthetic chemicals have become essential to our way of life. The manufacture and use of some 80,000 chemicals have made our lives easier and, in some cases, safer. The chemical industry created many new jobs, introduced many new products, improved food production and strengthened the nation's economy. That is the good news.

The bad news is that large amounts of hazardous chemical wastes are produced during the manufacture of products we use, including cars, refrigerators, pesticides, plastics, gasoline, jewelry, and cosmetics. Industries release billions of pounds of toxic chemicals into the air and water each year.

Industries are required to report the release or transfer of more than 300 toxic chemicals to the EPA. According to the EPA, 4.8 billion pounds (2.2 billion kg) of the listed toxic chemicals were released into the environment or transferred off-site by industries in 1990. Some of these hazardous wastes were placed in lagoons, others were stored in metal drums and buried in landfills, and some were injected into deep wells. Until recently, we thought that these were acceptable ways to dispose of toxic chemicals.

After many years we have learned that we can not simply bury or dump unwanted chemicals and forget them. Sometimes the past comes back to haunt us. Many old landfills and lagoons are leaking, and there is concern that the toxic chemicals will contaminate water supplies nearby. In some cases the ground water is already contaminated.

The EPA has identified more than 37,000 sites that are contaminated with toxic chemicals. Of these sites, about 1,200 are included on the Superfund's National Priorities List for clean-up. The creation of a Superfund for the clean-up of contaminated sites and new regulations for disposal of hazardous waste were the result of events that occurred at a dump site known as Love Canal.

The Lesson Learned at Love Canal

From 1947 until 1952, the Hooker Chemical Corporation dumped about 22,000 tons (20×10^3 kg) of toxic chemicals into the abandoned Love Canal in Niagara Falls, New York. Later the canal was filled and sold for a token of $1 to the Niagara Falls school board. The school board built an elementary school and playground directly over the canal. The remaining land was sold to a developer who built single-family houses along the filled canal.

In 1976 heavy rains caused chemicals leaking from the rusting drums to rise to the surface and seep into basements. Residents were concerned about their health and the health of their children. They reported unexplained miscarriages, birth defects, various forms of cancer, and other health problems. In 1978, President Carter declared a federal emergency. The school was closed, and more than 2500 residents moved from the area — the largest environmental evacuation ever.

The school and about 200 homes nearest the dump were torn down and buried. The dump site has been covered with clay, and a special drainage system has been installed. Water draining from the site passes through a special treatment plant. A chain-link fence around the site holds a sign that reads: "Danger — hazardous waste area — keep out".

We may never know the actual risk to the residents who were exposed to a mixture of toxic chemicals. After millions of dollars in clean-up costs, the government says that in some sections the risk has been reduced to an acceptable level. Some of the homes that were bought by the government and boarded up are now declared safe. The 60 families that refused to sell and still live in the area are getting new neighbors.

Health studies of abnormal pregnancies, learning disabilities, and cancer continue, but they are complicated by the evacuation of such a large number of people. More than 50 lawsuits for wrongful deaths have been settled, but lawsuits can be filed and settlements made without proof that the chemicals were the cause of the medical problems. We will never know if these people would have lived longer and healthier lives if they had not lived at Love Canal.

Woburn's Wells

Two hazardous waste sites located in Woburn, Massachusetts, are filled with toxic chemicals from Woburn's industries. The town is also the site of a leukemia cluster. A cluster occurs when a number of people living or working in the same area develop the same disease. Cancer refers to a group of diseases, and some forms of cancer are relatively common. Cancer clusters are frequently observed within a community.

Some people believe that the leukemia was caused by pollutants in the town's water supply. Eight families sued W.R. Grace & Co., claiming that two organic chemicals, trichloroethylene and tetrachloroethylene, dumped by the company had contaminated two of the town's wells. The families also claimed that the chemicals were responsible for the deaths of five children and one adult. The chemicals, they said, had also caused leukemia in two other children.

The company maintained the position that they were not responsible for the contamination of the wells or the deaths, but the court found the company guilty of causing the pollution. Did the chemicals cause the deaths? The second part of the trial was to answer this question, but the company decided to settle the lawsuit instead of continuing the trial.

The cause of the leukemia is not known. The average number of children who develop leukemia is 3.74 per 100,000. Twenty-six cases of leukemia were diagnosed in Woburn's 36,000 residents between 1979 and 1985. Most of these were in East Woburn. A study done by Harvard's School of Public Health showed that there was a significant increase in leukemia, stillbirths, sudden infant deaths, and some types of birth defects among those people who drank water from wells G and H.

Will there be other Woburns? It certainly seems possible. The EPA reports that nearly one-third of American cities with populations over 10,000 have industrial chemicals in the ground water supplies. We do not know how these chemicals will affect the health of people who drink the water. Many more studies are needed to determine the long-term health effects of exposure to low levels of toxic pollutants.

What the Fish Tell Us

Once in the air, chemicals may travel for several thousand miles before the air is cleaned by rain or snow. Heavy metals, acids, and toxic chemicals are washed from the air by rain and deposited in our rivers, lakes, and reservoirs. Air pollution is the major source of several toxic metal pollutants in the Great Lakes. About 90 percent of the PCBs (polychlorinated biphenyls) in Lake Superior are deposited in the lake from the atmosphere — **atmospheric deposition**.

Industries have spent billions of dollars to prevent pollution. They have eliminated the oxygen-demanding wastes that once made sewers of our rivers and streams. The fish have returned, but some species have high levels of toxic chemicals stored in their bodies. It is not safe to eat certain species of fish caught in some lakes and rivers.

Anglers fishing in Lake Superior, the cleanest of the Great Lakes, are warned not to eat lake trout larger than 30 inches (76 cm) because they are contaminated with PCBs. Approximately 30 percent of Wisconsin's lakes and 50 percent of Florida's lakes that were analyzed, had fish with mercury levels that exceeded the state health standard. In remote Michigan lakes, 15% of fish contain mercury in excess of the state health advisory level (0.5 ppm).

Michigan's state fishing licenses contain this warning:

"Certain Great Lakes fish should not be eaten by children or by women who are pregnant, nursing, or expect to bear children. Limit consumption by all others to no more than one meal per week."

The National Cancer Institute reports that carcinogens affect fish livers in the same way that they affect human livers. In five areas where fish with high numbers of tumors were found, the human cancer rates were significantly above the national average.

Scientists have begun to look at fish as an indicator of the health of the environment. At EPA's research laboratory in Gulf Breeze, Florida, scientists use the sheepshead minnow to identify cancer-causing pollutants. In only 14 weeks, scientists can identify developing tumors in minnows exposed to a carcinogen. Minnows are an ideal laboratory animal because they are small, and easy to keep.

Minnows may become biological monitors in our environment. Since they must constantly take in water, they are continuously exposed to the pollutant. If scientists find a high frequency of tumors, they will suspect carcinogenic chemicals in the water. If the fish are healthy, there is a good chance that the water is not polluted with carcinogens. Scientists hope that fish will help determine the level of a specific chemical that could be harmful to humans.

Water, Water, Everywhere, but . . .

Each minute of the day nine million gallons (3.4×10^7 L) of water flows down the Hudson River past Manhattan. There is also a large acquifer located beneath Brooklyn and Queens. New York City is surrounded by water, so why does the city transport water from upstate? The city grew fast. There were too many people and too much pollution. Even if the supply were adequate, the water is contaminated with toxic chemicals including PCBs and mercury. Ground water in some wells is contaminated with salt water.

New York City built three water tunnels to ensure an adequate and safe water supply for its residents. The third tunnel has been a costly project — more than $1 billion and twenty human lives, but the completion will ensure that when you are in New York City, you can drink some of the finest water in the world. You need not be concerned about toxic chemicals in the Hudson as long as you don't fall in or eat certain species of fish taken from the river.

New Orleans — City on a River

Between Baton Rouge and New Orleans there are more than 100 major industries along the Mississippi River. In 1987, the industries released 196 million pounds (8.9×10^7 kg) of toxic chemicals directly into the river. Unlike New York City, New Orleans doesn't own a protected watershed in the mountains. The city gets its drinking water from the Mississippi River.

THINK ABOUT IT

Why does development and paving of a floodplain inevitably lead to toxic pollution of rivers and streams? How does covering vast areas with impervious materials like pavement and sidewalks also lead to polluted waterways?

Could this pipeline have an impact on ground water?

As the river water travels through the city's waterworks, the water is cleaned up and levels of pollutants are reduced to meet the EPA drinking water standards. Yet there are some indications that the treated water may be bringing trouble to the river city. A study done in 1974 found higher than normal rates of bladder and gastrointestinal cancer in New Orleans and several other communities that use water from the Mississippi River.

In another study, the EPA found sixty-six chemical compounds in New Orleans' drinking water. The highest concentration was chloroform. Chloroform is one of a group of chemicals called THMs (trihalomethanes). **Trihalomethanes** are formed when naturally occurring organic chemicals react with chlorine in the water. Recent scientific studies suggest a strong link between THMs and the risk of human bladder and rectal cancers.

A study conducted by the US Public Health Service shows that expectant mothers exposed to THMs are at increased risk of bearing children with low birth weights. Other risks included premature birth, stillbirth, neural tube defects, and cleft palates. The highest risk was seen in women exposed to THM levels of 80 parts per billion (ppb) or more. The federal standard for total THMs in drinking water is 100 ppb.

To reduce levels of THMs, New Orleans stopped using chlorine as a disinfectant and switched to chloramines — a safer but more expensive disinfectant. THMs and other organic chemicals may also be removed by the addition of activated carbon during the treatment process or the use of activated carbon filters on the water faucet. The residents of New Orleans are paying the price of living downstream.

Problems with Underground Storage Tanks

Santa Clara Valley in northern California is better known as the "Silicon Valley". Many companies that make electronic parts, semiconductors, and computers are located in the valley. It is an important center of high-technology industry.

There are no smokestacks or buildings that look like factories. The major source of air pollution is the automobile. Although the air is cleaner, the valley is not free of pollution. The industries use organic chemicals in the manufacture of computers and other high-tech equipment. The chemicals are stored in underground storage tanks, and some of the tanks leaked.

Ground water is the source of half of the valley's drinking water, and the organic chemicals threaten the water supply. In 1984, the EPA added 19 sites in Santa Clara County to the Superfund's National Priorities List. Cleaning up the contamination is not an easy task. Each contaminated site must be evaluated and the best solution selected.

During the 1950s and 1960s many gasoline storage tanks were buried. The tanks were made of metal, and contact with the moist ground caused them to rust. Nearly 170,000, or 37 percent, of the tanks that have been checked are leaking. By law, underground storage tanks must be upgraded to corrosion-resistant models before 1998. The EPA estimates that it may cost $41 billion to clean up the contamination resulting from leaking underground storage tanks.

The gasoline that floats on the surface of the ground water can be pumped out and used, but gasoline contains some toxic chemicals that dissolve in the water. One of these is benzene, a chemical known to cause cancer in humans. The benzene can be removed by passing the water through an activated carbon filter, but it is expensive. (See Case Study: Before You Drink the Water)

Down on the Farm

The quality of the ground water beneath the Nebraska Sandhills is excellent, but that may be changing. For years the tall prairie grasses held the sandy soil in place and absorbed most of the rain that fell. Until the invention of the center-pivot irrigation system, there was not enough moisture to grow crops.

Large amounts of nitrogen fertilizer must be added to grow crops in sandy soils. Rain water may leach the nitrogen from the soil and transport it into the aquifer below. The problem is not limited to Nebraska. The nitrate levels in many wells exceed the "safe" standard of 10 milligrams of nitrate per litre of water. The EPA estimates that 4.5 million Americans drink water with nitrate levels exceeding the drinking water standard of 10 mg/L.

Nitrates are dangerous when they are changed into nitrites. The digestive system of human infants harbors bacteria that change nitrates to nitrites. If water contains more than 10 mg/L of nitrates it should not be given to infants or children less than one year old or to pregnant women.

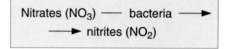

Nitrites interfere with hemoglobin's ability to carry oxygen. Babies with nitrate poisoning have a bluish color, especially around the eyes and mouth — a **blue baby syndrome**. Instead of the usual red color, the blood is chocolate brown. A blood test must be taken to confirm the diagnosis. Unless nitrate poisoning is treated, the baby will die.

Older children have more hydrochloric acid in their stomach. The acid kills most of the bacteria that convert nitrates to nitrites. Nitrates are not dangerous to older children and adults. Horses, sheep, cattle, baby pigs, and baby chickens also have bacteria in their digestive systems that change nitrates to nitrites. Although no standard is set for livestock, researchers suggest a maximum of 100 mg/L of nitrates in their drinking water.

Until the 1970s, scientists thought that pesticides were attracted to and held by soil particles until they were broken down. Now we know that certain pesticides travel through the soil and into ground water. The pesticide DBCP, that caused sterility in males, was banned by the EPA in 1977. The pesticide has contaminated wells in Califor-

What effect might pesticides applied by airplane have on ground water?

nia's Central Valley, and officials have closed more than 1,400 wells. In 1988, the EPA reported that 46 pesticides were detected in ground water in 26 states. Additional studies showed that only 1 percent of the wells exceeded the drinking water standard for any pesticide.

New pesticides must be tested to determine how readily they are leached from the soil before they can be registered for use. Registration of a pesticide may be denied, or its use restricted to specific soil types, in order to prevent ground water contamination.

Problems at Kesterson

In dry climates where ground water is used for irrigation, the water leaves behind a deposit of salt as it evaporates. The salt deposits eventually make the soil unsuitable for farming. The United States Department of Agriculture estimates that **salinization** — a buildup of salts and toxic elements in the soil of irrigated cropland may be costing farmers $5 billion per year in reduced crop yields.

Much of California's farmland was once a part of the sea floor, and the soil naturally has a high concentration of mineral salts. In California's San Joaquin Valley, a layer of clay lies beneath the topsoil. To prevent the clay from trapping the irrigation water and flooding the plant roots, farmers installed drainage systems.

A 207-mile-long (331 km) canal was proposed to carry the wastewater into the San Francisco Bay. With only 82 miles (131 km) of the canal finished money ran out, and the canal ended at the Kesterson National Wildlife Refuge. Engineers built a series of evaporation ponds that covered 1200 acres (480 hectares). When the canal and ponds were completed, the wastewater was diluted with fresh surface water. Soon the farmers needed the fresh water, so the only water entering the evaporation ponds was the wastewater.

In the spring of 1983 biologists found that 42 percent of the newly hatched birds and embryos in the unhatched eggs were deformed. The normal rate of deformed birds is 1 percent. Scientists had never seen anything like this before. Some birds had no eyes, feet, or wings. The bloated bodies of adult birds were found floating in the ponds.

Further investigation found that the problems were caused by **selenium**, a toxic element that had leached from the soil. While birds do need a few parts per billion of selenium in their diet, when it is present in a concentration of a few parts per million it is toxic. Breast tissue of adult coots at Kesterson contained between 3.5 and 9.5 ppm selenium.

Kesterson is a stopover and wintering ground for migrating ducks and geese. Studies have identified similar problems caused by a buildup of selenium at irrigation projects in Nevada, Utah, Wyoming, Arizona, Montana, Colorado, and Kansas. To minimize the problem in these areas, scientists have developed new irrigation techniques that reduce the amount of contaminated water draining from the soil.

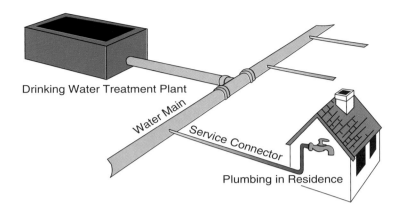

Drinking Water Treatment Plant

Water Main

Service Connector

Plumbing in Residence

Lead

Historians believe that the fall of the Roman Empire may have been caused by lead. Water pipes were made of lead. The origin of the words plumber and plumbing is the Latin word for lead — *plumbum*. The Romans used lead acetate, commonly called "sugar of lead," as a sweetener and preservative in wines and cider. The people of Rome may have suffered from lead poisoning.

Lead causes lower levels of intelligence and learning problems in children, complications in pregnant women, high blood pressure, strokes, and heart attacks in middle-aged men. According to an EPA report, lead contamination costs more than $1 billion a year in medical care, plumbing repairs, specialized education, and reduced future earnings among children with learning disabilities.

Lead rarely occurs naturally in drinking water sources, yet the levels of lead in some public water supplies exceed the proposed standard. The major source of contamination of drinking water is the corrosion of plumbing by acidic water. Lead from old pipes and the solder connecting copper pipes leaches into the water.

The current US EPA drinking water standard for lead is 5 ppb, measured at the tap. If lead exceeds the standard, water suppliers must take steps to control corrosion of the pipes. If lead levels still exceed the standard, all water pipes that contain lead must be replaced. Amendments to the Safe Drinking Water Act prohibit the use of lead in new public water systems or plumbing systems.

Under the City Streets

It is very expensive to dispose of hazardous wastes properly. In order to avoid the expense, some industries illegally dump their hazardous wastes. In Louisville, Kentucky, a recycling company dumped pesticides in the city's sewers. The sewage treatment plant had to be shut down for several months because the chemicals irritated the eyes, skin, and respiratory systems of the workers.

A waste disposal company in Philadelphia rented a warehouse near the Delaware River. Inside the warehouse was an opening to a storm sewer. Haulers brought toxic wastes to the warehouse and poured them into the sewer that carried the waste to the river. A few miles down river from the sewer pipe, the Torresdale water treatment plant draws drinking water for the city of Philadelphia.

To discourage illegal dumping, the city of Los Angles has formed a special Strike Force to catch illegal dumpers. Judges are imposing heavy fines on companies that have carefully planned schemes to illegally dump their hazardous wastes. In some states the white-collar executives, who make the decision to illegally dump the wastes, are being sentenced to several months in jail. The "head" of the Philadelphia waste disposal company was sent to prison for six months and fined $20,000.

Facing the Issue

Our surface water is significantly cleaner than it was 20 years ago mainly because we no longer use our rivers as sewers, but toxic chemicals from farms and industries threaten our water supplies. The Clean Water Act prohibited the release of toxic chemicals into US waters by 1985, but we didn't meet the challenge.

While the release of toxic pollutants into the air is declining, industrial releases into water are increasing. In 1991, industries reported the release of 244 million pounds of toxic chemicals into rivers, lakes, and streams from point sources — mainly the production of chemicals, metals, paper, petroleum, rubber, and plastics.

Additional pollution enters the water from nonpoint sources — urban, and agricultural runoff, and the air. Until now, nonpoint sources of pollution have been largely ignored. Agricultural runoff is the largest unregulated source of water pollution. State officials in Iowa estimate that 93 percent of their streams are contaminated with pesticides. A model program in Iowa's Big Spring Basin has reduced the amount of pesticides and fertilizers that farmers use.

Progress is also being made in industry. Industries have begun to modify processes to produce less waste and to recycle waste products. Although production of chemicals continues to increase, off-site shipment of wastes for treatment and disposal dropped 37 percent between 1987 and 1991.

While changing processes to reduce pollution often requires huge investments in equipment, the changes can save both money and the environment. Changes made by American Cyanamid in the production of a yellow dye eliminated the use of a toxic solvent. The changes required a $100,000 investment in equipment, but the new process saves the company $200,000 a year in disposal and energy costs.

Reducing or eliminating the use of the toxic chemicals may be the best way to reduce poisons in our air and water. Minnesota has passed a law that limits the amount of cadmium, hexavalent chromium, lead, or mercury in packaging. Minnesota incinerates much of its solid waste, and reducing the level of these metals in the waste reduces the metals that find their way into our water supplies.

Cleaning up our water will require greater attention to both point and nonpoint sources of toxic pollution. The goal of the Clean Water Act was zero discharge. We must continue to work toward that goal.

3.1 QUESTIONS FOR STUDY AND DISCUSSION

1. List at least three ways in which human-made chemicals are helpful.
2. What problem is created by the manufacture of products we use?
3. List three ways that have been used to dispose of toxic chemicals.
4. What resource is threatened by landfills and lagoons that are leaking?
5. After Congress became aware of the situation at Love Canal, how did they respond to make our country a safer place to live?

The Lesson Learned at Love Canal
6. For what purpose was the abandoned Love Canal used?
7. How was the land used after the canal was filled?
8. Why did President Carter declare a federal emergency in the Love Canal area?
9. What has been done to ensure that chemicals from the site don't contaminate the area's water supply?
10. Do you think that President Carter overreacted when he evacuated families from the Love Canal area? Would you buy a home in the area today? Explain your reasons for each answer.

Woburn's Wells
11. What is a cancer cluster?
12. What type of cancer was found in higher than normal rates among residents of Woburn?
13. According to the lawsuit filed by the families, what caused the increase in leukemia?
14. Did the court find that the company was responsible for pollution of the wells, or did the court find that the deaths were caused by chemicals polluting the wells?

15. Did the study done by Harvard's School of Public Health show a significant increase in leukemia?
16. The Harvard study showed a link between the water and effects that occurred during what time of a person's life?
17. What evidence is there that other situations like Woburn will occur?
18. Which statement is true?
   A. More studies are needed on long-term effects of low levels of pollutants.
   B. Studies have shown that low levels of pollutants are not dangerous.
   C. Studies have already shown that low levels of pollutants are dangerous and what we need to do now is to take action.

What the Fish Tell Us
19. What is the major source of most of the PCBs in Lake Superior?
20. The National Cancer Institute reports that:
   A. Carcinogens affect fish livers in the same way that they affect human livers.
   B. Areas with high numbers of fish tumors also have high numbers of human cancer.
   C. Both A and B.
21. What kind of fish is being used at the EPA lab to identify cancer-causing chemicals?
22. Give four reasons why minnows are ideal laboratory animals.
23. What is the goal of the EPA fish research project?

Water, Water Everywhere, but . . .
24. Why does the city of New York transport water from upstate when the city is surrounded by water?
25. How is the water transported to the city?

New Orleans — City on a River

26. What is the source of drinking water for the city of New Orleans?
27. According to the 1974 study, New Orleans has higher rates of what types of cancer?
28. What are THMs (trihalomethanes)?
29. What THM was present in high concentrations in New Orleans' drinking water?
30. Why is the EPA concerned about the level of THMs in the drinking water?
31. Why does it cost New Orleans residents more to live downstream?

Problems with Underground Storage Tanks

32. What is the major source of air pollution in the Santa Clara "Silicon Valley"?
33. What is the major industry in the "Silicon Valley"?
34. What type of pollution is threatening the valley? What resource is it threatening?
35. What pollutant is threatening ground water supplies in other locations?
36. Since gasoline is lighter than water, why can't the ground water contamination problem be solved by pumping water from the bottom of the well?
37. What chemical in gasoline is known to be a carcinogen?
38. How can benzene be removed from the water? What is the disadvantage of this method?

Down on the Farm

39. What pollutant threatens water supplies in the Nebraska Sandhills and other farming areas? What is the EPA "safe" drinking water standard for this pollutant?
40. Which nitrogen compound is dangerous?
41. What age group does this pollutant affect?
42. In what way does this pollutant affect humans and farm animals?
43. Why doesn't water with high levels of nitrates affect adult humans, pigs, or chickens?
44. What is the safe level of nitrates for infants? What level is thought to be safe for farm animals?

45. Before pesticides can be marketed they must be tested to determine how they will affect organisms such as fish, birds, and humans. What additional test is now required?
46. Are you concerned about pesticides in your water supply? How can the threat of pesticides in the water supply be reduced?

Problems at Kesterson

47. Explain how the irrigation of land sometimes makes the soil unsuitable for farming.
48. Why was it necessary to install a drainage system in the farmland in the San Joaquin Valley?
49. What was the original plan for the disposal of the wastewater?
50. Why wasn't the canal completed? Where did the canal finally end?
51. After the wastewater was no longer diluted with the surface water, what changes were observed in birds at the Refuge?
52. What toxic chemical caused these changes? What was the source of this toxic chemical?
53. What can be done to reduce the threat of salinization of the soil?

Lead

54. List at least three health effects of high levels of lead in the drinking water.
55. What is the major source of lead that contaminates drinking water supplies?
56. What changes made will in the future reduce the level of lead in the drinking water?

Under the City Streets

57. What has the city of Los Angeles done to discourage companies from dumping hazardous wastes illegally?
58. What actions have been taken by the court to discourage companies from dumping hazardous wastes illegally?

Facing the Issue

59. Identify the major sources and describe steps that are being taken to reduce the level of toxins in our water supply.
60. Do you think a zero discharge of toxins is a realistic goal? If not, how should the water supply be protected?

Protecting the Ground Water

Part of the price we must pay for the products of modern technology is the price of toxic waste disposal.

There is no question that water is one resource we can't afford to lose. A spokesman for the chemical industry told a senate subcommittee investigating toxic substances, "Ground water protection should be one of the nation's highest priorities."

It will cost several million dollars each year to properly dispose of toxic wastes, but failure to do so will cost even more. It is becoming clear that it is less expensive to prevent pollution of our ground water than it is to clean up once it has become polluted.

Since the Clean Water Act was passed in 1972, our rivers and lakes have become much cleaner, but some of the actions that were taken to clean up rivers and lakes have increased the threat of polluted ground water. What is industry to do with pollutants that can't be discharged into rivers and lakes? One answer is to put them underground.

Deep Well Injection — Is It the Answer?

The air in the cottonwood forest at Pennsylvania's largest state park, near the town of Erie, smelled like rotten eggs. It was the odor of hydrogen sulfide — a chemical usually associated with industry, but there was no industry nearby. The source of the odor was a puddle of black gunk in one of the parking areas at the park. Excavation at the site revealed an abandoned oil well.

Mineral Water Analysis

Geologists reported that the abandoned well had been used to pump oil from a rock formation known as the Bass Island Formation. This rock formation did not contain hydrogen sulfide or any black fluids. Further investigation revealed that 4 miles (6.4 km) away on the other side of Erie, a paper company had pumped 1.1 billion gallons (4.2×10^6 L) of a black sulfur wastewater into the Bass Island Formation.

This method of waste disposal is called **deep-well injection**. A double pipe leading to a deep layer of sandstone or other porous rock is used to inject chemical wastes. A pump forces the liquid wastes down the inner pipe and into the layer of sandstone. The outer pipe is filled with cement to prevent contamination of any aquifers that the pipe passes through.

Deep-well injection has been used since the 1930s for disposing of mud and salt water from oil wells. Today there are more than 180,000 injection wells. Many of them are used for disposing of wastes from oil drilling, but some are used for wastes that are far more hazardous.

While deep-well injection may seem like a perfect answer to the problem of toxic wastes, it is a potential threat to the ground water supply. Problems may occur when pipes are corroded by acids in the wastewater. Wastes may also dissolve chemicals in the rock or move upward through fractures in the rocks.

The EPA is concerned that toxic wastes injected into deep wells may eventually enter aquifers that are important sources of drinking water. Some feel that deep-well injection is safer than other methods used in the past. Others feel that we don't know enough about the rock structure or the chemical reactions that may occur to predict what will happen to the wastes after they have been injected.

The Problem with Landfills

At **sanitary landfills**, garbage is compacted and covered each day with a layer of soil. Sanitary landfills provide several benefits over open dumps that are a suitable habitat for rats, flies, and other wild animals. The problem with sanitary landfills is that chemicals which are leached from the landfill, may enter the ground water. Many industries and cities have buried their liquid and solid wastes in landfills, but it has become evident that this method of burial is not an acceptable method for safe disposal of hazardous wastes.

According to the EPA, most of the nation's 6,000 landfills are not operated in an environmentally safe manner. The EPA issued the first federal rules for solid-waste landfills in 1991. The rules prohibit certain liquid and solid wastes in sanitary landfills. Landfills must be

Deep Well Injection ▶

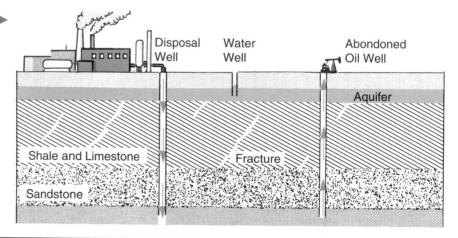

lined with a clay and plastic liner, they must be covered every day, and ground water must be monitored.

Engineers have designed **secure landfills** for storage of hazardous wastes. A chemical company in Montague, Michigan, spent $15 million to build a pyramid-shaped storage vault the size of fourteen football fields, to store toxic chemicals. Two permanent granite markers read *Hexachlorocyclopentadiene Toxic Production Waste*, while smaller signs inside the chain link fence read *WARNING KEEP OUT*.

The pit is lined and covered with a layer of clay that is more than 3 metres thick. The clay walls were designed so that it would take a molecule of water 100 years to pass through them. The vault is an example of a "secure" landfill, but how long will it keep the toxic wastes contained? Can we be certain that it will never leak? No.

The nation's largest clay-lined pit is located near Emelle, Alabama. It was designed to keep dangerous chemicals safely buried for thousands of years, but the EPA has reported that it is leaking. Studies show that certain chemicals change the clay. Scientists have found that chemicals will move through the clay walls more quickly than expected. The EPA now requires that new landfills be lined with clay and a synthetic liner, but chemical reactions or erosion can cause the synthetic lining to develop holes.

In the past, cost was frequently the most important factor in determining where a landfill would be located. Although there is no place that is completely safe, the possibility of danger can be reduced if the following factors are considered when a site is selected for a landfill.

Secure storage areas use large amounts of land, cost large amounts of money, and require constant care. The EPA requires that wells be drilled at all new landfill sites, and that the ground water be monitored for at least 30 years after the landfill is closed. Scientists feel that proper selection of a site, good engineering and long-term monitoring can reduce, but not eliminate, the risks of ground water contamination.

WHAT DO YOU THINK?

Many toxic pollutants in waterways "bind" to particles of sediment on the bottom of waterways. Some of the most polluted waterways in the nation are those that must be dredged periodically to improve navigation. These sites include New York's Hudson River and the harbors of Los Angeles, Seattle, and San Diego.

Shipping is vital to the economies of these cities. Yet maintaining harbors by dredging circulates the toxins throughout the water. What should be done with the toxic sediments?

◀ A Secure Landfill

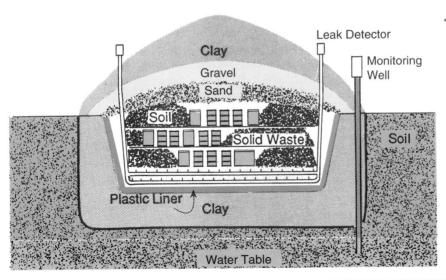

Leak Detector

Clay

Gravel

Sand

Monitoring Well

Soil

Soil

Solid Waste

Plastic Liner

Clay

Water Table

SUITABLE SITES	UNSUITABLE SITES
GEOLOGY	
• clay soils • stable bedrock	• rocks with fractures or folds • sandstone • limestone • faults • earthquakes
WATER	
• several miles from an important aquifer	• near an aquifer that is the source of drinking water • floodplains • wetlands • coastal areas
GEOGRAPHY	
• low population density	• high population density • large number of people less than 5 years or over 65 years old

In spite of the new rules and regulations, residents are often opposed to having a "secure" landfill in their community. "Not in my backyard" has become a familiar phrase. Many people feel that the potential for ground water contamination makes "secure" landfills an unacceptable method of hazardous waste disposal.

Some states are seeking other solutions. A hazardous waste act passed in Missouri prohibits the land filling of any hazardous wastes that can be disposed of by treating, recycling, detoxifying, or incinerating. California has banned six types of wastes, including PCBs and toxic metals, from landfills. States are beginning to encourage permanent destruction of wastes rather than permanent storage.

Treat, Recycle, and Reduce Wastes

As long as companies could place hazardous wastes in landfills, they did not investigate other alternatives. Today many industries are looking for methods to reduce the volume of wastes.

Paper companies use large quantities of water and produce large quantities of black sulfur wastewater. Today they are using a recycling process that not only prevents pollution, but also reduces the industry's huge demand for water. The black carbon is removed from the sulfur wastewater, and the sulfur liquid (wastewater) is reused to digest wood chips for making more paper. The carbon is heated with steam to make **activated carbon**. The activated carbon is then used to filter more wastewater.

The EPA is currently studying methods for the treatment and recovery of hazardous wastes that will be banned from landfills. Some of the treatment processes being studied are listed below:

Biological Treatment: Bacteria may be used to decompose certain hazardous wastes. Scientists are studying organisms collected from hazardous wastes sites to see if they will break down toxic substances into harmless waste products. One scientist has developed a bacterium that will "eat" or breakdown oil. Another type of bacteria has been used to digest the herbicide Agent Orange.

Carbon Adsorption: Specially treated carbon particles (activated carbon) can pick up (adsorb) certain chemicals from wastewater. This process is currently used to remove toxic chemicals as well as chemicals that cause color and odor from drinking water supplies.

Chemical Reactions: Some hazardous chemicals can be chemically changed into substances that are harmless, such as carbon dioxide and water. Toxic metals can be removed from water by chemical reactions that change them into compounds that are solids. The solids can then be filtered from the wastewater.

Human-Made Rocks

The idea is not new. The same process was used to build the Pantheon and Colosseum in Rome, and the oldest well-engineered roadway system in the world — the Appian Way. Volcanic ash and lime were mixed to make cement. The chemical reaction produced a mortar or concrete that is very hard and resistant to erosion.

Today the same process is being used to form waste materials into synthetic rocks. Instead of volcanic ash, fly ash from coal-burning power plants is mixed with certain hazardous wastes. Then lime is added, and the mixture is poured like concrete into a landfill. The synthetic rock may also be used to form the foundation for a road.

The process may be used to dispose of hazardous chemicals from the automotive, electroplating, steel-making, and mining industries. It can also be used for the waste from air pollution scrubbers. In fact, 90 percent of all hazardous waste materials may be permanently stored in synthetic rocks.

A specific recipe must be used for each type of waste material. Quality control is very important. The amount of each type of material must be carefully measured, and the correct amounts of fly ash and lime used. Sometimes other raw materials must be added to change the wastes into a usable form. The process cannot be used for all wastes. Some materials interfere with the chemical reactions or "hardening" of the rock. The process is not suitable for disposal of organic materials.

The EPA has developed chemical and physical tests that are run on samples of the product to ensure that it meets standards. The land filling process is also regulated by the EPA, and both runoff and ground water must be tested for possible chemicals that might leach from the synthetic rock.

Incineration at Sea or on Land

European countries have burned **organochlorines** (compounds that contain hydrogen, carbon, and chlorine) in specially built incinerators on ships at sea since 1969. The ships have double hulls and double bottoms to protect against loss of the toxic materials. Although there is a risk that the toxic material may leak from the ship, the risk is lower than the risk of losing toxic material from a transport vehicle on land.

Incineration at sea is controlled by national and international regulations. Regulations were adopted at the convention on the Prevention of Marine Pollution by Dumping of Wastes and Other Matter (commonly called the London Dumping Convention). Incinerators must meet minimum standards set at the convention. These standards require that 99.9 percent of the toxic material be destroyed.

Under the correct conditions, incineration changes organochlorines into simpler compounds. The major products of combustion are carbon dioxide, water and hydrochloric acid. Combustion is nearly complete (99.95 ± .05%) when the minimum flame temperature is 8,000°F (1250°C) and plenty of oxygen is available. The incineration is performed far away from land masses.

Nelson's column, London: before and after cleaning.

SCIENCE TECHNOLOGY & SOCIETY
ISSUES

A Pesticide Problem

Many Third World countries received donations of pesticides during the late 1960s. The donations exceeded the amount of pesticide needed, and the pesticides were stored. After many years in poor storage conditions, the pesticides are now a threat to the environment. North Africa has some 10,000 metric tonnes of pesticides, including banned organochlorines such as DDT and dieldrin.

- You are responsible for the safe disposal of the pesticides. Describe your plan for disposal and justify the method you chose.

Emissions from the smokestacks can be monitored for hydrochloric acid, total hydrocarbons, carbon monoxide, carbon dioxide, nitrogen oxides, and oxygen. Scrubbers are not required because the hydrochloric acid is spread over broad areas of the ocean, and the ocean contains chemicals that neutralize the acid.

The Environmental Protection Agency (EPA) regulates ocean incineration and dumping in US waters. The agency has conducted tests to determine the effect of oceanic incineration of organochlorines on the ocean ecosystem. The tests have included long-term effects on ocean life. Incineration at sea is less expensive than incineration on land because incinerators on land must have scrubbers to remove gases that form acid rain (H_2SO_4 and HCl).

According to the EPA, incineration is the most environmentally safe method available for disposing of organochlorine wastes. Emissions from the proper incineration of these hazardous wastes will have very little effect upon the environment.

Incineration is the method preferred by the American Society of Mechanical Engineers for managing hazardous organic chemicals because it permanently destroys the hazardous organic chemicals and prevents any future environmental problems. The engineering society says that incineration at high temperatures is the best technology available to control hazardous organic chemicals.

Grassroots environmental groups work to prevent the construction of incinerators. A statewide campaign by Alabamians for a Clean Environment stopped the construction of a hazardous waste incinerator. The group Friends of the Environment was organized to defeat a proposed incinerator in Georgia. Both groups feel the focus of waste treatment should be on hazardous waste reduction and recycling.

3.2 QUESTIONS FOR STUDY AND DISCUSSION

1. Choose the statement that best reflects the opinion of the chemical industry:
   A. It is important that ground water be protected from toxic chemicals.
   B. Toxic chemicals in ground water are not a major problem because the filters are available to remove them form water used for drinking.
2. Which of the following is less expensive?
   A. Preventing pollution of ground water.
   B. Cleaning polluted ground water once it is polluted.

Deep Well Injection — Is It the Answer?
3. What caused the "rotten egg" odor in the state park near Erie, Pennsylvania?
4. Describe the Bass Island Formation and explain how it was used by a paper company in Erie.
5. How are aquifers protected from the chemical wastes that are injected into deep wells?
6. Deep well injection is used for what types of wastes?
7. List three ways that toxic wastes injected into deep wells could enter the ground water supply.

8. Give two types of information needed to determine if a site is safe for injection of toxic wastes.

The Problem with Landfills
9. Describe the difference between a federally approved sanitary landfill and a "dump".
10. What type of wastes should not be placed in a sanitary landfill? Explain why.
11. Describe how a secure landfill differs from a sanitary landfill.
12. What are the two materials that must be used to line a secure landfill?
13. Give two changes that might occur that could result in a leak at a secure landfill.
14. Describe the soil and rock structure that would make a site most suitable for a secure landfill.
15. Would a desert be a good site for a secure landfill? Give reasons to support your answer.
16. List three factors that must be considered when selecting a site for a secure landfill.
17. List three disadvantages of secure landfills as a means of disposal of hazardous wastes.
18. Give three ways in which the risks of ground water contamination at a secure landfill can be reduced.
19. Why do people say "Not in my backyard" to a proposal for a secure landfill in their community? What do they fear will happen?
20. What are several alternatives to a secure landfill for hazardous wastes?

Treat, Recycle, and Reduce Wastes
21. Why did companies choose landfills instead of other means of hazardous waste disposal?
22. List the two substances that can be reclaimed from the wastewater produced by paper companies, and describe how they are used.
23. Give two advantages of recycling the wastewater.
24. What kind of organism may be used to breakdown or digest hazardous wastes?
25. What substance is presently being used to remove toxic chemicals from drinking water supplies?
26. Explain how chemical reactions can be used to remove toxic metals from water.

Human-Made Rocks
27. What two substances were mixed to produce the cement used to build the Pantheon, the Colosseum, and the Appian Way?
28. Why was this method of making cement superior to others?
29. For what purpose is this process being used today?
30. What material can be used in place of the volcanic ash?
31. In what ways are the synthetic rocks being used?
32. What industries may find the man-made rock a useful way to dispose of their hazardous wastes?
33. Is this process suitable for all hazardous waste materials? If not, what portion of hazardous wastes can be disposed of by using this process? What type of waste cannot be disposed of by using this process?
34. Why is this process much more expensive than disposal in a sanitary landfill?
35. How can we be assured that the human-made rock is not poisoning the environment?

Incineration At Sea or on Land
36. What type of hazardous material can be destroyed by incineration?
37. What was the purpose of the London Dumping Convention?
38. What are the products of the combustion of organochlorines?
39. What two conditions must be met to ensure complete combustion?
40. Why aren't scrubbers required for incinerators on ships?
41. What does research tell us about the long-term effect of oceanic incineration of organochlorines on the ocean ecosystem?
42. What are the advantages of oceanic incineration?
43. According to each of the following groups, what is the best way to destroy hazardous organic wastes?
   A. Environmental Protection Agency
   B. American Society of Mechanical Engineers

Before You Drink the Water

To the list of rights guaranteed by the constitution, we might add the right to a reliable supply of safe drinking water.

Beluga are beautiful white whales, living in the St. Lawrence River. At the beginning of the century, there were about 5,000 belugas in the river; by the 1950s, they numbered about 1,200. Today there are about 450. Autopsies of dead belugas show that whales have extremely high levels of more than 30 toxic chemicals. Are the toxic chemicals causing the low reproduction rates and premature deaths of these beautiful whales?

A spokesperson for the Canadian Department of Fisheries and Oceans stated that there was "insufficient evidence or data" to blame declines in beluga whale populations on toxic pollution. By the time we know the reasons for the decline, it may be too late.

In the year 1900 an estimated 27,000 Americans died of typhoid fever, an infection caused by bacteria carried in water that has been contaminated with human waste. Today most cities and towns in the United States, Canada, and Europe provide their residents with a good supply of safe drinking water. Because of better sanitation and the chemical and physical water treatment processes used today, typhoid fever has almost vanished from these countries.

Still several million Americans lack a safe supply of drinking water. Most of these people live in small towns or rural regions. According to a water resources specialist from the Pennsylvania State University, "The water tapped from about half of the single-user wells and springs in Pennsylvania is unsuitable for drinking."

Many rural homes in Pennsylvania have septic systems, but 80 percent of the land is not suitable for on-site sewage treatment. Officials estimate that the single largest source of ground water pollution caused by human activity is inadequate or malfunctioning on-site sewage systems. In 1983 and 1984, Pennsylvania reported more cases of water-related disease than any other state.

People in other countries are even less fortunate. In the developing world more than 95 percent of urban sewage is discharged untreated into surface waters. Each year diarrhea, caused by organisms transmitted in contaminated drinking water or food, kills more people than cancer or AIDS.

During a two-month epidemic in 1984, nearly 3000 people died from drinking contaminated water in India. In 1985, a cholera epidemic killed more than 1,500 people in an Ethiopian refugee camp in Somalia. In 1991, a cholera epidemic in South America caused 3,259 deaths. If all people had a safe supply of drinking water, about 2 million fewer children would die from diarrhea each year.

Many areas in the developing countries lack the sanitary conditions needed to guarantee a water supply that is safe to drink. The United Nations is taking steps to change this, but they did not meet their goal to provide safe water to all by 1990. With rising populations in some of the developing countries, the number of people lacking adequate water supplies and sanitation facilities will increase significantly.

The Safe Drinking Water Act

In the United States, the Safe Drinking Water Act was passed in 1974. It requires that water suppliers test the water for substances that, according to scientific research, may threaten health. The Environmental Protection Agency has set **Maximum Contaminant Levels (MCLs)** for these substances. The MCL is the highest amount of the pollutant allowed in the drinking water. The supplier must notify the public if the MCLs are exceeded. If necessary, the water supply may be shut off.

More than 200 chemicals have been detected in ground water supplies. For most of these chemicals, the EPA has not determined a level that is considered safe in drinking water. Studies are now being conducted to find the amount that will cause harmful effects. After studies are completed, the EPA will set MCLs for those chemicals that are found to be harmful.

In 1986 the EPA had set MCLs for 22 foreign substances found in drinking water. **Inorganic contaminants** include arsenic, barium, cadmium, chromium, fluoride, lead, mercury, nitrates, selenium, and silver. **Organic contaminants** include pesticides and trihalomethanes (THMs). Long-term exposure to THMs and other organic chemicals may increase the chance of cancer. (For more information on some of these substances see Section 3.1 Poisons in the Water.)

Organisms in the Water

Because they are difficult and expensive to identify in water supplies, the EPA has not set MCLs for any disease-causing organisms. Instead, the contamination of water supplies is based on identification of a group of bacteria called coliforms.

Coliform bacteria are **indicator organisms** because their presence tells us something about water quality. Coliform bacteria are normally found in the intestines of humans and other warm-blooded animals. If they are present in drinking water, the water has been contaminated with animal waste. Although coliform bacteria are not usually harmful, they serve as a warning that the water may also contain other harmful organisms.

No water supply is safe to drink unless it has been tested, and the laboratory report shows that it is free of bacteria. Wells and springs should be tested once each year. The number of samples for public water supplies is based on the size of the system. When the water samples taken during a month are averaged, the MCL for coliform bacteria must average less than 1 bacterium in 100 millilitres of water.

In addition to bacteria, water may contain tiny parasitic protozoans. A change in the water treatment procedure at a Milwaukee water treatment plant in 1993 allowed a protozoan called cryptosporidium to enter the city's water system. Once inside the human intestine, the tiny organism causes **cryptosporidiosis**, a flu-like illness accompanied by diarrhea. The outbreak of disease sent thousands of people to stores for antidiarrheal medications. The disease can be life-threatening to infants, the elderly, and people with certain medical conditions such as AIDS.

The most commonly identified cause of water-related disease in the US today is a one-celled protozoan parasite *Giardia lamblia*. The parasite lives in the intestines of humans and other mammals — including beaver, deer, cattle, raccoons, dogs, and cats. It causes **giardiasis**, an illness affecting the stomach and intestines. The symptoms are painful abdominal cramps, nausea, gas, and diarrhea. Although some people who have the cyst are not affected by it, others may require hospitalization.

Giardia form a foot-ball shaped cyst, or protective capsule, which can survive for two months or longer in water, especially cold mountain streams. The cysts have been found in surface water supplies in all regions of the United States and in other countries.

Is Your Water Safe?

Potable water refers to water that is suitable for drinking. All surface water supplies are probably contaminated with organisms and are not safe to drink unless treated. Water from a well or spring may be safe to drink without treatment. This depends upon the soil type, depth, and the distance from any source of pollution.

Increased public concern about the safety of water supplies has increased the popularity of home filter systems. Should you use a home filter system, and if so, what type of filter should be used? The first step in answering this question is to identify the source of your drinking water.

If the source of water is a reliable public water system, the water should be of high quality when it comes from the faucet. Water systems that serve 15 or more connections must notify customers if their water violates EPA standards. If you should experience water problems such as an unusual taste, odor, or the presence of sediment, you should call the water company.

Even though the water company is supplying water that meets EPA standards, there is the possibility that, in homes with lead plumbing or copper plumbing joined by lead solder, the water is being contaminated with lead. The only way to detect the presence of lead is to have the water tested by a qualified laboratory.

If you have a private well or your water system has less than 15 connections, you should have your water tested to see if a filter or other type of treatment is necessary. The EPA recommends that well

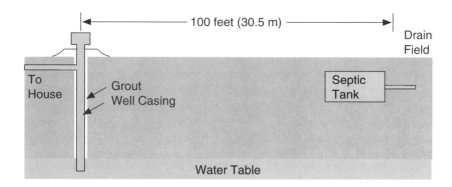

100 feet (30.5 m)

Drain Field

To House

Grout

Well Casing

Septic Tank

Water Table

owners have their water tested annually for nitrates and coliform bacteria. Spring is the best time to have the water tested since rain and melting snow leach the excess nitrates from the soil. The water should be tested more frequently if the water's taste, color, or odor changes. Additional testing is also recommended if there are heavy rains.

The EPA also recommends that well owners have their water tested for lead and radon at least once. Testing for pesticides is recommended if the well is near land where certain pesticides are being used.

Wells should be located up the slope from any possible pollution source such as a septic tank or barnyard. The US Public Health Service suggests that a minimum of 100 feet (30.5 m) should separate the well from a septic drain field. The steel casing of the well should extend 6 to 12 inches above the ground level, and cement grout should fill the space between the soil and the casing. The ground level should slope away from casing. This will prevent the well water from being contaminated by runoff.

Making the Water Safe

Surface water and well water that is contaminated can be made safe by the following chemical and physical treatment processes that remove certain chemicals and kill and/or remove the disease-causing organisms. Water test results will show which type of treatment, if any, is necessary.

Chlorination: Chlorine is used to disinfect most public and private surface water supplies. If wells are contaminated with Coliform bacteria, chlorinators may be installed. The **chlorine demand**, the amount of chlorine needed to treat the water, is affected by certain chemicals in the water. Water containing hydrogen sulfide and/or iron requires more chlorine.

The EPA recommends that the water be allowed to stand for 30 minutes after the chlorine has been added. This is called the **contact time**. The contact time can be reduced to 5 minutes if the amount of chlorine is increased. If the contact time is 30 minutes, there should be 0.4 parts per million of free chlorine in the water, after treatment.

If the contact time is 5 minutes, there should be 2-5 ppm chlorine left in the water after treatment.

Although some people object to the taste of chlorine, it is an inexpensive and effective disinfectant. Another advantage is that the water can easily be tested to ensure that it is safe to use. An inexpensive test kit can be used to measure the **chlorine residual** — the amount of free chlorine remaining in the water.

Giardia and other protozoan parasites can survive the normal amount of chlorine used to disinfect water supplies. The cysts may be killed by higher doses of chlorine — **superchlorination**, or they may be removed by filtration. Usually the soil acts as an effective filter for well water. Graded sand filters that are used at water treatment plants will remove the cysts, but the filtering systems must be properly operated and maintained. Outbreaks of *giardiasis* and *cryptosporidiosis* occur in areas with water systems that lack filters or have poorly maintained filters. (See Case Study: The Public Waterworks)

Ultarviolet Light: Water passes through a sealed chamber with ultraviolet lights. Bacteria exposed to the ultraviolet light are destroyed. The water must be filtered before it enters the light chamber to ensure that bacteria will not be hidden from the light. Although this method of disinfection is fast and does not give the water any taste or odor, it does have some drawbacks.

Ultraviolet light treatment is more expensive than chlorination. The lights must be kept clean and should be replaced each year. The water has no residual chemical that can easily be measured to see if the water is safe. UV treatment may not be effective against spores or cysts.

Heat: When test results show that water samples exceed the EPA standard of 1 coliform bacterium per 100 millilitres of water, the water supplier must issue a **Boil Water Advisory**. An advisory is also issued when an outbreak of protozoan parasites is identified or when a break or repair of a water main increases the potential for contamination of the water supply.

To kill bacteria or protozoan cysts, water must be boiled for at least one full minute. Only boiled water should be used for drinking and preparing food, washing fruits and vegetables, making ice, and washing dishes, unless dishes are thoroughly air-dried.

Filtration: Potable water should be clear and free of color. Well water is usually free of color although chemicals dissolved in it may stain plumbing fixtures and clothing. Algae and tannins from decaying organic matter may give color to surface water. Water may also be contaminated with dyes used in industry.

If the color is caused by organic chemicals dissolved in the water, it can be removed by an **activated carbon filter**. The organic chemicals stick or adhere to the surface of the carbon particles. The EPA requires all water supply systems serving populations over 10,000 people to install carbon filtration systems if their water supplies are contaminated with organic chemicals.

Most **activated carbon filters** are designed to remove organic chemicals that cause strange tastes and odors. They also remove some inorganic chemicals such as chlorine. In a limited test done by EPA, **line-bypass filters**, installed under the kitchen sink, removed more TCE (trichloroethylene) than units attached to the kitchen faucet.

The length of time that the water is in contact with the activated charcoal determines how much of the organic chemicals will be removed. If there are high concentrations of organic chemicals in the water, the filter must be changed more often. Home water filters must be changed regularly to be effective and to limit the growth of bacteria.

Small particles suspended in the water make the water cloudy or **turbid**. Although the particles themselves may not be harmful, they provide places for disease-causing organisms to hide from disinfectants. The MCL for **turbidity** is 5 TU (units of turbidity). Turbidity is a measure of the amount of light scattered or absorbed by particles suspended in water.

Particles may be physically removed by installing cartridge-type **sediment filters** in the water line. These filters work in the same way as a coffee filter or tea bag. They allow the water to pass through and hold back the particles. They do not remove chemicals dissolved in the water. Large water treatment systems use **graded sand filters.** (See Unit IV Section 3.4 "The Waterworks")

Some chemicals, such as hydrogen sulfide or copper, give water an objectionable odor and/or taste. A high concentration of iron gives water a metallic taste, and it leaves yellow or rust-colored stains. Humans are not the only animals to object to strange taste or odor. If cattle don't like the way water tastes or smells, they won't drink the water. If there is too much iron in the water at the dairy barn, the cows may not drink enough to maintain maximum milk production.

Iron present in ground water is dissolved in the water and is colorless. Once well water is exposed to the air, or chlorine is added to the water, the iron changes into red particles. The red particles (iron oxide) may be removed by a sediment filter or a sand filter. If there is a large amount of iron (more than 10 mg/L) dissolved in the water, it must be chemically changed into iron oxide and then filtered.

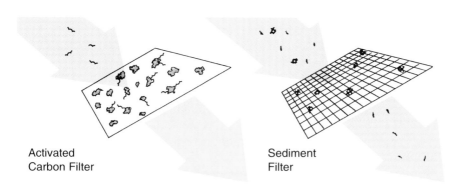

Activated
Carbon Filter

Sediment
Filter

● Activated Carbon

∿ Organic Chemical

⧺ Sediment

𝓝 Bacteria

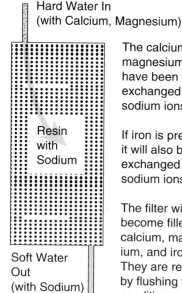

Hard Water In
(with Calcium, Magnesium)

Resin with Sodium

The calcium and magnesium ions have been exchanged for sodium ions.

If iron is present it will also be exchanged for sodium ions.

The filter will become filled with calcium, magnesium, and iron ions. They are removed by flushing the conditioner with a salt solution.

Soft Water Out
(with Sodium)

Inside a Water Softener

Water Conditioners (Softeners)

If the amount of iron dissolved in water is less than 3.0 mg/L, it may be removed by the same type of water softener used to remove calcium and magnesium. Calcium and magnesium dissolved in the water do not make it unsuitable for drinking. Instead they are removed because they form deposits called **scale** in water heaters, pipes, bathtubs, and on clothing.

Calcium and magnesium are both needed by the body. Some studies indicate that drinking hard water is better for you than drinking soft water. People who have high blood pressure, or for other reasons must limit the sodium in their diet, should not drink water that has been treated in an ion-exchange water softener. This type of water conditioner is filled with a material called a **resin**. The calcium and magnesium ions in the water are exchanged for sodium ions attached to the resin.

Homeowners who have hard water often install an ion-exchange water softener in the hot water line. Water passing through the cold water pipes is not treated. It can be safely used for drinking and watering plants.

Although the technology is available to remove nitrates from the water, the treatment processes are expensive. An ion exchange system similar to a water softener can remove nitrates. In a nitrate removal system, nitrate and sulfate ions are exchanged for chloride ions. The same methods used to remove salt from sea water — distillation and reverse osmosis — can also be used to remove nitrates. (See Case Study: Making More Fresh Water)

In an Emergency

If you must drink water and do not know whether it is contaminated with bacteria or protozoan cysts, you should treat it in one of the following ways:

- boil it for at least five minutes.
- Add 8 drops of household liquid chlorine bleach per gallon (3.8 L) of clear water, and let stand for 30 minutes. Make sure that the only ingredient in the bleach is sodium hypochlorite.
- add 8-10 drops of 2 percent tincture of iodine to a litre of water and allow to stand for twenty minutes.
- Treat it with water purification tablets, which contain tetraglycine hydroperiodide, a form of iodine.

The tincture of iodine and iodide tablets are available at drug or sporting goods stores. Although iodine is an effective way to kill disease-causing organisms including Giardia, health authorities recommend that it be used only for short periods of time. If it is used for long periods of time, it may have undesirable effects upon unborn children or people with thyroid problems.

3.3 QUESTIONS FOR STUDY AND DISCUSSION

1. Explain how diseases like typhoid fever are passed from person to person.
2. In many countries diseases carried by water have declined drastically. Give two reasons for this decline.
3. Where do most Americans who lack a safe supply of drinking water live?
4. What percent of the water wells and springs used by individual families in Pennsylvania are not safe to drink prior to treatment?
5. Give one reason why Pennsylvania has reported more cases of water-related disease than other states.
6. In addition to lack of food, what caused the death of Ethiopians in some refuge camps during the 1980s?
7. What part of the world does not have a safe supply of drinking water? How many children die each year because of diseases transmitted in drinking water?
8. What national organization is working to provide people in developing countries with a safe supply of drinking water? Why is the task of providing safe drinking water becoming more difficult?

The Safe Drinking Water Act
9. What does the Safe Drinking Water Act require of water suppliers?
10. What is the Maximum Contaminant Level or MCL? Who determines the MCL?
11. What is the basis for the MCL level?
12. How many chemicals have been found in ground water? Has the EPA set the MCL for all of these chemicals? If not, why?
13. List three inorganic contaminants that the EPA has regulated by setting an MCL. List two types of organic contaminants which are regulated by a MCL.
14. Why does the EPA regulate organic chemicals in drinking water supplies?

Organisms in the Water
15. Why didn't the EPA set an MCL for bacteria that cause typhoid fever? What type of bacteria has an MCL? Why did the EPA choose this bacteria?

16. How can you tell if a water supply is safe to drink? How often should wells and springs be tested?
17. What is the MCL for coliform bacteria?
18. Identify two water-related diseases caused by parasitic protozoans.
19. What are the symptoms of diseases caused by bacteria and parasitic protozoans found in drinking water?
20. During a hiking trip in an area identified as National Wilderness, would it be safe to drink the water without treating it first? Explain.

Is Your Water Safe?
21. Water that is drinkable is called _____.
22. Is it safer to assume that surface water and well water that has not been tested is contaminated. (True/False)
23. List three factors that determine whether organisms will be filtered out of ground water before reaching the well.
24. What should you do first before you decide to purchase a water filter?
25. Do you need to have your water tested if you are drinking water supplied by a public water supplier? If so, what kind of test would you request?
26. If your water comes from a well or spring, what should the water be tested for and how often should the water be tested?
27. What two factors should be considered when locating the well?
28. Describe how to prevent the well water from being contaminated by surface water.

Making the Water Safe
29. What method is used to disinfect most surface water supplies?
30. Define and explain the importance of the following terms:
   A. contact time
   B. chlorine demand
   C. chlorine residual

31. What is the required chlorine residual for water that has had a contact time of five minutes? How does it compare to the required chlorine residual for water that has had a contact time of thirty minutes?

32. Give one disadvantage of using chlorine as a disinfectant.
What are the advantages of using chlorine as a disinfectant?

33. Give two methods of disinfecting water with *Giardia* parasites.
Which method is used at water treatment plants?
Why aren't *Giardia* parasites usually found in well water?

34. What type of light is sometimes used to disinfect water? Why must the water be filtered first?

35. What are the advantages of ultraviolet disinfection?
List three disadvantages of ultraviolet disinfection.

36. Give three situations that would require a Boil Water Advisory.
Must water used for washing dishes be boiled?

37. Identify two natural substances that give color to surface water.

38. What type of filter is used to remove organic chemicals from water?
Explain how the chemicals are removed.

39. If you live in a town with a population greater than 10,000, do you need an activated carbon filter under your sink?

40. Putting an activated carbon water filter on the faucet may not do much good. Why?

41. Give two reasons why activated carbon water filters must be changed often.

42. What makes the water turbid?
How is the turbidity of water measured?
If the particles are not harmful, why did the EPA set an MCL for turbidity?

43. How are particles removed from single-user water systems?
How are particles removed at water treatment plants?

44. Give two reasons why people object to water with high levels of iron.
Why might dairy farmers be concerned about the amount of iron in the water?

45. If water contains more than 10 mg/L of iron, what procedure must be used to remove it from the water?

Water Conditioners (Softeners)

46. List three chemicals that can be removed from water by a water softener.

47. Why do homeowners want to remove calcium and magnesium from the water?

48. Should people who have high blood pressure drink softened water? Explain.

49. How can people who want soft water for washing and bathing install a water softener and yet have hard water for drinking?

50. Why do you think softened water makes house plants die?

51. How can excess nitrates be removed from a water supply?
What is the disadvantage of these treatments?

In An Emergency

52. How long must water be boiled to kill some bacteria?

53. Which has a longer contact time, chlorine or iodine?

54. Does iodine kill the *Giardia* parasite?

55. Why don't water treatment plants that lack filtration equipment use iodine instead of chlorine?

3.4 The Waterworks

The ancient Romans built **aqueducts** — canals to carry water from the mountains to the city. Some 260 miles (420 km) of aqueducts carried water to Rome. Some of these canals are still in use today.

The first municipal waterworks in America was built by the Moravians who settled in Bethlehem, Pennsylvania. At first, workers carried water in wooden buckets from a spring near the Lehigh River. When the waterworks was completed, a water-powered pump freed them from this task. The pump moved water up the hill through a system of hollow log pipes.

Industry developed along the river. A tannery and a flour mill were located close to the waterworks. Eventually the spring became polluted, and the city's leaders had to search for a new water source. Today gravity carries water to the city, through 23 miles (37 km) of pipes, from two reservoirs in the Pocono Mountains. Other modern cities, including New York City, Denver, and Los Angeles, have gone far beyond the city limits to obtain an adequate water supply.

Have a Drink in New York City

The source of New York City's water supply is primarily rain and snow that fall on some 1,950 square miles (5.1×10^9 km^2) of watersheds located in upstate New York. The water is stored in reservoirs and flows to the city by gravity through large pipes — some more than 20 feet (6 m) in diameter. State law allows local communities along the pipeline to draw their water supply from the pipes as long as they pay for the costs involved.

The water quality is constantly monitored. Watershed inspectors check the reservoirs, streams, and treated wastewater that flow into the reservoirs. In the summer the reservoirs are treated with a chemical, usually copper sulfate, to control the growth of algae. Bacteriologists and chemists collect and analyze more than 40,000 water samples each year. Chemists check the water samples for more than 80 substances, including traces of heavy metals and organic chemicals.

Urban Planner

While large cities may have a team of planners, small cities usually employ only one urban planner. Their responsibilities include planning for future industrial and residential development, transportation needs, and developing programs to provide adequate health and welfare services. They must consider the conservation of natural resources, adequate water supply, flood control, and regulations concerning water and air quality. Plans must include approved methods of disposal of hazardous and solid waste. Planners must have leadership qualities, be able to organize and analyze data, and communicate ideas effectively. Graduates of bachelor's degree programs will normally be placed with experienced planners as a part of a training program.

At the Waterworks

Public and private water companies must ensure that drinking water meets certain criteria set by the EPA. When reservoirs or rivers are the source of drinking water, the water must be treated to remove certain substances. At most water treatment plants, the treatment processes occur in the sequence described below.

Intake: Water enters the treatment plant through an intake pipe in the reservoir or river. The pipe is covered with a screen to prevent large objects, such as fish, sticks, and plants from entering. Algae and

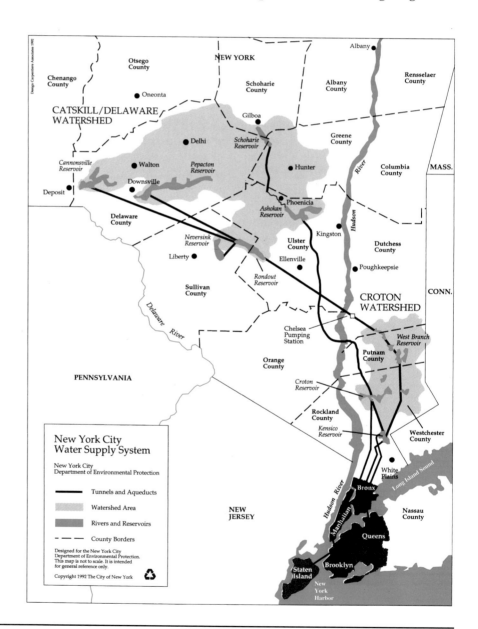

other small organisms that enter the pipe are removed during the treatment process.

Primary Chlorination: As the water enters the water treatment plant, **chlorine** is usually added to prevent the growth of algae and bacteria in the water pipes.

Chemical Treatment and Mixing: Several chemicals are added to the water to help clean it. The plant operator determines the amount of each chemical that is needed. **Alum** (aluminum sulfate) is added to cause the small particles suspended in the water to stick together. These clumps of particles are called **floc**. The best floc formation occurs when the pH of the water is near 6.0. **Lime** is added to adjust the pH to the proper level.

Activated carbon is sometimes added, especially in the summer months, to remove chemicals that cause strange taste, odor, or color. In some locations activated carbon is needed to remove trihalomethanes (THMs) and other organic chemicals that may cause cancer or other health problems. Trihalomethanes form when chlorine combines with organic chemicals in the water. Studies suggest that THMs may cause bladder and colorectal cancer.

Sodium zinc polyphosphate is often added to form a thin coating on the pipes. This helps prevent corrosion.

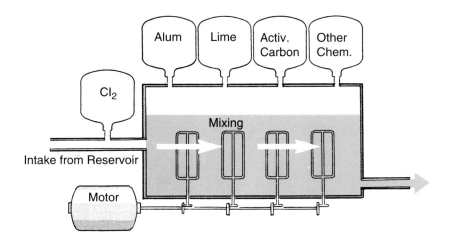

◀ Chemical Treatment

Flocculation: After the chemicals are mixed with the water, the water flows into a large tank that contains a series of dividers or **baffles**. The baffles are arranged so that the water moves over one baffle and under the next baffle. As the water moves through the tank, the **floc** grows bigger and bigger until it looks like big dirty snowflakes.

Sedimentation: From the flocculation tank, the water moves into a large storage tank. The floc is heavy, and it sinks to the bottom of the settling tank. The water must remain in the tank for a long period of time to allow the floc to settle.

Flocculation Tank ▶

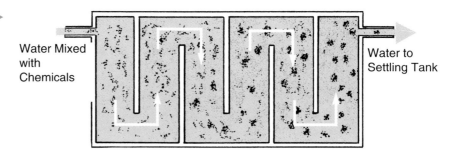

Water Mixed with Chemicals

Water to Settling Tank

Filtration: In some treatment plants, the water is pumped from the settling tanks to a **graded sand filter**. The sand filters out any remaining particles, including microscopic organisms, that were not removed in the settling tank. As the particles are trapped in the sand, they slow the flow of water. The treatment plant operators monitor the flow and clean the filters when necessary.

The graded sand filter is cleaned by reversing the flow of water and the stirring the sand. The process, called a **backwash**, removes the solids that are trapped between the particles of sand. The filters must be backwashed more frequently in the summer months because of the heavier growth of algae.

The water used to wash the filter is pumped to a lagoon to allow the solids to settle. To conserve water, some treatment plants recycle the wash water to the plant where it is treated to meet drinking water standards. At other plants, once the solids settle out, the wash water is returned to the river.

Graded sand filters reduce the risk of illness from tiny protozoans such as giardia and cryptosporidia. Water treatment systems without graded sand filters must use much high levels of chlorine to kill these organisms.

Settling Tank ▶

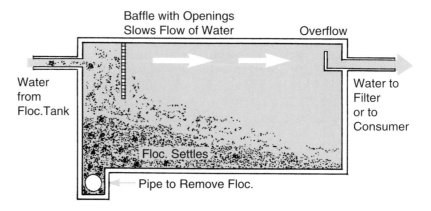

Baffle with Openings Slows Flow of Water

Overflow

Water from Floc. Tank

Water to Filter or to Consumer

Floc. Settles

Pipe to Remove Floc.

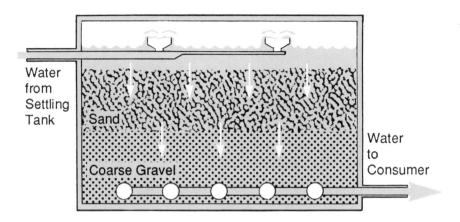

◀ Graded Sand Filter

Water from Settling Tank

Sand

Coarse Gravel

Water to Consumer

Final Chlorination: Before the water leaves the treatment plant, a small amount of **chlorine** is added to kill any bacteria that may have survived the treatment processes or that may be in the water system. Additional **lime** may be added to adjust the pH of the water and reduce the corrosion of the pipes. In some cities, **fluoride** is added fluoride is added to help prevent tooth decay. (See Unit IV Case Study 3.9: Fluoride in Your Water Supply — How Much is Enough?)

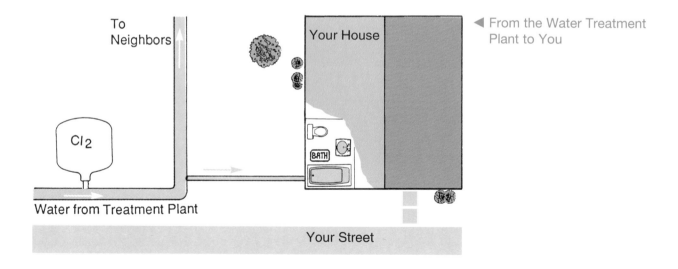

◀ From the Water Treatment Plant to You

To Neighbors

Your House

Cl₂

Water from Treatment Plant

Your Street

1. Give the source of drinking water used by residents of Bethlehem, Pennsylvania, during each of the following periods:
   A. when first settled
   B. after first waterworks was completed
   C. today
2. During which period in Bethlehem's history does the source of drinking water compare to the source of drinking water in Rome, Italy?

Have a Drink in New York City

3. What is the source of drinking water for New York City? your City?
4. When the chemists check water samples, what types of chemicals are they looking for?
5. Why is copper sulfate added to New York City's reservoirs?

At the Waterworks

6. What does water entering the treatment plant contain?
7. Why is chlorine first added when the water first enters the plant?
8. What is floc? What chemical is added to cause the formation of floc? Why is lime added to the water before it enters the flocculation tank?
9. Give two reasons why activated charcoal may be added to the water. What time of the year is activated charcoal most likely to be used?
10. What chemical is added to protect the plumbing from corrosion?
11. What is the purpose of the baffles in the flocculation tank?
12. What treatment process follows flocculation?
13. What is the purpose of the baffle in the settling tank?
14. Explain how water is filtered at some treatment plants.
15. Describe how a filter is cleaned when it becomes filled with particles.
16. Why must the filters be backwashed more often in the summer?
17. Identify three chemicals that may be added immediately before the water leaves the water treatment plant and give the reason for adding each chemical.
18. Do you think that water treatment facilities should be required to install graded sand filters? Justify your position.

Science **T**echnology **S**ociety

ISSUES

WATER FOR LAS VEGAS

Should there be limits on the water rights that cities can buy? The population in Clark County, Nevada, grew from 463,087 in 1980 to 741,459 in 1990. The county includes Las Vegas — the fastest growing city in the United States. The city of Las Vegas will outgrow its current water supplies by 1995. Landscaping in the city provides the illusion that water is abundant. Industry and city officials say that water provides the fantasy that makes Las Vegas what it is, and more water is necessary for the continued success of the tourist industry. Most of the water is used for fountains, artificial lakes, golf courses, and conventional lawns.

Las Vegas Valley Water District charges 91 cents for the first 1500 gallons a day and $1.01 for additional water. Most of the water comes from Lake Mead on the Colorado River. The water district has applied for permits to drill 146 wells that would yield 846,000 acre-feet per year. Some of the wells are 300 miles away from Las Vegas.

- Discuss the possible impacts on the surrounding counties if the permits are granted.
- Discuss the possible impacts on Las Vegas and the state of Nevada if the permits are not granted.
- Do you think the permits should be granted? What additional information do you need to make a decision?

3.5 Will there be Enough?

"When the well's dry, we know the worth of water."
Benjamin Franklin

Water is one of Earth's most abundant resources. There are 1.4 billion cubic kilometres of water on Earth. Streams carry an average of 1.2 trillion gallons (4.6×10^{12} L) of water to the oceans every day. If water is so abundant and is a renewable resource, how can we possibly run out of water?

Most of Earth's water — 97.2 percent — is in the oceans. Together the oceans, ice caps and glaciers contain 99.6 percent of Earth's total water supply. The usable supply of fresh water — ground water and surface water — is only four-tenths of one percent — 0.4 percent — of the world's total water supply.

If the volume of water in the oceans is represented by a one inch (2.5 cm) cube, a one-fourth inch (0.6 cm) cube would represent the water stored in the ice caps and glaciers, a one-eighth inch (0.3 cm) cube would represent ground water, and a one-sixteenth inch (0.15 cm) cube would represent surface water.

To put it another way, Earth's total water supply can be represented as 100 drops of water. Salt water in the ocean is represented by slightly more than 97 of the drops. Slightly more than two of the three remaining drops represent ice. Less than one half of the last drop represents the ground and surface water supply.

The three drops of fresh water are not equally distributed or readily available. Eighty-five percent of the fresh water is frozen in polar ice caps and glaciers. Fourteen percent is buried beneath the ground. Half of the ground water is more than 2,600 feet (800 metres) beneath Earth's surface. Fresh water also occurs as a film of moisture covering particles of soil and as water vapor high in the atmosphere. Less than one percent (0.66%) of Earth's supply of fresh water is found in lakes, rivers and streams.

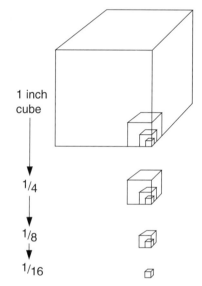

The Earth's Water Supply

The Distribution of Water

If all of the water in the atmosphere were to fall evenly as rain, Earth would be entirely covered with one inch (2.5 cm) of water. But when it rains it pours. Rain doesn't fall equally on everyone. Unusual

Twenty percent of the world's supply of fresh surface water is found in the Great Lakes.

weather patterns sometimes create long periods of drought or disastrous floods. California experienced its worst drought in the last century from 1987 to 1991. The Great Flood of 1993 caused billions of dollars in damage to property in eight Midwestern states.

The average annual rainfall in the United States is 30 inches (76 cm), but it is not evenly distributed. Less than 4 inches (10 cm) of rainfall each year on parts of the Southwest while parts of the Pacific Northwest receive 200 inches (508 cm) a year. The wettest place on Earth is Mt. Waialeale on the island of Kauai, Hawaii, where it rains almost every day. The yearly rainfall on Mt. Waialeale averages 451 inches (1,150 cm) a year.

Most of the rain falling on the United States falls in the East. West of the 100th Meridian — a line extending from North Dakota through western Texas — there are few major sources of freshwater. Two major rivers draining the Rocky Mountains supply most of the surface water. The Southwest gets much of its water from the Colorado River, and the Northwest taps the Columbia River. The **Ogallala Aquifer**, a 156,000 square mile (4.0×10^5 km^2) underground reservoir, provides water for irrigated agriculture in the High Plains states.

The survival and success of a community frequently depend upon the water it can provide for agriculture and industry. Water has often become the limiting factor in the growth of communities. Although the eastern part of the United States is wet, water supplies are sometimes not sufficient to meet the demand. The high population density along the eastern coast puts great demands upon the region's water supply.

The Demand for Water

In poor tropical countries, where women must walk several miles for water, each person may use less than one gallon (3.8 litres) of water per day. It is estimated that Californians use about 100 to 200 gallons (3.8-7.6×10^2 L) a day per person. During recent droughts in New Jersey and California, some residents were required to limit water use to 50 gallons (1.9×10^2 L) per person per day.

Average Daily Water Use for a Family of Four			
Water use	**Gallons**	**litres**	**Percent of Total Daily Use**
Toilet	100	380	39
Bathing & Hygiene	88	334	34
Laundry	35	133	14
Kitchen	27	103	11
Housekeeping	5	9	2
Totals	255	969	100

Our demand for water is great, and it continues to grow. World water demand has grown faster than the population. Water use is nearly 50 percent more per person than in 1950. Each day during 1985, nearly 1.3 trillion litres of water flowed through complex systems of pipes to homes, factories, farms, and power plants in the United States.

Most water — 141 billion gallons (5.3×10^{11} L) per day — is used for agriculture. A large supply of water is necessary to produce the food that we eat. One hundred and twenty gallons (4.6×10^2 L) of water is required to produce an egg for your breakfast. A steak for dinner requires 3,500 gallons (1.3×10^4 L).

Irrigated agriculture is the number one user of water in the western United States. In California, farmers use about 85 percent of the available water supply. They grow about half the fruits and vegetables produced in the United States. In California, cotton, rice, and alfalfa rely most heavily on irrigated water. In Kern County, a farmer can make seven cuttings of alfalfa in an irrigated field. Without water for irrigation, the fields may produce only one cutting.

The second major use of water in the United States is production of electricity at thermoelectric power plants. Power plants use 131 billion gallons (5.0×10^{11} L) of water per day, but most of this water (97%) is returned to the lake or the river and immediately available to be used again.

The charts below show how water was used in the United States in 1985. The charts include only water that is withdrawn from a source. They do not include recreation, hydroelectric power generation, transportation, or wildlife uses that do not remove water from the stream.

Daily Water Withdrawal Uses in the Entire United States — 1985			
Use	Litres Per Day	Consumed	Returned
Agricultural	534	54%	46%
Thermoelectric	496	3%	97%
Domestic and Commercial	118	20%	80%
Industrial and Mining	117	16%	84%

Some industries use huge amounts of water while others use very little. Paper companies are always located along rivers that provide the large amounts of water required for the production of paper products. Producing one ton of paper for books may require as much as 184,000 gallons (7×10^5 L) of water. Steel mills and oil refineries also require large volumes of water, and many are located along the coast. Some 60,000 gallons (2.3×10^5 L) of water is needed to make the steel for an automobile. More than 450 gallons (1.7×10^3 L) of water is needed to refine a barrel of crude oil. This includes 10 gallons of water for each gallon (3.8 litres) of gasoline produced.

East versus West — Water Usage Ranked in Descending Order	
The West	The East
Irrigated agriculture	Energy
Domestic and Commercial	Manufacturing
Energy	Irrigated agriculture
Minerals	Minerals

Water use in the East differs from its use in the West. The chart below shows how the water is used in each region of the country.

The Mining of Water

At least fourteen homes in Pittsburgh, Pennsylvania, have been abandoned because the land they were built on was sinking, and the houses were no longer safe. The houses in Pittsburgh are just a few of the thousands built above abandoned coal mines in Pennsylvania, Kentucky and West Virginia.

Subsidence — sinking of land — occurs when the resources beneath the land have been removed, and the ground above can no longer support its own weight. The mine subsidence in Pittsburgh prompted more than 2,500 people to call Pennsylvania's Department of Environmental Resources to apply for mine-subsidence insurance.

Mining is the removal of a natural substance from an ecosystem at a rate that is faster than the substance is being replaced. Like coal, ground water is sometimes mined. In Mexico City, the pumping of ground water exceeds the rate of recharge by more than 50 percent. Ground water helps support the land above it. The sagging of Mexico City's famous Metropolitan Cathedral was not caused by the mining of coal. It is sagging because of the mining of water.

In some regions of Texas, Louisiana, and Arizona where water has been mined the land is sinking. In Baytown, Texas, the pumping of ground water caused the land to sink, and the area is now below sea level. Homes along the coast have been abandoned as water from Galveston Bay invaded the area.

The annual rainfall in southeastern Arizona is only 12 inches (30 cm) per year. Farmers in the region have been mining water from **aquifers** — water-filled layers of porous rock — to irrigate their crops. The land is sinking, and where it does not sink evenly, large cracks appear. In Arizona there are hundreds of such cracks. One developer spent a half-million dollars filling a 400-foot-long (120 m) crack caused by subsidence.

Subsidence is not the only problem caused by mining of ground water. Roughly a third of today's harvest comes from cropland that is irrigated. Although less than 10 percent of US farmland is irrigated with ground water, these acres are very important to our food production. According to the World Resources Institute, one fifth of the total irrigated farm land in the United States relies on the mining of ground water.

The cost of energy to pump the water increases as the **water table** — the level of the water in the aquifer — drops. Farmers cannot earn a living growing crops when the cost of pumping the water rises above $200 to $300 per acre-foot (one acre of land receiving 12 inches or 1.2×10^9 L of rainfall). The US Department of Agriculture officials estimate that Texas may not be able to irrigate half of its six million acres of farmland by the year 2000, and Texas is not alone.

The **Ogallala or High Plains Aquifer** lies beneath the High Plains — a region stretching 800 miles (1,280 km) from South Dakota to northern Texas. The aquifer contains **fossil ground water** — water that has slowly been absorbed by Earth over the last three million years. Fossil aquifers receive little, if any, water from the surface and are considered a nonrenewable resource.

More than 170,000 wells tap the Ogallala Aquifer. The wells provide water to irrigate land that produces 25 percent of the nation's cotton, 15 percent of the grain and 40 percent of the beef cattle. In the early eighties, the mining of ground water caused the water table to fall four to six feet (1.2-1.8 m) each year. By 1990, it was no longer economical to pump water from 24 percent of the Ogallala aquifer in northern Texas. Many wells in Kansas, Colorado, and Texas have gone dry.

Rivers and Water Rights

Water is **consumed** if it is not returned to the natural body of water where it may be used again. Water that is consumed may be evaporated, or it may become a part of the finished product. Only about 16 percent of the water used in industry and mining is consumed. Unlike industry and mining, agriculture consumes more than half of the water withdrawn from wells or rivers.

The Colorado River flows only 7.6 miles (12 km) from where it begins in the Rocky Mountains until the first irrigation ditch diverts part of the water to four ranches. By 1886 arguments over water in the Colorado and Arkansas Rivers were so heated that the state government was forced to make laws to determine who had the right to withdraw water from the rivers.

An agreement between Colorado and Kansas assigned 60 percent of the water in the Arkansas River to Colorado. The other 40 percent must be allowed to flow into Kansas. Demand for the river's water is greater than the supply. When there is little rain and farmers begin to irrigate, the river begins to shrink. At times the Arkansas River flows no more than fifty miles (80 km) from the Colorado state line before the water has been consumed, and the river bed is dry.

The courts used the "first come, first served" rule as the basis to assign water rights. One treaty guaranteed water rights to Native Americans. The Supreme Court has ruled that five Native American reservations must be guaranteed enough water from the Colorado River to irrigate their land.

Another treaty signed in 1944 guaranteed Mexico 1.5 million **acre-feet** of Colorado river water per year. An acre-foot is the volume of water needed to cover one acre (0.4 hectare) of land twelve inches (30 cm) deep. This represents about 326,000 gallons (1.2×10^6 L), or the average amount of water used by a family of five in one year.

Studies were done, and the Colorado River's water flow was divided during a wet period. Since that time the Colorado River has not carried so much water, but until recently there was no problem.

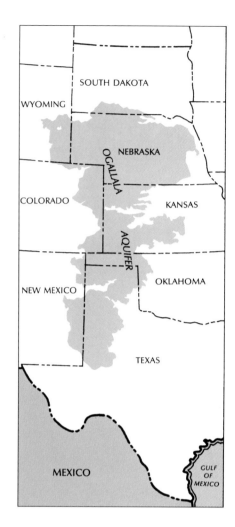

Above Ground Irrigation System

Some of the states along the upper Colorado and some Native American tribes did not demand their share of the river's water supply.

Completion of two projects will make the demand for water greater than the supply. Irrigation of 110,000 acres on the Navajo Reservation, and a 310 mile (496 km) channel that will carry water to Phoenix and Tucson, Arizona, will force southern California to give up 60 percent of the Colorado River water it has been using.

Where will dry regions, like southern California and western Kansas, get the water they need? The Army Corps of Engineers proposed a plan to build a canal from the Missouri River to Western Kansas. Construction costs would be more than $16 billion, and operation costs would also be high since the water must be lifted 2,000 feet (600 m).

California has already begun an educational program to promote conservation, but this won't be enough. Southern California must find additional water supplies — perhaps in northern California or maybe from the sea. Unless Californians can find another source of water, they will be forced to choose between water for the densely populated cities and water for irrigated agriculture. In some places, farmers are selling their water rights to the cities.

3.5 QUESTIONS FOR STUDY AND DISCUSSION

1. Three-fourths of Earth's surface is covered by water, yet the usable supply of fresh water is less than one percent. Explain why.
2. Match the following volumes of water with the proper description.

Description	Volumes of Water
A. glaciers and ice caps	1. less than 1 percent
B. oceans (saltwater)	2. 2.4 percent
C. usable fresh water	3. 97.2 percent
A. glaciers and ice caps	1. 1 inch (2.5 cm) cube
B. ground water	2. 1/4 inch (0.6 cm) cube
C. surface water	3. 1/8 inch (0.3 cm) cube
D. oceans (saltwater)	4. 1/16 inch (0.15 cm) cube
A. glaciers and ice caps	1. less than 1 drop
B. ground and surface water	2. about 2 drops
C. salt water (oceans)	3. 97 drops

The Distribution of Water

3. What is the average annual rainfall in the United States? What is the average annual rainfall where you live?
4. Remembering what you have learned about weather, explain why rainfall is not distributed evenly.
5. Identify the region of the US that normally receives the most rainfall.
6. Identify the major source of surface water in the Southwest and in the Northwest. What is the major source of water used to irrigate crops in the High Plains states?
7. If the eastern part of the US is the wettest, why do parts of the East sometimes experience water shortages?
8. What is often the major limiting factor in the growth of a community?

The Demand for Water

9. Compare the amount of water used by each person living in a poor tropical country to the amount used by each person in America.

10. Do you think that the amount of water allowed for each resident during the droughts in New Jersey and California was sufficient to meet their needs?

11. Rank the following uses of water beginning with the use that requires the greatest amount of water.

    bathing   household cleaning
    cooking   washing clothes
    flushing the toilet

12. During the 1970s there were energy conservation programs to reduce the amount of energy we used. Have similar programs reduced the amount of water used by each person?

13. Identify "instream" uses of water that could be affected by withdrawing large amounts of water from rivers or streams.

14. The largest amount of water used in the United States is used to produce _____.
    The second largest use of water in the US is for the production of _____.

15. Which withdrawal use of water would have the most impact on instream use and use by other communities downstream? Why would this use have the greatest impact?

16. Who is the major user of water in the East? Who is the major user of water in the West? Is more water used for manufacturing in the East or the West?

17. Identify two industries that use huge amounts of water.

18. Explain how it is possible that 2,000 gallons of water per day is used for the average person in the United States.

The Mining of Water

19. Define the terms aquifer, mining, subsidence, and water table.

20. Describe the events that led to homes being abandoned in Pittsburgh, Pennsylvania and Baytown, Texas.

21. What percentage of US farmland is irrigated with ground water? How much of this farmland depends upon mining of ground water?

22. Give the location of the Ogallala aquifer. Explain why it is called a "fossil" aquifer.

23. Explain why the Ogallala aquifer is so important to so many people in the United States.

24. Although water is a renewable resource, the Ogallala aquifer is considered a nonrenewable resource. Explain why.

Rivers and Water Rights

25. Explain what happens to water that is consumed. Who consumes more water — agriculture or industry?

26. What two rivers flowing out of Colorado have been rationed by the courts?

27. What is the basis for the water rights given to Native Americans?

28. During part of the year, the Arkansas River is dry. Where does the water go?

29. States in the upper Colorado River valley are guaranteed 7.5 million acre-feet of water annually. States in the lower river valley are also guaranteed 7.5 million acre feet. Mexico is guaranteed how many acre-feet of water? Do you think that the United States should be obligated to send more of the Colorado River's flow on to Mexico?

30. Define acre-foot. On the basis of average use in the US an acre-foot of water meets the annual needs of how many people? Research your community's water use. Is water use in your community above or below the national average?

31. In the past, southern California has been using more Colorado River water than is allotted to them by court order. Describe the two projects that forced southern California to give up some of this water.

32. Identify potential water sources for western Kansas; for southern California. What are alternatives to these expensive water projects?

3.6 Making More Water Available by Using Less

It's a matter of when, not if we must adopt water conservation measures.

TRY TO FIND OUT

Many of the household products you use every day contain toxic chemicals. When poured down the drain, they may contaminate ground water. When dumped in landfills, they add to leachate that may pollute our ground water or surface water. Are there natural, non-polluting substitutes for many of the poisonous products we commonly use? Find out about effective substances you can use as substitutes for toxic household products.

Water is still one of our cheapest natural resources. For only a few cents a family can get a ton of water delivered to their home. They would have to pay more for a ton of dirt (topsoil) or a load of rocks. Because water has been readily available, most Americans take water for granted, and we have become a nation of water-wasters. With the increasing population growth we are reaching a point where water conservation must become a way of life.

Meters

Most people who draw water from their own private well must pay for drilling the well and installing a pump, but there is no charge for the water that they use. Some cities with older water systems do not have water meters, and people pay a **flat rate** for each residence regardless of the amount of water used.

All commercial and industrial properties in New York City are required to have water meters, but few residential buildings have meters. Water bills for residences without a meter are based on a **frontage rate**. The frontage rate is determined by the size of the building and the number of sinks, showers, and toilets.

People with private wells and people who pay flat or frontage rates for water do not pay an increased cost for taking a longer shower. The only additional cost is for the energy needed to heat the water. Studies show that the use of water declines as water rates increase. Water use dropped 36 percent after Boulder, Colorado, installed water meters. Making people pay more for the water they use encourages them to use the water more efficiently.

Arizona has passed a law that requires people to put water meters on their wells and to report the amount of water used. The water is no longer free. Farms larger than two acres (0.8 hectare) must pay a small fee for each acre-foot of water used.

Residents of Tucson, Arizona, use about 160 gallons (6.0×10^2 L) of water per person per day. Residents of Phoenix use 260 gallons (9.9×10^2 L) per person per day. The cities are only 100 miles apart and have the same climate. Why is the demand for water so much greater in Phoenix? One factor is the lifestyle; another factor is cost.

The water supply for Phoenix is the Salt River. With a readily available supply of water for irrigation, lawns in Phoenix were planted with shade trees, hedges and a carpet of grass — a type of landscape that is normal in much wetter climates.

The water supply for Tucson is ground water, and residents pay significantly more for each gallon of water. Water costing $14 in Phoenix might cost $24 in Tucson. Lawns in Tucson are planted with cactus and other desert plants. Industries in Tucson recycle water. When faced with increased costs, industries are encouraged to recycle water. In some industries, the use of water has been reduced by 90 percent.

Leaky Water Systems

Much water is wasted. Water distribution systems in many big cities are old and need to be replaced. Needed repairs and replacements are so expensive that the faulty systems are still in use. New York City loses at least 20 percent of its water supply through the city's 6,000 miles (9.6×10^3 km) of leaky water lines. Newer systems have their share of leaks, too. Houston loses 13 percent of its water through leaks in the city's water lines.

In most cities, the city water department is responsible for the major water pipes or water mains, and homeowners are responsible for the house connection — the pipe running from the building to the water main. When New York City's Bureau of Water Supply discovers a leak in a house connection, the owner is given a three-day notice to repair the leak. If the leak is not repaired within three days, the city shuts off the water supply to the building.

While repairs to water pipes and plumbing fixtures may be expensive, they are an effective way to conserve water. Each leaky faucet or toilet wastes water. A faucet with a slow leak can waste 12 gallons (46 litres) of water per day, while a leaking toilet can waste 200 gallons (7.6×10^2 L) of water a day. Toilet leaks can easily be detected by adding food coloring to the water in the tank. If the colored water appears in the toilet bowl, the toilet is leaking.

Water Saving Fixtures

A typical family of four consumes 255 gallons (9.7×10^2 L) of water inside the home each day. By installing water saving fixtures this amount can be reduced by 90 to 140 gallons ($3-5 \times 10^2$ L) each day. Depending on water rates, installation of water-saving fixtures may save $100 to $300 per year.

By installing a high-quality low-flow showerhead, a family can reduce water use in the shower by more than half and still enjoy a good shower. Not only does this save water, but it also saves more than $150 annually if the water is heated with electricity. Flow control aerators on kitchen and bathroom faucets can save additional water

Fixture	Water Flow
Conventional Toilet	4-6 gal (15-23 L) /flush
Water Saving Toilet	4.5 gal (13 L) /flush
Low-Flow Toilet	1.6 gal (6 L) /flush
Conventional Showerhead	3-15 gal (10.5-57 L) /minute
Low-Flow Showerhead	2-3 gal (7.5-11 L) /minute
Low-Flow (1994 standard)	2.5 gal (9.5 L) /minute
Regular Faucet Aerator	2.5-6 gal (9.5-23 L) /minute
Flow Regulating Aerator	0.5-2.5 gal (2-9.5 L) /minute

and energy by reducing the flow rate from 6 to 2 gallons (23-28 litres) per minute.

Nearly 40 percent of all water used in the home is flushed down the toilet. Placing bottles or dams in conventional toilet tanks can reduce water use by 1.5 gallons (5.7 litres) of water per flush, without affecting the performance of the toilet. This can save 8,500 gallons (3.2×10^4 L) of water each year.

Regulations included in the 1992 energy bill set federal standards for new plumbing fixtures manufactured after January 1, 1994. Showerheads and faucets must limit flow to 2.5 gallons (9.5 litres) per minute. Toilets manufactured for domestic use must limit flow to 1.6 gallons (6 litres) per flush. These changes are expected to reduce domestic indoor water use by 30 percent.

Saving water can also reduce problems with some on-lot septic systems and sewage treatment plants. Many sewage treatment plants are too small to handle the amount of wastewater that passes through the plant. Reducing the amount of water used in each home reduces the volume of wastewater that must be treated. This results in more efficient treatment and cleaner **effluent** — treated wastewater entering a stream.

A Change in Lifestyle

There are many ways to reduce the water used in your household without spending money on new plumbing fixtures.

- Use a dishpan or stopper in the sink when washing and rinsing dishes. Wash the dishes only once a day.
- Use the dishwasher only when fully loaded and use the short cycle.
- Use the proper water level when using the washing machine.
- Avoid letting water run when brushing your teeth or shaving.
- Take a 3-minute shower.

During drought conditions, restaurants may be required to serve water to customers only if they specifically ask for it. When drought-like conditions occurred in Longview City, Washington, after the eruption of Mt. St. Helens, the district health officer recommended that food services use disposable cups, glasses, and tableware.

Replacing dishes with disposables saves water by eliminating the use of automatic dishwashers. Commercial dishwashers use between 70 and 500 gallons (2.7×10^2-1.9×10^3 L) per hour. During a drought, facilities that can't switch to disposables may be asked to close.

Great amounts of water are not used in the manufacture of paper or plastic disposables. Although making the paper requires large amounts of water, paper mills are located on rivers and streams where water is usually plentiful. The water used in making paper is treated and put back in the streams. Thus, it is not consumed; it is only borrowed and then returned. Water conservation measures at some paper mills have reduced use of water by more than 90 percent.

The watering of lawns and gardens can double the normal household water use during the summer. A standard garden hose can apply more than 6 gallons (23 litres) of water per minute. More than 620 gallons (2.4x10³ L) of water is required to apply an inch (2.5 cm) of water to 1,000 square feet (90 square metres) of lawn or garden.

In Cape Coral, Florida, a separate system of pipes will soon carry treated wastewater to homes for irrigation of lawns. Communities in eight states are changing to **Xeriscape landscaping** — landscaping that uses native, drought-tolerant plants. A lawn that is Xeriscaped uses 30-80 percent less water than a conventional lawn.

Irrigation

As the world population has increased to 5.6 billion, irrigation has become an important part of food production, but much of the water used for irrigation is wasted. Agriculture uses 70 percent of global water supplies. By improving the efficiency of irrigation, farmers will also reduce erosion, prevent loss of fertilizer and save the cost of pumping the excess water.

Farmers using conventional gravity-flow systems can reduce their need for water by 30 percent by capturing the water that normally runs off the field. Computerized irrigation systems that detect leaks and adjust flow for wind speed and soil moisture make more efficient use of water. The University of California at Davis is building a statewide computer network to provide customized irrigation plans for farmers.

The most efficient method of irrigation is a **subsurface drip irrigation system** where buried perforated plastic pipes feed water directly to the plant roots. While it can conserve huge amounts of water, few farmers are using this method of irrigation. Most farmers cannot afford to install the system that can cost $1,200 per acre, and maintenance can be a problem because the holes in the pipes tend to clog.

Farmers in Texas have cut water losses from evaporation by using **low-energy precision application** — a more efficient center-pivot irrigation system that delivers water closer to the ground. Improved irrigation systems and other water conservation measures in Texas have reduced demand for water by nearly 30 percent. Savings in energy costs and increased crop yields pay for installation of the system.

From Farm to City

With ever increasing populations, cities need more water and more food. The Metropolitan Water District of Southern California is financing irrigation conservation projects in exchange for rights to the water that is saved. This farm to city transfer of water will meet the water demands of 800,000 Californians. More efficient use of water can provide water for crops and people too.

In Arizona, cities like Tucson and Phoenix are "water ranching." In Arizona, the water rights are tied to ownership of the land. Cities are buying farms to obtain rights to their water supply. As cities purchase more irrigated farmland and divert the water from the farms

Self seeding annual larkspur are flowering in the back of this Xeriscape garden in Dallas, Texas. Perennial iris bulbs are sprouting in front.

Subsurface drip irrigation systems in orange groves like this one conserve both energy and water.

to the cities, the production of food decreases. Irrigated agriculture is expected to disappear in the area around Tucson by the year 2020.

Perhaps one day another water conservation project will send the wastewater from the cities in Arizona and California back to the farms. Sewage is mostly water — water that contains important plant nutrients.

The water cycle makes only a certain amount of water available each year. As the human population continues to expand and the demand for water grows, water conservation will be essential to ensuring a sustainable water supply.

3.6 QUESTIONS FOR STUDY AND DISCUSSION

1. Does the saying "cheaper than dirt" apply to water? Explain.

Meters

2. Explain why people who pay a flat rate or a frontage rate often waste more water than people who have water meters.
3. How does a flat rate differ from a frontage rate? Which type of rate more accurately reflects water use? Explain.
4. What method used to determine the amount of money charged for water use most accurately reflects the amount actually used? Which method encourages water conservation?
5. People living in cities usually receive a monthly water bill. Should people living in the country who get water from a private well have to pay for the water they use? Justify your opinion.
6. Give two reasons why residents and industries in Phoenix, Arizona, use much more water than residents and industries in Tucson, Arizona.

Leaky Water Systems

7. Explain why older water systems waste more water than newer water systems. Why don't cities repair old leaky water pipes?
8. Describe how toilet leaks can be detected.

Water Saving Fixtures

9. What other natural resource can be saved by saving water?
10. List three changes that can be made in plumbing to decrease the amount of water used.
11. Explain how water conservation can result in cleaner streams.

A Change in Lifestyle

12. How can water be saved in the following situations:
    A. washing dishes by hand
    B. washing dishes or clothing by machine
    C. brushing your teeth
13. List two ways that restaurants can save water.
14. Explain why the water used to wash a china dish is "consumed," but the water used to make a paper dish is "borrowed."
15. What is xeriscaping, and how might residents of Phoenix reduce their demand for water?
16. What other water conservation measures might allow people in Phoenix to maintain their conventional lawns?

Irrigation

17. In addition to the cost of the water, list two additional ways that farmers will save money by using more efficient method of irrigation.
18. Explain how more efficient irrigation systems can also save other natural resources.
19. Explain how a computerized irrigation system can reduce water use.
20. Describe the most efficient method of irrigation. Give two disadvantages of this system.
21. How does a low-energy precision application irrigation system (LEPA) reduce water use? Identify two ways that the LEPA system benefits the farmer.

From Farm to City

22. How is the Metropolitan Water District of Southern California getting additional water to meet the needs of its customers?
23. What is "water ranching"? What negative impact might it have on cities in the future?

Making More Fresh Water — Desalting the Sea

The sea is a very large reservoir. It holds 97 percent of Earth's water supply, but sea water is not fit to drink. It contains large amounts of dissolved minerals (35,000 ppm). This is 70 times the amount of salts allowed in public drinking water supplies (500 ppm).

The most abundant mineral in sea water is sodium chloride (table salt), but sea water also contains dissolved salts of calcium, magnesium, and potassium. These salts come from the weathering of rocks and erosion of the soil. Water carries the dissolved substances to the sea. When the water evaporates, it leaves the minerals behind, and the sea becomes saltier.

How to . . .

There are several methods that can be used to remove dissolved minerals from sea water. The sea water can be forced through a membrane that has openings large enough to allow water to pass through, but too small to allow the ions to pass through. This process is called **reverse osmosis**.

In another process, called **electrodialysis**, sea water flows through a container that is divided into three chambers. One chamber contains an electrode with a positive charge. Another chamber contains an electrode with a negative charge. As water passes through the chambers, ions with a positive charge are attracted to the negative electrode, and ions with a negative charge are attracted to the positive electrode. After it passes through a series of these chambers, water in the center chamber is demineralized, or desalted.

Membranes used for electrodialysis have much larger pores than membranes used for reverse osmosis. Both mineral ions and water molecules can easily pass through the membrane used in electrodialysis.

Electrodialysis works best if the water has only small amounts of salt. In Webster, South Dakota, the ground water is only twice as salty as the government standards allow. A desalting plant in Webster, uses electrodialysis to produce 250,000 gallons (9.5×10^5 L) of water a day. If the water were as salty as sea water, this process would be too expensive.

TRY TO FIND OUT

The Safe Drinking Water Act prescribes safe levels of chemicals and potential contaminants in the nation's drinking water. Does the act include regulation of contaminants that may enter your drinking water from water pipes?

After World War II, some cities such as Seattle installed asbestos cement water pipes under the streets. Asbestos is a known carcinogen.

Old water pipes are often made of lead. Lead can leach from the pipes and contaminate your drinking water. What kind of pipes carry your drinking water into your house?

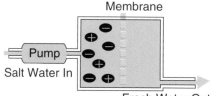

Reverse Osmosis of Sea Water

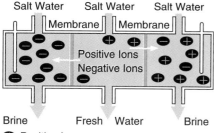

Salt Water   Salt Water   Salt Water

Positive Ions
Negative Ions

Brine   Fresh   Water   Brine

➕ Positive Ion
➖ Negative Ion

Electrodialysis of Sea Water

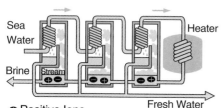

Sea
Water   Heater

Brine   Stream

Fresh Water

➕ Positive Ions
➖ Negative Ions

Flash Distillation of Sea Water

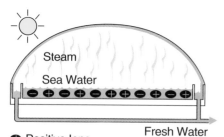

Steam

Sea Water

Fresh Water

➕ Positive Ions
➖ Negative Ions

Solar Distillation of Sea Water

In 1958, the US government built an experimental desalting plant in Freeport, Texas. Water from the Gulf of Mexico is pumped through a heater that heats it to 250°F (121°C). The super-heated water enters a series of chambers where the reduced pressure causes it to flash into steam. The steam condenses on coils of pipe that are cooled by sea water on its way to the heater. The demineralized water dripping from the pipes is collected and drained into a storage tank.

The flash distillation process removes too many minerals from sea water, and the water tastes flat. To improve the flavor, the water is mixed with salty water from local wells before it is piped to consumers. At another plant, water is run over broken coral to replace some of the minerals and give it a more pleasant taste.

Another method of distillation uses the sun's energy. Water is piped into a large flat container that is covered with a transparent plastic dome. The trapped solar energy (greenhouse effect) causes the water to evaporate. The water vapor condenses on the surface of the dome, and flows down the sides of the dome into collecting troughs. The minerals left behind are flushed away.

It Can Be Done but . . .

Although the technology exists to desalt the sea, and more than 200 desalting plants are now in operation, there are problems that must be faced. All of the processes except solar distillation require huge amounts of energy. The cost of energy makes desalted water very expensive compared to water from a fresh water supply. Solar distillation is much less expensive, but it is does not produce the large amounts of water needed in most areas.

A study by the Metropolitan Water District of Southern California showed that desalting sea water would cost five times as much as treating sewage for reuse. Communities in Southern California without adequate fresh water supplies may choose to reuse wastewater rather than desalting the sea.

Israel may have no choice. Israel is using 100 percent of the available surface and ground water, and as much as 67 percent of the water used is recycled sewage water.

It is unlikely that desalted water will ever be used to make the deserts bloom, because deserts are not located near the sea. Like the deserts, most of the farmland that requires irrigation is far from the sea and higher than sea level. The cost of pumping the desalted water to the farmland would make the water too expensive to be used for irrigation.

Another major problem with the desalting processes is disposal of the brine, or wastewater that contains large amounts of salt. A desalting plant that would produce enough water for New York City would produce 60 million tons (54 million metric tonnes) of salt each year. This represents the amount of salt normally consumed by the US every two years.

1. How much of the world's water supply is in the sea?
2. List four minerals that are dissolved in sea water. What is the source of these minerals?
3. Explain why the sea is becoming saltier.

How to . . .
4. Match the correct process with the statements below.

   Processes
   1. electrodialysis
   2. flash distillation
   3. reverse osmosis
   4. solar distillation

   Statements
   A. Ions are attracted to positive and negative electrodes.
   B. Water must be heated to 250°F (121°C).
   C. Pressure forces water through a membrane with small openings.
   D. Super-heated water passes through chambers with reduced pressure.
   E. Sea water evaporates because of the greenhouse effect.
   F. This is not a good method for desalting sea water, but is effective when used to remove smaller amounts of salt from ground water.
   G. Fresh water condenses on a dome-shaped surface.
   H. Mineral ions move through large openings in the membrane toward positively or negatively charged rods.
   I. Fresh water condenses on pipes carrying the cooler sea water.
5. List three reasons why the sea is not likely to become a major source of fresh water for most regions which need additional water supplies.
6. If you lived in a southern California community that lacked an adequate supply of fresh water, would you be in favor of building a desalination plant or a system to recycle water? Justify your position.

3.8 CASE STUDY
Water in a Bottle

Why do people buy bottled water when they can get it from the tap for practically nothing? In most cities 1,000 gallons of tap water costs less than a dollar — the price you might pay for one gallon of bottled water. In spite of the difference in cost, sales of bottled water are booming. Customers are spending nearly $3 billion a year for bottled water.

What is so special about water from a bottle, and where do companies get it? According to the geological definition, **spring water** comes to the surface naturally from underground aquifers. To be sold as "spring water" in North Carolina and several other states, it must flow from the ground, but in other states "spring water" may be pumped from a well. Most spring water is not bottled directly from a spring, but is first filtered and disinfected.

According to a report by the Environmental Policy Institute more than one-third of all bottled water comes from public water systems. Usually the water is further purified or treated

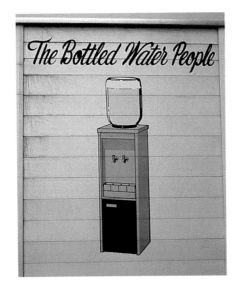

before being bottled. **Seltzer water** is water, probably from a municipal water supply, that has been filtered and carbonated. If minerals are added it is called **club soda**. **Sparkling water** also contains carbon dioxide.

There are about 700 brands of bottled water sold in the United States, and many companies sell their water under several different labels. One company markets as many as 50 brands of bottled water from the same source. Although the water is the same, prices of the different brands vary. In some states, bottlers are not required to list the source of the water.

Water from a Bottle — Is It Safe?

As water travels through the ground it is filtered, but it also leaches or dissolves certain chemicals from the soil and rocks. Some of these chemicals such as pesticides, arsenic, sodium, nitrates, and mercury may be present in amounts that are harmful. The water may also become contaminated by bacteria that cause diseases such as infectious hepatitis, cholera, typhoid fever, and dysentery.

Water and gases bubble from a famous spring, in southern France. The spring is the source of Perrier sparkling mineral water. The natural spring water contains benzene in a concentration of 10 ppm. Benzene — a colorless chemical with a distinctive odor — is a known carcinogen. Before the water is bottled and sold, it is purified and filtered.

The filtration process is usually so effective that no benzene can be detected in the water, but in January 1990, traces of benzene were discovered in the bottled water. The problem was caused by workers who failed to replace filters on schedule. Although the contamination was not a health threat, it did create an image problem for a product that was known for its purity. To protect its image, the company voluntarily recalled 160 million bottles and put extra controls in place to assure that the problem would not happen again.

After the Perrier incident, a government investigation tried to answer the question "Is bottled water a safe, consumable product?" Representing the Food and Drug Administration, Dr. Fred Shank testified that "we have no reason to question the safety of bottled water. Bottled water has a low potential for contamination or for causing sickness."

The Food and Drug Administration (FDA) regulates bottled water in much the same way that it regulates food that is transported across state lines for sale in another state. State governments regulate bottled water that is bottled and sold within the state. State regulations are more demanding than federal regulations in 14 states. Generally bottled water must meet the same EPA drinking water quality standards as tap water. Both bottled water companies and public water suppliers are required to test for bacteria at least once a week. This ensures that the water does not contain any disease-causing organisms.

The FDA also requires bottled water companies to have specific tests performed by an independent laboratory each year. Although the information is not readily available to consumers, the company must maintain records of the test results. Bottled water that does not meet the standards for drinking water quality must be labeled to notify the consumer that the water is below standard.

Water from the Tap — Is It Safe?

Tap water is not always fit to drink. Most problems with water contamination are not with public water supplies, but with private wells and small water companies. Bottled water is safer than tap water that has not been properly treated to remove contaminants.

If a farm well contains nitrates or coliform bacteria, drinking bottled water is an alternative to installing expensive filters. Some wells are contaminated with toxic organic chemicals from leaking underground gasoline tanks or landfills. Other wells are contaminated with pesticides. Removal of these chemicals may be prohibitively expensive or impossible. In that case, bottled water may be the only safe supply of water available.

The US Environmental Protection Agency estimated in 1986 that some 40 million Americans were using drinking water containing potentially hazardous levels of lead. If the level of lead in the drinking water is more than 5 parts per million, steps should be taken to reduce the level. If the lead levels cannot be reduced sufficiently, bottled water should be considered. The health benefits may justify the cost.

The only way to determine if bottled water is safer to drink than water from the faucet is to compare the results of the laboratory tests. The results of tests for substances regulated by the EPA should be available from the municipality or private water company that supplies the tap water. You may be able to obtain the test results from the company that bottles the water. If the source of tap water is a private well, the owner should have a water sample analyzed by an approved laboratory.

Is It Healthier?

The Fair Packaging and Labeling Act prohibits bottlers from making claims that bottled water is healthier than tap water. The Food and Drug Administration (FDA) requirements prohibit bottled water labels from listing the minerals the water contains because they believe that the amounts are so small that there is little if any added benefit from drinking bottled water.

WHAT DO YOU THINK?

New York City seems to be engaged in a perpetual battle with the upstate rural counties where the city's drinking water reservoirs are located. The relatively poor rural areas want to develop the land around the reservoir's watershed to bring in extra revenue. New York City must protect these watersheds from development to protect the purity of its water supply. If it does not protect the watershed, the city would be forced, by law, to build multi-billion dollar water purification plants. New York City recently purchased thousands of acres around crucial upstate watersheds. Though some concessions were granted to the rural towns, little development will be allowed near the watersheds. Do you think the water needs of New York City should take precedence over the development wishes of the rural communities?

Some buyers may feel that the minerals in bottled water make it healthier. According to the American Medical Association (AMA), there may be a slight chance that bottled water is more healthful, but any benefit would be very small when compared to exercising, eating properly, or not smoking. Some customers have switched from high calorie drinks like soda or beer to bottled water. Others drink bottled water because it is a socially acceptable alternative to alcohol.

Unless your tap water is contaminated, bottled water may offer few, if any, health or safety benefits. It may simply be draining money from your wallet. In fact some brands of bottled water may not be as healthy as your own tap water. A study by *Consumer Reports* magazine tested more than forty bottled water products as well as tap water from six different cities. While they rated tap water from New York City, New Orleans, San Francisco, and some parts of Los Angles as flawless or nearly flawless, they found the levels of arsenic and fluoride in a few brands of bottled water exceeded the federal standards.

Does It Taste Better?

Some brands of bottled water do taste better than water from some taps. Most public and private water suppliers use chlorine as a disinfectant. Most bottling companies purify the water with ozone. Ozone, like chlorine, kills bacteria. It is more expensive to use, but the water has a better flavor. Some people drink water from a bottle because they prefer the taste.

The taste of water usually depends upon the tiny amounts of minerals that have been dissolved from rocks. The only water that is likely to be free of minerals is distilled water. Distilled water is generally not purchased for drinking, but for use in batteries and steam irons where minerals could corrode the metal. Distilled water is also used in chemical laboratories where minerals might interfere with chemical reactions.

Although bottled water does not taste better than water from most deep wells, some deep wells are drilled into rock formations with a high sulfur content. The taste of sulfur may make water from these wells unacceptable for drinking. Although the sulfur can be removed by filters, some people may prefer to use the well water for other purposes and buy bottled water for drinking. It may even be a cheaper alternative in office buildings where very little water is used for drinking.

There are several reasons why more and more people are buying bottled water. For some people it is a safety issue, but for most it is a matter of taste.

1. After reading the case study "Water in a Bottle" list several reasons why some people prefer to drink bottled water instead of tap water.
2. Explain the difference between water labeled "mountain spring water" and "spring-fresh".
3. What is the source of most bottled water?
4. How does club soda differ from seltzer water?
5. What name is given to water that is naturally carbonated? Can this name be used for bottled water when carbon dioxide has been added?
6. The source of bottled water must be listed on the label. (True/False)
7. There are approximately 700 different sources of bottle water in the United States. (True/False)

Is It Safe?

8. Spring water is always pure because water is filtered as it travels through the soil. (True/False)
9. Water may become contaminated with high levels of certain chemicals dissolved from rocks as it travels through the soil. (True/False)
10. A consumer is usually correct in the assumption that bottled water is safe to drink. (True/False)
11. Bottled water is subject to more rigid water quality standards than tap water because bottled water is used only for drinking, but tap water is also used for many other purposes. (True/False)
12. The results of water quality tests do not appear on the label of bottled water. (True/False)
13. Information concerning the quality of water from a private well can be obtained from the state's department of environmental resources. (True/False)

14. The only reliable way to tell if well water is safe to drink is to have the water tested. (True/False)

Is It Healthier?

15. By comparing the labels consumers can easily tell which brand of bottled water best meets their needs. (True/False)
16. Bottled water is a good source of calcium and other minerals needed in the daily diet. (True/False)
17. According to the AMA, most consumers would probably be healthier if they spent more time exercising rather than consuming bottled water. (True/False)
18. If your lifestyle requires that you drink something from a bottle, bottled water is a healthy alternative to high calorie drinks. (True/False)
19. People living in New York City drink bottled water to avoid the high levels of lead in their tap water. (True/False)
20. Some city water supplies are healthier for you than some brands of bottled water. (True/False)

Does it Taste Better?

21. What chemical is frequently used to purify bottled water?
22. What is the advantage of using this chemical?
23. Why don't more cities use this chemical?
24. What usually determines the taste of untreated water?
25. Why does distilled water taste different from other types of bottled water?
26. Although their well water is safe, some people buy bottled water for drinking. What may be present in the well water that would make it "unfit" for drinking?
27. Under what circumstances would you buy bottled water rather than drinking water from the tap?

CASE STUDY
Fluoride in Your Water Supply —
How Much Is Enough?

Forty years ago children dreaded the dentist's drill, but today millions of children greet their parents with "Look Ma — No Cavities."

Some people living in certain parts of Colorado, and some other areas of the United States, have developed tooth enamel that is permanently discolored. In Colorado the condition became known as the **Colorado Brown Stain**. In Texas the discolored teeth were called **Texas Teeth**.

In the early 1900s a young dentist in Colorado Springs noticed that people whose teeth were stained had fewer cavities. A search began for the substance that caused the stains and might be making the teeth more resistant to decay. In 1931 the cause of the stains was found to be fluoride.

Fluorides — compounds that contain the element fluorine — are found in most foods, water supplies, and soils. Most natural water supplies contain 0.1-0.2 ppm fluoride. Natural water supplies in some areas of the Northeast contain only 0.05 ppm fluorides. In a few areas of the United States natural water supplies contain higher levels of fluoride — in some parts of the Southwest water supplies contain as much as 8 ppm of fluoride.

Scientific Studies

The proof that Colorado Brown Stain was due to high levels of fluoride came from experiments in which rats were fed fluoride or phosphate rock that contains fluoride. As expected, these rats developed the same tooth structure that is seen in children who live in areas where there are naturally high concentrations of fluoride in the water. These changes in tooth structure were not observed in rats that were in the control groups and were not fed fluoride.

Once scientists knew what caused the changes in tooth structure, they began a 10-year study of humans. The purpose of the study was to examine the effects of water supplies that had different amounts of fluoride. This study, and others that have followed, have shown that people who drink water that contains between 1.0 and 2.5 ppm fluoride from infancy to the age of 10 or 12 have fewer cavities in their permanent teeth.

Fluoride — How It Works

More recent studies have shown how fluoride works. The part of a tooth that is exposed is covered by a substance called

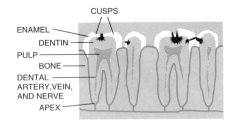

CUSPS
ENAMEL
DENTIN
PULP
BONE
DENTAL ARTERY,VEIN, AND NERVE
APEX

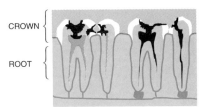

CROWN
ROOT

Dental Decay

enamel. Although tooth enamel is the hardest substance in the body, it can be dissolved by acids. Bacteria in the mouth digest sugar in the food we eat, and acids are a waste product of this digestion.

There are millions of tiny spaces between the rods that form tooth enamel. The acids seep into the tiny spaces between the rods and begin to dissolve the minerals (calcium and phosphorus) in the enamel. At the same time, more minerals move from the saliva into these spaces and begin to rebuild the enamel. Tooth enamel is constantly being dissolved and rebuilt. If the enamel is dissolved faster than it can be rebuilt the result is tooth decay or cavities.

It is believed that fluoride helps prevent cavities in the following ways.

- reducing the ability of bacteria to digest sugar and produce acid
- changing the enamel so that it is not as easily dissolved by acids
- increasing the rebuilding of enamel in areas where it has been weakened by the action of acids.

Fluoridation of Water Supplies

Studies in several states and in several other countries showed that water with 1 ppm natural fluoride reduced the level of decay by 50 to 60 percent. Since natural fluoride reduces tooth decay, scientists thought it might be possible to reduce tooth decay by adding fluoride to water supplies that have less than 1 ppm natural fluoride.

In 1945, scientists began a ten-year study of the effects of fluoride. Four cities that had low levels of fluoride in the water supply were selected as "experimental cities." Fluoride compounds were added to the water supply to increase the fluoride level to 1 ppm. Nearby cities that had low levels of fluoride in the water supply served as "control cities."

Children living in the "experimental" and the "control" cities were provided with extensive dental and medical examinations during the study. The experiment was declared a success after only five years. In all four experimental cities, the number of decayed, missing, or filled permanent teeth was reduced by 55 to 60 percent in children who were given fluoridated water from birth.

Today more than sixty percent of the nation's people live in communities with fluoridated water supplies. This means that the fluoride level of the water is adjusted to about 1 ppm. EPA regulations prohibit fluoride levels greater than 4 ppm in community water supplies. If the natural fluoride level is greater than 4 ppm, fluoride must be removed.

People living in warmer climates will be exposed to more fluoride because they are likely to drink more fluids. People living in colder climates will receive less fluoride because they are likely to drink less. When fluoride is added to a community water supply, the amount is adjusted for the temperature of the region. The recommended levels range from 1.2 ppm, for cold climates, to 0.7 ppm fluoride, for warm climates.

About 23 percent of the US population lives in rural regions without a central water supply. Studies have shown that fluoridation of the school water supply will improve the dental health of those children living in regions where the natural fluoride level is low. Children who are forming their permanent teeth receive the greatest benefits from drinking fluoridated water, but fluoride also provides adults with protection from tooth decay.

Too Much of a Good Thing — Fluorosis

Emissions from some industrial processes involving rock phosphate, that also contains fluorides, have caused widespread damage to plants and animals. A level of only 0.1 parts per billion (ppb) fluoride will cause the death of some plant species. Other plant species, including alfalfa, can change fluoride into a harmless chemical that is stored.

Fluoride can cause sickness and even the death of animals when high concentrations enter the food chain. Cattle and other animals that eat plants containing very high levels of fluorides (40 ppb) will develop **fluorosis** or fluoride poisoning. Dairy cattle are the most sensitive to fluoride poisoning. High levels of fluoride reduce the amount of milk produced and cause the animals to become lame. In the 1950s fluoride emissions from facilities processing phosphate rock led to the death of some thirty-thousand dairy cattle in Florida.

In those regions where the level of fluoride in the water supply is greater than 1.5 ppm some people develop **dental fluorosis**. Mild fluorosis causes paper white areas on teeth. Moderate to severe cases of fluorosis occur when the level of fluoride in water supplies is greater than 4 ppm. Colorado Brown Stain and pitted teeth are the evidence of moderate to severe fluorosis. Scientists disagree about whether moderate to severe dental fluorosis is a health effect or a cosmetic effect.

Large amounts of fluoride may lead to more serious health problems and possibly death. **Skeletal fluorosis** is caused by too much fluoride in the bones. The disease has several stages that begin with pain in the bones and joints. Bone spurs and fusion of vertebrae make moving the joints difficult in the advanced or crippling stage.

In regions of Asia and Africa where water is naturally fluoridated, large numbers of people have skeletal fluorosis. More than a dozen cases of skeletal fluorosis have been reported in the United States. Most victims live in areas where natural fluoride levels are greater than 2 ppm. The risk of skeletal fluorosis is difficult to determine. In addition to fluoride intake, it depends upon other nutritional factors including vitamin D, protein, calcium, and magnesium intake.

Research shows that people with dysfunctioning kidneys may have an increased risk of developing skeletal fluorosis. The National Kidney Foundation has recommended that doctors monitor the fluoride intake of kidney patients. It is also recommended that fluoride-free water be used for kidney dialysis. During a dialysis treatment, a patient is exposed to between 50 and 100 times more water than the average person consumes.

The Anti-fluoridation Campaign

Eight states have laws that require fluoridation of approved public water supplies. The Public Health Service had a goal of 95 percent fluoridation by the year 1990. Despite the fact that some 75 national health and science organizations support fluoridation of water supplies, the 95 percent goal was not met, and it is unlikely that it will be met by the year 2000.

Although ninety-nine percent of the dentists in Allentown, Pennsylvania, think the water supply should be fluoridated, the city government decided against fluoridation. The Coalition for Pure Water and other antifluoridation groups have been successful in persuading local governments in many cities to decide against fluoridation of the community water supply.

There have been reports of illness from drinking fluoridated water, but few scientific studies have found evidence to support these claims. In 1945 the newspaper in Newburgh, New York, reported that cases of nausea and skin rashes were caused by fluoridation of the drinking water. These symptoms were reported before fluoride was added to the water supply. When fluoride was added to the water supply a few weeks later, there were no complaints.

Although fluoride is poisonous in large amounts, there is no evidence that controlled fluoridation of water supplies is harmful. A 1975 study that linked fluoridation of water supplies in large cities to higher rates of cancer was discredited by the National Cancer Institute. A study reported in 1990 found four male rats receiving large doses (79 ppm) of fluoride in their drinking water developed a rare form of bone cancer. None of the female rats and none of the mice in the study developed bone cancer.

Animal studies that have linked fluoride to birth defects and infertility have involved far higher doses of fluoride that humans are exposed to. Some critics question the value of high-dose cancer tests in animals. A person would have to consume 20,000 gallons of water a day to consume the amount of fluoride in the water given to the mice in the cancer study.

Health studies of people who have lived their entire lives in areas that have high levels of fluoride in the water supply have shown no differences in bone cancer. The National Research Council says there is no credible evidence that fluoride causes cancer, kidney disease, or birth defects. Yet some people remain opposed to fluoridation. The Coalition for Pure Water is opposed to fluoridation because they feel it is a violation of individual rights to "medicate" the water supply.

Some people who have supported fluoridation are becoming concerned that fluoridation of water supplies is introducing too much fluoride into the food chain. Phosphate fertilizers and fluoridated water increase the amount of fluoride in food. If fruit juice, infant formula, and baby foods are made with fluoridated water, children under the age of two will receive more fluoride than the amount recommended by the American Dental Association.

Other Ways to Get Fluoride

It is a fact that when fluoride is available during the first ten to fifteen years of life, tooth enamel will become more resistant to acids. It is also a fact that fluoridation of the community water supply is the most effective and the least expensive way of providing fluoride to everyone. According to the American Dental Association, children living in communities with fluoride-adjusted water have 17 to 40 percent fewer cavities than children living in communities without fluoridated water. But fluoridation of the water supply is not the only means of increasing the fluoride available to the tooth enamel.

Some toothpastes contain 1000 ppm fluoride. According to the American Dental Association (ADA), toothpaste with fluoride is effective in preventing tooth decay. Brands of toothpaste that have been proven effective are given the Seal of Acceptance of the American Dental Association.

Many schools have fluoride mouth rinse programs that have proved effective. The dentist or dental hygienist may apply a fluoride solution or gel to the teeth. They may also prescribe fluoride solutions or tablets for use at home.

Swallowing too much fluoride can result in death. The ADA has recommended that manufacturers limit the size of packages containing fluoride. This could prevent the accidental death of a child.

Dr. Horowitz, of the National Institute for Dental Research, suggests that children under five years old not be given fluoride mouth rinses, and that they be given only a pea-sized amount of fluoride toothpaste. Daily swallowing of fluoride rinses or toothpaste could lead to dental fluorosis. By the time the symptoms appear, the changes in the tooth structure are permanent.

Fluoride is commonly found in baby vitamins. Dr. Horowitz suggests that infants getting one bottle of fluoridated water or formula made with fluoridated water should not be given any fluoride supplements. Children older than six are not likely to develop dental fluorosis.

A National Research Council committee, studying the effects of fluoride, reported that it was unable to determine the true exposure of Americans to fluoride because the chemical is present in foods, beverages, and a variety of dental products. The committee recommended continued study to determine if lifetime exposure to low levels of fluoride could be harmful.

THINK ABOUT IT

Some arid regions of California have been planted in water-loving rice. Though it's increasingly difficult to provide water for its huge human population, California appropriates rice farmers enormous quantities of irrigation water so they can grow this crop. What are the environmental impacts of growing rice in California?

3.9 QUESTIONS FOR STUDY AND DISCUSSION

1. Explain why some children who were born and raised in Texas and Colorado developed teeth that were stained.
2. Identify the region of the US having high levels of fluoride.

Scientific Studies

3. Describe the difference in treatment between the rats in the experimental group and the rats in the control group.
4. What conclusion was drawn from the study of human consumption of naturally fluoridated water supplies?
5. Drinking fluoridated water will reduce cavities in permanent teeth if it is consumed during these years: _____ to _____.

Fluoride-How It Works

6. The part of the tooth affected by fluoride is the _____.
7. Describe the structure of tooth enamel and explain how a cavity is formed.
8. List three ways that fluoride helps to prevent cavities.

Fluoridation of Water Supplies

9. Fluoride is sometimes added to water supplies when the natural level is less than _____ ppm.

10. What were the results of the fluoridation study begun in 1945?
11. What percent of people in the United States live in communities with fluoridated water supplies?
12. What is the maximum level of fluoride that is permitted in a community water supply?
13. What is the recommended level of fluoride in the water supply of Phoenix, Arizona? in Portland, Maine? in your city? Why do the recommended levels differ?

Too Much of a Good Thing — Fluorosis

14. Identify the source of fluoride that caused fluorosis in cattle in Florida. Describe the changes that occur in cattle that develop fluorosis.
15. Describe the changes that may occur in children who live in areas with more than 1.5-2.0 ppm fluoride in the water supply.
16. Describe the changes that occur in children's teeth who drink water with a fluoride level greater than 4 ppm.
17. What other health effects are seen in people who drink water with naturally high levels of fluoride? Why is it difficult to determine the risk of this condition?
18. What are the recommendations of the National Kidney Foundation?

19. State the position of the following groups concerning the issue of fluoridation of public water supplies:
    A. American Dental Association
    B. Coalition for Pure Water
    C. Public Health Service
20. Which of the following symptoms may be observed in people who live in areas that have 5-8 ppm fluoride in their water supply?
    bone spurs   higher rates of cancer
    nausea   skin rashes
21. What were the results of research studying the link between fluoride and cancer?
22. Why are some people who once supported fluoridation becoming concerned about fluoridation?

Other Ways to Get Fluoride
23. List five ways in which fluoride is available.
24. Which of these ways of getting fluoride is the most effective and least expensive?
25. Why shouldn't children under five years of age be given fluoride mouth rinses?
26. Should babies that live in areas with fluoridated water supplies be given vitamin drops with fluoride?
27. Is your community water supply fluoridated? Do you think that it should be? Explain why you feel this way.

Review Question
28. Match the level of fluoride to the statements on the left. One answer will be used twice:

Statements

A. This level found is in most natural water supplies.
B. This level is found in the water supplies of some southwestern states.
C. Natural fluoridation within this range has been shown to reduce the number of cavaties in permanent teeth.
D. This level is considered the best range for community water supplies.
E. This amount of fluoride is found in some toothpastes.
F. This level will cause the death of some very sensitive plants.
G. If present in plants, this level will cause fluorosis in cattle.
H. This level will cause some mild cases of dental fluorosis.
I. Levels greater than this cause cases of severe dental fluorosis and may cause skeletal fluorosis.
J. This is the maximum amount of fluoride allowed in drinking water by EPA standards

Level of Fluoride

1. < 1 ppm
2. 0.1-0.2 ppm
3. 1.5 ppm
4. 4 ppm
5. 8 ppm
6. 0.7-1.2 ppm
7. 1.0-2.5 ppm
8. 40 ppm
9. 1,000 ppm

Satellite Composite Image of the Sun

You are looking at a composite image of the Sun. The energy of some parts of the Sun are hotter or more energetic. This difference in energy is indicated by the spotty areas covering the Sun.

Streaming off the edge of the Sun is the solar corona. The particles forming the corona give off light that can only be seen on Earth during an eclipse. The solar corona is primarily composed of helium ions.

Energy — The Rest of the Story

1.1

Life depends upon a constant flow of energy. Unit I examined energy as it flows through food chains in an ecosystem, but that is only part of the story. Humans, at least in some societies, have become dependent upon tremendous amounts of matter and energy to maintain a "comfortable" life style.

Like other animals, we depend upon the sun's energy to produce our food. But in our modern agricultural society, additional energy is needed to plant, grow, harvest, store, transport, prepare, and cook our food. Growing and preparing the food is much easier now than it once was. The grower uses mechanical equipment for planting and harvesting. Once the food reaches the kitchen, the cook stores it in the refrigerator, peels it with an electric peeler, chops it in the food processor, heats it in the microwave, and afterwards puts the dishes in the dishwasher. We depend upon many labor-saving devices to make our life easier — to do our work for us. All of these devices consume energy.

It's the Law

Energy is the ability to do work, and work is the movement of matter. After many observations of energy, scientists made two statements or "laws" that describe what happens to energy. The first law states: Energy can not be created or destroyed, but it can be changed in form. This is sometimes called the law of Conservation of Energy.

Light energy can be changed into chemical energy. The energy in chemical compounds can be changed into heat energy. Heat energy can be changed into mechanical energy, and mechanical energy can be changed into electrical energy. These are just some of the changes that occur. You can think of others.

The second energy law states: When energy is changed from one form to another, some of the usable energy is lost. In other words, some of the energy cannot do any work. This energy is usually in the form of heat that cannot be recovered and may become a pollutant in our environment. (See Unit V Case Study 1.4 "Brunner Island and Other Solutions To Thermal Pollution.")

Hunter-gatherers had modest energy needs that were easily met by burning wood. Since the days of the earliest human societies, energy needs have steadily increased. Consider the following chart indicating the amount of energy, in kilojoules (KJ) used daily, on average, by each person in the world throughout human history.

Societies

Hunter-gatherer	21 000 KJ
Early agricultural	50 000 KJ
Pre-industrial agricultural	104 000 KJ
Post-industrial agricultural	290 000 KJ
Modern industrial	766 000 KJ

As developing countries industrialize, what can you predict will happen to the amount of energy used by each person? Think about what worldwide industrialization may mean for societies dependent on fossil fuels.

The energy efficiency of an invention is a measure of the amount of energy it can convert to useful work. A model with a higher energy efficiency will require less fuel to do the same amount of work. The energy efficiencies of several important inventions are shown in the table below:

Net Energy Efficiency of Some Common Inventions			
Steam Locomotive	8%	Diesel Locomotive	35%
Internal Combustion Engine	10%	Fuel Cell (electric vehicle)	60%
Oil Furnace	53%	Wood Stove (high efficiency)	26%
Natural Gas Furnace	70%	Natural Gas Furnace (high efficiency)	84%
Electric Heat from Coal-fired Plant	25%	Electric Heat from Nuclear Plant	14%
Incandescent Lamp	5%	Fluorescent Lamp	22%

A Little History

Animals and slaves provided most of the energy to do the work their masters required in early societies. By the fourth century, the water-wheel had been developed and was mainly used for grinding grains. Later it supplied the power for machines that crushed ore, pumped air, sawed wood, and washed clothes.

The invention of the water-powered saw in the thirteenth century helped supply the wood required by the increasing population and the growing industries in Europe. Soon the forests in Europe were devastated and Europeans turned to coal as a source of energy. Later the water-powered saw was used to cut the logs taken from forests in the American colonies.

The waterwheel and the windmill were the major sources of energy for Europe's Industrial Revolution. The location of the factories and cities was determined by the location of these energy sources. Waterwheels were also an important source of energy for industry in early America.

1776 Declaration of Independence. Most people burned wood for heating and cooking. Travel was by horse or on foot. The major use of coal was in the making of cannons. Because of the war against England, coal could no longer be imported from England and Nova Scotia, and there was a push for domestic mining.

Wood became more expensive as trees disappeared, and people turned to coal as the source of energy to heat their homes. Underground water in the coal mines often prevented the digging of deep deposits of coal. In 1698 a patent was granted to Thomas Savery for an engine that could pump water from the mines. Savery's wood-burning steam engine changed heat energy into the mechanical energy needed to move the water.

1786 — Fitch's Steamboat had a wood-burning boiler that powered mechanical oars.

1807 — Fulton's "Clermont" made a 150-mile (240 km) trip up the Hudson River. The trip took 32 hours, but it won support for the wood-burning steamboat.

1830 — In a race between the "Tom Thumb" steam locomotive and a horse-drawn rail car, the horse won.

1868 — Steam engines and waterwheels are equally important as power source for industry.

Steamboat

The first new source of power since the invention of the windmill 600 years earlier was the invention of the steam engine. Later inventors produced more powerful steam engines, and by the late 1800s steam engines had replaced the waterwheel as the major source of power for industry. The new steam engines burned coal, and coal quickly replaced wood as the major source of energy.

On the farm, steam engines were used to power threshing machines, and windmills were used to pump water. But horses, mules, and humans supplied most of the energy for agriculture until after World War I. More than 25 million horses and mules supplied the power for agriculture in 1918. One fourth of the land being cultivated was used to produce feed for the animals. As tractors replaced horses, farmers could grow more food for people. With less human power needed on the farm, the migration of people from farm to city began.

The discovery of new energy sources and the development of the technology to make use of them was necessary for the development of our modern industrial and agricultural society. Modern agriculture requires huge inputs of energy from other off-the-farm sources. This energy is needed to manufacture and transport chemical fertilizers and pesticides, to pump water for irrigation, and to power the machines that have replaced the animals.

As the cities and industries grew, so did the demand for energy and the pollution produced by its use. People migrated from the dirty cities to the suburbs. As the miles between home and work increased, so did the energy required for transportation. The economy (industrial growth) of the United States and the "comfortable" life style of its people have been built upon an abundant — seemingly endless — supply of inexpensive energy.

In 1952, President Truman's Materials Policy Commission warned that United States would be dependent upon oil from the Middle East by the 1970s. Although few people paid any attention, the prediction that had been made by President Truman's administration was correct. By the 1970s, with only 6 percent of the world's population, more than one third of the world's energy was consumed by the United States. Much of this energy was imported oil.

By the 1990s, the United States had only 5 percent of the world's population and consumed 25 percent of the energy used by the world's population. The nation's dependence on foreign oil became quite obvious during the Arab Oil Embargo in the 1970s and the Persian Gulf War.

1. Make a list of the food served the last time your family ate dinner together. Identify the types of energy that were required and describe how they were used to produce and prepare the dinner.

It's the Law

2. Define the following words:
   energy
   energy efficiency
   work

3. Energy cannot be created or destroyed, and it can't be recycled. Explain why.

4. Give an example of each of the following changes:
   A. light energy to chemical energy
   B. chemical energy to mechanical energy
   C. mechanical energy to electrical energy
   D. mechanical energy to heat energy

5. Identify the form energy is usually in when it is "lost" (can no longer be used to do work).

6. In each of the following pairs, identify the invention that is more energy efficient.
   A. gas furnace — oil furnace
   B. fuel cell — internal combustion engine
   C. steam locomotive — diesel locomotive
   D. incandescent lamp — fluorescent lamp
   E. wood stove — oil furnace
   F. nuclear power plant — coal fired power plant

A Little History

7. Identify the first form of technology that reduced the amount of human labor needed to saw wood and grind grain. Describe other ways in which this technology was later used.

8. Identify the major source of energy used to heat homes in 1776 and identify the source which had replaced it by 1900.

9. Identify the major sources of energy used by factories during Europe's Industrial Revolution. What invention replaced these sources as the major source of energy for industry?

10. Explain how the steam-engine was first used in the mining of coal, and identify the energy source used to produce steam. Identify the agricultural invention that was powered by the steam engine.

11. List as many reasons as you can that might explain why the inventors of later models of the steam engine designed the engine to burn coal instead of wood.

12. Identify the major sources of energy used on farms prior to World War I.

13. Identify the invention that replaced the horse as the major source of energy on farms. Give two reasons why fewer farmers are needed today than were needed when horses were the major source of energy on the farm.

14. Give examples of how farmers depend upon the oil driller and the coal miner.

15. What is your home address? What is the work address of either your mother or father? Do you think you would live where you live now if energy supplies were more limited and/or more expensive?

16. The US has only ____ % of the world's population, but is using ____ % of the energy consumed. Do you think people in the US are "energy hogs"?

17. It has been estimated that people living in the suburbs use 42% more energy than people living in the city. List as many reasons as you can why the demand for energy is greater in the suburbs.

18. President Truman's administration predicted that we would:
    A. develop the technology for renewable energy sources by the 1970s.
    B. become dependent upon oil from the Middle East by the 1970s.
    C. have a major accident at a nuclear power plant during the 1970s.

1.2 Fossil Fuels — Energy for a Nation

There was an energy crisis in the 1970s. Shortages of gasoline meant car owners often sat in line at the service station. A natural gas shortage caused schools and industries to shut down. The price of gasoline and fuel oil began a steep climb. In 1980 OPEC set the price of crude oil at $32.00 a barrel. A barrel of crude oil had cost only $3.00 in 1973. What was happening? Were we running out of fuel?

There was a flurry of activity in Washington, D.C. An Energy Research and Development Administration was established. Congress passed the Energy Policy and Conservation Act and the Solar Heating and Cooling Demonstration Act. The speed limit on interstate highways was reduced to 55 miles (88 km) per hour. The federal government promoted energy efficient technology.

Car manufacturers were required to develop cars that would get better gas mileage. Manufacturers of appliances were required to label certain electrical appliances with an **EnergyGuide** that provides the information needed to compare the energy efficiency of different models. Homeowners were allowed tax breaks for making their homes more energy efficient.

Then during the 1980s the lines at service stations disappeared, and the prices of gasoline and fuel oil declined. Congress even voted to allow states to increase the speed limit on interstate highways. Does this mean that our energy problems are over? No. Another crisis can occur any time there is an interruption in the supply of any energy source, especially oil.

The Changing American Scene

A **renewable resource** is one that is produced at least at the same rate it is used. In 1850 almost all energy was derived from renewable sources — wood, wind, and water. But our demand for wood became greater than nature's ability to replace it. In effect, wood became a nonrenewable resource. Today most of the energy we use is derived from nonrenewable fossil fuels — oil, natural gas, and coal. For a long time it seemed that there was an endless supply of inexpensive energy, and the demand steadily increased.

DID YOU KNOW?

As early as 1802, the Italians used natural gas in street lamps to light the streets of Genoa.

DID YOU KNOW?

Each year, about 3.2 million metric tonnes of oil spew into the world's oceans. About 50 percent of this oil comes from natural seepage from offshore deposits.

Coal is an important fuel for the production of electricity. The giant machines which remove the coal from deep beneath the soil can quickly destroy the environment. But new laws force coal companies to restore the land.

By 1958 our need for energy resources was greater than our nation could supply. We became dependent upon imported oil. By 1973 the United States was importing 35 percent of the petroleum used. Then the Arab oil-producing countries shut off all shipments of oil to the United States — the **Arab Oil Embargo**. Government officials began making policy changes to try to decrease our dependence on foreign oil. As a result, the amount of petroleum imported in 1983 was 7 percent less than in 1973.

Consumption of oil in the United States has increased dramatically since 1985, but our production has declined since 1986. As a result, the United States remains the world's largest importer of petroleum. In 1985 the United States imported 4.3 million barrels of oil a day. In 1990 the U.S. imported about 8 million barrels of oil a day.

Two-thirds of the world's proven and easily accessible oil reserves are located in the region surrounding the Persian Gulf. The political stability of this region is important to the United States, Japan, and other countries that have become dependent upon imported petroleum. The Persian Gulf is the major supplier of imported oil to the United States. Without oil imported from the Middle East, the United States would not have enough oil to meet the demand.

On August 2, 1990, Iraq invaded Kuwait. Armed forces were sent to the Persian Gulf, in part to protect the free flow of oil. Political disputes may once again interfere with the movement of oil tankers and create temporary shortages. But politics and the immediate future should not be our only concern. Petroleum is a fossil fuel, and fossil fuels are nonrenewable resources. Combustion of fossil fuels creates pollution. Its time we began to face the environmental impacts as well as the political issues.

It Began a Long Time Ago

Millions of years ago giant ferns and trees grew in great swamps that covered much of Earth. As the plants died and fell into the water, they formed layers of partially decayed plant material called **peat**. Earth's movements caused the swamps to sink, and they were covered with layers of mud, silt, sand, and water. The weight of the water and sediments created heat and pressure that changed the peat into coal. **Coal** refers to any black or brown rock that contains hydrocarbons formed from decayed plants. The mud, silt, and sand deposits were changed into other rocks such as sandstone or shale.

When coal is first formed from peat, it is very soft and crumbles easily. This soft coal is called **lignite**. The formation of lignite may take more than one million years. Most of the lignite in the United States is in North and South Dakota, Montana and Texas. Lignite is less than 40 percent carbon, and its heat content is lower than the heat content of other coals.

Subbituminous, with a carbon content between 40 and 60 percent, has a higher heat content than lignite. Large deposits of this coal are found in the western states, especially Montana and Wyoming. **Bituminous coal**, sometimes called soft coal, is formed when more heat and pressure are placed on lignite. The formation of bituminous coal may take more than 100 million years. Its carbon content is between 60 and 80 percent, thus it has a greater heat content than subbituminous. Most of the coal in the United States is bituminous coal.

More intense heat and pressure change bituminous coal into **anthracite**, or hard coal. Anthracite has the highest percentage of carbon (80-98 percent). Thus it has the highest heating value. Nearly all of the anthracite in the United States is in Pennsylvania, although some small deposits exist in other states.

Layers of plant material 3 to 7 feet (0.9-2.1 meters) thick produced a one-foot (0.3 meter) thick seam of bituminous coal. In some places where coal-forming swamps formed over buried swamps, several seams of coal were formed. Some seams are more than 400 feet (120 meters) thick.

Other fossil fuels: As plants and animals living in the ancient seas died, they drifted down to the bottom. Here they mixed with sand, mud, and silt. Layers of sandstone, shale, and limestone that were rich in organic matter (the decayed remains) were formed. As the older layers were buried deeper and deeper, the heat and pressure caused chemical changes. Mixtures of hydrocarbons — natural gas and petroleum — were formed from the organic matter.

The formation of petroleum and natural gas does not always result in deposits that can be found and recovered. The first requirement is a source rock. A **source rock** is a rock that is rich in organic matter. Second, sufficient heat and pressure must be present for a period of time that allows the organic matter to be changed into hydrocarbons.

The oil and gas must then move into a reservoir rock. A **reservoir rock** is a rock that contains many tiny pores with connecting passageways through which the oil and gas can move. A **trap**, or rock without pores, forms a dam or a lid that keeps the oil and gas from escaping. This lid must be tightly sealed in order for oil and gases to collect in the reservoir.

Finding these rock formations is the job of a petroleum scientist. Before drilling, these scientists use instruments that measure gravity, magnetic properties, and sound waves to determine what is beneath Earth's surface. A deposit of oil or gas that can economically be recovered with present technology is called a **reserve**. The process of selecting the site and drilling the well may cost more than $10 million. Depending on the location and the rock structure, well drilling may take a few weeks or several months. Only one out of three wells drilled in areas with known gas deposits yields gas.

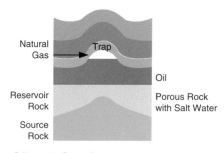

Oil and Gas Deposits

NATURAL GAS

Supply and Demand: Nearly 80 percent of the known natural gas reserves in the world are owned by the former countries of the Soviet Union (59 percent) and Iran (20 percent). The United States has 6 percent of the world's reserves. Most of the natural gas in the US lies beneath five states — Kansas, Oklahoma, Louisiana, Texas, and New Mexico. At the current rate of consumption, proven reserves are expected to last 15 years.

For years natural gas was considered worthless and burned off at the oil well. Natural gas supplies about 23 percent of the nation's energy. Now demand for natural gas is increasing. Improved drilling technology and federal tax incentives increased the production of natural gas in 1990. An additional 1300 new wells were producing gas. About 8 percent of the natural gas used in the US is imported, mainly from Canada. There are plans to increase gas imports. Liquefied natural gas (LNG) can be transported from other countries in tankers.

- **Industrial:** An amount of natural gas equal to the amount used to heat a home all year is required to manufacture the parts needed to make one automobile. Natural gas is used by the food industry to pasteurize milk and bake bread. Textile mills use the heat from natural gas to pre-shrink cloth, and paper companies use it to dry paper. By-products of natural gas are used to make many products including synthetic fibers, ink, photographic film, adhesives, explosives, antifreeze, synthetic rubber, and plastics. Agriculture uses vast quantities of natural gas to make fertilizer containing nitrogen.
- **Residential:** More than 45 million households depend upon natural gas. Most of the gas used in the home is for space heating. Other uses include water heating, cooking, and clothes drying.
- **Electricity:** The use of natural gas for the production of electricity is expected to increase during the 1990s. Electrical power plants are installing gas-fired turbines to increase their capacity to generate electricity at peak periods. Using natural gas allows power plants to increase production of electricity without installing expensive air pollution controls.
- **Commercial**: Most of the natural gas is used for heating and cooling office buildings, apartments, and stores. The rest is used for cooking.
- **Transportation**: In Oklahoma, United Parcel Service has converted 140 delivery trucks to run on compressed natural gas (CNG). The delivery route of vehicles converted to CNG must be less than 70 miles (112 km). Natural gas is a clean-fuel alternative to gasoline. The use of natural gas in fleet of vehicles can help urban areas meet air quality standards.

Processing: As it comes from the well, natural gas is mostly methane, but it also contains small amounts of other hydrocarbons, such as propane and butane, water vapor, and other elements, including sulfur. Before it is shipped to the customer, the gas is processed to remove these impurities.

Transportation: By weight, natural gas produces 50 percent more heat energy than coal, and 30 percent more than oil. This means that less energy is used to transport each unit of energy. An underground network of pipes delivers natural gas to customers across the nation. Pipelines are the most efficient means of transport because it requires the least amount of energy to move the gas.

Where pipelines don't exist, natural gas can be changed to a liquid by compressing and cooling it to -161°C (-260°F). This reduces its volume by 615 times. It is then transported in insulated tanker ships or trucks. Some liquefied natural gas (LGN) is imported from Africa. This method is much more hazardous and expensive than pipeline transport.

Environment and Health: Natural gas is the cleanest-burning fossil fuel. It produces much smaller quantities of pollutants than coal or oil. It can be burned without installing expensive air pollution controls. This makes it an ideal fuel for heating homes. The ability to control the flame makes natural gas the perfect fuel for cooking and for other industrial processes where temperature control is important.

Natural gas has no odor or color. As a safety precaution, a chemical is mixed with the gas to create an odor similar to the smell of rotten eggs. This allows gas leaks to be detected. Although the risk of a gas leak is small, leaking gas is dangerous. The vapors may be ignited by a spark, and the resulting explosion and fire are destructive and sometimes deadly.

The Future: New technology is being used to increase the yield from existing wells, and a $10 billion pipeline is being built to transport gas from wells to the densely populated areas.

Proven reserves in the US are estimated to be 165 trillion cubic feet. At the current rate of use, this is enough to meet demands for approximately 15 years. This number will change as more reserves are discovered and improved technology increases the ability to recover gas. The search for reserves has intensified. Using new drilling methods natural gas can now be recovered from some coal deposits.

PETROLEUM (CRUDE OIL)

Supply and Demand: Two-thirds of the world's proven oil reserves are located in the region surrounding the Persian Gulf. Other important reserves are located in Latin America, countries in the former Soviet Union, Africa, and North America.

Oil supplies about 40 percent of the U.S. energy needs. In 1990 the US used nearly 17 million barrels a day, but produced only 7.3 million barrels. The additional oil was imported. Although the consumption of oil declined in the 1980s, the demand for oil is once

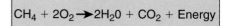

$$CH_4 + 2O_2 \rightarrow 2H_2O + CO_2 + Energy$$

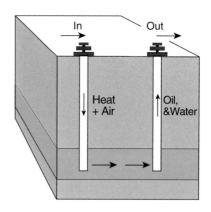

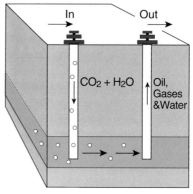

Secondary Recovery Methods

again increasing. The amount of oil imported has increased dramatically since 1985.

Products made from crude oil, gasoline, and diesel provide the energy for most methods of transportation. Crude oil also provides the raw materials used to make many products including:

deodorants	panty hose	rugs	video cassettes
lipstick	house paint	detergent	sun glasses
aspirins	bubble gum	shampoo	perfumes
soft contact lenses	credit cards	shoes	golf balls

Production: When a well is drilled, the petroleum is usually under pressure, and it may flow from the well without being pumped. When the well cannot flow by itself, pumps bring the oil to the surface.

Technology has been developed to remove more of the oil from the rock. Methods that allow more oil to be removed are called **secondary recovery methods**. In one method, acid is injected into the well to dissolve channels in the rock. In another method, fluids are pumped into the well under high pressure to fracture the rock. A third method involves pumping water, carbon dioxide, or other gases into the well to force the oil toward the opening. A fourth method uses solvents to dissolve the oil from the rock. Still other methods involve heating the oil so that it flows more freely. Each of these methods is expensive, but they may allow as much as 80 percent of the oil to be recovered.

Processing: The processing of crude oil begins with distillation. The crude oil is heated to 650°F (340°C). As the oil is heated, the vapors pass through a series of perforated trays in a fractionating tower. The different hydrocarbons condense at different temperatures. The lighter compounds condense near the top of the tower, and the heaviest compounds condense at the bottom of the tower.

An offshore oil rig in the Gulf of Mexico. A constant threat to the environment, oil wells and tankers carrying oil are essential to our way of life.

Simplified Diagram of an ▶
Oil Refinery

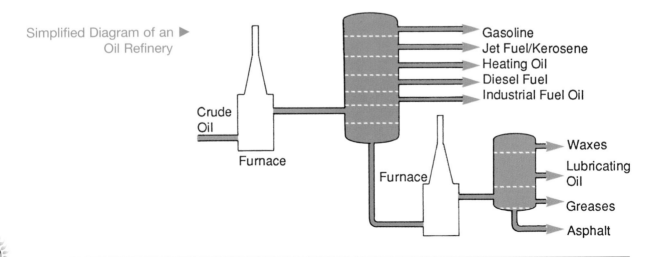

Some of the chemicals separated by distillation require further processing. By rearranging the atoms of molecules, more useful chemicals can be produced. More than 10,000 products are produced from the chemicals removed from crude oil and natural gas. The processes that are used to separate crude oil into its parts and to produce petroleum products are called **refining**.

In the production of gasoline, smaller molecules are combined to make larger ones. This produces the high octane fuel needed for automobiles. Modern refineries use chemicals called **catalysts** to speed up these chemical reactions. Catalysts allow refineries to produce gasoline 7,000 times faster than they could by the older methods.

Transportation: Crude oil may be transported to the refinery through pipelines or by tanker. The method of transporting products from the refinery is determined by their destination. Pipelines are the most energy efficient means of transport, and are used to transport 60 percent of the crude oil and petroleum products.

Ships and barges transport another one-third of the supply. Transport by ship or barge is more efficient than railroads, but railroads can move the oil faster and transport it to locations that are not near waterways. Tank trucks require four times more energy to transport fuels than that used by railroads. They are used for short distance hauls in areas without access to railroads.

Environment and Health: A large quantity of oil is spilled into the environment each year from shipping, oil drilling operations, and pipeline breaks. Although major oil spills do not occur often, when they do occur they cause massive kills of marine animals that live near the shore. The damage to wildlife is most easily seen by observing the birds that cannot swim or fly. When their feathers become matted with oil they cannot keep themselves warm.

Oil spills may also affect water supplies. It was a bitterly cold January day when a storage tank holding 3.85 million gallons (1.8x 10^7 L) of diesel fuel burst at the Ashland Oil Company near Pittsburgh. About 1 million gallons (4.5 million litres) of oil flowed over the dike, and through a sewer into the Monongahela River. Some 23,000 Pittsburgh residents were without water when water companies closed their intake valves. The extremely cold weather hampered cleanup efforts, and the huge oil slick moved down the Ohio River affecting wildlife and communities along the river.

Burning oil produces less pollution than the burning of coal, but oil is not a clean fuel. The automobile is the major source of air pollution produced by the burning of petroleum. As older cars are replaced by newer models with better pollution controls, the pollution levels are being reduced. Cleaner fuels are being tested in urban areas that do not meet air quality standards.

Future: Rock formations in the US have been extensively studied by the US Geological Survey. Most experts agree that the shallow oil and gas reservoirs have already been found, and the prospects for finding large reserves of oil are not good. Production of oil in the US has declined

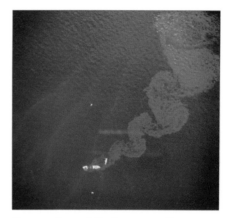

Image from Nimbus weather satellite showing an oil spill at sea.

Nature can clean up an oil spill without human intervention. When crude oil spills into the sea, about 25 percent of it (the more volatile components) will evaporate within 3 months. About 60 percent of the less volatile components are lighter than water and float on the surface. Over a period of several months, this light oil will be eaten by natural bacteria. The remaining heavy oil forms globs that sink to the bottom where they decompose very slowly. Since oil spills will be remedied eventually by nature, why are some people so concerned about, quick to respond to, and anxious to clean up oil spills?

since 1986. Worldwide production is increasing, but new reserves being discovered are not sufficient to replace the oil being consumed.

As of 1982 oil companies had drilled 85,800 wells in the United States. Nearly 8,000 of these were **wildcat wells**. A **wildcat well** is a well drilled in an unexplored area. More than 6,500 of the wildcat wells were dry. Only 755 of the wells produced enough oil to pump. The chance of finding a well that will be productive in an unexplored area is less than 10 percent.

Oil companies recently drilled for oil in an unexplored area near Alaska's Prudhoe Bay oil fields. Sound wave evidence suggested that there was a large reservoir of oil — maybe as much as 1.5 billion barrels. Rocks were stained with oil. After drilling for 13 months, at a depth of 1.5 miles (2.4x103 m), drillers found water but no oil. At one time the reservoir contained oil, but there was no trap and the oil had escaped. No one knows what happened to the oil. The dry hole cost the oil companies $1.7 billion.

Our need for oil will continue to increase, even with efforts to conserve. It will become necessary to drill deeper, use secondary recovery methods, and turn to other forms of energy. The American Petroleum Institute suggests that the government should permit exploration and development of oil and gas reserves in protected areas such as National Parks and National Wilderness Areas. At least for now, the government refuses. Even if these protected lands were explored and reserves were found, it will not change the fact that someday there will be no more oil.

When will we run out of oil? It depends on how much we use and what we're willing to pay. We won't suddenly run out of oil in the same way that you might run out of milk. An oil well is not like a carton of milk that can be emptied all at once. Only about 10 percent of the oil remaining in the reserve can be recovered each year. Each year the amount of oil pumped declines until it no longer produces enough oil to pay for pumping, and the oil company shuts down the well. The secondary recovery techniques may be used to recover more oil when oil prices rise.

As the price of oil increases, users begin to look for cheaper alternatives. For some uses, the most abundant and least expensive fossil fuel is coal.

COAL

Supply and Demand: Coal is our most abundant fossil fuel. Nearly seventy-five percent of all known coal reserves are in three regions — the United States, countries of the former Soviet Union, and China. The United States has 12 percent of the world's coal reserves. The US is the largest exporter of coal. The country exports over 100 million tons of coal each year.

In 1990, more than 1 billion tons of coal was mined to supply 22 percent of the energy used in the United States. Coal is used mainly for the generation of electricity. In 1990, 55 percent of the nation's electricity was produced at steam-turbine plants that burn bituminous coal. Coal is also used by industries as a source of heat for manufacturing processes. As the price of natural gas and crude oil increased, more power plants and industries switched to coal.

Some coal is used for heating homes, offices, and factories. Because it is the cleanest-burning, anthracite is preferred for heating homes. Since anthracite is more expensive, factories and commercial buildings often use bituminous coal. Subbituminous and lignite must be burned in large amounts because of their lower heat content. They are used for production of electricity or manufacturing processes. Lignite is also used to produce coal gases and liquids.

Steel mills heat bituminous coal to about 2000°F (1100°C) in air-tight ovens. Without oxygen the coal does not burn, but the heat changes some of the solids into gases. The remaining solid mass that is almost pure carbon is called **coke**. The coke is burned with iron ore and limestone to produce the iron needed for making steel. When the coal cools, some of the gases condense to form ammonia (NH_3) that is used in fertilizer. Other byproducts are used to make dyes, drugs, synthetic fibers and film, adhesives, insecticides, varnish, plastics, and other products. The gases that remain are burned to provide heat for the coke making process.

Mining: Most coal is produced from two major types of mining — surface and underground. Surface mining is safer, less expensive, and allows more coal to be recovered than underground mining.

Most surface mining is **strip mining** in which the soil and rock which lie over the coal deposit are removed by huge earth moving machines. In the past, strip mining often left pits that were ugly and useless. A law passed in 1977 requires coal companies to restore all land that is strip mined.

The process of restoring the land to the condition that existed before mining is called **reclamation**. Before mining begins, scientists study the soil, plants, wildlife, and water resources. When mining begins, the topsoil is removed and stored in piles that are graded and planted to prevent erosion. After the coal is dug, and the pits are filled with rock, the soil is replaced and prepared for planting. If necessary, the land is irrigated. Reclaimed land can be used for lakes or reservoirs, agriculture, or recreation. A special tax, paid on each ton of coal produced is used to help restore old abandoned coal mines (strip pits).

Some coal which is buried very deeply can only be recovered by deep mining. The most common type of underground mining uses the **room and pillar system**. As the miners dig large rooms, they leave pillars of coal to support the roof. Long bolts are also placed in the roof to bind the layers of rock together and keep the roof from falling. Only 50 to 60 percent of the coal can be removed when the room and pillar system is used.

The **longwall system** is used in deeper mines. Workers cut coal from a wall 300 to 700 feet (91 to 210 metres) long which joins the

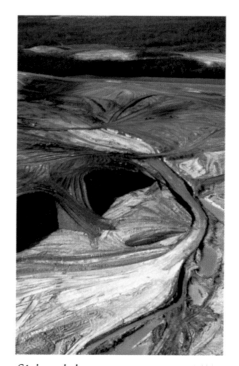

Strip mining

main tunnel. Movable steel supports are used to hold the roof in place over the area being mined. As the coal is mined, the supports are moved, and the roof over the mined area is allowed to fall. Up to 80 percent of the coal can be recovered in a longwall mine.

Processing: Most users of coal require that coal be a specific size. At a processing plant near the coal mine, coal is crushed and sorted according to size. It is then washed to remove impurities. Most of the impurities are heavier than the coal, and they settle to the bottom of the washing bin. Some forms of sulfur are removed by washing, but some sulfur is bound to the carbon and is released when the coal is burned. Bituminous coal is often high in sulfur content, and special equipment is necessary to control air pollution when it is burned.

Transportation: Coal from a mine in Arizona is carried by a pipeline to a power plant in Nevada. The coal is crushed and mixed with water to form a **slurry** that is pumped through the pipeline. Additional pipelines may be built, but in some locations water is not available, and in other cases pumping of the slurry may be less efficient than transport by train or barge.

Frequently coal must be shipped long distances. Barges provide the cheapest way of shipping coal. If shipment must be made over land, railroads offer the most economical means of transport. An increasing number of power plants located east of the Mississippi River are using subbituminous coal from the West, to meet the demand for low sulfur coal.

Environment and Health: Since 1900, more than 100,000 workers have been killed in coal mine accidents in the US. The federal government passed the Coal Mine Health & Safety Act in 1969, and the number of mine deaths has been greatly reduced. Most workers are killed by accidents involving equipment. The federal government now requires each mine to have a training program for miners and a scientific plan for the roof support of each underground mine.

Methane is an explosive gas that occurs naturally in coal seams. Automatic detectors are used to warn workers of a build up of this gas. Blasting may produce high levels of carbon monoxide if the mine is not properly ventilated. Thousands of miners have developed a condition known as **black lung** as a result of breathing coal dust. Coal dust is also explosive. Now federal law requires that walls in deep mines be sprayed with powdered limestone. Water is sprayed on surfaces being mined to control the dust. The process is called **rock dusting**.

Water pollution occurs when water pumped from underground mines or water from open pits left during strip mining enters a stream without first being treated. In the past, thousands of fish and aquatic organisms have been killed as slugs of acid water move down nearby streams. Today mines are required to treat water and remove sediments before it is released into the natural environment.

In 1977 Congress passed a law requiring all US electric power plants built after 1971 to meet federal pollution standards by 1982.

To meet the standards, pollution control devices must be used when burning coal that contains more than one percent sulfur. (See Unit II Case Study 6.1 "Clearing the Air — Stationary Sources") But pollution controls do not remove all pollutants from the air, and there is concern about the respiratory damage that may be caused by air pollution that results from burning coal.

Subsidence, or the sinking of land, occurs when the resources beneath the land have been removed, and the ground above can no longer support its own weight. Fourteen homes in Pittsburgh, Pennsylvania, have recently been abandoned because the land they were built on is sinking, and the houses are no longer safe. The houses in Pittsburgh are just a few of the thousands built above abandoned coal mines in Pennsylvania, Kentucky, and West Virginia.

After more than twenty years, and $7 million, government officials gave up their attempts to try to stop the fire burning in the abandoned coal mine beneath the streets of Centralia, Pennsylvania. The town's only gas station had been forced to close when temperatures in the basement reached 142°F (61°C). Carbon monoxide and other gases seeped into basements. The heat from the fire melts snow in the winter. In 1983, most of the citizens sold their houses to the government and left the town. Although Centralia has been the only town threatened by a mine fire, there are more than 500 fires burning in coal deposits and waste heaps which remain at abandoned coal mines in the US.

Future: As production of crude oil and natural gas declines, coal will become a more important source of energy for America and the world. Each ton of coal used to generated electricity or manufacture goods saves four barrels of oil. Although the supply of coal is limited, at the present rate of use, the reserves are sufficient to last more than two hundred years.

Synthetic Fuels from Fossil Fuels

History: Coal may one day be used to replace oil and natural gas. The technology for conversion is not new. Many European and American cities were lit with coal gas or "town gas" during the 1800s and early 1900s. But production of coal gas was dirty and its heat value was low. When long-distance pipelines were built, coal gas could not compete with natural gas that was cheaper, cleaner, and had a higher heating value.

During World War II, many of Germany's fuel needs were supplied by synthetic fuel plants that changed coal into liquid fuels. After the war, the US government organized a team of more than one hundred scientists to study the process. Two coal-liquefaction plants were built, and they succeeded in making a fuel that was used in a diesel locomotive. Then cheap oil from the Middle East became available, and the plants shut down.

Fuels that are produced by chemically changing fossil fuels or

> ### TRY TO FIND OUT
>
> The Oil Pollution Act stipulates that by the year 2015 all oil tankers must have double hulls. What are double hulls and why are they so important in preventing pollution from spilled oil? What event led to the passage of the Oil Pollution Act?

other organic materials are called **synthetic fuels** or **synfuels.** Synthetic fuels are comparable in chemical structure and energy value to petroleum products and natural gas. Fossil fuels which can be converted to synfuels are coal, oil shale, and tar sands.

Liquid Coal: Crushed coal is mixed with a solvent to form a slurry. Hydrogen is then added to the slurry as it is heated to a high temperature under pressure. The coal is changed into a liquid that resembles crude oil. This process can be used to produce as much as 3 barrels of synthetic oil from one ton of coal. The synthetic oil contains only 70 percent of the energy in the coal. At this time the only commercial liquefaction plant in operation is in South Africa, but a demonstration plant has been built in Morgantown, West Virginia.

Coal Gas: In West Virginia, North Dakota, and Pennsylvania, pilot plants have produced a high-quality gas from coal. Coal is heated in a large reactor with oxygen and steam. Impurities are removed, and the gases react with hydrogen to form methane (natural gas). Some large industries have built gasification plants. The gasifiers must be operated continuously, and the gas must be used as it is produced.

Rocks that Burn: Liquid oil lies trapped in rock formations known as **oil shales** and **tar sands**. Large deposits of oil shale reserves are located in Alberta, Colorado, Utah, and Wyoming. The problem is getting it out. The settlers found Indians making campfires with oil shales. But to provide the oil needed for today's lifestyle, vast amounts of the rocks must be mined, crushed, and heated in order to release the oil or tar. Another technology for recovery involves removing some of the rock and using a controlled burn to release the oil from the remaining oil shale in the mine. About one ton of oil shale will produce 25 gallons (112L) of oil.

Problems: A serious problem is cost. It is expensive to build the huge plants needed to produce synfuels, and the production process is expensive. Mines to provide the huge amounts of coal needed to heat the rocks and to provide the oil shale for processing would have to be far larger than any mines existing today.

Another problem is the need for water. About two quarts (2.2 L) of water are needed for each pound (2.2 kg) of coal processed. Three barrels of water are needed for each barrel of oil extracted from oil shale. Many of the coal and oil shale deposits are in areas where water is not plentiful. Since the coal will most likely be strip mined, water will also be necessary for reclamation.

Although synfuels burn clean, the process of production is dirty. Gases produced may cause air pollution. Millions of tons of ash containing traces of cadmium, lead, and mercury would have to be disposed of without polluting water supplies.

The production of synfuels from oil shale would require thousands of workers. Exposure of workers to toxic chemicals is a serious concern. A number of chemicals produced are carcinogens. Complaints of skin problems occur at the coal liquefaction plant in South Africa and at petroleum refineries.

1. Define the following terms:
   anthracite
   Arab Oil Embargo
   black lung
   bituminous
   coal
   coke
   EnergyGuide
   lignite
   longwall system
   peat
   reclamation
   refining
   renewable resource
   reserve
   reservoir rock
   rock dusting
   room and pillar
     system
   secondary recovery
     method
   slurry
   source rock
   strip mining
   subbituminous
   subsidence
   synfuels
   trap
   wildcat well

2. What two types of energy were in short supply during the 1970s?
3. How did the price of crude oil change during the 1970s?
4. List the changes made by Congress to encourage the conservation of energy.

The Changing American Scene
5. Identify the three sources that provided most of the energy used in 1850. Which of these were renewable resources?
6. Identify the three major sources of energy used today. Which of these are renewable resources?
7. When did the United States begin to import oil? How much of the oil used in 1973 was imported?
8. How did the Arab Oil Embargo affect life in the United States? How did the government respond to the embargo? How did the amount of oil imported in 1983 compare to the amount imported in 1973?
9. Compare the change in consumption of oil with the change in production of oil in the United States for the period between 1986 and 1990. Describe how these changes affect our dependence on foreign oil.
10. Explain why the United States is concerned about the political stability of the Middle East.

11. In addition to reducing our dependence on foreign oil, give two additional reasons for seeking alternatives to fossil fuels.

It Began a Long Time Ago
12. Describe the conditions which change peat into coal.
13. Match the statements below to the correct type of coal.
    Types of Coal
    1. anthracite   3. lignite
    2. bituminous   4. subbituminous
    Statements
    A. This is a very soft coal which crumbles easily.
    B. Large deposits are found in western states.
    C. This type of coal has the highest carbon content.
    D. Most of the coal found in the United States is of this type.
    E. This coal contains the lowest heat content.
    F. This coal first formed from peat.
    G. Nearly all of this coal is found in Pennyslvania
14. Describe the conditions which produced natural gas and petroleum deposits.
15. Identify the three types of rocks that must be present for a recoverable deposit of petroleum or natural gas to form.
16. Identify three physical properties that petroleum scientists measure when searching for oil.
17. What percent of the wells drilled in an area with known gas deposits will produce gas?

Natural Gas
18. Give the geographical location of most of the world's natural gas reserves. Identify the region of the US that has the largest natural gas reserves.
19. What part of our energy needs are supplied by natural gas?
20. Explain why there is an increasing demand for natural gas as an energy source for electrical power plants and commercial fleets of vehicles.

21. Identify the ways in which natural gas is used for each of the following: bread, clothing, newspaper, other consumer products, and automobiles.
22. What is the major residential and commercial use of natural gas?
23. What is the major hydrocarbon in natural gas? What element must be removed from natural gas so that it will burn without polluting the environment?
24. How is natural gas transported? Which means is the safest and least expensive?
25. Give one advantage of using natural gas for heating homes; for cooking; for certain industrial processes.
26. Why do gas companies add a foul-smelling chemical to natural gas?
27. Are we running out of natural gas? Explain.

Petroleum (Crude Oil)
28. In addition to the Middle East, what other regions might export oil to the United States?
29. What percent of the energy used is supplied by oil? What percent of the oil used in 1990 was imported?
30. Give two reasons why crude oil is so important to our lifestyle.
31. What is the purpose of using secondary recovery methods? What materials are injected into the wells? What two physical processes aid in removal of the oil?
32. What physical process is used to separate chemicals during the refining of crude oil?
33. What type of chemical is used to increase the speed of the chemical reactions in the manufacture of high octane gasoline and other products of petroleum?
34. What methods of transportation are used to transport most petroleum products long distances?
35. Rank the methods used to transport oil and other chemicals from most energy efficient to least energy efficient.
36. If tank trucks require so much more energy than railroads why aren't more petroleum products shipped by rail?

37. Give two ways in which oil pollutes the environment. What is the major source of pollution produced by the burning of oil? How can we reduce this source of pollution without a major change in lifestyle?
38. Indicate whether each of the following statements is true or false.
    A. Scientists expect to find major oil reserves that have yet to be discovered.
    B. Production of oil in the US is declining
    C. On a worldwide basis production of oil is increasing.
    D. On a world wide basis discovery of oil is increasing.
    E. The chance of finding a wildcat well which is productive is about 10%.
39. Do you think that oil companies should be permitted to drill for oil and gas in National Parks and National Wilderness Areas? Give reasons to support your opinion.
40. Why do oil companies cap a well when production declines instead of using secondary recovery methods? What determines whether they will reopen the well and use secondary recovery methods?
41. What cheaper alternative fuel replaced oil when oil prices increased?

Coal
42. Identify the regions with the largest coal reserves. How do the US coal reserves compare to the reserves found in the other countries? What country is the largest exporter of coal?
43. What percent of our energy needs are supplied by coal? What is the major use of coal?
44. Identify the type of coal used for each of the following processes:
    Types of Coal
    1. anthracite   3. lignite/subbituminous
    2. bituminous
    Processes
    A. used by most electric power plants
    B. mainly used for heating homes
    C. use is limited to manufacturing or production of electricity
    D. heating commercial buildings and factories
    E. production of coke for steel industry

45. Describe the physical conditions that must be present to make coke from coal. What manufacturing process requires coke? How does the making of coke benefit the farmer?
46. Identify the two major types of mining. List three advantages of surface mining.
47. What type of mining requires reclamation? How has the process of mining changed since the reclamation law was passed? How can reclaimed land be used?
48. Are owners of abandoned coal mines required to pay for reclaiming? If not, who is paying the costs of reclaiming this land?
49. How is the roof supported in a coal mine which is mined by the room and pillar system?
50. Explain how the longwall system of coal mining permits miners to remove a larger percent of the coal supply.
51. What happens to the coal at the processing plant?
52. Identify the type of coal that often contains high amounts of sulfur. Explain why this sulfur is not removed during the washing process.
53. Why aren't pipelines used more often for shipping coal long distances?
54. Which is the cheaper way to ship coal over long distances — land transport or water transport? What type of land transport is the most efficient?
55. Why do power plants located east of the Mississippi import coal from Montana?
56. What is the leading work-related cause of death of coal miners? Explain how each of the following changes in coal mining procedures reduced mine accidents:
    A. training program for miners
    B. scientific plan for roof support
    C. automatic detectors
    D. ventilation
    E. rock dusting
    F. use of water during mining
57. What pollutant causes the death of aquatic organisms when water is released without treatment from some coal mines? What pollutant damages the respiratory system and enters the air when coal is burned? What steps have been taken to reduce this pollution?

58. Identify the problems associated with abandoned coal mines that forced people from their homes in Pittsburgh and Centralia, Pennsylvania.
59. Will coal become more or less important in the future? What fossil fuels will still be available for your grandchildren?

Synthetic Fuels from Fossil Fuels
60. What fuel replaced the coal gas used for lighting city streets? What were the advantages of this new fuel? Why weren't the coal-liquefaction plants built after World War II successful?
61. Compare the energy content of liquid coal and crushed coal. In 1990 the US imported more than 8 million barrels of crude oil each day. Assuming that a barrel of liquid coal would produce the same products as a barrel of crude oil, how many tons of coal would have to be mined each day to produce the oil imported in 1990?
62. You might heat your home or cook your dinner with natural gas. Coal gas is the same chemical (methane) as natural gas. Why won't it be possible for you to heat your home with coal gas?
63. Describe two methods of getting the oil out of oil shale.
64. How do you think the cost of synfuels will compare to the cost of petroleum products we use today? Why?
65. Identify two environmental problems that may occur during the production of large amounts of synfuels from oil shale.
66. How will the production of oil from oil shale affect the level of carbon dioxide?
67. The production of oil from oil shale will require thousands of workers. Oil shale deposits are located in a region of the US that has a low population density. What environmental changes may result from the increasing population?

"By the end of the decade we will ... meet our own energy needs without depending on any foreign energy sources."

Thomas Edison might be amazed at the complexity of a control room at a modern coal-burning power plant.

President Nixon spoke those words when he introduced Project Independence at the time of the Arab Oil Embargo. Two decades later about 17 percent of the energy used in the United States is still imported.

Hawaii may have felt the effects of the Arab Oil Embargo to a greater extent than any other state. The Hawaiian islands were formed by volcanic action. They have no oil, no coal, and no natural gas. In the 1970s more than 90 percent of the energy used on the islands was imported. The major imported energy resource is crude oil.

To achieve President Nixon's goal of independence from foreign oil, the United States must develop alternative sources of energy. Following the energy shortages of the 1970s, Hawaii began to develop the technology needed to produce electricity without using foreign oil. By the year 2000, the state hopes to produce all of its electricity by using resources found on the islands.

Thank You, Thomas Edison

The production of most electricity depends upon a spinning turbine. A **turbine** is a machine with several curved blades on a larger rotating shaft. It looks something like a giant fan or paddle wheel. The spinning turbine is connected to a generator. The **generator** consists of stationary coils of copper wire and an electromagnet rotated by the turbine. When the electromagnet is rotated, it creates a magnetic field that causes the electrons to flow through the wire. This flow of electrons transmitted along wires is **electricity**.

The first commercial electric generating station, designed by Thomas Edison, burned coal to heat water and produce steam. The steam turned the turbines, and enough electricity was produced to light 1200 street lamps. The first hydroelectric power plant began operation the same year. This was the beginning of a new energy era. Now 35 percent of the energy used in the United States is in the form of electricity.

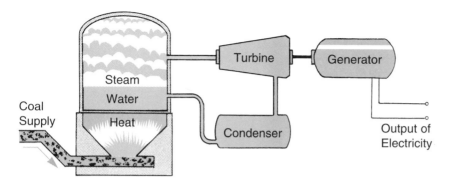

In 1991, nearly 68 percent of electricity in the United States was produced at power plants that burned fossil fuels, mostly coal. Hydroelectric power plants produced nearly 10 percent of electricity and nuclear power plants produced almost 22 percent. We can reduce our dependence on foreign oil and the air pollution caused by the combustion of coal if we use alternative energy sources. As you will see, each energy source has advantages and disadvantages.

Energy Sources for the Production of Electricity in the United States			
Fossil Fuel Plants	Percent	Other Energy Sources	Percent
Coal	54.8	Nuclear	21.8
Gas	9.3	Hydro	9.9
Oil	3.8	Solar, Wind, other	0.4

U.S. Council for Energy Awareness — 1991 Data

Electric Power Plant Operator

In modern power plants much of the equipment is controlled by computers and the workers primary responsibility is to monitor the equipment, record readings, and detect any malfunctions. Operators must have an understanding of mechanics and electricity. They must be alert, dependable, and willing to learn new skills. High school courses should include mathematics, industrial arts, and science. Power plants provide on-the-job training. Some cities and states require operators to be licensed.

Hydroelectric Power

Hydroelectric power is produced when the energy of falling water turns a water turbine. In the early 1900s falling water provided the energy for one-half of all electricity generated in the United States. The role of hydroelectric power has declined as other cheaper sources of energy became readily available.

Usually hydroelectric power is cheaper than power from fossil-fuel power plants. Another advantage is that hydroelectric power plants do not produce the air pollution or the heat associated with fossil-fuel power plants. But hydroelectric power plants cause major changes in the environment. (See Unit IV Case Study 2.5 "Dam the Rivers or Let Them Run Free?")

The amount of hydroelectric power produced in the US is not likely to increase significantly because most sites suitable for large plants have already been developed. Most additional electricity produced by hydroelectric power will be produced by facilities added

Hydroelectric station

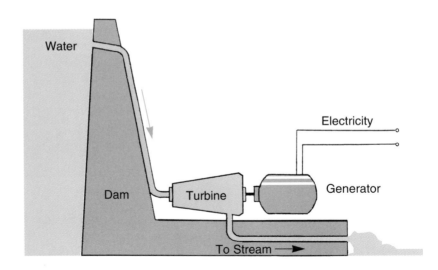

to dams that already exist. Canadian hydroelectric power plants sell electricity to utilities in the northern states. Since Canada has the potential to develop much more hydroelectric power, the US may import larger amounts of electricity in the future.

Some homeowners with streams flowing through their property have built small hydro systems to provide their own electricity. Small systems can be economical and efficient. The amount of power produced depends upon the **flow** — the volume of water, and the **head** — the vertical distance the water falls. Some systems can be built with little disturbance of the stream ecosystem. Since streams and rivers are protected by federal and state regulations, anyone planning to build a hydroelectric system must obtain the necessary permits.

Nuclear Power

Instead of the coal, oil, or natural gas used in a fossil-fuel power plant, the fuel used in nuclear power plants is mainly uranium. When the uranium atoms **fission** or split apart, they release huge amounts of energy. This energy heats water and creates steam that drives the turbines.

Nuclear power is considered a clean source of energy. Unlike a coal-burning power plant, a nuclear power plant does not release carbon dioxide and sulfur dioxide into the environment. In fact, the burning of coal releases more radioactive substances into the environment than the normal operation of a nuclear power plant.

Although it is a nonrenewable resource, the supply of uranium is large enough to last for many years. When President Nixon introduced Project Independence, nuclear energy was expected to play a major role in achieving energy independence. There are several reasons why the use of nuclear energy did not replace fossil fuels as the major source of energy for the production of electricity.

THINK ABOUT IT

Today's nuclear power plants create energy from nuclear fission — the splitting of atoms creating considerable amounts of radioactive waste. Scientists around the world are working feverishly to develop a way to use nuclear **fusion**—creating energy by uniting atoms—to generate energy. The sun's energy comes from nuclear fusion. Nuclear fusion is clean; it creates no pollution or radioactive waste. So far, scientists have been unable to design a system to sustain a nuclear fusion reaction.

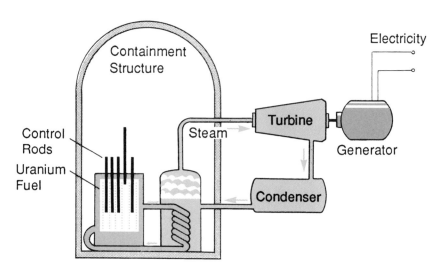

One factor is cost. Nuclear power plants are far more expensive to construct than fossil-fuel plants. Although the price of oil reached new highs in the 1970s, the prices began to fall in the 1980s. Nuclear energy could not compete with the low cost of fossil fuels. Electricity from nuclear power plants in the US costs about twice as much as electricity from coal-burning plants.

Another factor is the low demand for electricity. Some plants were canceled because the growth in the use of electricity has been much lower than expected. The growth rate was 7 percent each year in the early 1970s, but it has been only 1.8 percent since 1980.

Safety has been a major concern since the accident at Three Mile Island when the reactor's core partially melted in 1979. Although the reactor and the containment building were heavily contaminated, only very small amounts of radiation were released into the environment (less than the normal "background radiation" in Denver). The radiation did not cause any immediate damage. Long-term studies are still being conducted. (See Unit V Case Study 1.5: "Three-Mile-Island")

Unfortunately this was not the case at the Chernobyl nuclear plant in the Soviet Union. Within 6 months of the accident, more than 30 people who were near the accident site had died. Thousands more are at increased risk of cancer. The 1986 accident resulted in the highest levels of radioactive fallout ever recorded in Europe.

In Western Europe, France is the only country still building nuclear power plants. South Korea and Japan are continuing to build plants, but at a slower rate. While some countries plan for increasing use of nuclear energy, other countries are phasing out plans for nuclear power plants. Sweden plans to phase out nuclear power by 2010. A number of countries have established a no-nuclear policy.

Chernobyl Nuclear

Although the type of reactor involved in the Chernobyl incident — a water-cooled, graphite-moderated RBMK — is not exported or made by any other country, any type of reactor runs the risk of a similar accident.

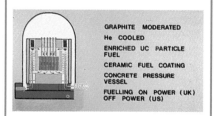

GRAPHITE MODERATED
He COOLED
ENRICHED UC PARTICLE FUEL
CERAMIC FUEL COATING
CONCRETE PRESSURE VESSEL
FUELLING ON POWER (UK)
OFF POWER (US)

The cores of all reactors are cooled in some way and the nuclear reaction is slowed by a moderator. At Chernobyl, the coolant — in this case water — was lost, allowing the reactor core to overheat and melt. The graphite which acted as a moderator caught fire and sent clouds of radioactive smoke into the atmosphere.

Solar Energy Technician

Solar energy technicians design, construct, install, and maintain solar energy systems. Technicians must be able to follow blueprints and have a knowledge of carpentry, sheet metal work, masonry, and electricity. Technicians may be responsible for preparing cost estimates for installation and repairs. Technicians must be able to follow oral and written instruction and work without constant supervision. Training may be completed as an apprenticeship or on-the-job. Courses in high school should include science, industrial arts, and mathematics.

Geothermal Energy ▶

People are still concerned over possible accidents and lack of a permanent storage site for the **spent fuel**. Spent fuel is the remains of uranium fuel that is still radioactive but can no longer be used to produce energy. Most experts consider it unlikely that nuclear energy will play a major role in the US plan for energy independence.

Geothermal Energy

Although Hawaii and Iceland have very different climates, they share a common energy source — geothermal energy. **Geothermal energy** is the natural heat or hot water trapped below Earth's surface. Some of the heat was trapped when Earth was formed. Additional heat energy is produced by radioactive substances, chemical reactions, and friction that is created by the moving continents.

In most places the heat is too deep to be tapped, but in Hawaii the pools of water lie only 6,000 feet (1800 m) below Earth's surface. Geothermal energy can be used to heat homes, produce electricity and power industrial plants. One city in Iceland taps 140°F (60°C) from deep wells and pipes it to nearly all the homes and office buildings.

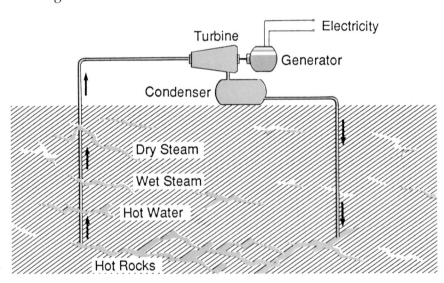

Dry steam is found at shallow depths in only a few places in the United States. **Wet steam** is a mixture of steam and hot water. The steam from **pressurized hot water** and dry steam systems can be used to drive a turbine and produce electricity. The production of energy from **hot dry rock** systems will require more advanced technology.

Each geothermal site presents a unique set of problems that must be solved. Often the pipes and the turbine can be damaged by corrosive minerals dissolved in the steam. At some sites, harmful gases such as radon, hydrogen sulfide, and ammonia must be vented into the atmosphere.

Electric power plants must be located at the geothermal field because too much heat and pressure are lost if the energy is transported more than one mile (1.6 km). Sites can be damaged by earthquakes and lava flows from volcanoes. In Hawaii one geothermal plant has been designed so that it can be easily dismantled in case of a lava flow.

Only four states have the potential to develop geothermal energy — Hawaii, California, Nevada, and Utah. The Geysers Geothermal Field in California produces 75 percent of the world's electricity that is generated by geothermal energy, but the output is declining. Due to overdevelopment of the field the power production has declined by 28 percent, and it is expected to decline further.

In Hawaii, a completed geothermal power plant has been unable to start operating because of opposition from conservationists and native Hawaiians. The drilling of explorations wells to determine the ability of molten magma to produce energy for a geothermal power plant has also been halted.

Solar Energy

The sun is the source of most energy on Earth. We have always depended upon solar energy to produce our food. Solar energy powers the water cycle and creates the temperature differences that cause the wind to blow. Before 1850 solar energy was responsible for the creation of the three major sources of energy — wood, wind, and water.

Today new houses are designed with windows facing the sun to take advantage of the sun's rays for warming rooms in winter. This form of **passive solar heating** occurs when the light energy passes through glass and is trapped (the greenhouse effect). Roof overhangs shade the windows from the sun's rays in the summer reducing the amount of passive solar heating and the need for air conditioning.

Silicon Solar Cells

Silicon solarcell arrays are being used in a remote village in Tunisia. This study will determine the effectiveness of a photovoltaic system in remote areas. The primary solar array provides 30 kilowatts of peak power for this residential population of 120, a commercial area of two stores, a barber shop and a café, plus the public area including street lights, a mosque, clinic, meeting house and a school.

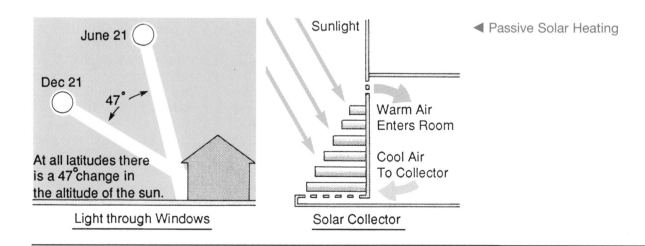

June 21

Dec 21

47°

At all latitudes there is a 47° change in the altitude of the sun.

Light through Windows

Sunlight

Warm Air Enters Room

Cool Air To Collector

Solar Collector

◀ Passive Solar Heating

Solar Water Heater

A single solar water heater can provide 40 to 70% of the hot water needs for a typical family of four. With two units in tandem it can provide 70 to 90% of their hot water needs. These units utilize a heat exchanger coupled with a latent heat storage technique originally developed for the Skylab spacecraft. This system alternately freezes and melts thus absorbs and releases heat through an indefinite number of cycles. The solar panels are also coated with a glazing material developed by Dupont for the Apollo Lunar Module.

Objects in direct sunlight absorb solar energy. The amount of solar energy stored as heat energy can be increased by adding **thermal mass** — large containers of water in floors or walls made of brick, stone, or concrete. These materials may be placed in passive collectors attached to a wall facing the sun. As the air in the collector is heated, it rises and flows through a vent at the top of the collector. Cool air enters the collector through a vent near the bottom.

Active solar heating systems require electricity for pumps or fans that distribute the heat. Often energy is collected in **flat plate collectors** that are shallow insulated boxes covered with glass and containing a black metal plate. Air or water flowing through the collector is heated and pumped to a storage tank. If the system is designed for space heating, the heat is pumped throughout the building in the same way it is from a conventional furnace. Active solar systems used for domestic water heating are smaller and more cost effective than active space heating systems.

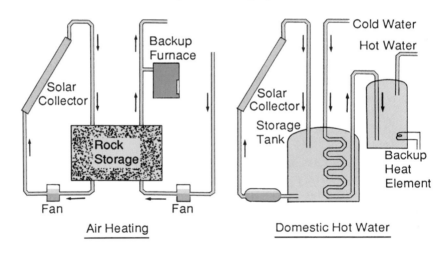

Active Solar Heating Systems ▲

In **photovoltaic cells** (solar cells) sunlight is directly changed into electricity. When sunlight strikes a thin layer of silicon, electrons are released creating an electric current. Photovoltaic cells have been available since the 1950s. They have been used to produce electricity on the space shuttles. Although the technology is available, it is more expensive than other energy sources. Another disadvantage of solar cells is that they require large amounts of space.

Solar thermal technology uses mirror-lined dishes or panels that rotate with the sun and collect solar energy. Water, heated by the concentrated solar energy, runs an electrical generator. According to the Edison Electric Institute, to supply electricity for a city the size of Pittsburgh would require solar collectors covering an area about 900 square miles (2340 km²).

Ninety percent of the world's solar thermal electricity is produced by one company in California. Natural gas-fired boilers are used to supplement solar power during the winter months and at night. The electricity is sold to Southern California Edison. The cost is about the same as the cost of electricity from a coal-fired power plant.

Without major technological developments, increased efficiency and reduced costs of installation, solar energy will not become a major source of energy for the production of electricity.

Wind Machines

Technology that uses the power of the wind has been used for centuries. Before power plants provided electricity to farms, small ten-kilowatt windmills were used to pump water and generate electricity. In 1941 a giant windmill, which could produce 1,250 kilowatts was built in Vermont. For three years it provided electricity for the local power plant, but cheap oil and gas were more reliable than the wind.

At many sites the wind is not reliable enough to generate power. Where it does blow, windpower is not without problems. The equipment to trap wind energy is expensive, and it can be damaged by powerful gusts of wind. The trade winds on the island of Oahu, Hawaii, provide some of the best wind conditions for power generation. Wind farms are a part of Hawaii's energy plan.

California has several wind farms that produce commercial power. The energy they produce is equal to the energy produced by a large nuclear power plant. Nationwide the contribution of wind energy is not expected to be large, but in specific locations it can help reduce the need for other energy sources.

Researchers are trying to find ways to improve the technology, reduce the cost, and store energy for use when the wind doesn't blow. One storage system would use wind energy to pump water into a reservoir located at a higher level. The falling water can be used to produce electricity if it is needed.

Biomass

Biomass is currently producing nearly 40 percent of the electricity on two of Hawaii's islands. **Biomass** refers to any substances produced by living organisms and used as a source of energy. Biomass includes wood, agricultural wastes, algae, and sewage.

The Forest Service believes that our forests can replace one third of the oil we import each year. Wood currently supplies 2 percent of our energy needs. Wood and wood products are a major source of energy for the forest products industry. Wood has once again become an important source of heat for many homes. More than 4.3 million wood stoves were sold in the US between 1980 and 1987.

There are no electric lines leading to Amish farms in Lancaster County, Pennyslvania. Here wind often supplies the power to pump water and horse power supplies farm labor and transportation.

Wind Farm

Most families spend about $1000 per year on appliances and heating and cooling equipment. The electricity you use to run these major appliances over their lifetimes can cost three times as much as the appliances themselves. With this in mind more energy efficient appliances are being built. For example, the latest refrigerators use only one-third as much electricity as older models. New federal energy efficiency standards are in effect for dishwashers, clothes dryers, water heaters, and air conditioners too. You can find more information in the *Consumer Guide to Home Energy Savings*, put out by the American Council for an Energy-Efficient Economy, which should be in your local library.

The major source of biomass in Hawaii is **bagasse** — the fibrous waste produced during the processing of sugar cane. Bagasse is a dry fibrous material similar to the wood shavings produced by sharpening a pencil. When oil was abundant and cheap, the sugar companies disposed of the bagasse by bulldozing it off cliffs or burying it in a landfill. Today they pack it into pellets. The pellets have the same energy value as coal.

Using one system to produce both electricity and heat for an industrial process is called **cogeneration**. The sugar companies burn the pellets to produce steam for electric generators. The used steam still contains enough energy to process the sugar. At a conventional power plant, the used steam is waste. Because of the large amount of energy remaining in the steam, the energy efficiency of a conventional power plant is about 35 percent. Cogeneration systems can be 80 percent efficient.

After harvest, more than 60,000 tons of straw remains on the wheat fields in eastern Colorado. Most of it was burned so that another crop could be planted. Now the straw is shredded and compressed into "strawloggs." The "logs" contain almost as much energy as coal and twice the energy of pine. They burn at a high temperature and leave no residues in the chimney. The ashes contain potash and are an excellent garden fertilizer.

Biomass can also be used to produce alcohol or methane. During the energy crisis much attention was given to the use of **gasohol** — a blend of one part grain alcohol and nine parts of gasoline. Most alcohol used in gasohol is distilled from corn. Our corn production would have to increase by 50 percent to provide the 11 billion gallons of alcohol needed to reduce our consumption of gasoline by 10 percent. According to Lester R. Brown, president of the Worldwatch Institute, ". . . even converting the entire world grain crop to alcohol would not provide enough fuel to operate the current world automobile fleet."

The Economics of Alternative Energy Sources

Renewable energy sources are often thought of as free, but most renewables are expensive compared to fossil fuels. In the last decade there have been major improvements in the technologies associated with alternative energy sources. The cost of generating electricity using some of the alternative energy sources such as wind and photovoltaic cells has fallen since the early '80s. Still, electricity from photovoltaic cells costs 30 to 40 cents per kilowatt-hour and electricity produced by wind turbines costs about 8 cents per kWh. To compete with fossil fuels, new energy sources must generate electricity at a cost of about 5 cents per kWh.

Some alternative technologies require further research and testing or the construction of facilities to make the technology produce commercial quantities of energy. Research and construction can require the investment of billions of dollars. The risks are often bigger than private industry is willing to take.

The Department of Energy had set a goal of 20 percent of energy supplied by renewable resources by the year 2000. Due to a combination of several factors, it is unlikely that this goal will be met. These factors include the following:

- Energy efficiency has reduced the rate of growth in demand for electricity.
- Since the 1970s, oil prices dropped and have been relatively stable.
- There was a sharp cut in federal funding for research and development during the 1980s.
- There has also been a decline in private investment.

During the next decade, use of renewable energy sources will be expanded. The increased use of renewables will be due to a combination of three factors:

- There is a growing demand for electricity. In spite of conservation efforts, more electricity will be needed to meet the needs of the growing population.
- Federal funding has increased. The Energy Policy Act of 1992 includes incentives and tax credits for development and production of renewable energy.
- Environmental benefits of renewables is an important factor. Electrical power plants must now consider environmental impacts when considering energy sources. This makes renewables more competitive with conventional energy sources.

1.3 QUESTIONS FOR STUDY AND DISCUSSION

1. Define the following terms:
   active solar heating system
   bagasse
   biomass
   cogeneration
   dry steam
   electricity
   fission
   flat plate collector
   flow
   gasohol
   generator
   geothermal energy
   head
   passive solar heating
   photovoltaic cells
   spent fuel
   thermal mass
   turbine

2. Explain why the state of Hawaii is developing alternative sources of energy.

Thank You, Thomas Edison

3. Explain how a turbine converts heat energy into mechanical energy.
4. Explain how a generator produces electricity.

5. What is the relationship between the turbine and the generator?
6. Identify the two sources of energy used to turn turbines at the first commercial electric generating stations.
7. Why is electricity considered to be a secondary source of energy?
8. Rank the three major sources of energy used to produce electricity in 1991. Which of these energy sources is renewable?

Hydroelectric Power

9. Explain how electricity is generated at a hydroelectric power plant.
10. Why are hydroelectric power plants less important as a source of electricity than they were in the early 1900s?

11. Give two advantages of generating electricity at hydroelectric power plants over fossil fuel power plants.
12. What are the disadvantages of hydroelectric power production?
13. Is hydroelectric power a renewable resource?
14. Explain why hydroelectric power plants will not become a major source of electricity in the US.
15. Identify the three additional sources of hydroelectric power which will be used in the future.
16. What two factors will determine the amount of power that can be produced at hydroelectric power plants?
17. Why are permits required before a hydroelectric plant can be built?

Nuclear Power
18. Identify the major fuel used in nuclear power plants and explain how it releases energy.
19. Compare the pollution produced by a coal-burning power plant with the pollution produced during normal operation of a nuclear power plant.
20. Give three reasons why the construction of nuclear power plants is not progressing at the rate anticipated by President Nixon.
21. How has the accident at Chernobyl affected the use of nuclear energy in other countries?
22. What two concerns do people have about the use of nuclear energy?

Geothermal Energy
23. What source of energy is being tapped in both Hawaii and Iceland? How is this energy being used?
24. Identify the three ways in which geothermal energy is continually being produced. Is geothermal energy a renewable energy source?
25. Explain why geothermal energy will not become a major source of energy in most states.
26. Identify the forms of geothermal energy that are currently being used and the form which requires the development of more advanced technology.
27. Identify possible environmental problems associated with geothermal energy.

Solar Energy
28. Identify two renewable sources of energy that depend upon solar energy.
29. Explain why a house with large windows facing the sun and a large roof overhang is able to take advantage of passive solar heating in the winter and avoid excessive heat in the summer.
30. Give two ways that homeowners can use thermal mass to help heat their home.
31. Describe the scientific principles that must be considered when building a solar collector.
32. What is the major difference between a passive solar heating system and an active solar heating system?
33. Identify the major use of active solar heating systems which are currently used by homeowners.
34. Describe two ways that solar energy can be changed into electricity.
35. Explain how photovoltaic cells produce electricity. What material is often used to trap the solar energy?
36. What are the major disadvantages of producing electricity with photovoltaic cells? What is the major disadvantage of using solar panels to produce electricity?

Wind Machines
37. What factors caused the windmill to disappear from the energy picture in the 1940s?
38. What factors will prevent windmills from becoming a major source of energy in the future?
39. Describe possible systems that can be used to store wind energy.

Biomass
40. Identify several types of biomass that can be used as sources of energy.
41. How has the production of bagasse changed from a waste disposal problem to a resource?
42. Explain how cogeneration increases energy efficiency.
43. How did Colorado wheat farmers convert straw into a resource instead of a waste product?

44. Compare "strawloggs" to coal in the following ways:
    1. heat content
    2. pollution produced during production
    3. pollution produced by combustion.
45. Evaluate the following statement: "When we run out of oil we will use alcohol to fuel our automobiles."
46. Which renewable resources will be important sources of energy in the future?

The Economics of Alternative Energy Sources
47. Explain why alternative energy sources have not replaced fossil fuels as a major source of energy for the generation of electricity.
48. Imagine that you are the next President of the United States. What steps would you take to ensure an adequate supply of energy to meet our future needs?

Science
Technology
Society

ISSUES

IN SEARCH OF THE WIND

In California's Alamont Pass, there are 7,300 wind turbines. The turbines are near a major corridor for migrating birds. A study revealed that wind turbines are killing birds of prey, including protected golden eagles. During the two-year study, an estimated 500 birds of prey were killed.

In Solano County US Windpower has signed an agreement to build 167 wind turbines. The turbines would provide electricity for 15,000 to 17,000 homes in the Sacramento area. According to the California Energy Commission, the impact on birds will be as great in Solano County as in the Alamont Pass. Although the size of the wind farm will be smaller, the area has larger populations of birds. One species that is likely to be affected is the endangered peregrine falcon.

US Windpower is studying the environmental impacts of the wind turbines. The company is testing a more efficient turbine that could produce four times the energy of most turbines. This would reduce the number of turbines needed. The blade of the new turbine is 2.23 times the area of other turbines.

Environmental groups such as The Sierra Club and The National Audubon Society could file lawsuits, if the company goes ahead with plans to build the turbines.

- Consider the economic and environmental impacts of wind power.
- Should wind power be banned in areas that serve as migration routes for birds?
- What impact on birds of prey is acceptable?
- What are the alternatives to wind power?
- What are the environmental and economic impacts of the alternative energy sources?

Fossil fuel and nuclear power plants produce electricity by heating water to form steam. The force of the steam turns the blades of a large fan-like, or paddle wheel structure called a **turbine**. The shaft of the turbine is connected to a **generator** that consists of a coil of wire in a magnetic field. Rotation of the coil forces the electrons in the wire to move. This flow of electrons is transmitted along wires as **electricity**.

Nuclear and older fossil-fueled power plants can only convert about one third of the fuel's energy into electricity. Modern fossil-fueled power plants are more efficient, but can convert only 40 percent of the fuel's energy into electricity. About 10-15 percent of the energy produced goes up the smoke stack as heat along with the products of combustion. The rest (45-50 percent) of the energy remains as heat energy in the steam that turned the turbine.

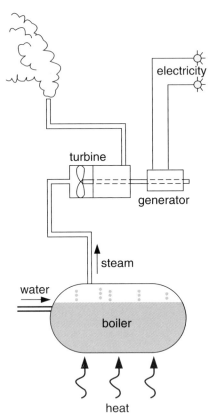

Basic Electric Generating System

Efficiency of a Fossil Fueled Steam-Electric Power Plant

Once the steam leaves the turbine, it passes through a condenser where it flows over pipes carrying cooler water. The cooler water in the pipes absorbs the heat. The steam condenses into water and is pumped back to the power plant's boiler or nuclear reactor. The cooling water is supplied to the condenser by one of three methods: once-through-cooling, cooling ponds, or cooling towers.

Once-Through-Cooling Method

The once-through-cooling method uses water from a river, lake, or ocean and returns it directly to the source. Because it is the least expensive, once-through-cooling has been the most commonly used method in the past. Although it is cheaper, this method creates problems in some aquatic ecosystems.

- Some species are not able to adapt to the warmer water temperatures. As the temperature of water increases, the ability of water to hold oxygen decreases. At the same time, the warmer temperatures increase the organism's metabolic rate, and the need for oxygen increases.
- Some types of algae and plants cannot grow in the warmer water. The result may be a decrease in certain species that are important producers. Many species of algae that are an important food source may be replaced by species of blue-green algae that organisms don't eat.

- **Synergistic effects** may also occur. The increased temperatures make some fish less resistant to disease. Some fish seem to be more sensitive to heavy metals and pesticides in warmer water.
- Those organisms that do survive may not be able to withstand the shock of cooler temperatures when the power plant is shut down for repairs.

Because of these effects, state and EPA water quality standards limit the increase in water temperature that may occur near a power plant discharge. Cooling water from the power plant must not raise the natural temperature of the river water more than 5°F (3°C). The temperature of the water must never be warmer than 90°F (32°C). This means that the cooling water can be returned directly to the river only if the flow has a very large volume.

Cooling Towers

Over 80 percent of the water used by industries is used for cooling. Large steam-electric power plants use as much as 500,000 gallons (2.3×10^6 L) of cooling water per minute. Some industries and power plants build cooling towers to prevent thermal pollution. There are two types of cooling towers: wet towers and dry towers.

Air enters the base of the hour glass-shaped cooling tower and rises as it is heated by the warm water. In **wet towers** the water is sprayed in a fine mist or allowed to fall over a series of wall-like structures called **baffles**. The major problem associated with wet towers is the loss of water through evaporation. Water loss is not a problem in a dry tower.

The heated water flows through a series of pipes in a **dry tower**. A fan at the base of the tower increases the flow of air. The water is cooled in the same way it is cooled in a car radiator. The major disadvantage of dry towers is that they are more expensive to build and operate.

Cooling Ponds or Reservoirs

An alternative to a cooling tower is a **cooling pond** or **reservoir**. Two large reservoirs in Missouri receive heated water from power plants. The Thomas Hill Power Plant near Macon discharges its water in a 4,500 acre (1800 hectare) cooling lake. The Kansas City Power and Light Company discharges water in the 1,600 acre (640 hectare) Montrose Reservoir. Both lakes are leased to the Missouri Department of Conservation. Bass, crappie, and catfish are attracted to the warm water near the power plants, and they provide good fishing through the winter months.

This heat recovery system recycles waste heat created during manufacturing processes.

Aquaculture

Waste-Heat Greenhouses

Some companies are finding that waste heat from power plants can be a valuable energy resource. Major food companies have leased greenhouses near a power plant owned by Pennsylvania Power and Light Company. They are using the waste heat to grow tomatoes and perform agricultural research. Waste heat is also being used to grow flowers, bedding plants and lettuce.

Some of the warm water (90-115°F/32-46°C) that would normally be sent to cooling towers is sent through insulated pipes to heat-exchange systems in the greenhouses. Back-up heat sources are needed when the power plant is shut down, in extremely cold weather and during seed germination. Even though the companies must pay for the waste heat and must have a back-up system, their energy costs are reduced by as much as 80 percent.

Aquaculture with Waste Water

Just a few miles down the Susquehanna River from Three Mile Island is another island that isn't as famous, but there is something important happening on Brunner Island. Brunner Island is the site of a coal-fired power plant owned by Pennsylvania Power & Light Company. It is also the site of PP&L's experimental fish farming called the **aquaculture** project.

A greenhouse heated by the warm wastewater is being used for hydroponics production of vegetables and to heat incubators for hatching catfish eggs. Once the small catfish are two inches (5 cm) in length, they are transferred to long concrete pools called raceways. The heat absorbed by the water as it passes through the power plant keeps the temperature of the raceways about 80°F (27°C). The optimum temperature for catfish is 84°F (29°C).

Raising catfish offers a solution to thermal pollution as well as an economical source of protein. In 36 weeks on Brunner Island catfish reach a size that would require two to three years in a natural environment. Since the diet and the conditions for growth can be controlled, the result is a fish that tastes better. Catfish have long been a favorite in the South. Through aquaculture they are available to markets in the northern part of the US.

Water from condensers in a nuclear power plant in Pickering, Ontario, Canada, was discharged into Lake Ontario, but now it is used to raise marketable rainbow trout and perch hatchlings. The water is not radioactive because it does not enter the nuclear reactor. It is used to cool steam from the turbines. Every day 10 million gallons (4.5×10^7 L) of water, which is 62°F (17°C) in the winter and 71°F (22°C) in the summer, is piped about a half mile (0.8 km) to Coolwater Farms. The fish farm was a former sewage treatment plant. The settling tanks at the plant are ideal for the fish.

1. Describe how a turbine and generator work together to produce electricity.
2. Match the following descriptions with the proper term.

   Terms
   1. condenser
   2. electricity
   3. generator
   4. turbine

   Descriptions
   A. a coil of wire in a magnetic field
   B. changes steam to water
   C. a large wheel with blades
   D. a flow of electrons
   E. structure turned by force of steam

3. Match the correct amount of energy to the following descriptions.
   A. The amount of energy converted to electricity in a nuclear power plant is:
      1. 15%   **2.** 33%   **3.** 40%   **4.** 45%
   B. The amount of energy converted to electricity in a fossil fueled power plant is:
      1. 15%   **2.** 33%   **3.** 40%   **4.** 45%
   C. The amount of unused energy remaining in steam after it has passed through the turbine is:
      1. 15%   **2.** 33%   **3.** 40%   **4.** 45%
   D. The amount of energy that is lost to the atmosphere as heat is:
      1. 15%   **2.** 33%   **3.** 40%   **4.** 45%
4. List the four methods power plants use to cool the "used" steam.

Once-Through-Cooling Method
5. What is the source of water for the once-through-cooling method?
6. What is the major advantage of the once-through-cooling method?
7. Explain how the warmer water causes shortages of oxygen and water.
8. How does the amount of oxygen needed by a fish change as the water is warmed?
9. Explain the synergistic effect between heated water and disease; between heated water and chemicals.
10. Why might there be a fish kill if the power plant shut down?
11. Explain why most industries and power plants cannot use the once through cooling method.

Cooling Towers
12. Describe how water is cooled in a wet tower; in a dry tower.
13. Give one disadvantage of each type of cooling tower.

Cooling Ponds or Reservoirs
14. What is the added benefit of the cooling ponds that receive warm water from power plants in Missouri?

Waste-Heat Greenhouses
15. Explain how one electric company, PP&L, has turned waste-heat into a product that can be sold.

Aquaculture
16. Give two advantages of combining aquaculture and power production.
17. What type of fish is being raised at Brunner Island, Pennsylvania? What type of fish is being raised at Coolwater Farms in Pickering, Ontario, Canada?

Candu Nuclear Reactor

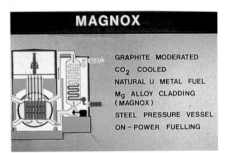

MAGNOX

GRAPHITE MODERATED
CO_2 COOLED
NATURAL U METAL FUEL
Mg ALLOY CLADDING
(MAGNOX)
STEEL PRESSURE VESSEL
ON-POWER FUELLING

*High Temperature Gas-Cooled
Reactor*

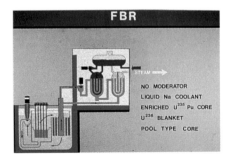

FBR

NO MODERATOR
LIQUID Na COOLANT
ENRICHED U^{235} Pu CORE
U^{238} BLANKET
POOL TYPE CORE

Fast Breeder Reactor

A study by researchers at Columbia University released in September 1990 found no associations between emissions from the Three-Mile Island accident and leukemia or other childhood cancers.

In the years since the March 1979 accident at the Three-Mile Island Nuclear Power Plant, many people have been concerned about the possible effects of the low levels of radiation that escaped during the accident. More than five years after the accident, the Pennsylvania Department of Health conducted a study to determine if the number of new cancer cases and if the number of deaths due to cancer was larger than expected. Why had they waited this long?

Cancer caused by radiation usually takes a long time to develop. It may take ten to twenty years before cancer caused by radiation is diagnosed. Even leukemia, a cancer that has a relatively short period of development, usually isn't detected until five years after exposure to radiation.

The best way to analyze the effect of radiation on the health of a population is a **before-and-after study**. A before-and-after study would compare cancer rates before the TMI accident to cancer rates after the accident. To make a valid comparison, adjustments must be made for the differences in age and sex make-up of the population studied. Since data was not available for the period prior to the accident, a before-and-after study could not be made.

Another problem in the study came from the mobility of the human population. Some people who had lived near Three-Mile Island moved away and could not be included in the study. Migrations out of the area cause some cancer cases to be missed that should have been included in the study. Other people were new to the area. This might cause cancers that had begun to develop before the people moved into the area to be included in the study.

The best method available was to compare the number of cancers that developed after the TMI accident to the number that would have been "expected" in the area prior to the accident. This is known as an **observed versus expected study**. The population used for this study was the 1980 population of the area surrounding TMI. No adjustment was made for the changes in ages or sex make-up of the population studied.

The department of health began a review of many records, including the cancer registry files that were set up in 1982. Other sources of information were the TMI census data, school records, death certificates, and surveys of physicians.

The state health department identified a total of 154 cancer deaths that had occurred since the accident in the "downwind communities" of Goldsboro and York Haven Boroughs, and Fairview and Newberry townships. The population of these communities is about 25,000. If the TMI accident had not occurred, scientists would have expected 152.5 cancer deaths in this region during the same period of time.

Within a 10-mile radius of TMI, the health department found 2,892 cancer deaths from 1979 to 1985. This was only a few less than the 2,909 that scientists would have expected. Within a 20-mile radius, 7,924 cancer deaths were recorded. Scientists would have expected 8,177.

The study of new cancer cases was limited to the four communities downwind from TMI — Goldsboro and York Haven Boroughs, and Fairview and Newberry townships. Results of the study showed 133 new cancer cases in those communities between July 1982 and June 1984. Scientists would have expected 121.4. Even though this is an additional twelve cases of cancer, scientists consider this number too small to be "statistically significant." In other words, these cancers may be due to factors other than the Three-Mile Island accident.

Newberry Township had ten cancer cases more than would have been expected. Further examination of the cases showed that nine of the ten were cancers that are not associated with radiation. Such a cluster of cancer cases is not unusual. This is because cancer is not one disease but a group of diseases that are common in the United States. One out of every four or five people will develop cancer during their lifetime.

Nine leukemia deaths were reported in the four communities after the accident. Only three leukemia deaths had occurred during the same time period before the TMI accident. Neither nine nor three deaths are significantly different from the expected number of six. Two of the nine cases were diagnosed before the accident. In a third case medical reports suggest the onset of leukemia also occurred before the accident.

Four cases of cancer were found among 3,582 mothers studied who were pregnant at the time of the accident, or who became pregnant shortly after the accident. At the time of the accident, all of these women were living within a 10-mile radius of the plant. Four cases of cancer were diagnosed nearly identical to the number normally expected (3.9) for females in the 10-44 year-old age group.

Two of the children born to these mothers were diagnosed with cancer. One case would normally be expected. This difference is not considered to be statistically significant.

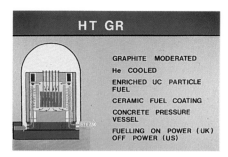

High Temperature Gas-Cooled Reactor

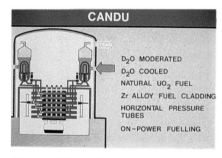

Pressurized Water Reactor

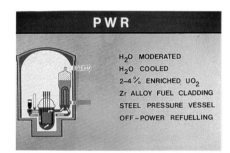

Heavy Water Reactor

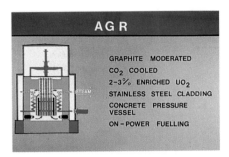

High Temperature Gas-Cooled Reactor

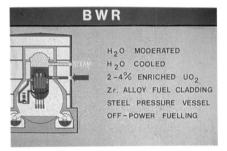

Boiling-Water Reactor

The study discussed above had been requested by the Advisory Panel for Decontamination of TMI Unit 2. After the study was completed, it was reviewed by nationally recognized physicians and scientists who expressed agreement with the findings as well as the validity of the methods used. It was not the first study of cancer deaths after the TMI accident.

The results of another study had been made public on June 21, 1984. Newspaper headlines read "Anti-nuke group's study finds higher cancer rates near TMI." The study, known as the Aamodt Survey, was a health survey conducted by a group of local residents.

A door-to-door survey found 20 cancer deaths in three communities "downwind" from Three-Mile Island. According to the survey this is several times higher than the normal rate of cancer deaths for the area. The accident at TMI was given as the cause of this increase in the cancer death rate. The report gave little information about the methods used to conduct the survey.

The Centers for Disease Control and the US Public Health Service reviewed the Aamodt Survey, at the request of the US Nuclear Regulatory Commission. Analysis of the data presented in the Aamodt survey, along with additional data available from the State Health Department, resulted in the following conclusion: "(The available data) does not support the claim that the TMI accident caused an increase in cancer deaths."

The most important and serious defect in the Aamodt Survey was the "selection bias" in the data collected. There is evidence that the selection was influenced by the pre-existing knowledge of cancer deaths. Only those streets where cancer deaths were known to have occurred were chosen for the survey. Other streets in the same area where there were no cancer deaths were excluded from the survey.

Following are other deficiencies in the Aamodt survey.
- a lack of information about new cancer cases
- no consideration of age and sex distribution in the local populations
- no attempt to include former residents and exclude newcomers
- a difference in time periods for the expected number of cancer deaths (five years) and the observed number of cancer deaths (five years and ten months)
- of the 20 reported cancer deaths, one died before the accident in 1978, one who died of a cause other than cancer was apparently confused with a relative who had died of cancer before the accident, six were diagnosed as having cancer before the accident, and two were long-term heavy smokers who died of lung cancer.

An increase in the number of cancer cases was expected for

the area, even without an accident at TMI. This increase was expected because of these factors:
- an increase in the population of many of the areas included in the study
- an overall increase in cancer cases throughout Pennsylvania as well as other regions in recent years
- Improved methods of reporting cancer cases, such as the new cancer registry
- improvements in diagnosis
- an increase in life span, since older people are more susceptible to cancer.

Cancer can be caused by many environmental factors including radiation exposure, diet, tobacco, microorganisms, food additives, and occupational-industrial exposure. Genetic factors also determine a person's susceptibility to cancer. Because of these complex relationships, we can not make quick conclusions about the cause of new cancer cases.

Previous studies indicate that certain forms of cancer are more likely to occur following exposure to high levels of radiation. The remaining ten cancer deaths in the Aamodt survey represented many different types of cancer. These cancers are normally found in any population. This suggests the absence of a single cause.

As of 1985 there is no evidence that suggests that the accident at TMI has caused an increase in the cancer death rate. Additional studies will be necessary because of the long period of time it may take for cancers caused by radiation to develop. "Did the accident at Three-Mile Island cause an increase in the number of cancer cases?" That question can only be answered by saying "Not yet."

1.5 QUESTIONS FOR STUDY AND DISCUSSION

1. Why wasn't a study of cancer rates made until five years after the accident at Three-Mile Island?
2. What kind of cancer might you expect to increase five years after exposure to radiation?
3. What method of study would have been the best? Why wasn't this method used?
4. What were two major problems that affected the results of the study?
5. What method did the Pennsylvania Department of Health use in the study?
6. What sources of information did the Department of Health use to find the number of cancer cases and cancer deaths that had occurred since the TMI accident?

7. Copy and complete the following chart:

Cancer Deaths	OBSERVED	EXPECTED
"Downwind Communities"		
10-mile radius of TMI		
20-mile radius of TMI		

8. In which region was the number of cancer deaths observed greater than the number expected? Considering the population of 25,000, do you think this difference is due to the accident at Three-Mile Island?

9. Copy and complete the following chart:

New Cancer Cases	OBSERVED	EXPECTED
"Downwind Communities"		
Leukemia		
Pregnant Women		
Babies		

10. Based on what you have read, are any of the differences shown above thought to be due to the accident at Three-Mile Island?

11. Give two reasons why the additional ten cases of cancer found in Newberry Township are not thought to be related to the accident at TMI.

12. How many people develop cancer during their lifetime?

13. Of the nine leukemia deaths reported after the TMI accident, at least three probably were not caused by the radiation released at the time of the accident. Why?

14. Give five reasons why the number of cancer cases expected would increase in the area of TMI, with or without an accident.

15. Do you think that a person who was a long-term heavy smoker and died of lung cancer should have been included in the study? Why or why not?

16. The study conducted by the Pennsylvania Department of Health and the study known as the Aamodt survey led to different conclusions about the increase in the rates of cancer. Identify the study described by each of the following descriptions.

Study	Descriptions
1. Aamodt survey	A. a door to door survey
2. Dept. of Health	B. lacked information about new cancer cases
3. both studies	C. did not consider age and sex of the population studied
4. neither	D. included cancer deaths although the cancer had been diagnosed before the TMI accident
	E. included cancers that occurred in women who were pregnant at the time of the TMI accident
	F. considered all cancers to be related to the TMI accident, even those that are not thought to be caused by radiation
	G. was requested by the Advisory Panel for Decontamination of TMI Unit 2
	H. a study done by an anti-nuclear group
	I. study that is considered valid by most scientists
	J. data collected was biased
	K. did not include former residents and did not exclude former residents
	L. used the 1980 population of the TMI area

17. Has the accident at TMI caused an increase in the death rate of cancer?

18. Why are more studies needed?

"A child born in the United States will have 30 times more impact on the earth's environment during his or her lifetime than a child born in India. The affluent of the world have a responsibility to deal with their disproportionate impact."

Vice-President Al Gore
in a speech before the UN
Sustainable Development Commission

The United States uses more energy per person than any other country. Our high standard of living is directly related to our ability to produce products, and our ability to produce products depends upon available energy supplies.

Oil and natural gas are important sources of energy. Nearly 46 percent of each barrel of crude oil becomes gasoline. A Russian chemist once suggested that oil and natural gas are too valuable to burn. He compared the burning of oil and natural gas to heating your house with bank notes (money).

These fossil fuels are also the sources of many industrial chemicals — **petrochemicals**. Less than 3 percent of each barrel of crude oil is converted to petrochemicals. These petrochemicals are used to make some 3,000 different products. Some petrochemicals are used to manufacture soaps, pesticides, and medicines. Others are important raw materials for making synthetic fibers, rubber, and plastics.

Disposable diapers are an indicator of our life style. We live in a "buy it — use it — throw it away" society. We have changed from a society that once used "returnables," such as glass milk jugs, to a society that prefers "disposables" such as plastic jugs and paper cartons. Diapers and shirts are no longer "natural" products made of 100 percent cotton. Today these products are often made of synthetic materials or a blend of natural and synthetic materials.

While many consumer items are made from petrochemicals, the consumer sometimes has a choice. Which is the better choice — a plastic bag or a paper bag? Should the exterior of the house be wood, or should it be covered with vinyl or aluminum siding? Should the football field be covered with artificial turf, or should it be natural grass? Should the baby's diapers be made of 100% cotton or disposable paper?

Every day people make decisions regarding the use of products. Personal preference plays an important role in their deci-

The geothermal energy plant in Hawaii is built in the Puna rain forest, the last rain forest remaining in the US. Construction and building of the plant has destroyed a large tract of the remaining rain forest. Thermal pollution further threatens the unique organisms that live in this fragile environment. Environmentalists have been fighting completion of the geothermal plant to save the rain forest. Yet geothermal energy is less polluting and more environmentally friendly than other forms of energy generation. How do you make a decision when two environmentally sound issues appear to be in conflict with each other?

sions. Convenience is the most important consideration for some people. Others would prefer to use the product that has the least environmental impact, but they often lack the information necessary for this decision. In this section we will examine some of the environmental impacts associated with a variety of consumer products made from petrochemicals. What are the alternatives? Which has the greatest environmental impact?

The Housing Project

Many construction materials that are made of plastic were once made of metal. Today builders are using plastic pipe made of polyvinylchloride (PVC) or high density polyethylene (HDPE) instead of copper or steel. Window frames and siding are made of vinyl instead of aluminum. Metals are produced by smelting huge amounts of rocks that contain minerals and are known as **ores**. Vinyl and other plastics are petrochemicals made from petroleum.

Both mineral ores and petroleum are nonrenewable resources. While some ores are plentiful, supplies of others are more limited. Although there is no shortage of most important minerals, some must be extracted from low-grade ores. Mining and processing of ores requires large amounts of energy. Petroleum supplies much of this energy.

What is the total environmental impact of a construction project? The environmental impact of the drilling and transportation of oil and natural gas must be weighed against the impacts of mining and transporting the ore. The air and water pollution caused by the manufacture of the plastic resin must be compared with the pollution caused by smelting the ore. The energy required for the production and transportation of metal pipes or window frames must be weighed against that needed to produce and transport the plastic pipes or window frames.

This information is not readily available for most products. One study by the Midwest Research Institute provides some useful information. This study compared the environmental impacts of various materials used to make containers. The data given in the chart on page 500 represents the impact of making one million of each type of container. This data allows us to compare the environmental impact of certain metals and plastics.

The increasing use of plastics in building and construction has led to the prediction that people may one day live in all-plastic houses. Why is the use of plastics increasing? One reason is the increased cost of energy. The production of plastic pipes made of PVC uses less than half the energy required to produce metal pipes. The production of plastic has a lower environmental impact on air and water resources. In addition to the environmental impacts identified in the chart on page 500, the use of plastic products offers a number of other advantages.

Design engineers and builders often prefer plastics because they have a high strength-to-weight ratio. Thus they are lighter and easier to install than the metal or stone counterpart. Pipes, window frames, and siding made of plastic are much more resistant to corrosion than those made of metal. Decks made from plastic "timbers" do not require treatment with toxic chemicals to prevent attack by fungi.

Plastic products can imitate more expensive products made of wood or marble. Insulation made of plastics lowers the cost of heating and cooling. Products made of plastics are durable and require little maintenance. These advantages make plastic the material of choice for many building materials.

The sleeve around the refueling noozle recovers gasoline vapors that escape during refueling. This vapor recovery technology is used in areas having high levels of air pollution such as southern California.

The Tiger in Your Tank

The average car produced in the early 1970s traveled only 13 miles per gallon of gasoline. As a result of the energy crisis in the 1970s, Congress passed a law that required car manufacturers to produce cars with better gas mileage. New cars produced in the United States today are almost twice as efficient as the gas-guzzlers of the early 1970s. The 1990 models produced by an auto company must average 27.5 m.p.g. or the company must pay stiff penalties.

To improve mileage, car makers are making cars that are smaller, lighter, and designed to reduce air resistance. Fenders and other body parts once made of steel are made of high-density polyethylene, polypropylene, and other plastics. A new engine has been designed that contains as much as 60% reinforced plastic (by weight).

Due to the high strength-to-weight ratio, manufacturers can replace 3.5 pounds of metal parts with 1 pound of plastic materials. By 1995, 75 percent of American cars will be equipped with fuel tanks blow-molded from high-density polyethylene. They are lightweight, durable, corrosion-resistant, and they can be designed to fit in almost any available space.

A 10 percent weight reduction of a vehicle will provide a 6 percent gain in fuel economy. Further gains in fuel efficiency will most likely result from greater substitution of lighter-weight materials for steel and cast iron. Due to low cost, plastics have made the greatest contribution to construction of lighter weight automobiles. Parts made of plastics accounted for 8 to 11 percent of the weight of automobiles made in 1985. Automobiles of the future may be as much as 20 percent plastic.

The Shirt in Your Closet

It's time to buy a shirt and you're faced with the choice of 100% cotton or a blend of polyester and cotton. What do you think is the better choice? More than 70 percent of the fibers used in fabrics made in the USA are synthetic. Cotton and wool are both natural fibers — renewable resources. Synthetic fibers, like polyester, are made from crude oil are non renewable.

Which requires more energy — a shirt made of 100% cotton or one made of a blend that is 35% cotton/65% polyester? A group of scientists examined this question. They calculated the energy required to produce the material, make the shirt, and maintain it (washing and ironing) in kilowatt-hours of fossil fuel equivalents. A **watt** is a unit of electrical power. A **kilowatt-hour** (kWh) is one thousand watts of power used for one hour. To produce one kWh of electrical energy requires ten ounces (30 mL) of oil or thirteen ounces (370 g) of coal.

Choosing a Shirt — Is a shirt made of natural fibers a better choice?		
Energy (in kWh) Needed to:	100% Cotton	65-35 Blend
produce the fiber	5.0	9.6
manufacture the cloth	18.5	20.2
sew the shirt	2.8	2.8
TOTAL MANUFACTURING (kWh)	26.3	32.6
wash the shirt (automatic)	32.2	15.8
dry the shirt (automatic)	40.8	18.7
iron the shirt	16.2	5.3
TOTAL MAINTENANCE (kWh)	39.8	89.2
TOTAL kWh per 50 WASHINGS	4486.3	2022.6

The growing of cotton is dependent upon fossil fuels. Large amounts of coal are used to make the steel needed for farm machinery. Oil supplies the energy to run the machines used for preparing the ground, planting and harvesting. Natural gas is used to synthesize the nitrogen fertilizer needed to grow the cotton. The cotton farmer also depends upon herbicides and pesticides that are made from petrochemicals.

It takes less energy to produce an all-cotton shirt, but maintenance of the shirt is another matter. Over the life of the shirt, the all-cotton shirt will require more energy to maintain than the 65/35 blend. Thus the life-time energy requirement for an all-cotton shirt is greater than the energy required for the blend.

The chart gives the energy in kilowatt-hours of fossil fuel equivalents. In many areas, the electricity required to maintain the shirt is produced by burning coal. In other areas the source of energy for electricity is hydropower or nuclear. Check with your utility company to determine if oil or natural gas is used for the production of electricity in your area.

To Market, To Market

On the way home from shopping you stop at the grocery store. One of the items on your list is "disposable beverage cups." Stopping the cart beside the display, you realize that you have a decision to make. There are several brands of cups in various designs and colors. Then there is the choice of paper or plastic.

You read the label on the package of plastic cups but the type of plastic isn't listed. The only hint is that the outside of the cup is colored and the rim and inside are white. The fact that the cups are not clear indicates the resin may be high-impact polystyrene (HIPS). Using the information in the chart on page 500 try to determine which cup will have the least environmental impact.

The figures in the chart reveal that there is not a significant difference between the HIPS cup and the paper cup. Dr. Jan Beyea, author of the Audubon Energy Plan, suggests choosing the plastic cup only if it weighs the same or less than the paper cup. Since a pound of most plastic is produced with less pollution than a pound of paper, the production of a plastic cup that weighs less than a paper cup will have the lower environmental impact.

With the disposable cups of your choice in your basket, you head for the dairy case. Another decision! Should you buy a gallon of milk in a plastic jug or two one-half gallon paper containers of milk? Check the data in the chart on page 500 and select the type of container that has the least environmental impact.

There are at least two additional factors you might want to consider before making your selection. Some studies have shown that the level of vitamin D declines when milk is exposed to light. Milk sold in high-density polyethylene jugs is exposed to light. Thus milk in polyethylene coated paper containers may provide more vitamin D per serving.

Dioxins and furans are members of a class of chemicals that causes cancer in laboratory animals. The EPA classifies these compounds as probable human carcinogens and capable of inducing reproductive and immune-system effects.

Recent studies have found that bleached paper products, including paper milk cartons, contain minute quantities of dioxins and furans. A Canadian study found that dioxins apparently migrate from the paper carton into the milk. Although the study involved only a few samples, the findings are considered to be very important.

SCIENCE TECHNOLOGY & SOCIETY
ISSUES

Environmental Impacts of Serving Food in a School Cafeteria

Take a survey of the dishes and containers used to serve food in your school's cafeteria. Make a chart listing the items used.

Classify each item as reusable or disposable.

List the advantage and disadvantages of each item.

List the alternatives for each item.

Consider the environmental impacts of the alternatives.

Sample Item: Milk container

- Is it disposable or refillable?
- What are the advantages and disadvantages of using this type of container?
- What alternatives are available? — Cartons may be available in plastic-coated paper, glass, or plastic.
- Research some alternatives and evaluate the environmental impacts. What information do you need to make an informed decision?
- Do this for each type of dish or container used.

There is considerable controversy about the risk associated with exposure to dioxins and furans. While more studies are being conducted, the following information is available:

- The tissues of all people living in Western industrialized societies contain dioxins and furans.
- The EPA estimates that dioxins and furans in the emissions from municipal-waste incinerators contribute two to 40 cases of cancer each year.
- The dioxin TCDD has been found in paper towels, paper plates, bond paper, coffee filters, and packaging used for frozen foods and cereal boxes.
- The quantities of dioxins and furans found are small — only 2 to 13 parts per trillion.
- Richard J. Ronk, acting director of the FDA's Centers for Food Safety and Applied Nutrition, believes that the very low levels of dioxins and furans found in paper products do not pose a significant risk to health.
- Charles Elkins, director of EPA's Office of Toxic Substances, would not describe the paper products as "safe." The position of the EPA is that any level of exposure above zero presents a possible risk. One EPA analysis indicates the risk factor may be in the one-in-a-million range.

Considering the information presented on page 500, choose milk in the type of carton you prefer and head for the meat counter. It's getting late and you forgot to thaw meat for dinner, so pick up some hamburger to put on the grill. Check the meat tray. Is it made of pulp or polystyrene foam? Although you may not have a choice of paper or plastic, check the chart on page 500 to compare the environmental impacts.

Before heading to the check-out counter you need to replenish your supply of soft drinks. You may find that your favorite drink is packaged in aluminum, glass, and plastic. Which type of container is the best buy? Which one has the greatest environmental impact? Compare the information in the following chart.

The Economic and Environmental Impacr of Carbonated Beverages			
Container	Consumer's Cost	Energy*	Solid Waste**
Returnable glass	$0.21	1.4	1.4
Non-returnable glass	$0.35	6.3	5.8
Plastic bottle	$0.40	3.1	7.0
Aluminum can	$0.48	8.5	4.0

*oz. of gas equivalent used to make, transport, etc.
**cubic inches of crushed solid waste
Source: Wisconsin Dept. of Natural Resources.

The container with the least economic and environmental impact is the returnable glass container. When returnable glass bottles are refilled 8 times, the total energy requirement per gallon of bottled beverage is 19,000 Btu. The energy needed to bottle a gallon of beverage in throw-a-way bottles is 58,000 Btu.

Although a refillable glass bottle requires more energy to manufacture than a throwaway bottle, the refillable bottle is more energy efficient. The energy saving for refillable containers is due to the reduction in the amount of raw materials that must be acquired and transported and the reduction in the amount of energy needed to manufacture bottles.

In 1958, 98 percent of all carbonated beverages sold in the US were packaged in refillable containers. In 1986, only 15 percent of carbonated beverages were sold in refillables. One way to reduce the energy used for one-use bottles is recycling. Recycling one ton of glass saves nine gallons of fuel oil.

Even though it is the most energy efficient, the use of glass is declining. Some stores no longer carry carbonated beverages in refillable glass bottles. You may have to choose between plastic bottles made of the polymer polyethylene terephthalate (PET) and HDPE or 12 ounce aluminum cans. The chart below provides an estimate of the energy-savings that results from using recycled glass, plastic, and aluminum containers.

Potential Energy-Savings from Recycling		
	Energy required for virgin materials (million Btu/ton)	Energy saved by use of recycled containers (percentage)
Aluminum	250.0	95.0%
Glass	15.6	5.0%
Plastic (PET)	98.0	88.0%

More than 60 percent of aluminum beverage cans are recycled. Aluminum from a Coke® can may reappear on the grocery store shelf as a can of Pepsi®. The same is true for throw-a-way glass bottles. The Proctor & Gamble Company is packaging Spic & Span® in bottles made from recycled PET. The plastic resin is also recycled into polyester fibers for carpets, cushions, sleeping bags, and clothing.

To make a pound of polyethylene terephthalate (PET) from raw materials requires 49,000 Btus of energy. Recycling the PET from beverage bottles into a pound of resin requires only 6,000 Btus — a savings of 43,000 Btus. Recycling one pound of HDPE from the base cups of soft drink bottles, milk jugs, oil, and detergent bottles saves another 38,000 Btus.

We've only just begun to recycle plastics. PET is the plastic most often recycled. In 1987, about 20 percent of the beverage bottles made of PET were recycled. The recycling rate for HDPE in 1987 was only 2 percent.

Finally you're at the check-out counter. Pointing to the grocery bags, the person bagging the groceries asks, "Paper or plastic?" If you were in Europe you wouldn't have to make this decision. You would pull out your own "personal carrier." The European method of using the same bag again and again is obviously the best choice. But faced with no bag of your own and no over-sized pockets, which bag should you choose? Consider the following data. Which bag has the lower environmental impact?

Everything we do, every choice we make, has certain environmental impacts. We can step more lightly on planet Earth by considering these choices before we act. An important question to consider is: How do our choices affect the sustainability of planet Earth?

MANUFACTURING ONE MILLION UNITS

The data given represents the impact of making one million of each container.

Container	Type of Material	Raw Material (pounds)	Energy (Million BTU)	Water (thousand gallons)	Solid wastes (cubic ft)	Atmos. emissions (pounds)	Wastes in water (pounds)	Post use wastes (cubic ft)
8-ounce dairy tub	ABS plastic	1,631	1,928	491	75	6,892	1,135	706
	Aluminum	32,183	5,813	1,032	2,026	24,764	18,095	239
Gallon oblong	HDPE	25,925	16,093	1,824	918	60,437	7,973	5,952
	Steel	1,140,789	20,328	21,126	40,066	80,596	196,923	1,570
9-ounce cup	HIPS	577	550	215	13	1,689	418	226
	Paper	8,315	324	304	38	1,515	740	226
Gallon of milk	HDPE	8,712	7,515	726	306	27,385	4,081	3,175
	Paper	190,375	7,204	6,755	918	34,054	16,527	4,762
Meat trays	PS Foam	303	879	118	37	3,691	327	266
	Pulp	35,559	847	339	130	3,509	1,759	806
Gallon bag	LDPE	384	540	44	21	1,983	248	194
	Paper	22,542	612	532	81	3406	1371	536

1. Define the following terms:
   kilowatt-hour (kWh) ore
   watt petrochemical
2. Describe the relationship between standard of living and energy.
3. Identify six products that you use which are made from petrochemicals.
4. Describe how the lifestyle of the 1970s and 1980s has changed from the lifestyle of the 1940s and 1950s. Explain how this change in lifestyle has affected energy use.

The Housing Project

5. What is the source of aluminum? What is the source of vinyl (PVC)?
6. Compare the environmental impacts caused by making a canoe of ABS plastic with the impacts caused by making the canoe of aluminum. If your only concern in the purchase of a canoe was the environmental impact caused by its manufacture, which canoe would you buy? Justify your choice.
7. Compare the environmental impacts of making a pipe of high density polyethylene (HDPE) to the impacts of making a steel pipe.
8. Why do builders often prefer to use construction materials made of plastic?
9. Why do homeowners often prefer patio furniture made of plastic rather than metal or wood?

The Tiger in Your Tank

10. What characteristics of plastics make them desirable for use in the manufacture of a car?
11. How has the use of plastics (that are made from crude oil) helped reduce the amount of crude oil that the US needs to import?

The Shirt in Your Closet

12. Give examples of fibers that are natural and fibers that are synthetic.

13. Which requires more energy to manufacture — a shirt made of material that is 100% cotton or material that is a blend of cotton and polyester?
14. Which shirt requires more energy to maintain — one made of 100% cotton or one made of a blend of cotton and polyester?
15. List the ways in which the cotton shirt in your closet depends upon fossil fuels.

To Market, To Market

16. Compare the environmental impacts caused by making a plastic cup with the impacts caused by making a cup of paper. If your only concern in the purchase of the cups was the environmental impact caused by its manufacture, which would you choose — paper or plastic? Justify your choice.
17. Which milk carton has the least environmental impact — paper or plastic? Which milk carton did you choose? What was the most important factor that influenced your decision?
18. Given a choice of a paper or polystyrene meat tray, which would you choose? What factors influenced your decision?
19. Which type of beverage container has the least environmental impact? Which did you choose? What factors influenced your decision?
20. Which material saves the most energy when recycled — aluminum, glass, or plastic?
21. Which grocery bag has a lower environmental impact? Which did you choose? Justify your choice.
22. What changes could or should you make to reduce your impact on planet Earth?

Although it was storm sewers that caused most of the trash on the beaches in 1988, the barges of trash heading out to sea provided an image that was hard for environmental groups and law-makers to ignore.

Burn it or Bury It? That is the Question!

Solid wastes include household garbage and other discarded materials. For each person living in the United States, 4 pounds (2 kg) of solid waste is discarded each day. If solid waste from construction sites and sewage treatment plants is included, the waste-per-person rises to 6 pounds per day. In 1991 seventy-six percent of the solid waste produced in the United States was buried in sanitary landfills. But we are quickly running out of usable landfill space. The National Solid Waste Management Association reports that more than half of the landfills in the United States will run out of room within the next ten years.

Other countries have refused to accept our garbage. In some cases, after spending months on a barge the garbage was returned to the United States and buried in a sanitary landfill. So it appears that unless we can find ways to use our solid waste, we will have to find a place to bury it here at home — where it will use our valuable land and threaten our water supplies.

EPA regulations for landfills that took effect in 1993, require installing plastic and clay liners, collecting and treating the **leachate** — the liquids that drain from the landfill, monitoring ground water and surface water quality, and monitoring for escaping methane gas. Protection of the environment will cause an increase in the cost of solid waste disposal in landfills.

According to the EPA, the amount of waste going to landfills should be about 30 percent of the solid waste produced. What are we going to do with the waste? If there is not enough room to bury it, then burn it. Most of the waste is paper, and the amount of plastics is increasing. A plastic soft drink bottle contains slightly more heat content than the same mass of coal. It seems that solid waste might be a good alternative to fossil fuels. In addition to providing energy, burning reduces the volume of waste by as much as 90 percent.

Heat Content of Selected Wastes in BTU per Pound			
food waste	2000	rubber	10000
paper	7200	grass	2800
plastics	14000	wood	8000

Ten percent of solid waste produced in the US is burned at 140 waste-to-energy incinerators. Denmark, Japan, Sweden, and Switzerland burn more than half of their domestic waste. Some of these waste-to-energy plants produce electricity while others produce steam that is used by industries or residential developments.

The EPA recommends that local governments reduce waste going into landfills by burning 20 percent of their solid waste. Not everyone is convinced that solid wastes should be burned. When some plastics and bleached paper are burned, they produce toxic compounds containing chlorine. Some of these chemicals are dioxins that can affect the immune system, fetal development, and cause skin acne. Dioxins are found in the fatty tissues of most humans and in the milk of nursing mothers. No one knows how much the incinerators contribute to the dioxin contamination.

Another concern about burning solid waste is ash disposal. The ash contains heavy metals — cadmium, mercury, and lead. Sweden considers it to be hazardous waste. In the US each incinerator operator must determine if the ash is hazardous. If ash contains high levels of heavy metals, it must be disposed of in licensed hazardous-waste landfills. Cost of disposal in licensed landfills may be as much as ten times higher than in other landfills.

Pulp and Paper Hill

Resource Recovery

Resource recovery refers to the salvaging of usable materials from solid waste. Resource recovery and **recycling** — the use of these "waste" materials in the manufacturing process — are increasing. Fourteen percent of the solid waste produced in the United States was recycled in 1991.

Until 1975 most soft drinks were sold in glass bottles that were returned to the bottling company and reused. Today only 16 percent of soft drinks are sold in "returnable" bottles; most are packaged in aluminum or plastic. Recycling of containers saves raw materials and energy, and it reduces air and water pollution. Producing an aluminum can from another aluminum can uses only 5 percent of the energy needed to produce aluminum from bauxite, and it reduces the emissions of aluminum fluoride.

According to ALCOA (Aluminum Company of America), recycling aluminum also creates jobs. In 1991 twice as many people worked in aluminum recycling as in aluminum manufacturing. Since 1983 the state of New York has required a deposit on beverage containers. A study of the effects showed that the law has saved millions of dollars spent for clean up and disposal. It has also provided nearly 4000 jobs. Nine states have passed "bottle bills."

Recycling of steel, glass, and paper also saves energy and reduces pollution. Paper can be burned to help generate elec-

The recycling of aluminum saves energy and reduces pollution. "Recycling two aluminum beverage cans saves as much energy as one can filled with gasoline."

tricity, but high-grade paper is more valuable as a raw material than as a fuel. The recycling of old newspapers has increased 90 percent since 1983.

Benefits of Recycling Solid Waste				
Benefit	Aluminum	Steel	Paper	Glass
Energy saved (%)	90-97	47-74	23-74	4-32
Reduce Air Pollution (%)	95	85	74	20
Reduce Water Pollution (%)	97	76	35	—
Reduce Mining Wastes (%)	—	97	—	80
Reduce Water Use (%)	—	40	58	50

Not all materials are suitable for recycling. Materials composed of several different substances may not be easily separated. Some paper products are covered with plastic or foil that cannot be easily separated. Some states have passed laws that ban the sale of certain forms of packaging such as juice boxes. Denmark banned the sale of almost all one-way soft drink containers — including aluminum cans.

Resource Recovery Facility ▶

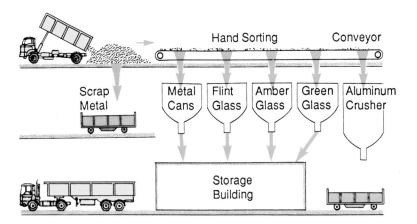

Several states have passed mandatory recycling laws. Large communities must collect materials for recycling, and smaller communities must provide drop-off sites for materials to be recycled. Residents are required to recycle certain materials including paper, glass, aluminum, or plastic. In some states, leaves and grass clippings are no longer permitted in landfills. Instead they are turned into compost. Some communities now have a "pay-as-you-throw" policy to encourage recycling and reduce solid waste going to landfills. Residents are charged by the bag or by the pound to dispose of trash.

With decreasing supplies of natural resources, limited space and concerns about the environmental effects of landfills, and waste-to-energy plants, recycling is no longer merely a way for boy scouts and other organizations to make money. "Reduce, reuse, and recycle" must be more than a slogan, if we are to provide for our growing population and have a healthy environment. These actions must become an important part of our lifestyle.

Reduce and Reuse

Citizens in the United States and Canada produce twice as much solid waste per person as people in other industrialized countries. Farm communities produce far less solid waste than people living in cities. But even in farm communities more people are working away from home, and the demand for convenience products is increasing. More energy is often used to package convenience products than is used to produce the product in the package. Getting rid of the packaging materials also consumes energy.

Energy Consumed for Manufacture of Certain Packaging Materials (in kWh)			
steel can (16 oz/454 mL)	1.17	polystyrene tray	0.25
aluminum can (12 oz/354 mL)	1.91	molded fiber tray	0.45
plastic bag (2 QT/2.2L)	1.23	aluminum TV tray	1.74

In addition to conserving energy, reducing packaging also conserves other valuable resources. The Worldwatch Institute reports that packaging uses 50 percent of all paper and 25 percent of all plastics sold. Packaging materials contribute 50 percent of the volume of domestic waste.

The ultimate answer to the solid waste problem is prevention — reduce the amount of solid waste created. McDonald's Corporation reduced its solid waste by 70 percent simply by changing the way that it packaged hamburgers. The US Environmental Protection Agency (EPA) has made **source reduction** — decreasing the amount of waste produced — the top priority in the management of solid waste.

One way to reduce the solid waste is to reuse, that is, to buy products that can be used again and again. Yvon Chouinard, President of Patagonia Outdoor Clothing, recommends that you, "Buy fewer products, but buy excellent products that you know are going to last."

Recycling is the next best thing, but recycling does have environmental impacts. Although recycling resources saves energy when compared to using virgin resources, recycling does require energy. Recycling also contributes to air and water pollution.

Large containers at convenient locations can be usd to separate garbage. This is one way of reducing the amount of solid waste ending up in Landfills.

WHAT DO YOU THINK?

Packaging is one of the largest contributors to our solid waste stream and to our landfill problems. Yet plastic and other kinds of packaging have advantages. For example, the United States has the lowest rate of food spoilage in the world. This is largely due to the efficient way foods are packaged to prevent spoilage. Do you think packaging that uses nonrenewable resources should be banned? How would you distinguish between "good" packaging and environmentally "bad" packaging?

DID YOU KNOW?

Around 500 BC the first "solid waste law" was passed in Athens, Greece. Prior to the law, sewage and garbage were disposed of inside the city, sometimes contaminating water and causing disease. The law required Athenians to dump their garbage no closer than 1.6 kilometres outside the city walls.

1. Define the following terms:
   recycling   reuse
   reduce   solid waste
   resource recovery waste-to-energy plant

Burn it or Bury It — That is the Question!

2. How many people share your home? Assume that each member of your family produces an average amount of solid waste. Calculate the amount of waste produced by your family during one year.
3. What happens to most of this waste?
4. Identify problems associated with the use of landfills as a means of disposal.
5. What actions must landfill owners take to protect the ground water? the air?
6. In each of the following pairs, identify the waste that is the best fuel source (has the highest BTU content).
   A. paper or plastic
   B. yard waste or food waste
   C. old tires or wood
7. Compare the amount of solid waste burned in waste-to-energy plants in the United States to the amount burned in Japan and Switzerland.
8. Compare the amount of solid waste burned in waste-to-energy plants in the United States with the amount recommended by the EPA.
9. Give two advantages of burning as a method of disposing of solid wastes.
10. Give two reasons why some people are concerned about waste-to-energy plants.

Resource Recovery

11. What is the difference between resource recovery and recycling?
12. How have the types of containers used to package soft drinks changed since 1975?
13. Give three advantages of recovering and recycling aluminum, steel, and paper.
14. Explain how reducing the water used to produce a product will save energy.
15. Identify types of products that cannot be recycled.
16. What policy changes are helping to increase the rate of recycling?
17. Discuss the importance of resource recovery and recycling to the sustainability of planet Earth.

Reduce and Reuse

18. Compare the solid waste produced per person in North America with the solid waste produced per person in other industrialized countries.
19. Compare the solid waste produced by farm societies with the solid waste produced by urban lifestyles.
20. Which packaging material requires the most energy to produce — paper, plastic, aluminum, or steel?
21. What is the EPA's top priority in waste management?
22. Compare the environmental impacts of the "reuse" and "recycle" methods of reducing solid waste.
23. Evaluate your lifestyle. What changes could you make to help make planet Earth sustainable?

Acid (acidic) — any chemical compound that will dissolve and produce hydrogen ions (Hy⁺).

Acid deposition — both wet and dry substances in the atmosphere that produce a pH lower than natural rainfall — more commonly called acid rain.

Acid rain — the commonly used term for acid deposition.

Acid shock — a condition that occurs in fish when there is a sudden increase in the amount of acid in the water. It may kill an entire population of fish.

Acid tolerant — species that can survive and reproduce in water with a low pH.

Acre-foot — the amount of water that covers one acre of land to a depth of one foot.

Activated carbon filter — a filter that contains carbon that has been heated with steam, and is used to remove organic chemicals from water.

Activated sludge — type of secondary sewage treatment in which waste water is mixed with oxygen.

Active solar heating system — a heating system that uses pumps or fans to distribute heat collected and trapped by the greenhouse effect.

Aeration — the ability of air to move through the soil.

Aerosols — fine droplets of liquid.

Agricultural Stabilization and Conservation Service (ASCS) — a federal agency created to help pay for conservation work.

Agriculture — the process of planting and harvesting of crops for food.

Air quality standard — the maximum amount of pollutant allowed in either ambient air or emissions.

Air — a colorless, odorless, tasteless mixture of gases.

Algal bloom — excessive growth of algae that can be observed by the color of the water.

Alkaline (basic) — refers to any solution that has the properties of a base.

Alloy — two metals or a metal and a nonmetal that are fused together. An example is brass.

Alpha radiation — particles of radiation that can be stopped by a sheet of paper

Alum — a chemical that is added to cause small particles in water to clump or stick together.

Ambient air — air outdoors from ground level to about 10 miles (16 km) above Earth's surface.

Anthracite — a bright and shiny hard coal that is formed under intense heat and pressure. It has the highest percentage of carbon and the highest heat content.

Aquaculture — fish farming.

Aqueducts — canals that carry water.

Aquifer — water-filled layers of porous or fractured rock.

Arab Oil Embargo — during the Arab-Israeli War in 1973, Arab oil-producing nations cut off oil supplies to the United States and the Netherlands because they supported Israel.

Archaeologist — scientist who studies things that were made or used by early humans.

Artifact — objects modified by early humans.

Asbestos — a group of natural minerals that are heat resistant, very durable, and are found in certain types of rock formations .

Asbestosis — a disease of the lungs caused by the presence of asbestos in the lungs.

Atmosphere — the mixture of gases that forms a blanket around a planet.

Atmospheric deposition — the process in which air pollutants enter the water with precipitation or by diffusion.

Attrition — the wearing or grinding of a substance by friction.

Background level — the level of naturally occurring radiation for a given location.

Backwash — the process in which the direction of the water flow through a filter is reversed in order to clean the filter.

Baffles — a series of wall-like structures over which water falls in cooling towers — a series of dividers in a water tank that slows the flow of water.

Bagasse — fibrous waste produced during the processing of sugar cane.

Bark rights — the right to continue cutting trees and selling bark from land that had been sold.

Base — any chemical compound that will dissolve and give hydroxyl ions (OH⁻) or accept hydrogen (H⁺) is a base.

Basin — the watershed or area of land that drains into a river.

Before-and-After Study — a study in which data is gathered before an event and a second set of data is gathered after an event in an attempt to determine cause and effect.

Best Management Practices — BMP — agricultural practices that reduce pollution and reduce the cost of producing a crop.

Beta radiation — fast moving particles of ionizing radiation that may be stopped by a thin sheet of aluminum.

Binder twine — a type of string used to tie bundles of grain.

Bioaccumulation — the increasing concentration of chemicals as they are stored in the bodies of organisms and passed up the food chain.

Biodegradable — chemicals that can be broken down by organisms in the environment.

Biodiesel — sometimes called Soydiesel — an alternative fuel that is made from soybeans rather than petroleum.

Biodiversity — the variety of plant and animal species in an ecosystem — the variety of ecosystems in the biosphere.

Biogeochemical cycles — the flow of chemicals between the environment and the organisms in it.

Biologist — a scientist who studies living things.

Biomass — the total mass of all organic matter at any level in a food chain.

Biome — a large geographic region determined by the climate and soil type. Examples: Arctic tundra, tropical rain forest, desert.

Biosphere — the large masses of air, water, and land that support a thin layer of life on planet Earth.

Bituminous coal — a type of soft coal with a relatively high heat content — the most common type of coal found in the US.

Black blizzards — Dark skies created when strong winds picked up and carried large amounts of topsoil.

Black lung — a lung condition resulting from the breathing of coat dust. Symptoms of the disease include excess mucus, shortness of breath, and a chronic cough.

Blue-baby syndrome — a syndrome in which babies develop a bluish color, especially around the eyes and mouth because the blood does not carry enough oxygen — may be due to nitrite poisoning.

Bog — a poorly drained area that is acidic and contains characteristic acid-tolerant plants such as sphagnum moss, carnivorous plants, and sedges.

Boil Water Advisory — a notification made by a water supplier to customers when the water exceeds the EPA standard of 1 coliform bacterium per 100 milliliters of water or when a water main break increases the potential for contamination of the water supply.

Bordeaux mixture — a fungicide made of calcium hydroxide and copper sulfate.

Boreal — a type of bog that exists in Canada and the northern United States.

Bottomland hardwood forests — often called swamps, forests on river floodplains that are periodically flooded.

Bounty — money paid for a dead predator.

Broadcast seeder — a piece of equipment that uses a small fan to scatter seeds.

Broad-spectrum pesticide — chemicals that kill many different kinds of organisms.

Bronchial asthma — a respiratory disease caused by an allergic reaction of the membranes lining the bronchial tubes.

Buffer — a substance that when placed in water, prevents large changes in the pH — chemicals that help neutralize acids and bases and maintain pH.

Cancer — a disease of the lungs or other tissues that results when cells grow and divide at an unusually fast rate.

Canopy — the leafy roof that is created by the tops of the mature trees in the forest.

Captex — an experiment in which a tracer substance was released and air samples were collected to plot the path of air pollutants.

Carbon dioxide — a compound that contains one atom of carbon and two atoms of oxygen — a product of combustion and respiration and an important greenhouse gas.

Carbon monoxide — a compound consisting of one atom of oxygen and one atom of oxygen, when absorbed by the blood it interferes with hemoglobin's ability to transport oxygen.

Carbonic acid — chemical that is formed when carbon dioxide combines with water.

Carcinogen — a substance that causes cancer.

Carcinogenic — cancer-causing.

Carnivore — consumers (animals) that eat other animals (meat).

Carrion — the carcass of a dead animal.

Carrying Capacity — the size of the population that an ecosystem can support at any given time without damage to the ecosystem.

Catalyst — a special chemical that speeds up a chemical reaction.

Catalytic converter — a stainless steel container about the size of a litre of soda that contains a platinum catalyst that reduces two of the three major air pollutants produced by internal combustion engines.

Cavity Nester — birds that make their nest in the hollow spaces in a dead or dying tree.

Center-pivot irrigation — a self-propelled sprinkler system that is used to spray water over field crops.

Chaff — protective sheaths that cover individual kernels of grain.

Channel — the natural bed of a river or a stream in which the water usually flows — human-made channels are straight box-like ditches dug to move water more efficiently.

Chemistry — the study of matter (and energy), its composition, and changes in its composition.

Chesapeake Bay Agreement — a cooperative effort between the states that surround the Chesapeake Bay to improve and protect the water quality and living resources of the Bay.

Chestnut blight — a fungus that grows beneath the bark of the American chestnut tree and cuts off the flow of nutrients and water.

Chisel plow — a method of conservation tillage in which chisels loosen the soil without turning under the sod or other plant material.

Chlorinated hydrocarbon — a chemical compound made by removing hydrogen atoms from a hydrocarbon and adding chlorine atoms.

Chlorine demand — the amount of chlorine needed to treat the water.

Chlorine residual — the amount of free chlorine remaining in the water at the end of the contact period.

Chlorine — a disinfectant used to treat water supplies.

Chlorofluorocarbons — also known as CFCs —compounds containing carbon, fluorine and chlorine that destroy the ozone layer and act as a greenhouse gas.

Chronic bronchitis — a respiratory disease in which the bronchial tubes are damaged, excess mucus interferes with the exchange of air and causes a chronic cough.

Clean coal technology — refers to methods of reducing the air pollution that results from the burning of coal.

Clean fuels — fuels that reduce the emissions of some pollutants. Clean fuels include compressed natural gas, methanol, ethanol, electricity.

Clearcutting or **clearcut logging** — the cutting or felling of every tree on a specific tract of forest.

Climate — the average weather of a region described by the amount and pattern of precipitation and the normal range of temperatures — the long-term weather patter of a place over a period of years.

Cloud — airborne masses of microscopic water droplets of ice crystals.

Club soda — a form of bottled water that contains added minerals and carbon dioxide.

Cluster — group of people living or working in the same area that develop the same disease.

Coal — a black or brown rock that contains hydrocarbons formed from decayed plants.

Cogeneration — the use of only one system to produce electricity and heat for industrial processes.

Coke — a solid mass of nearly pure carbon that is formed by burning coal at high temperatures without oxygen. It is used in the manufacture of steel.

Coliform bacteria — type of bacteria normally found in the intestines of humans and other warm-blooded animals.

Colorado Brown Stain — discoloration of teeth due to high levels of fluoride in the water supply; also called Texas Teeth.

Combine harvesters — a modern self-propelled machine that reaps and threshes grain of all types.

Combined sewers — pipes that carry both sewage and storm water.

Combustion — burning — the chemical reaction in which certain substances combine with oxygen and release light and energy.

Combustion — the oxidation (burning) of compounds containing carbon — the burning of a mixture of fuel and oxygen.

Compost — a mixture of soil and decomposed organic materials (humus).

Condensation — the process in which water vapor changes into liquid water.

Conservation district — a geographic area, usually a county, in which a group of local people help plan and implement conservation projects.

Conservation tillage — planting crops without using a moldboard plow.

Consumed — a natural resource that is used and not returned to the source.

Consumers — organisms that cannot make their own food and must depend directly or indirectly on producers.

Contact time — period of time that is needed for chlorine to react with the water in order to disinfect it.

Contaminant — pollutant, especially those found in drinking water or food.

Contour planting — plowing and planting across a slope rather than up and down the slope — "horizontal planting"

Control — a group of subjects that does not receive the experimental treatment in a controlled experiment.

Controlled experiment — an experiment that has two groups of subjects with only one difference between the two groups.

Cooling pond — a reservoir that is used as an alternative to a cooling tower.

Corn peg — a hand-held instrument used to husk corn.

Corn picker — a mechanical harvester that replaced the binder.

Corn sheller — a machine that removes corn kernels from the cob.

Corps of Engineers — (COE) — engineers employed by the federal government to maintain navigable waterways, control floods, and regulate wetlands.

Cosmic radiation — ionizing radiation that enters Earth's atmosphere from outer space.

Coulter — a circular steel blade that is attached in front of the plow and cuts through sod or debris.

Cover crops — grasses or legumes that are planted to hold the soil in place.

Cover — a place where animals can hide from predators and be protected from the weather.

Cradle — a wooden attachment for a scythe that catches the stalks of grain.

Crop rotation — planting a series of crops such as corn-beans-wheat-clover-corn.

Crumb — soil structure in which clumps are described as irregular with a diameter less than 1.5 cm.

Cryptosporidiosis — a flu-like illness accompanied by diarrhea that is caused by a tiny parasitic protozoan called cryptosporidium.

Cull trees — trees that will not yield high quality lumber and may be removed to provide space for other trees or left standing to become snags.

Curie — an amount of radiation equal to the decay of 3.7×10^{10} atoms per second — the amount of radiation from one gram of radium.

Cyclones — vertical tube with circular air flow that removes large particles from flue gases before they leave the smoke stack.

Days to harvest — the number of days between the last application of the pesticide and the day the crop can be legally harvested.

DDT — the first chlorinated hydrocarbon used as an insecticide.

Decomposer — organisms that feed on the waste products or bodies of other dead organisms.

Deep forest species — species that live in the interior of the forest.

Deep-well injection — method of waste disposal in which liquid wastes are pumped into a layer of sandstone or other porous rock.

Delaware River Basin Commission — body created to manage the Delaware River as a natural resource.

Delaware River Basin Compact — a document, signed by the governors of New York, New Jersey, Pennsylvania, and Delaware, recognizing the Delaware River as a regional resource and creating a commission to manage the resource.

Delta — a mass of land that forms at the mouth of a river as the river drops its load of silt and clay particles.

Dental fluorosis — a condition that occurs in areas in which the level of fluoride is greater than 1.5 ppm. In mild form teeth have paper white areas, and in more severe forms the teeth are stained brown and may be pitted.

Development rights — refers to the right of the owner of a parcel of land to construct buildings on (develop) the land.

Dew — water that condenses on a cool surface.

Die casting — forcing heated metal into a die to make parts for equipment.

Die — a mold or pattern that determines the shape of an object.

Diesel engine — a type of internal combustion engine in which the fuel is ignited by the heat created by the compression of the fuel.

Diffusion — the movement of a substance from an area of high concentration to an area of lower concentration.

Digesters — heated tanks used for treatment of sewage sludge.

Digging stick — used for digging root and bulbs and later planting seeds, it may have been the first farm tool.

Dike — hard rock that is resistant to erosion forms ridges when the softer material is eroded away — massive sloping concrete walls built along a stream to protect a developed area from a flood.

Discs — a piece of farm equipment made of iron or steel that is used to cut through clods before using a harrow.

Dissolved oxygen — **DO** — oxygen gas that is dissolved in the water and available to aquatic organisms through their skin or special respiratory structures.

Diversion terrace — ridges of soil that are constructed along the contours to slow the speed of the flowing water.

Dose rate — the amount of radiation given per unit of time.

Dose — quantity of radiation.

Drip irrigation — a method of watering plants through a series of subsurface pipes.

Drought-resistant — crops that can tolerate long periods without water.

Dry steam — steam created by geothermal energy and trapped at shallow depths in some locations.

Dry tower — a method of cooling water in which the hot water flows through pipes and a fan is used to increase the flow of air.

Dust Bowl — the southern part of the Great Plains including parts of Kansas, Oklahoma, Texas, New Mexico, and Colorado.

Dutch elm disease — an imported fungus that clogs the sap-carrying tubes of the American elm tree.

Ecologist — a scientist who studies organisms interacting with their environment and with other organisms in it — a scientist who studies organisms within an ecosystem.

Ecology — the study of organisms in their natural environment. — the study of living things in relation to their physical environment and to each other.

Ecosystem — a group of plants, animals, and other organisms that live together, and that interact with the surrounding physical environment.

Ecotone — the place where two ecosystems meet — sometimes call an edge.

Edge Effect — the result that occurs when a large number of species and larger populations of each of these species are present at the place were two ecosystems meet (edge) because of the increase in the amount of food and cover.

Edge — the place where two ecosystems meet.

Effluent — treated waste water from a sewage treatment plant or industry.

El Niño — a dramatic warming of water in the eastern Pacific Ocean.

Electricity — the flow of electrons transmitted along wires.

Electrodialysis — a method of removing salt from sea water by passing the water through a chamber that contains electrodes with positive and negative charged.

Electromagnetic radiation (EMR) — a form of energy that all objects (living and nonliving) absorb, reflect, and emit. Each type of object can be identified by a distinctive pattern of EMR.

Electrostatic precipitators — a series of charged metal plates that attract particles in flue gases before they leave the smokestack.

Emerging plant stage — stage of succession of a pond or lake that is characterized by larger plants such at cattails and water lilies.

Emigrate — organisms moving to other areas often due to stress from overcrowded conditions.

Emission standards — the maximum amount of a pollutant that is allowed to enter the atmosphere from exhaust pipes, chimneys, or smokestacks.

Emissions cap — a maximum amount of sulfur dioxide that can be released in the atmosphere from all electrical power plants.

Emissions — gases and particles entering the air from smoke stacks, chimneys, and exhaust pipes.

Emphysema — a respiratory disease in which the air sacs lose their elasticity and lose the ability to push the air out of the lungs.

Enamel — the hard substance that covers the teeth above the gum line.

Endangered species — animals whose chances of survival and reproduction are in immediate jeopardy.

Energy efficiency — a measure of the amount of energy that an appliance or other invention can convert to useful work.

Energy — the ability to do work.

EnergyGuide — labels that contain the information needed to compare the energy efficiency of different models of appliances.

EPA — Environmental Protection Agency — the branch of the federal government that sets and enforces standards for air and water pollution.

Erosion — the movement of soil or mineral particles from one location to another by wind or water.

Estuary — an area where fresh water from a river mixes with salt water from the ocean.

Ethylene — a hydrocarbon that is present in auto exhaust. It causes damage to some flowering plants.

Even-aged trees — a stand of trees that mature and are ready for harvest at the same time.

Experimental group — a group of subjects that receives the treatment being tested in a controlled experiment.

Expiratory reserve volume — the amount of air that can be forced out after a normal breath is exhaled.

Extinct species — animals that are no longer surviving on Earth.

Eye of the bog — the last remaining area of open water in the lake that is changing to a bog.

Felling — refers to the cutting of trees.

Fertile soils — soils that have chemicals that plants require for growth.

Fertilizer — any substance that is added to the soil to provide nutrients for plant growth.

Filamentous algae — algae that grows as long strands instead of individual floating cells.

Filtration — the process of passing water through a substance in order to remove certain types of chemicals or solid particles.

Fish kill — the death of many fish at one time.

Fish ladder — pools of water arranged as a series of steps to allow fish to move around a dam.

Fission — the splitting apart of atoms.

Flail — a long-stick with a heavy beater-stick fastened to the end for threshing grain.

Flat plate collector — shallow insulated boxes that are covered with glass and contain a black metal plate to absorb heat.

Flat rate — a system of payment that requires the same payment regardless of the amount of the resource used.

Floating plants — plants that have leaves and flower that lie on the surface or rise only slightly above the surface but whose roots and stems are submerged.

Floc — clumps of particles that form in the water during the treatment process.

Flood — the condition that exists when water flows over the top of the river's bank and across the low land that lies along the river.

Floodplain — low, flat land that lies along a river.

Flow — the volume of water in a river or stream.

Fluidized bed combustion — a technology for burning coal and other low-grade fuels, including high-sulfur coal using injected air and crushed limestone.

Fluorides — compounds that contain the element fluorine and are found in most soils, water supplies, and foods. Fluorides are also compounds added to toothpaste to prevent tooth decay.

Fluorosis — fluoride poisoning that reduces milk supply in cattle. The severe form causes lameness in cattle and skeletal deformation in humans. It can be fatal.

Fly ash — small particles containing minerals that are released during the burning of fuels, especially coal.

Fog — water vapor that condenses to form clouds near the surface of the earth.

Food chain — a diagram that shows the flow of energy from green plants through a series of consumers in an ecosystem.

Food web — a diagram that shows many possible food chains that exist in an ecosystem.

Forage — nonwoody and new woody growth that is eaten by browsing and grazing animals.

Forest decline — a forest condition in which many trees show signs of stress such as a thinning of the foliage, premature yellowing or loss of foliage, and an increase in the number of dead and dying trees.

Fossil fuels — goal, oil, natural gas.

Fossil ground water — water that has slowly been absorbed by Earth over millions of years and is essentially not being replaced as it is used.

Fragmentation — the carving of an ecosystem into small isolated tracts.

Friable — the condition of substances that can be easily crumbled by the hand when dry.

Frontage rate — system of payment based on the size of the building and number of bathrooms and sinks.

Frost — water that forms ice crystals on a cool surface.

Fusion — joining of the nuclei of two atoms to form one atom of a different element; the process of heating two substances to form a metal alloy.

Galvanizing — the process of coating iron or steel with zinc to prevent rusting.

Game management — the science that includes measuring the size of the population, determining the carrying capacity of the habitat, and determining the number that can be harvested.

Game species — those species that can be legally hunted.

Gamma rays — energy waves that travel at the speed of light.

Gang plow — a piece of farm equipment with several coulters and moldboard plows.

Gas bubble disease — condition that occurs in fish when too much air is dissolved in the water and small bubbles of air form in the blood and tissues.

Gasohol — a blend of one part grain alcohol and nine parts gasoline.

Generator — stationary coils of copper wire with electromagnets that can be rotated to create a flow of electrons.

Genetics — the study of inherited traits.

Geothermal energy — the energy from the natural heat or hot water trapped below the earth's surface.

Giardiasis — an illness affecting the stomach and intestines causing abdominal cramps, nausea, gas, and diarrhea and caused by a one-celled protozoan parasite *Giardia lamblia*.

Global warming — an increase in the planet's average temperature; an accelerated greenhouse effect.

Graded sand filter — bed made of layers of rock and sand that is used to filter water.

Grain drill — a planter that has a long box with planting tubes that deliver seed into a shallow ditch made by two discs.

Granular — the soil structure in which clumps are described as rounded with a diameter less than 1.5 cm.

Green manure crops — crops that are grown for the purpose of adding organic matter to the soil.

Green Revolution — the development of high-yielding, disease-resistant varieties of wheat and rice during the 1970s.

Greenhouse effect — the warming of Earth's atmosphere caused by the sun's radiation (light energy) passing into the atmosphere and being changed to heat energy that is absorbed (trapped) by gases in the atmosphere.

Greenhouse gases — gases that act as a blanket to trap heat and keep the planet warm.

Grinder — a large garbage disposal-type structure that reduces the size of solids entering the sewage treatment plant.

Ground water — the layer of water that accumulates within the soil due to an impermeable layer of rock or clay blocking its flow.

Growing degree days — the daily accumulation of heat calculated using the average daily temperature and the minimum and maximum temperatures for the development of a species.

Gully erosion — the formation of large ditches by water as it moves down a steep slope.

H^+ — hydrogen ion

Habitat — the place in an ecosystem where an organism prefers to live.

Half-life — the amount of time it takes for one half of a radioactive element to break down.

Hard coal — a form of coal, also known as anthracite, contains little sulfur compared to other coal.

Hard water — water that contains a high concentration of dissolved minerals.

Harrow — a piece of farm equipment that breaks up the clods and levels the soil before planting.

Head — the vertical distance water falls at a dam.

Header — a part on a combine or corn picker that guides the stalks into the machine.

Hellgrammite — the common name for a dobsonfly larvae.

Herbicides — chemicals used to kill "weed" species.

Herbivore — organisms (consumers) that eat plants.

Host — an organism that a parasite lives in or on and that provides the parasite with food.

Hot dry rock system — a technology used to produce electricity from geothermal energy.

Humidity — the amount of moisture (water vapor) in the air.

Humus — decayed matter consisting of the remains of dead organisms — partly decomposed organic matter that was once living or was produced by a living thing.

Hunters and gatherers — people who depend upon wild plants and animals for food.

Hydrocarbon — compounds that contain only hydrogen and carbon. Examples include methane, propane, and benzene.

Hydroponics — method of growing plants with roots suspended in a solution of nutrients (fertilizers).

Index species — a species whose presence in large numbers tells us that the water is clean or polluted.

Indicator organisms — an organism whose presence tells something about the condition of the environment.

Indicator species — a species whose presence is a sign that the ecosystem is healthy and can provide for the needs of many species.

Indicator — chemicals that change color at a specific pH.

Infertile — soil that is lacking certain chemicals (nutrients) and unable to support good plant growth.

Infiltration — the process in which the soil absorbs water or the process of water soaking into the soil.

Inspiratory reserve volume — the amount of air that can be taken in following a normal breath.

Integrated Pest Management — IPM — an approach to controlling pests that involves the use of not one but several methods of insect control.

Intensively managed forests — increasing the yield of a forest by growing trees from high quality seedlings, using chemicals to control insects and weed species and provide nutrients.

Internal combustion engine — an engine in which the fuel burns or explodes inside a closed cylinder.

Introduced species — a species that has been accidentally or intentionally introduced to a new ecosystem.

Inversion — a layer of cold air is trapped by a layer of warm air above it.

Ion — a charged atom or group of atoms.

Ionizing radiation — high-energy radiation that can knock electrons from atoms. Includes Alpha, Beta, and Gamma radiation.

Irrigation — artificial application of water to aid growing crops.

Jab planter — a mechanical device used for making a hole and planting corn seeds.

Jet stream — a 200-mile-an-hour river of air that flows 20,000 to 30,000 above Earth's surface.

Kettle lake — a lake with no streams carrying water into or out of it, usually formed by glaciers.

Keystone species — a species that keeps the ecosystem in balance.

Kilowatt-hour — one thousand watts of power used for one hour.

Lactic acid — waste product produced by muscle cells when there is a lack of oxygen.

Lagoon — a shallow pond where sewage is held for treatment.

Lake — a standing body of water with an area that is too deep for rooted plants to grow.

Landslide — a straight piece of metal that guides the moldboard plow.

Latent period — the time between exposure to a substance and the appearance of damage.

Leachable — chemicals that are soluble in water.

Leachate — the liquids that drain from a landfill.

Leaching — the process in which water dissolves and removes minerals from rock or soil — the process in which chemicals are dissolved and carried away by the water.

Lead — a heavy metal that interferes with the normal activity of the nervous system.

Legumes — a large family of plants, including peas, beans, and alfalfa, that have nodules with nitrogen-fixing bacteria on the roots.

Lignite — a very soft coal formed from peat. It has a lower percent of carbon and a lower heat content that other forms of coal.

Lime — calcium carbonate — a chemical added to adjust the pH of water.

Limiting Factor — anything that prevents the population size from increasing. Examples include weather, food, and living space.

Line-bypass filter — a filter installed under the sink to remove contaminants from the water supply.

Load — the clay and silt particles that are carries by water in a stream or river.

Loam — soils that contain less than 20% clay and nearly equal parts of sand and silt.

Lock — an area, between two massive steel gates in which the water level can be raised or lowered to allow ships and barges to pass around a dam.

Longwall system — a method of mining coal in deep mines in which the coal is removed along a wall several hundred feet long and the roof is allowed to collapse behind the mined area.

Low-energy precision application — a more efficient center-pivot irrigation system that delivers water closer to the ground.

Lower reaches — sections of the stream with a gentle, steady flow containing no rapids, riffles, or water falls and with a layer of mud or sand on the bottom.

Machete — a big knife used for clearing brush.

Mark-release-recapture method — a method used to determine the population density of a species.

Marsh — an area of shallow water with grasses and other rooted plants.

Mass erosion — also called slumping; a movement of a mass of soil that is saturated with water down a slope due to the force of gravity.

Mast — acorns and other nuts and fruits that lie on a forest floor and become food for animals.

Matter — anything that takes up space and has mass.

Maximum Contaminant Level — the highest amount of the pollutant that is allowed in drinking water.

Meander — a path that has large curves.

Mercury — a chemical that may be absorbed by the body and cause damage to the nervous system and the kidneys.

Mesothelomia — cancer in the lining of the chest and abdomen caused by asbestos fibers.

Meteorology — the study of the physics and chemistry of the atmosphere.

Methane — a hydrocarbon produced by the decomposition of organic material in wet, oxygen-deficient environments; an important greenhouse gas.

Methemoglobinemia — a "blue baby" condition in which nitrites in the blood prevent hemoglobin from combining with oxygen.

Micronutrients — elements that are needed by plants in very small amounts.

Middle reaches — sections of the stream with less slope than the upper reaches, larger pools and silt deposits.

Millirem — one one-thousandth of a rem.

Mineral — certain compounds found in rocks and soil — naturally occurring solids with specific chemical and physical structures.

Mining — removal of a natural substance from an ecosystem faster than it can be replaced by natural processes.

Minute volume — the total amount of air taken in during one minute.

Moldboard — a piece of curved metal that is attached to a plow share and turns the soil.

Molting — the process by which birds shed old feathers.

Monoculture — growing of only one plant species in a large area.

Mortar — a bowl-shaped container in which foods are pounded into a powder.

Muck soil — soils that contain more than 20% humus.

Multiple uses — the principle that is the basis for management of federal land. Uses include timbering, mining, watershed protection, grazing, recreation, and fish and wildlife habitat.

NAAQS — the maximum amount of specific air pollutants allowed in the ambient air.

National Forest Management Act — a law passed in 1976 that requires management plans for all national forests to include sufficient habitat for all native vertebrate species.

National Wildlife Refuge System — land purchased with money from the migratory bird hunting stamp (duck stamp) and set aside for wildlife.

Natural increase — the change in size of the population due to a greater number of births than deaths.

Natural regeneration — restoring a forest by the germination of seeds from trees remaining after logging.

Natural Resources Defense Council — an environmental organization that works to protect the environment by hiring lawyers to argue cases against polluters in court.

Natural Valley Storage Plan — method of flood protection that involved the purchase of wetlands to absorb the excess water in the Charles River watershed.

Nature Conservancy — a conservation organization whose goal is the preservation of the best examples of a wide variety of ecosystems.

Neutral — a solution with a pH of 7 (10^{-7} H ions and 10^{-7} OH ions).

Niche — an organism's role or job in the ecosystem usually described by its position in the food chain.

Nicotine sulfate — a pesticide made from tobacco plants.

Nitrate poisoning — a condition that cattle develop if high levels of nitrates accumulate in plants during dry periods.

Nitrogen dioxide — a brownish red gas (NO_2) formed in the atmosphere when oxygen reacts with nitrogen oxide; a major ingredient in photochemical smog.

Nitrogen fixers — organisms (algae or bacteria) that change nitrogen into a form of fertilizer (nitrate or ammonium ions) that plants can use.

Nitrogen — an element that exists in the atmosphere as N_2 and is the most frequently the nutrient that is a limiting factor for plant growth.

Nitrous oxide — a compound consisting of two atoms of nitrogen and one atom of oxygen; a potent greenhouse gas.

No-till drill — a type of grain planter that eliminates the need to prepare the soil before planting.

Nodules — enlargements on the roots of legumes that contain nitrogen-fixing bacteria.

Nongame species — species that are protected and can not be legally hunted.

Nonpoint sources — pollutants that flow directly into the water with runoff from the land.

Nonwithdrawal use — water that is removed from a river or lake and immediately returned.

Nurse log — a fallen log that becomes a nursery for new trees.

Nutrients — chemicals that plants need for growth.

Observed vs. Expected Study — a method of scientific study in which the number of cases of a disease that occurs in an area is compared to the number of cases that are normally expected to occur based on the population of the area.

Obsidian — a type of stone formed when hot volcanic lava cools quickly, used to make arrows.

Ogallala Aquifer — also known as the High Plains Aquifer, this large reservoir of ground water lies beneath the High Plains states, extending from South Dakota to Texas.

OH⁻ — hydroxyl ion

Oil shale — a rock formation that contains liquid oil.

Oil slick — a layer of oil on the surface of a body of water.

Old-growth forests — virgin stands of timber whose ancient trees have never been cut.

Omnivore — organisms that eat both plants and animals.

Once-through-cooling — a method in which water flows through a condenser, is warmed by the steam in the pipes in the condenser, and is returned to the source.

Open water — an area where rooted plants do not reach the surface of the water.

Ore — a rock that is mined to extract a useful mineral.

Organic chemicals — chemicals produced by plants that contain carbon. Also refers to synthetic chemicals made from fossil fuels such as coal or oil.

Organic fertilizer — natural products that provide plant nutrients.

Organic matter — the decomposing organisms or waste products that provide nutrients for plants, feed the organisms in the soil, and maintain good soil structure.

Organism — a living thing.

Organochlorines — compounds that contain hydrogen, carbon, and chlorine.

OSHA — (Occupational Safety and Health Administration) — regulates the use of toxic chemicals in the work place and enforces the proper safety requirements.

Oxygenated fuel — fuel that contains alcohol or other compounds that reduce the amount of carbon monoxide produced during combustion.

Ozone shield — a layer of ozone within Earth's stratosphere that forms a protective shield against UV radiation.

Ozone — a compound that consists of three atoms of oxygen; an important greenhouse gas and an air pollutant in the lower atmosphere.

Parasite — a consumer that feeds on another organism while it is still living.

Parching — the process used to dry grain by heating it in drums over slow fires.

Parent material — fractured bedrock that lies beneath the subsoil and that is the source of minerals in the soil.

Particulates — small particles often created by attrition or incomplete combustion.

Passive solar heating — the use of building design and collectors to increase the amount of heating caused by light energy that is trapped by glass.

Peat — partially decayed plant material (sphagnum moss) formed in swamps or bogs.

Pedestal — odd mushroom shaped structures that are formed when rocks that are more resistant to erosion protect a column of softer material below.

Percolation rate — rate at which water moves through the soil.

Percolation — movement of water through the soil.

Permafrost — a layer of permanently frozen soil found in the Arctic Tundra biome.

Persistent pesticide — pesticides that are not easily broken down by organisms in the environment, and that may remain in the environment for many years.

Pest — any troublesome, destructive, or annoying organism.

Pesticide — chemicals that kill birds, insects, fungi, nematodes, and weeds.

Petrochemical — chemicals that come from oil and natural gas.

pH scale — a scale used to measure a solution's acidity or alkalinity. It is based on the number of hydrogen ions.

Phosphorus — a primary plant nutrient necessary for good root growth and flower and seed formation.

Photochemical smog — a brown-colored haze produced when sunlight provides the energy for chemical reactions that result in the formation of nitrogen dioxide.

Photosynthesis — the process in which green plants trap the sun's energy and use it to make food — process in which plants use light energy to combine water and carbon dioxide to form sugar.

Photovoltaic cells — a device that converts sunlight directly into electricity.

Physics — the study of matter (and energy), its position and changes in its position.

Pico — prefix meaning one-trillionth (1×10^{-9}).

Picocurie — the amount of radiation given off by a trillionth of a gram of radium.

Pioneer stage — first stage of succession of a pond, lake, or other ecosystem such as a plowed field.

Piston — a movable plunger tightly fitted into the cylinder of an internal combustion engine.

Pittman-Robertson Act — a law that placed a tax on firearms and ammunition and required that this money plus the money collected for hunting license fees be used for wildlife conservation.

Planet Earth — a body orbiting the sun that is a complex environmental system with constant interactions between its atmosphere, oceans, and land masses.

Plankton — microscopic plants and animals that float in the open water.

Plant manager — the person in charge of the operations of a chemical plant including the safety of the processes and the equipment.

Plantlings — young plants that are produced by tissue culture from selected parent plants.

Platy — soil structure in which clumps are glued into thin horizontal plates.

Plot — an area of the organism's habitat that is marked off for the purpose of counting the organisms during a sample census.

Plow share — a blade that cuts through the soil.

Plow — large digging sticks that were pulled by oxen and used to turn the soil.

Pneumonia — an infection of the respiratory tract that often occurs when pollutants kill the bacteria-destroying cells.

Poaching — the taking of wildlife by any method that is illegal.

Pod corn — the type of corn that has each kernel wrapped separately.

Point sources — pipes or ditches that carry pollutants into the water.

Pole size — trees that are six to ten inches (15-20 cm) in diameter.

Pollutant — any natural or human-made substance that is present in quantities that make it undesirable or harmful..

Polluted — water or air that contains substances in amounts that are harmful to the organisms living in or using the water or air.

Pond scum — a floating mat of filamentous algae.

Pond — a body of standing water that is shal-

low enough for sunlight to penetrate so that plants can grow across the entire bottom.

Pools — areas of the stream with slower moving water.

Popeye — a symptom of gas bubble disease caused by bubbles collecting behind the fish's eye and pushing it out of its socket.

Population density — number of a species per unit area of living space.

Population growth rate — the percentage change in the population over time.

Population — the total number of a species living in a defined region.

Potable water — water that is suitable for drinking.

Potassium — a primary plant nutrient that is necessary for proper growth and resistance to disease.

Potato digger — a modified moldboard plow that digs and picks up potatoes.

Prairie potholes — shallow basins in the Great Plains states that fill with water each spring and are important habitat for migrating waterfowl.

Prairie — a grassland without trees.

Precipitation — moisture falling from the atmosphere including rain, snow, sleet, and hail.

Predator — an organism that feeds on other animals that it must first hunt and kill.

Pressurized hot water — a technology used to drive turbines and produce electricity that may use geothermal energy.

Prey — an organism that is killed and eaten by a predator.

Primary chlorination — the initial treatment of water to prevent the growth of algae and bacteria in the water pipes at the water treatment plant.

Primary consumer — an herbivore or first consumer in a food chain.

Primary nutrients — chemicals needed by plants in large amounts.

Primary settling tanks — large tanks in which sewage is allowed to stand for a certain period of time to allow the physical separation of solids and liquids.

Producer — an organism that can use the sun's energy to make its own food.

Productivity — the biomass of plants that an ecosystem can produce in a unit area.

PVC system — a positive crankcase ventilation system that recirculates the vapors that squeeze past the pistons in an internal combustion engine.

Pyramid of biomass — a diagram that shows the decrease in biomass with each step in a food chain.

Pyramid of numbers — a diagram showing the number of organisms at each step in a food chain.

Pyrethrum — a pesticide made from the dried flowers of chrysanthemums.

Rad — (radiation absorbed dose) — a measure of energy deposited in any material by radiation.

Radiation — the transfer of heat or light waves of energy.

Radiocarbon dating — the process used to determine the age of once-living objects.

Radon daughters — solid particles that are produced when radon decays.

Radon — a naturally occurring radioactive gas

that is produced by the decay or uranium and radium in the earth.

Rapids — areas of water that appear white because the surface is broken by the water flowing over rocks.

Reading Prong — a granite rock formation that extends from Reading, PA into New York and New Jersey.

Reaper — a machine that was pulled by horses and cut and tied the bundles of grain.

Reclamation — the process of restoring land to the condition that existed before mining operations took place.

Recycling — use of "waste" materials in the manufacturing process.

Refining — the processes used to separate crude oil into its parts.

Rem — (roentgen equivalent man) — a measure of the result of energy deposited in tissue.

Renewable resource — a natural resource that is replaced by ecological cycles at least at the same rate it is used.

Reserve — a deposit of oil or gas that can economically be recovered with present technology.

Reservoir rock — a porous rock through which oil and gas can move.

Reservoir — lakes that are used to store a supply of water for future use.

Resin — material in a water softener that contains sodium ions.

Resistant — organisms that have become immune to a chemical. Also refers to plants that have built-in protection from pests.

Resource recovery — salvaging of usable materials from solid waste.

Respiration — the process in which organisms break down compounds containing carbon (organic chemicals) and release carbon dioxide or other organic chemicals.

Respiratory irritants — substances that irritate the lining of the respiratory system.

Restricted — classification for pesticides that are only available to farmers and commercial applicators who have been certified by the state's department of agriculture.

Reverse osmosis — a method of removing salt from sea water by forcing it through a membrane that has openings large enough to allow water to pass through but too small to allow the ions to pass through.

Riffles — shallow areas of swiftly flowing water.

Right-to-pollute — an legal allowance owned by a utility company that may be sold if the company reduces its emissions below the legal limit.

Rill erosion — the formation of small ditches by water as it moves down gentle slopes.

River control structure — a set of levees and water control gates that are designed to keep water in the Mississippi River and prevent it from flowing into the Atchafalaya River.

River — a large body of flowing water that receives water from many streams and lakes.

Rock dusting — a process in which the walls of the coal mine are sprayed with powdered limestone to control dust.

Rock — a collection of minerals.

Room and pillar system — a method of coal mining in which columns of coal are left to support the mine roof.

Rotenone — a pesticide made from legumes that grow in the East Indies.

Row crops — crops that are planted with enough distance between rows for mechanical cultivation.

Salinization — increased levels of salts in the soil often due to evaporation of irrigation water.

Salt front — the location where fresh water from the river meets the ocean water.

Sample census — an estimate of the population that is made by counting the organisms or signs of the organism in a number of plots.

Sanitary landfill — method of garbage disposal in which garbage is covered with a layer of soil or other material each day and special liners and drainage systems may be required.

Scale — deposits of minerals on pipes, water heaters, bathtubs, clothing, and furnaces.

Scavenger — carnivores that feed on organisms that died naturally or were killed by other predators.

Screens — structures that sewage flows through as it enters sewage treatment plants to remove large items such as sticks.

Scrubber — sometimes called a wet scrubber —a device in which water is mixed with gases to remove sulfur dioxide from the emissions.

Scythe — a curved blade on a long handle used for harvesting grain.

Secondary consumer — a carnivore that is the second consumer in a food chain.

Secondary nutrients — elements needed by plants in smaller amounts than the primary nutrients.

Secondary recovery method — technology developed to remove more of the oil from the rock than can be removed by normal pumping processes.

Secondary settling tanks — large tanks which hold sewage after primary treatment for the purpose of letting the remaining solids settle out.

Secure landfill — the method of disposal of hazardous wastes in which a pit is lined with clay and plastic and covered with a layer of clay.

Sediment filters — filters that remove small particles from the water.

Sedimentation — the process of allowing water to stand in order for the solids to sink to the bottom.

Seed tree logging — a form of clearcutting in which selected mature trees are left to provide seed for regeneration of the cut area.

Selective cutting — cutting or felling only certain trees to harvest high-quality sawlogs or provide room for other trees to grow.

Selective pesticide — chemicals that kill only one type of organism.

Selenium — a trace element that is essential in the diet of many organisms, but at a few parts per million is toxic and causes deformities in developing birds and the death of adult birds.

Seltzer water — a type of bottled water that has been filtered and carbonated.

Septage — mixture of fluid and solids pumped from the septic tank.

Septic tank — a tank buried in the ground to treat sewage from individual homes.

Septic tank-soil absorption system — the most common type of wastewater treatment used in rural areas.

Settling tank — tank in which water is held in order to allow particles to settle.

Sex attractant — chemicals that are used to draw insects to traps.

Sheet erosion — a thin layer of soil removed from very gentle slopes.

Shelling board — an instrument, first made of wood, that was used to remove kernels of corn from the cob.

Shelterwood logging — a method of harvesting mature trees over a period of years to provide a seed source and protection for shade tolerant species.

Shin — a metal plate attached to the front edge of the moldboard that cuts through the soil.

Shocks — groups of bundles (sheaves) of grain that were stood in the field to dry.

Sick building syndrome — health effects due to a build-up of indoor air pollutants when buildings are sealed.

Sickle — a curved blade on a short handle used for reaping.

Skeletal fluorosis — a serious condition caused by fluoride poisoning affecting the bones and joints that may advance to a crippling form.

Slash burning — using fire to clear duff and slash from logged areas.

Slash — limbs, tree tops, and other waste that remains after logging.

Sludge — solids in sewage that settle to the bottom of the treatment tanks.

Slumping — also called mass erosion — movement of a mass of soil that is saturated with water down a slope due to the force of gravity.

Slurry — a mixture of water and crushed coal that is pumped through a pipeline.

Smelting — heating the ore to high temperatures to separate the impurities from the metal.

Smog — a mixture of smoke and fog.

Snag — a dead tree that is still standing.

Sodium zinc polyphosphate — a chemical added to water supplies to prevent the corrosion of pipes.

Soft water — water that contains low concentrations of dissolved minerals.

Soil absorption field — an area with pipes that carry effluent from the septic tank and allow it to percolate through the soil

Soil Conservation Service — a federal agency of the US Department of Agriculture created to help people understand and protect the soil.

Soil survey maps — maps that show the location of soil types in an specific region.

Soil — that thin layer on the surface of Earth that is made by the interaction of rocks, sunlight, water, air, and living organisms.

Solar thermal technology — the use of mirror-lined dishes or panels that rotate with the sun to collect solar energy and heat water to run electrical generators.

Solid waste — garbage and other discarded materials.

Soot — small carbon particles released by the burning of fuels.

Source reduction — decreasing the amount of solid waste produced.

Source rock — a rock rich in organic matter that is changed into hydrocarbons if

conditions provide sufficient heat and pressure.

Spark plug — a plug that ignites the air-fuel mixture in the cylinder of a gasoline engine.

Sparkling water — a type of bottled water that contains carbon dioxide.

Species — a group of organisms that are very much alike and that breed to produce fertile offspring in their natural environment.

Spent fuel — the remains of uranium fuel that is still radioactive but can no longer be used to produce energy at a power plant.

Spirometer — an instrument used to measure respiratory volumes.

Spring water — in some states, water that comes to the surface naturally from underground aquifers. In other states, the water may be pumped from the underground aquifer.

Stalactites — icicle-like mineral deposits that are formed as the dripping water evaporates from the cave ceilings.

Stalagmites — mineral deposits that build up as the mineral-laden water evaporates from the floor of the cave.

Stonewort algae — algae that is often found in lakes with limestone soil. Sometimes called muskgrass algae, it is identified by whorls of branches that may grow one meter in length.

Stratified internal combustion engine — a type of internal combustion engine that has two combustion chambers — a high temperature ignition chamber and a main chamber in which fuel burns at lower temperatures.

Stream — bodies of flowing water that are usually more shallow than a pond. Sometimes called brooks or creeks.

Strip mining — the most common type of surface mining of coal where the soil and rock covering the coal deposits are removed by huge earth-moving machines.

Strip-cropping — planting of alternating bands of close-growing crops with row crops.

Structure — physical characteristic of the soil that is formed when particles are glued together to form larger particles.

Subbituminous — a type of soft coal with 40 to 60 percent carbon and a heat content higher than lignite, but lower than bituminous.

Submerged plant stage — the stage of succession of a pond or lake in which plants growing on the bottom of the pond do not reach the surface.

Subsidence — the sinking of land that occurs once the resources beneath the land have been removed.

Subsoil — layer of soil beneath the topsoil that does not contain humus.

Subsurface drip irrigation system — method of irrigation that uses buried perforated plastic pipes to feed water directly to the plant roots.

Succession — the series of changes that occur in an ecosystem with the passing of time.

Sulfur dioxide — a compound consisting of one atom of sulfur and two atoms of oxygen. Sulfur dioxide and an air pollutant are produced during the combustion of fuels, especially coal.

Superchlorination — higher than normal doses of chlorine used to disinfect the water.

Superfund — the Comprehensive Environmental Response, Compensation, and Liability Act of 1980 (CERCLA) a law enacted to provide a nationwide program to address the threat of hazardous substances in the environment.

Superphosphate — a synthetic fertilizer made by treating rock phosphate with sulfuric acid to make phosphate more readily available to plants.

Supersaturated — a liquid in which more gas or solid is dissolved than would normally be dissolved at a given temperature.

Surface film — the place where the water meets the air.

Suspended particulates — any solid particles or droplets that are small enough to remain in the air for long periods of time.

Sustainable — the ability to keep in existence or maintain. A sustainable ecosystem is one that can be maintained.

Sustained yield — the ability to maintain production of a product such as timber.

Swamp Lands Act — a law passed by Congress in the mid-1800s gave federal wetlands to states to be reclaimed.

Swamp — an area of trees that is often wet and may flood in spring and fall.

Synergistic effect — the total damage caused by a combination of pollutants is greater than the total damage that is caused by the pollutants when acting separately.

Synfuels — synthetic fuels that are produced by chemically changing fossil fuels or other organic materials.

Synthetic fertilizer — man-made soil additives that provide plant nutrients.

Tannic acid — a waste product produced when bacteria break down plant material.

Tannin — a bitter chemical found in acorns.

Tar sands — a rock formation that contains liquid oil.

Taxol — a chemical extracted from the bark of a Pacific yew that is used in the treatment of certain forms of cancer.

Technology — knowledge that is used to make products or develop objects that make life easier.

Terraces — ridges of soil across a slope that slow the speed of water moving down the slope.

Texas teeth — discoloration of teeth due to presence of high levels of fluoride; also called Colorado Brown Stain.

Texture — the size of particles in the soil. Also the proportions of sand, silt, and clay particles in the soil.

Thermal mass — materials that absorb sunlight and store it as heat energy, such as brick, stone, concrete, or water.

Thinning — removing poorly formed and overcrowded trees to give other trees space to grow.

Threatened species — a species that is likely to become endangered and possibly extinct unless it gets help.

Threshing floor — the floor of a barn where grain was beat with flails to separate the grain from the straw and the chaff.

Threshing machine — a machine that separated the grain from the straw and the chaff.

Tidal volume — the amount of air taken in or pushed out during one breath.

Tile drainage — a method of improving the ability of water to percolate through the soil by burying porous pipes beneath the soil help carry water away from the area.

Tissue culture — cells grown in laboratory dishes for the purpose of studying the effects of poisonous substances.

Tolerance level — the maximum amount of pesticide residue that is allowed in or on food or in drinking water.

Tolerance value — the rate at which topsoil can be replaced.

Topsoil — the upper layer of soil that contains humus.

Total Ozone Mapping Spectrometer (TOMS) — an instrument aboard an orbiting satellite that monitors the ozone levels in the upper atmosphere.

Toxic substance — chemicals that can harm living organisms.

Toxicology — the study of the effects of poisonous compounds.

Tracer — a chemical that is usually absent or present in the atmosphere in very small amounts, and that is used to follow the movement of chemicals in the atmosphere.

Transect — a straight line made through an ecosystem.

Transpiration — the loss of water vapor from openings (stomates) in the leaves of plants.

Trap — a rock without pores that forms a cap or lid that keeps the oil and gas from escaping from the reservoir rock.

Tributary — a stream that flows into a river.

Trickling filter — a bed of stones or specially made structures that are covered with algae and bacteria that filter chemicals out of sewage as it is sprayed over the rocks.

Trihalomethanes — carcinogenic chemicals formed when naturally occurring organic chemicals, such as those in humus, react with chlorine in the water.

True census — an actual count of all the individuals of a species in a given area.

True cost — the cost of a product including the cost of technology that prevent pollution during the manufacture, use and disposal of the product.

Truffle — a kind of fungus that produces a massive network of filaments that grow through the soil and penetrate the outer cells of tree roots.

Tufa towers — irregular columns of calcium carbonate that form in Mono Lake and are exposed by the lowering of the water level.

Turbid — cloudiness caused by small particles suspended in the water.

Turbidity — a measure of the amount of light scattered or absorbed by particles suspended in the water.

Turbine — a machine with a series of curved blades on a large rotating shaft — connected to a generator at electrical power plant.

Uneven-aged trees — a stand of trees that are of different ages.

Upper reaches — regions of the stream with the greatest slope.

Urea — a nitrogen-containing waste product that is produced by the kidneys and returned to the soil when animal bedding is dug into the soil (organic fertilizer). Also refers to a synthetic fertilizer that is synthesized from atmospheric nitrogen and natural gas.

USDA — United States Department of Agriculture.

Vaporization — the process in which a substance is changed from a liquid into a gas.

Variable — the factor that differs in the treatment of two groups in a controlled experiment.

Virgin forest — a forest that has not been changed by human activity; sometimes called an old-growth forest.

Visibility — the greatest distance that one can see without the aid of technology.

Vital capacity — the maximum amount of air that can be forced out after the biggest breath possible.

Volatile organic compounds (VOCs) — compounds containing carbon that readily vaporize at normal temperatures.

Waste-to-energy plants — systems that burn solid waste to produce electricity or steam that is used by industries or residential developments.

Water table — the level of the water in the aquifer.

Water vapor — water in a gaseous state, the most important atmospheric greenhouse gas.

Water's edge — the location where water meets the land provides habitat for the greatest number of species of plants and animals

Waters of the United States — navigable waterways, streams, and lakes that flow into navigable waterways, and wetlands that lie beside these bodies of water.

Watershed — the drainage area that surrounds a body of water.

Waterway — a wide shallow ditch planted with a permanent grass cover to prevent gully erosion.

Watt — a unit of electrical power

Weather — the atmospheric conditions that result from interactions between temperatures, moisture, winds and clouds.

Weathering agent — chemical and physical forces that break apart rocks and/or remove minerals from them.

Weathering — the process of physical and chemical forces releasing minerals from rocks. Also refers to the action of wind, water, and changing temperatures on substances such as rocks.

Weed — any plant that is growing where it is not wanted.

Wet meadows — grassy areas that are seldom flooded but have soil that is usually waterlogged.

Wet scrubbers — see scrubbers.

Wet towers — the method of cooling in which hot water from a power plant is sprayed in a fine mist or allowed to fall over a series of baffles.

Wetlands — areas with plants that are adapted for life in soil that is saturated with water.

Wildcat well — oil or natural gas wells drilled in unexplored areas.

Windbreak — strips of trees, shrubs, or tall grasses that are planted perpendicular to the direction of the prevailing wind.

Winnowing — the process in which the hulls are separated from the kernels of grain.

Work — the movement of matter.

Xeriscape landscaping — landscaping that uses native, drought-tolerant plants.